Study Guide

Cornelius Rea Douglas College

Study Guide

to accompany

PSYCHOLOGY

Third Edition

Don H. Hockenbury
Sandra E. Hockenbury

WORTH PUBLISHERS

Study Guide
by Cornelius Rea
to accompany
Hockenbury and Hockenbury: **Psychology**, Third Edition

Copyright © 2003, 2000, 1997 by Worth Publishers

Printed in the United States of America

ISBN 0-7167-5125-9

Printing: 5 4 3 2 1
Year: 05 04 03 02

Worth Publishers
41 Madison Avenue
New York, NY 10010
www.worthpublishers.com

Contents

To the Student

This Study Guide is designed to help you to study effectively and to learn the important concepts in *Psychology*, Third Edition, by Don and Sandy Hockenbury. Use this study guide in an active manner and as a complement to the textbook, not as a substitute for it. By actively interacting with the text material and this study guide, you will be able to master the chapter concepts in a straightforward and enjoyable manner. Our goal is to create independent, motivated students who enjoy learning for its own sake, who can think critically, and who have a deep conceptual understanding of the information presented in the text.

Your first course in psychology is very exciting but it is also challenging. Besides the volume of new information you will be asked to learn, you are faced with learning new terminology, novel concepts, unfamiliar theories, and, most important, the scientific way of thinking. "How to Use This Guide," which outlines this study guide, explains how best to use the study guide to learn all the new material. "Study Tips" (p. ix) provides some practical suggestions for improving your ability to learn, understand, and remember.

HOW TO USE THIS GUIDE

Scanning

Scanning is a useful strategy that can facilitate learning. When you scan a chapter, you get a better idea of what lies ahead. So survey the text chapter first. Spend some time looking at the graphics, and examine the special features, boxed inserts, and concept reviews; note the parts that look interesting to you. Pay attention to the diagrams, graphs, photographs, cartoons, and tables. This preview will give you a clearer impression of what is going to be covered in the chapter. Don't worry about the details at this point; just try to get the big picture.

Next read the chapter overview (Chapter . . . At a Glance) in the study guide. This will give you a general, but more detailed, summary of what you are about to encounter in the chapter. This type of previewing activity will help you to develop a conceptual framework (or cognitive map) that will allow you to more readily understand the details of what you are about to read and will make learning the material easier. For example, imagine trying to put together a large jigsaw puzzle without knowing what the finished picture looked like. Do you think it would be easier if you could see the finished picture? Of course it would! Likewise, when you scan the chapter and read the preview, you will have some idea of the big picture and of how the various pieces of the chapter fit together.

Advance Organizers and Preview Questions

The text authors have provided advance organizers at the beginning of each major section of a chapter. These will help you to start thinking about the material and will give you an overview of what lies ahead. The preview questions at the beginning of each main section in the study guide are derived from these advance organizers. Read these preview questions before you read each section of the text chapter and before you start the exercises in the study guide. Both the advance organizers and the preview questions are directly linked to the concept checks, true/false tests, matching exercises, progress tests, and graphic organizers in the study guide. Successful completion of these activities will prepare you for tests, quizzes, exams, and other evaluation procedures.

Structured Note Taking

Good note taking is very important to learning. So we encourage you to take notes. The study guide structures your note taking by prompting you to write definitions, to paraphrase information, and to integrate concepts. Simply highlighting sentences in the textbook is not sufficient. Highlighting does not involve active cognitive processing of the information, whereas writing, especially using your own words, does.

Graphic Organizers

An important aid to better understanding text material is the use of visualization. Completing the graphs, charts, and flow diagrams will provide a visual synopsis that will help you understand and remember the material. So be sure to complete all these exercises, and practice making up your own graphic organizers.

Corrective Feedback: Concept Checks, Matching Exercises, True/False Tests, and Progress Tests

At the end of each major section in the study guide are learning checks in the form of conceptual questions, matching exercises, and true/false tests. These exercises provide you with feedback as you progress through the chapter. Be sure to complete each of these before going on to the next section. Three progress tests containing multiple-choice questions conclude each chapter. These are designed to help you assess your mastery of the material. If you don't know the answers to these questions, go back and study the parts of the text that you didn't understand.

If your instructor gives a quiz or test after each chapter, complete all three progress tests before the exam. Testing, and the corrective feedback it provides, will give you a more realistic idea of how well prepared you actually are and thus reduces the tendency for "overconfidence."

If your exam covers a number of chapters, it is a good idea to complete progress tests 1 and 2 after you have studied each chapter, then create a "comprehensive pretest" from progress test 3 in all the relevant chapters. Taking this larger test will give you a better idea of what the exam is going to be like. Also, be sure to ask your instructor if material other than that covered in the textbook (e.g., material from lectures, videos, lab demonstrations, and tutorials) will be on the exam.

One additional point: It is important not to confuse your recognition ability with your ability to recall and write about a topic. Multiple-choice questions tap your ability to recognize the correct answer, but do not assess your ability to express your ideas logically and coherently. You need to develop both types of skills.

Something to Think About

Each study guide chapter concludes with a special feature called Something to Think About, which contains thought-provoking questions about the material. We encourage you to think actively about what you have read in the chapter. Discuss these topics with friends and family members. This will help you remember the concepts and make learning more enjoyable.

You can also use the ideas from these sections as a guide for writing short essays or papers or for preparing for a presentation.

Answers   The answers to all the questions are included at the end of each chapter. Check your answers as you work your way through the material: Getting immediate corrective feedback facilitates the learning process.

STUDY TIPS   What are the five or ten most effective ways to improve your ability to learn, comprehend, and remember the material in this course? The truth is that there is probably no single list of techniques, no matter who develops it, that will work for all learners all the time. Everyone has a different way or style of learning; becoming familiar with your own unique learning style is the first step in becoming a successful student. However, we can all improve our ability to learn and to remember what we have learned. On that optimistic note, here are some general strategies that can be of value and can benefit almost anyone who makes the effort to use them. So, when faced with the challenge of mastering a large amount of new material try some, or all, of the following.

Use Distributed Practice   You know that you should not cram. Cramming, or what psychologists called massed practice, is not good for long-term retention of material. Spacing out your studying, or distributed practice, on the other hand, enhances your ability to remember. This is one of the most well-established principles in psychology—the spacing effect. Instead of studying for five straight hours at one time, you would be much better off studying one hour a day over five days. This technique also works at shorter intervals. For example, if you have to memorize a formula, you will probably repeat it over and over (say, ten times) until you feel confident you have it memorized. This, of course, is massed practice, and the sense of confidence that typically accompanies it is often misleading. A better way to maximize the benefits of those ten rehearsals is to space them over time, allowing a longer interval after each rehearsal than the one before.

Reduce Interference   One reason we tend to forget new information is that other information (either previously learned or learned later) can interfere with the material we are trying to master. So, if you are studying for a number of courses at the same time, try to study subjects that are different from each other. The more similar they are, the greater the interference. Another source of interference comes from social activities, such as watching TV or interacting with friends. When you engage in these activities after studying, you increase the risk of interference. In addition, playing loud music, having the TV on, or listening to other people's conversations while you are studying can cause distraction and interfere with learning. The best advice? Go to sleep after studying. A good sleep is the best way to cut down on interference and it helps consolidate memories. The worst thing to do? Stay up all night cramming for an exam that is being given the next day.

Try Overlearning   Overlearning is another very effective, and relatively simple, technique for preventing forgetting. When you feel you have mastered the material in a chapter, and you have just answered all the progress test questions correctly, you usually feel relieved and put away the books. It is at this point, however, that overlearning is useful. If you had spent, say, an hour and a half getting to this level, what you need to do now is spend another 10 to 15 minutes reviewing the material one more time. These few extra minutes of studying are the most beneficial minutes you can spend in terms of consolidating your memory and preventing the forgetting of material you have just learned. Hermann Ebbinghaus showed, over a hundred years ago, that most of the information is lost very soon after it is learned. He was the first to demonstrate the powerful effect of overlearning as a way of dealing with this problem.

Get Corrective Feedback

If you studied hard and felt you really knew the material, it is a bit of a shock to find that you did poorly on the test. What could have happened? One possibility is that you only thought you knew the material and you were suffering from "the overconfidence effect." A simple way of preventing this is to get corrective feedback on what you know before taking the exam. For example, using the True/False tests and the Matching Tests, completing the Graphic Organizers, and, of course, taking the Progress Tests will give you the feedback you need.

Be aware, however, that this is not necessarily a perfect gauge of how you will do on the real exam. When you are testing yourself, you tend to be in a much more relaxed state: You have just studied the material and you are in no particular rush. If you make a mistake, it is no big deal; you can simply look up the answers at the end of the chapter (this is not something that you can do in the exam!). These factors often lead students to the false conclusion that the questions on the real exam were much harder than the ones in the progress tests, sample exams, and so forth. Try to make your self-testing as real as possible (get a little anxious); that way you will benefit most from corrective feedback.

Use Mnemonics

Use of memory aids, called mnemonics, can help in memorizing new material and in preventing forgetting. Visual imagery, in particular, is very effective with some material. Try to vividly imagine what it is you are attempting to memorize. A picture is worth a thousand words and is much more memorable. For other material, try making up a story that links elements together. Create acronyms for lists of terms or complex concept names, for example (it is easier to remember SCUBA than self-contained underwater breathing apparatus). Look ahead in your textbook to Chapter 6 and read about how memory works, why we forget, and how we can make memories last; specifically, read the Application for more study tips.

Develop Good Study Habits

Most top students get good grades because of effective study habits (not sheer brilliance). Evaluate your current study habits. Manage your time effectively. Remember, we are usually poor judges about how long things take to do (late papers are a typical example that is the result of our poor judgment). So, after you have made your plans, allow yourself some extra time.

Make studying a priority and firmly commit to doing well in school. Don't let other people interfere with your goal of mastering the material and getting good grades. Study by yourself (too much socializing takes place in study groups). Reward yourself with social activities, if that's what is important to you, AFTER you have successfully completed your study and have achieved an A+ on the progress tests. If you like music, play soft instrumental music. Take a short break after an hour or so of studying—walk around for a few minutes. Do some exercise. Don't study when you are sleep deprived, very tired, or stressed out. If you are getting nowhere and can't concentrate on the material, do something else for a while (a breath of fresh air, a brief nap, a little walk, a chat with a friend, a little meditation or exercise, can all be helpful).

Try Exercise   Exercising before you study will help relieve stress and will induce a more relaxed state. This is because exercise causes the brain to release pain-killing chemicals called endorphins (you have your own little drug-producing factory). It is also a good idea to exercise before a major exam for the same reasons. If aerobic exercise is not your thing (if it makes you tired and unable to concentrate), try something less strenuous, like walking. Anxiety interferes with performance, so anything you can do to effectively control and reduce your anxiety will help. Have fun, good luck, and enjoy your introductory psychology course.

Study Guide

chapter 1

Introduction and Research Methods

PREVIEW

Reading the section below first will give you a general sense of the chapter's contents and an initial introduction to some of the major concepts and terms. This will prime you for what you are about to read and help you to develop a "cognitive map" that will guide your study of the material in this chapter. Likewise, reading the **preview questions** at the beginning of each major section will improve your ability to understand, learn, and retain the information.

CHAPTER 1 . . . AT A GLANCE

Chapter 1 first defines psychology, then gives a brief history of the people and events that influenced its development. Beginning with the contributions of philosophy and physiology, the chapter discusses the two early schools, structuralism and functionalism, the emergence of the major perspectives in twentieth-century psychology, and the major specialty areas.

The four goals of psychology are used to introduce the scientific method. The descriptive and experimental research methods are outlined, and the advantages and disadvantages of each arc discussed.

Important issues such as the need for representative sampling and random selection are raised. The section concludes with a discussion of the uses and limitations of correlational studies. The concepts of correlation, the correlation coefficient, and negative and positive correlations are described and explained.

The experimental method is explained in detail, using a specific study to illustrate important concepts such as dependent and independent variables, experimental and control groups, and random assignment. Also presented are variations in experimental design.

The chapter concludes with an important discussion of the ethical guidelines that regulate psychological research and the role played by the American Psychological Association.

Introduction: The Origins of Psychology

Preview Questions

Consider the following questions as you study this section of the chapter.

- How is psychology defined today?
- Which two disciplines influenced the emergence of psychology as a science?
- Who founded psychology?
- What were the first two schools of psychology called, who is associated with their founding, and how do they differ?
- Who founded psychoanalysis, and what was its main focus?
- What are the goals of behaviorism, and who were the three main proponents of this perspective?
- What is the emphasis of humanistic psychology, and what are the names of its two major advocates?

*Read the section "Introduction: The Origins of Psychology" and **write** your answers to the following:*

1. Psychology is defined as _____
   _____

2. The two disciplines that influenced the emergence of psychology were _____
   _____

3. The founder of psychology was
   _____

4. The first two schools of psychology were
   _____ ,
   and the people associated with their beginnings
   were _____

5. Structuralism emphasized _____
   _____

   _____

   Functionalism stressed the importance of
   _____

   _____

6. Psychoanalysis was founded by
   _____ , and its main focus

was on _____
_____

7. Behaviorism focused on _____
_____

_____

and rejected _____
_____

_____

8. The main proponents of behaviorism were
_____

9. Humanistic psychology emphasizes _____
_____

Its two major advocates were
_____

After you have carefully studied the preceding section, complete the following exercises.

Concept Check 1

Read the following and write the correct term in the space provided.

1. A psychologist who stresses the importance of how behavior enables organisms to adapt to their environment would be classified as belonging to the _____ school of psychology.

2. Dr. Levine adheres to the theory that emphasizes the role of unconscious conflicts in determining behavior and personality. This viewpoint is most consistent with the _____ school of psychology.

3. Environmental influences and overt measurable behavior are to _____ as conscious experience, psychological growth, and self-determination are to

   _____ .

4. While researching a paper on the history of psychology, John discovered that René Descartes, a seventeenth-century philosopher and mathematician, promoted the idea that the mind and body are separate entities that interact to produce sensations, emotions, and other conscious

experiences. Descartes's view is called

_____ .

5. Dr. Brunac's research focuses on the question of the degree to which heredity and environment influence the development of human abilities such as intelligence and personality characteristics. Dr. Brunac is interested in the

_____ issue.

6. Alvira believes that our most complex conscious experiences can be broken down into elemental structures, or basic components, of sensations and feelings through the research method of introspection. Alvira's view is most consistent with the school of thought in psychology called

_____ .

Review of Terms, Concepts, and Names 1

Use the terms in this list to complete the Matching Test, then to help you answer the True/False items correctly.

psychology	Mary Whiton Calkins
interactive dualism	Margaret Floy
nature–nurture issue	Washburn
(heredity versus	Sigmund Freud
environment)	psychoanalysis
physiology	behaviorism
Wilhelm Wundt	Ivan Pavlov
Edward B. Titchener	John B. Watson
structuralism	B. F. Skinner
introspection	humanistic psychology
William James	Carl Rogers
functionalism	Abraham Maslow
G. Stanley Hall	

Matching Exercise

Match the appropriate term/name with its definition or description.

1. _____ American psychologist who established the first psychology research laboratory in the United States and founded the American Psychological Association.

2. _____ Looking inward in an attempt to reconstruct feelings and sensations experienced immediately after viewing a stimulus object.

3. _____ School of psychology and theoretical viewpoint that emphasizes each

person's unique potential for psychological growth and self-direction.

4. _____ American psychologist who founded behaviorism, emphasizing the study of observable behavior and rejecting the study of mental processes.

5. _____ Early school of psychology that emphasized studying the purpose, or function, of behavior and mental experiences.

6. _____ The scientific study of behavior and mental processes.

7. _____ The idea that the mind and body are separate entities that interact to produce sensations, emotions, and other conscious experiences.

8. _____ German physiologist who founded psychology as a formal science and opened the first psychology research laboratory in 1879.

9. _____ British-born American psychologist who founded structuralism, the first school of psychology.

10. _____ School of psychology and theoretical viewpoint that emphasizes the study of observable behaviors, especially as they pertain to the process of learning.

11. _____ American psychologist who was the major founder of the school of humanistic psychology.

True/False Test

Indicate whether each statement is true or false by placing T or F in the blank space next to each item.

1. ____ Margaret Floy Washburn was the American psychologist who conducted research on memory, personality, and dreams and was the first women president of the American Psychological Association.

2. ____ Structuralism was an early school of psychology that emphasized studying the most basic components, or structures, of conscious experience.

3. ____ Physiology is a branch of biology that studies the functions and parts of living organisms, including human beings.

4. ____ William James was an American philosopher and psychologist who was instrumental in establishing psychology in the United States and whose ideas became the basis for the psychological school called functionalism.

5. ___ The issue of heredity versus environment is the same as the nature-nurture issue and refers to the debate over which is more important, the inborn characteristics of the individual or the impact of the environment.

6. ___ Mary Whiton Calkins was an American psychologist who published research on mental processes in animals and was the first woman in the United States to earn a doctorate in psychology.

7. ___ Ivan Pavlov was an Austrian physician whose work focused on the unconscious causes of behavior and personality formation and who founded psychoanalysis.

8. ___ B. F. Skinner was a famous American psychologist who championed behaviorism.

9. ___ Abraham Maslow was a humanistic psychologist who developed a theory of motivation that emphasized psychological growth.

10. ___ Psychoanalysis is a personality theory and form of psychotherapy that emphasizes the role of unconscious factors in personality and behavior.

11. ___ Sigmund Freud was a Russian physiologist whose pioneering research on learning contributed to the development of behaviorism and who discovered the basic learning process that is now called classical conditioning.

Check your answers and review any areas of weakness before going on to the next section.

Contemporary Psychology

Preview Questions

Consider the following questions as you study this section of the chapter:

- What are the seven major perspectives in contemporary psychology, and how do they differ?
- What are the main specialty areas in contemporary psychology?
- How do clinical psychologists and psychiatrists differ?
- What is a psychoanalyst?

*Read the section "Contemporary Psychology" and **write** your answers to the following:*

1. The seven major perspectives in psychology are

   _____

   _____

   _____

2. The main specialty areas in contemporary psychology are _____

   _____

   _____

   _____

   _____

3. The difference between a clinical psychologist and a psychiatrist is _____

   _____

   _____

   _____

   _____

4. A psychoanalyst is _____

   _____

   _____

After you have carefully studied the preceding section, complete the following exercises.

Concept Check 2

Which specialty area is represented by each of the following?

1. Dr. Matthews studies the relationship between behavior and the nervous system. She would most likely be classified as a(n) _____ psychologist.

2. Michele wants to study physical, social, and psychological changes that occur over the lifespan when she attends graduate school. Michele is planning to be a(n) _____ psychologist.

3. Dr. Bowman studies the causes, treatment, and prevention of different types of psychological disorders. Dr. Bowman is most likely a(n) _____ psychologist.

4. Dr. Ying explores how individuals are affected by people and situations and the factors that influence conformity and obedience. Dr. Ying is a(n) _____ psychologist.

5. Dr. Steinberg examines individual differences and the characteristics that make each person unique. He is most likely a(n) _____ psychologist.

6. Ingrid is interested in investigating mental processes such as reasoning, thinking, and problem solving. Ingrid is probably planning a career as a(n) _____ psychologist.

7. Dr. Whinney develops instructional methods and materials used to train people in both educational and work settings; she also studies how people of all ages learn. She is a(n) _____ psychologist. Her colleague, Dr. Marx, focuses on designing programs that promote the intellectual, social, and emotional development of children, including those with special needs. He is a(n) _____ psychologist.

8. Dr. Barton is concerned with stress and coping, the relationship between psychological factors and well-being, and ways of promoting health-enhancing behaviors. Dr. Barton is probably a(n) _____ psychologist.

9. Pitor, who just completed his Ph.D., applied for a job concerned with the relationship between people and work, including the study of job satisfaction, worker productivity, personnel selection, and the interaction between people and equipment. Pitor has applied for a job as a(n) _____ psychologist.

10. Dr. Manhas has a medical degree plus years of specialized training in the treatment of psychological disorders. He typically prescribes medication for his patients' psychological problems. Dr. Manhas is a _____ .

Graphic Organizer 1

The statements in the table below represent some of the major perspectives and specialty areas in contemporary psychology. Which perspective is reflected by each statement, and which specialty area is being described? Write your answers in the spaces provided.

Statement	Perspective	Specialty
1. I'm interested in how different parenting styles and techniques influence each child's individual potential for growth and self-determination.		
2. I study the relationship between people and work and, more specifically, how to increase productivity. I believe that by changing environmental factors, increasing the use of rewards and praise for correct behavior, and providing corrective feedback, workers' overt behavior can be changed.		
3. I study how people of all ages learn, and I develop instructional methods and materials to help the learning process. In particular, I stress the roles played by thinking, problem solving, memory, and mental imagery.		
4. I work mostly with people who suffer from mental disorders, and I believe that the main causes of mental illness are either genetic or due to some malfunction in the central nervous system or endocrine system. I often prescribe medications and order medical procedures such as electroshock treatment.		
5. I often travel to different countries to research people's attitudes and group relations. My research tends to show that many behavioral patterns—for instance, the amount of personal space people require to feel comfortable—vary from one country to another.		
6. I believe that unconscious conflicts, early childhood experiences, and repressed sexual and aggressive feelings make us who we are, and I use this point of view in my work on individual differences and in trying to determine which characteristics make each of us unique.		
7. I focus on the relationship between psychological factors and health, in particular on how people cope with stress in their lives. It is not what happens to us that is important; rather, how we perceive and think about potentially stressful events determines our well-being.		
8. My research keeps me in the lab most of the time, and I focus on the principles and conditions of learning and motivation. Recently, I have been investigating how quickly rats learn the layout of a maze as a function of either large or small amounts of reinforcement.		
9. Psychological processes that have helped individuals adapt to their environment have also helped them to survive, reproduce, and pass those abilities on to their offspring. I adopt this point of view in my investigations of interpersonal attraction, prejudice, and aggression.		

Graphic Organizer 2

Origins of Psychology, First Schools, and Key Figures

Flow diagram exercise: To help you develop the technique of creating your own graphic organizers, we encourage you to try making a flow diagram/ timeline, using boxes, lines, and arrows, that contains the following information. Using a separate sheet of paper, generate your own graphic organizer, then compare it to the sample in the answer section. To help you in this early stage of your study, we've filled in portions of the first two boxes.

```
┌─────────────────────┐   ┌─────────────────────┐
│     Philosophy      │   │     Physiology      │
│  (list key figures) │   │  (list key figure)  │
│                     │   │                     │
└─────────────────────┘   └─────────────────────┘
```

1. Two areas that influenced the beginnings of psychology and the key figures in each.

2. The founder of psychology and the year the first psychology research lab was established.

3. First school in psychology and key figure.

4. First American school in psychology and key figures.

5. Two new approaches (and key figures in each) that challenged the first two schools in psychology.

6. New school that emerged in the 1950s and key figures.

Review of Terms, Concepts, and Names 2

Use the terms in this list to complete the Matching Test, then to help you answer the True/False items correctly.

perspective
specialty area
biological perspective
neuroscientists
psychodynamic
   perspective
behavioral perspective
humanistic perspective
cognitive perspective
cross-cultural
   perspective
social loafing
culture
cross-cultutral
   psychology
ethnocentrism

individualistic cultures
collectivistic cultures
evolutionary perspective
evolutionary psychology
Charles Darwin
natural selection
phobia
biological psychology
cognitive psychology
experimental psychology
developmental
   psychology
social psychology
personality psychology
health psychology
educational

psychology
school psychology
industrial/organizational
   psychology

clinical psychologist
counseling psychologist
psychiatrist
psychoanalyst

Matching Exercise

Match the appropriate term/name with its definition or description.

1. _____ Psychologist who has a doctorate in psychology and intensive training in diagnosing and treating people with psychological disorders.

2. _____ The study of physical, social, and psychological changes over the lifespan, from infancy to old age.

3. _____ Mental health professional who has a medical degree plus years of specialized training in the diagnosis and treatment of psychological disorders.

4. _____ Specialty area in psychology that studies how people of all ages learn.

5. _____ General term that describes research focused on such basic psychological topics as learning, emotion, and motivation.

6. _____ Point of view or general framework that reflects a psychologist's emphasis in investigating psychological topics.

7. _____ Specific area in psychology in which psychologists are trained and in which they work or practice.

8. _____ Broad term that refers to the attitudes, values, beliefs, and behaviors shared by a group of people and communicated from one generation to another.

9. _____ Specialty area that investigates mental processes, including reasoning, thinking, language, and memory.

10. _____ British naturalist and scientist whose theory of evolution through natural selection was first published in *On the Origin of Species by Means of Natural Selection* in 1859.

11. _____ Area of psychology that examines individual differences and may also study the origins and development of those differences.

12. _____ Perspective in psychology that studies how behavior is acquired or modified by environmental consequences and whose

focus is on observable behavior and the fundamental laws of learning.

13. _____ The tendency to use your own culture as the standard for judging other cultures.

14. _____ Perspective in psychology that emphasizes studying the physical bases of human and animal behavior, including the nervous system, endocrine system, immune system, and genetics.

15. _____ Branch of psychology that studies the effects of culture on behavior and mental processes.

16. _____ An extreme fear of a particular object or situation.

17. _____ Principle that organisms that inherit characteristics that increase their chances of survival in their particular habitat are more likely to survive, reproduce, and pass on their characteristics to their offspring.

True/False Test

Indicate whether each statement is true or false by placing T or F in the blank space next to each item.

1. ____ Biological psychology studies the physical bases of human and animal behavior.

2. ____ Evolutionary psychology refers to the application of the principles of evolution, including natural selection, to explain psychological processes and phenomena.

3. ____ Counseling psychology is concerned with the relationship between people and work, and it includes the study of job satisfaction, worker productivity, personnel selection, and the interaction between people and equipment.

4. ____ The cross-cultural perspective stresses the importance of cultural and ethnic influences on behavior.

5. ____ School psychology focuses on designing programs that promote the intellectual and social development of children in school.

6. ____ Psychologists who explore how individuals are affected by people and situations and what factors influence conformity, obedience, persuasion, interpersonal attraction, and other related phenomena work in a specialty area called social psychology.

7. ____ Individualistic cultures emphasize the needs and goals of the group over the needs and goals of the individual.

8. ____ Health psychology focuses on the role of psychological factors in health, illness, medical treatment, and health-related behaviors.

9. ____ Industrial/organizational psychology aims to improve everyday functioning by helping people to cope more effectively with everyday problems and challenges.

10. ____ Psychologists who take the humanistic perspective emphasize the importance of unconscious influences, early life experiences, and interpersonal relationships in explaining the underlying dynamics of behavior or treating people with psychological problems.

11. ____ Collectivistic cultures emphasize the needs and goals of the individual over the needs and goals of the group.

12. ____ The psychodynamic perspective focuses on the motivation of people to grow psychologically, the influence of interpersonal relationships on a person's self-concept, and the importance of choice and self-direction in striving to reach one's potential.

13. ____ The cognitive perspective stresses the important role of mental processes in how people process information, develop language, solve problems, and think.

14. ____ A psychoanalyst is a clinical psychologist, psychiatrist, or other mental health professional with extensive training in Freud's psychoanalytic method of psychotheraphy.

15. ____ Social loafing refers to a psychological finding that people in Western cultures exert less effort on a task when working as part of a group than when working alone.

16. ____ The evolutionary perspective analyzes behavior in terms of how it increases a species' chance of surviving and reproducing; it has been applied to many different areas of psychology, including human relationships, mate selection, eating behavior, and emotional responses.

17. ____ Biological psychologists who specialize in the study of the brain and the rest of the nervous system are called neuroscientists.

Check your answers and review any areas of weakness before going on to the next section.

The Scientific Method

Preview Questions

Consider the following questions as you study this section of the chapter.

- What are the four goals of psychology?
- What is the scientific method?
- What assumptions and attitudes guide psychologists?
- What is meant by empirical evidence, and what are the four basic steps of the scientific method?
- What are theories, how do they differ from hypotheses, and what principle do they reflect?

*Read the section "The Scientific Method" and **write** your answers to the following:*

1. The four basic goals of psychology are to _____

   _____

   _____

2. The scientific method refers to _____

   _____

   _____

3. Psychologists are guided by the basic assumptions that _____

   _____

   _____

   _____

4. Psychologists share a set of attitudes, including

   _____

5. Empirical evidence refers to _____

   _____

   The four basic steps of the scientific method are _____

   _____

   _____

   _____

6. A theory is _____

   _____

   It is different from a hypothesis _____

   _____

   _____

   _____

7. The role of statistics in psychological research is to _____

   _____

   _____

8. Theories can evolve and change because they reflect the _____

   _____

   _____

After you have carefully studied the preceding section, complete the following exercises.

Concept Check 3

Read the following and write the correct term in the space provided.

1. Dr. Marlow is interested in drinking and driving behavior and wants to know the frequency with which people will drive after receiving feedback from a Breathalyzer test. In one condition, she sets up her equipment in a bar and administers the test to patrons who are leaving and planning to drive and then observes whether feedback on their level of intoxication influences their decision to drive. Dr. Marlow is using _____ research.

2. In the above example, Dr. Marlow makes this prediction: the majority of people who are told that they are over the legal limit will still drive; the higher the level on the Breathalyzer test, the more likely it is that they will drive. Dr. Marlow has formulated a _____ .

3. After collecting data over many weeks, Dr. Marlow performs calculations and mathematical tests to see if her prediction was correct. Dr. Marlow is using _____ to analyze her data.

4. Dr. Marlow next writes a report describing the background of this research and details her research design, data collection methods, results, analyses, and conclusions. She submits her report to a respected psychology journal for peer review and publication. She is following step _____ of producing scientific evidence by _____ .

Review of Terms and Concepts 3

Use the terms in this list to complete the Matching Test, then to help you answer the True/False items correctly.

scientific method
critical thinking
empirical evidence
hypothesis
variable
operational definition
descriptive method

experimental method
statistics
statistical significance
meta-analysis
replicate
theory

Matching Exercise

Match the appropriate term/name with its definition or description.

1. _____ Statistical technique that involves combining and analyzing the results of many research studies on a specific topic in order to identify overall trends.

2. _____ To repeat or duplicate a scientific study in order to increase confidence in the validity of the original findings.

3. _____ A set of assumptions, attitudes, and procedures that guide researchers in creating questions to investigate, in generating evidence, and in drawing conclusions.

4. _____ Tentative statement about the relationship between two or more variables.

5. _____ Precise description of how the variables in a study will be manipulated or measured.

6. _____ Method of investigation used to demonstrate cause-and-effect relationships by purposely manipulating a factor thought to produce change in a second factor.

7. _____ Mathematical methods used to summarize data and draw conclusions based on the data.

True/False Test

Indicate whether each statement is true or false by placing T or F in the blank space next to each item.

1. ____ A statistically significant finding is one that is likely to have occurred by chance.

2. ____ Empirical evidence is evidence that is the result of observation, measurement, and experimentation.

3. ____ A theory is a tentative explanation that tries to integrate and account for the relationships among various findings and observations.

4. ____ Descriptive methods are research strategies for observing and describing behavior and include naturalistic observation, surveys, case studies, and correlational studies.

5. ____ A variable is a factor that can vary, or change, in ways that can be observed, measured, and verified.

6. ____ Critical thinking is the active process of trying to minimize the influence of preconceptions and biases while rationally evaluating evidence, determining what conclusions can be drawn from the evidence, and considering alternative explanations.

Check your answers and review any areas of weakness before going on to the next section.

Descriptive Methods

Preview Questions

Consider the following questions as you study this section of the chapter.

- What are descriptive methods?
- How is naturalistic observation typically conducted?
- What are case studies, and when are they normally used?
- What is the survey method, and how do researchers ensure that their sample closely parallels the larger group on relevant characteristics?
- What is random selection, and why is it important for obtaining accurate results?
- What does a correlational study involve, and what are its limitations?
- What is the correlation coefficient, and how does a negative correlation differ from a positive correlation?

*Read the section "Descriptive Methods" and **write** your answers to the following:*

1. Descriptive methods are _____

_____

_____

2. Naturalistic observation involves the _____

_____

_____

3. A case study is _____

_____

Case studies are typically used to _____

_____

_____

4. In the survey method, the researcher _____

_____

_____

_____

5. Researchers ensure that their sample closely parallels the population of interest by

_____

_____

6. Random selection refers to _____

_____

_____

It is important because _____

_____

_____

7. Correlational studies show _____

_____

_____

They are limited because _____

_____

8. The correlation coefficient is _____

_____

_____

The correlation coefficient has two parts:

_____

_____

_____

9. A positive correlation is one in which _____

_____

A negative correlation is one in which _____

_____

After you have carefully studied the preceding section, complete the following exercises.

Concept Check 4

Read the following and decide which term applies in each case.

1. If a researcher found a correlation coefficient of –0.85 between amount of exercise and weight, this would indicate that the _____ people exercise, the _____ they weigh.

2. If an organization wants to find out about the spending habits of high-income people, they would be advised to conduct a _____ , using a representative _____ that would be _____ selected from this population.

3. Dr. Klatz is interested in whether there is a difference in the way males and females carry objects such as textbooks, bags, and other large items, so she sets up a hidden camera on the main concourse of a large university and videotapes people at various times throughout the day. Dr. Klatz is using

_____ .

4. A psychologist discovers that the more control people feel they have over what happens in their work environments, the more productive they are. The psychologist has discovered a _____ correlation between perceived control and productivity.

5. A psychologist who is interested in finding out about the lives and experiences of people who claim to have been abducted by aliens and who wants to know how these people are viewed by

their families, friends, and coworkers would be advised to use the _____ method of research.

6. Dr. Hamashima's correlational research discovered that university graduates earn significantly more money than high school graduates. In addition, he found that the more education people had, the less likely they were to be diagnosed with psychological problems. In this research, it appears that there is a _____ correlation between education and income and a _____ correlation between education and psychological health.

Graphic Organizer 3
Positive and Negative Correlations

The following box shows both positive and negative correlations between variables. In cells A through D the arrows indicate a relationship between the amount students study (variable X) and their grade point average (GPA) (variable Y). Fill in the appropriate term in each space provided.

Amount of Study (X)

	High	Low
High	Cell A ↑↑	Cell B ↓↑
Low	Cell C ↑↓	Cell D ↓↓

GPA (Y)

1. Cell A indicates a _____ correlation, and cell D indicates a _____ correlation.

2. Cell C indicates a _____ correlation, and cell B indicates a _____ correlation.

3. Cell A: _____ amounts of X are associated with _____ levels of Y.

Cell D: _____ amounts of X are associated with _____ levels of Y.

4. Cell C: _____ amounts of X are associated with _____ levels of Y.

Cell B: _____ amounts of X are associated with _____ levels of Y.

Review of Terms and Concepts 4

Use the terms in this list to complete the Matching Test, then to help you answer the True/False items correctly.

descriptive methods
naturalistic observation
case study
multiple case study
case study research
survey
sample

representative sample
random selection
correlational study
correlation coefficient
positive correlation
negative correlation

Matching Exercise

Match the appropriate term with its definition or description.

1. _____ A questionnaire or interview designed to investigate the opinions, behaviors, or characteristics of a particular group.

2. _____ General term for scientific procedures that involve systematically observing behavior in order to describe the relationships among behaviors and events.

3. _____ Selected segment of the population under study.

4. _____ Selected segment of a population that very closely parallels the larger group being studied on relevant characteristics.

5. _____ Research strategy that allows the precise calculation of how strongly related two factors are to each other.

6. _____ Process in which participants are selected randomly from the larger group such that every member has an equal chance of being included in the study.

7. _____ Type of research in which psychologists combine information from several case studies that focus on the same type of behavior.

True/False Test

Indicate whether each statement is true or false by placing T or F in the blank space next to each item.

1. ____ A case study is an intensive, in-depth investigation of an individual.

2. ____ A negative correlation between two variables means that the two factors are totally unrelated.

3. ____ Naturalistic observation is the systematic observation and recording of behaviors as they occur in their natural setting.

4. ____ A correlation coefficient is a numerical indication of the magnitude and direction of the relationship between two variables.

5. ____ A positive correlation is one in which the two variables move in opposite directions; as one factor increases, the other decreases.

6. ____ In a multiple case study, a small group of individuals is intensively studied.

Check your answers and review any areas of weakness before going on to the next section.

The Experimental Method

Preview Questions

Consider the following questions as you study this section of the chapter.

- What is the experimental method, and what is its main purpose?

- What are independent and dependent variables, and why do researchers use random assignment?

- What is the experimental group, the control group, and the placebo control group?

- What is a double-blind study, why do researchers use this technique, and what is meant by demand characteristics?

- How do natural experiments differ from laboratory experiments?

- What are the five key provisions of the APA guidelines for research using humans?

Read the section "The Experimental Method" and **write** *your answers to the following:*

1. The experimental method of investigation is used to _____ _____ _____

2. The independent variable is the _____ _____

   The dependent variable is the _____ _____

3. Random assignment means that _____ _____ _____

   It helps ensure that _____ _____ _____

4. The experimental group (or experimental condition) is _____ _____

   The control group (or control condition) is ____ _____ _____

   The placebo control group is _____ _____ _____

5. Natural experiments are different from laboratory experiments in that _____ _____ _____

6. A double-blind study is one in which _____ _____

   It is used to _____ _____ _____

7. Five key provisions of the APA ethical guidelines regulating research with human participants are

(a) _____

(b) _____

(c) _____

(d) _____

(e) _____

After you have carefully studied the preceding section, complete the following exercises.

Concept Check 5

Read the following and decide which term applies in each case.

Dr. Denton studies the effects of marijuana on memory. He designs an ethically approved experiment that consists of two groups: group A gets the active ingredient in cannabis, THC, and group B gets a harmless inert substance. Neither the researcher nor the participants know who is getting the drug and who is not. Subjects are assigned to each group by chance, and all subjects are given a long list of word pairs to learn and are later given a memory test.

1. The independent variable in this study is

_____ .

2. The dependent variable is the

_____ .

3. Group A is the _____ group, and group B is the

_____ group.

4. Dr. Denton has used a _____ technique in designing the experiment; along with the control procedure used, this should help guard against _____ .

5. Subjects ended up in group A or group B on the basis of _____ .

Review of Terms and Concepts 5

Use the terms in this list to complete the Matching Test, then to help you answer the True/False items correctly.

experimental method
independent variable
  (treatment of interest)
dependent variable
random assignment
experimental group (or
  experimental condition)
control group (or control
  condition)
placebo control group
placebo

expectancy effect
  (placebo effects)
double-blind study
single-blind study
demand characteristics
natural experiment
pseudoscience
paranormal phenomena
rule of falsifiability
illusory correlation

Matching Exercise

Match the appropriate term with its definition or description.

1. _____ Experimental technique in which the researchers, but not the participants, are aware of the critical information about the experiment.

2. _____ Method of investigation used to demonstrate cause-and-effect relationships by purposely manipulating a factor thought to produce change in a second factor.

3. _____ The factor that is observed and measured for change in an experiment.

4. _____ Alleged abilities that fall outside the range of normal experience and established scientific explanations.

5. _____ Changes in a participant's behavior produced by his or her belief that change should happen.

6. _____ A group of participants that is not exposed to the independent variable or treatment of interest and against which the experimental group is compared.

7. _____ Subtle cues or signals that communicate what is expected of particular participants in an experiment.

8. _____ An inert substance or a treatment that has no known effects.

9. _____ A fake or false science that makes claims based on little or no scientific evidence.

True/False Test

Indicate whether each item is true or false by placing T or F in the blank space next to each item.

1. ___ Random assignment means that all participants have an equal chance of being assigned to any of the conditions or groups in the study.

2. ___ Participants in the placebo control group receive a fake treatment or substance with no known effects.

3. ___ Participants in the experimental group (or condition) are exposed to the independent variable or treatment of interest.

4. ___ The independent variable (treatment of interest) in an experiment is purposely manipulated in order to cause a change in another variable.

5. ___ The experimental technique in which neither the participants nor the researcher is aware of the experimental conditions to which each subject has been assigned is called the double-blind technique.

6. ___ The rule of falsifiability is a basic rule of science which states that in order for a claim to be scientifically tested and proved true, there must be identifiable evidence that could prove the claim false.

7. ___ In a natural experiment, researchers carefully observe and measure the impact of naturally occurring events on their study participants.

8. ___ An illusory correlation is the mistaken belief that two factors are related when they are not.

Check your answers and review any areas of weakness before going on to the next section.

Something to Think About

1. When family and friends find out you are taking a psychology course, someone typically makes some comment about "headshrinking" and "psychoanalyzing," or notes that "psychology is just plain old common sense." To prepare yourself for these remarks, think about how you would explain what psychology really is and how you might "educate" your family and friends about the difference between psychiatry, clinical psychology, and psychoanalysis.

2. If you are like most introductory psychology students, you were probably motivated to take this course, at least in part, because of questions about human behavior and mental processes. For example, students often wonder if hypnosis can really help recover repressed memories and memories of past lives; if a lie detector really can detect lies; if "satanic messages" embedded in the lyrics of rock music can cause people to commit suicide; if ESP really exists; or whether subliminal tapes can really improve memory, clear up acne, or improve self-esteem. Now that you know more about the science of psychology, take one of your questions and think about how a psychologist would try to answer it.

Check your answers and review any areas of weakness before doing the following progress tests.

Progress Test 1

Review the complete chapter (including Concept Reviews and the boxed inserts), review all your study notes, and then test yourself on the following progress test. Check your answers. If you make a mistake, review your notes, check the relevant section in the study guide, and, if necessary, go back and read the appropriate part of your textbook.

1. Two disciplines influenced the founding of psychology. The discipline that concerns itself with questions such as mind-body dualism and the nature-nurture issue is _____ ; the discipline that is a branch of biology and studies functions and structures of living organisms is _____ .
   (a) chemistry; physics
   (b) neurology; sociology
   (c) physics; neurology
   (d) philosophy; physiology

2. A Japanese psychologist investigating the relationship between worker satisfaction and productivity was surprised to find that North American workers were less productive when working as part of a group than when working alone. In some Asian countries, he had found the opposite to be true. This researcher probably has a _____ perspective, and his specialty area is _____ psychology.
   (a) cross-cultural; developmental
   (b) behavioral; health
   (c) behavioral; developmental
   (d) cross-cultural; industrial/organizational

3. Dr. Hammersly focuses on the role of unconscious factors in his patients' behaviors and spends time analyzing their dreams and delving into their early childhood experiences. Dr. Finkleman is more concerned with the way her patients think and reason, and her psychotherapy involves teaching her patients how to recognize irrational thinking and to find different ways of thinking about their situation. Dr. Hammersly's perspective is _____ , and Dr. Finkleman's perspective is

   _____ .

   (a) cognitive; behavioral
   (b) psychodynamic; cognitive
   (c) humanistic; biological
   (d) cognitive; psychodynamic

4. Dr. Devries emphasizes the importance of unconscious influences, early life experiences, and interpersonal relationships in explaining the underlying dynamics of behavior. His approach is most consistent with the _____ perspective in psychology.
   (a) biological
   (b) behavioral
   (c) psychodynamic
   (d) cognitive

5. Dr. Lebel investigates how people differ on such characteristics as shyness, assertiveness, and self-esteem. It is most likely that she is a _____ psychologist.
   (a) clinical   (c) developmental
   (b) biological   (d) personality

6. To ensure that differences among participants are evenly distributed across all conditions in the experiment and that there is no bias in how participants are assigned to their respective groups, a researcher studying the behavioral effects of playing violent video games should
   (a) operationally define each participant's role and assign participants on the basis of how closely they fit the definition.
   (b) make sure that the most aggressive people are assigned to the experimental condition.
   (c) make sure that the most aggressive people are assigned to the control group.
   (d) randomly assign the participants to each condition in the experiment.

7. A researcher is interested in how sleep deprivation affects performance and cognitive abilities. She proposes that there is a relationship between the amount of sleep deprivation and the ability to solve complex mental tasks; the more sleep-deprived people are, the more mistakes they are likely to make. She has
   (a) developed a theory.
   (b) formulated a hypothesis.
   (c) produced empirical evidence.
   (d) merely stated the obvious.

8. In a study investigating emotional arousal and memory, Dr. Alves discovers a statistically significant difference in recall ability between the high-arousal group and the low-arousal group. This finding indicates that
   (a) the participants were not randomly assigned to the two groups.
   (b) the difference between the two groups is likely to have occurred by chance.
   (c) there is an illusory correlation between level of arousal and memory ability.
   (d) the difference between the two groups is not likely to have occurred by chance.

9. Dr. Barbone and his colleagues decide to repeat the essence of an earlier study using different participants. They are
   (a) replicating the previous study.
   (b) wasting their time.
   (c) doing a meta-analysis.
   (d) violating the rule of falsifiability.

10. In an experiment designed to test the effects of alcohol on motor coordination, group 1 participants are given a precise amount of alcohol in a mixed drink and group 2 participants are given a drink that smells and tastes exactly like the alcoholic drink but contains no alcohol. Which of the following is true?
    (a) Group 1 is the control group.
    (b) Group 2 is the experimental group.
    (c) Group 2 is the placebo control group.
    (d) Group 1 will have much more fun than group 2.

11. A researcher is interested in whether people talk when they are riding in elevators, so she and her research assistants spend many hours riding in elevators and unobtrusively noting when they hear a conversation. This researcher is using
    (a) naturalistic observation.
    (b) experimental research.
    (c) correlational research.
    (d) case study research.

12. In an attempt to understand how traumatic brain injuries affect behavior, Dr. Nicolai extensively and carefully observes and questions three accident victims who had suffered brain injuries. Which research method is Dr. Nicolai utilizing?
    (a) naturalistic observation
    (b) experimental research
    (c) correlational research
    (d) the case study method

13. In her research, Dr. Cranshaw focuses on the application of principles of natural selection to explain psychological processes and phenomena. Dr. Cranshaw is most likely a(n) _____ psychologist.
    (a) evolutionary   (c) behavioral
    (b) biological   (d) psychodynamic

14. According to Culture and Human Behavior 1.1, individualistic cultures emphasize the needs and goals of the _____ over the needs and goals of the _____ .
    (a) individual; group
    (b) country; company
    (c) group; individual
    (d) collective; group

15. According to Science Versus Pseudoscience 1.3, which of the following is true of pseudoscience?
    (a) It is a legitimate science that uses both established and unorthodox methods in the search for the truth.
    (b) It is a fake or false science that makes claims based on little or no scientific evidence.
    (c) It is not accepted by most of the scientific establishment because pseudoscientists have discovered truths that threaten all the fundamental laws and principles of science.
    (d) It does not use sophisticated jargon, impressive-looking statistical graphs, or elaborate theories, and virtually no pseudoscientist has impressive-sounding credentials.

Progress Test 2

After you have checked your understanding of the material in Progress Test 1 and have done a complete chapter review with special focus on any areas of weakness, you are ready to assess your knowledge on Progress Test 2. Check your answers. If you make a mistake, review your notes and the relevant section of the study guide and, if necessary, review the appropriate part of your textbook.

1. In an experiment, children were randomly assigned to a group that watched a violent video or to a group that watched a nonviolent video; later, the level of aggression in both groups was measured under controlled laboratory conditions. In this example, the measure of the children's aggression was the
    (a) dependent variable.
    (b) independent variable.
    (c) control variable.
    (d) naturalistic variable.

2. Dr. Ames researches changes in people's intellectual abilities as they grow older. Dr. Ames's specialty area is _____ psychology.
    (a) social   (c) developmental
    (b) educational   (d) clinical

3. While researching a paper for her history of psychology course, Sangeeta noted that behaviorism and psychoanalysis dominated psychology for many decades early in the twentieth century. However, in the 1950s a new school of thought emerged which emphasized conscious experience and each person's unique potential for psychological growth, self-determination, and free will. This school of psychology is called

   (a) structuralism.
   (b) functionalism.
   (c) humanistic psychology.
   (d) cross-cultural psychology.

4. Dr. Sandman investigates the relationship between sleep deprivation and cognitive abilities. He decides to test subjects in his sleep research lab under varying conditions. First, he allows all his subjects to get a number of uninterrupted nights' sleep and records how long each subject sleeps on average. Next, he decides that sleep deprivation would be either two, three, or four hours fewer than the average for each subject. Dr. Sandman

   (a) has operationally defined one of his variables.
   (b) is using cruel and unusual punishment.
   (c) is conducting correlational research.
   (d) has proposed a theory.

5. An educational psychologist is interested in whether having students evaluate instructors' performance is actually a good measure of teaching ability. A review of the literature showed some inconsistent findings across hundreds of different studies. To get a sense of the overall trends in this body of research, the investigator would be advised to use a technique called

   (a) the correlation coefficient.
   (b) meta-analysis.
   (c) the case study method.
   (d) replication.

6. Compared to clinical psychologists, psychiatrists are more likely to

   (a) prescribe drugs and other medical procedures for their clients.
   (b) assume that psychological disorders result from unconscious conflicts.
   (c) use a cognitively based therapy rather than a biologically based therapy.
   (d) favor a humanistic perspective rather than a psychoanalytic perspective.

7. In order to test the claim that listening to classical music improves cognitive functioning, researchers divided participants into three groups. Group A listened to classical music, group B listened to instrumental jazz, and group C spent the same amount of time in silence. All subjects were given a standard cognitive reasoning test before and after being exposed to the treatment of interest. In this experiment, the independent variable was _____ and the dependent variable was _____ .

   (a) group C; groups A and B
   (b) the music and silent conditions; scores on the pretest and posttest
   (c) Groups A and B; group C
   (d) scores on the prest and posttest; the music and silent conditions

8. In the above experiment, participants were randomly assigned to one of three conditions. The purpose of random assignment is to

   (a) increase the probability that the same number of participants end up in each condition.
   (b) increase the likelihood that the participants are representative of people in general.
   (c) decrease the probability of expectancy effects.
   (d) reduce the possibility of bias and ensure that differences among participants are spread out across all experimental conditions.

9. Neither the researchers nor the participants in a study examining the effects of marijuana on memory are aware of who actually received the active ingredient and who were given a placebo. This study involves the use of

   (a) replication.
   (b) the single-blind procedure.
   (c) the double-blind procedure.
   (d) correlational techniques.

10. Researchers using a form of descriptive research have found that the larger a person's line of credit, the more money he or she is likely to owe. The researchers have found _____ between the size of a credit line and the amount of debt.

   (a) a positive correlation
   (b) a negative correlation
   (c) an illusory correlation
   (d) a zero correlation

11. Mary is interviewed in depth, and her friends, family, and coworkers are contacted for further information. She also takes a number of psychological tests, and her behavior in various situations is observed. This is an example of
    (a) a survey.
    (b) correlational research.
    (c) the case study method.
    (d) experimental research.

12. In an attempt to predict the winner in the next election, The Kneed to Know Kompany contacts a randomly selected representative sample of the voting population and questions them about their voting plans. This is an example of
    (a) correlational research.
    (b) a survey.
    (c) the case study method.
    (d) experimental research.

13. Mr. and Mrs. Drachoola hang strings of garlic in their kitchen because they believe that garlic keeps away vampires. When asked if it works, they reply "Absolutely; we've never had a single vampire in the house!" The Drachoola's mistaken belief that the two factors, garlic and vampires, are related best illustrates
    (a) a strong positive correlation.
    (b) a strong negative correlation.
    (c) an illusory correlation.
    (d) the power of paranormal phenomena.

14. According to Culture and Human Behavior 1.1, ethnocentrism is
    (a) the tendency to use one's own culture as the standard for judging other cultures.
    (b) introspective, self-centered analysis.
    (c) much more common in individualistic cultures than in collectivistic cultures.
    (d) much more common in collectivistic cultures than in individualistic cultures.

15. When evaluating claims made in the media about psychology-related topics, the Application makes the point that
    (a) skepticism is the rule, not the exception, in science.
    (b) there is no way to sort out true claims from false claims.
    (c) testimonials are the most reliable source of information.
    (d) correlational research is the most valid type of research because it can clearly establish cause-and-effect relationships between two variables.

Progress Test 3

After you have checked your understanding of the material in Progress Tests 1 and 2 and have done a complete chapter review with special focus on any areas of weakness, you are ready to assess your knowledge on Progress Test 3. Check your answers. If you make a mistake, review your notes and the relevant section of the study guide and, if necessary, review the appropriate part of your textbook.

1. An emphasis on the physical bases of behavior is to the _____ perspective as an emphasis on the influence of culture on behavior is to the _____ perspective.
   (a) biological; evolutionary
   (b) behavioral; humanistic
   (c) biological; cross-cultural
   (d) behavioral; cognitive

2. The evolutionary perspective focuses on _____ , whereas the cognitive perspective emphasizes _____ .
   (a) the physical bases of behavior; environmental influences on behavior
   (b) unconscious influences on behavior and personality; psychological growth and personal potential
   (c) mental processes, information processing, problem solving, and thinking; the influence of culture on behavior
   (d) the application of principles of natural selection to explain psychological processes and phenomena; information processing, problem solving, and thinking

3. Psychologists went to Slogaria after the fall of the dictatorship. There they discovered that many children in orphanages had suffered extreme physical and psychological deprivation. Children from these orphanages, who were later adopted, were matched with a control group of children of the same ages, gender, and so on, who had not experienced deprived conditions. The psychological, emotional, cognitive, and physical development of each group was then measured and monitored over a number of years. This example best illustrates which kind of research?
   (a) correlational research
   (b) naturalistic observation
   (c) a natural experiment
   (d) a double-blind study

4. In the preceding example, the measurements of psychological and physical health taken over the years constitute the
   (a) independent variable.
   (b) expectancy effects.
   (c) dependent variable.
   (d) demand characteristics.

5. In conducting research on the effects of a new memory-enhancing drug, Dr. Simpleton used the double-blind technique. The purpose of doing so was to guard against the possibility that the researcher will inadvertently display
   (a) expectancy effects.
   (b) demand characteristics.
   (c) placebo effects.
   (d) ethnocentrism.

6. In order to learn students' opinions about the recent cutbacks at her university, Gira sent a questionnaire to every twentieth person on the list of currently enrolled students. Gira used the technique of
   (a) replication.　　(c) random sampling.
   (b) meta-analysis.　(d) interviewing.

7. Research showing that students with the highest GPAs study approximately twice as many hours per week as those with the lowest GPAs would indicate that
   (a) there is a positive correlation between study behavior and GPA.
   (b) there is a negative correlation between study behavior and GPA.
   (c) high GPA causes good study behavior.
   (d) that the correlation coefficient would probably exceed +1.50.

8. Ethical principles developed by the American Psychological Association require psychologists to
   (a) always tell the participants the exact nature of the experiment and inform them of the hypothesis that will be tested.
   (b) never, under any circumstances, use deception with potential participants.
   (c) withhold all information about the nature, results, and conclusions of the study because of the confidentiality principle.
   (d) obtain informed consent and voluntary participation of potential participants.

9. Dr. Joyce supports the view that the goal of psychology should be to discover the fundamental principles of learning and that psychologists should focus exclusively on overt behavior rather than on mental processes. Dr. Joyce would be classified as a _____ psychologist.
   (a) behavioral　　(c) psychodynamic
   (b) cognitive　　 (d) humanistic

10. An experimenter found that variable A and variable B had a correlation coefficient of +.55, and variable C and variable D had a correlation coefficient of −.75. She can conclude that
    (a) variables A and B have a stronger correlation than variables C and D.
    (b) variable A causes variable B, but C and D are unrelated.
    (c) variables A and B have a weaker correlation than variables C and D.
    (d) variables A and B are strongly correlated, but C and D have no relationship.

11. If researchers wanted to discover the extent to which education level can be used to predict political preferences, they would most likely use
    (a) correlational research.
    (b) naturalistic observation.
    (c) experimental research.
    (d) a natural experiment.

12. Dr. Angellino stated, "Psychology should study the purpose of behavior and mental processes and how they function to allow organisms to adapt to their environment." It is most likely that Dr. Angellino belonged to the _____ school of psychology
    (a) functionalist
    (b) structuralist
    (c) behaviorist
    (d) psychoanalytic

13. According to In Focus 1.4, animal research is condoned by the American Psychological Association as long as the research
    (a) has an acceptable scientific purpose.
    (b) will likely increase knowledge about behavior.
    (c) will likely increase understanding of the species under study.
    (d) produces results that benefit the health and welfare of humans or other animals.
    (e) will do all of the above.

14. Misha believes that in order for a claim to be proved true, you must be able to identify some type of evidence that would refute the claim or prove that it is false. According to Science Versus Pseudoscience 1.3, Misha is referring to a basic rule of science called
    (a) an operational definition.
    (b) the rule of replication.
    (c) the rule of falsifiability.
    (d) statistical significance.

15. According to Critical Thinking 1.2, critical thinking involves
    (a) minimizing the influence of preconceptions and biases while rationally evaluating evidence.
    (b) determining the conclusions that can be drawn from the evidence.
    (c) considering alternative explanations.
    (d) all of the above.

Answers

Introduction: The Origins of Psychology

1. *Psychology is defined as* the science of behavior and mental processes.
2. *The two disciplines that influenced the emergence of psychology were* philosophy and physiology.
3. *The founder of psychology was* Wilhelm Wundt.
4. *The first two schools of psychology were* structuralism and functionalism, *and the people associated with their beginnings were* Edward B. Titchener and William James.
5. *Structuralism emphasized* studying the most basic components, or structures, of conscious experience using a procedure called introspection. *Functionalism stressed the importance of* how behavior functions to allow people and animals to adapt to their environments.
6. *Psychoanalysis was founded by* Sigmund Freud, *and its main focus was on* the role of unconscious conflicts in determining personality and behavior.
7. *Behaviorism focused on* the scientific study of overt behavior that could be objectively measured and verified *and rejected* the emphasis on consciousness promoted by structuralism and functionalism, as well as Freudian notions of unconscious influences.
8. *The main proponents of behaviorism were* Ivan Pavlov, John. B. Watson, and B. F. Skinner.

9. *Humanistic psychology emphasizes* each person's unique potential for psychological growth and self-direction. *Its two major advocates were* Carl Rogers and Abraham Maslow.

Concept Check 1

1. functionalist
2. psychoanalytic
3. behaviorism; humanistic psychology
4. interactive dualism
5. nature–nurture
6. structuralism

Matching Exercise 1

1. G. Stanley Hall
2. introspection
3. humanistic psychology
4. John B. Watson
5. functionalism
6. psychology
7. interactive dualism
8. Wilhelm Wundt
9. Edward B. Titchener
10. behaviorism
11. Carl Rogers

True/False Test 1

1. F	7. F
2. T	8. T
3. T	9. T
4. T	10. T
5. T	11. F
6. F	

Contemporary Psychology

1. *The seven major perspectives in psychology are* biological, psychodynamic, behavioral, humanistic, cognitive, cross-cultural, and evolutionary.
2. *The main specialty areas in contemporary psychology are* biological, cognitive, experimental, developmental, social, personality, health, educational, school, industrial/organizational, clinical, and counseling psychology.
3. *The difference between a clinical psychologist and a psychiatrist is* that a clinical psychologist

typically has a doctorate in psychology, which includes intensive training in treating people with psychological disorders, and a psychiatrist has a medical degree plus additional specialized training in the treatment of psychological disorders. A psychiatrist also can prescribe medications and other biomedical treatments.

4. *A psychoanalyst is* a clinical psychologist, psychiatrist, or other mental health professional with extensive training in Freud's psychoanalytic method of psychotherapy.

Concept Check 2

1. biological

2. developmental

3. clinical

4. social

5. personality

6. cognitive

7. educational; school

8. health

9. industrial/organizational

10. psychiatrist

Graphic Organizer 1

PERSPECTIVE	SPECIALTY
1. humanistic	developmental
2. behavioral	industrial/organizational
3. cognitive	educational
4. biological	psychiatrist
5. cross-cultural	social
6. psychodynamic	personality
7. cognitive	health
8. behavioral	experimental
9. evolutionary	social

Graphic Organizer 2

Origins of Psychology, First Schools, and Key Figures

1.

<u>Philosophy</u> Aristotle René Descartes	and	<u>Physiology</u> Hermann von Helmholtz

2.

Wilhelm Wundt; 1879

3.

<u>Structuralism</u>
Edward B. Titchener

4.

<u>Functionalism</u>
William James
G. Stanley Hall
Mary Whiton Calkins
Margaret Floy Washburn

5.

<u>Behaviorism</u> Ivan Pavlov John B. Watson B. F. Skinner	<u>Psychoanalysis</u> Sigmund Freud

6.

<u>Humanistic Psychology</u>
Carl Rogers
Abraham Maslow

Matching Exercise 2

1. clinical psychologist
2. developmental psychology
3. psychiatrist
4. educational psychology
5. experimental psychology
6. perspective
7. specialty area
8. culture
9. cognitive psychology
10. Charles Darwin
11. personality psychology
12. behavioral perspective
13. ethnocentrism
14. biological perspective
15. cross-cultural psychology
16. phobia
17. natural selection

True/False Test 2

1. T	8. T	15.	T
2. T	9. F	16.	T
3. F	10. F	17.	T
4. T	11. F		
5. T	12. F		
6. T	13. T		
7. F	14. T		

The Scientific Method

1. *The four basic goals of psychology are to* describe, explain, predict, and control or influence behavior and mental processes.

2. *The scientific method refers to* a set of assumptions, attitudes, and procedures that guide researchers in creating questions to investigate, in generating evidence, and in drawing conclusions.

3. *Psychologists are guided by the basic assumptions that* all events are lawful, that behavior and mental processes follow consistent patterns, that events are explainable, and that behavior and mental processes have a cause or causes that can be understood through careful systematic study.

4. *Psychologists share a set of attitudes, including* open-mindedness, scientific skepticism, caution in making claims, and a willingness to critically evaluate the evidence for new findings.

5. *Empirical evidence refers to* evidence that is the result of objective observation, measurement, and experimentation. *The four basic steps of the scientific method are* formulate a specific question that can be tested, design a study to collect relevant data, analyze the data to arrive at conclusions, and, finally, report the results.

6. *A theory is* a tentative explanation that tries to account for diverse findings. *It is different from a hypothesis*—a specific question or prediction to be tested—in that a theory integrates and summarizes a large number of findings and observations and often generates predictions and new hypotheses that can be tested by further research.

7. *The role of statistics in psychological research is to* enable researchers to summarize, analyze, and draw conclusions about the data they have collected.

8. *Theories can evolve and change because they reflect the* self-correcting nature of the scientific enterprise; when new research findings challenge established ways of thinking about a phenomenon, theories are expanded, modified, or even replaced.

Concept Check 3

1. experimental (in a natural setting)
2. hypothesis
3. statistics
4. 4; reporting her findings

Matching Exercise 3

1. meta-analysis
2. replicate
3. scientific method
4. hypothesis
5. operational definition
6. experimental method
7. statistics

True/False Test 3

1. F	4. T
2. T	5. T
3. T	6. T

Descriptive Methods

1. *Descriptive methods are* scientific procedures that involve systematically observing behavior in order to describe the relationship among behaviors and events.

2. *Naturalistic observation involves the* systematic observation and recording of behaviors as they occur in their natural settings.

3. *A case study is* an intensive, in-depth investigation of a single individual or event. *Case studies are typically used to* develop a complete profile of a psychotherapy client and to investigate rare, unusual, or extreme conditions.

4. *In the survey method, the researcher designs a* questionnaire or conducts an interview designed to investigate the opinion, behaviors, or characteristics of a particular group.

5. *Researchers ensure that their sample closely parallels the population of interest by* selecting a representative sample that matches the larger group on relevant characteristics, such as age, sex, race, marital status, and educational level.

6. *Random selection refers to* the process in which subjects are selected randomly from a group such that every member has an equal chance of being included in the study. *It is important because* it ensures that the sample is representative of the larger population being studied on relevant characteristics.

7. *Correlational studies show* how strongly two factors, or variables, are related to one another and are used for making predictions. *They are limited because* they cannot be used to demonstrate cause-and-effect relationships (experimental research is used to do that).

8. *The correlation coefficient is* a numerical indication of the magnitude and direction of the relationship between two variables; it always falls in the range from −1.00 to +1.00. *The correlation coefficient has two parts:* the number indicates the strength of the relationship (the bigger the number, the stronger the relationship) and the sign (+ or −) indicates the direction of the relationship between the two variables.

9. *A positive correlation is one in which* the two factors vary in the same direction, increasing together or decreasing together. *A negative correlation is one in which* the two variables move in opposite directions, one increasing and the other decreasing.

Concept Check 4

1. more; less
2. survey; sample; randomly
3. naturalistic observation
4. positive
5. case study
6. positive; negative

Graphic Organizer 3

1. positive; positive
2. negative; negative
3. high; high; low; low
4. high, low, low; high

Matching Exercise 4

1. survey
2. descriptive methods
3. sample
4. representative sample
5. correlational study
6. random selection
7. case study research

True/False Test 4

1. T	4. T
2. F	5. F
3. T	6. T

The Experimental Method

1. *The experimental method of investigation is used to* demonstrate cause-and-effect relationships by purposely manipulating one variable and observing the effect on a second variable.

2. *The independent variable is the* purposely manipulated factor thought to produce change (also referred to as the treatment of interest). *The dependent variable is the* factor that is observed and measured for change as a result of the manipulation of the independent variable in an experiment.

3. *Random assignment means that* all participants in the study have an equal chance of being assigned to any of the groups or conditions in an experiment. *It helps ensure that* potential differences among participants are spread out across all experimental conditions and that assignment is done in an unbiased manner.

4. *The experimental group (or experimental condition) is* the group of participants that is exposed to the independent variable or treatment of interest. *The control group (or control condition) is* the group of participants that is not exposed to the independent variable or treatment of interest and against which the experimental group is compared. *The placebo control group is* a group of participants that are exposed to an inert substance or treatment with no known effects; this group serves as a check for expectancy effects.

5. *Natural experiments are different from laboratory experiments in that* researchers are able to study phenomena that would be impossible or unethical to duplicate in a controlled laboratory setting by taking advantage of naturally occurring events that involve such factors of interest.

6. *A double-blind study is one in which* neither the participants nor the researcher who interacts with the participants is aware of the treatment or condition to which the participants have been assigned. *It is used to* guard against the possibility that the researcher will display subtle cues or signals that communicate what is expected from the participants (demand characteristics).

7. *Five key provisions of the APA ethical guidelines regulating research with human participants are*
   (a) Informed consent and voluntary participation of subjects is required.
   (b) Students must be given the option of not participating in research involving credits without being penalized in any way.
   (c) Psychologists are restricted in their use of deception.
   (d) All records must be kept confidential.
   (e) Participants must be allowed the opportunity to obtain information about the study once it is completed and must be debriefed about the nature of their involvement in the study.

Concept Check 5

1. the drug and placebo conditions (more precisely, THC, the active ingredient in marijuana, and the harmless, inert substance constitute the independent variable)

2. participants' scores on the memory tests

3. experimental; placebo control

4. double-blind; expectancy effects and demand characteristics

5. random assignment

Matching Exercise 5

1. single-blind study
2. experimental method
3. dependent variable
4. paranormal phenomena
5. expectancy effects (placebo effects)
6. control group
7. demand characteristics
8. placebo
9. pseudoscience

True/False Test 5

1. T	5. T
2. T	6. T
3. T	7. T
4. T	8. T

Something to Think About

1. (a) Psychology tackles questions that people have grappled with for thousands of years. Instead of using anecdotal evidence, intuition, philosophical discussion, and speculation, psychology uses the scientific method to answer questions that are amenable to empirical testing. It uses four steps in generating empirical evidence. First, questions are formulated into testable hypotheses; next, the study is designed and the data are collected, then statistical analyses are prepared and conclusions are drawn, and finally, the results are reported. Psychologists operationally define all variables and precisely specify the method of measurement or manipulation. Following this process, they can have more confidence in the reliability and validity of their results.

(b) The difference between clinical psychologists and psychiatrists is training. Clinical psychologists have a doctorate in psychology and extensive training in the assessment, diagnosis, and treatment of people with psychological disorders. Psychiatrists, on the other hand, have an M.D. plus years of training in dealing with people with psychological disorders; because of their medical qualifications, they can prescribe drugs and order medical procedures such as electroshock therapy. A psychoanalyst can be a clinical psychologist, psychiatrist, or other mental health professional, who has extensive training in Freud's psychoanalytic method of psychotherapy.

2. Many of the questions of students coming into psychology can be tested empirically, and quite a few have, in fact, been answered. For example, how would you test the claim that subliminal messages can influence our behavior? It turns out that psychologists have done just that.

The essence of their experimental design was the use of two subliminal tapes, one claiming to improve self-esteem and the other claiming to improve memory. They randomly assigned subjects to one of four groups and gave them all pretests on measures of self-esteem and memory. Members of group 1 were given the memory tape to listen to for a set period of time and told it would help improve their memory; those in group 2 were given the same memory tape but were told it would improve their self-esteem. (Remember, on subliminal tapes you can't, by definition, hear the messages, only the surface music.) Group 3 was given the self-esteem tape and told it would improve self-esteem, and group 4 was given the same self-esteem tape but were told that it would improve memory. All subjects listened to their respective tapes for exactly the same length of time, at the same times of the day, etc. Later they were given another test of self-esteem and memory. The pretest and posttest scores for all conditions were compared.

What do you think the results showed? If you believe the claims of those who promote the power of subliminal tapes, then groups 1 and 3 should have shown significant improvement in memory and self-esteem scores, respectively. And, one would assume, if the results were not due to some placebo effect, then groups 2 and 4 should have shown some change—memory improvement for group 2 and self-esteem

improvement for group 4—because that is what they were actually exposed to.

The results were clear and unequivocal: there was no improvement in any of the groups between their pretest and posttest scores. In contrast to the claims of their promoters, subliminal tapes were shown to be of no value in improving memory or self-esteem.

This is a good example of how useful the scientific method is in answering questions of a psychological nature. Can you apply what you know about scientific psychology to answer other questions you may have?

Progress Test 1

1. d	6. d	11. a
2. d	7. b	12. d
3. b	8. d	13. a
4. c	9. a	14. a
5. d	10. c	15. b

Progress Test 2

1. a	6. a	11. c
2. c	7. b	12. b
3. c	8. d	13. c
4. a	9. c	14. a
5. b	10. a	15. a

Progress Test 3

1. c	6. c	11. a
2. d	7. a	12. a
3. c	8. d	13. e
4. c	9. a	14. c
5. b	10. c	15. d

Neuroscience and Behavior

PREVIEW

Reading the section below first will give you a general sense of the chapter's contents and an initial introduction to some of the major concepts and terms. This will prime you for what you are about to read and help you to develop a "cognitive map" that will guide your study of the material in this chapter. Likewise, reading the **preview questions** at the beginning of each major section will improve your ability to understand, learn, and retain the information.

CHAPTER 2 . . . AT A GLANCE

Chapter 2 first outlines the scope and diversity of biological psychology, and notes that it is one of the scientific disciplines that makes important contributions to neuroscience. Biological psychologists (or biopsychologists) investigate the physical processes underlying psychological experiences, mental processes, and behavior. The first section describes the structure and functions of the neuron. Next, neural activation, synaptic transmission, and the role of neurotransmitters are outlined. The functions and effects of several neurotransmitters are discussed.

The next section discusses the structures and functions of the divisions of the nervous system: the central nervous system, which consists of the brain and spinal cord; and the peripheral nervous system, with its two main subdivisions, the somatic and autonomic nervous systems. The sympathetic and parasympathetic systems, which make up the autonomic nervous system, are described. This section ends by focusing on the endocrine system, its glands, and its chemical messengers, called hormones.

The section on the brain begins with a Focus on Neuroscience that describes how the brain's complex operations are studied—through case studies, EEG, MRI, PET scans, and fMRI. A guided tour of the brain takes you through the regions of the hindbrain, midbrain, and forebrain, including their structures and functions. The different roles of the four lobes of the brain (temporal, occipital, parietal, and frontal) are explained, and the functions of forebrain structures in the limbic system—the thalamus, hypothalamus, hippocampus, and amygdala—are described.

The chapter ends with a discussion of hemispheric specialization and the part played by split-brain patients in discovering the specialized functions of the brain's hemispheres.

Introduction: Neuroscience and Behavior

Preview Questions

Consider the following questions as you study this section of the chapter.

- What is biological psychology?
- What is neuroscience?
- What systems and structures are of interest to biopsychologists?

*Read the section "Introduction: Neuroscience and Behavior" and **write** your answers to the following.*

1. Biological psychology is _____

   _____

2. Neuroscience is _____

   _____

   _____

3. The systems and structures that are of interest to biopsychologists are _____

   _____

The Neuron: The Basic Unit of Communication

Preview Questions

Consider the following questions as you study this section of the chapter.

- How is information in the nervous system transmitted?
- What are glial cells, and what are the three main types of neurons?
- What are the basic components of the neuron, and what are their functions?
- How is information communicated within and between neurons?
- What are some common neurotransmitters, and what are their primary roles?
- How can drugs affect synaptic transmission?

*Read the section "The Neuron: The Basic Unit of Communication" and **write** your answers to the following:*

1. Information is transmitted in the nervous system by the three basic types of neurons:

   _____

   _____

2. Glial cells are _____

   _____

3. The basic components of the neuron and their functions are _____

   _____

   _____

   _____

   _____

   _____

4. Within the neuron, information is communicated (describe the complete process) _____

   _____

   _____

   _____

   _____

   _____

   _____

   _____

5. Communication between neurons may be electrical or chemical. Chemically, it involves

   _____

   _____

   _____

6. Some important neurotransmitters (and their primary roles) are _____

   _____

   _____

   _____

   _____

   _____

   _____

7. Drugs can affect synaptic transmission by _____

   _____

   _____

   _____

   _____

After you have carefully studied the preceding sections, complete the following exercises.

Concept Check 1

Read the following and decide which neurotransmitter is most likely involved:

1. Mrs. Cartwright's memory functions have deteriorated, and she has been diagnosed as suffering from Alzheimer's disease.

   _____

2. The painkilling effect of the opiate, morphine, no longer worked after Hiu took the drug _____ , which blocked the opiate receptor sites in his brain.

3. When Gerald was bitten by a black widow spider, he suffered severe, uncontrollable muscle spasms and had great difficulty breathing.

   _____

4. When Melanie was suffering from severe depression, her doctor prescribed Prozac, which he said would help alleviate the symptoms of her mood disorder by increasing the availability of a particular neurotransmitter.

   _____

5. Patients afflicted with Parkinson's disease suffer from rigidity, muscle tremors, and poor balance and have trouble initiating movements. These symptoms are believed to result from diminished production of the neurotransmitter

   _____ .

6. George suffers from chronic anxiety. His doctor has prescribed the antianxiety drug Valium because it works by increasing _____ , which inhibits action potentials and slows brain activity.

7. Mr. Lee had his back pain treated by an ancient Chinese medical technique called acupuncture. Inserting needles in various parts of his body may have reduced his perception of pain because of the involvement of

   _____ .

8. After being injected with the drug curare, a rat becomes paralyzed. This occurred because curare mimics a neurotransmitter called _____ and blocks its receptor sites.

Graphic Organizer 1

Identify the parts of the neuron in the figure below:

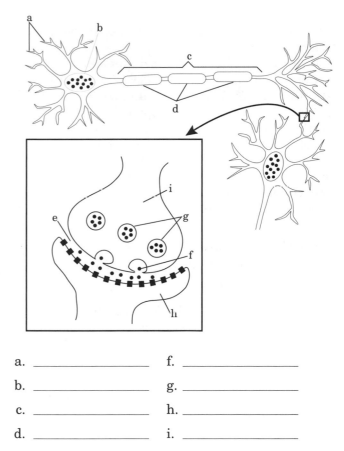

a. _____   f. _____

b. _____   g. _____

c. _____   h. _____

d. _____   i. _____

e. _____

Review of Terms and Concepts 1

Use the terms in this list to complete the Matching Test, then to help you answer the True/False items correctly.

biological psychology
  (biopsychology)
neuroscience
neuron
glial cells
sensory neuron
motor neuron
interneuron
cell body
dendrites
axon
nodes of Ranvier (nodes)
multiple sclerosis
myelin sheath
action potential
stimulus threshold
polarized
resting potential
all-or-none law
refractory period
synapse
presynaptic neuron/
  postsynaptic neuron

synaptic gap
axon terminals
synaptic vesicles
neurotransmitter
synaptic transmission
reuptake
excitatory and
  inhibitory messages
acetylcholine
Alzheimer's disease
dopamine
Parkinson's disease
serotonin
norepinephrine
GABA (gamma-
  amniobutyric acid)
opiates
endorphins
acupuncture
curare
naloxone

Matching Exercise

Match the appropriate term from the list with its definition or description.

1. _____ Highly specialized cell that communicates information in electrical and chemical form.

2. _____ Neurotransmitter that usually communicates an inhibitory message.

3. _____ Neurotransmitters that regulate pain perception.

4. _____ Small gaps that separate segments of the myelin sheath that surrounds the axons of many neurons

5. _____ Neurotransmitter that is involved in sleep, moods, and emotional states, including depression.

6. _____ The part of a neuron that contains the nucleus.

7. _____ Disease that involves the degeneration of patches of the myelin sheath that surrounds many neurons and causes such symptoms as muscular weakness, loss of coordination, and disturbances in speech and vision.

8. _____ Chemical messenger manufactured in the synaptic vesicles of a neuron.

9. _____ Neural condition in which the axon's interior is more negatively charged than the exterior fluid surrounding it, that occurs while the neuron is waiting for sufficient stimulation to activate it.

10. _____ The point of communication between two neurons.

11. _____ Tiny pouches, or sacs, in the axon terminals that contain chemicals called neurotransmitters.

12. _____ Neurotransmitter involved in the regulation of bodily movements and pleasurable or rewarding sensations.

13. _____ Minimum level of stimulation required to activate a particular neuron.

14. _____ The scientific study of the nervous system.

15. _____ Time period, lasting a thousandth of a second or less, that follows the action potential and during which the neuron is unable to fire.

16. _____ Disease characterized by progressive loss of memory and deterioration of intellectual functioning, caused by severe depletion of several neurotransmitters, most notably, acetylcholine.

17. _____ Specific group of painkilling drugs derived from the opium poppy that includes morphine, heroin, and codeine.

18. _____ Ancient Chinese medical technique that involves inserting needles at various locations in the body.

19. _____ Drug that eliminates the effects of both endorphins and opiates by blocking opiate receptor sites.

20. _____ Disease characterized by rigidity, muscle tremors, poor balance, and difficulty in initiating movements, caused by the degeneration of neurons in one brain area that produce dopamine.

True/False Test

Indicate whether each statement is true or false by placing T or F in the blank space next to each item.

1. ____ Norepinephrine is involved in activation of neurons throughout the brain, is critical in the body's response to danger, and is implicated in learning and memory retrieval.

2. ____ Biological psychology (biopsychology) is the specialized branch of psychology that studies the relationship between behavior and bodily processes and systems.

3. ____ Reuptake is the process in which neurotransmitters are released by one neuron, cross the synaptic gap, and affect adjoining neurons.

4. ____ Glial cells assist neurons by providing structural support, nutrition, and removal of cell wastes; they also enhance the speed of communication between neurons by manufacturing myelin.

5. ____ Interneurons communicate information from one neuron to the next.

6. ____ Synaptic transmission is the process by which neurotransmitter molecules detach from a postsynaptic neuron and are reabsorbed by a presynaptic neuron so that they can be recycled and used again.

7. ____ Axon terminals are branches at the end of the axon that contain tiny pouches, or sacs, called synaptic vesicles.

8. ____ Neurons that communicate information to the brain from specialized receptor cells in sense organs and internal organs are called motor neurons.

9. ____ Dendrites are multiple short fibers that extend from the neuron's cell body and receive information from other neurons or from sensory receptor cells.

10. ____ The myelin sheath is a white, fatty covering wrapped around the axons of some neurons that increases their speed of communication.

11. ____ The resting potential is a brief electrical impulse by which information is transmitted along the axon of a neuron.

12. ____ Acetylcholine is a neurotransmitter that produces muscle contractions and is involved in memory functions.

13. ____ The synaptic gap is a tiny space between the axon terminal of one neuron and the dendrite of an adjoining neuron.

14. ____ The all-or-none law states that either a neuron is sufficiently stimulated and an action potential occurs or a neuron is not sufficiently stimulated and an action potential does not occur.

15. ____ Sensory neurons are a type of neuron that signal muscles to contract or relax.

16. ____ The action potential is a state in which a neuron is prepared to activate and communicate its message if it receives sufficient stimulation.

17. ____ The long, fluid-filled tube that carries a neuron's messages to other body areas is called the axon.

18. ____ The message sending neuron is called the presynaptic neuron and the message receiving neuron is called the postsynaptic neuron.

19. ____ The drug curare mimics acetylcholine and blocks acetylcholine receptor sites, causing almost instantaneous paralysis.

20. ____ An excitatory message increases the likelihood that the postsynaptic neuron will activate, and an inhibitory message decreases the likelihood that the postsynaptic neuron will activate.

Check your answers and review any areas of weakness before going on to the next section.

The Nervous System and the Endocrine System: Communication Throughout the Body

Preview Questions

Consider the following questions as you study this section of the chapter.

- What are the two main divisions of the nervous system, and what does each include?

- What are spinal reflexes?

- What are the key components of the peripheral nervous system, and what are their functions?

- What is the endocrine system, and how does it transmit information?

- How does the endocrine system interact with the nervous system?

- What are the specific functions of the pituitary gland and the adrenal glands?

*Read the section "The Nervous System and the Endocrine System: Communication Throughout the Body" and **write** your answers to the following:*

1. The two main divisions of the nervous system and their components are _____

_____

_____

2. Spinal reflexes are _____
_____

3. The key components of the peripheral nervous system and their functions are_____
_____
_____
_____
_____

4. The two branches of the autonomic nervous system and their functions are _____
_____
_____
_____
_____

5. The endocrine system is made up of_____
_____
_____

6. The endocrine system interacts with the nervous system in a number of ways: _____
_____
_____
_____
_____
_____
_____
_____

7. The hypothalamus serves as _____
_____
_____

8. The pituitary gland's hormones _____
_____
_____

The adrenal glands (adrenal cortex and adrenal medulla) are involved in _____
_____
_____

After you have carefully studied the preceding section, complete the following exercises.

Concept Check 2

Read the following and complete the sentence with the correct term:

1. Allison accidentally touched a hot stove top and immediately withdrew her hand before becoming consciously aware of the sensation or movement. She was able to do this because of her
_____ .

2. Always a daredevil, Miguel dived off the cliff into the river below. Unfortunately, he landed on his head and is now paralyzed from the shoulders down. Apart from his paralysis, all his mental functions are intact, and he is attempting to complete his college degree. His present inability to move the lower part of his body is a result of permanent damage to his
_____ .

3. At home alone late one night, Jason had just finished watching the most frightening video he had ever seen when there was a sudden knock on the door. His heart rate suddenly increased, his breathing accelerated, and he began to sweat. These physiological changes were most likely triggered by his
_____ .

4. When Jason answered the door, he discovered it was only the pizza delivery, and before long he calmed down and his blood pressure, heart rate, and breathing returned to their normal state. These physical reactions were most likely regulated by his _____ .

5. Jason's initial reaction to the knock on the door (his fight-or-flight response) resulted in his adrenal glands (in particular, the adrenal medulla) releasing the two hormones
_____ and _____ .

6. When Munro tripped and fell headlong down the flight of stairs, he suffered only minor scrapes and bruises. His brain and spinal cord were protected from serious damage because they are suspended in _____ .

7. When Jannelle breast-feeds her baby, there is a complex interaction among the nervous system, the endocrine system, and behavior. The production of prolactin, which stimulates milk production, and oxytocin, which produces the let-down reflex, is a function of the _____ gland, which is under the direction of a brain structure called the _____ .

8. Tejinder read her book for about ten minutes after getting into bed. When she began to feel sleepy, she turned off the light, falling asleep soon after that. It is very likely that her _____ gland was involved in regulation of the hormone _____ that controls sleep and wakefulness.

9. Before entering ninth grade, Kristofer had to have most of his clothes replaced because he had grown almost five inches since finishing eighth grade the previous spring. This relatively sudden increase in height was probably the result of his _____ gland producing _____ .

10. In addition, Kristofer developed some secondary sex characteristics as a result of the pituitary gland secreting hormones called _____ , which increase levels of the male sex hormone _____ .

11. As Estelle was searching for some change in her purse she accidentally dropped her keys on the floor. She quickly reached down, retrieved her keys, and put them back in her purse. This voluntary reaction involved _____ (motor/sensory) signals that were communicated to her muscles via the _____ (somatic/autonomic) nervous system.

12. While Randolf is relaxing on the couch after lunch, his heart rate, blood pressure, breathing, and digestion, all are functioning without any conscious effort on his part. This is because a subdivision of the _____ nervous system called the _____ regulates these involuntary functions.

Graphic Organizer 2

Mapping the Divisions and Functions of the Nervous System

In the following organizational chart of the nervous system, write the name of each division and choose the appropriate function of each from the list below

(e.g., A is the appropriate choice for the nervous system).

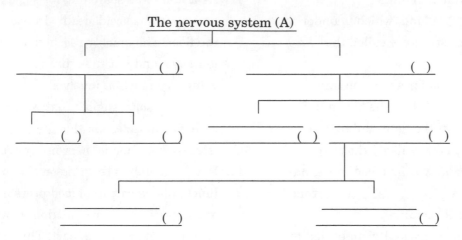

The nervous system (A)

A. Complex, organized communication system of nerves and neurons.
B. Maintains normal bodily functions and conserves physical resources.
C. Produces rapid physical changes to perceived threats and emergencies.
D. Includes all nerves lying outside the central nervous system.
E. Communicates sensory and motor information.
F. Consists of the brain and the spinal cord.
G. Regulates involuntary functions such as heartbeat and respiration.
H. Main organ of the nervous system; made up of billions of neurons.
I. System that handles both incoming and outgoing messages to and from the brain.

prolactin
oxytocin
adrenal glands
adrenal cortex
adrenal medulla
immune system
gonads

gonadotrophins
testosterone, estrogen, and progesterone
thyroid gland
pancreas
pineal gland
melatonin

Review of Terms and Concepts 2

Use the terms in this list to complete the Matching Test, then to help you answer the True/False items correctly.

nervous system
nerves
central nervous system
cerebrospinal fluid
spinal reflexes
peripheral nervous system
somatic nervous system
autonomic nervous system

sympathetic nervous system
parasympathetic nervous system
fight-or-flight response
endocrine system
hormones
hypothalamus
pituitary gland
growth hormone

Matching Exercise

Match the appropriate term with its definition or description.

1. _____ Bundles of neuron axons that carry information in the peripheral nervous system.

2. _____ System composed of glands located throughout the body that secrete hormones into the bloodstream.

3. _____ Simple, automatic behaviors that are processed in the spinal cord without any brain involvement.

4. _____ Pair of endocrine glands that are involved in the human stress response.

5. _____ Fluid in which the brain and spinal cord are suspended that protects them from being jarred.

6. _____ Brain structure that regulates the release of hormones by the pituitary gland.

7. _____ Hormone secreted by the pituitary gland that stimulates normal skeletal growth during childhood.

8. _____ Division of the nervous system that includes all the nerves lying outside the central nervous system.

9. _____ In nursing mothers, the hormone produced by the pituitary gland that stimulates milk production.

10. _____ Endocrine gland that controls metabolism.

11. _____ Endocrine glands (ovaries in females and testes in males) that secrete hormones that regulate sexual characteristics and reproductive processes.

12. _____ Hormone involved in the regulation of sleep and wakefulness.

13. _____ Endocrine gland that produces melatonin.

14. _____ Hormones secreted by the pituitary gland, which regulate the production of sex hormones by the gonads.

15. _____ Body's defense system against invading viruses and bacteria.

True/False Test

Indicate whether each statement is true or false by placing T or F in the blank space next to each item.

1. ____ The nervous system is the primary internal communication network of the body; it is divided into the central nervous system and the peripheral nervous system.

2. ____ The central nervous system is a major division of the nervous system and consists of the brain and the spinal cord.

3. ____ The pituitary gland is an endocrine gland attached to the base of the brain which secretes hormones that affect the function of other glands as well as hormones that act directly on physical processes.

4. ____ The fight-or-flight response refers to physiological changes such as increased heart rate, accelerated breathing, dry mouth, and perspiration that occur in response to perceived threats or danger.

5. ____ The parasympathetic nervous system is a branch of the autonomic nervous system that produces rapid physical arousal in response to perceived emergencies or threats.

6. ____ Hormones are chemical messengers that are secreted into the bloodstream by endocrine glands.

7. ____ The somatic nervous system is a subdivison of the peripheral nervous system that regulates involuntary functions such as heartbeat, digestion, breathing, and blood pressure.

8. ____ The adrenal medulla is the inner portion of the adrenal glands that secretes epinephrine and norepinephrine.

9. ____ The branch of the autonomic nervous system that maintains normal bodily functions and conserves the body's physical resources is called the sympathetic nervous system.

10. ____ The adrenal cortex is the outer portion of the adrenal glands.

11. ____ The autonomic nervous system is a subdivision of the peripheral nervous system that communicates sensory information to the central nervous system and carries motor messages from the central nervous system to the muscles.

12. ____ Oxytocin is a hormone secreted by the pituitary gland that produces the let down reflex, in which stored milk is "let down" into the nipple.

13. ____ Testosterone, estrogen, and progesterone are sex hormones, regulated by the release of gonadotrophins, that have a profound effect on sexual development, reproduction, and sexual behavior.

14. ____ The pancreas regulates blood sugar levels and plays a key role in hunger and eating.

Check your answers and review any areas of weakness before going on to the next section.

A Guided Tour of the Brain

Preview Questions

Consider the following questions as you study this section of the chapter.

- Why have scientists used case studies of brain-damaged people to study the brain?
- How has the production of *lesions* and the use of electrical stimulation been useful in advancing knowledge of the brain?
- (Focus on Neuroscience) What is cognitive neuroscience?

- (Focus on Neuroscience) What are main imaging techniques used to study the brain, and what are some limitations of this technology?
- How does the brain develop, and what are its three main divisions?
- What are the key structures of the hindbrain and midbrain, and what functions are associated with each structure?
- What are the two main structures of the forebrain, and what functions have been identified with each of the four lobes of the cerebral cortex?
- What are the key limbic system structures, and what role do they play in behavior?

Read the section "A Guided Tour of the Brain" and **write** *your answers to the following:*

1. Scientists used case studies to study the brain because _____

_____

_____

_____

2. The production of lesions and electrically stimulating areas of the brain have been useful because _____

_____

_____

_____

3. (Focus on Neuroscience) Cognitive neuroscience is _____

_____

_____

4. (Focus on Neuroscience) The major imaging techniques used to study the brain are _____

_____

_____

_____

_____

_____

5. (Focus on Neuroscience) Limitations of this technology are as follows: _____

_____

_____

_____

_____

6. The brain develops from _____

_____

_____

_____

7. The three divisions of the developing brain are

_____

_____

8. The key structures of the hindbrain and their functions are _____

_____

_____

_____

_____

9. The midbrain contains _____

_____

10. The forebrain includes _____

_____

11. The four lobes and their functions are _____

_____

_____

_____

_____

12. The main structures of the limbic system and their functions are _____

_____

_____

_____

_____

_____

After you have carefully studied the preceding sections, complete the following exercises.

Concept Check 3

Decide which area of the brain is most likely involved in each of the following.

1. Marcel had a stroke on the *right* side of his brain in an area that controls motor movement; as a result, he has trouble moving limbs on the *left* side of his body. This is because incoming sensory messages and outgoing motor messages cross over at the _____ level of the brain.

2. If this area of your brain was electrically stimulated while you were fast asleep, you would wake up instantly. _____

3. After Larry was hit in the head by a baseball, his movements became jerky and uncoordinated, and he could no longer type or play his guitar. _____

4. In the third round of a boxing match Bruno caught a right hook that snapped his head back; when he hit the canvas, his breathing stopped. _____

5. Ever since his automobile accident six months ago, Sam watches the same video day after day and each time responds to it as though he had never seen it before. All his other sensory functions appear to be intact, but it is clear that one brain area was damaged in the accident that prevents him from forming new memories.

   _____

6. Because of a tumor growing in her brain, Janna has lost her sense of taste, sight, hearing, and touch, but not her sense of smell. The area of the brain involved in regulating these behaviors is the _____ .

7. Following an industrial accident, Harinder has lost his ability to feel any sensation on the right side of his body. It is most likely that the accident damaged his _____ lobe.

8. Mr. Endo has been diagnosed with Parkinson's disease. Many of his movement-related symptoms are associated with the degeneration of dopamine-producing neurons in a midbrain structure called the _____ .

9. When researchers electrically stimulated a forebrain structure in a cat, its back arched, its fur fluffed, and it showed all the characteristic feline signs of rage and anger. The part of the cat's limbic system that was stimulated was the

   _____ .

10. Morgana believes that you can tell a lot about a man's personlity, character, and mental ability simply by examining the size and shape of his skull. Morgana's views are most like those of the popular nineteenth-century pseudoscience _____ , which, strangely enough, triggered scientific interest in the notion that specific psychological and mental functions are located or localized in specific brain areas, an idea called _____ .

11. Because of severe and persistent headaches, Dou Mu was given a number of tests, one of which involved having electrodes placed on various parts of her scalp. In this instance, her doctors are using a machine called the

    _____ to monitor and measure the electrical activity in her brain.

12. In her experimental research on brain function and mental activity, Dr. Ligeralde makes use of techniques such as the PET scan, MRI, and fMRI. She works in the relatively new field that incorporates aspects of psychology, neuroscience, and computer science called

    _____ .

13. During her ballet class, Emmalee executed a number of difficult moves, including a series of pirouettes on point. She is able to accomplish this difficult dance routine because somatosensory information about her muscles and joints, and the position of her arms and legs, are relayed to the _____ lobe in her brain.

Graphic Organizer 3

Chart Diagram Exercise: The Key Structures of the Limbic System

To help you develop the technique of creating your own graphic organizers, we encourage you to try to locate the structures listed below in the following outline of a brain. Then, on a separate piece of paper, write a description of each structure.

Locate and describe the following:
   (a)   Hypothalamus
   (b)   Thalamus
   (c)   Amygdala
   (d)   Hippocampus

Review of Terms and Concepts 3

Use the terms in this list to complete the Matching Test, then to help you answer the True/False items correctly.

case study
cognitive neuroscience
electroencephalograph
electroencephalogram
  (EEG)
magnetic resonance
  imaging scanner
  (MRI)
positron emission
  tomography (PET
  scan)
functional magnetic
  resonance imaging
  (fMRI)

ventricles
neurogenesis
brainstem
hindbrain
medulla
pons
cerebellum
reticular formation
  (reticular activating
  system)
midbrain
substantia nigra
forebrain (cerebrum)
cerebral cortex

cerebral hemispheres
corpus callosum
temporal lobe
primary auditory cortex
occipital lobe
primary visual cortex
parietal lobe
somatosensory cortex
frontal lobe
primary motor cortex
association areas

prefrontal association
  cortex
limbic system
thalamus
hypothalamus
suprachiasmatic nucleus
  (SCN)
hippocampus
amygdala
phrenology

Matching Exercise

Match the appropriate term with its definition or description.

1. _____ The nearly symmetrical left and right halves of the cerebral cortex.

2. _____ The area on each cerebral hemisphere located above the temporal lobe that processes somatic sensations.

3. _____ Midbrain area involved in motor control and containing a large concentration of dopamine-producing neurons.

4. _____ The part of the temporal lobe that enables hearing.

5. _____ Hindbrain structure that connects the medulla to the two sides of the cerebellum; helps coordinate and integrate movement on each side of the body.

6. _____ Forebrain structure that processes motor information and sensory information from all the senses except smell and relays it to higher brain centers.

7. _____ The part of the occipital lobe that receives information from the eyes.

8. _____ The curved forebrain structure that is part of the limbic system and is involved in learning and forming new memories.

9. _____ Region of the brain made up of the hindbrain and the midbrain.

10. _____ Band of tissue in the frontal lobe on which the movements of different parts of the body are represented.

11. _____ Large association area of the brain, situated in front of the primary motor cortex, that is involved in the planning of voluntary movements.

12. _____ Hindbrain structure that controls vital life functions such as breathing, circulation, heart rate, and digestion.

13. _____ Instrument that produces a graphic record of the brain's electrical activity by using electrodes placed on the scalp.

14. _____ Network of nerve fibers located at the center of the medulla and pons that helps regulate attention, arousal, and sleep.

15. _____ Imaging technique that generates computerized color-coded images of the brain's activity by tracking and measuring the amount of a radioactively tagged substance in various brain areas while the person engages in some kind of mental activity; an invasive procedure that involves injecting the person with the radioactive substance before the scan.

16. _____ Area of the hypothalamus that plays a key role in regulating daily sleep–wake cycles and other rhythms of the body.

17. _____ The development of new neurons.

18. _____ The study of the neural basis of cognitive processes that integrates contributions from psychology, neuroscience, and computer science.

19. _____ Pseudoscience based on the assumption that bumps on the skull reveal personality characteristics and abilities.

True/False Test

Indicate whether each statement is true or false by placing T or F in the blank space next to each item.

1. ____ The frontal lobe is the largest lobe of the cerebral cortex; processes voluntary muscle movement and is involved in thinking, planning, and emotional expression and control.

2. ____ The somatosensory cortex is a band of tissue on the parietal lobe that receives information from touch receptors in different parts of the body.

3. ____ The midbrain is a region at the base of the brain that controls several structures that regulate basic life functions.

4. ____ The cerebellum is an almond-shaped forebrain structure that is part of the limbic system and involved in emotion and memory.

5. ____ The forebrain, the largest and most complex brain region, contains centers for complex behaviors and mental processes.

6. ____ The cerebral cortex is the wrinkled outer portion of the forebrain that contains the most sophisticated brain centers.

7. ____ The amygdala is the large, two-sided hindbrain structure at the back of the brain that is responsible for muscle coordination and maintaining posture and equilibrium.

8. ____ The occipital lobe is a region at the back of each cerebral cortex hemisphere that is the primary receiving area for visual information.

9. ____ The association areas, which make up the bulk of the cerebral cortex and are the regions in which sensory and motor information is combined, produce complex, sophisticated human behaviors.

10. ____ The temporal lobe is an area on each hemisphere that is the primary receiving area for auditory information.

11. ____ The hindbrain is the middle and smallest brain region that is involved in processing auditory and visual sensory information.

12. ____ Magnetic resonance imaging (MRI) is a procedure that generates highly detailed images of the body or brain's internal structures by bombarding them with powerful but harmless magnetic fields; this causes the molecules of the body to create electromagnetic signals, which are analyzed by a computer.

13. ____ The limbic system is a group of forebrain structures that form a border around the brainstem and are involved in emotions, motivation, learning, and memory.

14. ____ The hypothalamus is a peanut-sized forebrain structure that is part of the limbic system and is involved in diverse functions such as eating, drinking, sexual activity, and fear and aggression; it exerts control over the secretion of endocrine hormones by directly influencing the pituitary gland.

15. ____ In the case study, researchers systematically observe and record the behavior of people whose brains have been damaged by illness or injury.

16. ____ Functional magnetic resonance imaging (fMRI) uses the same scanning hardware as an MRI to provide moment-by-moment color-coded images of the brain's ongoing activity by tracking changes in the brain's blood flow and

oxygen levels as the person engages in some kind of mental activity.

17. ____ The thick band of nerve fibers that connects the two cerebral hemispheres, and acts as a communication link between them, is called the corpus callosum.

18. ____ The graphic record of the brain's electrical activity that the electroencephalograph produces is called an electroencephalogram or EEG.

19. ____ Ventricles are the fluid-filled cavities at the core of the fully developed brain.

Check your answers and review any areas of weakness before going on to the next section.

Specialization in the Cerebral Hemispheres

Preview Questions

Consider the following questions as you study this section of the chapter.

- What did Broca and Wernicke contribute to our knowledge of the brain?
- What is lateralization of function?
- What is aphasia, Broca's aphasia, and Wernicke's aphasia?
- What is the split brain-operation, and what did tests on split-brain patients reveal about differences in the abilities of the two hemispheres?
- What are the most important functions of each cerebral hemisphere?

*Read the section "Specialization in the Cerebral Hemispheres" and **write** your answers to the following:*

1. Broca and Wernicke provided the first evidence that _____

    _____

2. Lateralization of function (or lateralization) is

    _____

    _____

3. Aphasia refers to _____

    _____

    Broca's aphasia results in _____

    _____

    _____

Wernicke's aphasia results in _____

_____

_____

4. The split-brain operation involves _____

_____

5. In a specialized procedure, split-brain subjects are directed to focus on a point in the middle of a screen and then_____

    _____

    Split-brain subjects can _____

    _____

    _____

    _____

6. Tests on split-brain patients revealed that the left hemisphere is specialized for _____

    _____

    _____

    and the right hemisphere is specialized for

    _____

    _____

    _____

After you have carefully studied the preceding section, complete the following exercises.

Concept Check 4

Complete the following examples by placing the term right *or* left *in each blank:*

1. A blindfolded split-brain patient would be able to verbally identify an object placed in her _____ hand but not in her _____ hand.

2. When the picture of an apple was flashed to the _____ of the midpoint during an experiment with a split-brain patient, the patient was not able to say what he saw. However, he could draw a picture of the object with his _____ hand.

3. When a swear word was flashed to her _____ hemisphere, a split-brain patient could not say what she saw but showed some nonverbal signs of embarrassment.

4. The fact that a split-brain patient had trouble assembling colored blocks to match a design with his left hand but not his right hand suggests that the _____ hemisphere is superior to the _____ hemisphere at perceptual tasks that involve deciphering visual cues, reading maps, copying designs, and so on.

Review of Terms, Concepts, and Names 4

Use the terms in this list to complete the Matching Test, then to help you answer the True/False items correctly.

cortical localization	Broca's aphasia
Pierre Paul Broca	Wernicke's aphasia
Broca's area	split-brain operation
Karl Wernicke	Roger Sperry
Wernicke's area	functional plasticity
lateralization of function	structural plasticity
aphasia	

Matching Exercise

Match the appropriate term/name with its definition or description.

1. _____ The American psychologist who received the Nobel Prize in 1981 for his pioneering research on brain specialization in split-brain patients.

2. _____ The partial or complete inability to articulate ideas or understand spoken or written language due to brain damage or injury.

3. _____ The language area on the left temporal lobe concerned with speech comprehension.

4. _____ The brain's ability to shift functions from damaged to undamaged areas.

5. _____ The notion that different functions are located, or localized, in different areas of the brain; also referred to as localization of function.

6. _____ The phenomenon in which brain structures physically change in response to environmental influences.

7. _____ The notion that specific psychological or cognitive functions are processed primarily on one side of the brain; also referred to as lateralization.

True/False Test

Indicate whether each statement is true or false by placing T or F in the blank space next to each item.

1. ____ Karl Wernicke was a German neurologist who discovered an area on the left temporal lobe that, when damaged, produces meaningless or nonsensical speech and difficulties in verbal or written comprehension.

2. ____ The split-brain operation is a surgical procedure that involves cutting the corpus callosum.

3. ____ People with Wernicke's aphasia find it difficult or impossible to produce speech, but their comprehension of verbal or written words is relatively unaffected.

4. ____ Pierre Paul Broca was a French surgeon and neuroanatomist who discovered an area on the lower left frontal lobe that, when damaged, produces speech disturbances but no loss of comprehension.

5. ____ Broca's area is a language area on the lower left frontal lobe of the cerebral cortex.

6. ____ Patients with Broca's aphasia can speak but may have problems finding the right words and typically have great difficulty understanding written or spoken communication.

Check your answers and review any areas of weakness before going on to the next section.

Something to Think About

1. A biological psychologist who specializes in the assessment and diagnosis of people with brain-related problems is faced with the following cases. Based on what you now know about biological psychology, the brain, and the functions of the nervous system, give some thought to what the specialist's assessment might be.

   (a) Fraser slipped on ice and hit the back of his head on the sidewalk, and now his vision is seriously affected. Which brain area is most likely affected?

   (b) Following an operation to remove a brain tumor, Yoko is able to read and understand written and spoken language but has difficulty speaking and expressing herself clearly. It is likely that she has damage in which part of the brain?

(c) Ever since a brain lesion destroyed part of her limbic system, Vanessa has had trouble controlling her appetite and has had a constant urge to eat and drink. Which structure was most likely damaged?

(d) Mr. Ashley has a disorder that is characterized by rigidity, muscle tremors, poor balance, and difficulty in initiating movements.

2. Family members and friends who know you are taking a psychology course may ask you some interesting and curious questions. One often-asked question is, "I know that regular exercise helps keep me in shape physically, but is there anything I can do to prevent mental deterioration?" What advice would you give in response to that question?

Check your answers and review any areas of weakness before doing the following progress tests.

Progress Test 1

Review the complete chapter (including Concept Reviews and all boxed inserts), review all your study notes, and then test yourself on the following progress test. Check your answers. If you make a mistake, review your notes, the appropriate section in the study guide, and, if necessary, the relevant part of the chapter in your textbook.

1. A hunter in a South American jungle uses the poison called curare on the tip of his arrow; when the arrow strikes an animal, the animal becomes almost instantly limp and quickly suffocates because its respiratory system has become paralyzed. The curare has _____ the neurotransmitter_____ .

    (a) blocked the release of; acetylcholine
    (b) blocked the receptors for; acetylcholine
    (c) increased the release of; acetylcholine
    (d) increased the reuptake of; acetylcholine

2. Miguel has been diagnosed with schizophrenia. His psychologist believes that Miguel's hallucinations and perceptual distortions may, in part, be caused by _____ amounts of the neurotransmitter _____ .

    (a) diminished; dopamine
    (b) excessive; dopamine
    (c) diminished; serotonin
    (d) excessive; serotonin

3. Jenny has just finished running a very tough marathon (26.22 miles) but seems to be very happy and elated. One cause of her "runner's high" may be due to abnormally high levels of chemical substances in her brain called

    (a) acetylcholines.   (c) endorphins.
    (b) serotonins.   (d) dopamines.

4. Mrs. Danvers has multiple sclerosis. She experiences muscle weakness, loss of coordination and speech, and visual disturbances that result from the slowdown or interruption of neural transmission. The cause of these symptoms probably involves the degeneration of the

    (a) dendrites.   (c) myelin sheath.
    (b) corpus callosum.   (d) synaptic vesicles.

5. When Dr. Maxwell electrically stimulated a specific area of a patient's right cerebral hemisphere, the patient's left hand twitched. The part of the cortex that was stimulated was

    (a) Broca's area.
    (b) the primary motor cortex.
    (c) Wernicke's area.
    (d) the somatosensory cortex.

6. While Rupert was reading a poem, researchers studied his brain activity by using a noninvasice procedure that tracked changes in his brain's blood supply as a function of fluctuations in blood oxygen levels. They were most likely using an imaging technique called

    (a) functional magnetic resonance imaging (fMRI).
    (b) electroencephalography (EEG).
    (c) positron emission tomography (PET scan).
    (d) psycography.

7. Neurotransmitters are to hormones as _____ is to _____ .

    (a) nervous system; endocrine system
    (b) nerves; neurons
    (c) hypothalamus; pituitary gland
    (d) brain; spinal cord

8. When Mike was faced with a final exam worth 80 percent of his grade in his graduate statistics class he was totally stressed out. The particular gland(s) in his endocrine system that is (are) likely to be stimulated is (are) the

    (a) thyroid gland.   (c) adrenal glands.
    (b) pituitary gland.   (d) nervous glands.

9. If researchers electrically stimulate the reticular formation in a sleeping cat, it is most likely that the cat will
   (a) aggressively attack the researchers.
   (b) stop breathing.
   (c) become paralyzed on both sides of the body.
   (d) instantly wake up, fully alert.

10. If researchers destroy or lesion the amygdala of a timid cat, it is likely that the cat will
    (a) become even more fearful.
    (b) lose its timidity and fearfulness.
    (c) become a vicious predator and start attacking large dogs.
    (d) stop breathing and die.

11. If a normal right-handed individual sustained severe damage to the right cerebral hemisphere, this would most likely reduce a number of abilities. Damage to the right hemisphere is *not* likely to affect his ability to
    (a) manipulate blocks to match a particular design.
    (b) recognize people's faces.
    (c) appreciate art and music.
    (d) decipher visual cues related to emotional expression.
    (e) produce and understand written and spoken language.

12. The occipital lobe is to _____ as the temporal lobe is to _____ .
    (a) anticipatory thinking; seeing
    (b) seeing; anticipatory thinking
    (c) seeing; hearing
    (d) hearing; seeing

13. If someone taps you on the back, you sense the touch because the _____ cortex in the _____ lobe receives this tactile information.
    (a) primary motor; frontal
    (b) primary visual; occipital
    (c) primary somatosensory; parietal
    (d) primary auditory; temporal

14. According to In Focus 2.3, most left-handed people
    (a) process language in the left hemisphere.
    (b) process language in the right hemisphere.
    (c) are intellectually challenged.
    (d) are female.

15. According to the Application, rats were exposed to either an enriched environment or an impoverished environment. Researchers found that enrichment
    (a) increases the number and length of dendrites, enlarges the size of neurons, and produces more synaptic connections.
    (b) results in a dramatic increase in the number of neurons in the brain.
    (c) has profound effects on the brains of young rats but no effect on those of mature rats.
    (d) dramatically affects the limbic system but has little or no effect on the cerebral cortex.

Progress Test 2

After you have checked your understanding of the material in Progress Test 1 and have done a complete chapter review with special focus on any areas of weakness, you are ready to further assess your knowledge on Progress Test 2. Check your answers. If you make a mistake, review your notes, the appropriate parts of the study guide, and, if necessary, the relevant sections of your textbook.

1. A patient is suffering from a number of symptoms, including depression, sleep disturbances, and mood fluctuations, and has problems in learning and memory retrieval. Her doctor prescribes Prozac and some other drugs, because the patient's problems are probably due to abnormal levels of the neurotransmitters
   (a) dopamine and acetylcholine.
   (b) serotonin and endorphins.
   (c) acetylcholine and norepinephrine.
   (d) serotonin and norepinephrine.

2. Signal reception is to _____ as signal transmission is to _____ .
   (a) myelin sheath; cell body
   (b) dendrite; axon
   (c) action potential; resting potential
   (d) axon; dendrite

3. As a result of a stroke, 75-year-old Mrs. Yee suffered brain damage. While she is no longer able to speak, she can understand what is being said to her. Mrs. Yee suffers from
   (a) damage to her occipital lobe.
   (b) Wernicke's aphasia.
   (c) damage to her left temporal lobe.
   (d) Broca's aphasia.

4. Your brain is involved in every perception, thought, and emotion, as are its neurons and their neurotransmitters. Neurotransmitters are chemical messengers that

   (a) carry information primarily in the endocrine system.
   (b) travel from the cell body along the axon and create an action potential.
   (c) assist neurons by providing physical support, nutrition, and waste removal.
   (d) travel across the synaptic gap and affect adjoining neurons.

5. If a patient suffers damage to the hippocampus, she is likely to have problems

   (a) learning and forming new memories.
   (b) remembering events and things that happened before her brain injury.
   (c) comprehending spoken and written language.
   (d) controlling emotions such as aggression, fear, anger, and disgust.

6. After Eduardo's serious skiing accident, doctors detected damage to his cerebellum. Eduardo is most likely to have trouble

   (a) swallowing, coughing, and breathing.
   (b) sleeping.
   (c) staying awake.
   (d) playing tennis, typing, and walking with a smooth gait.

7. In a typical test situation with a split-brain patient, a picture of an apple is briefly presented to the right of the center point. If the patient is asked to name the object, she will

   (a) be unable to say what she saw.
   (b) be able to draw a picture of the object with her left hand.
   (c) report that she saw nothing.
   (d) say she saw an apple.

8. If a researcher anesthetizes the entire right hemisphere of a right-handed patient who is asked to recite the alphabet aloud while reclining on the operating table with both arms extended upward, it is most probable that the patient's

   (a) left arm will fall limp but she will continue saying the alphabet.
   (b) right arm will fall limp but she will continue saying the alphabet.
   (c) left arm will fall limp and she will become speechless.
   (d) right arm will fall limp and she will become speechless.

9. A champion athlete loses his medal after officials discover that he has taken anabolic steroids, a synthetic version of the male sex hormone testosterone. Anabolic steroids, like other hormones, circulate through the _____ and act as chemical messengers in the _____ .

   (a) cerebrospinal fluid; central nervous system
   (b) bloodstream; endocrine system
   (c) cerebrospinal fluid; peripheral nervous system
   (d) bloodstream; limbic system

10. In response to an exam question, Leilani carefully draws a picture of a neuron and indicates the sequence of events that are typically involved when a neuron communicates. She is likely to note that information is carried from

    (a) the axon terminals to the cell body and then down the dendrites to the synapse.
    (b) from the cell body to the dendrites and then down the axon to the axon terminals and the synapse.
    (c) from the dendrites to the axon and then down the axon to the cell body and the synapse.
    (d) the dendrites to the cell body and then along the axon to the axon terminals and the synapse.

11. Dr. Jones systematically observes and records the behavior of people whose brains have been damaged by illness or injury. He is using an investigative technique called

    (a) fMRI.   (c) PET scan.
    (b) MRI.   (d) the case study.

12. The parietal lobe is to _____ as the frontal lobe is to _____ .

    (a) anticipatory thinking; hearing
    (b) sensing touch; anticipatory thinking
    (c) seeing; hearing
    (d) tasting; smelling

13. The chapter prologue tells the story of Asha, who suffered a stroke. This story illustrates that the brain has a remarkable ability to gradually shift functions from damaged to undamaged areas, a phenomenon called

    (a) lateralization of function.
    (b) structural plasticity.
    (c) synaptic transmission.
    (d) functional plasticity.

14. According to the Application, structural plasticity refers to the capacity of some brain structures to
    (a) change in response to environmental stimulation.
    (b) remain rigid or "hard-wired" for life.
    (c) deteriorate with age and cause forgetfulness.
    (d) wear out if they are used too much.

15. Despite the fact that phrenology was eventually dismissed as a pseudoscience, it was pointed out in Science Versus Pseudoscience 2.1 that phrenology played a significant role in advancing the scientific study of the brain by triggering interest in
    (a) split-brain operations for epilepsy.
    (b) the role neurotransmitters play in regulating behavior.
    (c) cortical localization, or localization of function.
    (d) how drugs affect synaptic transmission.

Progress Test 3

After you have checked your understanding of the material in Progress Tests 1 and 2 and have done a complete chapter review with special focus on any areas of weakness, you are ready to further assess your knowledge on Progress Test 3. Check your answers. If you make a mistake, review your notes, the appropriate parts of the study guide, and, if necessary, the relevant sections of your textbook.

1. When doctors removed a tumor from Andrew's occipital lobe, they also had to remove healthy brain tissue from the same area. When he recovers, Andrew is most likely to suffer some loss of
   (a) language comprehension.
   (b) muscular coordination.
   (c) visual perception.
   (d) taste perception.

2. Nancy suffers from severe epilepsy that so far has not responded to any treatment. As a final resort, her doctor operates on her brain and surgically cuts the
   (b) amygdala.
   (b) hippocampus.
   (c) corpus callosum.
   (d) adrenal cortex.

3. After a police car with flashing lights and blaring siren passes him and pulls over another driver for speeding, Jerry's heartbeat soon slows down, his blood pressure decreases, and he stops sweating so much. These calming physical reactions are most directly regulated by his
   (a) sympathetic nervous system.
   (b) parasympathetic nervous system.
   (c) somatic nervous system.
   (d) central nervous system.

4. While cooking dinner for a large family gathering, Mindy was so distracted by the conversations around her that she forgot to use an oven mitt when she grabbed a very hot roaster pan. She instantly withdrew her hand before becoming consciously aware of the sensation or her own hand movement. Mindy was able to do this because of her
   (a) spinal reflexes.
   (b) parasympathetic nervous system.
   (c) high levels of endorphins.
   (d) limbic system.

5. As a result of a stroke, Mr. Nelson can no longer understand what he reads or what is being said to him, and he often has trouble finding the right words when he tries to speak. Mr. Nelson suffers from
   (a) Wernicke's aphasia.
   (b) Broca's aphasia.
   (c) Parkinson's disease.
   (d) Alzheimer's disease.

6. If a picture of a hammer is flashed to the left of the midpoint during an experiment with a split-brain patient and she is asked to indicate what she saw, the patient will
   (a) verbally report what she saw.
   (b) be able to draw a picture of the hammer with her right hand.
   (c) be unable to verbally report what she saw.
   (d) most likely draw a picture of a nail with her right hand.

7. In order to determine which area of Drucilla's brain was most active when she read a passage from a book, neuroscientists injected her with radioactively tagged glucose before using an imaging technique called a(n)
   (a) PET scan.
   (b) MRI.
   (c) fMRI.
   (d) EEG.

8. Sonny suffered brain damage when he was knocked down in a boxing match; he can no longer hear in one ear. It is most probable that one of his _____ lobes was injured.
   (a) ear
   (b) occipital
   (c) temporal
   (d) frontal
   (e) parietal

9. In an effort to relax after a stress-filled week, Joanne had a couple of glasses of wine, and her coworker Jim took a Valium. Both alcohol and Valium work by increasing the activity of the neurotransmitter _____ , which inhibits action potentials and slows brain activity.
   (a) GABA
   (b) dopamine
   (c) norepinephrine
   (d) serotonin

10. If Dr. Doonan's research showed that the left hemisphere is dominant for speech and language in virtually all right-handed people and the majority of left-handers, this would argue strongly for the notion of
   (a) lateralization of function.
   (b) the all-or-none law.
   (c) structural plasticity.
   (d) functional plasticity.

11. In his medical practice, Dr. Setiadi uses acupuncture, an ancient Chinese procedure, which involves inserting needles at various points in the body. This pain-killing technique is assumed to involve the production of _____ by the brain.
   (a) endorphins
   (b) dopamine
   (c) GABA
   (d) acetylcholine

12. During a lecture on the brain, Professor Chiga notes that an action potential will not occur unless a neuron is sufficiently stimulated. The principle that she is referring to is the
   (a) all-or-none law.
   (b) law of phrenology.
   (c) principle of lateralization.
   (d) principle of fight or flight.

13. A researcher plans to survey 1,000 randomly selected individuals about hand preference. According to In Focus 2.3, the results are likely to indicate that about
   (a) 50 percent will be left-handed.
   (b) 25 percent will be left-handed.
   (c) 8 percent will be left-handed.
   (d) one-third will be left-handed, one-third right-handed, and one-third ambidextrous.

14. During the early 1800s, Franz Gall developed a theory that the shape of the skull reflects abilities and personality characteristics. According to Science versus Pseudoscience, 2.1, this idea was called
   (a) philosophy.
   (b) bumpology.
   (c) phrenology.
   (d) physiology.

15. After a tamping iron accidentally went through his skull, Phineas Gage recovered physically, but his personality was profoundly changed. He could no longer make rational decisions, he became mentally unstable, and he could no longer do his job. According to In Focus 2.2, his _____ were damaged.
   (a) frontal lobes
   (b) occipital lobes
   (c) parietal lobes
   (d) temporal lobes

Answers

Introduction: Neuroscience and Behavior

1. *Biological psychology is* the specialized branch of psychology that studies the relationship between behavior and bodily processes and systems.

2. *Neuroscience is* the scientific study of the nervous system, especially the brain.

3. *The systems and structures that are of interest to biopsychologists are* the nervous system (the body's primary communication network), neurons (the basic cells of the nervous system) the major regions of the brain (hindbrain, midbrain, and forebrain), and the endocrine system (a communication system closely linked to the nervous system).

The Neuron: The Basic Unit of Communication

1. *Information is transmitted in the nervous system by the three basic types of neurons:* sensory neurons, motor neurons, and interneurons.

2. *Glial cells are* cells that assist neurons by providing structural support, nutrition, and removal of cell wastes; they also enhance the speed of communication between neurons by manufacturing myelin.

3. *The basic components of the neuron and their functions are* the cell body, which contains the nucleus and provides energy for the neuron to carry out its functions; the dendrites, which extend out from the cell body and receive messages from other neurons or specialized cells; and the axon (often surrounded by a myelin sheath), which carries information from the neuron to other cells in the body, including other neurons, glands, and muscles.

4. *Within the neuron, information is communicated* in the form of brief electrical impulses, called action potentials, which are produced by the movement of electrically charged particles, called ions, across the membrane of the axon. The resting potential is the state in which a neuron is prepared to activate and communicate its message if it receives sufficient stimulation. For an action potential to occur, stimulation must be above the stimulus threshold, the minimum level of stimulation required to activate a particular neuron. In addition, neurons either respond or they don't, the all-or-none law.

5. *Communication between neurons may be electrical or chemical. Chemically, it involves* neurostransmitters from one neuron crossing over the synapse, the junction between two neurons, and affecting adjoining neurons.

6. *Some important neurotransmitters (and their primary roles) are* acetylcholine, which is involved in memory, learning, general intellectual functioning, and muscle contraction; dopamine, which is involved in movement, attention, learning, and pleasurable or rewarding sensations; serotonin, which is involved in sleep, moods, and emotional states; norepinephrine, which is involved in the activation of neurons, memory, learning, and physical arousal; GABA, which inhibits brain activity; and endorphins, which affect pain perceptions and positive emotions.

7. *Drugs can affect synaptic transmission by* increasing or decreasing the amount of neurotransmitter released by the neuron, by blocking the reuptake of the neurotransmitter by the sending neuron, by mimicking specific neurotransmitters and producing the same effects, or by mimicking a neurotransmitter and blocking its effect by occupying its receptor sites and preventing it from acting.

Concept Check 1

1. acetylcholine
2. naloxone
3. acetylcholine
4. serotonin
5. dopamine
6. GABA
7. endorphins
8. acetylcholine

Graphic Organizer 1

a. dendrites
b. cell body
c. axon
d. myelin sheath
e. synaptic gap
f. neurotransmitter
g. synaptic vesicles
h. postsynaptic neuron
i. presynaptic neuron

Matching Exercise 1

1. neuron
2. GABA (gamma-amniobutyric acid)
3. endorphins
4. nodes of Ranvier
5. serotonin
6. cell body
7. multiple sclerosis
8. neurotransmitter
9. polarized
10. synapse
11. synaptic vesicles

12. dopamine
13. stimulus threshold
14. neuroscience
15. refractory period
16. Alzheimer's disease
17. opiates
18. acupuncture
19. naloxone
20. Parkinson's disease

True/False Test 1

1. T	6. F	11. F	16. F
2. T	7. T	12. T	17. T
3. F	8. F	13. T	18. T
4. T	9. T	14. T	19. T
5. T	10. T	15. F	20. T

The Nervous System and the Endocrine System: Communication Throughout the Body

1. *The two main divisions of the nervous system and their components are* the central nervous system, which includes the brain and spinal cord, and the peripheral nervous system, which includes all the nerves lying outside the central nervous system.

2. *Spinal reflexes are* simple, automatic behaviors that are processed in the spinal cord.

3. *The key components of the peripheral nervous system and their functions are* the somatic nervous system, which communicates sensory information to the central nervous system and carries motor messages from the central nervous system to the muscles, and the autonomic nervous system, which regulates involuntary functions, such as heartbeat, blood pressure, breathing, and digestion.

4. *The two branches of the autonomic nervous system and their functions are* the sympathetic nervous system, which produces rapid physical arousal in response to perceived threats or emergencies, and the parasympathetic nervous system, which maintains normal bodily func-

tions and conserves the body's physical resources.

5. *The endocrine system is made up of* glands that transmit information via chemical messengers called hormones.

6. *The endocrine system interacts with the nervous system in a number of ways:* by interacting with the nervous system and affecting internal organs and bodily tissue, hormones regulate such things as metabolism, growth rate, digestion, blood pressure, and sexual development and reproduction; endocrine hormones can promote or inhibit the generation of nerve impulses (the release of hormones, in turn, can be stimulated or inhibited by certain parts of the nervous system); and finally, because some hormones and neurotransmitters are chemically identical, the same molecules can act as either a hormone or a neurotransmitter.

7. *The hypothalamus serves as* the main link between the endocrine system and the nervous system and controls the pituitary gland.

8. *The pituitary gland's hormones* affect the function of other glands as well as regulate the production of other hormones. *The adrenal glands (adrenal cortex and adrenal medulla) are involved in* the human stress response.

Concept Check 2

1. spinal reflexes
2. spinal cord
3. sympathetic nervous system
4. parasympathetic nervous system
5. norepinephrine; epinephrine
6. cerebrospinal fluid
7. pituitary; hypothalamus
8. pineal; melatonin
9. pituitary; growth hormone
10. gonadotrophins; testosterone
11. motor; somatic
12. peripheral; autonomic nervous system

Graphic Organizer 2

Mapping the Divisions and Functions of the Nervous System

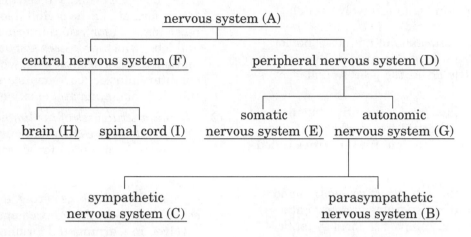

Matching Exercise 2

1. nerves
2. endocrine system
3. spinal reflexes
4. adrenal glands
5. cerebrospinal fluid
6. hypothalamus
7. growth hormone
8. peripheral nervous system
9. prolactin
10. thyroid gland
11. gonads
12. melatonin
13. pineal gland
14. gonadotrophins
15. immune system

True/False Test 2

1. T	5. F	9. F	13. T
2. T	6. T	10. T	14. T
3. T	7. F	11. F	
4. T	8. T	12. T	

A Guided Tour of the Brain

1. *Scientists used case studies to study the brain because* the brain is encased entirely by bone, and it was not possible to directly observe a normal, living brain in action; observing and recording the behavior of people whose brains have been damaged by illness or injury has provided valuable insights into behavior in such areas as memory, speech, emotion, movement, and personality.

2. *The production of lesions and electrically stimulating areas of the brain have been useful because* by surgically altering, removing, or destroying specific portions of the brain (in humans, usually for medical reasons) researchers can observe subsequent changes in behavior; electrical stimulation produces the opposite behavioral effect of a lesion in the same area.

3. *Cognitive neuroscience is* the study of the neural basis of cognitive processes and integrates contributions from psychology, neuroscience, and computer science.

4. *The major imaging techniques used to study the brain are* electroencephalography, magnetic resonance imaging (MRI), positron emission tomography (PET scan), and functional magnetic resonance imaging (fMRI).

5. *Limitations of this technology are as follows:* First, most brain imaging studies involve small groups of subjects, making it difficult to generalize the findings to a wider population. Second, most brain-imaging studies involve simple aspects of behavior and do not capture the extraordinary complexity of human behavior, Third, knowing what brain area is involved may reveal little about the process under investigation.

6. *The brain develops from* a fluid-filled neural tube, which forms about two weeks after conception, into separate fluid-filled cavities called ventricles; as the human fetus develops, brain cells multiply, differentiate, and migrate to their final locations; between conception and birth, the number of neurons increases at a dramatic rate and compete to form synaptic connections.

7. *The three divisions of the developing brain are* the hindbrain, midbrain, and forebrain.

8. *The key structures of the hindbrain and their functions are* the medulla, which controls breathing, heartbeat, digestion, and other vital life functions; the pons, which connects the medulla to the two sides of the cerebellum and helps coordinate and integrate movements on each side of the body; and the cerebellum, which is responsible for muscle coordination and maintaining posture and equilibrium. The reticular formation, which is a network of neurons at the core of the pons and the medulla, plays a role in regulating attention and sleep.

9. *The midbrain contains* centers important to the processing of auditory and visual sensory information, and an area involved in motor control, called the substantia nigra, which contains a large concentration of dopamine-producing neurons.

10. *The forebrain includes* the cerebral cortex (the wrinkled outer portion of the forebrain) and the limbic system structures, which are involved in emotion, motivation, learning, and memory.

11. *The four lobes and their functions are* the temporal lobe, the primary receiving area for auditory information; the occipital lobe, the primary receiving area for visual information; the parietal lobe, which processes somatosensory information; and the frontal lobe, which processes voluntary muscle movements and is involved in thinking, planning, and emotional control.

12. *The main structures of the limbic system and their functions are* the thalamus, which processes sensory information for all senses, except smell, and relays it to the cerebral cortex; the hypothalamus, which regulates behaviors related to survival, such as eating, drinking, and sexual behavior; the hippocampus, which is involved in learning and forming new memories; and the amygdala, which is involved in emotions such as fear, anger, and disgust, and in learning and memory.

Concept Check 3

1. hindbrain (more specifically, the medulla is the point at which neural messages cross over)

2. reticular formation

3. cerebellum

4. medulla

5. hippocampus

6. thalamus

7. left parietal

8. substantia nigra

9. amygdala

10. phrenology; cortical localization (or localization of function)

11. electroencephalograph

12. cognitive neuroscience

13. parietal

Graphic Organizer 3
Chart Diagram Exercise: The Key Structures
of the Limbic System

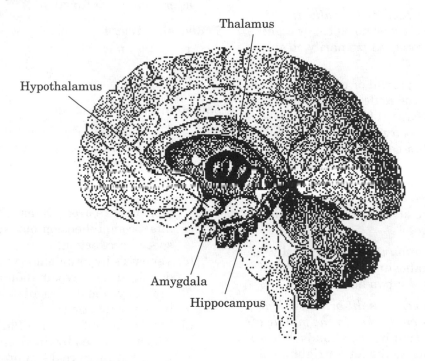

Thalamus

Hypothalamus

Amygdala

Hippocampus

(a) Hypothalamus: a peanut-sized forebrain structure that regulates both divisions of the autonomic nervous system as well as behaviors related to survival, such as eating, drinking, and sexual activity

(b) Thalamus: a forebrain structure that processes motor information and sensory information for all the senses except smell and relays it to the cerebral cortex

(c) Amygdala: an almond-shaped forebrain structure that is involved in emotion and in learning and forming memories

(d) Hippocampus: a curved forebrain structure that is involved in learning and forming new memories

Matching Exercise 3

1. cerebral hemispheres
2. parietal lobe
3. substantia nigra
4. primary auditory cortex
5. pons
6. thalamus
7. primary visual cortex
8. hippocampus
9. brainstem

10. primary motor cortex

11. prefrontal association cortex

12. medulla

13. electroencephalograph

14. reticular formation (reticular activating system)

15. positron emission tomography (PET)

16. suprachiasmatic nucleus (SCN)

17. neurogenesis

18. cognitive neuroscience

19. phrenology

True/False Test 3

1. T	7. F	13. T	19. T
2. T	8. T	14. T	
3. F	9. T	15. T	
4. F	10. T	16. T	
5. T	11. F	17. T	
6. T	12. T	18. T	

Specialization in the Cerebral Hemispheres

1. *Broca and Wernicke provided the first evidence that* the left and right hemispheres were specialized for different functions (cortical localiza-

tion or localization of function), and in particular that language is processed primarily in the left hemisphere.

2. *Lateralization of function (or lateralization) is* the notion that specific psychological or cognitive functions are processed primarily on one side of the brain.

3. *Aphasia refers to* the partial or complete inability to articulate ideas or understand spoken or written language because of brain injury or damage. *Broca's aphasia results in* the inability to produce speech, but comprehension is relatively unaffected. *Wernicke's aphasia results in* problems in finding the correct word and comprehension of written or spoken communication, but speech is relatively unaffected unless the damage is severe.

4. *The split-brain operation involves* surgically cutting the corpus callosum, the thick band of axons that connects the two hemispheres.

5. *In a specialized procedure, split-brain subjects are directed to focus on a point in the middle of a screen and then* visual information is differentially projected either to the left or right hemisphere. *Split-brain subjects can* verbally identify the object when it is projected to the left hemisphere but not the right; however, the left hand (which is controlled by the right hemisphere) can correctly pick out the object projected to the right hemisphere.

6. *Tests on split-brain patients revealed that the left hemisphere is specialized for* language abilities, speech, reading and writing, and *the right hemisphere is specialized for* nonverbal emotional expression, visual-spatial tasks, facial recognition, reading maps, copying designs, drawing, and musical appreciation or responsiveness (but not necessarily musical ability, which involves the left hemisphere as well).

Concept Check 4

1. right; left
2. left; left
3. right
4. right; left

Matching Exercise 4

1. Roger Sperry
2. aphasia
3. Wernicke's area
4. functional plasticity

5. cortical localization
6. structural plasticity
7. lateralization of function

True/False Test 4

1. T   3. F   5. T
2. T   4. T   6. F

Something to Think About

1. (a) The occipital lobe is most likely affected because it includes the primary visual cortex where visual information is received, so damage to this area could affect vision.
   (b) Yoko probably has damage to the left frontal lobe, Broca's area. Damage here would not affect comprehension but would influence speech production.
   (c) Vanessa's hypothalamus was most likely damaged. The hypothalamus is part of the limbic system and regulates appetite, among its many functions.
   (d) Mr. Ashley suffers from Parkinson's disease, which is caused by the degeneration of neurons that produce dopamine in one brain area. Symptoms can be alleviated by the drug L-dopa, which converts to dopamine in the brian.

2. In answer to this question, the news is good. Because of the brain's structural plasticity, some brain structures can change in response to environmental stimulation. Research with rats has demonstrated that, in addition to other changes, an enriched environment increases the number and length of dendrites, enlarges the size of neurons, and increases the number of neural connections. More important, there is an impressive amount of correlational research showing that the human brain also seems to benefit from enriched environments. Getting a good education, as long as the process is challenging, is one way to "exercise" the brain. Another piece of advice is to remain mentally active throughout the lifespan and to get involved in complex and stimulating activities rather than passively watching TV.

   It is important to point out that intellectual decline is not the inevitable result of aging. To increase the number of synaptic connections and dendritic growth, the best advice is to get involved in novel, challenging, and unfamiliar pursuits. Keep pumping those neurons and remember, "If you don't use it, you lose it!"

Progress Test 1

1. b	6. a	11. e
2. c	7. a	12. c
3. c	8. c	13. c
4. c	9. d	14. a
5. b	10. b	15. a

Progress Test 2

1. d	6. d	11. d
2. b	7. d	12. b
3. d	8. a	13. d
4. d	9. b	14. a
5. a	10. d	15. c

Progress Test 3

1. c	6. c	11. a
2. c	7. a	12. a
3. b	8. c	13. c
4. a	9. a	14. c
5. a	10. a	15. a

chapter 3

Sensation and Perception

PREVIEW   Reading the section below first will give you a general sense of the chapter's contents and an initial introduction to some of the major concepts and terms. This will prime you for what you are about to read and help you to develop a "cognitive map" that will guide your study of the material in this chapter. Likewise, reading the **preview questions** at the beginning of each major section will improve your ability to understand, learn, and retain the information.

CHAPTER 3 . . . AT A GLANCE   Chapter 3 describes both sensation and perception. Beginning with the basic principles of sensation—sensory threshold, Weber's law, and sensory adaptation—the chapter then explains the senses of vision, hearing, smell, taste, and touch. This is followed by a discussion of pain, pain perception, and the gate-control theory of pain. The section concludes with the kinesthetic and vestibular senses.

The discussion of perception first distinguishes between bottom-up and top-down processing. How we perceive shape and depth are explained, including a description of monocular and binocular cues. The perception of motion is explained, followed by the phenomenon of perceptual constancy. How we misperceive objects and events in our world is illustrated through various illusions and impossible figures. That perception is a psychological process is made clear through a discussion of how perceptual sets—expectations, learning experiences, and cultural factors—influence our interpretations.

The Application at the end of the chapter is devoted to how we can use various perceptual strategies and techniques in the control of pain.

Introduction: What Are Sensation and Perception?

Preview Questions

Consider the following questions as you study this section of the chapter.

- What are the definitions of sensation and perception?
- How do sensation and perception differ?

*Read the section "Introduction: What Are Sensation and Perception?" and **write** your answers to the following:*

1. The primary function of the nervous system is _____

2. Sensation refers to _____

   and perception occurs _____ _____

3. The difference between sensation and perception is _____ _____

Basic Principles of Sensation

Preview Questions

Consider the following questions as you study this section of the chapter.

- What are sensory receptors; how do they help us hear, taste, smell, feel, and see; and what is transduction?
- What are the two types of sensory thresholds?
- How does Weber's law relate to the just noticeable difference (jnd)?
- Why does sensory adaptation occur, and why is it important?

*Read the section "Basic Principles of Sensation" and **write** the answers to the following:*

1. Sensory receptors help us hear, taste, smell, feel, and see by_____ _____

2. Transduction is _____ _____

3. The two types of sensory threshold are _____ _____ _____ _____

4. Another name for the difference threshold is _____

5. Weber's law states _____ _____

6. Sensory adaptation occurs because _____ _____ _____

After you have carefully studied the preceding sections, complete the following exercises.

Concept Check 1

Read the following and write the correct term in the space provided.

1. When Anton went to have his hearing tested, he was presented with many different tones; in fact, some were at such a low level of intensity he could not detect them. These sounds were below Anton's _____ threshold.

2. When Jennifer was first presented with the auditory stimulus, she simply detected the sequence of sounds as a series of different tones. After hearing the tones a second time, she recognized the sequence of sounds as a melody. This example illustrates the overlapping processes of _____ and _____ .

3. Jan was exposed to a 100-watt light. When its brightness was increased by 5 watts, she was not aware of the increase. However, when a 20-watt light was increased by 5 watts, she detected the increase immediately. Jan's ability to detect this difference is called the _____ , or _____ , and this may vary as a function of the size of the initial stimulus, a principle of sensation called _____ .

4. The school bell rings at lunch time. The process by which our ears convert the sound waves from the bell into a coded neural signal that can be processed by the nervous system is called _____ .

5. Not realizing how cold it is after you have been on the ski slope for a while is an example of

_____ .

6. Dr. Jasenka's research demonstrated that simple information presented outside conscious awareness influenced emotions, thoughts, and attitudes. These effects, however, were weak and short-lived. More complex messages had no effect. Dr. Jasenka's research is concerned with

_____ .

Review of Terms and Concepts 1

Use the terms in this list to complete the Matching Test, then to help you answer the True/False items correctly.

sensation
perception
sensory receptors
transduction
threshold
absolute threshold

difference threshold
(just noticeable
difference or jnd)
Weber's law
sensory adaptation
subliminal perception

Matching Exercise

Match the appropriate term with its definition or description.

1. _____ The level at which a stimulus is strong enough to be detected by activating sensory receptors.

2. _____ The process by which a form of physical energy is converted into a coded neural signal that can be processed by the nervous system.

3. _____ The smallest possible strength of a stimulus that can be detected half the time.

4. _____ Specialized cells unique to each sense organ that respond to a particular form of sensory stimulation.

5. _____ The smallest possible difference between two stimuli that can be detected half the time; also called the just noticeable difference.

True/False Test

Indicate whether each statement is true or false by placing T or F in the blank space next to each item.

1. ____ Perception refers to the process of detecting a physical stimulus, such as sound, light, heat, or pressure.

2. ____ Sensory adaptation refers to the decline in sensitivity to a constant stimulus.

3. ____ Weber's law is a principle of sensation that holds that the size of the just noticeable difference will vary depending on its relation to the strength of the original stimulus.

4. ____ The process of integrating, organizing, and interpreting sensations is called sensation.

5. ____ The perception of stimuli that are below the threshold of conscious awareness is called subliminal perception.

Check your answers and review any areas of weakness before going on to the next section.

Vision: From Light to Sight

Preview Questions

Consider the following questions as you study this section of the chapter.

- How do we see, and what is the electromagnetic energy spectrum?

- What are the key structures of the eye?

- What are the functions of the rods and cones, and how do the bipolar and ganglion cells process visual information for transmission to the brain?

- What properties of light determine our experience of color, and how do the two theories of color vision explain the process?

Read the section "Vision: From Light to Sight" and **write** *your answers to the following.*

1. The process of seeing begins with _____

_____

_____

2. The electromagnetic spectrum is _____

_____

_____

3. The key structures of the eye are _____ _____ _____

4. The function of rods is to _____ _____

   the function of cones is to _____ _____

5. Bipolar cells process visual information by _____ _____

6. The optic disk is _____ _____

7. Our experience of color involves _____ _____ _____ _____

8. According to the trichromatic theory, _____ _____ _____ _____

   This theory explains_____ _____

9. According to the opponent-process theory, _____ _____ _____

   This theory explains_____ _____

After you have carefully studied the preceding section, complete the following exercises.

Concept Check 2

Read the following and write the correct term in the space provided.

1. According to the trichromatic theory, if Mr. Colorado's red- , green- , and blue-sensitive cones are stimulated simultaneously, he should see _____ .

2. Constantino, who has normal vision, stared at a red circle for a couple of minutes, then shifted his eyes to a white surface. The afterimage of the circle will be _____ .

3. The fact that Constantino experiences an after-image cannot be explained by the _____ theory of color vision, but it can be explained by the _____ theory.

4. Following an accident, the fovea in Harbinder's right eye was destroyed. Although he can still see with this eye, it is likely that he will have trouble seeing _____ and _____ when his left eye is closed.

5. According to the opponent-process theory, if certain cells in Dale's retina are stimulated by exposure to green light, they are likely to be inhibited by exposure to _____ light.

Graphic Organizer 1

Identify each part of the eye by writing the name on the appropriate line; then match its function by placing the corresponding number next to the name. (For example, "1. retina" is the first answer.)

1. A light-sensitive membrane located at the back of the eye that contains sensory receptors for vision.

2. The black opening in the middle of the eye that changes size to let in different amounts of light.

3. A clear membrane covering the visible part of the eye that helps gather and direct incoming light.

4. The colored part of the eye that is the muscle that controls the size of the pupil.

5. A transparent structure located behind the pupil that actively focuses, or bends, light as it enters the eye.

6. A small area in the center of the retina that contains cones but not rods.

7. The area of the retina without rods or cones, where the optic nerve leaves the eye.

Review of Terms and Concepts 2

Use the terms in this list to complete the Matching Test, then to help you answer the True/False items correctly.

wavelength
cornea
pupil
iris
iridology
lens
accommodation
retina
nearsightedness
  (myopia)
farsightedness
  (hyperopia)
presbyopia
astigmatism
rods
cones
fovea
optic disk

blind spot
ganglion cells
bipolar cells
visual acuity
optic nerve
optic chiasm
feature detectors
color
hue
saturation
brightness
trichromatic theory of
  color vision
color blindness
afterimage
opponent-process theory
  of color vision

Matching Exercise

Match the appropriate term with its definition or description:

1. _____ The visual ability to see fine details.

2. _____ Visual experience that occurs after the original source of stimulation is no longer present.

3. _____ Distance from one wave peak to another.

4. _____ Process by which the lens changes shape to focus incoming light so that it falls on the retina.

5. _____ Perceived intensity of color that corresponds to the amplitude of the light wave.

6. _____ Thick nerve that exits from the back of the eye and carries visual information to the visual cortex in the brain.

7. _____ Theory that the sensation of color is due to cones in the retina that are especially sensitive to red, green, or blue light.

8. _____ Short, thick, pointed sensory receptors of the eye that detect color and are responsible for color vision and visual acuity.

9. _____ Property of wavelengths of light, what we know as color, in which different wavelengths correspond to our subjective experience of different colors.

10. _____ Long, thin, blunt sensory receptors that are highly sensitive to light but not to color and are primarily responsible for peripheral vision and night vision.

11. _____ Specialized neurons in the retina that collect sensory information from the rods and cones and then funnel it to other specialized neurons before it is transmitted to the brain.

12. _____ Perceptual experience of different wavelengths of light, involving hue, saturation (purity), and brightness (intensity).

13. _____ Area of the retina without rods or cones, where the optic nerve exits the back of the eye.

14. _____ A form of farsightedness caused by the lens becoming brittle and inflexible during middle age.

15. _____ A visual disorder in which an abnormally curved eyeball results in blurry vision for lines in a particular direction.

16. _____ Specialized neurons in the visual cortex that detect, or respond to, particular aspects of more complex visual stimuli.

True/False Test

Indicate whether each statement is true or false by placing T or F in the blank space next to each item.

1. ____ The cornea is the transparent structure located behind the pupil that actively focuses, or bends, light as it enters the eye.

2. ____ The opponent-process theory states that color vision is the product of opposing pairs of color receptors, red-green, black-white, and blue-yellow; when one member of a color pair is stimulated, the other is inhibited.

3. ____ The lens is the clear membrane covering the visible part of the eye that helps gather and direct incoming light.

4. ____ A single ganglion cell might receive information from only one or two cones or it might receive information from a hundred or more rods.

5. ___ The retina is a small area in the center of the back of the eye that is composed entirely of cones, where visual information is most sharply focused.

6. ___ The colored part of the eye, which is actually a ring of muscles that controls the size of the pupil, is called the iris.

7. ___ The pupil is the opening in the middle of the iris that changes size to let in different amounts of light.

8. ___ The fovea is a thin, light-sensitive membrane located at the back of the eye that contains two kinds of sensory receptors for light and vision.

9. ___ The optic chiasm is the point in the brain where the optic fibers from each eye meet and partly cross over to the opposite side of the brain.

10. ___ Saturation is the property of color that corresponds to the purity of the light wave.

11. ___ Color blindness occurs because there are no receptor cells in the area where the optic nerve exits the eye.

12. ___ The blind spot is the point where the optic nerve leaves the eye, producing a small gap in the field of vision.

13. ___ Nearsightedness occurs when close objects are seen clearly but distant objects appear blurry because the light from distant objects is focused in front of the retina.

14. ___ Iridology is based on the unproven assumption that physical and psychological functioning are reflected in the iris, the colored part of the eye.

15. ___ Farsightedness occurs when distant objects are seen clearly but close objects appear blurry because the light from close objects is focused behind the retina.

Check your answers and review any areas of weakness before going on to the next section.

Hearing: From Vibration to Sound

Preview Questions

Consider the following questions as you study this section of the chapter.

- What is audition, and how do we hear?

- What properties of a sound wave correspond to our perception of sound?
- What are the key structures of the ear, and what are their functions?
- How do place theory and frequency theory explain pitch perception?

*Read the section "Hearing: From Vibration to Sound" and **write** your answers to the following:*

1. Audition is _____
   _____

2. Our perception of sound is directly related to the physical properties of _____
   _____
   _____

3. The key structures of the ear are _____
   _____
   _____

4. The process of hearing begins when _____
   _____

   It then involves _____
   _____
   _____

5. According to frequency theory, _____
   _____
   _____
   _____
   _____

   This theory explains_____
   _____
   _____

6. According to place theory, _____
   _____
   _____
   _____
   _____

   This theory explains_____
   _____
   _____

After you have carefully studied the preceding section, complete the following exercises.

Concept Check 3

Read the following and write the correct term in the space provided.

1. Golnaz became so totally engrossed in the movie that she lost track of time and place. Her enjoyment of the film was made possible, in part, because the light waves from the screen were transduced by receptors in her _____ , and the sound waves from the speakers were transduced by a structure in her ears called the _____ .

2. Rita, who has suffered damage to the bones in her middle ear, has been told by the experts that a hearing aid that artificially amplifies sounds will help restore her hearing. Rita probably has _____ deafness.

3. After a small area of his basilar membrane was damaged, Hamish could no longer hear high-pitched sounds. This loss of hearing can best be explained by the _____ theory.

4. Mrs. Newbold is 75 years old and has had some hearing loss due to stiffness of the tiny bones in her middle ear. It is possible that her deafness can be helped by a _____

5. Dr. Emison's research, which found that high-frequency sounds trigger activity near the stir-rup end of the basilar membrane, supports the _____ theory of pitch.

Graphic Organizer 2

Identify each part of the ear by writing the name on the appropriate line and then match its function by placing the corresponding number next to the name. (For example, "1. pinna" is the first answer.)

1. pinna

1. The oddly shaped flap of skin and cartilage that is attached to each side of the head.
2. A tightly stretched membrane at the end of the ear canal that vibrates when hit by sound waves.
3. A fluid-filled coiled structure that contains the sensory receptors for sound.
4. The tunnel through which sound waves travel to reach the eardrum.

5. The tightly stretched membrane that separates the middle ear from the inner ear.
6. The small structures of the middle ear whose joint action almost doubles the amplification of the sound.
7. The nerve that carries the neural information to the thalamus and the auditory cortex in the brain.

Review of Terms and Concepts 3

Use the terms in this list to complete the Matching Test, then to help you answer the True/False items correctly.

audition
sound waves
loudness
amplitude
decibel
pitch
frequency
hertz
timbre
outer ear
pinna
ear canal
eardrum

oval window
middle ear
hammer, anvil,
 and stirrup
conduction deafness
inner ear
cochlea
basilar membrane
hair cells
nerve deafness
frequency theory
place theory

Matching Exercise

Match the appropriate term with its definition or description.

1. _____ Type of deafness due to damage to the hair cells or auditory nerve.

2. _____ Technical term for the sense of hearing.

3. _____ Rate of vibration, or number of waves per second.

4. _____ Hairlike sensory receptors for sound embedded in the basilar membrane.

5. _____ Physical stimuli that produce our sensory experience of sound.

6. _____ The distinctive quality of a sound, determined by the complexity of the sound waves.

7. _____ Part of the ear that collects sound waves and consists of the pinna, the ear canal, and the eardrum.

8. _____ Relative highness or lowness of a sound, determined by the frequency of the sound wave.

9. _____ The view that different frequencies cause larger vibrations at different locations along the basilar membrane.

10. _____ Unit of measurement for loudness.

11. _____ Intensity or amount of energy of a wave, reflected in the height of the wave; determines a sound's loudness.

12. _____ The part of the ear that amplifies sound waves; consists of three small bones—the hammer, the anvil, and the stirrup.

True/False Test

Indicate whether each statement is true or false by placing T or F in the blank space next to each item.

1. ____ According to frequency theory, the basilar membrane vibrates at the same frequency as the sound wave, thereby enabling low-frequency sound to be transmitted to the brain.

2. ____ The oval window is a tightly stretched membrane that separates the middle ear from the inner ear.

3. ____ Conduction deafness results from damage to the bones of the middle ear that prevents any one of them from transmitting to the inner ear.

4. ____ The hammer, anvil, and stirrup are important transduction structures in the inner ear.

5. ____ The cochlea is a coiled, fluid-filled structure that contains the sensory receptors for sound.

6. ____ Hertz refers to the number of wave peaks per second.

7. ____ The ear canal is the fluid-filled section of the ear that contains the cochlea.

8. ____ The structure within the cochlea that contains the hair cells is called the basilar membrane.

9. ____ The eardrum is a tightly stretched membrane at the end of the ear canal that vibrates when sound waves hit it.

10. ____ The pinna is the oddly shaped flap of skin and cartilage that is attached to each side of your head.

11. ____ The inner ear is the part of the ear where sound is transduced into neural impulses; it consists of the cochlea and semicircular canals.

12. ____ Loudness is the intensity (or amplitude) of a sound wave measured in decibels.

Check your answers and review any areas of weakness before going on to the next section.

The Chemical and Body Senses: Smell, Taste, Touch, and Position

Preview Questions

Consider the following questions as you study this section of the chapter.

- How are olfaction and gustation defined, and what is meant by the chemical senses?
- How do airborne molecules result in the sensation of odor?
- What are the primary tastes, and how do we perceive different tastes?
- What are the skin and body senses, and what sensory receptors are involved in touch and temperature?
- How is the sensation of pain produced, and what causes pain?
- What is the gate-control theory of pain?
- What are the kinesthetic and vestibular senses, and where are their receptors located?

*Read the section "The Chemical and Body Senses: Smell, Taste, Touch, and Position" and **write** your answers to the following:*

1. Olfaction is the technical term for

   _____

   and gustation is the technical term for

   _____

2. They are called chemical senses because

   _____

   _____

3. Our sense of smell begins when _____

   _____

   It then involves _____

   _____

   _____

4. Our sense of taste begins when _____

   _____

   It then involves _____

   _____

   _____

5. The five primary taste qualities are

   _____

6. The skin and body senses include _____

   _____

7. The skin responds to _____

   _____

8. One receptor for touch is _____

   and it works by _____

   _____

   _____

9. Temperature is sensed _____

   _____

   _____

10. Pain is the sensation of _____

    _____

11. According to gate-control theory, _____

    _____

    _____

    _____

    _____

12. The experience of pain is also influenced by

    _____

    _____

13. Our kinesthetic sense involves _____

    _____

    _____

14. Our vestibular sense provides us with

    _____

15. The two sources of vestibular sensory information are _____

    _____

    _____

After you have carefully studied the preceding sections, complete the following exercises.

Concept Check 4

Read the following and write the correct term in the space provided.

1. After eating his salad with vinegar dressing, Mario thinks that his very expensive vintage wine tastes strange. This change in perceived taste is probably due to the vinegar causing some disruption to his

   _____ .

2. As a result of damage to her olfactory bulb, Danielle has lost the ability to detect the _____ of whatever she eats or drinks.

3. As the result of an accident, Chih Fan experienced damage to his thalamus. The one sense that will be least affected by this brain damage is his sense of_____ .

4. For dinner Klara had a salad with lemon dressing, a teriyaki steak with mushrooms, a potato with sour cream, and ice cream for dessert. It is very likely that she has experienced the five basic taste sensations of _____ , _____ , _____ , _____ , and _____ .

5. On the day of her final statistics exam, Nadia has a sore ankle. According to the gate-control theory, it is likely that Nadia's anxiety about the exam will _____ her perception of the pain in her ankle.

6. While fishing in a small boat, Mortimer becomes nauseated from the motion of the waves. Mortimer's _____ and _____ are most likely responsible for making him feel ill.

7. If Dr. Farnaz investigates certain aspects of gate-control theory, his research is concerned with the sensation of _____ .

8. If you are blindfolded and asked to touch your chin, nose, and forehead with your index finger, you probably will have no trouble doing so. This ability is due to your _____ sense.

9. Arleigh accidentally scrapes the skin off his knuckles while working on his car. The pain he feels following the injury is caused in part by the release of the neurotransmitter _____ .

Review of Terms and Concepts 4

Use the terms in this list to complete the Matching Test, then to help you answer the True/False items correctly.

olfaction
gustation
chemical senses
airborne molecules
olfactory receptor cells
olfactory nerves
olfactory bulb
olfactory cortex
olfactory tract
pheromones
taste buds
umami
skin senses

body senses
Pacinian corpuscle
pain
gate-control theory
free nerve endings
substance P
endorphins
kinesthetic sense
proprioceptors
vestibular sense
semicircular canals
vestibular sacs

Matching Exercise

Match the appropriate term with its definition or description.

1. _____ Technical term for our sense of taste.

2. _____ Fluid-filled sacs that are lined with hairlike receptor cells that shift in response to motion, changes in body position, or changes in gravity.

3. _____ Touch receptor located beneath the skin; when stimulated by pressure, it converts the stimulation into neural messages that are relayed to the brain.

4. _____ The name sometimes given to our senses of taste and smell because they both involve sensory receptors for chemical substances.

5. _____ Small-diameter sensory fibers in the skin, muscles, or internal organs that, when activated by an intense stimulus, begin the process of pain perception.

6. _____ Cells located high in the nasal cavity that are stimulated by inhaled molecules in the air.

7. _____ Enlarged ending of the olfactory cortex at the front of the brain, where the sensation of smell is registered.

8. _____ Specialized sensory receptors for taste that are located on the tongue and inside the mouth and throat.

9. _____ Tract formed by bundles of axons from the olfactory bulb that projects to different brain areas, including the temporal lobe and structures in the limbic system.

10. _____ The sense of balance or equilibrium.

11. _____ The body's natural painkillers that are produced in many parts of the brain and the body.

12. _____ The sense of location and position of body parts in relation to one another.

13. _____ A taste category that involves the distinctive taste of monosodium glutamate, aged cheeses, mushrooms, seaweed, and protein rich foods such as meat.

True/False Test

Indicate whether each item is true or false by placing T or F in the space next to each item.

1. ___ Pain is the unpleasant sensation of physical discomfort or suffering that can occur in varying degrees of intensity.

2. ___ Gate-control theory suggests that pain is the product of both physiological and psychological factors that cause spinal "gates" to open and relay patterns of intense stimulation to the brain, which perceives them as pain.

3. ___ Airborne chemical molecules are emitted by the substances we are smelling; we inhale them through the nose and through the opening in the palate at the back of the throat.

4. ___ The olfactory nerves connect directly to the olfactory bulb, where smells are perceived by the brain.

5. ___ Proprioceptors are neurotransmitters that are involved in the transmission of pain messages to the brain.

6. ___ Olfaction is the technical term for our sense of smell.

7. ___ The semicircular canals are fluid-filled structures lined with hairlike receptors that shift in response to motion, changes in bodily position, and gravity and are a source of information for our vestibular sense.

8. ___ The olfactory cortex is at the front of the brain and is directly linked to the outside world via neural pathways.

9. ___ The body senses provide essential information about our physical status and our physical interaction with objects in our environment.

10. ___ Substance P is found in the muscles and joints and provides information about body position and movement.

11. ___ The skin senses keep us informed as to our position and orientation in space.

12. ___ Chemical signals used by animals to communicate boundaries and sexual receptiveness are called pheromones.

Check your answers and review any areas of weakness before going on to the next section.

Perception (Part 1)

Preview Questions

Consider the following questions as you study this section of the chapter.

- What is perception?
- How does bottom-up processing differ from top-down processing?
- What three questions does perception answer about the stimuli we sense?
- Who founded Gestalt psychology, and what is the main focus of this perspective?

Read the section "Perception" (the introduction only) and **write** *your answers to the following:*

1. Perception is the process of _____

   _____

2. Bottom-up processing refers to _____

   _____

   _____

3. Top-down processing refers to _____

   _____

   _____

4. The three basic questions of perception are

   _____

   _____

   _____

   _____

5. Gestalt psychology was founded by _____

_____

and is concerned with _____

Perception: The Perception of Shape (Part 2)

Preview Questions

Consider the following questions as you study this section of the chapter.

- What is the figure–ground relationship, and how significant is it to perception?
- What perceptual principles do we follow in determining figure–ground relationships?
- What perceptual principles do we follow when we group visual elements?
- What is the law of Prägnanz, and what does it explain?

Read the section "Perception: The Perception of Shape" (up to depth perception) and **write** *your answers to the following:*

1. The figure–ground relationship describes

_____

_____

It is important because it demonstrates that

_____

_____

2. The perceptual principles involved in grouping visual elements are _____

_____

_____

3. The law of Prägnanz states _____

_____

_____

It is important because it encompasses _____

_____

and suggests that_____

_____

_____

Perception: Depth Perception (Part 3)

Preview Questions

Consider the following questions as you study this section of the chapter.

- Why is depth perception important, and how is it defined?
- What are monocular cues, and how do they contribute to depth perception?
- What are binocular cues, and how do they differ from monocular cues?
- How is binocular disparity involved in our ability to see three-dimensional images in stereograms?

Read the section "Perception: Depth Perception" (up to motion perception) and **write** *your answers to the following:*

1. Depth perception refers to _____

_____

It is important because _____

_____

2. Monocular cues are defined as _____

_____

_____

and include _____

_____

_____

3. Binocular cues are defined as _____

_____

_____

and include _____

4. A stereogram is _____

_____

_____

After you have carefully studied the preceding sections, complete the following exercises.

Concept Check 5

Read the following and write the correct term in the space provided.

1. When Tsung looked at the 12 numbers on his credit card—2314 5634 8679 1357—he perceived them as four groups of four numbers each. The tendency to perceive things that are close together as a single unit is called the

   _____ .

2. At a noisy party, Ben focuses on his girlfriend's conversation, while tuning out the other conversations. Using a Gestalt perceptual principle to analyze this example, the noisy environment is the _____ and his girlfriend's voice is the _____ .

3. While viewing a stereogram, Nina experiences the perceptual illusion of three-dimensional depth from the two-dimensional scene. The binocular cue responsible for this phenomenon is _____ .

4. Chan knows that the red bicycle in the parking lot is closer to him than the green bicycle because the red one casts a larger retinal image. This illustrates the distance cue known as _____ .

5. Emily paints a long garden pathway bordered with flowers. She shows the flowers as decreasing in size as they approach the horizon, where they seem to meet; Emily is using

   _____ to convey depth on the canvas.

6. Although a number of individual lights had burned out on the flashing sign, Lizabet perceived the sign as complete and had no trouble reading the whole message. The tendency to fill in gaps in an incomplete image is called the

   _____ .

7. To make the task of completing the jigsaw puzzle more challenging, Zahra attempted to assemble it without the finished picture in front of her. Zahra is most likely to use _____ , or data-driven processing, to accomplish the task.

Review of Terms, Concepts, and Names 5

Use the terms in this list to complete the Matching Test, then to help you answer the True/False items correctly.

perception
bottom-up processing
  (data-driven
  processing)
top-down processing
  (conceptually driven
  processing)
extrasensory perception
  (ESP)
parapsychology
Gestalt psychology
Max Wertheimer
figure–ground
  relationship
figure–ground reversal
law of similarity
law of closure
law of good continuation

law of proximity
law of Prägnanz
  (law of simplicity)
depth perception
monocular cues
relative size
overlap
aerial perspective
texture gradient
linear perspective
motion parallax
pictorial cues
accommodation
binocular cues
convergence
binocular disparity
stereogram

Matching Exercise

Match the appropriate term with its definition or description.

1. _____ School of psychology founded in Germany in the early 1900s that maintained that our sensations are actively processed according to consistent perceptual rules that result in meaningful whole perceptions.

2. _____ Law that states that when several perceptual organizations are possible, the perceptual interpretation that will occur will be the one that produces the best, simplest, and most stable shape.

3. _____ Monocular cue that suggests that faraway objects often appear hazy or slightly blurred by the atmosphere.

4. _____ Binocular cue that relies on the fact that our eyes are set a couple of inches apart and thus cast slightly different images on the retina of each eye.

5. _____ Gestalt principle of perceptual organization that states that we automatically separate the elements of a perception into the feature that clearly stands out from its less distinct background.

6. _____ Monocular cue in which an object partially blocked or obscured by another object is perceived as being farther away.

7. _____ Distance or depth cues that require the use of both eyes.

8. _____ Monocular cue that utilizes information about changes in the shape of the lens of the eye to help us gauge depth and distance.

9. _____ Gestalt principle of organizaiton that refers to the tendency to perceive objects that are close to us as a unit or figure.

10. _____ The use of monocular or binocular visual cues to perceive the distance or three-dimensional characteristics of objects.

11. _____ The perception of an image in which the ground can be perceived as the figure and the figure as the ground; underscores that our perception of figure and ground is a psychological phenomenon.

12. _____ German psychologist who founded Gestalt psychology in the early 1900s.

13. _____ The scientific investigation of claims of various paranormal phenomena.

14. _____ Gestalt principle of organization that refers to the tendency to perceive objects of similar size, shape, or color as a unit or figure.

True/False Test

Indicate whether each item is true or false by placing T or F in the space next to each item.

1. ____ Perception is defined as the process of integrating, organizing, and interpreting sensory information in a meaningful way.

2. ____ The law of good continuation, a Gestalt principle of organization, is the tendency to group elements that appear to follow in the same direction as a single unit or figure.

3. ____ The monocular cue of linear perspective refers to the fact that if two or more objects are assumed to be similar in size, the object that appears larger is perceived as being closer.

4. ____ Monocular cues are distane or depth cues that can be processed with either eye alone.

5. ____ The depth cue that occurs when parallel lines seem to meet in the distance (and the closer together the lines appear to be, the greater the perception of depth) is called relative size.

6. ____ Convergence is a binocular cue that relies on the degree to which muscles rotate the eyes to focus on an object; the less convergence, the farther away the object appears to be.

7. ____ When we are in motion, we can use the speed of passing objects to estimate their distance; nearby objects will appear to move much faster relative to distant objects. This monocular cue is called motion parallax.

8. ____ Texture gradient is a monocular cue in which the details of a surface with distinct texture become gradually less clearly defined as the surface extends into the distance; it appears crisp and distinct when close, and fuzzy and indistinct when farther away.

9. ____ Monocular cues used by artists to create the perception of distance or depth in paintings are called pictorial cues.

10. ____ Top-down processing is information processing that emphasizes the importance of sensory receptors in detecting the basic features of a stimulus in the process of recognizing a whole pattern; it involves analysis from the parts to the whole.

11. ____ A stereogram is a picture that uses the principle of binocular disparity to create the perception of a three-dimensional image.

12. ____ Bottom-up processing is information processing that emphasizes the importance of the observer's knowledge, expectations, and other cognitive processes in arriving at meaningful perceptions and involves analysis from the whole to the parts.

13. ____ Extrasensory perception (ESP) is based on the idea that sensory information can be detected by some means other than through the normal processes of sensation.

14. ____ The law of closure, a Gestalt principle of organization, is the tendency to fill in gaps or contours in an incomplete image.

Check your answers and review any areas of weakness before going on to the next section.

Perception: The Perception of Motion (Part 4)

Preview Questions

Consider the following questions as you study this section of the chapter.

- Which sources of information contribute to our perception of motion?

- Who first studied induced motion, and how did he go about demonstrating this phenomenon?
- How does stroboscopic motion work, and how does it relate to the perception of motion?
- What role do auditory cues play in perceiving distance and direction?

Read the section "Perception: The Perception of Motion" (up to perceptual constancies) and **write** *your answers to the following:*

1. The perception of motion involves _____

_____

_____

_____

2. Induced motion refers to _____

_____

It was first studied by _____

3. Stroboscopic motion creates _____

_____

It is caused by _____

_____

_____

_____

_____

4. Auditory cues are used to judge distance and direction in a couple of ways: _____

_____

_____

_____

Perception: Perceptual Constancies (Part 5)

Preview Questions

Consider the following questions as you study this section of the chapter.

- What is perceptual constancy?
- What principles guide our perception of size constancy?
- What are shape constancy and brightness constancy?

Read the section "Perception: Perceptual Constancies" and **write** *your answers to the following:*

1. Perceptual constancy refers to _____

_____

_____

2. Size constancy is _____

_____

_____

An important aspect of size constancy is _____

_____

_____

3. Shape constancy is _____

_____

_____

_____

4. Brightness constancy is _____

_____

_____

Perceptual Illusions and The Effects of Experience on Perceptual Interpretations

Preview Questions

Consider the following questions as you study this section of the chapter.

- What are perceptual illusions, and why are psychologists interested in them?
- How are the Müller-Lyer and moon illusions explained?
- What do illusions and impossible figures reveal about normal perceptual processes?
- How do perceptual sets influence the perceptual conclusions we reach?

Read the sections "Perceptual Illusions" and "The Effects of Experience on Perceptual Interpretations" and **write** *your answers to the following:*

1. Perceptual illusions involve _____

_____

_____

2. The Müller-Lyer illusion is _____

_____

_____

3. The moon illusion is _____

_____

_____

_____

and may be the result of _____
_____
_____

4. Perceptual illusions and impossible figures reveal that _____
_____
_____

5. Perceptions can be influenced by _____
_____
_____

6. A perceptual set is _____
_____
_____

After you have carefully studied the preceding sections, complete the following exercises.

Concept Check 6

Read the following and write the correct term in the space provided.

1. Stereotypes are mental conceptions that we have about individuals belonging to specific racial or ethnic groups and can influence how we interpret their behaviors. Stereotypes are most similar to the perceptual phenomenon of _____ .

2. William noticed that the full moon seemed to be much larger on the horizon than when it was overhead. His friend Jane, a psychology major, explained that the illusion results from distance cues that make the horizon moon seem _____ (farther away/closer) than an overhead moon.

3. Your unopened introductory psychology textbook produces a trapezoidal retinal image, but you typically perceive the book as a rectangular object. This is due to _____ constancy.

4. When asked to judge the length of two equal lines, Desiree judged the one with outward-pointing arrows as being longer than the one with inward-pointing arrows. Desiree has experienced the _____ illusion.

5. When Dave's dog runs down the lane to greet him after work, the image of the dog on his retinas gets bigger and bigger, yet Dave does not perceive Rex as the incredible growing dog. This tendency to perceive objects, particularly familiar objects, as constant and unchanging despite changes in sensory input is called _____ .

6. Ricardo uses sequentially flashing Christmas lights in front of his house to make it look as though Santa and his sleigh are moving from the garden to the roof. Ricardo is using the perceptual illusion of _____ .

Review of Terms and Concepts 6

Use the terms in this list to complete the Matching Test, then to help you answer the True/False items correctly.

induced motion
Karl Dunker
stroboscopic motion
auditory cues
perceptual constancy
size constancy

shape constancy
brightness constancy
perceptual illusion
Müller-Lyer illusion
moon illusion
perceptual set

Matching Exercise

Match the appropriate term with its definition or description.

1. _____ The influence of prior assumptions and expectations on perceptual interpretations.

2. _____ The tendency to perceive objects, especially familiar objects, as constant and unchanging despite changes in sensory input.

3. _____ Famous visual illusion involving the misperception of the identical length of two lines, one with arrows pointed inward and one with arrows pointed outward.

4. _____ The perception of an object as maintaining the same size despite changing images on the retina.

5. _____ German Gestalt psychologist who is best known for his studies on the perception of motion.

6. _____ An illusion of movement that results when two separate, carefully timed flashing lights are perceived as one light moving back and forth.

True/False Test

Indicate whether each item is true or false by placing T or F in the space next to each item.

1. ___ When we misperceive the true characteristics of an object or image, we experience a perceptual illusion.

2. ___ The moon illusion involves the misperception that the moon is larger when it is on the horizon than when it is directly overhead.

3. ___ The perception of a familiar object as maintaining the same shape regardless of the image produced on the retina is called shape constancy.

4. ___ Brightness constancy is the perception that the brightness of an object remains the same even though the lighting conditions change.

5. ___ Induced motion occurs because we have a strong tendency to assume that the background is stationary while the object or figure moves.

6. ___ In addition to monocular and binocular visual cues, auditory cues can be used to judge distance and direction.

Check your answers and review any areas of weakness before going on to the next section.

Something to Think About

1. Many people have reported strange experiences that they interpret as extrasensory perception, or ESP. Suppose that a friend or family member told you about such an experience. This person might be convinced that something extraordinary has occurred. Based on what you have learned in this chapter, how would you go about explaining to your friend what has most likely taken place?

2. Imagine that you have decided to become an artist. You want to paint a picture that includes a variety of elements such as buildings, fields, a river, a mountain, and some people and animals. Using what you know about sensation and perception, think of all the monocular cues that you could use to give your masterpiece a sense of depth. In addition, can you think of any perceptual components that might add interest to your canvas?

Check your answers and review any areas of weakness before doing the progress tests.

Progress Test 1

Review the complete chapter (including Concept Reviews and all boxed inserts), review all your study notes, and then test yourself on the following progress test. Check your answers. If you make a mistake, review your notes, the appropriate section in the study guide, and if necessary, the relevant part of the chapter in your textbook.

1. Dr. Kandola's research showed that the vibrations of hair cells in the basilar membrane were at the same frequency as the low-frequency sound waves that stimulated them. This research supports the _____ theory of pitch.
   (a) place
   (b) frequency
   (c) timbre
   (d) amplitude

2. Dr. Frankenstein's younger brother built a monster but omitted a very important part of his anatomy. As a result, the monster cannot transform sounds into neural messages. The missing part is the
   (a) eardrum.
   (b) middle ear with its tiny bones.
   (c) vestibular sacs.
   (d) basilar membrane.

3. A red pen is displayed in Roger's peripheral vision while he stares straight ahead. He correctly identifies the object but is unable to name the color. The reason for this is that
   (a) there are many rods but very few cones in the periphery of the retina.
   (b) there are many cones but very few rods in the periphery of the retina.
   (c) there are no receptor cells for vision in the periphery of the retina.
   (d) the stimulus was below Roger's difference threshold.

4. After staring at a blue light for a few minutes, Yoko shifts her gaze to a white wall and experiences an afterimage in the color _____; Yoko's experience provides support for the _____ theory of color vision.
   - (a) red; opponent-process
   - (b) yellow; opponent-process
   - (c) red; trichromatic
   - (d) yellow; trichromatic

5. Neville is color-blind and cannot see red or green, yet he can see blue with no problem. Which theory of color vision can most easily explain this?
   - (a) trichromatic theory
   - (b) place theory
   - (c) opponent-process theory
   - (d) frequency theory

6. Ever since her operation, Madame Burgundi can no longer experience the flavors of the gourmet foods and wines she serves in her restaurant. It is most likely that she has suffered damage to her
   - (a) kinesthetic sense.
   - (b) sense of smell.
   - (c) sense of humor.
   - (d) vestibular sense.

7. The dizziness and disorientation Shelly felt after she rolled down the hill are a function of her
   - (a) basilar membrane.
   - (b) Pacinian corpuscles.
   - (c) semicircular canals and vestibular sacs.
   - (d) proprioceptors.

8. As Pancho gazed down the railway tracks it seemed to him that the two parallel rails actually met in the distance. Pancho is experiencing the monocular depth cue
   - (a) linear perspective.
   - (b) aerial perspective.
   - (c) motion parallax.
   - (d) texture gradient.

9. Many people have mistaken a floating log for Ogopogo, the alleged Okanagan Lake monster. The most likely reason for this misperception is
   - (a) a perceptual set.
   - (b) monocular vision.
   - (c) rye whisky.
   - (d) extrasensory perception.

10. If Fred holds a letter he is reading very close to his nose and Charlie holds it at arm's length when he reads it, Fred will experience _____ Charlie.
    - (a) more convergence than
    - (b) the identical level of convergence as
    - (c) less convergence than
    - (d) more motion parallax than

11. In an experiment, you are seated in a darkened room and shown a large lighted frame with a single dot of light inside it. The frame slowly moves to the left, and the dot remains stationary. It is very probable that you will perceive
    - (a) induced motion.
    - (b) the dot moving to the right.
    - (c) the frame as remaining stationary.
    - (d) all of the above.

12. As Demi moves away from the camera, her image on the screen grows smaller and smaller, yet viewers do not perceive Demi as the incredible shrinking woman. This illustrates
    - (a) convergence.
    - (b) binocular disparity.
    - (c) size constancy.
    - (d) motion parallax.

13. Nedzad claims that by examining the color and markings of your iris he can determine your level of mental stress, personality characteristics, genetic tendencies, nutritional deficiencies, and personal history of illness and injuries; he can also tell whether you presently have a disease and what it is. According to Science versus Pseudoscience 3.2, Nedzad is probably
    - (a) a Gestalt psychologist.
    - (b) an iridologist.
    - (c) suffering from mental illness.
    - (d) a gate-control theorist.

14. Whether perceptual principles are universal and inborn (nativist position) or vary from culture to culture and are influenced by experience and learning (empiricist position) has been the subject of a longstanding debate. According to Culture and Human Behavior 3.5, research using the Müller-Lyer illusion tends to support.
    - (a) the nativist position.
    - (b) the empiricist position.
    - (c) neither the nativist nor the empiricist position.
    - (d) the nativist position slightly more than the empiricist position.

15. According to Science versus Pseudoscience 3.1, if advertisers were to expose moviegoers to the subliminally flashed words EAT POPCORN and DRINK COKE during a movie
    - (a) sales of popcorn and Coke would increase dramatically.
    - (b) the moviegoers would feel hungry and thirsty for days after seeing the movie.
    - (c) the subliminal messages are not likely to have any discernible effect on the sale of popcorn and Coke.
    - (d) the moviegoers will have recurring nightmares involving popcorn and Coke.

Progress Test 2

After you have checked your understanding of the material in Progress Test 1 and have done a complete chapter review with special focus on any areas of weakness, you are ready to further assess your knowledge on Progress Test 2. Check your answers. If you make a mistake, review your notes, the relevant sections of the study guide, and if necessary, the appropriate parts of your textbook.

1. Detection of stimulus energy is to the interpretation of the information as _____ is to _____ .
    - (a) transduction; accommodation
    - (b) hue; saturation
    - (c) hearing; vision
    - (d) sensation; perception

2. When Julius returns from getting a drink of water, he resumes weightlifting a 150-pound free weight and doesn't notice that someone has added a five-pound ring to each end. For Julius the additional ten pounds
    - (a) is not a just noticeable difference (jnd).
    - (b) is below his absolute threshold.
    - (c) is not sensed because of sensory adaptation.
    - (d) is easy to lift because water releases endorphins.

3. When Vincent arrived home, the first thing he noticed was the smell of freshly baked bread. The process by which the odor of baking bread was converted into neural signals that Vincent's brain could interpret is called
    - (a) sensory adaptation.
    - (b) transduction.
    - (c) accommodation.
    - (d) conduction.

4. In an experimental situation, Malgorzata is able to detect a very small difference in the loudness of two tones. It is very likely that the researchers are investigating
    - (a) the difference threshold.
    - (b) sensory adaptation.
    - (c) the absolute threshold.
    - (d) subliminal perception.

5. When Tony was painting a landscape, he used many different colors. The technical term for each of the different wavelengths of light that produce the subjective sensation of different colors in Tony's painting is
    - (a) saturation.
    - (b) hue.
    - (c) brightness.
    - (d) timbre.

6. As Rodney was setting up the equipment for the concert, he adjusted the amplitude of the speaker system. This is most likely to affect the _____ of the music.
    - (a) pitch
    - (b) frequency
    - (c) timbre
    - (d) loudness

7. Eight-year-old Sean can hear sounds close to 20,000 hertz. This sensory capacity is best explained by
    - (a) extrasensory perception (ESP) theory.
    - (b) opponent-process theory.
    - (c) frequency theory.
    - (d) place theory.

8. When Derrick removed all visual distance cues, he noticed that the moon on the horizon looked to be the same size as it was when directly overhead. Derrick concluded correctly that the distance cues make the horizon moon seem _____ the overhead moon.
    - (a) farther away than
    - (b) closer than
    - (c) smaller than
    - (d) the same size as

9. In terms of the transduction of physical energy into coded neural messages, the _____ is to the eye as the _____ is to the ear.
    - (a) lens; oval window
    - (b) fovea; auditory nerve
    - (c) retina; cochlea
    - (d) iris; eardrum

10. On the day of an important job interview, Madeline wakes up with a slight toothache. As the time for the stressful interview approaches, her anxiety increases and so does her perception of the pain from her tooth. When the interview is over, Madeline is elated because she feels it has gone well and, to her surprise, she feels hardly any pain from her tooth. Madeline's experience is best explained by the _____ theory and the contribution of her psychological and emotional state.
    - (a) opponent-process
    - (b) gate-control
    - (c) place
    - (d) frequency

11. Astrid holds a pencil quite close to her nose and opens and closes her left and right eyes a couple of times in succession. She notices that the images are quite different. When she views the same pencil in a similar manner from across the room, she sees almost identical images. Astrid has demonstrated the _____ cue of _____ .
    - (a) binocular; binocular disparity
    - (b) monocular; motion parallax
    - (c) binocular; overlap
    - (d) monocular; convergence

·12. With his eyes closed, Shahin can accurately touch his nose, lips, and ears with his right index finger. Shahin's ability to do this is due to specialized sensory neurons called _____ that are involved in his _____ sense.
    - (a) Pacinian corpuscles; vestibular
    - (b) ganglion cells; visual
    - (c) proprioceptors; kinesthetic
    - (d) pheromones; olfactory

13. As dusk descends, Carmen thinks that the yellow tulips are just as yellow as they had been earlier when there was more daylight. Despite the changing lighting conditions, Carmen's perception of the color of the flowers did not change. This is best explained by _____ constancy and the fact that objects always reflect the same _____ of available light.
    - (a) brightness; amount
    - (b) brightness; proportion
    - (c) size; degree
    - (d) shape; amount

14. According to the Application, the process of learning voluntary control over largely autonomic body functions such as heart rate, blood pressure, and muscle tension by using specialized sensitive equipment is called
    - (a) proprioception.
    - (b) psychokinesis.
    - (c) acupuncture.
    - (d) biofeedback.

15. Willard believes he can influence the mechanical systems within slot machines with the power of his mind alone. According to Critical Thinking, 3.4, Willard is claiming to possess the power of
    - (a) telepathy.
    - (b) clairvoyance.
    - (c) psychokinesis.
    - (d) precognition.

Progress Test 3

After you have checked your understanding of the material in Progress Tests 1 and 2 and have done a complete chapter review with special focus on any areas of weakness, you are ready to further assess your knowledge on Progress Test 3. Check your answers. If you make a mistake, review your notes, the appropriate parts of the study guide, and if necessary, the relevant sections of your textbook.

1. During a psychology lab demonstration, the instructor set up two flashing lights about three feet apart in a darkened room. About one-tenth of a second after the first light flashed, the second light flashed, and then the first light flashed again, and so on. Most of the students experienced the illusion of apparent motion, perceiving just one light traveling back and forth. The instructor is most likely to explain this phenomenon in terms of
    - (a) the principles of stroboscopic motion.
    - (b) the kinesthetic sense.
    - (c) motion parallax.
    - (d) binocular disparity.

2. You have just arrived at the beach and the texture of the sand toward the water appears smooth, even, and perfectly flat, yet the sand beneath your feet is rough and uneven and you can see individual small stones, seashells, and other debris. You are experiencing the monocular distance cue of
    - (a) motion parallax.
    - (b) aerial perspective.
    - (c) linear perspective.
    - (d) texture gradient.

3. José notices that near the horizon the moon appears larger than when it is overhead in the sky. The effect is mainly the result of
   (a) distance cues that make the horizon moon seem farther away.
   (b) the retinal image of the horizon moon being larger than the retinal image of the overhead moon.
   (c) distance cues that make the horizon moon seem nearer.
   (d) having to tilt your head upward when looking at the overhead moon.

4. While carrying out a sensory demonstration in which a small object is positioned so that its retinal image would be cast on the exact spot where her optic nerve exits the eye, Deidre should expect the image of the object to
   (a) change to its opposite color.
   (b) look twice as large as it had before.
   (c) produce an afterimage if she shifts her gaze to a white surface.
   (d) disappear from sight.

5. Analysis that moves from the parts to the whole is to _____ as analysis that moves from the whole to the parts is to
   _____ .
   (a) figure–ground relationship; figure–ground reversal
   (b) bottom-up processing; top-down processing
   (c) size constancy; shape constancy
   (d) the moon illusion; the Müller-Lyer illusion

6. While strolling through the garden, Jamal suddenly noticed the beautiful odor of roses. Jamal is using her _____ sense, and the process by which the odor is converted into neural signals that her brain can understand is called _____ .
   (a) gustatory; saturation
   (b) olfactory: transduction
   (c) gustatory; adaptation
   (d) olfactory; accommodation

7. Whenever Robyn looks at her boyfriend, her pupils dilate. The eye structure responsible for this response is called the
   (a) retina.   (c) iris.
   (b) fovea.   (d) optic disk.

8. When looking carefully at a picture of a country scene we are able to detect fine visual details, especially those that are focused on the fovea. One reason for this visual acuity is that
   (a) the fovea contains rods, which have many individual neural connections to the cortex.
   (b) the fovea contains cones, which have many individual neural connections to the cortex.
   (c) the fovea is the spot where the optic nerve leaves the eye.
   (d) there are only bipolar cells in the fovea, and these are specialized for feature detection.

9. After Jackson has been in the hot tub for a few minutes, he no longer notices how hot the water is. This is because of
   (a) sensory adaptation.
   (b) the just noticeable difference.
   (c) Jackson's thick skin.
   (d) sensory saturation.

10. After playing in a heavy metal rock band for most of his young adult life, Edwin has suffered a significant hearing loss. Unfortunately for Edwin, his hearing problem cannot be helped by a hearing aid. It is most likely that he is suffering from
    (a) damage to the auditory cortex in his left temporal lobe.
    (b) nerve deafness.
    (c) damage to his proprioceptors.
    (d) conduction deafness.

11. Graham is nearsighted and Grace is farsighted. Corrective lenses work for both of them because their respective visual disorders are caused by
    (a) the lack of rods and cones in the visual disk.
    (b) clouding or occlusion of the cornea.
    (c) smaller than normal ganglion and bipolar cells in the retina.
    (d) a failure of the lens to properly focus incoming light on the retina.

12. Mehnroosh believes that the size of the just noticeable difference varies depending on its relation to the strength of the original stimulus. Her views are most consistent with
    (a) Weber's law.
    (b) place theory.
    (c) the opponent-process theory.
    (d) gate-control theory.

13. To reduce the experience of pain, Dexter looks away and focuses on a picture on the wall as a nurse sticks a hypodermic needle into his arm. According to the Application, Dexter is using the pain control technique of
    - (a) counterirritation.
    - (c) biofeedback.
    - (b) relaxation.
    - (d) distraction.

14. Dr. Frederick believes that people living in urban, industrialized environments have a great deal of perceptual experience in judging lines, corners, edges, and other rectangular, manufactured objects; thus, they should be more susceptible to the Müller-Lyer illusion than people in cultures whose experience has been primarily with more natural objects. According to Culture and Human Behavior 3.5, this idea is called
    - (a) Weber's law.
    - (b) gate-control theory.
    - (c) the carpentered-world hypothesis.
    - (d) the opponent-process theory.

15. Maxwell is a male pig and, like most male pigs, he releases a chemical substance in the sweat glands to communicate territorial boundaries and sexual receptiveness. According to In Focus 3.3, these chemical signals, common in the animal kingdom, are called _____ .
    - (a) chemosignals
    - (c) substance P
    - (b) pheromones
    - (d) umami

Answers

Introduction: What Are Sensation and Perception?

1. *The primary function of the nervous system is* communication—the transmission of information from one part of the body to another.

2. *Sensation refers to* the detection and basic sensory experience of environmental stimuli, *and perception occurs* when we integrate, organize, and interpret sensory information in a way that is meaningful.

3. *The difference between sensation and perception is* that sensation involves responding to stimulation and transmitting it to the brain, whereas perception involves the organization and interpretation of sensation. However, there is no clear definitive boundary between the two.

Basic Principles of Sensation

1. *Sensory receptors help us hear, taste, smell, feel, and see by* using specialized cells called sensory receptors that respond to stimulation by some form of energy (e.g., sound waves, chemicals, pressure, light waves, etc.).

2. *Transduction is* the process by which a form of physical energy is converted into a coded neural signal that can be processed by the nervous system.

3. *The two types of sensory threshold are* the absolute threshold, which is the smallest possible strength of a stimulus that can be detected half the time, and the difference threshold, which is the smallest possible difference between two stimuli that can be detected half the time.

4. *Another name for the difference threshold is* the just noticeable difference (jnd).

5. *Weber's law states* that the size of the just noticeable difference (jnd) will vary depending on its relation to the strength of the original stimulus.

6. *Sensory adaptation occurs because* sensory receptor cells become less responsive to a constant stimulus; it is relative to the duration of exposure.

Concept Check 1

1. absolute
2. sensation; perception
3. difference threshold; just noticeable difference (jnd); Weber's law
4. transduction
5. sensory adaptation
6. subliminal perception

Matching Exercise 1

1. threshold
2. transduction
3. absolute threshold
4. sensory receptors
5. difference threshold

True/False Test 1

1. F   3. T   5. T
2. T   4. F

Vision: From Light to Sight

1. *The process of seeing begins with* stimulation of visual receptors cells in the eye, which are sensitive to the physical energy of light.

2. *The electromagnetic spectrum is* made up of many different forms of electromagnetic energy, which vary in wavelength; humans are capable of visually detecting only a tiny portion of the spectrum (visual light).

3. *The key structures of the eye are* the cornea, pupil, iris, lens, and retina (rods and cones).

4. *The function of rods is to* detect light (but not color); *the function of cones is to* detect color and fine details (most cones are concentrated in the fovea, the point of central focus in the retina).

5. *Bipolar cells process visual information by* collecting information from the rods and cones and funneling it to the ganglion cells, whose bundled axons form the optic nerve; from the optic chiasm (the point of partial crossover of the optic nerves from each eye) information is sent to the thalamus and then on to the visual cortex.

6. *The optic disk is* the point at which the fibers that make up the optic nerve exit the back of the eye and create a blind spot in our field of vision.

7. *Our experience of color involves* three properties of light waves: hue (color), saturation (purity), and brightness (intensity). Different wavelengths correspond to our subjective experience of different colors.

8. *According to the trichromatic theory,* there are three types of cones, each of which is especially sensitive to certain wavelengths: red light (long wavelengths), green light (medium wavelengths), or blue light (short wavelengths); other colors are a result of stimulation of a combination of cones. *This theory explains* the most common form of color blindness, red–green color blindness.

9. *According to the opponent-process theory,* there are four basic colors, which are divided into two pairs of color-sensitive neurons, red–green and blue–yellow (black and white also act as an opposing pair), and when one member of a pair is stimulated, the other member is inhibited. *This theory explains* afterimages.

Concept Check 2

1. white

2. green

3. trichromatic; opponent-process

4. color; fine detail

5. red

Graphic Organizer 1

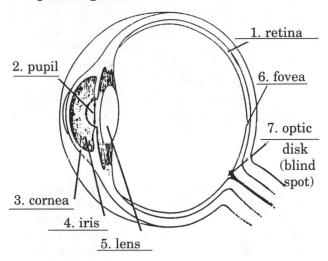

1. retina
2. pupil
3. cornea
4. iris
5. lens
6. fovea
7. optic disk (blind spot)

Matching Exercise 2

1. visual acuity
2. afterimage
3. wavelength
4. accommodation
5. brightness
6. optic nerve
7. trichromatic theory of color vision
8. cones
9. hue
10. rods
11. bipolar cells
12. color
13. optic disk
14. presbyopia
15. astigmatism
16. feature detectors

True/False Test 2

1. F	5. F	9. T	13. T
2. T	6. T	10. T	14. T
3. F	7. T	11. F	15. T
4. T	8. F	12. T	

Hearing: From Vibration to Sound

1. *Audition is* the technical term for the sense of hearing.

2. *Our perception of sound is directly related to the physical properties of* sound waves and involves intensity (amplitude, measured in decibels), pitch (the relative highness or lowness of a sound, determined by frequency), and timbre (the distinctive quality of a sound).

3. *The key structures of the ear are* the outer ear (pinna, ear canal, and eardrum), the middle ear (the hammer, anvil, and stirrup), and the inner ear (cochlea and semicircular canals).

4. *The process of hearing begins when* sound waves are caught by the pinna and funneled down the ear canal. *It then involves* the sound waves being amplified in the middle ear and transformed into neural messages by hair cells in the basilar membrane, which runs the length of the cochlea in the inner ear.

5. *According to the frequency theory,* the basilar membrane vibrates at the same frequency as the sound waves. *This theory explains* how low-frequency sounds (up to about 1,000 hertz) are transmitted to the brain but cannot explain the transmission of higher-frequency sounds.

6. *According to place theory,* different frequencies cause larger vibrations at different locations along the basilar membrane. *This theory explains* our discrimination of higher-pitched sounds; for intermediate frequencies, both place and frequency theories are involved.

Concept Check 3

1. retina; cochlea
2. conduction
3. place
4. hearing aid
5. place

Graphic Organizer 2

1. pinna
6. hammer, anvil, and stirrup
3. cochlea
7. auditory nerve
2. eardrum
5. oval window
4. ear canal

Matching Exercise 3

1. nerve deafness
2. audition
3. frequency
4. hair cells
5. sound waves
6. timbre
7. outer ear
8. pitch
9. place theory
10. decibel
11. amplitude
12. middle ear

True/False Test 3

1. T	5. T	9. T
2. T	6. T	10. T
3. T	7. F	11. T
4. F	8. T	12. T

The Chemical and Body Senses: Smell, Taste, Touch, and Position

1. *Olfaction is the technical term for* the sense of smell, *and gustation is the technical term for* the sense of taste.

2. *They are called chemical senses because* the sensory receptors for taste and smell are specialized to respond to different types of chemical substances.

3. *Our sense of smell begins when* airborne molecules emitted by substances we smell stimulate olfactory receptor cells high in the nasal cavity. *It then involves* the resulting neural messages being passed along the olfactory nerves, which are directly connected to the olfactory bulb (the enlarged ending of the olfactory cortex). From there, the messages pass along the olfactory tract to various brain areas, including the temporal lobe and structures in the limbic system.

4. *Our sense of taste begins when* specialized receptors in the taste buds located on the tongue and inside the mouth and throat are stimulated. *It then involves* neural messages being sent along neural pathways to the thalamus, which, in turn, directs the information to several regions in the cortex.

5. *The five primary taste qualities are* sweet, sour, salty, bitter, and umami.

6. *The skin and body senses include* touch and temperature, pain, position, and balance.

7. *The skin responds to* stimulation such as pressure, warmth, and cold.

8. *One receptor for touch is* the Pacinian corpuscle, *and it works by* converting pressure stimulation into a neural message that is relayed to the brain. If pressure is constant, sensory adaptation takes place.

9. *Temperature is sensed* depending on whether warm or cold spots are stimulated. When these spots are stimulated simultaneously, we sense hot.

10. *Pain is the sensation of* physical discomfort or suffering that can occur in varying degrees of intensity. It occurs when an intense stimulus activates free nerve endings, which carry their messages to the spinal cord, releasing substance P.

11. *According to the gate-control theory,* the sensation of pain is controlled by a series of gates that open (pain is experienced) and close (pain is not experienced) in the spinal cord. It results from both physiological and psychological factors.

12. *The experience of pain is also influenced by* both negative and positive emotions, and by social and cultural learning experiences about the meaning of pain and how people should react to pain.

13. *Our kinesthetic sense involves* stimulation of proprioceptors, which constantly communicate information to the brain about changes in body position and muscle tension and provide information about the location and position of body parts in relation to one another.

14. *Our vestibular sense provides us with* a sense of balance, or equilibrium, by responding to changes in gravity, motion, and body position.

15. *The two sources of vestibular sensory information are* the semicircular canals and the vestibular sacs, both of which are located in the ear.

Concept Check 4

1. taste buds
2. smell (olfaction)
3. smell (olfaction)
4. sweet; salty; sour; bitter; umami
5. intensify
6. semicircular canals; vestibular sacs
7. pain
8. kinesthetic
9. substance P

Matching Exercise 4

1. gustation
2. vestibular sacs
3. Pacinian corpuscle
4. chemical senses
5. free nerve endings
6. olfactory receptor cells
7. olfactory bulb
8. taste buds
9. olfactory tract
10. vestibular sense
11. endorphins
12. kinesthetic sense
13. umami

True/False Test 4

1. T	5. F	9. F
2. T	6. T	10. F
3. T	7. T	11. F
4. T	8. T	12. T

Perception (Part 1)

1. *Perception is the process of* integrating, organizing, and interpreting sensory information in a meaningful way.

2. *Bottom-up processing refers to* the flow of information from the sensory receptors to the brain; this type of analysis moves from the parts to the whole (data-driven processing).

3. *Top-down processing refers to* analysis that moves from the whole to the parts; it occurs when we use our knowledge, experience, expectations, and other cognitive processes to arrive at meaningful perceptions (conceptually driven processing).

4. *The three basic questions of perception are* What is it?, How far away is it?, and Where is it going? (Bottom-up and top-down processing are both necessary for arriving at perceptual conclusions.)

5. *Gestalt psychology was founded by* Max Wertheimer *and is concerned with* the fact that we tend to perceive whole objects or figures (gestalts) rather than isolated bits and pieces of sensory information.

Perception: The Perception of Shape (Part 2)

1. *The figure–ground relationship describes* how we automatically separate the elements of perception into the feature that clearly stands out (the figure) and its less distinct background (the ground). *It is important because it demonstrates that* the separation of a scene into figure and ground is not a property of the actual elements in the scene but instead is a psychological accomplishment.

2. *The perceptual principles involved in grouping visual elements are* similarity, closure, good continuation, and proximity.

3. *The law of Prägnanz states* that when several perceptual organizations of an assortment of visual elements are possible, the perceptual interpretation that occurs will be one that produces the best, simplest, and most stable shape (also called the law of simplicity). *It is important because it encompasses* all other Gestalt principles, including the figure–ground relationship *and suggests that* we actively and automatically construct a perception that reveals the essence of something.

Perception: Depth Perception (Part 3)

1. *Depth perception refers to* the ability to perceive the distance of an object as well as its three-dimensional characteristics. *It is important because* being able to perceive the distance of an object has obvious survival value, especially regarding potential threats or danger.

2. *Monocular cues are defined as* distance or depth cues that can be processed by either eye alone *and include* relative size, overlap, aerial perspective, texture gradient, linear perspective, motion parallax, and accommodation. (Monocular cues used by artists are called pictorial cues.)

3. *Binocular cues are defined as* distance or depth cues that require the use of both eyes *and include* convergence and binocular disparity.

4. *A stereogram is* a picture that uses the principles of binocular disparity to create the perception of a three-dimensional image.

Concept Check 5

1. law of proximity
2. ground; figure
3. binocular disparity
4. relative size
5. linear perspective
6. law of closure
7. bottom-up processing

Matching Exercise 5

1. Gestalt psychology
2. law of Prägnanz
3. aerial perspective
4. binocular disparity
5. figure–ground relationship
6. overlap
7. binocular cues
8. accommodation
9. law of proximity
10. depth perception
11. figure–ground reversal

12. Max Wertheimer
13. parapsychology
14. law of similarity

True/False Test 5

1. T	6. T	11. T
2. T	7. T	12. F
3. F	8. T	13. T
4. T	9. T	14. T
5. F	10. F	

Perception: The Perception of Motion (Part 4)

1. *The perception of motion involves* the integration of information from several sources, including microfine eye muscle movements, the changing retinal image, and the contrast of the moving object with its stationary background.

2. *Induced motion refers to* our strong tendency to assume that the background is stationary and that it is the object or figure that moves. *It was first studied by* Karl Dunker.

3. *Stroboscopic motion creates* an illusion of movement with two carefully timed flashing lights going on and off in succession. *It is caused by* the brain's visual system combining the rapid sequence of visual information (the two lights going on and off and being detected at two different points on the surface of the retina) and arriving at the conclusion of movement, even though no movement has occurred (the perception of smooth motion in movies is due to the same phenomenon).

4. *Auditory cues are used to judge distance and direction in a couple of ways:* First, the louder a sound is, the closer in distance it is perceived to be. Second, when a sound comes from one side, it reaches the nearer ear a few thousandths of a second before it reaches the other ear; the brain calculates the time difference between the arrival of the sound stimulus at each ear and thus determines the direction of the sound.

Perception: Perceptual Constancies (Part 5)

1. *Perceptual constancy refers to* the tendency to perceive objects as unchanging despite changes in sensory input.

2. *Size constancy is* the perception that an object remains the same size despite its changing image on the retina. *An important aspect of size constancy is* that if the retinal image of an object does not change, but the perception of its distance increases, the object is perceived as larger.

3. *Shape constancy is* the tendency to perceive familiar objects as having a fixed shape regardless of the image they cast on the retina.

4. *Brightness constancy is* the perception that the brightness of an object remains the same even though the lighting conditions change.

Perceptual Illusions and the Effects of Experience on Perceptual Interpretations

1. *Perceptual illusions involve* the misperception of a stimulus; they are used to study perceptual principles.

2. *The Müller-Lyer illusion is* a famous illusion involving the misperception of the length of two identical lines, one with arrows pointing outward and one with arrows pointed inward.

3. *The moon illusion is* a visual illusion involving the misperception that the moon is larger when it is on the horizon than when it is overhead *and may be the result of* the misapplication of the principle of size constancy—distance cues make the horizon moon seem farther away, and thus we perceive the moon as being larger, even though the retinal image of the moon remains constant.

4. *Perceptual illusions and impossible figures reveal that* what we see is not merely a reflection of the real world, but instead, it is our subjective interpretation of it; we actively construct perceptual conclusions about the information detected through our senses (in a way, believing is seeing).

5. *Perceptions can be influenced by* a variety of learning experiences, including educational, cultural, and social factors.

6. *A perceptual set is* the tendency for prior assumptions and expectations to influence our perceptual interpretations.

Concept Check 6

1. perceptual set
2. farther away
3. shape
4. Müller-Lyer
5. perceptual constancy
6. stroboscopic motion

Matching Exercise 6

1. perceptual set
2. perceptual constancy
3. Müller-Lyer illusion
4. size constancy
5. Karl Dunker
6. stroboscopic motion

True/False Test 6

1. T	3. T	5. T
2. T	4. T	6. T

Something to Think About

1. First, you would note that these strange experiences happen to many people, that there is nothing particularly unique about them. The problem arises in the way people interpret these experiences. These experiences, of course, do not constitute proof of ESP, no matter how strongly someone believes they do. Two less extraordinary concepts can explain these occurrences: coincidence and the fallacy of positive instances. Coincidence, which refers to an event occurring simply by chance, can account for many of the experiences reported by people. Combine coincidence with our tendency to remember coincidental events that seem to confirm our belief about unusual phenomena—the fallacy of positive instances—and the feeling that something unusual has happened can be very strong, even though there are no rational grounds for it. Finally, there is no strong scientific evidence for the existence of ESP, despite years of intensive study by psychologists interested in this topic. To date, no parapsychology experiment that has claimed to show evidence of ESP has been successfully replicated. This, of course, does not prove conclusively that ESP does not exist; however, although one should keep an open mind, there is not a shred of evidence or any rational reason to believe in its existence.

2. Some of the most common monocular or pictorial cues that are useful in conveying a sense of depth on the canvas are overlap, in which "nearer" objects are depicted as blocking or obscuring more "distant" objects; linear perspective, in which parallel lines are depicted as converging toward the top of the painting, for instance; and texture gradient, in which surfaces that are supposed to be close to the observer have distinct, clearly defined textures and those that are gradually less and less clearly defined depict distance. Relative size and aerial perspective are also useful devices to convey depth.

To make your picture more interesting you might want to attempt to incorporate some of the elements from impossible figures (such as the Escher drawings) or perceptual illusions.

Progress Test 1

1. b	6. b	11. d
2. d	7. c	12. c
3. a	8. a	13. b
4. b	9. a	14. b
5. a	10. a	15. c

Progress Test 2

1. d	6. d	11. a
2. a	7. d	12. c
3. b	8. a	13. b
4. a	9. c	14. d
5. b	10. b	15. c

Progress Test 3

1. a	6. b	11. d
2. d	7. c	12. a
3. a	8. b	13. d
4. d	9. a	14. c
5. b	10. b	15. b

Consciousness and Its Variations

chapter **4**

PREVIEW

Reading the section below first will give you a general sense of the chapter's contents and an initial introduction to some of the major concepts and terms. This will prime you for what you are about to read and help you to develop a "cognitive map" that will guide your study of the material in this chapter. Likewise, reading the **preview questions** at the beginning of each major section will improve your ability to understand, learn, and retain the information.

CHAPTER 4 . . . AT A GLANCE

Chapter 4 examines the different forms of human consciousness, beginning with how biological and environmental "clocks" regulate our circadian rhythms and sleep-wake cycles. The discovery of REM sleep and how the EEG is used to measure brain-wave activity are discussed. This is followed by an examination of the different stages of sleep and their associated brain-wave activity and behavioral patterns, including the various sleep disorders. The section concludes with an exploration of dreams and mental activity during sleep. Two major theories of the meaning of dreams and their relevance to psychological and physiological functioning are presented.

Altered states of consciousness are introduced next, and both hypnosis and meditation are discussed in this context. Under hypnosis, profound sensory and perceptual changes may be experienced. This section focuses on phenomena such as posthypnotic suggestion, posthypnotic amnesia, and hypermnesia. Hilgard's notions of dissociation and the hidden observer are examined, and the controversy surrounding how to explain hypnosis is discussed. Finally, meditation is defined, and techniques for inducing a meditative state are presented along with research findings on transcendental meditation, or TM.

The final section of the chapter is concerned with using drugs to alter consciousness. The psychoactive drugs are classified and listed along with their various effects on brain activity and physiological and psychological functioning. Drug dependence, drug tolerance, withdrawal symptoms, and drug abuse are discussed.

The Application offers some practical suggestions for improving your mental alertness.

Introduction: Consciousness: Experiencing the "Private I"

Preview Questions

Consider the following questions as you study this section of the chapter.

- How is consciousness defined, and what did William James mean by "stream of consciousness"?
- Why was research on consciousness abandoned for a time, and why did it regain legitimacy?

*Read the section "Introduction: Consciousness: Experiencing the 'Private I'" and **write** your answers to the following:*

1. Consciousness is defined as the _____

   _____

2. William James's idea of "stream of consciousness" refers to the fact that _____

   _____

   _____

3. Research on consciousness was abandoned because _____

   _____

   Psychologists turned instead to _____

   _____

4. Psychologists returned to studying consciousness in the late 1950s for two reasons: _____

   _____

   _____

Biological and Environmental "Clocks" Regulating Consciousness

Preview Questions

Consider the following questions as you study this section of the chapter.

- What are circadian rhythms?
- What roles do the suprachiasmatic nucleus (SCN), sunlight, and melatonin play in regulating circadian rhythms?
- How do "free-running" conditions affect circadian rhythms?
- Why do people suffer jet-lag symptoms, and what role does melatonin play in producing these symptoms?

*Read the section "Biological and Environmental 'Clocks' Regulating Consciousness" and **write** the answers to the following:*

1. Circadian rhythms are _____

   _____

2. The suprachiasmatic nucleus (SCN) is _____

   _____

   _____

   Its role in sleep–wake cycles and other circadian rhythms is to _____

   _____

   _____

3. Melatonin is a _____

   _____

4. Free-running conditions are created by _____

   They have two distinct effects: First, _____

   Second, _____

   _____

5. People suffer from jet lag symptoms because

   _____

   _____

6. Melatonin plays a key role in jet lag symptoms by _____

   _____

After you have carefully studied the preceding sections, complete the following exercises.

Concept Check 1

Read the following and write the correct term in the space provided.

1. Sheena works night shifts and has found that she can sleep quite well during the day now that she has hung heavy curtains in her bedroom that effectively block out any daylight. She is able to get restful sleep in the daytime because her _____ are staying in sync with her night work schedule, and she has prevented sunlight from resetting her _____ .

2. Although Marvin was very tired after pulling an "all-nighter" to finish a paper, he began to feel much less drowsy as the morning proceeded. His reaction is probably due to decreased levels of the hormone _____ .

3. David typically experiences a slump in his mental alertness around midafternoon but feels very energetic in the early evening. These daily highs and lows are examples of _____ .

4. During a history lecture, Alfie is listening and taking notes but at times he is also thinking about his girlfriend and the argument they had last night. He wonders what he will say to her when he phones her that afternoon, which gets him thinking about how often his parents fight and whether arguing is genetic, which reminds him about his biology exam next week. This description reflects Alfie's _____ .

5. Dr. Parizeau arranges for volunteers to spend several weeks in underground bunkers without exposure to sunlight, clocks, or other environmental time cues, and during this time he monitors their sleep–wake cycles and other biological events. Dr. Parizeau is attempting to create _____ in his research on circadian rhythms.

Review of Terms, Concepts, and Names 1

Use the terms in this list to complete the Matching Test, then to help you answer the True/False items correctly.

consciousness
William James
introspection
circadian rhythm
suprachiasmatic nucleus
  (SCN)

melatonin
pineal gland
free-running condition
jet lag
biorhythms
chronobiology

Matching Exercise

Match the appropriate term/name with its definition or description:

1. _____ Personal awareness of mental activities, internal sensations, and the external environment.

2. _____ Subjective verbal reports that try to capture the structure of conscious experience through examining one's present mental state.

3. _____ Cluster of neurons in the brain's hypothalamus that governs the timing of circadian rhythms.

4. _____ Symptoms such as physical and mental fatigue, depression, irritability, disrupted sleep, and fuzziness in concentration, thinking, and memory that result from circadian rhythms being out of sync with daylight/darkness cues.

5. _____ Hormone manufactured by the pineal gland that produces sleepiness.

6. _____ Pseudoscience based on the unproven notion that from birth onward, three rigidly fixed natural biorhythms reflect high, low, and critical periods of a person's physical, emotional, and intellectual functioning.

True/False Test

Indicate whether each statement is true or false by placing T or F in the blank space next to each item.

1. ___ Chronobiology is the scientific study of biological rhythms over time.

2. ___ William James was the American psychologist and philosopher who proposed that the subjective experience of consciousness is an ongoing stream of mental activity.

3. ___ The pineal gland is an endocrine gland located in the brain that regulates the production of the hormone melatonin.

4. ___ Researchers have had volunteers live in underground bunkers, depriving them of all environmental time cues for various periods of time, in order to create free-running conditions.

5. ___ Circadian rhythm refers to a cycle or rhythm that is roughly 24 hours long and involves cyclical daily fluctuations in biological and psychological processes.

Check your answers and review any areas of weakness before going on to the next section.

Sleep

Preview Questions

Consider the following questions as you study this section of the chapter.

- How did the invention of the electroencephalograph and the discovery of REM sleep contribute to modern sleep research?

- What are the characteristics of the sleep stages?
- How do sleep patterns change over the lifespan?

*Read the section "Sleep" (up to "Why Do We Sleep?") and **write** your answers to the following:*

1. An electroencephalograph is _____

   _____

   _____

2. By studying EEGs, sleep researchers have established that _____

   _____

3. Use of the EEG led to the discovery of _____

   _____

4. Beta brain waves are associated with _____

   _____

   Alpha brain waves are associated with_____

   _____

5. Hypnagogic hallucinations are _____

   _____

6. The four NREM sleep stages are characterized by different brain and body activity:

   Stage 1 NREM: _____

   _____

   Stage 2 NREM: _____

   _____

   Stage 3 and 4 NREM: _____

   _____

7. REM sleep is characterized by _____

   _____

   _____

8. Over the course of the lifespan, the quantity and quality of our sleep _____

   _____

   _____

Why Do We Sleep?

Preview Questions

Consider the following questions as you study this section of the chapter.

- Why do we need to sleep?
- How do the restorative and adaptive theories of sleep explain the function of sleep?

*Read the section "Why Do We Sleep?" and **write** your answers to the following:*

1. Sleep deprivation studies demonstrate that

   _____

   _____

2. The phenomena of REM and NREM rebound seem to indicate that _____

   _____

3. The restorative theory of sleep suggests that

   _____

   _____

4. The adaptive theory of sleep suggests that

   _____

   _____

   _____

Sleep Disorders: Troubled Sleep

Preview Questions

Consider the following questions as you study this section of the chapter.

- What are sleep disorders, who suffers from them, and how common are they?
- How is insomnia defined, and what is restless leg syndrome (RLS)?
- What are parasomnias, and what are the characteristics of sleep apnea, sleepwalking, night terrors, REM sleep behavior disorder, and narcolepsy?

*Read the section "Sleep Disorders: Troubled Sleep" and **write** your answers to the following:*

1. Sleep disorders are_____

   _____

   _____

   _____

2. Insomnia is _____

   _____

Many complaints of insomnia are related to restless leg syndrome (RLS), which is _____

_____

_____

3. With sleep apnea, _____

_____

_____

4. Sleepwalking is characterized by _____

_____

5. A night terror is characterized by _____

_____

_____

6. In REM sleep behavior disorder, _____

_____

7. Parasomnias are _____

_____

_____

_____

8. Narcolepsy is characterized by _____

_____

_____

After you have carefully studied the preceding sections, complete the following exercises.

Concept Check 2

Read the following and write the correct term in the space provided.

1. James went to bed a short while ago; although his eyes are closed and he is very relaxed, he has not yet fallen asleep. If James's brain is relatively normal, it is probably generating _____ brain waves.

2. Shortly after falling asleep, James experiences a muscle spasm that jolts him awake. James has most likely experienced the most common hypnagogic hallucination of _____ accompanied by a _____ .

3. Bjorn, who has been under a lot of stress ever since he started college, is having trouble sleep-

ing. He repeatedly complains about the quality and duration of his sleep, and worry about not sleeping well often keeps him awake at night. Bjorn is most likely to be diagnosed as suffering from _____ .

4. In an attempt to deal with his sleep disturbance, Bjorn decides to try an over-the-counter sleep medication combined with alcohol. Bjorn's approach is most likely to make his problem _____ (better/worse) in the long run.

5. After being asleep for about 2 hours, eight-year-old Soo Mee suddenly sits up in bed screaming incoherently. Her mother has trouble waking her and calming her down. Soo Mee is experiencing a(n) _____ and is probably in stage _____ or _____ of NREM sleep.

6. Salim is enjoying a night out with a bunch of his college friends at Yuk Yuks comedy club. While laughing heartily at a very funny act, he suddenly goes limp and falls asleep for a few minutes. It is likely that Salim is suffering an attack of _____ and has instantly entered REM sleep and experienced

_____ .

7. Mrs. Eastman has just turned 65 and is worried because she is waking up more easily nowadays, sleeps less than 7 hours most nights, and feels less rested and less satisfied after sleeping. A sleep specialist is most likely to say that she _____

_____ .

8. Azra has been asleep for about ten minutes and is now in stage 2 sleep. Her brain-wave activity is likely to be predominantly _____ waves and to be marked by

_____ .

Graphic Organizer 1

The diagram below shows the brain waves typical of each stage in a 90-minute (approximately) sleep   *cycle. Match the term or description with the correct brain-wave pattern.*

A. Brain waves associated with dreaming

B. Sleep spindles and K complexes

C. Beta brain waves

D. Mixture of theta and delta brain waves

E. Alpha brain waves

F. Delta brain waves

G. Mixture of alpha and theta brain waves

Review of Terms and Concepts 2

Use the terms in this list to complete the Matching Test, then to help you answer the True/False items correctly.

electroencephalograph

electroencephalogram
  (EEG)

REM sleep (active or
  paradoxical sleep)

NREM sleep (quiet
  sleep)

beta brain waves

alpha brain waves

hypnagogic
  hallucinations

myoclonic jerk
  (sleep starts)

theta brain waves

sleep spindles

K complex

slow-wave sleep

delta brain waves

microsleeps

REM rebound

NREM rebound

restorative theory of
  sleep

adaptive (evolutionary)
  theory of sleep

sleep disorders

insomnia

restless legs syndrome
  (RLS)

periodic limb movement
  disorder

stimulus control

sleep apnea

nocturnal enuresis

sleepwalking
  (somnambulism)

night terrors
  (sleep terrors)

sleep bruxism

parasomnias

REM sleep behavior
  disorder

narcolepsy

modafinil

Matching Exercise

Match the appropriate term with its definition or description.

1. _____ Condition in which a person regularly is unable to fall asleep, stay asleep, or feel adequately rested by sleep.

2. _____ Type of sleep during which rapid eye movements and dreaming occur, and voluntary muscle activity is suppressed; also called active sleep or paradoxical sleep.

3. _____ The view that sleep and dreaming are essential to normal physical and mental functioning.

4. _____ Brain-wave pattern associated with relaxed wakefulness and drowsiness.

5. _____ Sleep disorder in which the person repeatedly stops breathing during sleep.

6. _____ Graphic record of brain activity produced by an electroencephalograph.

7. _____ Short bursts of brain activity that characterize stage 2 NREM sleep.

8. _____ Vivid sensory phenomena that can occur during the onset of sleep.

9. _____ Term applied to the combination of stage 3 and stage 4 sleep.

10. _____ Involuntary muscle spasm of the whole body that jolts the person completely awake and often accompanies the hypnagogic hallucination of falling.

11. _____ Single but large high-voltage spike of brain activity that characterizes stage 2 NREM sleep.

12. _____ Sleep disorder in which the sleeper acts out his or her dreams.

13. _____ Phenomenon in which a person who is deprived of REM sleep greatly increases the amount of time spent in REM sleep at the first opportunity for uninterrupted sleep.

14 _____ Instrument that uses electrodes placed on the scalp to measure and record the brain's electrical activity.

15. _____ Condition characterized by unpleasant creeping, crawling, tingling, itching, or prickling sensations deep inside the lower legs and an irresistible urge to move.

16. _____ Behavior therapy for insomnia in which the person is conditioned to associate the bed only with sleepiness and sleep, rather than with watching television, talking on the phone, or other nonsleep activities.

True/False Test

Indicate whether each statement is true or false by placing T or F in the blank space next to each item.

1. ___ NREM rebound is a phenomenon in which a person who is deprived of stage 3 and 4 NREM sleep spends less time in these stages when permitted to sleep undisturbed.

2. ___ The adaptive (evolutionary) theory of sleep suggests that unique sleep patterns of different animals evolved over time to help promote survival and environmental adaptation.

3. ___ Sleep disorders are serious disturbances in the normal sleep pattern that interfere with daytime functioning and cause subjective distress.

4. ___ Narcolepsy is a sleep disorder characterized by excessive daytime sleepiness and brief lapses into sleep throughout the day.

5. ___ Nocturnal enuresis is a sleep disorder in which people grind their teeth loudly during sleep.

6. ___ Sleepwalking (somnambulism) is a sleep disturbance characterized by an episode of walking or performing other actions during stage 3 or stage 4 NREM sleep.

7. ___ Parasomnias are sleep disorders characterized by arousal or activation during sleep or sleep transitions; they include sleepwalking, night terrors, sleep bruxism, and REM sleep behavior disorder.

8. ___ Beta brain waves are patterns of electrical activity that begin in stage 1 NREM sleep and predominate in stage 2 NREM sleep.

9. ___ Episodes of sleep lasting only a few seconds that occur during wakefulness are called microsleeps; they can occur after as little as one day's sleep deprivation.

10. ___ Night terrors typically occur during stage 3 or stage 4 NREM sleep and are characterized by increased physiological arousal, intense fear and panic, frightening hallucinations, and no recall of the episode the next morning.

11. ___ NREM sleep is quiet sleep, which is divided into four stages and does not involve dreaming.

12. ___ Theta brain waves are small, fast brain waves that reflect an awake and reasonably alert state of consciousness.

13. ___ *Sleep bruxism* is another name for bedwetting and typically occurs in children during deep sleep.

14. ___ Delta brain waves are the long, slow waves associated with stage 3 and stage 4 of NREM sleep.

15. ___ Periodic limb movement disorder is characterized by sudden jerks of the legs, ankle flexing, or flexing of the knees and hip during sleep.

16. ___ Modafinil is a new drug used in the treatment of narcolepsy that reduces daytime sleepiness.

Check your answers and review any areas of weakness before going on to the next section.

Dreams and Mental Activity During Sleep

Preview Questions

Consider the following questions as you study this section of the chapter.

- What is the difference between sleep thinking and dreaming?

- What are the main characteristics of dreams, and what are the most common themes in dreams?
- Why do we remember some dreams and forget others?
- How does Freud's theory of the meaning of dreams differ from the activation–synthesis model?
- What conclusions can we draw about the meaning of dreams?

*Read the section "Dreams and Mental Activity During Sleep" and **write** your answers to the following:*

1. Sleep thinking refers to_____

_____

whereas a dream is _____

_____

2. The main characteristics of dreams are

_____

_____

_____

3. Most dreams are _____

_____

_____

with the most common themes being _____

_____

_____

4. We are most likely to remember a dream if

_____

_____

5. We are more likely to forget dreams because

_____

_____

_____

6. Freud's explanation for dreams suggests that

_____

_____

7. The manifest content refers to _____

_____

The latent content is the _____

_____

_____

8. The activation–synthesis model of dreaming maintains that_____

_____

9. Current research concludes that dreams reflect

_____

_____

_____

_____

After you have carefully studied the preceding section, complete the following exercises.

Concept Check 3

Read the following and write the correct term in the space provided.

1. Meredith recalls having a dream about dancing in a ballet with a very big, strong, muscular male dancer when suddenly the music switches to loud rock music and the man disappears. According to Freud, Meredith's account represents the _____ of the dream.

2. Dr. Dormo believes that Meredith's dream could be the result of a burst of neural activity that spread upward from the brainstem and activated more sophisticated brain areas. This interpretation is most consistent with the _____ model of dreaming.

3. After falling asleep, Ricardo finds that his mind keeps returning to the material he has been studying all day in preparation for his exam the next morning. Ricardo is experiencing the most common form of mental activity during sleep, called _____ .

4. Dr. Roach is a cross-cultural psychologist interested in investigating sleep and dreams. His cross-cultural data are likely to show that the dreams of people in various parts of the world have _____ (common/no common) themes.

5. Maxwell claims that he has no recollection of any dream when he wakes up in the morning, and he is convinced that he never dreams. One way to demonstrate to Maxwell that he does dream is to wake him up after he has been asleep for about _____ minutes, when he is clearly in _____ sleep.

6. After a visit to the natural history museum, young Jamila had a scary dream about dinosaurs, which caused her to wake up in a very frightened state. Jamila has experienced an unpleasant anxiety dream called a(n) _____ .

Review of Terms, Concepts, and Names 3

Use the terms in this list to complete the Matching Test, then to help you answer the True/False items correctly.

sleep thinking	manifest content
dream	latent content
memory consolidation	J. Allan Hobson
procedural memories	activation–synthesis
nightmare	model
Sigmund Freud	

Matching Exercise

Match the appropriate term/name with its definition or description:

1. _____ Neuroscientist who extensively researched sleep and dreaming; proposed the activation–synthesis model of dreaming.

2. _____ The founder of psychoanalysis, who proposed that dream images are disguised and symbolic expressions of unconscious wishes and urges.

3. _____ Repetitive, bland, and uncreative ruminations about real-life events during sleep.

4. _____ The gradual process of converting new memories into a long-term, relatively permanent form.

5. _____ A frightening or unpleasant anxiety dream that occurs during REM sleep.

True/False Test

Indicate whether each item is true or false by placing T or F in the space next to each item

1. ___ Procedural memories are memories of how to perform sequences of behaviors.

2. ___ In Freud's psychoanalytic theory, the latent content of a dream refers to the elements that are consciously experienced and remembered by the dreamer.

3. ___ A dream is a storylike episode of unfolding mental imagery during sleep.

4. ___ The activation–synthesis model of dreaming states that brain activity during sleep produces dream images (*activation*), which are combined by the brain into a dream story (*synthesis*).

5. ___ In Freud's psychoanalytic theory, the manifest content of a dream refers to the unconscious wishes, thoughts, and urges that are concealed in the latent content of a dream.

Check your answers and review any areas of weakness before going on to the next section.

Hypnosis

Preview Questions

Consider the following questions as you study this section of the chapter.

- What is hypnosis, and what are the characteristics of the hypnotic state?
- What are the main characteristics of people who are susceptible to hypnosis?
- What are the effects of hypnosis, and what are its limits?
- How has hypnosis been explained?

*Read the section "Hypnosis" and **write** your answers to the following:*

1. Hypnosis is a _____

_____

2. Hypnosis is characterized by _____

_____

_____

_____

3. The best candidates for hypnosis are _____

_____

_____

_____

4. The effects of hypnosis include _____

_____

_____

_____

5. The limits of hypnosis are that _____

_____

_____

_____

6. Hilgard's neodissociation theory of hypnosis suggests that _____

_____

_____

_____

_____

Meditation

Preview Questions

Consider the following questions as you study this section of the chapter.

- What is meditation, and what is it intended to accomplish?
- What are the two general categories of meditation?
- What are the effects of meditation?

*Read the section "Meditation" and **write** your answers to the following:*

1. Meditation refers to _____

_____

_____

2. The two general types of meditation differ in that _____

_____

_____

_____

_____

3. The effects of meditation include _____

_____

_____

_____

After you have carefully studied the preceding sections, complete the following exercises.

Concept Check 4

Read the following and write the correct term in the space provided.

1. Janna quickly becomes deeply absorbed while reading novels or watching movies. It is very likely that Janna is among the 15 percent of adults who are _____ to hypnosis.

2. While under hypnosis, Karl describes a very frightening experience of being lost at the fairgrounds when he was six years old. When his therapist makes the suggestion that Karl will soon forget this traumatic event, he is attempting to induce _____ .

3. During every final exam period, Declan gets uptight and anxious. At the suggestion of a friend, he has tried using a meditation technique in which he focuses his awareness and attention by repeating a simple phrase over and over to himself. Declan is using a _____ technique of meditation.

4. A researcher suggests to a hypnotized subject that the letter D does not exist. After being brought out of the trance, the subject is asked to recite the alphabet; when she does, she skips the letter D. This example illustrates the use of

_____ .

5. An eyewitness to a robbery (who couldn't remember much of the incident) was hypnotized. When the hypnotherapist suggested that there had been three white men and one black woman involved in the robbery, the subject agreed and described them in some detail. All the other five witnesses reported that only one white male robber was involved. The hypnotherapist has created a

_____ .

6. Lynda has an irrational fear and dislike of cats but has no conscious memory of when or how her phobia developed. In an attempt to enhance her memory, Lynda's therapist hypnotizes her. If the therapist's hypnotic suggestions actually work, this would demonstrate

_____ .

7. Neuroscientists investigating brain activity during meditation used an imaging technique called single photo emission computed tomography (SPECT) on a number of highly practiced meditators. If their results are consistent with those reported in the Focus on Neuroscience, they are likely to observe increased blood flow to both _____ lobes, and decreased blood flow to the _____ .

Review of Terms, Concepts, and Names 4

Use the terms in this list to complete the Matching Test, then to help you answer the True / False items correctly.

hypnosis
posthypnotic suggestion
posthypnotic amnesia
hypermnesia
pseudomemory
age regression
Ernest R. Hilgard
dissociation
neodissociation theory of
  hypnosis
hidden observer
meditation
concentration technique
opening-up techniques
transcendental
  meditation (TM)
single photon emission
  computed tomography
  (SPECT)

Matching Exercise

Match the appropriate term / name with its definition or description.

1. _____ Theory proposed by Ernest Hilgard that explains hypnotic effects as being due to the splitting of consciousness into two simultaneous streams of mental activity, only one of which is available to the consciousness of the hypnotized subject.

2. _____ Meditative technique that has been widely used in research in which practitioners sit quietly with eyes closed, mentally repeat the mantra they have been given, and practice a strategy for getting rid of distracting thoughts.

3. _____ A cooperative social interaction in which the hypnotized person responds to the hypnotist's suggestions with changes in perception, memory, and behavior.

4. _____ The splitting of consciousness into two or more simultaneous streams of mental activity.

5. _____ Suggestion made during hypnosis that the person carry out a specific instruction following the hypnotic session.

6. _____ Hypnotic suggestion that supposedly enhances the person's memory for past events.

7. _____ Hilgard's term for the hidden, or dissociated, stream of mental activity during hypnosis.

8. _____ Imaging technique that measures the brain's blood-flow patterns by detecting a radioactive tracer, injected into the bloodstream, that locks into brain cells.

True/False Test

Indicate whether each item is true or false by placing T or F in the space next to each item.

1. ___ Ernest Hilgard is the American psychologist who extensively studied hypnosis and advanced the neodissociation theory of hypnosis.

2. ___ A concentration meditative technique involves a present-centered awareness of the passing moment without mental judgment and does not involve concentrating on a mantra or object or activity.

3. ___ In posthypnotic amnesia, the result of a posthypnotic suggestion, the subject is unable to recall specific information or events that occurred before or during hypnosis.

4. ___ Pseudomemories are false memories (even though the person may be very confident that the memories are real) that result when suggestions are made during hypnosis that create distortions and inaccuracies in recall.

5. ___ The opening-up meditative techniques involve focusing awareness on a visual image or your breathing, or mentally repeating a sound called a mantra.

6. ___ Meditation is any of a number of sustained concentration techniques that focus attention and heighten awareness.

7. ___ The use of hypnosis to recall or reexperi-
ence an earlier developmental period is called
age regression.

---

*Check your answers and review any areas of
weakness before going on to the next section.*

Psychoactive Drugs

Preview Questions

*Consider the following questions as you study this
section of the chapter.*

- What are psychoactive drugs, and what properties do they have in common?
- What factors influence the effects of a drug, and what factors influence drug-taking behavior?
- How do depressants work, and what effects do alcohol, barbiturates, tranquilizers, and inhalants have?
- What are opiates, and what effects do they have?
- How do stimulants affect the brain and psychological functioning?
- How do the most common psychedelic drugs influence perception, mood, and thinking?
- What are "club drugs," and what effects do they have?

*Read the section "Psychoactive Drugs" and **write** your answers to the following:*

1. Psychoactive drugs are _____

   _____

   _____

2. Addiction is a broad term that refers to _____

   _____

   _____

   More specific terms for addiction-related conditions are _____

   _____

3. The effects of a drug may be influenced by

   _____

   _____

   _____

   _____

4. Drug abuse refers to_____

   _____

   _____

   Factors that influence drug-taking behavior are

   _____

5. Depressants have several effects: _____

   _____

   _____

   Examples include_____

6. Alcohol depresses _____

   _____

   and impairs _____

   _____

   _____

   _____

7. Barbiturates are depressant drugs that _____

   _____

   _____

8. Tranquilizers are depressants that _____

   _____

   _____

9. Inhalants are chemical substances that _____

   _____

   _____

   Examples include _____

   _____

   _____

10. The opiates are a group of addictive drugs that

    _____

    _____

    Examples include_____

    _____

11. Stimulant drugs_____

    _____

    Examples include_____

    _____

12. The psychedelic drugs create _____

    _____

    _____

    Examples include_____

    _____

13. Marijuana and its active ingredient, THC, produce _____

    _____

    _____

    THC has been shown to be useful in _____

    _____

    _____

14. "Club drugs" are _____

    _____

    Examples (and their effects) include _____

    _____

    _____

    _____

    _____

    _____

    _____

    _____

    *After you have carefully studied the preceding
    section, complete the following exercises.*

Concept Check 5

*Read the following and write the correct term in the
space provided.*

1. Sian regularly drinks five or six cups of strong
   coffee a day. If she is like most people, she
   would probably be surprised to find out that
   caffeine is a _____
   drug and is _____ addictive.

2. Zachary has been using a mood-altering, eupho-
   ria-enhancing psychoactive drug; with continued use, he needs to take larger and larger
   doses in order to experience its original effects.
   Zachary is developing _____ for
   the drug.

3. At a party where he has had too much to drink,
   the normally shy Darryl keeps people enter-
   tained for quite a while with his silly antics.

Darryl's unusual behavior is probably caused by
the fact that alcohol lessens inhibitions by
depressing the brain centers responsible for
_____ and _____ .

4. If he continues drinking at the party, Darryl
   will probably lose his coordination and balance;
   the next day, he might _____
   (remember/not remember) very clearly the
   events of the evening before.

5. While undergoing chemotherapy for cancer,
   Brendan is given marijuana to help prevent
   nausea and vomiting. It is very likely that
   Brendan _____ (will/will not) develop
   drug tolerance and physical dependence.

6. Dora has been suffering from severe anxiety, so
   her doctor prescribes a depressant drug called
   Valium, which is a commonly prescribed

   _____ .

7. Shortly after "snorting" an illegal psychoactive
   drug, Samuel experiences intense euphoria,
   mental alertness, and self-confidence that lasts
   for several minutes. It is most likely that
   Samuel has inhaled the stimulant drug

   _____ .

8. Nadine noticed that after she took a designer
   drug at a party, she experienced a combination
   of stimulant and mild psychedelic effects. It is
   most likely that Nadine has taken a club drug
   called _____ or _____ .

9. After an accident, Trent was given medication
   to reduce his perception of pain. It is probable
   that he has been prescribed Percodan or
   Demerol, drugs that belong to the category of
   psychoactive drugs called _____
   or _____ .

Graphic Organizer 2

Read the following examples, identify the drug involved, and indicate the type of drug it is.

Example	Drug Name	Drug Class
1. During a party Jordy becomes less and less inhibited as the night wears on, and by the time the party is nearly over, he is very unco-ordinated and unbalanced and has trouble walking.		
2. After taking her prescription drug for a number of weeks, Janet no longer feels the intense anxiety she used to suffer.		
3. Mrs. Smothers, who suffers from glaucoma, and Mr. Hartley, who has asthma, have both been given an ordinarily illegal drug at the university hospital.		
4. Harold has used a powerful synthetic drug for a number of years to create sensory and perceptual distortions and to alter his mood, but now he is experiencing flashbacks, depression, and occasional psychotic reactions.		
5. Henrietta was a very heavy coffee drinker until she quit cold turkey. She is now experiencing headaches, irritability, drowsiness, and fatigue.		
6. Following surgery, Gregory was given a common prescription drug under medical supervision in order to alleviate his pain.		
7. Just before his exam, Juan smokes a couple of cigarettes and finds he is less tired, more mentally alert, and yet fairly relaxed.		

Review of Terms and Concepts 5

Use the terms in this list to complete the Matching Test, then to help you answer the True/False items correctly.

psychoactive drug
physical dependence
drug tolerance
withdrawal symptoms
drug rebound effect
drug abuse
depressants
binge drinking
delirium tremens (DTs)
barbiturates
tranquilizers
inhalants
opiates (narcotics)
opium

morphine
stimulants
caffeine
nicotine
amphetamines
cocaine
stimulant-induced
    psychosis
psychedelic drugs
mescaline
psilocybin
LSD
marijuana
THC

hashish
designer drugs
MDMA (ecstasy)

dissociative anesthetics
    (PCP and ketamine)
sleep inertia
    (morning brain fog)

Matching Exercise

Match the appropriate term with its definition or description.

1. _____ The active ingredient of marijuana and other preparations derived from the hemp plant.

2. _____ Category of psychoactive drugs that depress or inhibit brain activity.

3. _____ Stimulant drug found in tobacco products.

4. _____ Recurrent drug use that results in disruptions in academic, social, or occupational functioning or in legal or psychological problems.

5. _____ Drug that alters normal consciousness, perception, mood, and behavior.

6. _____ Schizophrenia-like symptoms that can occur as the result of prolonged amphetamine or cocaine use.

7. _____ Psychedelic drug derived from the peyote cactus.

8. _____ Condition in which increasing amounts of a physically addictive drug are needed to produce the original, desired effect.

9. _____ Potent form of marijuana made from the resin of the hemp plant.

10. _____ Unpleasant physical reactions, combined with intense drug cravings, that occur when a person abstains from a drug on which he or she is physically dependent.

11. _____ Stimulant drug derived from the coca tree.

12. _____ Class of stimulant drugs that arouse the central nervous system and suppress appetite.

13. _____ The collective term for withdrawal symptoms associated with high levels of alcohol dependence; may involve confusion, hallucinations, severe tremors, or seizures.

14. _____ Feelings of grogginess upon waking from sleep that interfere with the ability to perform mental or physical tasks.

15. _____ Chemical substances that are inhaled to produce an alteration in consciousness.

16. _____ Synthetic "club drug" that combines stimulant and mild psychedelic effects.

True/False Test

Indicate whether each item is true or false by placing T or F in the space next to each item.

1. ___ Marijuana is a psychoactive drug derived from the hemp plant.

2. ___ Opiates are a category of depressant drugs that reduce anxiety and produce sleepiness.

3. ___ The occurrence of withdrawal symptoms that are the opposite of a physically addictive drug's action is referred to as the drug rebound effect.

4. ___ Caffeine is the stimulant drug found in coffee, tea, cola drinks, chocolate, and many over-the-counter medications.

5. ___ Opium is a natural opiate derived from the opium poppy.

6. ___ Binge drinking is defined as five or more drinks in a row for men, or four or more drinks in a row for women.

7. ___ Psilocybin is a psychedelic drug derived from the psilocybe mushroom, which is sometimes called "magic mushroom."

8. ___ LSD is a synthetic psychedelic drug.

9. ___ Morphine is the active ingredient of the natural opiate called opium.

10. ___ Tranquilizers such as Valium and Librium are depressants that are prescribed to relieve anxiety.

11. ___ Psychedelic drugs are a category of psychoactive drugs that increase brain activity, as reflected in aroused behavior and increased mental alertness.

12. ___ Physical dependence is a condition in which a person who has physically adapted to a drug must take the drug regularly in order to avoid withdrawal symptoms.

13. ___ Barbiturates are a category of psychoactive drugs that have strong pain-relieving properties and are chemically similar to morphine.

14. ___ Stimulants are a category of psychoactive drugs that create sensory and perceptual distortions, alter mood, and affect judgment by altering brain chemistry or activity.

15. ___ Designer drugs are drugs that are synthesized in a laboratory rather than being derived from naturally occurring compounds.

16. ___ Dissociative anesthetics are a class of drugs that reduce sensitivity to pain and produce feelings of detachment and dissociation.

Check your answers and review any areas of weakness before going on to the next section.

Something to Think About

1. We've all heard the complaint, "There's so much to do, and so little time!" When people are busy and feel pressured, they often end up sleep-deprived, making them less efficient or productive than well-rested people. More important, they are more likely to make potentially dangerous mistakes. Those most at risk are shift workers or people who suffer jet-lag symptoms for other reasons.

   Imagine you are a consultant and have been asked to prepare a report for an organization concerned with these problems among its employees. Based on what you have learned about the sleep–wake cycle, circadian rhythms, biological and environmental clocks, and so on, what would you recommend in your report?

2. Almost everybody has some fascination with dreams and what they mean. Some people believe that dreams can foretell the future or are important in other mysterious ways. Suppose a friend tells you that she has dreamed that she could not understand a single question on a very important math exam. She just stared at the exam until the professor announced the exam was over and removed the paper from in front of her. At this point, she awoke in a very anxious state. Now she is worried that when she takes the real exam next week, her dream will come true. What would you say to her about dreams and their meaning, theories of dreams, and such?

Check your answers and review any areas of weakness before doing the progress tests.

Progress Test 1

Review the complete chapter (including Concept Reviews and the boxed inserts), review all your study notes, and then test yourself on the following progress test. Check your answers. If you make a mistake, review your notes, the relevant section of the study guide, and, if necessary, the appropriate part of your textbook.

1. Nightmares are to _____ as night terrors are to _____ .
   (a) sleep spindles; beta waves
   (b) alpha waves; beta waves
   (c) REM sleep; slow-wave NREM sleep
   (d) slow-wave NREM sleep; REM sleep

2. Bernita witnessed a robbery, but her recall of the event was vague. Police investigators therefore used hypnosis in an attempt to enhance her memory. The hypnotic effect that the investigators hope for is called _____ , which research shows is _____ to be successful.
   (a) hypermnesia; very likely
   (b) posthypnotic suggestion; not very likely
   (c) hypermnesia; not very likely
   (d) posthypnotic suggestion; very likely

3. After ingesting a small dose of a psychoactive drug, Graham experiences vivid visual halluci-

nations and other perceptual distortions; he feels as if he is floating above his body. Graham is most likely experiencing the effects of
   (a) cocaine.   (d) LSD.
   (b) barbiturates.   (e) cappuccino.
   (c) tranquilizers.

4. "Consciousness is like a stream or river; it is continuous and cannot be divided or broken down into component parts." The person most likely to have made that statement is
   (a) Sigmund Freud.   (c) Ernest Hilgard.
   (b) William James.   (d) J. Allan Hobson.

5. After flying from San Diego to New York, Jasmine experiences a restless, sleepless night; the next day, she is irritable and cannot concentrate on her work. Jasmine's problems are likely due to
   (a) disruption in her circadian rhythms.
   (b) high blood levels of melatonin.
   (c) jet lag.
   (d) all of the above.

6. Justine believes that dreaming is simply our subjective awareness of the brain's internally generated signals during sleep, which start with automatic activation of brain stem circuits that then arouse more sophisticated brain areas. Justine's views are most consistent with which theory of dreams?
   (a) adaptive theory
   (b) restorative theory
   (c) activation-synthesis theory
   (d) wish-fulfillment theory

7. In order to find out what goes on in people's brains during a typical night's sleep, researchers are most likely to
   (a) ask people to try to remember as much as possible when they awake in the morning
   (b) closely watch the actions of subjects sleeping in the sleep research lab.
   (c) wake people up every fifteen minutes and ask them what is going on in their minds.
   (d) use an electroencephalograph to measure their brain-wave activity throughout the night.

8. Just as you are about to fall asleep, you have the sudden feeling of falling and your body gives an involuntary spasm. You have experienced

   (a) a sleep spindle.
   (b) a myoclonic jerk.
   (c) sleep apnea.
   (d) a K complex.

9. Harry has been asleep for about an hour or so, and his heart begins to beat faster, his breathing becomes irregular, his voluntary muscle activity is suppressed, and his closed eyes move rapidly back and forth. It is most probable that Harry is in _____ and is therefore experiencing _____ .

   (a) REM sleep; a myoclonic jerk
   (b) NREM: sleep spindles
   (c) REM; paradoxical sleep
   (d) NREM; quiet sleep

10. Eight-year-old Billy gets out of bed at 1 A.M. and starts to sleepwalk. He is most likely

    (a) in slow-wave stage 3 or 4 NREM sleep.
    (b) suffering from narcolepsy.
    (c) in REM sleep.
    (d) suffering from sleep apnea.

11. After Zufina has been asleep for a period of time in the sleep lab, the EEG monitor indicates the presence of theta waves, sleep spindles, and K complexes. Zufina is in _____ sleep.

    (a) stage 3 NREM   (c) stage 2 NREM
    (b) REM   (d) stage 4 NREM

12. Mr. Jensen repeatedly complains about the quality and duration of his sleep; he claims that he can't fall asleep and stay asleep and usually wakes up before it is time to get up. Mr. Jensen apparently suffers from

    (a) sleep apnea.   (c) nocturnal enuresis.
    (b) narcolepsy.   (d) insomnia.

13. People have no problem staying up a little later each night on the weekend. The most likely explanation for this is that

    (a) the SCN naturally tends toward a 25-hour day.
    (b) the SCN naturally tends toward a 23-hour day.
    (c) there are no obvious environmental time cues during the weekend.
    (d) there are much better late-night movies on TV during the weekend.

14. According to the Application, Improving Sleep and Mental Alertness, sleep inertia refers to

    (a) feelings of grogginess upon awakening from sleep that interfere with the ability to perform mental or physical tasks.
    (b) a sleep disorder in which the person stops breathing during sleep and awakens momentarily, only to return immediately to sleep.
    (c) the paralysis that accompanies stage 3 and 4 deep sleep.
    (d) the sudden involuntary spasm of the whole body during stage 1 sleep.

15. According to Critical Thinking 4.5, _____ theory suggests that hypnotic subjects are responding to social demands by acting the way they think good hypnotic subjects should act and by conforming to expectations and situational cues.

    (a) neodissociation
    (b) social-cognitive
    (c) imaginative suggestibility
    (d) adaptive

Progress Test 2

After you have checked your understanding of the material in Progress Test 1 and have done a complete chapter review with special focus on any areas of weakness, you are now ready to assess your knowledge on Progress Test 2. Check your answers. If you make a mistake, review your notes, the relevant section of the study guide, and, if necessary, the appropriate part of your textbook.

1. Dr. Benjamin hypnotizes a client and suggests that she will no longer feel a craving for chocolates. Dr. Benjamin is making use of

   (a) posthypnotic suggestion.
   (b) hypermnesia.
   (c) posthypnotic amnesia.
   (d) meditation.

2. Amber sits in a relaxed position, closes her eyes, and begins to recite her mantra. Amber is practicing

   (a) hypnosis.   (d) dissociation.
   (b) meditation.   (e) laziness.
   (c) sleep inertia.

3. Researchers who have found evidence that subjects appear to have a "hidden observer" are likely to suggest that hypnosis involves
   (a) dissociation.
   (b) social factors.
   (c) stages 3 and 4 NREM sleep.
   (d) experimenter bias.

4. John drinks five or six cups of coffee every day; if he doesn't, he feels irritable, drowsy, and fatigued. John is _____ a(n) _____ drug.
   (a) addicted to; psychedelic
   (b) physically dependent on; opiate
   (c) addicted to; depressant
   (d) physically dependent on; stimulant

5. Richard has just finished his fourth night shift and is driving home from work in the bright morning light. The most likely effect of this exposure is that
   (a) the bright light will reset his body clock to a day schedule.
   (b) he will become very drowsy and sleepy.
   (c) he will experience an increase in the production of melatonin.
   (d) all of the above will occur.

6. Nancy's parents took her to the doctor because she grinds her teeth loudly in her sleep. The doctor is likely to diagnose her with _____ called _____ .
   (a) a parasomnia; nocturnal enuresis
   (b) a hypermnesia; somnambulism
   (c) a parasomnia; sleep bruxism
   (d) a hypermnesia; sleep inertia

7. Phelan has just had a very painful operation. His doctors are most likely to prescribe _____ for pain relief.
   (a) a tranquilizer   (c) morphine
   (b) marijuana   (d) alcohol

8. Mr. Godfrey has cancer and was given marijuana to counter the nausea and vomiting following chemotherapy. The active ingredient that makes this a useful drug in such cases is
   (a) psilocybin.   (c) LSD.
   (b) cannabis.   (d) THC.

9. Sleep researchers deprive subjects of REM sleep for a number of nights but allow them an otherwise normal sleep; the subjects are likely to experience _____ when next allowed to sleep uninterrupted.
   (a) narcolepsy   (c) sleep inertia
   (b) REM rebound   (d) NREM rebound

10. Harold dreams that he is on a train traveling through mountains in what he thinks is Switzerland. He can see the train very clearly going in and out of tunnels over and over again. Harold's therapist suggests that the dream is not about travel in a foreign country but about Harold's concern with his sexual performance. The therapist adheres to the _____ theory of dreams and is attempting to reveal the _____ of Harold's dream.
    (a) evolutionary; adaptive aspects
    (b) Freud's wish-fulfillment; manifest content
    (c) Freud's wish-fulfillment; latent content
    (d) activation–synthesis; restorative aspects

11. During a very intense game of pool, Gary attempts a very difficult shot that will win him the game when he suddenly collapses and falls fast asleep on the pool table. Gary probably suffers from _____ and is experiencing _____ .
    (a) sleep apnea; sleep paralysis
    (b) narcolepsy; a sleep attack
    (c) insomnia; sleep inertia
    (d) REM sleep behavior disorder; sleep paralysis

12. Nicotine is to alcohol as a _____ drug is to a _____
    (a) stimulant; depressant
    (b) psychedelic; stimulant
    (c) depressant; stimulant
    (d) depressant; psychedelic

13. Dr. Tirian's research is concerned with the effects of psychedelic drugs on brain functioning. Which of the following is she most likely to test in her experiments?
    (a) LSD, psilocybin, and mescaline
    (b) amphetamines and cocaine
    (c) alcohol, nicotine, and caffeine
    (d) barbiturates and tranquilizers

14. According to In Focus 4.2, which of the following is true?
    (a) Research suggests that very low levels of a naturally occurring compound in the body called adenosine cause sleepiness.
    (b) It is extremely dangerous to awaken a sleepwalker.
    (c) If you dream you are falling and you hit the ground, you will wake up dead.
    (d) In a relatively common phenomenon called sleep paralysis, the paralysis of REM sleep carries over to the waking state for up to 10 minutes.

15. According to In Focus 4.4, What You Really Want to Know About Dreams, which of the following is true?
    (a) People who have been blind all their lives don't dream.
    (b) Up until the widespread use of color TV, most people dreamed in black and white.
    (c) Virtually all mammals experience sleep cycles in which REM sleep alternates with slow-wave NREM sleep, and it is reasonable to conclude that they all experience dreams.
    (d) People who frequently experience sleep thinking have more nightmares than normal because they have little or no control over their dreams.

Progress Test 3

After you have checked your understanding of the material in Progress Tests 1 and 2, and have done a complete chapter review with special focus on any areas of weakness, you are ready to further assess your knowledge on Progress Test 3. Check your answers. If you make a mistake, review your notes, the appropriate parts of the study guide, and if necessary, the relevant sections of your textbook.

1. Mrs. Cadogan complains that her overweight sixty-five-year-old husband snores and snorts throughout the night and appears to be gasping for breath. She notes that this happens most often when he is sleeping on his back. Mr. Cadogan suffers from
   (a) sleep apnea.   (c) sleep inertia.
   (b) sleep terrors.   (d) sleep bruxism.

2. Dr. Gerhardt believes that sleep promotes physiological processes that repair and rejuvenate the body and mind. Dr. Gerhardt's view is consistent with the _____ theory of sleep.
   (a) evolutionary
   (b) activation–synthesis
   (c) wish-fulfillment
   (d) restorative

3. Brianna, who has a very warm, loving relationship with her husband, dreamed that she had an intense, emotional argument with him in which she shouted and screamed and called him horrible names. Her psychoanalyst suggested that Brianna must have some deeply repressed anger and frustration toward her father that is expressed symbolically in the dream about her husband. Brianna's account of the dream represents the _____ , and her therapist's account represents the _____ .
   (a) latent content; manifest content
   (b) activation phase; synthesis phase
   (c) manifest content; latent content
   (d) synthesis phase; activation phase

4. Stage 2 sleep is to _____ as stage 4 is to _____ .
   (a) beta waves; alpha waves
   (b) alpha waves; beta waves
   (c) sleep spindles and K complexes; delta waves
   (d) dreams; nightmares

5. Dr. Hayward uses hypnosis on a patient during a root canal procedure. When he asks her to raise her hand if some part of her can feel pain, she raises her hand. This illustrates
   (a) the hidden observer.
   (b) paradoxical sleep.
   (c) posthypnotic amnesia.
   (d) tolerance.

6. In a class discussion of sleep and dreams, Anouk suggests that different sleep patterns exhibited by various animals, including humans, evolved as a way of preventing a particular species from interacting with the environment when it is most dangerous to do so. Anouk is promoting the
   (a) restorative theory.
   (b) the activation–synthesis model.
   (c) the adaptive theory.
   (d) the neodissociation theory.

7. Due to prolonged and heavy use of cocaine, Andrew suffered schizophrenia-like symptoms, including auditory hallucinations of "voices," bizarre paranoid ideas, and the "cocaine bugs" hallucination in which he felt that insects were crawling under his skin. Andrew's symptoms suggest that he has
   (a) stimulant-induced psychosis (cocaine psychosis).
   (b) delirium tremens (DTs).
   (c) hypermnesia.
   (d) a parasomnia.

8. During a rave, Drake was given a substance that reduced his sensitivity to pain and produced feelings of detachment and dissociation. He is most likely to have used a class of club drug called _____ , and, in particular, either _____ or _____ .
   (a) psychedelics; LSD; mescaline
   (b) the dissociative anesthetics; PCP (angel dust); ketamine (Special K)
   (c) depressants; methaqualone; quaalude
   (d) tranquilizers; Valium; Librium

9. After he abruptly stops taking a depressant psychoactive drug, Ernie suffers from sleep problems, excitability, and restlessness. Ernie is suffering from
   (a) drug rebound effect. (c) inertia.
   (b) parasomnia.   (d) apnea.

10. Maya uses the zazen, or the "just sitting" technique of Zen Buddhism, in which she engages in quiet awareness of the "here and now" without any distracting thoughts. Maya is using a type of _____ meditation.
    (a) opening-up
    (b) inertia
    (c) concentration
    (d) parasomnia

11. According to his wife, seventy-year-old Hugo sometimes jumps out of bed during the night and appears to be acting out his dreams. It is very likely that Hugo suffers from a sleep disorder called
    (a) narcolepsy.
    (b) REM sleep behavior disorder.
    (c) sleep apnea.
    (d) nocturnal enuresis.

12. Jason frequently experiences morning brain fog. One way to deal with his sleep inertia, according to the Application, is to
    (a) stay in bed, in a deep sleep, until the last possible minute after the alarm has gone off.
    (b) get up very gradually and spend the first 30 minutes or so in very low-level light conditions.
    (c) set his alarm clock 15 minutes earlier than usual, get up as soon as it goes off, sip some coffee, and expose himself to bright light.
    (d) stay up about 15 minutes later than usual each night for a week, but get up at the same time each morning.

13. According to Culture and Human Behavior 4.3, having siestas or afternoon naps
    (a) is a normal, even beneficial, aspect of our daily sleep–wake circadian rhythm.
    (b) is positively correlated with high birth rates.
    (c) is the leading cause of insomnia.
    (d) leads to lethargy, low energy levels, and ultimately, low productivity levels in the workplace.

14. Biorhythms are discussed in Science Versus Pseudoscience 4.1. Which of the following point(s) were made?
    (a) Biorhythms is a popular pseudoscience.
    (b) The notion that there are three "natural biorhythms" rigidly fixed from birth on is unproved.
    (c) Although "biorhythms" and "biological rhythms" sound very similar, they have virtually nothing in common.
    (d) The legitimate scientific study of biological rhythms examines the consistent but potentially varying cycles of living organisms over time.
    (e) All of the above points were made.

15. In Focus 4.2 presents information about sleep. Which of the following is (are) true according to this section?
    (a) Deaf people who use sign language sometimes "sleep sign" during sleep.
    (b) Yawning is caused by too little oxygen or too much carbon dioxide and is highly contagious.
    (c) It is possible to learn foreign languages, chemistry, etc., by listening to tape recordings while fast asleep.
    (d) All of the above are true.

Answers

Introduction: Consciousness: Experiencing the "Private I"

1. *Consciousness is defined as the* personal awareness of mental activities, internal sensations, and the external environment.

2. *William James's idea of "stream of consciousness" refers to the fact that* although consciousness is always changing, it is perceived as unified and unbroken, in much the same way that a river or stream is seen as one thing, yet is constantly changing.

3. *Research on consciousness was abandoned because* introspective self-reports were not objectively verifiable. *Psychologists turned instead to* overt behavior that could be directly observed and measured.

4. *Psychologists returned to studying consciousness in the late 1950s for two reasons:* first, because it became clear that a complete understanding of behavior would not be possible without considering the role of conscious mental processes in behavior, and second, because psychologists devised more objective ways to study the phenomenon (technological advances in studying brain activity and more objective means of inferring conscious experience from behavior).

Biological and Environmental "Clocks" Regulating Consciousness

1. *Circadian rhythms are* biological and psychological processes that systematically vary over a 24-hour period

2. *The suprachiasmatic nucleus (SCN) is* a cluster of neurons in the hypothalamus that governs the timing of circadian rhythms, including the sleep–wake cycle and the mental alertness cycle; thus, it is considered the master biological clock. *Its role in sleep–wake cycles and other circadian rhythms is to* detect, through its connections with the visual system, decreases in sunlight and, in turn, to trigger an increase in the production of melatonin, which makes you sleep. Exposure to sunlight suppresses melatonin levels.

3. *Melatonin is a* hormone manufactured by the pineal gland (an endocrine gland in the brain), which produces sleepiness.

4. *Free-running conditions are created by* the absence of environmental time cues like sunlight and clocks. *They have two distinct effects: First,* in the absence of normal light, darkness, and other time cues, people tend to drift to the natural rhythm of the SCN, which is approximately a 25-hour day, and consequently people go to sleep about an hour later each night. *Second,* circadian rhythms lose their normal synchronization with one another.

5. *People suffer from jet lag symptoms because* time cues are out of sync with their internal biological clocks; these symptoms can be produced by travel across multiple time zones, working night shifts, or working rotating shifts.

6. *Melatonin plays a key role in jet lag symptoms by* causing sleepiness, grogginess, etc., at a time when the external environmental cues suggest that you should be alert and awake (your internal body clock says it is 3:00 A.M., so melatonin levels are high, but the external time is 10:00 A.M. and you need to be awake).

Concept Check 1

1. circadian rhythms; SCN (the body's clock)
2. melatonin
3. circadian rhythms
4. consciousness
5. free-running conditions

Matching Exercise 1

1. consciousness
2. introspection
3. suprachiasmatic nucleus (SCN)
4. jet lag
5. melatonin
6. biorhythms

True/False Test 1

1. T	3. T	5. T
2. T	4. T	

Sleep

1. *An electroencephalograph is* an instrument that uses electrodes placed on the scalp to measure and record the brain's electrical activity and produces an electroencephalogram (EEG).

2. *By studying EEGs, sleep researchers have established that* brain-wave activity systematically changes throughout sleep.

3. *Use of the EEG led to the discovery of* rapid-eye-movement sleep, or REM sleep, and this marked the beginning of modern sleep research.

4. *Beta brain waves are associated with* being alert and awake. *Alpha brain waves are associated with* drowsiness and relaxation.

5. *Hypnagogic hallucinations are* vivid sensory phenomena that occur during the onset of sleep.

6. *The four NREM sleep stages are characterized by different brain and body activity:*

   Stage 1 NREM: a mixture of alpha and theta waves, lasts only a few minutes, and is a transitional stage from wakefulness to being asleep

   Stage 2 NREM: the appearance of sleep spindles (bursts of brain activity that last a second or two), K complexes (single but large high-voltage spikes of brain activity), and mainly theta brain waves with perhaps a few delta waves.

   Stages 3 and 4 NREM: delta brain-wave activity (20 percent in stage 3, and 50 percent in stage 4); in combination, these stages are referred to as slow-wave sleep.

7. *REM sleep is characterized by* increased brain activity (smaller, faster brain waves), dreaming, suppression of voluntary muscle activity, and considerable physiological arousal.

8. *Over the course of the lifespan, the quantity and quality of our sleep* changes considerably; from birth onward, the average amount of time spent sleeping gradually decreases, and the amount of time devoted to REM and slow-wave NREM also gradually decreases.

Why Do We Sleep?

1. *Sleep deprivation studies demonstrate that* we have a biological need to sleep; when people are deprived of sleep (either REM or stage 3 and 4 NREM), they will experience rebound effects if allowed to sleep undisturbed.

2. *The phenomena of REM and NREM rebound seem to indicate that* the brain needs to make up for missing components of sleep.

3. *The restorative theory of sleep suggests that* sleep promotes physiological processes that restore and rejuvenate the body and the mind.

4. *The adaptive theory of sleep suggests that* the sleep patterns exhibited by different animals, including humans, are the result of evolutionary adaptation and that different sleep patterns evolved as a way of preventing a particular

species from interacting with the environment when it may be dangerous to do so.

Sleep Disorders: Troubled Sleep

1. *Sleep disorders are* serious disturbances in the normal sleep pattern that interfere with daytime functioning and cause subjective distress. Virtually everyone is seriously troubled by the quality or quantity of their sleep at some point.

2. *Insomnia is* a condition in which a person regularly experiences an inability to fall asleep, to stay asleep, or to feel adequately rested by sleep; it is the most common sleep complaint among adults. *Many complaints of insomnia are related to restless leg syndrome (RLS), which is* a condition in which unpleasant sensations in the lower legs are accompanied by an irresistible urge to move the legs, temporarily relieving the unpleasant sensations but disrupting sleep (approximately 30% of people with RLS have periodic limb movement disorder).

3. *With sleep apnea,* the person repeatedly stops breathing during sleep; it is the second most common sleep disorder.

4. *Sleepwalking is characterized by* an episode of walking or performing other actions during stage 3 or stage 4 NREM sleep; it is also called somnambulism.

5. *A night terror is characterized by* an episode of increased physiological arousal, intense fear and panic, and frightening hallucinations, with no recall of the episode in the morning; it usually occurs during stage 3 or stage 4 NREM sleep.

6. *In REM sleep behavior disorder,* the sleeper acts out his or her dreams.

7. *Parasomnias are* a category of sleep disorders characterized by arousal or activation during sleep and include sleepwalking, night terrors, sleep bruxism, and REM sleep behavior disorder.

8. *Narcolepsy is characterized by* excessive daytime sleepiness and brief lapses into sleep throughout the day.

Concept Check 2

1. alpha
2. falling; myoclonic jerk
3. insomnia
4. worse
5. night terror; 3; 4

6. narcolepsy; sleep paralysis

7. is experiencing sleep disturbances that are normal for her age

8. theta; sleep spindles and K complexes

Graphic Organizer 1

1. C   4. B   6. F
2. E   5. D   7. A
3. G

Matching Exercise 2

1. insomnia
2. REM sleep
3. restorative theory of sleep
4. alpha brain waves
5. sleep apnea
6. electroencephalogram (EEG)
7. sleep spindles
8. hypnagogic hallucinations
9. slow-wave sleep
10. myoclonic jerk (sleep start)
11. K complex
12. REM sleep behavior disorder
13. REM rebound
14. electroencephalograph
15. restless legs syndrome (RLS)
16. stimulus control

True/False Test 2

1. F   6. T   11. T   16. T
2. T   7. T   12. F
3. T   8. F   13. F
4. T   9. T   14. T
5. F   10. T   15. T

Dreams and Mental Activity During Sleep

1. *Sleep thinking refers to* repetitive, bland, and uncreative ruminations about real-life events during sleep, *whereas a dream is* an unfolding episode of mental images that is storylike, involving characters and events.

2. *The main characteristics of dreams are* intense emotions, usually illogical content and organization, sometimes bizarre and uncritically accepted sensations, and difficult-to-remember dream images.

3. *Most dreams are* a reflection of everyday life including people we know and familiar locations, *with the most common themes being* falling, being chased, or being attacked, which are common across cultures.

4. *We are most likely to remember a dream if* we wake up during the dream; if it is vivid, bizarre, or emotionally intense; or if we minimize distractions upon awakening.

5. *We are most likely to forget dreams because* a fundamental change in brain chemistry during sleep makes the processing and storage of information in memory very difficult (neurotransmitters needed to acquire new memories, including serotonin, norepinephrine, and dopamine, are greatly reduced), the frontal lobe areas involved in memory are shut down during REM sleep, and the brain is largely programmed to forget not only the vast majority of dreams but also any experiences that happen during sleep.

6. *Freud's explanation for dreams suggests that* because the sexual and aggressive instincts that motivate human behavior are so unacceptable to the conscious mind, they are pushed into the unconscious mind, or repressed.

7. *The manifest content refers to* the elements of a dream that are consciously experienced and remembered by the dreamer; *the latent content is the* disguised psychological meanings of the dream that are concealed in the manifest content.

8. *The activation–synthesis model of dreaming maintains that* dreaming is our subjective awareness of the brain's internally generated signals during sleep; brain activity produces dream images (activation), which are combined by the brain into a dream story (synthesis).

9. *Current research concludes that dreams reflect* the waking concerns and preoccupations of the dreamer and the active process of trying to make sense of stimuli produced by the brain during sleep; dream interpretation occurs when we are awake, and it may reveal more about the psychological characteristics of the interpreter than about the dream itself.

Concept Check 3

1. manifest content
2. activation-synthesis
3. sleep thinking

4. common

5. 70; REM

6. nightmare

Matching Exercise 3

1. J. Allan Hobson

2. Sigmund Freud

3. sleep thinking

4. memory consolidation

5. nightmare

True/False Test 3

1. T   3. T   5. F

2. F   4. T

Hypnosis

1. *Hypnosis is a* cooperative social interaction in which the hypnotized person responds to the hypnotist's suggestions with changes in perception, memory, and behavior.

2. *Hypnosis is characterized by* highly focused attention, increased responsiveness to suggestions, vivid images and fantasies, and a willingness to accept distortions of logic or reality; during hypnosis, the person temporarily suspends a sense of initiative and voluntarily accepts and follows the hypnotist's instructions.

3. *The best candidates for hypnosis are* individuals who approach the experience with positive, receptive attitudes and expect it to work and people who are fantasy prone and easily become absorbed in reading fiction, watching movies, or listening to music.

4. *The effects of hypnosis include* sensory and perceptual changes (blindness, deafness, or loss of sensation in some body part), hallucinations, carrying out posthypnotic suggestions, posthypnotic amnesia, hypermnesia, and the possibility of creating false memories or pseudomemories.

5. *The limits of hypnosis are that* you cannot be hypnotized against your will, you cannot become physically stronger than you are, you cannot exhibit talents that you don't already possess, and you cannot be made to perform behaviors that are contrary to your morals and values.

6. *Hilgard's neodissociation theory of hypnosis suggests that* hypnotic effects are due to the splitting of consciousness into two simultaneous streams of memory activity, only one of which the hypnotic participant is consciously aware of during hypnosis (the dissociated stream is called the hidden observer).

Meditation

1. *Meditation refers to* techniques used to control or retrain attention so as to induce an altered state of focused attention and heightened awareness.

2. *The two general types of meditation differ in that* concentration techniques involve focusing awareness on a visual image, your breathing, a word, or a phrase, and opening-up techniques involve a present-centered awareness of the passing moment, without mental judgment.

3. *The effects of meditation include* a state of lowered physiological arousal, lowered blood pressure, changes in brain waves, and enhanced physical and psychological functioning (beyond that provided by relaxation alone).

Concept Check 4

1. highly susceptible

2. posthypnotic amnesia

3. concentration

4. posthypnotic suggestion

5. pseudomemory

6. hypermnesia

7. frontal; left parietal lobe

Matching Exercise 4

1. neodissociation theory of hypnosis

2. transcendental meditation (TM)

3. hypnosis

4. dissociation

5. posthypnotic suggestion

6. hypermnesia

7. hidden observer

8. single photon emission computed tomography (SPECT)

True/False Test 4

1. T   4. T   7. T

2. F   5. F

3. T   6. T

Psychoactive Drugs

1. *Psychoactive drugs are* chemical substances that alter consciousness, perception, mood, and behavior; they include depressants, opiates, stimulants, and psychedelic drugs.

2. *Addiction is a broad term that refers to* a condition in which a person feels psychologically and physically compelled to take a specific drug. *More specific terms for addiction-related conditions are* physical dependence, drug tolerance, withdrawal symptoms, and the drug rebound effect.

3. *The effects of a drug may be influenced by* psychological and environmental factors, including personality characteristics, mood, expectations, experience with the drug, and the setting in which the drug is taken.

4. *Drug abuse refers to* recurrent drug use that leads to disruptions in academic, social, or occupational functioning and to legal or psychological problems. *Factors that influence drug-taking behavior are* social and cultural norms that are favorable toward drug taking; availability and cost of the drug; drug-taking behavior of role models and family members; occupational, social, and academic problems; association with drug-taking peers; and rebelliousness or alienation from society as a whole.

5. *Depressants have several effects:* they inhibit central nervous system activity; produce drowsiness, sedation, or sleep; relieve anxiety; and lower inhibitions. *Examples include* alcohol, barbiturates, and tranquilizers.

6. *Alcohol depresses* the activity of neurons throughout the brain *and impairs* cognitive abilities, such as concentration, memory, and speech, and physical abilities, such as muscle coordination and balance.

7. *Barbiturates are depressant drugs that* reduce anxiety and promote sleep by depressing activity in the brain centers that control arousal, wakefulness, and alertness. They also depress the brain's respiratory centers.

8. *Tranquilizers are depressants that* relieve anxiety and, while chemically different from barbiturates, produce similar, although less powerful, effects.

9. *Inhalants are chemical substances that* are inhaled to produce an alteration in consciousness. *Examples include* paint solvents, model-airplane glue, gasoline, nitrous oxide, and certain aerosol sprays.

10. *The opiates are a group of addictive drugs that* relieve pain and produce euphoria by mimicking the brain's own natural painkillers called endorphins. *Examples include* opium, morphine, heroin, methadone, and the prescription painkillers Percodan and Demerol.

11. *Stimulant drugs* increase brain activity, arouse behavior, and increase mental alertness. *Examples include* caffeine, nicotine, amphetamines, and cocaine.

12. *The psychedelic drugs create* sensory and perceptual distortions, alter mood, and affect judgment by mimicking the neurotransmitter serotonin (which is involved in regulating moods and sensations) and stimulating serotonin receptor sites. *Examples include* mescaline, psilocybin, and LSD.

13. *Marijuana and its active ingredient, THC, produce* a sense of well-being, mild euphoria, and a dreamy state of relaxation. *THC has been shown to be useful in* the treatment of pain, epilepsy, hypertension, nausea, glaucoma, and asthma.

14. *"Club drugs" are* synthetic drugs used at dance clubs, parties, and "raves." *Examples (and their effects) include* MDMA (ecstasy), which acts as a stimulant and produces mild psychedelic effects, and the dissociative anesthetics, PCP (angel dust) and ketamine (Special K), which reduce sensitivity to pain and produce feelings of detachment and dissociation.

Concept Check 5

1. psychoactive; physically
2. tolerance
3. judgment; self-control
4. not remember
5. will not
6. tranquilizer
7. cocaine
8. MDMA; ecstasy
9. opiates; narcotics

Graphic Organizer 2

1. alcohol; depressant
2. tranquilizer; depressant
3. marijuana; psychedelic
4. LSD; psychedelic

5. caffeine; stimulant

6. morphine; opiate

7. nicotine; stimulant

Matching Exercise 5

1. THC

2. depressants

3. nicotine

4. drug abuse

5. psychoactive drug

6. stimulant-induced psychosis

7. mescaline

8. drug tolerance

9. hashish

10. withdrawal symptoms

11. cocaine

12. amphetamines

13. delirium tremens (DTs)

14. sleep inertia

15. inhalants

16. MDMA (ecstasy)

True/False Test 5

1. T	6. T	11. F	16. T
2. F	7. T	12. T	
3. T	8. T	13. F	
4. T	9. T	14. F	
5. T	10. T	15. T	

Something to Think About

1. Generally speaking, humans are very adaptable; in fact, most people can easily adapt to shift work. If shifts are scheduled to take into account our natural tendencies and use knowledge about sleep–wake cycles, circadian rhythms, and the role of the SCN, they need not produce the usual jet-lag symptoms.

   Begin your report with a discussion of how to rotate a person's shifts. Because we tend to drift to longer days (the 25-hour day rather than the 24-hour day), as we often do on weekends, it would seem best to rotate shifts forward: first shift, 8 A.M. to 4 P.M., second shift 4 P.M. to 12 midnight, and then midnight to 8 A.M. for the third shift.

The length of the shift rotation is the next issue to address. Every shift change is going to take some time to get used to and will be accompanied by some jet-lag symptoms, so the less someone has to change the better. It would probably be best to have people do the same shift for at least a month before changing to the next shift.

Shift workers should be given as much information as possible about circadian rhythms, sleep–wake cycles, and the role of the SCN in the production of melatonin. People finishing a night shift, for example, could be told the value of black-out curtains to avoid having their biological clock reset by bright light; those suffering from sleep inertia could be given the information presented in the Application (Improving Sleep and Mental Alertness). For instance, for the midnight to 8 A.M. shift, having bright lights, especially in the early part of the shift, can help people adjust to the night shift.

Finally, present the organization with a somewhat radical idea. Introduce the idea of the siesta or nap and explain how the low points in our circadian rhythms produce fatigue, especially in sleep-deprived people. Taking a nap is a normal, even beneficial, aspect of our daily sleep–wake cycle. In fact, research has shown that naps reduce fatigue and sleepiness, improve mood and mental alertness, and can improve overall productivity.

2. This dream sounds like a real nightmare. The first thing to tell your friend is that dreams cannot predict the future. She is not likely to fail the exam because of her dream. Her dream reflects the fact that she is concerned and worried about the course. The best way to do well on the exam, and to deal with exam anxiety, is to study the material completely. The text presents two theories of dreams. Freud's view is that the manifest content is relatively unimportant; he would suggest looking for disguised symbolic meaning that reflects the latent content. The activation–synthesis theory suggests that if someone is worried and anxious, these concerns are likely to show up in a dream if these well-worn neural pathways are activated. In other words, the brain produces dream images that are synthesized into a meaningful story, using memories about daily events, past experiences, concerns, and worries.

   The person's interpretation of the dream may tell us more about the dreamer than anything else. If that is the case, it would be fairly safe to assume that this dreamer is experiencing some perceived difficulty with the course (or some aspect of it) and/or the course material itself.

Progress Test 1

1. c	6. c	11. c
2. c	7. d	12. d
3. d	8. b	13. a
4. b	9. c	14. a
5. d	10. a	15. b

Progress Test 2

1. a	6. c	11. b
2. b	7. c	12. a
3. a	8. d	13. a
4. d	9. b	14. d
5. a	10. c	15. c

Progress Test 3

1. a	6. c	11. b
2. d	7. a	12. c
3. c	8. b	13. a
4. c	9. a	14. e
5. a	10. a	15. a

Learning

PREVIEW	Reading the section below first will give you a general sense of the chapter's contents and an initial introduction to some of the major concepts and terms. This will prime you for what you are about to read and help you to develop a "cognitive map" that will guide your study of the material in this chapter. Likewise, reading the **preview questions** at the beginning of each major section will improve your ability to understand, learn, and retain the information.

CHAPTER 5 . . . AT A GLANCE

Chapter 5 answers the question "What is learning?" in its discussions of classical conditioning, operant conditioning, and observational learning. Conditioning focuses on how we form associations between environmental events and behavioral responses. Classical conditioning (discovered by Ivan Pavlov) involves repeatedly pairing a neutral stimulus with a stimulus that naturally elicits a response until the neutral stimulus elicits the same response. Behaviorism was founded by John B. Watson and was concerned with the scientific study of observable behaviors, especially as they pertain to learning. Classical conditioning is used to explain conditioned emotional reactions, placebo responses, and conditioned drug side-effects. Classically conditioned compensatory responses are implicated in the development of drug tolerance, withdrawal symptoms, addiction, and accidental overdoses. Contemporary psychology has modified the basics of classical conditioning to account for cognitive functioning and biological predispositions.

Operant conditioning (developed by B. F. Skinner) demonstrates how voluntary, active behaviors are acquired through shaping, reinforcement (positive and negative), and punishment (by application and by removal). Once acquired, behaviors are maintained through different schedules of reinforcement. Behaviors that are partially reinforced are more resistant to extinction than are behaviors that are continuously reinforced. Behavior modification is the application of principles of operant conditioning to help people develop more adaptive behaviors. Operant conditioning theory has also been modified by contemporary cognitive and biological views.

Observational learning (studied by Albert Bandura) shows how new behaviors can be acquired through watching the actions of others; it involves the processes of attention, memory, motor skills, and motivation. This type of learning is not limited to humans but has been demonstrated in many nonhuman animals as well. Applications involve education, vocational and job training, psychotherapy, and counseling.

Introduction: What Is Learning?

Preview Questions

Consider the following questions as you study this section of the chapter.

- How is learning defined?
- What is conditioning?
- What are three basic types of learning?

*Read the section "Introduction: What Is Learning?" and **write** your answers to the following:*

1. Learning refers to _____
   _____

2. Conditioning is the _____
   _____

3. The three basic types of learning are
   _____
   _____

Classical Conditioning: Associating Stimuli

Preview Questions

Consider the following questions as you study this section of the chapter.

- Who discovered classical conditioning, and how did he investigate it?
- What is the basic process of classical conditioning?
- What factors can affect the strength of a classically conditioned response?
- What phenomena did Pavlov discover when he varied the stimuli during conditioning?

*Read the section "Classical Conditioning: Associating Stimuli" and **write** your answers to the following:*

1. The person who discovered classical conditioning was _____
   He investigated the phenomenon by_____
   _____
   _____
   _____

2. Classical conditioning is the process of (describe the elements involved in the process)
   _____
   _____
   _____
   _____

3. The two factors that can affect the strength of a classically conditioned response are _____
   _____
   _____

4. Pavlov also discovered four other phenomena when additional stimuli were presented:
   _____
   _____
   _____
   _____

From Pavlov to Watson: The Founding of Behaviorism

Preview Questions

Consider the following questions as you study this section of the chapter.

- Who founded behaviorism, and what were its basic assumptions?
- How can classical conditioning be used to create and explain conditioned emotional responses?

*Read the section "From Pavlov to Watson: The Founding of Behaviorism" and **write** your answers to the following:*

1. Behaviorism was founded by _____
   and was defined as _____
   _____
   _____
   _____

2. The fundamental assumptions of behaviorism are _____
   _____
   _____
   _____
   _____

3. Watson identified three innate emotions, which

   are _____

   each of which could be _____

   _____

   With regard to these emotions, Watson showed
   that classical conditioning could be used to

   _____

   _____

4. Classical conditioning can be used to create a
   conditioned emotional response (CR) to a previously neutral stimulus by_____

   _____

   _____

5. The classical conditioning components in the
   Little Albert study were as follows:

   CS: _____

   UCS: _____

   UCR: _____

   CR: _____

Classical Conditioning and Drug Use

Preview Questions

*Consider the following questions as you study this
section of the chapter.*

- How is classical conditioning involved in
  responses to drugs, especially psychoactive
  drugs?

- What are placebo responses, and what role does
  classical conditioning play in producing them?

- What are conditioned compensatory responses,
  and what drug effects are they implicated in?

*Read the section "Classical Conditioning and Drug
Use" and write your answers to the following:*

1. Some people acquire classically conditioned
   responses to drugs such as caffeine, an active
   ingredient in coffee. In this example the CS is

   _____ ; the UCS is

   _____ ; the UCR is

   _____ ; and the CR is

   _____ .

2. A placebo response is _____

   _____ .Use classical con-

ditioning terms to identify each of the following
components in the acquisition of the placebo
response:

Particular situational cues, including the act
of taking the drug, the sight and taste of the
drug, and so on, constitute _____ ;
the active ingredient in the real drug is

_____ ; the effect of the

real drug on the person is _____ ;
following a number of pairings, the response to
a fake pill is _____ .

3. A conditioned compensatory response (CCR) is

   a _____

   _____ . These CCRs are

   implicated in drug effects such as

   _____

Contemporary Views of Classical Conditioning

Preview Questions

*Consider the following questions as you study this
section of the chapter.*

- How does the cognitive explanation of learning
  differ from the behavioral explanation?

- What kinds of cognitive processes are involved
  in classical conditioning, and how have they
  been demonstrated experimentally?

- How does the evolutionary perspective account
  for the conditioning process?

- How do taste aversions challenge the principles
  of classical conditioning, and how can they be
  explained?

- What is biological preparedness?

*Read the section "Contemporary Views of Classical
Conditioning" and **write** your answers to the following:*

1. According to the cognitive perspective, learning

   _____

   On the other hand, the traditional behavioral

   perspective holds that _____

   _____

   _____

2. In his research with rats, Robert Rescorla demonstrated that _____

_____

_____

3. According to the evolutionary perspective,

_____

This is because_____

_____

_____

4. Taste aversion is a _____

_____

Taste aversions violate two basic principles of classical conditioning: _____

_____

_____

_____

5. John Garcia demonstrated that taste aversions could be produced under controlled laboratory conditions by _____

_____

He found that _____

_____

_____

6. Biological preparedness refers to _____

_____

_____

After you have carefully studied the preceding sections, complete the following exercises.

Concept Check 1

Read the following and write the correct term in the space provided.

1. Dr. Munchausen believes that the general principles of learning apply to virtually all species and all learning situations, whereas his colleague Dr. Milstein believes that an animal's natural behavioral patterns and unique characteristics can influence what it is capable of learning. Dr. Munchausen supports the _____ perspective, and

Dr. Milstein's views are consistent with an _____ perspective.

2. Dr. Wells decided to classically condition some rats. He used a tone (CS) followed by a shock (UCS) for group 1; for group 2, he used a taste (CS) followed by a shock. It is very _____ (likely/unlikely) that the rats in group 1 will be classically conditioned; it is very _____ (likely/unlikely) that the rats in group 2 will be classically conditioned.

3. It appears that Dr. Wells in the above example is investigating how _____ affects learning through classical conditioning.

4. Dr. Manly believes that classical conditioning depends on the information the CS provides about the UCS and that for learning to occur, the CS must be a reliable signal that predicts the presentation of the UCS. Dr. Manly's views are most consistent with the _____ perspective.

5. About 5 hours after extinguishing the classically conditioned response (CR) in an experimental animal, Dr. Taylor presented the conditioned stimulus (CS) and obtained a CR. Dr. Taylor has demonstrated

_____ .

6. Fido drools whenever he hears the sound of the electric can opener but does not drool when he hears the sound of the blender, which makes a similar noise. It appears that Fido has learned to _____ between the two sounds.

7. Ahmood, who has recently started drinking a lot of hot chocolate, notices that he now feels a positive emotional reaction at just the sight and smell of hot chocolate. In classical conditioning terms, Ahmood's response to these cues is called a _____ .

8. Ahmood also observes that he has a similar emotional response to the smell of other beverages such as herbal tea and coffee. In this situation, he is experiencing a phenomenon called

_____ .

9. Tremaine regularly takes a psychoactive drug while lying on the couch in his living room. Over time, however, he has had to increase the amount taken in order to experience the original "high." Tremaine has developed

_____ as a result of

acquiring a _____

10. In a research study, patients with high blood pressure regularly received a drug that reduced their hypertension. The drug was always administered in the same location. When a similar-looking fake pill was administered in the same place, the patients' blood pressure was reduced, much as it had been with the real drug. This example illustrates

_____ .

Graphic Organizer 1

In his classic experiment Pavlov repeatedly presented a neutral stimulus, such as a tone, just before putting food in the dog's mouth, which automatically elicited salivation. After several repetitions the tone alone triggered the salivation. Label the following graph using the correct terms (UCS, UCR, CS, CR):

Before Conditioning

| Food in the mouth is the ____ and the salivation is the ____ . | The neutral stimulus is the ___. It elicits no salivation before conditioning. |

During Conditioning

| The neutral stimulus is the ___ . | + | Food in the mouth is the ____ . | → | The salivation is the ____ . |

After Conditioning

| The tone alone is the ___ . | → | The salivation is now the ___ . |

Review of Terms, Concepts, and Names 1

Use the terms in this list to complete the Matching Test, then to help you answer the True/False items correctly.

learning
conditioning
Ivan Pavlov
classical conditioning
elicit
unconditioned stimulus
unconditioned response
conditioned stimulus
conditioned response
stimulus generalization
stimulus discrimination
extinction
spontaneous recovery

John B. Watson
behaviorism
placebo response
conditioned
  compensatory response
  (CCR)
Shepard Siegel
cognitive perspective
Robert A. Rescorla
taste aversion
John Garcia
biological preparedness
phobia

Matching Exercise

Match the appropriate term/name with its definition or description.

1. _____ The gradual weakening and disappearance of conditioned behavior; in classical conditioning, it occurs when the conditioned stimulus is repeatedly presented without the unconditioned stimulus.

2. _____ The process of learning associations between environmental events and behavioral responses.

3. _____ A relatively enduring change in behavior or knowledge as a result of past experience.

4. _____ Classically conditioned dislike for and avoidance of a particular food that develops when an organism becomes ill after eating the food.

5. _____ School of psychology and theoretical viewpoint that emphasizes the scientific study of observable behaviors, especially as they pertain to the process of learning.

6. _____ American psychologist who founded behaviorism in the early 1900s.

7. _____ Natural stimulus that reflexively elicits a response without the necessity of prior learning.

8. _____ Russian physiologist who first described the basic learning process of associating stimuli that is now called classical conditioning.

9. _____ Extreme, irrational fear of a specific object, animal, or situation.

10. _____ Unlearned, reflexive response that is elicited by an unconditioned stimulus.

11. _____ In learning theory, the idea that an organism is innately predisposed to form associations between certain stimuli and not others.

12. _____ A classically conditioned response in which stimuli that reliably precede the administration of a drug elicit a physiological reaction that counteracts or is opposite to the drug's effects.

True/False Test

Indicate whether each statement is true or false by placing T or F in the blank space next to each item.

1. ___ Classical conditioning is the basic learning process that involves repeatedly pairing a neutral stimulus with a response-producing stimulus until the neutral stimulus elicits the same response.

2. ___ "Elicit" means to draw out or bring forth and causes an existing behavior to occur.

3. ___ The American psychologist who experimentally demonstrated the involvement of cognitive processes in classical conditioning is John Garcia.

4. ___ The occurrence of a learned response not only to the original stimulus but to other similar stimuli as well is called stimulus discrimination.

5. ___ The conditioned stimulus is a formerly neutral stimulus that acquires the capacity to elicit a reflexive response.

6. ___ The reappearance of a previously extinguished conditioned response after a period of time without exposure to the conditioned stimulus is called spontaneous recovery.

7. ___ Stimulus generalization occurs when a learned response is made to a specific stimulus but not to other similar stimuli.

8. ___ Robert A. Rescorla is the American psychologist who experimentally demonstrated the learning of taste aversions in animals.

9. ___ The conditioned response is the learned, reflexive response to a conditioned stimulus.

10. ___ The cognitive perspective holds that mental processes as well as external events are an important component in the learning of new behaviors.

11. ___ The Canadian psychologist who has extensively studied the role of classical conditioning and conditioned compensatory responses in the development of drug tolerance, drug withdrawal symptoms, and drug relapse is Shepard Siegel.

12. ___ The placebo response is an individual's psychological and physiological response to what is actually a fake treatment or drug.

Check your answers and review any areas of weakness before going on to the next section.

Operant Conditioning: Associating Behaviors and Consequences (Part 1)

Preview Questions

Consider the following questions as you study the first three parts of this section of the chapter (up to and including Punishment).

- What was Thorndike's contribution to learning theory?
- What were B. F. Skinner's key assumptions, and what is the fundamental premise of operant conditioning?
- How are positive and negative reinforcement similar, and how are they different?
- What is punishment, and what factors influence its effectiveness?
- What negative effects are associated with the use of punishment?

Read the section "Operant Conditioning: Associating Behaviors and Consequences" (up to Discriminative Stimuli) and **write** *your answers to the following:*

1. Edward L. Thorndike was the first person to
_____

He concluded that _____

2. B. F. Skinner believed that _____

3. Operant conditioning is _____

It explains _____

4. The basic premise of operant conditioning is _____

5. Reinforcement refers to _____

6. Positive reinforcement involves _____

Negative reinforcement involves _____

Negative and positive reinforcement are similar in that _____

They differ in that _____

7. A primary reinforcer is_____

and a conditioned reinforcer (secondary reinforcer) is_____

8. Punishment is a _____

9. The factors that influence the effectiveness of punishment are _____

The drawbacks of punishment are that _____

After you have carefully studied the preceding section, complete the following exercises.

Concept Check 2

Read the following and write the correct term in the space provided.

1. Ashley holds the view that responses followed by a satisfying state of affairs are strengthened and are more likely to occur again in the same situation and that responses followed by an unpleasant or annoying state of affairs are less likely to recur. This view is most consistent with a fundamental principle of learning called the _____ .

2. April burned her fingers when she picked up a hot saucepan with her bare hands. She now always dons her oven mitts before touching any hot pan or pot. The aversive stimulus of getting burned reduced her tendency to pick up pots with her bare hands and is therefore an example of _____ ; her increased tendency to use oven mitts because doing so reduces the possibility of getting burned is an example of _____ .

3. Whenever young Simon wants something, such as a new toy or candy, he cries and screams until his parents give in and give him what he wants. Simon's whining behavior is _____ reinforced by his parents giving in, and the parents' behavior is _____ reinforced because it stops the annoying crying and screaming.

4. While researching a term paper for his history of psychology class, Rupert discovered the name of the first psychologist to investigate how voluntary behaviors are influenced by their consequences. That psychologist was _____ .

5. The following are examples of negative reinforcement. Decide which illustrate *escape* and which illustrate *avoidance*.

   (a) You go to the dentist on a regular basis; as a result, you don't experience problems such as toothaches. This an example of _____ .

   (b) Your partner is complaining about your messy habits, so you put on your running gear and go for a five-mile jog. This is an example of _____ .

   (c) You study hard all semester because you don't want to end up with a low grade-point average. This is an example of _____ .

   (d) You turn the air conditioner on when the temperature in your room gets too hot and uncomfortable. This is an example of _____ .

6. For each of the following, decide whether the example illustrates negative reinforcement (NR), punishment by application (P/A), or punishment by removal (P/R).

   (a) _____ Marco always wears his seatbelt when he drives his car because he doesn't want to be thrown against the windshield if his car is hit from behind.

   (b) _____ Darryl has tried some new aftershave lotion. "It smells like diesel oil!" complains his girlfriend. Darryl never uses that aftershave lotion again.

   (c) _____ Maria does not misbehave at the dinner table because she knows that misbehavior will result in her forfeiting dessert.

   (d) _____ Greta's cigarette lighter ignites the hair spray she has just put on her hair and burns her bangs and eyebrows. Greta no longer smokes when she is doing her hair.

   (e) _____ Jim no longer picks up hitchhikers after the last one robbed him at gun point.

   (f) _____ Before pouring milk on her cereal, Carmelita smells the carton to make sure the milk has not gone sour.

   (g) _____ Astrid brushes her teeth after every meal because she wants to cut down on the number of visits she needs to make to the dentist.

Graphic Organizer 2

The following is a very useful way to organize the procedures used in operant conditioning. The arrow

(↑ or ↓) indicates whether the behavior increases or decreases. Fill in the blanks in cells 1, 2, 3, and 4.

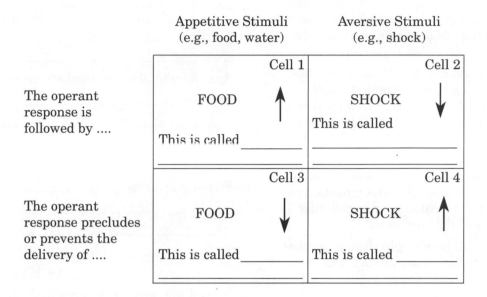

Appetitive Stimuli (e.g., food, water)   **Aversive Stimuli** (e.g., shock)

The operant response is followed by ....

Cell 1 FOOD ↑ This is called _____

Cell 2 SHOCK ↓ This is called _____

The operant response precludes or prevents the delivery of ....

Cell 3 FOOD ↓ This is called _____

Cell 4 SHOCK ↑ This is called _____

Review of Terms, Concepts, and Names 2

Use the terms in this list to complete the Matching Test, then to help you answer the True/False items correctly.

Edward L. Thorndike
law of effect
B. F. Skinner
operant
operant conditioning
reinforcement
positive reinforcement
negative reinforcement
aversive stimuli

primary reinforcer
conditioned reinforcer
punishment
punishment by application (positive punishment)
punishment by removal (negative punishment)

Matching Exercise

Match the appropriate term/name with its definition or description.

1. _____ American psychologist who developed the operant conditioning model of learning.

2. _____ Situation in which a response results in the removal of, avoidance of, or escape from an aversive stimulus, increasing the likelihood of the response being repeated in similar situations.

3. _____ American psychologist who was the first to study animal behavior experimentally and document how active behaviors are influenced by their consequences.

4. _____ Presentation of a stimulus or event following a behavior that acts to decrease the likelihood of the behavior being repeated.

5. _____ Stimulus or event that has acquired reinforcing value by being associated with a primary reinforcer; also called a secondary reinforcer.

6. _____ Occurrence of a stimulus or event following a response that increases the likelihood of the response being repeated.

7. _____ Skinner's term for an actively emitted behavior that operates on the environment to produce consequences.

True/False Test

Indicate whether each statement is true or false by placing T or F in the blank space next to each item.

1. ___ A primary reinforcer is a stimulus or event that is naturally or inherently reinforcing for a given species; examples include food, water, and other biological necessities.

2. ___ Punishment by application involves the removal or subtraction of a reinforcing stimulus following a response.

3. ____ Positive reinforcement refers to a situation in which a response is followed by the addition of a reinforcing stimulus, increasing the likelihood of the response being repeated in a similar situation.

4. ____ Punishment by removal involves the presentation or addition of an unpleasant or aversive event or stimulus following a response.

5. ____ The law of effect states that responses followed by a satisfying effect become strengthened and are more likely to recur in a particular situation, whereas responses followed by a dissatisfying effect are weakened and less likely to recur in a particular situation.

6. ____ Operant conditioning is the basic learning process that involves changing the probability of a response being repeated by manipulating the consequences of that response.

7. ____ Aversive stimuli involve physical or psychological discomfort that an organism seeks to escape or avoid.

Check your answers and review any areas of weakness before going on to the next section.

Operant Conditioning: Associating Behaviors and Consequences (Part 2)

Preview Questions

Consider the following questions as you study the last parts of this section of the chapter (up to and including Applications of Operant Conditioning).

- What are discriminative stimuli, and what important role do they play in operant conditioning?

- What is shaping, and how does it work?

- How does partial reinforcement affect behavior?

- What are the four basic schedules of reinforcement?

- What are some practical applications of operant conditioning principles?

- How has behavior modification been used to change human behavior?

*Read the section "Operant Conditioning: Associating Behaviors and Consequences" and **write** your answers to the following:*

1. Discriminative stimuli are _____
   _____
   _____
   _____

   According to Skinner, they are important
   because _____
   _____
   _____

2. Shaping involves _____
   _____
   _____
   _____
   _____

3. Partial reinforcement is more effective than continuous reinforcement because it _____
   _____
   _____

4. The four basic schedules of reinforcement are
   _____
   _____
   _____
   _____

5. Behavior modification is _____
   _____
   _____
   _____
   _____

After you have carefully studied the preceding section, complete the following exercises.

Concept Check 3

Read the following and write the correct term in the space provided.

1. Your instructor, Dr. Jones, decides to give surprise quizzes throughout the semester. Your studying will be reinforced on a

   _____ schedule.

2. A ringing telephone is a

_____ for picking up

the receiver.

3. Your instructor, Dr. Wong, schedules a quiz

every two weeks throughout the semester. Your

studying will be reinforced on a

_____ schedule.

4. A rat gets a food pellet for every 20 responses.

It is reinforced on a

_____ schedule.

5. If parents use praise and encouragement to

gradually teach a child how to dress herself,

they are using a _____ procedure.

6. Maria sells magazine subscriptions over the

phone. She makes many calls but only gets paid

for making a sale. She is reinforced on a

_____ schedule.

7. Juanita and her colleagues assemble TV sets in

a factory. They get paid a bonus for every ten

TVs they produce. They are being rewarded on

a _____ schedule.

Graphic Organizer 3

Fill in each cell with the name of the appropriate partial reinforcement schedule.

	Based on the number of responses made	Based on the elapsed time
Fixed	Cell 1 _____	Cell 2 _____
Variable	Cell 3 _____	Cell 4 _____

Review of Terms, Concepts, and Names 3

Use the terms in this list to complete the Matching Test, then to help you answer the True/False items correctly.

discriminative stimulus

operant chamber

  (Skinner box)

shaping

continuous

  reinforcement

partial reinforcement

extinction

partial reinforcement

  effect

schedule of

  reinforcement

fixed ratio

variable ratio

fixed interval

variable interval

behavior modification

Matching Exercise

Match the appropriate term/name with its definition or description:

1. _____ The application of learning principles to help people develop more effective or adaptive behaviors.

2. _____ Schedule of reinforcement in which every occurrence of a particular response is reinforced.

3. _____ The name of the experimental apparatus invented by B. F. Skinner to study the relationship between environmental events and active behaviors.

4. _____ Reinforcement schedule in which a reinforcer is delivered after a fixed number of responses has occurred.

5. _____ Operant conditioning procedure in which successively closer approximations of a goal behavior are selectively reinforced until the goal behavior is displayed.

6. _____ Reinforcement schedule in which a reinforcer is delivered for the first response that occurs after a fixed time interval has elapsed.

7. _____ The delivery of a reinforcer according to a preset pattern based on the number of responses or the time interval between responses.

True/False Test

Indicate whether each statement is true or false by placing T or F in the blank space next to each item.

1. ____ Partial reinforcement refers to a situation in which the occurrence of a particular response is only sometimes followed by a reinforcer.

2. ____ A variable-ratio schedule is one in which a reinforcer is delivered for the first response that occurs after an average time interval has elapsed, but the time varies unpredictably from trial to trial.

3. ____ A discriminative stimulus is a specific stimulus in the presence of which a particular response is more likely to be reinforced.

4. ____ A variable-interval schedule is one in which a reinforcer is delivered after an average number of responses, but the number varies unpredictably from trial to trial.

5. ___ The partial reinforcement effect refers to the fact that continuously reinforced behaviors are more resistant to extinction than behaviors that are only sometimes reinforced.

6. ___ The gradual weakening and disappearance of conditioned behavior in operant conditioning is called extinction; it occurs when an emitted behavior is no longer followed by a reinforcer.

Check your answers and review any areas of weakness before going on to the next section.

Contemporary Views of Operant Conditioning

Preview Questions

Consider the following questions as you study this section of the chapter.

- What factors do contemporary learning researchers suggest are involved in operant conditioning?
- How did Tolman's research demonstrate the involvement of cognitive processes in learning?
- What are cognitive maps, latent learning, and learned helplessness?
- How is operant conditioning influenced by an animal's natural behavior pattern?
- How does the phenomenon of instinctive drift challenge the traditional behavioral view of operant conditioning?

*Read the section "Contemporary Views of Operant Conditioning" and **write** your answers to the following:*

1. Contemporary learning researchers confirm the basic principles of operant conditioning but also acknowledge _____

2. Unlike Skinner and Thorndike, Tolman believed that _____

3. A cognitive map is _____

   Latent learning refers to _____

4. Learned helplessness demonstrates the role of cognitive factors in learning in that _____

5. Operant conditioning may also be influenced by _____

6. The phenomenon of instinctive drift challenged the traditional behavioral view by _____

Observational Learning: Imitating the Actions of Others

Preview Questions

Consider the following questions as you study this section of the chapter.

- What type of learning is indirect?
- What four mental processes are involved in observational learning?
- How has observational learning been applied?

*Read the section "Observational Learning: Imitating the Actions of Others" and **write** your answers to the following:*

1. Observational learning is _____

   The person most strongly identified with work in this area is _____

2. The four cognitive processes that interact to determine if imitation will occur are _____

3. Observational learning has been applied in a variety of settings, including _____

After you have carefully studied the preceding sections, complete the following exercises.

Concept Check 4

Read the following and write the correct term in the space provided.

1. Maria watches the cooking show Cucina Amore on public TV on Saturday afternoon and often cooks one of the dishes she sees the chef prepare. Maria's culinary ability is the result of _____ learning.

2. Dr. Bristow believes that reinforcement is not necessary for learning to occur but that the *expectation* of reinforcement can affect the performance of what has been learned. Dr. Bristow is emphasizing the importance of _____ factors in learning.

3. If a rat has been allowed to explore a maze for a number of trials without ever getting a reinforcer, it is very _____ (likely/unlikely) that when food is made available in the goal box, the rat will find it very quickly with few errors.

4. An animal trainer has a hard time operantly conditioning a pig to pick up a large wooden penny and put it in a big "piggy bank" because the pig seems to prefer to push the coin with its snout even though it is not reinforced for this behavior. The Brelands called this phenomenon _____ .

5. Mr. and Mrs. Delbrook both stopped smoking when they started a family because they wanted to model healthy behavior patterns for their children. They are apparently aware of the importance of _____ learning in children's development.

Review of Terms, Concepts, and Names 4

Use the terms in this list to complete the Matching Test, then to help you answer the True/False items correctly.

Edward C. Tolman
cognitive map
latent learning
learned helplessness
instinctive drift
Albert Bandura
observational learning

Matching Exercise

Match the appropriate term/name with its definition or description:

1. _____ Learning that occurs through observing the actions of others.

2. _____ Tolman's term for learning that occurs in the absence of reinforcement but is not behaviorally demonstrated until a reinforcer becomes available.

3. _____ American psychologist who used the terms *cognitive map* and *latent learning* to describe experimental findings that strongly suggested that cognitive factors play a role in animal learning.

4. _____ Tolman's term for the mental representation of the layout of a familiar environment.

5. _____ American psychologist who experimentally investigated observational learning, emphasizing the role of cognitive factors.

6. _____ The tendency of an animal to revert to instinctive behaviors, which can interfere with the performance of an operantly conditioned response.

7. _____ A phenomenon in which exposure to inescapable and uncontrollable aversive events produces passive behavior.

Check your answers and review any areas of weakness before going on to the next section.

Something to Think About

1. Imagine that you are a behavioral therapist whose client has a real fear of going to the dentist. Despite the need for some important dental work, he can't bring himself to make an appointment. Using what you know about classical conditioning, explain how his phobia might have come about, and describe how to extinguish the fear.

2. Mrs. Denton can't understand why scolding her ten-year-old son for misbehaving only seems to make the problem worse. Using what you know about operant conditioning techniques, what advice would you give Mrs. Denton about how she might (a) reduce the disruptive behavior and (b) encourage more appropriate behavior.

3. Imagine that your family has decided to adopt a puppy. Using what you know about operant conditioning techniques, what advice would you give them about how they should train the dog to be obedient and do some neat pet tricks?

Check your answers and review any areas of weakness before doing the progress tests.

Progress Test 1

Review the complete chapter (including Concept Reviews and all the boxed inserts), review all your study notes, and then test yourself on the following progress test. Check your answers. If you make a mistake, review your notes, review the relevant section of the study guide, and, if necessary, go back and read the appropriate part of your textbook.

1. Dr. Ramos is a behavioral psychologist who conducts basic research using animals in carefully controlled laboratory studies. The goal of his research is most probably to
   (a) train animals to do tricks.
   (b) collect and sell saliva from dogs and other animals.
   (c) identify the general principles of learning that apply across a wide range of species, including humans.
   (d) observe changes in animal behavior that result from biological maturation.

2. Dr. Frolov classically conditioned a dog to flex his hind leg at the sound of a bell by pairing the ringing of a bell with a mild electric shock to the leg. In this example, the ringing bell is the
   (a) unconditioned stimulus (UCS).
   (b) conditioned response (CR).
   (c) unconditioned response (UCR).
   (d) conditioned stimulus (CS).

3. Some forms of chemotherapy make patients sick. A patient who has eaten vegetarian pizza just before the therapy (and is then sick) later feels ill when she sees or smells pizza. In this example of taste aversion learning, the conditioned response is the
   (a) vegetarian pizza.
   (b) chemotherapy.
   (c) illness induced by the therapy.
   (d) nausea felt at the sight or smell of pizza.

4. Zoran has a classically conditioned fear of rivers and lakes after he was attacked by an alligator while swimming in a river near his home. A behavioral psychologist is likely to suggest that his conditioned response (CR) can be weakened and may eventually disappear through a process called
   (a) spontaneous recovery.
   (b) extinction.
   (c) instinctive drift.
   (d) stimulus generalization.

5. Dr. Redner believes that classical conditioning depends on the information the conditioned stimulus provides about the unconditioned stimulus and that for learning to occur, the conditioned stimulus must be a reliable signal that predicts the presentation of the unconditioned stimulus. Dr. Redner's views are most consistent with those of the learning theorist
   (a) Robert A. Rescorla.
   (b) Edward L. Thorndike.
   (c) Ivan Pavlov.
   (d) B. F. Skinner.

6. Ricardo always gets nervous and apprehensive whenever his professor uses the word "exam" but he seldom feels the same anxiety when the word "quiz" is mentioned. Assuming that classical conditioning is involved in these two different reactions at the mention of tests, it appears that Ricardo is exhibiting
   (a) stimulus discrimination.
   (b) spontaneous recovery.
   (c) latent learning.
   (d) stimulus generalization.

7. About five hours after she had successfully extinguished a dog's classically conditioned response of salivating to the sound of a bell, Dr. Sheckenov discovered that the dog once again salivated in the presence of the bell. This example illustrates the phenomenon of
   (a) stimulus generalization.
   (b) spontaneous recovery.
   (c) latent learning.
   (d) instinctive drift.

8. Dr. Radersched conducts research on the phenomenon of biological preparedness. She is most likely to discover that
   (a) organisms are innately predisposed to form associations between some stimuli and responses and not others.
   (b) the general principles of learning apply to virtually all animal species and all learning situations.
   (c) classical conditioning occurs because two stimuli are associated closely in time and that frequency and contiguity are the only variables that affect learning.
   (d) mental processes, but not innate predispositions, are the crucial variables involved in classical conditioning.

9. After studying very hard last semester Sasha got very good grades in all her courses. This semester, Sasha is once again studying very hard. It appears that good grades are _____ for Sasha's studying behavior.
   (a) conditioned stimuli
   (b) discriminative stimuli
   (c) positively reinforcing
   (d) negatively reinforcing

10. Rachel studies very hard to avoid getting bad grades because for her a bad grade is a devastating experience. Rachel's studying behavior is maintained by
    (a) negative reinforcement.
    (b) primary reinforcement.
    (c) positive reinforcement.
    (d) punishment by removal.

11. Helmut is employed by his university as a telephone solicitor for a fund-raising drive. He is paid a set amount of money for every ten calls he makes regardless of whether he is successful in raising funds. Helmut's telephoning is reinforced on a _____ schedule of reinforcement.
    (a) fixed-interval (FI)
    (b) variable-interval (VI)
    (c) fixed-ratio (FR)
    (d) variable-ratio (VR)

12. Ever since Thelma got her new fax machine and hooked up her computer to the Internet, her phone line is often busy. It is difficult for her parents to know when to call her so they try at random times. It appears that phoning Thelma is reinforced on a _____ schedule.

    (a) fixed-interval (FI)
    (b) variable-interval (VI)
    (c) fixed-ratio (FR)
    (d) variable-ratio (VR)

13. After they had been watching Superman cartoons all morning, 5-year-old Jim and 6-year-old John, each using a beach towel as a cape, climbed on top of the garage roof and got ready to fly. Their startled mother stopped them in time and realized the powerful influence of _____ on behavior.
    (a) observational learning
    (b) classical conditioning
    (c) operant conditioning
    (d) stimulus generalization

14. According to Critical Thinking 5.4, B. F. Skinner maintained that
    (a) human freedom is an illusion.
    (b) all behavior arises from causes that are within the individual, and environmental factors have little or no influence.
    (c) cognitive factors are the crucial elements in all learning.
    (d) the evolutionary perspective best explains animal behavior but can't be applied to human beings.

15. According to Critical Thinking 5.5, the amount of violence depicted on American television
    (a) has decreased dramatically, year by year, over the past decade.
    (b) is so low today, compared to a decade or two ago, that there should be no cause for concern about its effects on children or adults.
    (c) is very high and should be of concern because the criteria that are more likely to lead to imitation, especially by children, are fulfilled in these depictions of violence on television.
    (d) does both (a) and (b).

Progress Test 2

After you have checked your understanding of the material in Progress Test 1 and have done a complete chapter review with special focus on any areas of weakness, you are now ready to assess your knowledge on Progress Test 2. Check your answers. If you make a mistake, review your notes, the relevant section of the study guide, and, if necessary, the appropriate part of your textbook.

1. Which of the following best illustrates classical conditioning?
   (a) Henry feels ill at the sight or smell of peanut butter because it once made him sick.
   (b) Annalee studies hard because she wants to get good grades.
   (c) Virginia goes shopping for new clothes fairly frequently because it makes her feel good.
   (d) Lyndle drives at the posted speed limit after getting a number of speeding tickets.

2. Erv developed a fear of attics after he was accidentally locked in his own attic by his wife. Erv's present fear and apprehension of the attic is a(n)
   (a) example of instinctive drift.
   (b) conditioned emotional response.
   (c) form of observational learning.
   (d) conditioned compensatory response.

3. Little Richard receives attention from his teacher in the form of a scolding every time he misbehaves. As a result, Richard misbehaves quite frequently. In this instance, it would appear that the teacher's scolding is a
   (a) form of punishment by application.
   (b) positively reinforcing stimulus.
   (c) form of punishment by removal.
   (d) negatively reinforcing stimulus.

4. A group of 4-year-old children watch a video showing an adult hitting, kicking, and punching a large Bobo doll. These children are later asked to imitate the model and are promised a reward for every behavior they can imitate. It is very probable that the children will
   (a) not imitate the adult model.
   (b) verbally describe what they saw but will refuse to imitate the adult model.
   (c) quite readily imitate the adult's aggressive behavior.
   (d) become very upset as a result of watching the aggressive behavior.

5. Lauren spent the first week of the semester exploring the campus. Later, she had no trouble locating the library, although she had never been there before. According to Tolman, Lauren
   (a) has developed biological preparedness.
   (b) has formed a cognitive map.
   (c) is suffering from instinctive drift.
   (d) has developed a sense of direction.

6. Gerry puts up her umbrella soon after it starts to rain in order prevent her clothes from getting any wetter. This example illustrates _____ behavior and _____ reinforcement.
   (a) avoidance; positive
   (b) escape; negative
   (c) avoidance; negative
   (d) escape; positive

7. When Juanita gets paid, she uses her money to buy food to feed her family. For Juanita, money is a _____ reinforcer and food is a _____ reinforcer.
   (a) conditioned; primary
   (b) primary; negative
   (c) conditioned; secondary
   (d) primary; positive

8. At dinner one night, Amanda created quite a disturbance using her spoon as a drumstick. Her mother told her that she would get no dessert if she persisted with her unruly behavior. Amanda soon stopped the banging. This example most clearly illustrates
   (a) negative reinforcement.
   (b) punishment by removal.
   (c) positive reinforcement.
   (d) punishment by application.

9. Dr. Glendening and his colleagues believe that people with damaged prefrontal lobes are unable to use information from rewarding and punishing outcomes to guide their behavior. According to the Focus on Neuroscience, some supporting evidence for this view was obtained by researchers who scanned the brains of participants in a reinforcing or punishing situation. The results of the fMRI scans showed
   (a) reinforcement and punishment activated different areas of the orbitofrontal cortex (OFC).
   (b) reinforcement activated the middle region of the OFC.
   (c) punishment activated areas on both sides of the OFC.
   (d) the greater the reward or punishment, the higher the level of activation in the OFC areas.
   (e) all of the above.

10. Zeno tried to train his potbellied pig to pick up the newspaper on the doorstep and bring it into the house. However, the pig pushed the paper with his snout into the garden, even though this behavior would not be rewarded. It appears that Zeno's attempt to operantly condition his pig has been subject to
(a) instinctive drift.
(b) stimulus discrimination.
(c) spontaneous recovery.
(d) extinction.

11. Greta loves playing the slot machines even though she wins money only once in a while. Greta's gambling behavior is likely to be very resistant to extinction because of
(a) the partial reinforcement effect.
(b) spontaneous recovery.
(c) the law of effect.
(d) instinctive drift.

12. Dalbir believes that reinforcement is not necessary for learning to occur but it does affect the performance of what has been learned. Dalbir's view is most consistent with the phenomenon of
(a) instinctive drift.
(b) biological preparedness.
(c) shaping.
(d) latent learning.

13. Harold, a regular heroin user, typically injects the drug while listening to music in his living room. Once, however, when he injected the usual amount of the drug while watching TV in the kitchen, he almost died. According to Siegel, this situation most likely illustrates
(a) a placebo response.
(b) spontaneous recovery.
(c) a conditioned compensatory response (CCR).
(d) instinctive drift.

14. According to the Application, we often choose a short-term reinforcer over a more valuable long-term goal. Your text suggests that we do this because
(a) the relative value of a reinforcer can shift over time.
(b) as the availability of a reinforcer gets closer, the subjective value of the reinforcer increases.
(c) when we make our decision, we'll choose whichever reinforcer has the greatest subjective value.
(d) of all of the above reasons.

15. According to Seligman (In Focus 5.2), people are more likely to develop phobias of spiders, snakes, or heights—as compared to doorknobs, knives, washing machines, and ladders—because
(a) of instinctive drift.
(b) we are biologically prepared to do so.
(c) doorknobs, knives, and ladders are inherently safer than spiders, snakes, and heights.
(d) of latent learning.

Progress Test 3

After you have checked your understanding of the material in Progress Tests 1 and 2, and have done a complete chapter review with special focus on any areas of weakness, you are ready to further assess your knowledge on Progress Test 3. Check your answers. If you make a mistake, review your notes, the appropriate parts of the study guide, and, if necessary, the relevant sections of your textbook.

1. Arturo, a psychology major, was asked by his roommate to explain conditioning. He is most likely to point out
(a) that conditioning is the process of learning associations between environmental events and behavioral responses.
(b) that there are two basic types of conditioning, operant conditioning and classical conditioning.
(c) that contemporary learning theorists also consider the process of observational learning.
(d) all of the above.

2. Habitual coffee drinkers, such as Don and Sandy, often acquire a classically conditioned response (CR) to the smell, sight, or taste of coffee. Even after drinking a cup or two of decaffeinated coffee, which is obviously missing the active ingredient caffeine, they experience increased arousal and alertness. In this example the smell, taste, and sight of the decaffeinated coffee is the _____ and the response to the decaffeinated coffee is called _____ .
(a) UCS; a conditioned compensatory response (CCR)
(b) CS; learned helplessness
(c) CS; a placebo response
(d) UCS; an unconditioned response (UCR)

3. Justine got sick after eating a chicken burger. Now she not only has an intense dislike of chicken burgers but feels nauseated at the sight of beef burgers, fish burgers, soybean burgers, or anything that even resembles a burger. It would appear that Justine has experienced the phenomenon Pavlov called
   (a) stimulus discrimination.
   (b) spontaneous recovery.
   (c) extinction.
   (d) stimulus generalization.

4. By presenting the CS over and over again without the UCS, Dr. Laslove discovered that the subject's conditioned response (CR) gradually weakened and disappeared. Dr. Laslove has carried out a procedure called
   (a) latent learning.
   (b) spontaneous recovery.
   (c) extinction.
   (d) stimulus discrimination.

5. Rolando got very sick after eating a big dish of oysters. Ever since that experience Rolando feels ill whenever he sees or smells oysters. It appears that Rolando
   (a) has developed a taste aversion.
   (b) has experienced latent learning.
   (c) is suffering from instinctive drift.
   (d) is experiencing spontaneous recovery.

6. Dr. Alonzo takes a cognitive perspective in his research on learning. He is most likely to suggest that classical conditioning
   (a) involves learning the relations between events and that the CS must be a reliable predictor of the UCS.
   (b) results from simply pairing the CS with the UCS for a number of trials.
   (c) is constrained by biological predispositions.
   (d) follows general principles of learning that apply to virtually all animal species and all learning situations.

7. Positive reinforcement is to _____ as negative reinforcement is to _____ .
   (a) increased responding; decreased responding
   (b) decreased responding decreased responding
   (c) increased responding; decreased responding
   (d) increased responding; increased responding

8. When Billy used his knife to release a piece of toast that was jammed in the toaster he got a severe electric shock. Billy has never used his knife to get toast out of the toaster again. It appears that Billy's behavior has been changed by
   (a) punishment by application.
   (b) negative reinforcement.
   (c) punishment by removal.
   (d) extinction.

9. Whenever the doorbell rings, Rex runs to the door and barks and growls. For Rex the ringing doorbell is a(n) _____ for his growling and barking behavior.
   (a) discriminative stimulus
   (b) unconditioned stimulus
   (c) reinforcing stimulus
   (d) primary reinforcer

10. Tammy wants to train her dog to "shake hands" with people, so she reinforces closer and closer approximations to the desired behavior. First she rewards him for sitting on command, then for slightly raising his front paw, then for fully raising his paw, then for moving his paw up and down until it is grasped, and so on. Tammy has used a process called
    (a) latent learning.
    (b) extinction.
    (c) partial reinforcement.
    (d) shaping.

11. Arnie always drives at the posted speed limit and obeys all the rules of the road because he can't afford to pay fines for driving offenses. Arnie's good driving habits are maintained by
    (a) positive reinforcement.
    (b) partial reinforcement.
    (c) secondary reinforcement.
    (d) negative reinforcement.

12. Harry works on an assembly line as part of a team of eight workers. They get paid a bonus for every one hundred products they assemble. Harry and his coworkers are being rewarded on a _____ schedule of reinforcement.
    (a) fixed-interval (FI)
    (b) variable-interval (VI)
    (c) fixed-ratio (FR)
    (d) variable-ratio (VR)

13. Wilma's psychology instructor schedules tests every two weeks throughout the semester, but her sociology instructor has surprise quizzes throughout the semester. The psychology instructor is using a _____ schedule and the sociology instructor is using a _____ schedule.
    (a) fixed-interval (FI); variable-interval (VI)
    (b) variable-interval (VI); variable-ratio (VR)
    (c) fixed-ratio (FR); variable-ratio (VR)
    (d) variable-ratio (VR); fixed-interval (FI)

14. According to In Focus 5.1, John B. Watson
    (a) believed that punishment was the best and most desirable way to change behavior.
    (b) vehemently opposed Skinner's idea that freedom is just an illusion.
    (c) was a pioneer in the application of classical conditioning principles to advertising.
    (d) discovered the phenomenon of latent learning.

15. According to In Focus 5.3, which of the following is true?
    (a) Punishment is the most effective way to change undesirable behavior.
    (b) Punishment works better than any other behavioral strategy in changing undesirable behavior.
    (c) There are no effective strategies for reducing undesirable behaviors.
    (d) Several strategies other than punishment can be used to change undesirable behavior.

Answers

Introduction: What Is Learning?

1. *Learning refers to* a relatively enduring change in behavior or knowledge as a result of past experience.

2. *Conditioning is the* process of learning associations between environmental events and behavioral responses.

3. *The three basic types of learning are* classical conditioning, operant conditioning, and observational learning.

Classical Conditioning: Associating Stimuli

1. *The person who discovered classical conditioning was* Ivan Pavlov. *He investigated the phenomenon by* studying how dogs learned to salivate to the presence of a stimulus (that would not normally elicit saliva) after it had been associated with food in the mouth, which reflexively elicits saliva.

2. *Classical conditioning is the process of (describe the elements involved in the process)* learning an association between two stimuli: the neutral stimulus (later to be the conditioned stimulus, or CS) that does not normally produce the response of interest and the natural stimulus (the unconditioned stimulus, or UCS), which automatically elicits the response (the unconditioned response, or UCR). Following this association, the CS will elicit a new learned response (the conditioned response, or CR).

3. *The two factors that can affect the strength of a classically conditioned response are* the frequency of the presentations of the two stimuli (the more frequently the CS and UCS are paired, the stronger the conditioning) and the timing of the stimulus presentations (the CS needs to be presented about a half-second before the UCS).

4. *Pavlov also discovered four other phenomena when additional stimuli were presented:* generalization, the ability to respond to new stimuli that were similar to the CS; discrimination, the ability to distinguish between two stimuli, responding only to the one that had been followed by food; extinction, the gradual weakening and disappearance of the CR after repeated exposure to the CS alone (without the UCS); and spontaneous recovery, the reappearance of a previously extinguished conditioned response following a rest period when the CS is again presented.

From Pavlov to Watson: The Founding of Behaviorism

1. *Behaviorism was founded by* John B. Watson *and was defined as* the scientific study of observable behaviors, especially as they pertain to learning.

2. *The fundamental assumptions of behaviorism are* that psychology is an objective science, the goals of which are the prediction and control of behavior; introspection and the study of consciousness are not part of scientific psychology; overt, observable, measurable behavior is the subject matter; and virtually all human behavior can be explained in terms of conditioning and learning.

3. *Watson identified three innate emotions, which are* fear, rage, and love, *each of which could be* reflexively triggered by a small number of specific stimuli. *With regard to these emotions, Watson showed that classical conditioning could be used to* deliberately establish a conditioned emotional response (i.e., a new learned response).

4. *Classical conditioning can be used to create a conditioned emotional response (CR) to a previously neutral stimulus by* pairing the neutral stimulus (now called the CS) with a stimulus (the UCS) that naturally and reflexively elicits the emotion in question (the UCR).

5. *The classical conditioning components in the Little Albert study were as follows: CS:* the sight of the white rat (initially neutral); *UCS:* the loud noise caused by hitting the steel bar with a hammer; *UCR:* the fear experienced to the loud noise; *CR:* the fear experienced to the white rat after conditioning had taken place.

Classical Conditioning and Drug Use

1. *Some people acquire classically conditioned responses to drugs such as caffeine, an active ingredient in coffee. In this example the CS is* the smell, taste of coffee; *the UCS is* the caffeine; *the UCR is* increased arousal and alertness elicited by the caffeine; *and the CR is* the increased arousal and alertness in response to the CS (smell, taste of coffee) following a number of pairings of the CS and UCS.

2. *A placebo response is* an individual's psychological and physiological response to what is actually a fake treatment or drug, and is also referred to as the placebo effect. *Use classical conditioning terms to identify each of the following components in the acquisition of the placebo response: Particular situational cues, including the act of taking the drug, the sight and taste of the drug, and so on, constitute* the CS; *the active ingredient in the real drug is* the UCS; *the effect of the real drug on the person is* the UCR; *following a number of pairings, the response to a fake pill is* the CR.

3. *A conditioned compensatory response (CCR) is a* classically conditioned response in which stimuli that reliably precede the administration of a drug elicit a physiological reaction that counteracts or is opposite to the drug's effects. *These CCRs are implicated in drug effects such as* physical dependence, drug tolerance, withdrawal, and addiction.

Contemporary Views of Classical Conditioning

1. *According to the cognitive perspective, learning* involves mental processes as well as external events. *On the other hand, the traditional behavioral perspective holds that* conditioning results from a simple association of the CS and the UCS.

2. *In his research with rats, Robert Rescorla demonstrated that* classical conditioning involves cognitive processes such as learning the relationship between events and assessing the reliability of signals and that organisms actively process information about the predictive value of stimuli they encounter in their environments.

3. *According to the evolutionary perspective, bio-*logical predispositions, shaped by evolution, affect the conditioning process. *This is because* animals have developed unique forms of behavior to adapt to their natural environment, and so some responses and behavioral patterns are more readily conditioned than others.

4. *Taste aversion is a* classically conditioned dislike for and avoidance of a particular food that develops when an organism becomes ill after eating the food. *Taste aversions violate two basic principles of classical conditioning:* first, conditioning requires only a single pairing of the CS and UCS, not multiple pairings; second, the time span between the CS and UCS can be several hours, not necessarily a matter of seconds, as Pavlov claimed.

5. *John Garcia demonstrated that taste aversions could be produced under controlled laboratory conditions by* pairing saccharin-flavored water (the CS) with poison (the UCS), which produced illness (the UCR). *He found that* even though the interval between the presentation of the two stimuli was several hours, the rats developed a taste aversion (CR) to the CS and refused to drink the saccharin-flavored water.

6. *Biological preparedness refers to* the idea that organisms are innately predisposed to form associations between certain stimuli and not others.

Concept Check 1

1. behavioral; evolutionary
2. likely; unlikely
3. biological preparedness
4. cognitive
5. spontaneous recovery
6. discriminate
7. conditioned response (CR)
8. generalization
9. drug tolerance; conditioned compensatory response (CCR)
10. a placebo response or placebo effect

Graphic Organizer 1

Before Conditioning

| Food in the mouth is the <u>UCS</u> and the salivation is the <u>UCR</u>. | The neutral stimulus is the <u>CS</u>. It elicits no salivation before conditioning. |

During Conditioning

The neutral stimulus is the <u>CS</u>. + Food in the mouth is the <u>UCS</u>. → The salivation is the <u>UCR</u>.

After Conditioning

The tone alone is the <u>CS</u>. → The salivation is now the <u>CR</u>.

Matching Exercise 1

1. extinction
2. conditioning
3. learning
4. taste aversion
5. behaviorism
6. John B. Watson
7. unconditioned stimulus (UCS)
8. Ivan Pavlov
9. phobia
10. unconditioned response (UCR)
11. biological preparedness
12. conditioned compensatory response (CCR)

True/False Test 1

1. T	5. T	9. T
2. T	6. T	10. T
3. F	7. F	11. T
4. F	8. F	12. T

Operant Conditioning: Associating Behaviors and Consequences (Part 1)

1. *Edward L. Thorndike was the first person to* experimentally study how voluntary behaviors are influenced by their consequences. *He concluded that* (according to his law of effect) animals use the process of trial and error, rather than reasoning, to acquire new behaviors and that behaviors followed by satisfying outcomes were "strengthened" (more likely to occur again), and behaviors followed by unpleasant consequences were "weakened" (less likely to occur).

2. *B. F. Skinner believed that* psychology should restrict itself to studying only overt observable behavior that could be objectively measured and verified, that subjective factors such as internal thoughts, expectations, and perceptions should not be included in psychology, and that the most important form of learning was demonstrated by new behaviors that were actively emitted by the organism (operants).

3. *Operant conditioning is* the learning of active, nonreflexive behavior. *It explains* how we acquire everyday voluntary behaviors.

4. *The basic premise of operant conditioning is* that behavior is shaped and maintained by its consequences.

5. *Reinforcement refers to* the occurrence of a stimulus or event following a response that increases the likelihood of that response being repeated.

6. *Positive reinforcement involves* following an operant with a reinforcing stimulus, thus increasing the likelihood that the response will be repeated. *Negative reinforcement involves* the removal of an aversive or unpleasant stimulus from a situation, thereby increasing the future probability of the behavior that brought about the removal of the stimulus (can involve escape from, or avoidance of, the stimulus). *Negative and positive reinforcement are similar in that* they both increase the probability of the behavior occurring again. *They differ in that*

positive reinforcement involves the addition of a reinforcing stimulus, and negative reinforcement involves the removal of an aversive stimulus.

7. *A primary reinforcer is* one that is naturally reinforcing for a given species, *and a conditioned reinforcer (secondary reinforcer) is* one that has acquired reinforcing value by being associated with a primary reinforcer.

8. *Punishment is a* process that decreases the occurrence of behavior and may involve punishment by application (of an aversive stimulus), or punishment by removal (of a reinforcing stimulus).

9. *The factors that influence the effectiveness of punishment are* the consistency and immediacy of the delivery of the punishment following the response. *The drawbacks of punishment are that* it doesn't teach the correct response, it may produce undesirable results, and its effects are likely to be temporary.

Concept Check 2

1. law of effect

2. punishment by application; negative reinforcement

3. positively; negatively

4. Edward L. Thorndike

5. (a) avoidance
   (b) escape
   (c) avoidance
   (d) escape

6. (a) NR   (e) P/A
   (b) P/A   (f) NR
   (c) P/R   (g) NR
   (d) P/A

Graphic Organizer 2

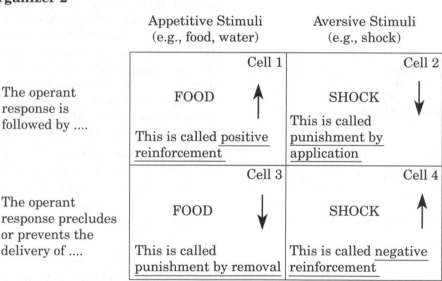

Matching Exercise 2

1. B. F. Skinner

2. negative reinforcement

3. Edward L. Thorndike

4. punishment

5. conditioned reinforcer

6. reinforcement

7. operant

True/False Test 2

1. T   3. T   5. T   7. T
2. F   4. F   6. T

Operant Conditioning: Associating Behaviors and Consequences (Part 2)

1. *Discriminative stimuli are* specific stimuli in the presence of which a particular response is likely to be reinforced, and in the absence of

which a particular response is not reinforced. *According to Skinner, they are important because* behavior is determined and controlled by the stimuli that are present in a given situation (discriminative stimuli) and not by personal choice or conscious decisions.

2. *Shaping involves* reinforcing successively closer approximations of a behavior until the correct behavior is displayed; it works by allowing the animal to gradually learn the correct response by making reinforcement dependent on getting closer and closer to the target behavior with each attempt.

3. *Partial reinforcement is more effective than continuous reinforcement because it* makes the target behavior more resistant to extinction than behavior that has been continuously reinforced (called the partial reinforcement effect).

4. *The four basic schedules of reinforcement are* fixed-ratio (FR), in which a fixed number of responses are required for reinforcement; variable-ratio (VR), in which an average number of responses, which varies from trial to trial, are needed for reinforcement; fixed-interval (FI), in which a reinforcer is delivered for the first response after a fixed amount of time; and variable-interval (VI), in which a reinforcer is delivered for the first response after an average, and unpredictable, amount of time.

5. *Behavior modification is* the application of learning principles to help people develop more effective or adaptive behaviors, and it has been used in such diverse situations as improving worker performance, increasing social skills, and in the specialized training of animals to help the physically challenged.

Concept Check 3

1. variable-interval (VI)
2. discriminative stimulus
3. fixed-interval (FI)
4. fixed-ratio (FR)
5. shaping
6. variable-ratio (VR)
7. fixed-ratio (FR)

Graphic Organizer 3

	Based on the number of responses made	Based on the elapsed time
Fixed	Cell 1 — Fixed ratio	Cell 2 — Fixed interval
Variable	Cell 3 — Variable ratio	Cell 4 — Variable interval

Matching Exercise 3

1. behavior modification
2. continuous reinforcement
3. operant chamber (Skinner box)
4. fixed-ratio (FR)
5. shaping
6. fixed-interval (FI)
7. schedule of reinforcement

True/False Test 3

1. T	3. T	5. F
2. F	4. F	6. T

Contemporary Views of Operant Conditioning

1. *Contemporary learning researchers confirm the basic principles of operant conditioning but also acknowledge* the importance of both cognitive and evolutionary factors in operant conditioning.

2. *Unlike Skinner and Thorndike, Tolman believed that* cognitive processes played an important role in the learning of complex behavior, and he demonstrated their importance with his research on cognitive maps and latent learning.

3. *A cognitive map is* Tolman's term for the mental representation of the layout of a familiar environment. *Latent learning refers to* learning that occurs in the absence of reinforcement but is not demonstrated in overt behavior until a reinforcer becomes available.

4. *Learned helplessness demonstrates the role of cognitive factors in learning in that* this behavior reflects a cognitive expectation that the organism cannot avoid the painful stimulus, no matter what it does to avoid or escape it. Exposure to inescapable and uncontrollable aversive events produces passive behavior.

5. *Operant conditioning may also be influenced by* biological predispositions to perform natural, or instinctive, behaviors that can interfere with the performance of an operantly conditioned response, a tendency called instinctive drift.

6. *The phenomenon of instinctive drift challenged the traditional behavioral view by* demonstrating that reinforcement is not the sole determinant of behavior and that instinctive behavior patterns can interfere with the operant conditioning of arbitrary responses.

Observational Learning: Imitating the Actions of Others

1. *Observational learning is* learning that occurs through observing the action of others. *The person most strongly identified with work in this area is* Albert Bandura.

2. *The four cognitive processes that interact to determine if imitation will occur are* attention (you must pay attention to the model), memory (you must remember the model's behavior), motor skills (you must be able to transform the mental representation into actions that you are capable of reproducing), and motivation (you must have some expectation of the outcome of your imitation of the behavior).

3. *Observational learning has been applied in a variety of settings, including* education, vocational and job training, psychotherapy, and counseling.

Concept Check 4

1. observational
2. cognitive
3. likely
4. instinctive drift
5. observational

Matching Exercise 4

1. observational learning
2. latent learning
3. Edward C. Tolman

4. cognitive map
5. Albert Bandura
6. instinctive drift
7. learned helplessness

Something to Think About

1. The first assumption that someone who adheres to the behavioral perspective would make is that the irrational fear, or phobia, was the result of a classical conditioning process. In the past, the client had a very unpleasant experience at a dentist's office. One could speculate that as a child he was taken to the dentist and experienced pain and fear when a hypodermic needle was inserted into his gum or a drill struck a nerve. If this were the case, the dentist (CS) has become associated with the needle or drill (UCS), which elicited pain and fear (UCR). The dentist (CS) now evokes a fear response (CR), which may have generalized to all dentists.

   One way to get rid of the irrational fear would be to use an extinction procedure in which the CS (the dentist) is presented over and over without the UCS until the fear subsides. This might mean that the client will have to find a very understanding dentist who will allow him to make many visits to the office without having any work done. The behavioral perspective predicts that this would eventually result in a reduction of the irrational fear and therefore allow the client to get some much-needed dental work done. It would also be important to point out that following a prolonged absence from the dentist, spontaneous recovery may occur.

2. It is possible that Mrs. Denton's "scolding" may in fact be reinforcing the undesirable behavior. Attention, in almost any form, from an adult can be a powerful positive reinforcer for a child. If this is the case, then withholding reinforcement (scolding) will tend to extinguish the target behavior, but only if it is consistent. Inconsistent or intermittent reinforcement will make the behavior very resistant to extinction.

   In addition, she should encourage desirable behavior. She should pay attention to any instance of good behavior, or any close approximation of the goal behavior, by praising her son or providing some other positive reinforcer. In other words, she should use a shaping procedure initially, then use partial reinforcement to ensure that the desirable behavior becomes resistant to extinction. It is also important that she model the appropriate behavior and avoid punishing the child, especially using punishment by application.

3. Operant conditioning techniques can be used to train animals. Decide on the target behavior(s) and start by using a shaping procedure and continuous positive reinforcement. Pick one of the behaviors you want to train—for example, having the dog sit at the command "sit"—and use a reinforcer such as "good dog!" while patting the dog on the head or chest. The command "sit" should be followed with gentle pressure on the dog's rear end to make him sit; he should be reinforced immediately. After just a few trials, the dog will sit on command without the application of pressure to his back; he should always be immediately reinforced. It is important to let the dog know who is in command at all times without using punishment. After the dog is obeying the commands regularly, then switch to a partial reinforcement schedule, only occasionally reinforcing the dog for obeying. This will ensure greater resistance to extinction. Dogs can be trained to do many tricks in this manner, but remember to work with the animal's natural repertoire of behaviors (biological predispositions). Dogs can learn some behaviors more easily than others.

Progress Test 1

1. c	6. a	11. c
2. d	7. b	12. b
3. d	8. a	13. a
4. b	9. c	14. a
5. a	10. a	15. c

Progress Test 2

1. a	6. b	11. a
2. b	7. a	12. d
3. b	8. b	13. c
4. c	9. c	14. d
5. b	10. a	15. b

Progress Test 3

1. d	6. a	11. d
2. c	7. d	12. c
3. d	8. a	13. a
4. c	9. a	14. c
5. a	10. d	15. d

chapter 6

Memory

PREVIEW

Reading the section below first will give you a general sense of the chapter's contents and an initial introduction to some of the major concepts and terms. This will prime you for what you are about to read and help you to develop a "cognitive map" that will guide your study of the material in this chapter. Likewise, reading the **preview questions** at the beginning of each major section will improve your ability to understand, learn, and retain the information.

CHAPTER 6 . . . AT A GLANCE

Chapter 6 examines memory and the mechanisms involved in remembering and forgetting. The first section begins with the fundamental processes of encoding, storage, and retrieval, followed by a discussion of the capacity, duration, and function of each of the three stages of memory: sensory memory, short-term memory, and long-term memory. Next, maintenance rehearsal, elaborative rehearsal, the levels-of-processing framework, and the three categories of long-term memory (procedural, episodic, and semantic memory) are explained. Two dimensions of long-term memory, explicit memory (memory with awareness) and implicit memory (memory without awareness), are explored. The section concludes with a discussion of the ways in which information is organized in long-term memory (clustering and the semantic network model).

How retrieval works and the problems associated with retrieval failure, as in the tip-of-the-tongue phenomenon, are examined. The serial position effect, encoding specificity principle, and flashbulb memories contribute to our ability to remember—or not remember—information, and these are explored next. An explanation of the fact that memories are constructed and reconstructed lays the groundwork for a discussion of the sources of potential memory problems resulting from schema distortion, source confusion, and the misinformation effect. The influence of such problems on eyewitness testimony and in creating false memories are also considered in this section.

Forgetting, theories of forgetting, and relevant research findings are explored next. Finally, the biological basis of memory is explained and the contributions of empirical research and case studies of people with amnesia are presented. The chapter ends with an examination of the role played by brain structures such as the hippocampus, the amygdala, and the prefrontal cortex. The Application presents several effective strategies for improving memory.

Introduction: What Is Memory?

Preview Questions

Consider the following questions as you study this section of the chapter.

- How is memory defined?
- What are encoding, storage, and retrieval?
- What is the three-stage model of memory, and what are the characteristics of each stage?
- How do the stages differ, and how do they interact?

*Read the section "Introduction: What Is Memory?" and **write** your answers to the following:*

1. Memory refers to _____
_____
_____

2. Encoding is the process of _____
_____

   Storage is the process of _____
_____

   Retrieval is the process of _____
_____

3. The stage model of memory describes memory
   as _____
_____
_____
_____

4. The three stages differ in three ways: _____
_____
_____
_____

   They interact by_____
_____
_____

Sensory Memory: Fleeting Impressions of the World

Preview Questions

Consider the following questions as you study this section of the chapter.

- How long is information from the environment held in sensory memory?
- How did Sperling's experiment establish the duration of visual sensory memory?
- What are the functions of sensory memory?

*Read the section "Sensory Memory: Fleeting Impressions of the World" and **write** your answers to the following:*

1. Information is held in sensory memory for
_____

2. Sperling's classic experiment demonstrated
_____
_____
_____

3. An important function of sensory memory (iconic and echoic) is _____
_____
_____

Short-Term, Working Memory: The Workshop of Consciousness

Preview Questions

Consider the following questions as you study this section of the chapter.

- What is the main function of short-term, or working, memory?
- What is the duration and capacity of short-term memory?
- How do we overcome the limitations of short-term memory?

*Read the section "Short-Term, Working Memory: The Workshop of Consciousness" and **write** your answers to the following:*

1. Short-term, working memory is the stage of
   memory in which _____
_____

2. The duration of short-term memory is _____
_____

3. The capacity of short-term memory is _____
_____

   It can be increased by _____
_____

Long-Term Memory

Preview Questions

Consider the following questions as you study this section of the chapter.

- How much information can be stored in long-term memory?
- What factors increase the efficiency of encoding?
- What is the levels-of-processing framework?
- What characterizes procedural, episodic, and semantic memory?
- What is the difference between explicit memory and implicit memory?
- How is information organized in long-term memory, and what is one of the best-known models of organization?

*Read the section "Long-Term Memory" and **write** your answers to the following:*

1. The amount of information that can be held in long-term memory is _____

2. Three ways to increase the efficiency of encoding are _____ _____ _____

3. According to the levels-of-processing framework, information_____ _____ _____

4. Procedural memory refers to _____ _____

   Episodic memory refers to _____ _____

   Semantic memory refers to _____ _____

5. Explicit memory is _____ _____

   Implicit memory is _____ _____

6. Information is organized in long-term memory by_____ _____

7. The best-known model of how information is organized in memory is _____ _____ which describes long-term memory as _____ _____ _____ _____

After you have carefully studied the preceding sections, complete the following exercises.

Concept Check 1

Read the following and write the correct term in the space provided.

1. During a math exam, Trevor is desperately trying to think of the correct formula for the area of a triangle. Although he knew the formula when he was studying last week, it just won't come to mind, despite all his efforts. Trevor is experiencing trouble with one of the three fundamental processes of memory, called

   _____ _____ .

2. To help learn the number of days in each month, eight-year-old Gloria has been reciting a short rhyme over and over: "Thirty days hath September, April, June, and November; all the rest have thirty-one except February, which has twenty-eight." She is using the fundamental process of _____ to transform the information into a form that can be entered and retained by the memory system.

3. In the above example, Gloria is using a type of rehearsal that is giving some meaning to an otherwise hard-to-remember string of numbers; this is called _____ rehearsal.

4. After looking up a phone number, Alysha is able to remember it only long enough to press all the correct numbers on the keypad. The phone number is in her _____ memory and is briefly stored there by the use of _____ rehearsal.

5. Vito is an excellent chess player and can easily recall the exact positions of most of the chess pieces after a brief glance at the board. He explains his ability by pointing out that he does not try to memorize the locations of all the individual pieces but instead focuses on their relatively few attack patterns. Vito is using

_____ to improve the capacity of his short-term memory.

6. Fifty-five-year-old Mr. Adams puts on roller skates for the first time in over forty years; much to his surprise, he has no trouble remembering how to skate. In this instance, Mr. Adams is using one of the three categories of long-term memory, called

_____ memory.

7. When Stephan was consciously reviewing the information he had researched for a term paper, he was using a dimension of long-term memory called _____ (or declarative memory); later, when he was typing his paper without conscious awareness of the exact layout of the letters on the keyboard, he was using _____ (or nondeclarative memory).

8. During an interview about his military accomplishments, General Rooyakkers described specific wartime episodes in which he was directly involved; he went on to reminisce about events in his early life that eventually led him to a career in the army. In the first instance, he was using _____ memory to recall the time and place of wartime events; in the second case, he was using _____ memory to recall his personal life history.

Review of Terms, Concepts, and Names 1

Use the terms in this list to complete the Matching Test, then to help you answer the True/False items correctly.

memory	self-reference effect
encoding	visual imagery
storage	levels-of-processing
retrieval	framework
stage model of memory	procedural memory
sensory memory	episodic memory
short-term memory	autobiographical
(working memory)	memory
long-term memory	semantic memory
George Sperling	explicit memory
visual sensory memory	(declarative memory)
(iconic memory)	implicit memory
auditory sensory	(nondeclarative
memory	memory)
(echoic memory)	clustering
maintenance rehearsal	association
chunking	semantic network model
elaborative rehearsal	

Matching Exercise

Match the appropriate term/name with its definition or description.

1. _____ Rehearsal that involves focusing on the meaning of information to help encode and transfer it to long-term memory.

2. _____ Model that describes units of information in long-term memory as being organized in a complex network of associations.

3. _____ The process of recovering information stored in memory so that we are consciously aware of it.

4. _____ Organizing items into related groups during recall from long-term memory.

5. _____ The use of mental representations, or pictures, especially vivid ones, to enhance encoding.

6. _____ Active stage of memory in which information is stored for about 30 seconds.

7. _____ Category of long-term memory that includes memories of particular events.

8. _____ The process of transforming information into a form that can be entered into and retained by the memory system.

9. _____ Model that describes memory as consisting of three distinct stages: sensory memory, short-term memory, and long-term memory.

10. _____ The mental processes that enable us to retain and use information over time.

11. _____ Category of long-term memory that includes memories of different skills, operations, and actions.

12. _____ American psychologist who identified the duration of visual sensory memory in a series of classic experiments in 1960.

13. _____ The view that information that is processed at a deeper (more meaningful) level is more likely to be remembered than information that is processed at a shallow (less meaningful) level.

True/False Test

Indicate whether each statement is true or false by placing T or F in the blank space next to each item.

1. ____ Information or knowledge that can be consciously recollected is called implicit, or nondeclarative, memory.

2. ____ Auditory sensory memory is sometimes referred to as iconic memory because it is a brief memory of an image, or icon.

3. ____ Applying information to yourself to help you remember that information is called the self-reference effect.

4. ____ Semantic memory is the category of long-term memory that includes memories of general knowledge of facts, names, and concepts.

5. ____ When people are presented with the stimulus word *salt*, they frequently respond with the word *pepper*, and this suggests that there is some logical association between bits of information in long-term memory.

6. ____ Storage is the process of retaining information in memory so that it can be used at a later time.

7. ____ Sensory memory is the stage of memory that registers information from the environment and holds it for a very brief period of time.

8. ____ Maintenance rehearsal involves the mental or verbal repetition of information in order to maintain it beyond the usual 30-second duration of short-term memory.

9. ____ Increasing the amount of information that can be held in short-term memory by grouping related items together as a single unit is called chunking.

10. ____ Visual sensory memory is sometimes referred to as echoic memory, because it is a brief memory that is like an echo.

11. ____ Information or knowledge that affects behavior or task performance but cannot be consciously recollected is called explicit, or declarative, memory.

12. ____ Long-term memory is the stage of memory that represents the storage of information over extended periods of time.

13. ____ Autobiographical memory, which is closely related to episodic memory, refers to memories of events in our lives, our personal life history.

Check your answers and review any areas of weakness before going on to the next section.

Retrieval: Getting Information from Long-Term Memory

Preview Questions

Consider the following questions as you study this section of the chapter.

- How is retrieval defined, and what is a retrieval cue?

- What does the TOT experience tell us about the nature of memory?

- How is retrieval tested, and what is the serial position effect?

- What is the encoding specificity principle, and how is it reflected in context effects, state-dependent retrieval, and mood congruence?

- What role does distinctiveness play in retrieval, and how accurate are flashbulb memories?

*Read the section "Retrieval: Getting Information from Long-Term Memory" and **write** your answers to the following:*

1. Retrieval refers to _____
_____

A retrieval cue is _____
_____

Retrieval cue failure refers to _____
_____

2. The tip-of-the-tongue (TOT) experience is

_____

_____

It illustrates the fact that_____

_____

_____

3. Retrieval is tested by _____

_____

_____

_____

4. The serial position effect is _____

_____

_____

5. The encoding specificity principle states that

_____

_____

_____

6. The context effect, an encoding specificity phe-
    nomenon, refers to _____

_____

_____

State-dependent retrieval is a form of encoding
specificity in which _____

_____

_____

Mood congruence, another example of encoding
specificity, refers to _____

_____

7. Distinctiveness plays a role in retrieval because

_____

_____

8. A flashbulb memory is _____

_____

Reconstructing Memories: Sources of Potential Errors

Preview Questions

Consider the following questions as you study this section of the chapter.

- Why do errors and distortions in memory occur during the process of retrieval?

- What are schemas, and what has research shown about their contribution to memory distortion?

- What is source confusion, and how can it produce false memories?

- What factors can reduce the accuracy of eyewitness testimony?

*Read the section "Reconstructing Memories: Sources of Potential Errors" and **write** your answers to the following:*

1. Errors and distortions occur during the process of retrieval because _____

_____

_____

2. A schema is _____

_____

Research has demonstrated that _____

_____

_____

3. Source confusion is _____

_____

It can produce false memories because_____

_____

_____

4.   The misinformation effect (one phenomenon
    that can reduce the accuracy of eyewitness tes-
    timony) refers to _____

_____

_____

_____

After you have carefully studied the preceding sections, complete the following exercises.

Concept Check 2

Read the following and write the correct term in the space provided.

1. When Cathy feels depressed, she remembers certain sad childhood events that she otherwise never thinks about. Cathy is experiencing the effects of _____ .

2. Hendrik vividly remembers exactly what he was doing when he felt the vibrations of the earthquake shake his house. This example illustrates a _____ memory.

3. Although elderly Mrs. Haggerty always answers her family's questions completely, she appears to be filling in blanks with logical, though often incorrect, information. This example illustrates the _____ nature of memory.

4. Jessie cannot remember the newer name of the small Central American country that was formerly called British Honduras until she is told it starts with the letter B. The letter B acts as a _____ for the name *Belize*.

5. Professor Patheiger's exams consist of both multiple choice questions and short essay questions. The multiple choice questions are retrieval tests that involve _____ whereas the short essay questions measure the ability to _____ information from long-term memory.

6. When Mr. Melvin questioned a witness, he deliberately kept referring to the murder weapon as large scissors instead of garden shears. When the witness was later asked to identify the garden shears as the murder weapon, he appeared slightly confused and said that he believed the weapon was a large pair of scissors. Mr. Melvin has successfully used the

_____ .

7. Research subjects memorized long lists of words while in a room full of fresh flowers. Later, half the subjects were tested in the same room, and half were tested in a room with no flowers. Those tested in the same room recalled significantly more words than those in the different room. This is one form of the _____ principle, called the _____ .

8. When Beata was given a free recall test of a list of twenty words, she recalled words from the beginning and the end of the list more easily than those in the middle of the list. The tendency to remember the first items is called the _____ , and the tendency to remember the final items is called the

_____ .

Graphic Organizer 1

Read the definitions and fill in the correct term next to the appropriate number in the puzzle below (items 1–6). When you have finished, the letters in the boxes will spell a significant memory term. Write out the definition of this term (item 7).

1. The tendency to remember items at the beginning and end of a list better than the items in the middle.

2. The inability to recall long-term memories because of inadequate or missing retrieval cues.

3. The recall of very specific images or details surrounding a vivid, rare, or significant personal event.

4. A memory phenomenon that involves the sensation of knowing that specific information is stored in long-term memory but being temporarily unable to retrieve it.

5. An encoding specificity phenomenon in which a given mood tends to evoke memories that are consistent with that mood.

6. A test of long-term memory that involves retrieving information without the aid of retrieval cues.

7. Write the definition of the memory term:

_____

_____

_____

Review of Terms, Concepts, and Names 2

Use the terms in this list to complete the Matching Test, then to help you answer the True/False items correctly.

retrieval
retrieval cue
retrieval cue failure
tip-of-the-tongue (TOT)
  experience
recall (free recall)
cued recall
recognition
serial position effect
primacy effect
recency effect
serial recall
encoding specificity
  principle

context effect
state-dependent
  retrieval
mood congruence
distinctiveness
flashbulb memory
schema
false memory
source confusion
Elizabeth Loftus
misinformation effect
cryptomnesia

Matching Exercise

Match the appropriate term with its definition or description.

1. _____ Tendency to recover information more easily when the retrieval occurs in the same setting as the original learning of the information.

2. _____ The process of accessing stored information.

3. _____ Organized cluster of information about a particular topic.

4. _____ The tendency to remember items at the beginning and end of a list better than items in the middle.

5. _____ A memory distortion that occurs when the true source of the memory is forgotten.

6. _____ American psychologist who has conducted extensive research on the memory distortions that can occur in eyewitness testimony.

7. _____ Test of long-term memory that involves remembering an item of information in response to a retrieval cue.

8. _____ Memory distortion in which people's existing memories can be altered by exposing them to misleading information.

9. _____ Clue, prompt, or hint that helps trigger recall of a given piece of information stored in long-term memory.

10. _____ Encoding specificity phenomenon in which a given mood tends to evoke memories that are consistent with that mood.

11. _____ Principle that when the conditions of information retrieval are similar to the conditions of information encoding, retrieval is more likely to be successful.

12. _____ Memory distortion in which "hidden," or unremembered, memory becomes the basis for a seemingly "new" memory.

True/False Test

Indicate whether each statement is true or false by placing T or F in the blank space next to each item.

1. ____ The primacy effect refers to the tendency to recall the final items in a list during serial recall.

2. ____ A test of long-term memory that involves retrieving information without the aid of retrieval cues is called recall, or free recall.

3. ____ The tip-of-the-tongue (TOT) experience involves the sensation of knowing that specific information is stored in long-term memory but being temporarily unable to retrieve it.

4. ____ Serial recall refers to remembering a list of items in their original order.

5. ____ When the encoded information represents a unique, different, or unusual memory, it is said to be characterized by a high degree of distinctiveness.

6. ____ A distorted or inaccurate memory that feels completely real and is often accompanied by all the emotional impact of a real memory is called a false memory.

7. ____ The inability to recall long-term memories because of inadequate or missing retrieval cues is called retrieval cue failure.

8. ____ The recency effect refers to the tendency to recall the first items in a list during serial recall.

9. ____ Recognition refers to a test of long-term memory that involves identifying correct information from several possible choices.

10. ____ Flashbulb memory refers to recall of very specific images or details surrounding a vivid, rare, or significant personal event.

11. ___ State-dependent retrieval is an encoding specificity phenomenon in which information that is learned in a particular drug state is more likely to be recalled while the person is in the same drug state.

_____

Check your answers and review any areas of weakness before going on to the next section.

_____

Forgetting: You *Forgot* the Tickets?!

Preview Questions

Consider the following questions as you study this section of the chapter.

- How is forgetting defined?
- What did Ebbinghaus contribute to the study of forgetting?
- What are the four potential causes of forgetting?

Read the section "Forgetting: You Forgot *the Plane Tickets?!" and* **write** *your answers to the following:*

1. Forgetting is the _____

_____

2. The Ebbinghaus forgetting curve reveals two distinctive patterns about forgetting:

    (a) _____

    _____

    (b) _____

    _____

3. Encoding failure refers to_____

_____

4. Interference theory is the theory that _____

_____

The two basic types of interference affect memory in the following ways:_____

_____

_____

5. Motivated forgetting refers to the idea that

_____

_____

There are two forms of motivated forgetting:

_____

_____

6. According to decay theory_____

_____

_____

The Search for the Biological Basis of Memory

Preview Questions

Consider the following questions as you study this section of the chapter.

- How did research by Lashley and Thompson contribute to our understanding of the physical basis of memory?
- How do neurons change when a memory is formed?
- How have case studies of people with retrograde and anterograde amnesia provided important insights into the brain structures involved in memory?
- What brain structures are involved in normal memory, and what roles do they play?

Read the section "The Search for the Biological Basis of Memory" and **write** *your answers to the following:*

1. Lashley and Thompson contributed to our understanding of the physical basis of memory by_____

_____

2. When a new memory is formed, neurons change in two ways: _____

_____

_____

3. Amnesia refers to_____

Retrograde amnesia is _____

_____

Anterograde amnesia is _____

_____

_____

4. The brain structures (and their functions) involved in normal memory are _____

_____

_____

_____

After you have carefully studied the preceding sections, complete the following exercises.

Concept Check 3

Read the following and write the correct term in the space provided.

1. When he first moved to his new apartment, Adam could not remember his new phone number; instead, he would give people his old phone number. Adam's inability to remember his new number is due to _____ interference.

2. At a recent orientation meeting, Juan was introduced to five of the directors; much to his embarrassment, after a short while he could not remember their names. Juan's memory lapse is probably due to _____ .

3. Later that night, while thinking about his embarrassment at the meeting, Juan decided that because it was normal to forget names under such circumstances, he was just not going to think about it any more. Juan is using a form of motivated forgetting called

_____ .

4. Bruno, who was knocked out in his last boxing match, cannot remember anything about the fight or events that happened before the bout. Bruno is most likely suffering from a form of amnesia called _____ amnesia.

5. Mrs. O'Meara, whose hippocampus was removed during a recent brain operation, is most likely to have trouble forming

_____ memories.

6. Jackson has just finished a course in Spanish and is experiencing problems in remembering the Italian he learned last semester. Jackson's memory problem is a result of

_____ .

7. After many training trials, Pookie the dog will now sit on her hind legs and "beg" for food. Learning this new behavior has probably involved functional and structural neuronal changes in her brain that are collectively called

_____ .

8. Mr. Usselman has been diagnosed with a condition characterized by impairment of memory and intellectual functions. He is likely suffering from _____ a condition most often caused by _____ .

Graphic Organizer 2

Use the following to review forgetting due to interference in the test phase. Write in the type of interference that is responsible for forgetting in the test phase.

Memorizing Phase	Test Phase	Type of Interference
1. Learn A first; later learn B	Test A	
2. Learn A first; later learn B	Test B	

Review of Terms, Concepts, and Names 3

Use the terms in this list to complete the Matching Test, then to help you answer the True/False items correctly.

forgetting
Hermann Ebbinghaus
nonsense syllable
forgetting curve
encoding failure
interference theory
retroactive interference
proactive interference
motivated forgetting
suppression
repression
decay theory
memory trace (engram)
Karl Lashley

Richard F. Thompson
Eric Kandel
long-term potentiation
amnesia
retrograde amnesia
memory consolidation
anterograde amnesia
hippocampus
infantile amnesia
prefrontal cortex
amygdala
senile dementia
Alzheimer's disease

Matching Exercise

Match the appropriate term/name with its definition or description.

1. _____ Motivated forgetting that occurs consciously.

2. _____ American physiological psychologist who attempted to find the specific brain locatiton of particular memories.

3. _____ The brain changes associated with a particular stored memory.

4. _____ Severe memory loss.

5. _____ American psychologist and neuroscientist who conducted extensive research on the neurobiological foundations of learning and memory.

6. _____ The inability to recall previously available information.

7. _____ Theory that forgetting is due to normal metabolic processes that occur in the brain over time.

8. _____ Motivated forgetting that occurs unconsciously.

9. _____ The theory that forgetting is caused by one memory competing with or replacing another.

10. _____ German psychologist who originated the scientific study of forgetting; plotted the first "forgetting curve," which describes the basic pattern by which learned information is forgotten over time.

11. _____ Inability to recall specific information because of insufficient encoding for storage in long-term memory.

12. _____ The inability to remember infant experiences during adulthood.

13. _____ A brain structure that plays an important role in memory involving the sequence of events, but not the events themselves.

14. _____ American neurobiologist, born in Austria, who won the Nobel Prize in 2000 for his work on the neural basis of learning and memory in the sea snail *Aplyoia*.

True/False Test

Indicate whether each item is true or false by placing T or F in the space next to each item.

1. ___ Anterograde amnesia is the loss of memory, especially for episodic information; backward-acting amnesia.

2. ___ With retroactive interference, an old memory interferes with remembering a new memory; forward-acting memory interference.

3. ___ The idea that forgetting occurs because an undesired memory is held back from awareness is called motivated forgetting.

4. ___ Memory consolidation is the gradual, physical process of converting new long-term memories to stable, enduring long-term memory codes.

5. ___ Retrograde amnesia is the loss of memory caused by the inability to store new memories; forward-acting amnesia.

6. ___ Damage or destruction of the hippocampus can affect the ability to transfer short-term memories into long-term memories.

7. ___ Hermann Ebbinghaus used nonsense syllables to study memory and the forgetting of completely new material and to avoid the potential bias of using words that had preexisting associations in memory.

8. ___ Proactive interference is forgetting in which a new memory interferes with remembering an old memory; backward-acting memory interference.

9. ___ Damage or destruction of the amygdala will make monkeys lose their normal fear of snakes and other natural predators.

10. ___ The forgetting curve reveals two distinct patterns in the relationship between forgetting and the passage of time; much of what is learned is forgotten relatively quickly, and the amount of forgetting eventually levels off.

11. ___ Senile dementia is a condition characterized by impairment of memory and intellectual functions.

12. ___ Long-term potentiation refers to a long-lasting increase in synaptic strength between two neurons.

13. ___ The symptoms of Alzheimer's disease are caused by the progressive degeneration of neurons in the brain; this disease is the most common cause of senile dementia.

Check your answers and review any areas of weakness before going on to the next section.

Something to Think About

1. You may have met that rare person who seems to have a perfect memory—rarely forgetting anything. Most of us, however, have to struggle to learn and retain at least some of the vast amount of material we are constantly exposed to in the "information age." If someone were to ask you what you have learned about memory and forgetting that could help them, what would you say?

2. Suppose a friend of yours is falsely identified as being the culprit in a grocery store hold-up and comes to you for help. Based on what you know about eyewitness testimony and related phenomena, what advice would you give him?

Check your answers and review any areas of weakness before doing the progress tests.

Progress Test 1

Review the complete chapter (including Concept Reviews and the boxed inserts), review all your study notes, and then test yourself on the following progress test. Check your answers. If you make a mistake, review your notes, the relevant section of the study guide, and, if necessary, the appropriate part of your textbook.

1. In preparation for his biology exam, Lionel repeats the list of terms and their definitions over and over. Lionel's rehearsal strategy involves the fundamental memory process of
   (a) encoding.   (c) retrieval.
   (b) storage.   (d) wasting his time.

2. Michael, whose aggressive, arrogant behavior and indifferent attitude have resulted in the break-up of many relationships, is contemplating getting married for the third time. Michael is confident that this time it will work and that his previous relationship problems were never his fault. Michael is either actively _____ or unconsciously _____ memory of his own behavior.
   (a) consolidating; schematizing
   (b) schematizing; consolidating
   (c) suppressing; repressing
   (d) repressing; suppressing

3. Five-year-old Betty can recite the alphabet perfectly every time she is asked to do so. Betty's ability to do this involves the fundamental memory process of
   (a) repression.   (c) retrograde amnesia.
   (b) retrieval.   (d) encoding.

4. Sarina repeated the ten-digit telephone number over and over in her mind as she walked over to the phone booth to make her call. Paige created an acronym for the names of the different brain waves associated with various states of wakefulness and sleep, BATD—Beta, Alpha, Theta, Delta. According to the levels-of-processing framework, Sarina is using _____ rehearsal, and Paige is using _____ rehearsal.
   (a) distributed; massed
   (b) maintenance; elaborative
   (c) massed; distributed
   (d) elaborative; maintenance

5. Dirk can remember in vivid detail where he was and what he was doing when he heard about the terrorist attacks in New York City and Washington, D.C. Dirk's flashbulb memory is stored in his

(a) iconic memory.   (c) long-term memory.
(b) short-term memory. (d) echoic memory.

6. Whenever Killian is introduced to someone, he usually remembers the name by repeating it over and over to himself. Killian is using a memory strategy called

(a) rehearsal.
(b) retroactive interference.
(c) clustering.
(d) chunking.

7. One conclusion that can be drawn from Ebbinghaus's work on forgetting is that

(a) we can remember only about seven non-sense syllables at one time.
(b) when we memorize new information, most forgetting occurs relatively soon after we learn it.
(c) the duration of visual sensory memory is less than half a second.
(d) the capacity of long-term memory is large but fleeting.

8. Mrs. Carson was very busy when she phoned her husband and quickly listed the twelve items she wanted him to pick up at the store. After she hung up, Mr. Carson attempted to write down the items. It is likely that he will

(a) forget the items in the middle.
(b) remember only the middle and the last items.
(c) remember only the first and middle items.
(d) forget the first and last items and remember the items in the middle.

9. At her high school reunion, Chychi met a girl who used to sit next to her in tenth grade, but she could not recall the girl's name. In an attempt to jog her memory, Chychi began reciting the alphabet. When she came to the letter M, she immediately remembered that her schoolfriend's name was Maureen. In this example, the letter of the alphabet

(a) eliminated source confusion.
(b) served as a retrieval cue.
(c) provoked a flashbulb memory.
(d) reversed encoding failure.

10. Charlie finds it easier to remember a list of words that includes *automobile, cigarettes, encyclopedia, lampshade, geranium,* and *seashell,* compared to a list of the same length that includes *philosophy, processes, justice, abstraction, fundamental,* and *inherent,* because with the first list it is easier to use

(a) echoic processing.
(b) maintenance rehearsal.
(c) procedural memory.
(d) visual imagery.

11. Karen can remember very clearly when and where she met Jim and how she felt when he first spoke to her. This information, which is stored in Karen's long-term memory, is called

(a) procedural memory.
(b) episodic memory.
(c) semantic memory.
(d) retroactive memory.

12. After his hippocampus was destroyed by a tumor, Mr. Locke is likely to experience problems

(a) forming procedural memories.
(b) recognizing common objects.
(c) correctly repeating items over and over.
(d) transferring short-term memories into long-term memory.

13. Mr. Locke (in the above example) is likely to be classified as suffering from

(a) retrograde amnesia.
(b) anterograde amnesia.
(c) Alzheimer's disease.
(d) cryptomnesia.

14. According to the Application, one way to make memories last is to learn material over several sessions rather than cramming learning into one long session. This method of study is called

(a) distributed practice.
(b) massed practice.
(c) maintenance rehearsal.
(d) serial position learning.

15. According to Critical Thinking 6.3, which of the following regarding childhood sexual abuse is true?
    (a) Physical and sexual abuse in childhood can contribute to psychological problems in adulthood.
    (b) It is possible that memories of abuse can become repressed in childhood and surface later in life.
    (c) Repressed memories recovered in therapy need to be regarded with caution.
    (d) A person's confidence in a memory is no guarantee that the memory is accurate.
    (e) All of the above are true.

Progress Test 2

After you have checked your understanding of the material in Progress Test 1 and have done a complete chapter review with special focus on any areas of weakness, you are ready to assess your knowledge on Progress Test 2. Check your answers. If you make a mistake, review your notes, the relevant section of the study guide, and, if necessary, the appropriate part of your textbook.

1. When Gary was preparing for an exam, he tried to make the material more meaningful by using strategies such as visual imagery, creating short stories involving the terms, self-referencing, and so on. Gary is using _____ to help him remember the information.
    (a) elaborative rehearsal
    (b) maintenance rehearsal
    (c) retroactive interference
    (d) proactive interference

2. Shortly after he finished reading an exciting novel, Sean fell down the stairs and suffered a concussion; now, he has no recall of ever having read the novel. Sean's memory problem is probably the result of
    (a) retrieval cue failure.
    (b) source confusion.
    (c) disruption of memory consolidation.
    (d) mood incongruence.

3. Sean (in the above example) is most likely to be classified as suffering from
    (a) anterograde amnesia.
    (b) proactive forgetting.
    (c) retrograde amnesia.
    (d) retroactive forgetting.

4. Richard F. Thompson classically conditioned rabbits to eye-blink to a tone; he later found that the brain activity in the rabbit's cerebellum changed. This result suggests that some long-term memories
    (a) are stored in a localized region of the brain.
    (b) are distributed and stored across multiple brain locations.
    (c) have no biological or physical basis in the brain.
    (d) are very vulnerable if they are not given enough time to consolidate.

5. Dr. Dement believes that forgetting is due to memory traces being eroded by normal metabolic processes in the brain. Dr. Dement supports the
    (a) interference theory.
    (b) motivated forgetting theory.
    (c) semantic network theory.
    (d) decay theory.

6. When Manfred, who used to be a compulsive gambler, is asked how much money he won or lost, he recalls losing much less money than was actually the case. Manfred's memory failure best illustrates
    (a) motivated forgetting.
    (b) retrieval cue failure.
    (c) retroactive interference.
    (d) proactive interference.

7. Natasha has memorized the new personal identity code she was given by security; now, she can't remember her old personal identity code. Natasha is experiencing the effects of
    (a) mood congruence.
    (b) source confusion.
    (c) proactive interference.
    (d) retroactive interference.

8. Jeffery, who was an eyewitness to a robbery, initially thought the robber looked like a female. During questioning, a police detective suggested to him many times that the robber was probably a man with long hair. Later, when he was giving testimony on the witness stand, Jeffery was quite sure that it was a man who robbed the store. This example illustrates
    (a) the serial position effect.
    (b) mood congruence.
    (c) a flashbulb memory.
    (d) the misinformation effect.

9. Arvind believes that recall of information will be better when the pharmacological, or drug, state of learning and retrieval match. Arvind believes in an encoding specificity principle called
   (a) state-dependent retrieval.
   (b) the serial position effect.
   (c) the context effect.
   (d) maintenance retrieval.

10. The smell of cherry blossoms awakened in Mrs. Yamomoto vivid memories of her childhood in Osaka. The aroma of the blossoms apparently acted as an effective
    (a) schema.   (c) flashbulb cue.
    (b) echoic cue.   (d) retrieval cue.

11. During a discussion about old movies, Grace could not bring to mind the name of the actor who played Sidney Greenstreet's sidekick in *The Maltese Falcon*, despite the fact that she felt she knew the name and had, in fact, talked about his role in the movie on other occasions. Grace is experiencing
    (a) the serial position effect.
    (b) encoding failure.
    (c) the tip-of-the-tongue (TOT) phenomenon.
    (d) anterograde amnesia.

12. Harold, who was in the kitchen, asked Jane, who was reading a book in the living room, whether she wanted a diet or a regular soft drink. Jane replied, "What did you say?" Before Harold could respond, Jane said, "Make it a regular Coke, please." This example illustrates
    (a) iconic memory.   (c) echoic memory.
    (b) repression.   (d) a flashbulb memory.

13. According to Culture and Human Behavior 6.1, which of the following is true?
    (a) Autobiographical memories may be shaped by cultural and social contexts.
    (b) American and Chinese college students' earliest memories were very similar in content, and both groups had their earliest memories at an average age of three and half years.
    (c) Autobiographical memories are relatively independent of culture and context and reflect universal and innate biological developments in the brain.
    (d) The memories of Chinese students tended to be longer, more elaborate, and more self-focused than those of the American students.

14. The Application lists a number of strategies that can be used to improve memory for important information. Which of the following is *not* one of those strategies?
    (a) Use visual imagery.
    (b) Organize the information.
    (c) Counteract the serial position effect.
    (d) Use contextual cues to jog memories during a test.
    (e) Always use massed practice, especially during all-night cramming sessions before a test.

15. According to Science Versus Pseudoscience 6.2, which of the following is true?
    (a) There is ample scientific evidence that people can remember actual past lives.
    (b) There is good reason to believe that many memories of past lives are examples of cryptomnesia.
    (c) Most reincarnation memories can only be recovered by a skilled hypnotherapist.
    (d) Most people cannot recall memories of past lives because of repression.

Progress Test 3

After you have checked your understanding of the material in Progress Tests 1 and 2 and have done a complete chapter review with special focus on any areas of weakness, you are ready to further assess your knowledge on Progress Test 3. Check your answers. If you make a mistake, review your notes, the appropriate parts of the study guide, and, if necessary, the relevant sections of your textbook.

1. Memory with awareness is to _____ as memory without awareness is to
   _____ .
   (a) explicit memory; implicit memory
   (b) retroactive interference; proactive interference
   (c) implicit memory; explicit memory
   (d) proactive interference; retroactive interference

2. Dr. Rhodes believes that when the conditions of information retrieval are similar to the conditions of information encoding, retrieval is more likely to be successful. This view is most consistent with
   (a) the stage model of memory.
   (b) the semantic network model.
   (c) the encoding specificity principle.
   (d) interference theory.

3. Elizabeth Loftus's story, presented in the Prologue, demonstrates how it is possible to form an extremely vivid, but inaccurate, memory. A common cause of such false memories is
   (a) retrograde amnesia.
   (b) source confusion.
   (c) anterograde amnesia.
   (d) retrieval cue failure.

4. The _____ is to encoding emotional aspects of memory as the _____ is to the encoding and transfer of new information from short-term to long-term memory.
   (a) amygdala; hippocampus
   (b) prefrontal cortex; amygdala
   (c) hippocampus; amygdala
   (d) cerebellum; hippocampus

5. Research participants were first presented with a visual stimulus (a picture of a cat and the word *cat*); later, they heard an auditory stimulus (the sound of a dog barking and the word *dog*). Next, they were given a retrieval cue (cat or dog) and asked to recall the original stimulus (visual or auditory). If these results are similar to those in the Focus on Neuroscience, fMRI scans during the recall phase are likely to show that remembering the sound activates the _____ and remembering the picture activates the _____ .
   (a) visual cortex; auditory cortex
   (b) prefrontal cortex; cerebellum
   (c) auditory cortex; visual cortex
   (d) hippocampus; amygdala

6. Neddy cannot accurately remember the order of the numbers on the small calculator he has owned for ten years and uses quite frequently. Neddy's problem in recall is most likely a function of
   (a) retrieval cue failure.
   (b) proactive interference.
   (c) encoding failure.
   (d) retroactive interference.

7. Most subjects in an experiment responded with *sky* and *grass* to the stimulus words *blue* and *green*. Results such as these support
   (a) the semantic network model.
   (b) decay theory.
   (c) the tip-of-the-tongue (TOT) experience.
   (d) interference theory.

8. Emelia can quite easily list all fifty U.S. states and Canada's ten provinces and two territories. This type of information in long-term memory is called _____ information.
   (a) procedural   (c) semantic
   (b) episodic   (d) implicit

9. Marcus, like most adults, cannot recall events and experiences from the first few years of his life. His infantile amnesia most likely reflects
   (a) the fact that early childhood events were never effectively encoded and stored in the first place.
   (b) motivated repressed memories.
   (c) the fact that childhood memories are forgotten after they have been encoded and stored.
   (d) the fact that the brain does not contain brain structures, such as the hippocampus and amygdala, until after the age of three.

10. Lisa took a strong mood-altering prescription medication while studying for her exam; the following week, she took the same pills before the exam because she wanted to be in the same positive emotional state on both occasions. Lisa appears to believe in the effects of
    (a) maintenance rehearsal.
    (b) elaborative rehearsal.
    (c) mood congruence.
    (d) source confusion.

11. When Kirk was given a long list of items to memorize, he found it easier to remember them when he regrouped all the items according to whether they were vegetables, furniture, animals, and so on. Kirk is using a memory aid called
    (a) the serial position effect.
    (b) the self-referencing technique.
    (c) the context effect.
    (d) chunking.

12. When she first transferred from a college to a university, Kelly had trouble remembering her new student number; she would always recall her old college student number instead. Kelly's memory problem is an example of
    (a) retrograde amnesia.
    (b) proactive interference.
    (c) anterograde amnesia.
    (d) retroactive interference.

13. Mrs. Kahn experienced no trouble skiing despite the fact that she had not been on the slopes for almost fifteen years. Mrs. Kahn's current skiing ability is probably due to a category of long-term memory called _____ memory.
    - (a) procedural
    - (b) episodic
    - (c) semantic
    - (d) repressed

14. According to Culture and Human Behavior 6.4, declines in memory ability
    - (a) are due entirely to a natural, biological aging process.
    - (b) may be influenced by cultural expectations about aging and memory abilities.
    - (c) are predominantly the function of diseases such as Alzheimer's.
    - (d) are most evident in members of the deaf culture who communicate with American Sign Language.

15. According to Science Versus Pseudoscience 6.2, cryptomnesia refers to
    - (a) memories of being buried in a mausoleum or crypt.
    - (b) a memory distortion in which a seemingly "new" or "original" memory is actually based on an unrecalled previous memory.
    - (c) loss of memory caused by the inability to store new memories.
    - (d) severe memory loss following a near-death experience.

Answers

Introduction: What Is Memory?

1. *Memory refers to* the group of related mental processes that enable us to acquire, retain, and use information over time.

2. *Encoding is the process of* transforming information into a form that can be entered into and retained by the memory system. *Storage is the process of* retaining information in memory so that it can be used at a later time. *Retrieval is the process of* recovering information stored in memory so that we are consciously aware of it.

3. *The stage model of memory describes memory as* consisting of three distinct stages, sensory memory (the stage that registers information from the environment for a brief period of time), short-term, working memory (the active

stage in which information is stored for about 30 seconds), and long-term memory (the stage that represents the long-term storage of information).

4. *The three stages differ in three ways:* capacity (how much information can be stored), duration (how long the information can be stored), and function (what is done with the stored information). *They interact by* transferring information from one to another. Transfer between short-term and long-term memory goes two ways.

Sensory Memory: Fleeting Impressions of the World

1. *Information is held in sensory memory for a few* seconds or less.

2. *Sperling's classic experiment demonstrated that* our visual sensory memory holds a great deal of information very briefly (for about half a second); this information is available just long enough for us to pay attention to specific elements that are significant to us at that moment.

3. *An important function of sensory memory (iconic and echoic) is* to store sensory impressions very briefly so that they overlap slightly with one another; consequently, we perceive the world around us as continuous, rather than as a series of disconnected images or disjointed sounds.

Short-Term, Working Memory: The Workshop of Consciousness

1. *Short-term, working memory is the stage of memory in which* information transferred from sensory and long-term memory is temporarily stored.

2. *The duration of short-term memory is* approximately 30 seconds, unless the information is rehearsed (maintenance rehearsal).

3. *The capacity of short-term memory is* limited to about seven items, or bits of information (plus or minus two). *It can be increased by* maintenance rehearsal and by chunking (grouping related items together into a single unit or chunk).

Long-Term Memory

1. *The amount of information that can be held in long-term memory is* essentially unlimited.

2. *Three ways to increase the efficiency of encoding are* to engage in elaborative rehearsal (focus on

the meaning of information), use self-referencing (apply information to yourself), and use
visual imagery.

3. *According to the levels-of-processing framework,
information* processed at a deeper (more meaningful) level is more likely to be remembered
than information that is processed at a shallow
(less meaningful) level.

4. *Procedural memory refers to* the long term-
memory of how to perform different skills, operations, and actions. *Episodic memory refers to*
the long-term memory of specific events or
episodes, including the time and place that they
occurred (autobiographical memory is closely
related and refers to memory of events in your
life). *Semantic memory refers to* memory of general knowledge that includes facts, names, definitions, concepts, and ideas.

5. *Explicit memory is* information or knowledge
that can be consciously recollected (also called
declarative memory). *Implicit memory is* information or knowledge that affects behavior or
task performance, but cannot be consciously
recollected (also called nondeclarative memory).

6. *Information is organized in long-term memory
by* clustering and association.

7. *The best-known model of how information is
organized in memory is* the semantic network
model, *which describes long-term memory as*
units of information organized in a complex
network of associations.

Concept Check 1
1. retrieval
2. encoding
3. elaborative
4. short-term; maintenance
5. chunking
6. procedural
7. explicit memory; implicit memory
8. episodic; autobiographical

Matching Exercise 1
1. elaborative rehearsal
2. semantic network model
3. retrieval
4. clustering
5. visual imagery
6. short-term memory
7. episodic memory

8. encoding
9. stage model of memory
10. memory
11. procedural memory
12. George Sperling
13. levels-of-processing framework

True/False Test 1

1. F	6. T	11. F
2. F	7. T	12. T
3. T	8. T	13. T
4. T	9. T	
5. T	10. F	

Retrieval: Getting Information from Long-Term Memory

1. *Retrieval refers to* the process of accessing
stored information. *A retrieval cue is* a clue,
prompt, or hint that helps trigger recall of a
given piece of information stored in long-term
memory. *Retrieval cue failure refers to* the
inability to recall long-term memories because
of inadequate or missing retrieval cues.

2. *The tip-of-the-tongue (TOT) experience is* a
memory phenomenon that involves the sensation of knowing that specific information is
stored in long-term memory but being temporarily unable to retrieve it. *It illustrates the
fact that* retrieving information is not an all-or-
nothing process; in many instances, information
is stored in memory but is not accessible without the right retrieval cues. It also shows that
information stored in memory is organized and
connected in relatively logical ways.

3. *Retrieval is tested by* recall (retrieving information without the aid of retrieval cues), cued
recall (remembering an item of information in
response to a retrieval cue), and recognition
(identifying correct information out of several
possible choices).

4. *The serial position effect is* the tendency to
remember items at the beginning of a list (primacy effect) and at the end of a list (recency
effect) better than items in the middle of the
list.

5. *The encoding specificity principle states that*
when the conditions of information retrieval are
similar to the conditions of information encoding, retrieval is more likely to be successful.

6. *The context effect, an encoding specificity phenomenon, refers to* the tendency to recover information more easily when retrieval occurs in the same setting as the original learning of the information. *State-dependent retrieval is a form of encoding specificity in which* information that is learned in a particular drug state is more likely to be recalled when the person is in the same drug state. *Mood congruence, another example of encoding specificity, refers to* the idea that a given mood tends to evoke memories that are consistent with that mood.

7. *Distinctiveness plays a role in retrieval because* highly unusual, surprising, or even bizarre experiences are easier to retrieve from memory than are routine events.

8. *A flashbulb memory is* the recall of very specific images or details surrounding a vivid, rare, or significant event; although confidence about the recollection is usually high, accuracy is not (confidence in a memory is no guarantee of accuracy).

Reconstructing Memories: Sources of Potential Errors

1. *Errors and distortions occur during the process of retrieval because* retrieval involves the active construction and reconstruction of memories and may be affected by the information stored before and after the memory occurred.

2. *A schema is* an organized cluster of information about a particular topic. *Research has demonstrated that* our schemas can influence what we remember; that once a memory is formed, it has the potential to be changed by new information; and that memories can quite easily become distorted.

3. *Source confusion is* a memory distortion that occurs when the true source of the memory is forgotten. *It can produce false memories because* one of the most easily forgotten parts of a memory is its source (how, when, or where it was acquired), and we are capable of confusing something we only heard about, read about, or even seen in a film with something that really happened.

4. *The misinformation effect (one phenomenon that can reduce the accuracy of eyewitness testimony) refers to* a memory-distortion phenomenon in which a person's existing memories can be altered if the person is exposed to misleading information.

Concept Check 2

1. mood congruence
2. flashbulb
3. reconstructive
4. retrieval cue
5. recognition; recall
6. misinformation effect
7. encoding specificity; context effect
8. primacy effect; recency effect

Graphic Organizer 1

Crossword:
1. SERIAL POSITION EFFECT
2. RETRIEVAL CUE FAILURE
3. FLASHBULB MEMORY
4. TIP OF THE TONGUE EXPERIENCE
5. MOOD CONGRUENCE
6. RECALL

7. A schema is an organized cluster of information about a particular topic

Matching Exercise 2

1. context effect
2. retrieval
3. schema
4. serial position effect
5. source confusion
6. Elizabeth Loftus
7. cued recall
8. misinformation effect
9. retrieval cue
10. mood congruence
11. encoding specificity principle
12. cryptomnesia

True/False Test 2

1. F	5. T	9. T
2. T	6. T	10. T
3. T	7. T	11. T
4. T	8. F	

Forgetting: You *Forgot* the Plane Tickets?!

1. *Forgetting is the* inability to recall information that was previously available.

2. *The Ebbinghaus forgetting curve reveals two distinct patterns about forgetting: (a)* much of what we forget is lost relatively soon after we originally learned it; *(b)* the amount of forgetting eventually levels off, with information that is not quickly forgotten remaining quite stable in memory over long periods of time.

3. *Encoding failure refers to* the inability to recall specific information because of insufficient encoding for storage in long-term memory.

4. *Interference theory is the theory that* forgetting is caused by one memory competing with or replacing another memory. *The two basic types of interference affect memory in the following ways:* in retroactive interference, a new memory interferes with remembering an old memory (backward-acting memory interference); in proactive interference, an old memory interferes with remembering a new memory (forward-acting memory interference).

5. *Motivated forgetting refers to the idea that* we forget because we are motivated to forget, usually because a memory is unpleasant or disturbing. *There are two forms of motivated forgetting:* suppression (a conscious or deliberate effort to forget) and repression (unconscious motivation to forget).

6. *According to decay theory,* forgetting is due to normal metabolic processes that occur in the brain over time.

The Search for the Biological Basis of Memory

1. *Lashley and Thompson contributed to our understanding of the physical basis of memory by* demonstrating that memories have the potential to be both localized and distributed: very simple memories are localized in a specific area, and more complex memories appear to be distributed throughout the brain.

2. *When a new memory is formed, neurons change in two ways:* functionally, they increase the amount of neurotransmitters they produce, and structurally, they show an increase in the number of interconnecting branches between neurons as well as in the number of synapses on each branch.

3. *Amnesia refers to* severe memory loss. *Retrograde amnesia is* loss of memory, especially for episodic information (backward-acting amnesia). *Anterograde amnesia is* loss of memory caused by the inability to store new memories (forward-acting amnesia).

4. *The brain structures (and their functions) involved in normal memory are* the cerebellum (memories involving movement), amygdala (associates memories involving different senses and encodes the emotional aspects of memories), prefrontal cortex (memories of sequences of events), and the hippocampus (encodes and transfers new explicit memories to long-term memory).

Concept Check 3

1. proactive
2. encoding failure
3. suppression
4. retrograde
5. long-term
6. retroactive interference
7. long-term potentiation
8. senile dementia; Alzheimer's disease

Graphic Organizer 2

1. retroactive interference
2. proactive interference

Matching Exercise 3

1. suppression
2. Karl Lashley
3. memory trace (engram)
4. amnesia
5. Richard F. Thompson
6. forgetting
7. decay theory
8. repression
9. interference theory
10. Hermann Ebbinghaus
11. encoding failure
12. infantile amnesia

13. prefrontal cortex
14. Eric Kandel

True/False Test 3

1. F	5. F	9. T	13. T
2. F	6. T	10. T	
3. T	7. T	11. T	
4. T	8. F	12. T	

Something to Think About

1. We are all vulnerable to forgetting, and sometimes the consequences can be serious. What can we do to improve memory? Fortunately, a number of strategies can help us to remember important information. You might begin your answer with a discussion of the fundamental processes of encoding, storage, and retrieval, then explain the function, capacity, and duration of each of the three stages of memory. Of course, no discussion of the topic of memory would be complete without mentioning Ebbinghaus's work on forgetting as well as the contributions of the various theories of forgetting to our understanding of memory. Finally, mention the ten most important strategies that could help improve memory, as described in the Application.

2. It is a real nightmare to contemplate the prospect of being falsely accused of a crime and having an eyewitness point at you and say very confidently, "Yes, that is the person. There's no doubt about it, he did it!" What can be done in such a situation? If you don't have an alibi, the jury is very likely to believe a confident eyewitness who, under oath, points a finger at the accused. First, you might consider hiring an expert witness, such as Elizabeth Loftus, to testify to the problems inherent in eyewitness testimony. Such testimony, based on scientific evidence, is difficult to refute. If your friend cannot afford the testimony of an expert witness, then we suggest he try to educate his defense lawyer about the relevant research findings in this important area of psychology. These include source confusion, the personal schema of the eyewitness, the power of the misinformation effect, evidence related to false memories, and relevant aspects of the encoding specificity principle. An additional source of information is a 1999 report published by the United States Department of Justice, which contains guidelines for use of eyewitness evidence based on years of psychological research into eyewitness testimony (see textbook reference list for complete information about this report).

Progress Test 1

1. a	6. a	11. b
2. c	7. b	12. d
3. b	8. a	13. b
4. b	9. b	14. a
5. c	10. d	15. e

Progress Test 2

1. a	6. a	11. c
2. c	7. d	12. c
3. c	8. d	13. a
4. a	9. a	14. e
5. d	10. d	15. b

Progress Test 3

1. a	6. c	11. d
2. c	7. a	12. b
3. b	8. c	13. a
4. a	9. a	14. b
5. c	10. c	15. b

Thinking, Language, and Intelligence

PREVIEW

Reading the section below first will give you a general sense of the chapter's contents and an initial introduction to some of the major concepts and terms. This will prime you for what you are about to read and help you to develop a "cognitive map" that will guide your study of the material in this chapter. Likewise, reading the **preview questions** at the beginning of each major section will improve your ability to understand, learn, and retain the information.

CHAPTER 7. . . AT A GLANCE

Chapter 7 combines thinking, language, and intelligence, three closely related cognitive functions. The section on thinking begins with discussions of the use of mental imagery and concept formation. This leads to a description of problem-solving strategies, followed by an explanation of two common obstacles to effective problem solving, functional fixedness and mental sets. The section concludes with a discussion of different decision-making models.

The next section, on our remarkable cognitive capacity for language, first explains the character of language, then explores the various ways in which language influences thought. Animal communication and the controversial debate over whether animals are capable of language finishes up this section.

Our ability to think and use language are aspects of what we call intelligence. Because the measurement of intelligence has been a controversial issue, this section provides some background into the development of intelligence testing and the contributions of various psychologists. The difference between aptitude tests and achievement tests is explained, and the requirements of standardization, reliability, and validity are described as a way of understanding the problems of testing.

The debate over the nature of intelligence centers on whether intelligence is a single, general ability or a cluster of different abilities, and on whether intelligence should be narrowly or broadly defined. Four theories regarding this issue are presented. The heredity–environment debate regarding the origins of intelligence is examined in detail. The Application presents a number of suggestions for enhancing our ability to think creatively.

Introduction: Thinking, Language, and Intelligence

Preview Questions

Consider the following questions as you study this section of the chapter.

- What is cognition?
- How is thinking defined, and what does it typically involve?
- What are mental images, and how do we manipulate them?
- What are concepts, and how are they formed?
- What is a prototype, and what role do prototypes play in concept formation?

*Read the section "Introduction: Thinking, Language, and Intelligence" and **write** your answers to the following:*

1. Cognition is _____

   _____

2. Thinking is defined as _____

   _____

   It typically involves _____

   _____

3. A mental image is _____

   _____

4. We manipulate mental images

   _____

   Mental images are potentially subject to error and distortion because _____

   _____

   _____

5. Concepts are _____

   _____

   The two ways of forming concepts are _____

   _____

   _____

6. A prototype is _____

   _____

   The more closely an item matches a prototype,

   _____

Solving Problems and Making Decisions

Preview Questions

Consider the following questions as you study this section of the chapter.

- How is problem solving defined?
- What are four problem-solving strategies, and what are the advantages and/or disadvantages of each?
- What are functional fixedness and mental sets, and how do they interfere with problem solving?

*Read the section "Solving Problems and Making Decisions" and **write** your answers to the following:*

1. Problem solving is defined as _____

   _____

2. The trial-and-error strategy involves _____

   _____

   _____

3. An algorithm involves _____

   _____

   _____

4. A heuristic is a _____

   _____

   _____

5. Insight is the _____

   _____

   _____

6. Functional fixedness is _____

   _____

   _____

7. A mental set is _____

   _____

   _____

Decision-Making Strategies

Preview Questions

Consider the following questions as you study this section of the chapter.

- What are the single-feature, additive, and elimination-by-aspects models of decision making?

- Under what conditions is each strategy appropriate?
- When are the availability and representativeness heuristics used, and what potential problems are associated with each?

Read the section "Decision-Making Strategies" and **write** *your answers to the following:*

1. The single-feature model involves _____

   _____

   It is appropriate when _____

   _____

2. Using the additive model, you first _____

   _____

   It is appropriate for _____

   _____

3. Using the elimination-by-aspects model, you

   _____

   _____

   _____

   It is appropriate when _____

   _____

4. The availability heuristic is a strategy _____

   _____

   _____

5. The representativeness heuristic is a strategy

   _____

   _____

After you have carefully studied the preceding sections, complete the following exercises.

Concept Check 1

Read the following and write the correct term in the space provided.

1. After a chimpanzee tries unsuccessfully to get bananas that are out of reach, she sits for a long time staring at them. Suddenly, she looks around the cage, picks up a stick, and uses it to pull the bananas within her reach, something she has never done before. Her solution to the banana problem is probably the result of

   _____ .

2. You learn that one of the Russell children is taking ballet classes; you immediately conclude that it is their one daughter rather than any of their three sons. You reached a possibly erroneous conclusion by using the

   _____ .

3. Dr. Mendleson studies how people manipulate mental representations to draw inferences and conclusions. Dr. Mendleson is most likely a _____ psychologist interested in people's _____ ability.

4. You are asked to decide which city is farther north, Edinburgh, Scotland, or Stockholm, Sweden, so you try to picture a map of Europe in your mind. You are using a

   _____ .

5. Marisa has learned the rules and features that define a square, a rectangle, and a right-angle triangle. Marisa has learned a _____ concept.

6. Henry had trouble recognizing that a seahorse is a fish because it does not closely resemble his _____ concept of fish.

7. In order to convert liters into U.S. gallons, Natalie multiplies the number of liters by 0.264178. She is using a(n) _____ to arrive at the correct answer.

8. Hilda is asked to complete the sequence "J, F, M, A, _, _, _, _, _, _, _, _." After trying a few different possibilities, she comes up with the correct answer—M, J, J, A, S, O, N, D (the first letter of the months of the year). It appears that Hilda is using a(n)

   _____ strategy to solve the problem.

9. Anatole is trying to decide which of two equally affordable and attractive cars to purchase, so he makes a list of the advantages and disadvantages of each using an arbitrary rating scale. Anatole is using the _____ model to help him make a decision.

Review of Terms and Concepts 1

Use the terms in this list to complete the Matching Test, then to help you answer the True/False items correctly.

cognition
thinking
mental image
fusiform facial area
   (FFA)
parahippocampal place
   area (PPA)
concept
formal concept
natural concept
prototype
problem solving
trial and error
algorithm
heuristic

subgoals
working backward
insight
intuition
guiding stage,
   integrative stage
functional fixedness
mental set
single-feature model
additive model
elimination-by-aspects
   model
availability heuristic
representativeness
   heuristic

Matching Exercise

Match the appropriate term with its definition or description.

1. _____ Decision-making model in which all the alternatives are evaluated one characteristic at a time, starting with the most important feature and scratching each alternative off the list of possible choices if it fails to meet the criterion.

2. _____ The manipulation of mental representations of information in order to draw inferences or conclusions.

3. _____ Most typical instance of a particular concept.

4. _____ Sudden realization of how a problem can be solved.

5. _____ Decision-making strategy in which the choice among many alternatives is simplified by basing the decision on a single feature.

6. _____ Strategy in which the likelihood of an event is estimated by comparing how similar it is to the typical prototype of the event.

7. _____ An area of the brain that is activated when we look at faces.

8. _____ Problem-solving strategy that involves attempting different solutions and eliminating those that do not work.

9. _____ Mental category that is formed by learning the rules or features that define it.

10. _____ The mental activities involved in acquiring, retaining, and using knowledge.

11. _____ Mental category of objects or ideas based on properties that they share.

12. _____ Problem-solving strategy that involves following a general rule of thumb to reduce the number of possible solutions.

13. _____ An area of the brain that is activated when we look at pictures of places.

True/False Test

Indicate whether each statement is true or false by placing T or F in the blank space next to each item.

1. ____ Working backward is a common heuristic used to break a problem down into a series of smaller problems; as each subproblem is solved, you get closer to solving the larger problem.

2. ____ A mental representation of objects or events that are not physically present is called a mental image.

3. ____ Problem solving is thinking and behavior directed toward attaining a goal that is not readily available.

4. ____ The tendency to persist in solving problems with solutions that have worked in the past is called functional fixedness.

5. ____ The additive model of decision making involves generating a list of the most important factors, then using an arbitrary rating scale to rate each alternative on each factor, and finally adding the ratings together for comparison purposes.

6. ____ The availability heuristic is a strategy in which the likelihood of an event is estimated on the basis of how easily other instances of the event are available in memory.

7. ____ A natural concept is a mental category that is formed as a result of everyday experience.

8. ____ A useful heuristic in which you start at the end point and determine the steps necessary to reach your goal uses the analysis of subgoals.

9. ____ A mental set is the tendency to view objects as functioning only in their usual or customary manner.

10. ____ Intuition refers to the process of coming to a conclusion or making a judgment without conscious awareness.

11. ____ A problem-solving strategy that involves following a specific rule, procedure, or method that inevitably produces the correct solution is referred to as an algorithm.

12. ____ The two-stage model of intuition involves a guiding stage (a pattern in the information is perceived unconsciously) and an integrative stage (a representation of the pattern becomes conscious).

Check your answers and review any areas of weakness before going on to the next section.

Language and Thought

Preview Questions

Consider the following questions as you study this section of the chapter.

- How is language defined?
- What are the five most important characteristics of language?
- In what ways does language influence thinking?
- Can animals use language?

*Read the section "Language and Thought" and **write** your answers to the following:*

1. Language is defined as _____

2. The five most important characteristics of language are as follows:

   (a) _____

   (b) _____

(c) _____

(d) _____

(e) _____

3. An important way in which language can influence thought has to do with _____

4. Animals communicate with each other and with other species, but _____

Measuring Intelligence

Preview Questions

Consider the following questions as you study this section of the chapter.

- How is intelligence defined?
- What roles did Binet, Terman, and Wechsler play in the development of intelligence tests?

*Read the section "Measuring Intelligence" and **write** your answers to the following:*

1. Intelligence is defined as _____

2. Alfred Binet, along with psychiatrist Theodore Simon, devised _____

3. Lewis Terman translated and adapted _____

4. David Wechsler developed a new intelligence test, _____

_____

_____

_____

Principles of Test Construction: What Makes a Good Test?

Preview Questions

Consider the following questions as you study this section of the chapter.

- How do achievement tests differ from aptitude tests?

- What does it mean to standardize a test?

- What is the role of norms in standardization, and what is the normal curve?

- How are reliability and validity defined, and how are they determined?

*Read the section "Principles of Test Construction: What Makes a Good Test?" and **write** your answers to the following:*

1. Achievement tests are designed to _____

_____

Aptitude tests are designed to _____

_____

2. Standardization refers to _____

_____

_____

3. The normal curve, or normal distribution, is

_____

_____

4. Reliability is defined as _____

_____

It is determined by _____

_____

5. Validity is defined as _____

_____

One way to determine validity is by _____

_____

After you have carefully studied the preceding sections, complete the following exercises.

Concept Check 2

Read the following and write the correct term in the space provided.

1. A Norwegian visitor to England asks the hotel clerk, "Can you please my key to my room give me?" This visitor has apparently not yet mastered the _____ of the English language.

2. When Elinore's husband refers to her psychiatrist as a "headshrinker" during discussions with friends or family, he may be influencing their _____ perceptions of Elinore and her therapist.

3. Ten-year-old Jean performed at the same level as most 12-year-olds on Binet's test. Her _____ age is different from her _____ age.

4. According to his score on the Standard-Binet test, Marcel's mental age is identical to his chronological age. Marcel's IQ score is likely to be _____ .

5. When 25-year-old Dagmar applied for a position with the Department of Defense, she was given a test; she scored slightly above the norm on overall verbal ability but well above the norm in overall performance for her age group. The test Dagmar was given was a(n) _____ called the _____ .

6. The test and retest scores on the new Zander jealousy scale were highly similar but lacked predictive value; furthermore, it was not clear exactly what human attribute it was measuring. The Zander test was high in _____ but low in _____ .

7. Marta is thoroughly enjoying reading the latest book in a series that recounts the adventures of children who attend a special school for wizards and witches. The author of these books has an extraordinary talent for telling interesting and exciting tales about nonexistent places and people. This ability to communicate meaningfully about imaginary events and characters demonstrates an important characteristic of language called _____.

8. Twelve year-old Golnaz was given a standardized intelligence test, specially designed for children. She is most likely to have taken the _____.

Review of Terms, Concepts, and Names 2

Use the terms in this list to complete the Matching Test, then to help you answer the True/False items correctly.

language
syntax
generative
displacement
linguistic relativity
  hypothesis
animal cognition
  (comparative cognition)
intelligence
Alfred Binet
mental age
Lewis Terman
Stanford-Binet
  Intelligence Scale
intelligence quotient
  (IQ)
David Wechsler
Wechsler Adult
  Intelligence Scale
  (WAIS)

verbal score
performance score
Wechsler Intelligence
  Scale for Children
  (WISC), Wechsler
  Preschool and
  Primary Scale of
  Intelligence (WPPSI)
achievement test
aptitude test
standardization
norms
normal curve (normal
  distribution)
reliability
validity

Matching Exercise

Match the appropriate term/name with its definition or description.

1. _____ Every language's unique rules for combining words.

2. _____ The French psychologist who, along with French psychiatrist Théodore

Simon, developed the first widely used intelligence test.

3. _____ The ability to communicate meaningfully about ideas, objects, and activities that are not physically present.

4. _____ Measure of intelligence in which an individual's mental level is expressed in terms of the average abilities of a given age group.

5. _____ Name of Lewis Terman's translation and revision of the Binet-Simon intelligence test.

6. _____ The ability of a test to measure what it is intended to measure.

7. _____ Characteristic of language that allows one to create an infinite number of new and different phrases and sentences.

8. _____ The study of animal learning, memory, thinking, and language.

9. _____ Bell-shaped distribution of individual differences in a normal population in which most scores cluster around the average score.

10. _____ The global capacity to think rationally, act purposefully, and deal effectively with the environment.

11. _____ System for combining arbitrary symbols to produce an infinite number of meaningful statements.

12. _____ Two tests developed by David Wechsler for testing children's intelligence.

True/False Test

Indicate whether each item is true or false by placing T or F in the space next to each item.

1. ____ Lewis Terman was the American psychologist who translated and adapted the Binet-Simon intelligence test for use in the United States.

2. ____ David Wechsler was the American psychologist who developed the Wechsler Adult Intelligence Scale (WAIS), the most widely used intelligence scale.

3. ____ An aptitude test is designed to measure a person's level of knowledge, skill, or accomplishments in a particular area, such as mathematics or a foreign language.

4. ____ The intelligence quotient (IQ) is a global measure of intelligence derived by comparing an individual's score to that of others in the same age group.

5. ____ The *verbal score* on the WAIS reflects scores on subtests such as identifying missing parts in incomplete pictures, arranging pictures to tell a story, or arranging blocks to match a given pattern.

6. ____ Reliability refers to the ability of a test to produce consistent results when administered on repeated occasions under similar conditions.

7. ____ Standardization is the process of administering a test to a large, representative sample of people under uniform conditions for the purpose of establishing norms.

8. ____ An achievement test is designed to measure a person's capacity to benefit from education or training.

9. ____ The *performance score* on the WAIS represents scores on subtests of vocabulary, comprehension, knowledge of general information, and other similar tasks.

10. ____ The Wechsler Adult Intelligence Scale (WAIS) is an adult intelligence test with scores on 11 subtests that are grouped to provide an overall verbal score and a performance score.

11. ____ The notion that differences among languages cause differences in the thoughts of their speakers is called the linguistic relativity hypothesis.

12. ____ The scores of the large number of representative subjects for whom the test is designed establish the norms or the standards against which an individual score is compared and interpreted.

Check your answers and review any areas of weakness before going on to the next section.

The Nature of Intelligence

Preview Questions

Consider the following questions as you study this section of the chapter.

- What are the two key issues involved in the debate over the nature of intelligence?
- What is the *g* factor (general intelligence), and who first proposed a theory regarding its existence?

- What was Louis L. Thurstone's contribution to the debate about the nature of intelligence?
- Who proposed the idea of "multiple intelligences," and what are the eight distinct intelligences?
- What is the triarchic theory of intelligence, and who proposed it?

Read the section "The Nature of Intelligence" and **write** *your answers to the following:*

1. The two key issues involved in the debate over the nature of intelligence are as follows:

   (a) _____

   _____

   (b) _____

   _____

2. The *g* factor (or general intelligence) is the notion _____

   _____

   It was proposed by _____

3. Louis L. Thurstone proposed the notion that _____

   _____

4. The idea of multiple intelligences was proposed by _____

   The eight intelligences are _____

   _____

   _____

   _____

5. The triarchic theory of intelligence proposes that _____

   _____

   _____

   It was developed by _____

The Roles of Genetics and Environment in Determining Intelligence

Preview Questions

Consider the following questions as you study this section of the chapter.

- What is the heredity-environment issue?
- How are twin studies used to measure genetic and environmental influences?

- What is heritability, and why can't heritability estimates be used to explain differences between groups?
- Are IQ tests culturally biased?

*Read the section "The Roles of Genetics and Environment in Determining Intelligence" and **write** your answers to the following:*

1. The basic heredity–environment issue is concerned with _____

   _____

   _____

   _____

2. Twin studies have been used because _____

   _____

   _____

3. Heritability is defined as _____

   _____

   Heritability estimates cannot be used to explain differences between groups because _____

   _____

   _____

   _____

4. It is virtually impossible to create a culture-free IQ test because _____

   _____

   _____

   _____

   _____

After you have carefully studied the preceding sections, complete the following exercises.

Concept Check 3

Read the following and write the correct term in the space provided.

1. Although Dr. Bowman recognizes that particular individuals might excel in specific areas, she believes that a factor, called general intelligence, or the *g* factor, is responsible for overall performance on mental ability tests. Her belief about the nature of intelligence is most consistent with the approach taken by psychologist

   _____ .

2. Jamal is a highly valued maintenance worker because of his almost uncanny ability to be able to fix almost any piece of equipment that breaks down. Jamal is demonstrating what Robert Sternberg would call _____ intelligence.

3. Selma is a very successful, highly motivated, goal-directed, and creative graphic designer. These aspects of her intelligence are _____ (not likely/very likely) to be assessed and measured on a conventional intelligence test.

4. Dicky and Ricky are identical twins and have almost identical IQ scores despite the fact that they were separated at birth and raised in different environments. Fraternal twins Joel and Joanna were raised together but their IQ scores are much less similar than Dicky and Ricky's scores. This example provides the most support for the _____ side in the heredity-environment debate.

5. As compared with the scores of two randomly selected unrelated people of the same age, Joel and Joanna's IQ scores are much more similar. This finding provides most support for the _____ side in the heredity-environment debate.

6. Dr. Yokomoto, like the majority of experts on intelligence testing, is most likely to attribute the finding that Japanese and Chinese children outperform American children on mathematics achievement tests to _____ factors.

7. When Dr. Parsei, an expert on intelligence testing, was asked if a completely culture-free intelligence test could be designed, he replied that it _____ (was/was not) because group ability tests reflect the values, knowledge, and communication strategies of their culture of origin.

8. Professor Kensington suggests that there are seven "primary mental abilities," which are relatively independent elements of intelligence. These abilities include verbal comprehension, numerical ability, reasoning, and perceptual speed. Dr. Kensington's views of intelligence are most consistent with those of

   _____ .

9. Yan is an expert chess player with an exceptional ability to mentally visualize the relationship of the various chess pieces following different moves. Howard Gardner labeled this type of intelligence _____ .

10. Constantino is a very successful salesperson. His success is due, in part at least, to his ability to understand and respond appropriately to other people's emotions, motives, and intentions. Constantino demonstrates _____ intelligence, one of the eight intelligences proposed by _____ .

11. Before taking a challenging math test Chung Yee was reminded of the cultural stereotype that Asian-Americans have superior math skills. She scored significantly higher than her equally gifted friend Jee Young, who was reminded before the same test of the stereotype that females are poor at math. The unexpected difference in their performance on the same test may be the result of what psychologist Claude Steele called _____ .

12. Researchers calculated that approximately 50 percent of the differences in IQ scores within a given population was due to genetic factors. They have calculated the _____ of the variation within that group that is due to heredity.

Graphic Organizer 1

Read the following statements and decide which psychologist is most associated with each.

Statement	Psychologist
1. I define intelligence as the global capacity to think rationally, act purposefully, and deal effectively with the environment; a good IQ test should have both verbal and performance scores representing subtests that measure a variety of abilities.	
2. My theory of intelligence emphasizes both universal aspects of intelligent behavior and the importance of adapting to the individual's particular social and cultural environment; there are essentially three forms of intelligence: analytical, creative, and practical intelligence.	
3. I'm not sure I have a fully developed theory of intelligence, but I do believe that we can help children do better in school if we devise tests that can identify those who need help and then provide that help. There is a great deal of variation in intelligence in any age group of children.	
4. I am convinced that a factor called general intelligence, or the *g* factor, is responsible for overall performance on mental ability tests. Furthermore, I would go so far as to say that intelligence can be accurately expressed as a single number that reflects an individual's intellectual abilities.	
5. I disagree with those who say that intelligence is a single, general mental capacity. On the basis of my observations of what is valued in different cultures, I've concluded that there are eight multiple intelligences, each independent of the other, and these must be viewed in the context of a particular culture.	
6. I tend to agree with statement 4 above. In addition, I believe that intelligence can best be expressed by a number I call the intelligence quotient, or IQ, which is derived by dividing the mental age by the chronological age and multiplying the result by 100.	
7. I do not agree with the notion that intelligence is a single general mental capacity. Instead, I believe that there are a number of different "primary mental abilities" such as verbal comprehension, numerical ability, reasoning, and perceptual speed, and that each one is a relatively independent element of intelligence. In my view the so-called *g* factor is simply an overall average score of these independent abilities and is therefore less important than an individual's specific pattern of mental abilities.	

Review of Terms, Concepts, and Names 3

Use the terms in this list to complete the Matching Test, then to help you answer the True/False items correctly.

Charles Spearman
general intelligence,
    or the *g* factor
Louis L. Thurstone
Howard Gardner
Robert Sternberg
triarchic theory of
    intelligence
successful intelligence
analytic intelligence

creative intelligence
practical intelligence
heredity
environment
identical twins
fraternal twins
heritability
creativity
stereotype threat

Matching Exercise

Match the appropriate term/name with its definition or description.

1. _____ Contemporary American psychologist whose triarchic theory of intelligence includes three forms of intelligence (analytical, creative, and practical).

2. _____ The percentage of variation within a given population that is due to heredity.

3. _____ Factor of intelligence that is responsible for a person's overall performance on tests of mental ability.

4. _____ Group of cognitive processes used to generate useful, original, and novel ideas or solutions.

5. _____ American psychologist who advanced the theory that intelligence is composed of several primary mental abilities and cannot be accurately described by a general intelligence, or *g*, factor.

6. _____ Sternberg's type of intelligence that involves the ability to adapt to the environment and often reflects what is commonly described as street smarts.

7. _____ British psychologist who advanced the theory that a general intelligence factor, called the *g* factor, is responsible for overall intellectual functioning.

8. _____ Form of intelligence that involves the ability to deal with novel situations by drawing on existing skills and knowledge.

9. _____ Psychological predicament in which fear that you will be evaluated in terms of a negative stereotype about a group to which you belong creates anxiety and self-doubt, lowering performance in a particular domain that is important to you.

True/False Test

Indicate whether each item is true or false by placing T or F in the space next to each item.

1. ____ Howard Gardner is a contemporary American psychologist whose theory of intelligence states that there is not one intelligence but multiple intelligences, the importance of each being determined by cultural values.

2. ____ Identical twins develop from two different fertilized eggs and are 50 percent genetically similar to each other.

3. ____ Heredity refers to the traits, capacities, and intellectual potential that we inherit from our parents, grandparents, and great-grandparents.

4. ____ Analytic intelligence refers to the mental processes used in learning how to solve problems, that is, in picking a problem-solving strategy and applying it to solve problems.

5. ____ In the debate over what determines intelligence, environment refers to factors such as type of upbringing, nutritional and health standards, social and cultural factors, and other influences that may have an impact on intellectual development.

6. ____ Fraternal twins share exactly the same genes because they developed from a single fertilized egg that split into two.

7. ____ Sternberg's theory that there are three forms of intelligence—analytic, creative, and practical—is called the triarchic theory of intelligence.

8. ____ Successful intelligence involves three distinct types of mental ability, analytic, creative, and practical.

Check your answers and review any areas of weakness before going on to the next section.

Something to Think About

1. Many people mistakenly believe that creativity is restricted to a few gifted, genius-level, artistic people. What would you tell someone who wants to be creative but does not believe he or she possesses an artistic temperament?

2. People vary in their IQ test scores, but about 68 percent of scores on tests such as the WAIS-III are between 85 and 115, the range for normal intelligence. A friend comes up to you and says, "Wouldn't it be great if we all had above-average IQ scores? Just think how wonderful life would be and how happy and successful we'd be!" How might you enlighten your friend about IQ tests and IQ scores?

Check your answers and review any areas of weakness before doing the progress tests.

Progress Test 1

Review the complete chapter (including Concept Reviews and all the boxed inserts), review all your study notes, and then test yourself on the following progress test. Check your answers. If you make a mistake, review your notes, review the relevant section of the study guide, and, if necessary, go back and read the appropriate part of your textbook.

1. In applying for a job at O'Hare Airport, Lynda is given a test to see if she is suited to be an air traffic controller. This is an example of _____ testing.
   - (a) intelligence
   - (b) achievement
   - (c) aptitude
   - (d) motivational

2. When Aaron is asked to define *weapon*, he responds that it is anything you could use to beat someone with. Aaron is using the word *weapon* as a
   - (a) natural concept.
   - (b) prototype.
   - (c) formal concept.
   - (d) heuristic.

3. When Michelle is asked the same question as Aaron, she replies that a weapon is one of a variety of instruments, or objects, that can be used to defend, attack, hurt, maim, or kill. Furthermore, the term *weapon* can even refer to words in a phrase, as in "the pen is mightier than the sword." Michelle is using the word *weapon* as a
   - (a) natural concept.
   - (b) prototype.
   - (c) formal concept.
   - (d) heuristic.

4. When three-year-old Claudia is asked which letter of the alphabet comes before *g*, she recites the alphabet from the beginning until she arrives at the solution. Claudia is using _____ to solve the problem.
   - (a) trial and error
   - (b) insight
   - (c) an algorithm
   - (d) a heuristic

5. Louis forgot to bring his pillow when he went camping for the weekend, so he spent a very uncomfortable night. It didn't occur to Louis that he could use his down-filled jacket as a pillow. This example best illustrates
   - (a) functional fixedness.
   - (b) mental set.
   - (c) the availability heuristic.
   - (d) use of an algorithm.

6. When Vasilis is faced with the decision of which of two equally attractive apartments to rent, he makes a list of what is most important and gives each factor a numerical rating. It appears that Vasilis is using the _____ model of decision making.
   - (a) elimination-by-aspects
   - (b) additive
   - (c) single-feature
   - (d) heuristic

7. Jerome recently saw a TV special in which most of the psychologists interviewed were middle-aged males. When he took his first psychology class, he was surprised to find that his professor was a young female rather than an older, bearded male. Jerome's surprise is probably due to his use of the
   - (a) availability heuristic.
   - (b) representativeness heuristic.
   - (c) single-feature model.
   - (d) additive model.

8. When Heidi tells Hans that she is going to enter a foot race to raise funds to end the arms race, he has no trouble understanding that she is going to run in a race to generate support for an anti-weapons cause. Hans's correct interpretation best illustrates the importance of
   - (a) syntax.
   - (b) displacement.
   - (c) generativity.
   - (d) prototypes.

9. When asked what she does for a living, Krista always replies that she is a sanitary engineer rather than a garbage collector. Krista is probably aware of the effect of language on
   (a) functional fixedness. (c) social perception.
   (b) gender bias.   (d) income level.

10. Six-year-old Bruce's performance on an intelligence test is at a level characteristic of an average four-year-old. Bruce's mental age is
    (a) eight.   (c) six.
    (b) four.   (d) five.

11. Scott is a very bright ten-year-old with a mental age of thirteen. If tested on the Stanford-Binet Intelligence Scale, his IQ score would most likely be
    (a) 100.   (c) 150.
    (b) 77.   (d) 130.

12. Twenty-year-old Val has just taken a test that includes vocabulary, comprehension, general knowledge, object assembly, and other subtests. Val has completed the
    (a) WAIS.   (c) WISC.
    (b) WPPSI.   (d) Stanford-Binet.

13. In his research on very young black children adopted into white middle-class families, Dr. Wilson found that their IQ scores were several points above the average of both blacks and whites. Dr. Wilson, like most experts in this area, is most likely to conclude that
    (a) intelligence is determined primarily by heredity.
    (b) IQ scores cannot be improved by environmental factors.
    (c) improved diet and health standards are the crucial factor in improving IQ scores.
    (d) socioeconomic conditions, cultural values, and other such environmental factors can affect IQ scores.

14. Dr. Shong was initially puzzled by her patient's unusual symptoms and was unable to arrive at a clear diagnosis. However, by integrating both obvious and subtle cues she began to recognize a pattern in the patient's symptoms and, thus, was able to formulate a tentative hypothesis that enabled her to order the appropriate lab tests. In this instance, Dr. Shong appears to be using _____ to diagnose her patient's illness.
    (a) an algorithm
    (b) the single feature approach
    (c) the elimination-by-aspects technique
    (d) insight or intuition

15. All of the following are obstacles to logical thinking that can account for much of the persistence of unwarranted beliefs in pseudo-sciences *except*
    (a) the belief bias effect.
    (b) confirmation bias.
    (c) the underestimation effect.
    (d) the fallacy of positive instances.
    (e) the overestimation effect.

Progress Test 2

After you have checked your understanding of the material in Progress Test 1 and have done a complete chapter review with special focus on any areas of weakness, you are now ready to assess your knowledge on Progress Test 2. Check your answers. If you make a mistake, review your notes, the relevant section of the study guide, and, if necessary, the appropriate part of your textbook.

1. As part of his overall vocational assessment, Steven took a test that measured his level of knowledge, skills, and accomplishments in particular areas such as mathematics and writing ability. Steven took a(n) _____ test.
   (a) aptitude   (c) intelligence
   (b) achievement   (d) motivational

2. When Katrina is asked to identify the letters of the alphabet that do not have curved lines, she tries to mentally picture each letter as she completes the task. Katrina is using
   (a) mental imagery.   (c) a formal concept.
   (b) a natural concept. (d) a prototype.

3. Shawn is asked to memorize a map of an island that has a hut, a lake, a tree, a beach, and a grassy area, all clearly marked at distinct locations. Later, he is asked to imagine a specific location, such as the hut; when a second location, the tree, is named, he has to press a button when he reaches the tree on the visual image in his mind. The results of this experiment will most likely reveal that the _____ the distance between the two points, the _____ time it will take to scan the mental image of the map.
   (a) greater; more
   (b) greater; less
   (c) shorter; more
   (d) All of the above are false; there is no relationship between distance and time taken to mentally scan points on a map.

4. When Earl is asked what object or objects come to mind in response to the word *vegetable*, he answers "potatoes and carrots." For Earl, potatoes and carrots are

(a) formal concepts.   (c) algorithms.
(b) prototypes.   (d) heuristics.

5. Dr. Naidu's research is concerned with the study of animal learning, memory, thinking, and language. Dr. Naidu is most likely interested in

(a) testing the linguistic relativity hypothesis.
(b) investigating the triarchic theory of intelligence.
(c) heritability and heritability estimates.
(d) animal cognition or comparative cognition.

6. When Elana got her new VCR, she spent hours trying different approaches to programming the machine rather than consulting the manual. Elana is using the _____ approach to problem solving.

(a) algorithm   (c) heuristic
(b) trial-and-error   (d) insight

7. After spending weeks studying a variety of sources and materials, Terry still couldn't decide on a topic for her seminar presentation. However, when she was out for her daily jog, she suddenly had a flash of inspiration about her topic. Terry solved her problem

(a) through insight.
(b) by using an algorithm.
(c) through functional fixedness.
(d) by using the representativeness heuristic.

8. Whenever his TV picture became fuzzy, Lloyd would bang the top of the TV set, which usually cleared the picture. Recently, when he was playing a video on his new VCR, tracking problems created a fuzzy picture; Lloyd banged the top of the TV over and over but to no avail. Lloyd appears to be experiencing a problem-solving obstacle called

(a) functional fixedness.
(b) subgoal analysis.
(c) a mental set.
(d) confirmation bias.
(e) prototypical male stupidity.

9. When writing term papers, assignments, and exams, Gary is very careful to use "he or she" in place of the masculine pronoun and "people" instead of "man." Gary is apparently aware of the relationship between language and

(a) prototypes.   (c) social perception.
(b) gender bias.   (d) functional fixedness.

10. Dr. Peerless has designed a test to measure the level of scientific knowledge in high school graduates. To establish a norm against which individual scores may be interpreted and compared, she is presently administering the test to a large representative sample of high school graduates. Dr. Peerless is in the process of

(a) establishing the test's reliability.
(b) establishing the test's validity.
(c) standardizing the test.
(d) determining the test's aptitude.

11. After completing the above process, Dr. Peerless needs to check whether her test measures what it was designed to measure. She does this by comparing scores on her test with the scores and grades obtained by students in high school science courses. In this instance, Dr. Peerless is in the process of

(a) establishing the test's reliability.
(b) establishing the test's validity.
(c) standardizing the test.
(d) determining the test's aptitude.

12. Arnie is very adept at dealing with novel situations by drawing on previous experience and can often find unusual ways to relate old information to solve new problems. Robert Sternberg would call this _____ intelligence.

(a) analytic   (c) creative
(b) practical   (d) motivational

13. As part of a bizarre experiment in a science fiction story, Dr. Igor places 100 genetically identical individual infants in different homes. Because the infants are all identical, the heritability of intelligence (that is, the percentage of variation within the group that is due to genetic factors) should be _____ percent.

(a) 0   (c) 65
(b) 50   (d) 100

14. According to In Focus 7.3, "Does a High IQ Score Predict Success in Life?," which of the following is true?

    (a) IQ scores reliably predict academic success.
    (b) Academic success is no guarantee of success beyond school.
    (c) Many different personality factors are involved in achieving success, such as motivation, emotional maturity, commitment to goals, creativity, and a willingness to work hard.
    (d) All of the above are true.

15. According to the Application, which of the following is *not* a way to increase your creative potential?

    (a) Focus almost exclusively on extrinsic motivation.
    (b) Choose the goal of creativity.
    (c) Try different approaches.
    (d) Acquire relevant knowledge.
    (e) Engage in problem finding.

Progress Test 3

After you have checked your understanding of the material in Progress Tests 1 and 2, and have done a complete chapter review with special focus on any areas of weakness, you are ready to further assess your knowledge on Progress Test 3. Check your answers. If you make a mistake, review your notes, the appropriate parts of the study guide, and, if necessary, the relevant sections of your textbook.

1. Adrian took the WAIS test. One aspect of his general cognitive ability that is *not* likely to have been measured is his

   (a) linguistic ability.
   (b) problem-solving ability.
   (c) general knowledge.
   (d) creativity.

2. Dr. Larch is a renowned researcher and theorist in the area of intelligence testing. Like most experts in his field, Dr. Larch is most likely to agree that

   (a) genetic factors, rather than environmental influences, are the primary cause of any IQ differences found between racial groups.
   (b) within a given racial group, the differences among people are due at least as much to environmental influences as they are to genetic influences.
   (c) the IQ of any individual, regardless of his or her race, is determined almost exclusively by genetic factors and is relatively uninfluenced by environmental influences.
   (d) the IQ of any given individual, regardless of his or her race, is determined almost exclusively by environmental factors and is relatively uninfluenced by genetics.

3. With little or no hesitation, Matthew was able to state that cats and dogs are both examples of the concept of mammal; he was slower to respond when asked whether dolphins and whales were also examples of mammals. This example suggests that

   (a) formal concepts have fuzzy boundaries and that cats and dogs are prototypes of the category.
   (b) natural concepts have fuzzy boundaries and that cats and dogs are prototypes of the category.
   (c) formal concepts have fuzzy boundaries and that dolphins and whales are prototypes of the category.
   (d) natural concepts have fuzzy boundaries and that dolphins and whales are prototypes of the category.

4. Tom created the novel sentence, "The faceless bureaucrat was finally faced with making a face-saving decision but could not face up to the fact that he was in a fatal face-off with his favorite facetious faculty." Tom's ability to do this illustrates the _____ nature of language.

   (a) syntactic
   (b) inflexible
   (c) generative
   (d) practical

5. Dr. Adatia, a cross-cultural psychologist, discovered that children of immigrant Buraku families living in the United States had IQ scores no different from other Japanese-Americans, but that the Burakumin in Japan had IQ scores 10 to 15 points lower than those of other Japanese. Dr. Adatia is most likely to conclude that

   (a) IQ scores are genetically determined.
   (b) social discrimination can affect IQ scores.
   (c) better nutrition is the main factor that influences IQ scores.
   (d) the U.S. educational system is better than that of Japan.

6. Dr. Bishop assesses the correlation between scores obtained on two halves of her new abstract reasoning test in order to measure the _____ of her test.
   - (a) reliability
   - (b) validity
   - (c) norms
   - (d) aptitude

7. Miguel is extremely adept at learning how to solve problems; that is, he is very good at picking problem-solving strategies and applying them to problems. Robert Sternberg would call this ability a form of
   - (a) analytic intelligence.
   - (b) creative intelligence.
   - (c) practical intelligence.
   - (d) general intelligence, or the *g* factor.

8. Dr. Welch believes that there are multiple independent intelligences that cannot be reflected in a single measure of mental ability and that each intelligence must be viewed within a cultural context. Dr. Welch's position is most consistent with the views of
   - (a) Charles Spearman.
   - (b) L. L. Thurstone.
   - (c) Howard Gardner.
   - (d) Robert Sternberg.

9. When Allison goes to graduate school, she plans to investigate aspects of the heredity–environment debate as it relates to intelligence. She is most likely to
   - (a) use animals, such as rats and pigeons, in her research.
   - (b) get involved in twin studies.
   - (c) study the language abilities of primates.
   - (d) explore creativity and intuition.

10. Maja is writing a paper for her course in comparative cognition. After reviewing all the relevant research on animal language, Maja is likely to conclude that
   - (a) only humans possess language capabilities.
   - (b) animals can communicate with each other but are not capable of mastering any aspect of language.
   - (c) some species have demonstrated an elementary understanding of syntax and certain other limited aspects of language.
   - (d) many animal species can "think," use language, and possess self-awareness.

11. Martin has had some difficulties in school and has fallen behind in academic achievement. His chronological age is ten and his IQ score on the Stanford-Binet is 70. Martin's mental age is therefore
   - (a) seven.
   - (b) ten.
   - (c) thirteen.
   - (d) five.

12. Cynthia always buys the brand of paper towels that is on sale, even if it is not the highest quality towel. Cynthia makes her decision about which paper towel to purchase based on the _____ model of decision making.
   - (a) single-feature
   - (b) additive
   - (c) elimination-by-aspects
   - (d) heuristic

13. Jan is orderly, neat, quiet, and shy. She enjoys reading in her spare time and is an avid chess player. Given this description, most people would guess that she is a librarian rather than a real estate agent. This tendency to classify Jan as a librarian illustrates the influence of
   - (a) the availability heuristic.
   - (b) belief bias.
   - (c) the representativeness heuristic.
   - (d) the elimination-by-aspects strategy.

14. According to Culture and Human Behavior 7.2, the linguistic relativity hypothesis (or Whorfian hypothesis)
   - (a) proposes that the differences among languages cause differences in the thoughts of their speakers.
   - (b) has been supported by the results of dozens of cross-cultural studies.
   - (c) accounts for the fact that the English language has more than a dozen words for *snow* but Eskimos have only one or two.
   - (d) holds that language does not determine cultural differences but instead language reflects cultural differences.

15. According to Culture and Human Behavior 7.4, which of the following is (are) true?

    (a) Older people always score lower on memory tests than younger people because forgetfulness and an inability to remember new material is the inevitable consequence of growing old.

    (b) Performance on relatively fair and objective tests may be susceptible to social and cultural influences such as the stereotype threat.

    (c) What other people expect and believe about a person's performance on a test will have no influence on his or her score as long as the test has been standardized.

    (d) Females always score lower than males on advanced math tests because they do not possess the same level of logical-mathematical intelligence as males.

    (e) All of the above are true.

Answers

Introduction: Thinking, Language, and Intelligence

1. *Cognition is* the general term that refers to the mental activities involved in acquiring, retaining, and using knowledge.

2. *Thinking is defined as* the manipulation of mental representations of information in order to draw inferences and conclusions. *It typically involves* the manipulation of mental images and concepts.

3. *A mental image is* a mental representation of objects or events that are not physically present.

4. *We manipulate mental images* in much the same way as we manipulate the actual objects they represent. *Mental images are potentially subject to error and distortion because* they are not perfect duplicates of our actual sensory experience; instead, they are memories of visual images and are actively constructed.

5. *Concepts are* mental categories of objects or ideas based on properties they share. *The two ways of forming concepts are* learning the rules or features that define the particular concept (formal concept) and as the result of everyday experiences (natural concept).

6. *A prototype is* the most typical instance of a particular concept. *The more closely an item matches a prototype,* the more quickly we can identify it as being an example of the concept.

Solving Problems and Making Decisions

1. *Problem solving is defined as* thinking and behavior directed toward attaining a goal that is not readily available.

2. *The trial-and-error strategy involves* attempting different solutions and eliminating those that do not work; it is useful when there is a limited range of possible solutions.

3. *An algorithm involves* following a specific rule, procedure, or method that inevitably produces the correct solution (such as mathematical formulas); using an algorithm may not always be practical because of the amount of time it can take to solve some problems.

4. *A heuristic is a* general rule of thumb that reduces the number of possible solutions; while it tends to simplify problem solving, it is not guaranteed to solve a given problem.

5. *Insight is the* sudden realization of how a problem can be solved, but insights, intuitions, or hunches are likely to be accurate only in contexts in which you already have a broad base of knowledge and experience.

6. *Functional fixedness is* the tendency to view objects as functioning only in their usual or customary way; it may prevent us from seeing the full range of ways in which an object can be used.

7. *A mental set is* the tendency to persist in solving problems with solutions that have worked in the past; it may prevent us from coming up with new and possibly more effective solutions.

Decision-Making Strategies

1. *The single feature model involves* making a decision based on a single feature. *It is appropriate when* the decision is a minor one.

2. *Using the additive model, you first* generate a list of factors that are most important to you, next you rate each alternative using an arbitrary rating scale, and finally, you add up the ratings for each alternative. *It is appropriate for* complex decisions and useful in identifying the most acceptable choice from a range of possible decisions.

3. *Using the elimination-by-aspects model, you* evaluate all the alternatives one characteristic at a time (starting with what you consider to be the most important feature) and systematically eliminate all alternatives that don't meet that criterion until only the one choice that satisfies your criteria remains. *It is appropriate when*

the decision is complex and there is a need to narrow down a range of choices with multiple features.

4. *The availability heuristic is a strategy* in which the likelihood of an event is estimated on the basis of how readily available other instances of the event are in memory.

5. *The representative heuristic is a strategy* in which the likelihood of an event is estimated by comparing how similar it is to the typical prototype of the event.

Concept Check 1

1. insight
2. representativeness heuristic
3. cognitive; thinking
4. mental image
5. formal
6. natural
7. algorithm
8. trial-and-error
9. additive

Matching Exercise 1

1. elimination-by-aspects model
2. thinking
3. prototype
4. insight
5. single-feature model
6. representativeness heuristic
7. fusiform facial area (FFA)
8. trial and error
9. formal concept
10. cognition
11. concept
12. heuristic
13. parahippocampal place area (PPA)

True/False Test 1

1. F	5. T	9. F
2. T	6. T	10. T
3. T	7. T	11. T
4. F	8. F	12. T

Language and Thought

1. *Language is defined as* a system for combining arbitrary symbols to produce an infinite number of meaningful statements.

2. *The five most important characteristics of language are as follows: (a)* The purpose of language is to communicate; to do so, language requires the use of symbols. *(b)* The meaning of these arbitrary symbols is shared by others. *(c)* Language is a highly structured system that follows rules for combining words (syntax). *(d)* Language is creative, allowing for the generation of an infinite number of new and different phrases and sentences (generative). *(e)* Language involves displacement, the ability to communicate meaningfully about ideas, objects, and activities that are not physically present.

3. *An important way in which language can influence thought has to do with* our social perception of others; when the nuances of words promote stereotypical thinking, language may encourage discrimination against women, the elderly, and members of racial or ethnic minorities.

4. *Animals communicate with each other and with other species, but* many psychologists question whether animals can learn to use language, and they caution against jumping to the conclusion that animals can think or that they possess self-awareness, on the basis of the few studies on animal cognition that demonstrated language ability in animals (e.g., bonobos and dolphins appear to have demonstrated an elementary grasp of the rules of syntax).

Measuring Intelligence

1. *Intelligence is defined as* the global capacity to think rationally, act purposefully, and deal effectively with the environment.

2. *Alfred Binet, along with psychiatrist Théodore Simon, devised* a series of tests to measure different elementary mental abilities, such as memory, attention, and the ability to understand similarities and differences; his research led to the concept of mental age.

3. *Lewis Terman translated and adapted* Binet's intelligence test (the Stanford-Binet Intelligence Scale) and developed the concept of the intelligence quotient, or IQ.

4. *David Wechsler developed a new intelligence test,* the Wechsler Adult Intelligence Scale (WAIS), which was designed specifically for adults, and its 11 subtest scores (measuring a variety of abilities) can be grouped to provide an overall verbal score and performance score. He also devised the WISC and WPPSI.

Principles of Test Construction: What Makes a Good Test?

1. *Achievement tests are designed to* measure a person's level of knowledge, skill, or accomplishment in a particular area. *Aptitude tests are designed to* assess a person's capacity to benefit from education or training.

2. *Standardization refers to* the administration of a test to a large, representative sample of people under uniform conditions for the purpose of establishing norms.

3. *The normal curve, or normal distribution, is* a bell-shaped distribution of individual differences in a normal population in which most scores cluster around the average.

4. *Reliability is defined as* the ability of a test to produce consistent results when administered on repeated occasions under similar conditions. *It is determined by* administering two similar, but not identical, versions of the test at different times, or by comparing the scores on one half of the test to the scores on the other half of the test.

5. *Validity is defined as* the ability of a test to measure what it is intended to measure. *One way to determine validity is by* demonstrating the predictive value of a test.

Concept Check 2

1. syntax
2. social
3. mental; chronological
4. 100
5. IQ test; WAIS
6. reliability; validity
7. displacement
8. Wechsler Intelligence Scale for Children (WISC)

Matching Exercise 2

1. syntax
2. Alfred Binet

3. displacement
4. mental age
5. Stanford-Binet Intelligence Scale
6. validity
7. generative
8. animal cognition (comparative cognition)
9. normal curve (normal distribution)
10. intelligence
11. language
12. Wechsler Intelligence Scale for Children (WISC) and Wechsler Preschool and Primary Scale of Intelligence (WPPSI)

True/False Test 2

1. T		5. F		9. F	
2. T		6. T		10. T	
3. F		7. T		11. T	
4. T		8. F		12. T	

The Nature of Intelligence

1. *The two key issues involved in the debate over the nature of intelligence are as follows: (a)* Is intelligence a single, general ability or is it better described as a cluster of different mental abilities? *(b)* Should the definition of intelligence be restricted to the mental abilities measured by IQ and other intelligence tests, or should it be defined more broadly?

2. *The g factor (or general intelligence) is the notion* of a general intelligence factor that is responsible for a person's overall performance on tests of mental ability. It was proposed by Charles Spearman.

3. *Louis L. Thurstone proposed the notion that* intelligence is a cluster of seven different primary mental abilities, each a relatively independent element of intelligence.

4. *The idea of multiple intelligences was proposed by* Howard Gardner. *The eight intelligences are* linguistic, logical-mathematical, musical, spatial, bodily-kinesthetic, interpersonal, intrapersonal, and naturalist intelligence.

5. *The triarchic theory of intelligence proposes that* there are three distinct forms of intelligence: analytic, creative, and practical. *It was developed by* Robert Sternberg.

The Roles of Genetics and Environment in Determining Intelligence

1. *The basic heredity–environment issue is concerned with* whether we inherit our intelligence from our parents (genes, or nature) or whether our intellectual potential is primarily determined by our environment and upbringing (nurture). (Because of research by molecular biologists, the issue has become one of how environment influences gene expression.)

2. *Twin studies have been used because* identical twins share exactly the same genes, and any differences between them must be due to environmental factors rather than to hereditary differences.

3. *Heritability is defined as* the percentage of variation within a given population that is due to heredity. *Heritability estimates cannot be used to explain differences between groups because* unless the environmental conditions of the two groups are identical, it is impossible to estimate the overall genetic differences between groups; even if intelligence were primarily determined by heredity, IQ differences between groups could still be due entirely to the environment (socioeconomic conditions, cultural values, and so on).

4. *It is virtually impossible to create a culture-free IQ test because* ability tests reflect the values, knowledge, and communication strategies of their culture of origin. Cultural differences in test-taking behavior may also affect results. Finally, the stereotype threat can cause students to perform as they think they are expected to perform.

Concept Check 3

1. Charles Spearman
2. practical
3. not likely
4. heredity
5. environment
6. environmental
7. was not
8. Louis L. Thurstone
9. spatial intelligence
10. interpersonal intelligence; Howard Gardner
11. the stereotype threat
12. heritability estimate

Graphic Organizer 1

1. David Wechsler
2. Robert Sternberg
3. Alfred Binet
4. Charles Spearman
5. Howard Gardner
6. Lewis Terman
7. Louis L. Thurstone

Matching Exercise 3

1. Robert Sternberg
2. heritability
3. *g* factor (general intelligence)
4. creativity
5. Louis L. Thurstone
6. practical intelligence
7. Charles Spearman
8. creative intelligence
9. stereotype threat

True/False Test 3

1. T	4. T	7. T
2. F	5. T	8. T
3. T	6. F	

Something to Think About

1. Many people would like to be more creative. Fortunately, much can be done to increase our creative potential. The first thing to tell someone is that creativity is hard to define precisely but that most cognitive psychologists agree that creativity is a group of cognitive processes used to generate useful, original, novel ideas and solutions. Creativity is not confined to artistic expression; as indicated in the definition, creativity involves usefulness as well as originality. Based on information in the Application, you could then conduct your own mini-workshop on creativity. You can summarize the workshop by using the letters of the word **CREATE** as an acronym: **C**hoose the goal of creativity; **R**einforce creative behavior; **E**ngage in problem finding; **A**cquire relevant knowledge; **T**ry different approaches; **E**xert effort and expect setbacks.

2. First, you could tell your friend that we can't all be above average. The distribution of intelli-

gence scores tends to follow a normal, or bell-shaped, curve, with about 50 percent above average and 50 percent below average. Next, you could talk a little about the problems involved in defining intelligence. Not even the experts agree. Some think that performance on mental ability tests reflects a general intelligence, or *g* factor; others think there are three forms of intelligence; and some postulate multiple intelligences. Despite these disagreements, psychologists do agree that intelligence involves such elements as abstract thinking, problem solving, and the capacity to acquire knowledge. They also tend to agree that aspects of intelligent behavior such as creativity, motivation, goal-directed behavior, and adaptation to one's environment are not measured by conventional intelligence tests. Thus, IQ scores reflect the limitations of existing intelligence tests. Finally, although IQ scores may predict academic success, doing well in school is no guarantee of success and happiness in life in general. Many different personality factors are involved in achieving success, such as motivation, emotional maturity, commitment to goals, creativity, and, perhaps most important of all, a willingness to work hard. None of these attributes are measured by traditional IQ tests.

Progress Test 1

1. c	6. b	11. d
2. a	7. a	12. a
3. c	8. a	13. d
4. c	9. c	14. d
5. a	10. b	15. c

Progress Test 2

1. b	6. b	11. b
2. a	7. a	12. c
3. a	8. c	13. a
4. b	9. b	14. d
5. d	10. c	15. a

Progress Test 3

1. d	6. a	11. a
2. b	7. a	12. a
3. b	8. c	13. c
4. c	9. b	14. a
5. b	10. c	15. b

chapter 8

Motivation and Emotion

PREVIEW

Reading the section below first will give you a general sense of the chapter's contents and an initial introduction to some of the major concepts and terms. This will prime you for what you are about to read and help you to develop a "cognitive map" that will guide your study of the material in this chapter. Likewise, reading the **preview questions** at the beginning of each major section will improve your ability to understand, learn, and retain the information.

CHAPTER 8 . . . AT A GLANCE

Chapter 8 is concerned with motivation and emotion. Motivation refers to the biological, emotional, cognitive, or social forces that activate and direct behavior, whereas emotion is defined as the complex psychological state that involves subjective experience, a physiological response, and a behavioral or expressive response. Motivational concepts and theories (e.g., instinct theories, drive theories, homeostasis, incentive motivation, arousal theory, and humanistic theories) are introduced.

Hunger is a biological motive, but eating behavior is influenced by psychological, biological, social, and cultural factors. This section starts with a discussion of how food is converted to energy in the body and describes the role played by the basal metabolic rate (BMR) and energy homeostasis. Physiological factors that are correlated with eating include small changes in glucose, insulin, body temperature, and metabolism; factors involved in satiation include cholecystokinin (CCK) and sensory-specific satiety. Chemical signals that regulate body weight include leptin, insulin, neuropeptide Y (NPY), and corticotropin-releasing hormone (CRH). Both set-point theory and settling-point theory are discussed.

Body weight status can be calculated by the body mass index (BMI). Factors involved in becoming overweight include the positive incentive value of foods, the cafeteria diet effect, preloading calories, and individual differences in BMR. Several factors contribute to obesity including genetic susceptibility, leptin resistance, and frequent dieting. A discussion of eating disorders (anorexia, bulimia, and binge-eating disorder) and their causes concludes the section.

The section on psychological needs as motivators includes Maslow's hierarchy of needs, self-determination theory (SDT), intrinsic motivation and extrinsic motivation, and the role of self-esteem in psychological functioning. Competence motivation, achievement motivation, and the Thematic Apperception Test (TAT) are introduced next.

Emotions have many functions, including triggering motivated behavior, and they contribute to rational decision making and purposeful behavior. Emotional intelligence, which is the capacity to understand and manage your own emotional experiences and respond appropriately to the emotional responses of others, is necessary for success in life. Evolutionary psychologists consider the capacity for emotion to be a product of evolution that helps us solve important adaptive problems and contributes to survival and reproductive success. Basic emotions are innate and universal and emotions can be classified in terms of degree of pleasantness and activation; additionally, the dimension of interpersonal engagement is recognized in collectivistic cultures. The neuroscience of emotion is introduced next, and the roles played by the sympathetic nervous system, the amygdala, the thalamus, the cortex, and the hypothalamus are outlined. Facial expressions for many basic emotions seem to be universal and innate, but expression of emotion is also influenced by cultural display rules.

The major theories of emotion—the James–Lange theory, the Cannon–Bard theory, the facial feedback hypothesis, Schachter and Singer's two-factor theory, and Richard Lazarus's cognitive-mediational theory—are examined. Emotion researchers today tend to agree that emotions can be triggered in multiple ways and that instinctive emotional responses may not require a conscious cognitive appraisal.

The Application discusses Albert Bandura's concept of self-efficacy and describes ways of improving the way we view our abilities.

Introduction: Motivation and Emotion

Preview Questions

Consider the following questions as you study this section of the chapter.

- How is motivation defined?
- What three characteristics are associated with motivation?
- How is emotion related to motivation?

*Read the section "Introduction: Motivation and Emotion" and **write** your answers to the following:*

1. Motivation refers to _____
   _____

2. The three characteristics associated with motivation are _____
   _____
   _____

3. Emotions are closely tied to motivational processes (and vice versa) because both topics involve _____
   _____
   _____

Motivational Concepts and Theories

Preview Questions

- What five theories have historically been included in the study of motivation?
- How does each theory explain motivation, and what are some of the limitations of these theories?
- What lasting ideas did each theory contribute to the study of motivation?

*Read the section "Motivational Concepts and Theories" and **write** your answers to the following:*

1. According to the earliest theories of motivation, instinct theories, people are motivated to
   _____
   _____

   The limitation of these theories is _____
   _____
   _____

2. According to drive theories, behavior is motivated by _____
   _____
   _____

Their limitations are _____
_____
_____

3. Incentive theories proposed that behavior is motivated by _____
_____

Their limitation is _____
_____

4. Arousal theory is based on the notion that people are motivated _____
_____

The limitation of this theory is that _____
_____
_____
_____

5. Humanistic theories emphasize the importance of _____
_____
_____

(Limitations of this model are covered later in the chapter.)

6. The key ideas and concepts from each theory that were incorporated into newer models include _____
_____
_____

_____

After you have carefully studied the preceding section, complete the following exercises.

Concept Check 1

Read the following and write the correct term in the space provided.

1. Amber is a graduate student studying the biological, emotional, cognitive, and social forces that activate and direct behavior. Her area of research is _____ .

2. When Trevor is hungry, he eats. The consumption of food serves to maintain

_____ .

3. Gurjinder loves bungee jumping, skydiving, and hang-gliding. Because of her need for novel and exciting sensory stimulation she is likely to be dubbed a _____ .

4. Mrs. Lewis gives a gold star to any child in her class who gets 100 percent on the weekly spelling test. This example illustrates _____ theory.

5. Bruno the bear hibernates every winter. This behavior is an example of a(n)

_____ .

6. When Bernice finished her first 10-mile race in less than 90 minutes, she felt totally exhilarated and overjoyed by having achieved her goal. Her intense feelings suggest that _____ are closely tied to motivation.

Review of Terms and Concepts 1

Use the terms in this list to complete the Matching Test, then to help you answer the True/False items correctly.

motivation	drive theories
emotion	homeostasis
activation	drive
persistence	incentive theories
intensity	arousal theory
instinct theories	sensation seeking
fixed action patterns	humanistic theories of
evolutionary perspective	motivation

Matching Exercise

Match the appropriate term/name with its definition or description.

1. _____ Theories that emphasize the importance of psychological and cognitive factors in motivation, especially the notion that people are motivated to realize their personal potential.

2. _____ The biological, emotional, cognitive, or social forces that activate and direct behavior.

3. _____ Basic characteristic commonly associated with motivation that is seen in a person's continued efforts or determination to achieve a particular goal, often in the face of obstacles.

4. _____ Automatic and innate instinctual behavior patterns, such as migration or mating rituals, displayed by animals.

5. _____ Need or internal motivational state that activates behavior to reduce the need and restore homeostasis.

6. _____ Theories that view certain human behaviors as innate and due to evolutionary programming.

7. _____ Degree to which an individual is motivated to experience high levels of sensory and physical arousal associated with varied and novel activities.

8. _____ Point of view that considers how our evolutionary heritage influences human behaviors such as eating habits or the expression of emotions.

True/False Test

Indicate whether each statement is true or false by placing T or F in the blank space next to each item.

1. ____ Incentive theories propose that behavior is motivated by the pull of external goals, such as rewards.

2. ____ Arousal theory is the view that people are motivated to maintain an optimal level of arousal that is neither too high nor too low.

3. ____ Activation, one of the basic characteristics commonly associated with motivation, is seen in the greater vigor of responding that usually accompanies motivated behavior.

4. ____ Drive theories propose that behavior is motivated by the desire to reduce internal tension caused by unmet biological needs.

5. ____ Homeostasis refers to the notion that the body monitors and maintains internal states, such as body temperature and energy supplies, at relatively constant levels; in general, the tendency to reach or maintain equilibrium.

6. ____ Intensity, one of the basic characteristics commonly associated with motivation, is seen in the initiation or production of behavior.

7. ____ Emotion is a complex psychological state that involves subjective experience, a physiological response, and a behavioral or expressive response.

Check your answers and review any areas of weakness before going on to the next section.

Biological Motivation: Hunger and Eating

Preview Questions

Consider the following questions as you study this section of the chapter.

- What factors interact and influence the motivation to eat?

- What is energy homeostasis and how does it relate to energy balance?

- What are glucose, insulin, the basal metabolic rate, and adipose tissue, and what role do they play in energy homeostasis?

- What are the short-term signals that regulate eating behavior and what roles do satiation, cholecystokinin (CCK), and sensory-specific satiety play?

- What are the long-term chemical signals that regulate body weight and what influences do leptin, insulin, neuropeptide Y (NPY), and corticotropin-releasing hormone (CRH) have in the long-term regulation of stable body weight?

- What are set-point and settling point theories, and how do they differ?

*Read the section "Biological Motivation: Hunger and Eating" and **write** your answers to the following:*

1. Eating behavior reflects the complex interaction of _____

   _____

2. Energy homeostasis refers to _____

   _____

3. Energy balance or homeostasis involves
   (a) glucose (blood sugar), which is a _____

   _____

   _____

   (b) insulin, which is a _____

   _____

   _____

(c) basal metabolic rate (BMR) which is

_____

_____

(d) adipose tissue, which is _____

_____

4. A positive energy balance occurs when

_____

_____

A negative energy balance occurs when

_____

_____

5. In terms of physiological changes, about 30
minutes before eating there is _____

_____

Once a meal has begun _____

_____

_____

6. Psychological factors that trigger eating
behavior involve
(a) classical conditioning, in which _____

_____

_____

(b) operant conditioning, in which _____

_____

_____

7. Satiation refers to   _____

_____

Satiation involves signals from
(a) _____ on the tongue, roof
of the mouth, and throat,
(b) _____ in the stomach, and
(c) _____ , a hormone/
neurotransmitter that promotes satiety effects.

8. Sensory-specific satiety refers to _____

_____

_____

9. Four long-term chemical signals that regulate
body weight are
(a) leptin, a hormone produced by_____

_____

_____

(b) insulin, which _____

_____

_____

(c) neuropeptide Y (NPY), a neurotransmitter
manufactured_____

_____

_____

(d) corticotropin-releasing hormone (CRH), a
hormone manufactured _____

_____

_____

10. According to set-point theory _____

_____

_____

_____

According to settling-point models of weight
regulation _____

_____

_____

_____

*After you have carefully studied the preceding
section, complete the following exercises.*

Concept Check 2
*Read the following and write the correct term in the
space provided.*

1. Although Farah was resting on the couch, her
body was still using energy to maintain vital
body functions, a process called

_____ .

2. By the end of her family's holiday dinner
Federicca declared that she was so full she
couldn't eat another bite. Federicca is experiencing _____ , a feeling that is
promoted, in part at least, by the chemical

_____ .

3. Although she was feeling full after her turkey dinner, Federicca was still able to eat a plate of her favorite dessert. It appears that her feeling of being full after eating the main course was a _____ satiety.

4. Although he leads a somewhat sedentary lifestyle, 35-year-old Joshua has been about the same weight, give or take a pound or two, since his late teens. Joshua's relatively consistent weight is called his _____ , and instances of stable weight over time, such as Joshua's, provide support for _____ theory.

5. The regulatory process of matching food intake with energy expenditure that allows Joshua to maintain his typical body weight over time is called _____ .

6. If Dr. Hamagoochi studies the long-term signals that regulate body weight, he is most likely to investigate the effects of the four chemical messengers _____ _____ .

7. When Maurice went on a diet, he experienced a negative energy balance and the desired weight loss. However, his decreased levels of leptin and insulin are likely to promote the secretion of _____ and decrease the activity of _____ , which may result in a greater desire to eat and a greater risk of weight gain.

8. Benjamin, a lively sixty-year-old, noted that as he aged his weight tended to increase somewhat, then stabilize, increase again, and stabilize once again, and so on. Now he is thirty pounds heavier than when he was a young adult. This phenomenon can best be accounted for by _____ theory.

Review of Terms and Concepts 2

Use the terms in this list to complete the Matching Test, then to help you answer the True/False items correctly.

glucose (blood sugar)
glycogen
insulin
basal (or resting)
   metabolic rate (BMR)
adipose tissue
baseline body weight
energy homeostasis
   (energy balance)
positive energy balance
negative energy balance
positive incentive value
satiation

stretch receptors
cholecystokinin (CCK)
sensory-specific satiety
leptin
neuropeptide Y (NPY)
corticotropin-releasing
   hormone (CRH)
set-point theory
set-point weight
settling point models of
   weight regulation
settling point weight

Matching Exercise

Match the appropriate term with its definition or description.

1. _____ An organism's typical body weight.

2. _____ When at rest, the rate at which the body uses energy for vital bodily functions.

3. _____ Compound formed and stored in the liver and the muscles that can easily be re-converted into glucose for energy.

4. _____ Neurotransmitter found in several brain areas, most notably the hypothalamus, that stimulates eating behavior and reduces metabolism, promoting positive energy balance and weight gain.

5. _____ Body fat that is the main source of stored or reserve energy.

6. _____ Hormone produced by the pancreas that regulates blood levels of glucose and signals the hypothalamus, regulating hunger and eating behavior.

7. _____ According to set-point theory, the natural or optimal body weight that the body defends from becoming higher or lower.

8. _____ In the stomach, specialized sensory receptors that detect the degree of distention of the stomach as food is consumed and that communicate sensory information to the brainstem.

9. _____ In eating behavior, the long-term matching of caloric intake and caloric energy expenditure.

10. _____ According to settling-point models of weight regulation, the body weight that will remain stable as long as the factors influencing food consumption and energy expenditure remain constant.

11. _____ Reduced desire to continue consuming a particular food.

True/False Test

Indicate whether each statement is true or false by placing T or F in the blank space next to each item.

1. ____ Set-point theory suggests that body weight settles, or stabilizes, around the point at which there is a balance between the factors influencing energy intake and energy expenditure.

2. ____ Glucose is the simple sugar that provides energy and is primarily produced by conversion of carbohydrates and fats.

3. ____ In eating behavior, a negative energy balance occurs when caloric intake exceeds calories expended for energy; produced by overeating or overconsumption.

4. ____ In eating behavior, satiation is the feeling of fullness and diminished desire to eat that accompanies eating a meal, and in general, refers to fully or excessively satisfying an appetite or desire.

5. ____ Leptin is a hormone produced by fat cells that signal the hypothalamus, regulating hunger and eating behavior.

6. ____ Cholecystokinin (CCK) is a chemical that is secreted primarily by the small intestines that promotes satiation; also found in the brain.

7. ____ Settling-point models of weight regulation propose that humans and other animals have a natural or optimal body weight that the body defends from becoming higher or lower by regulating feelings of hunger and metabolism.

8. ____ In eating behavior, positive incentive value is the anticipated pleasure of consuming a particular food and in general, the expectation of pleasure or satisfaction in performing a particular task.

9. ____ In eating behavior, a positive energy balance occurs when calories expended for energy exceed caloric intake; produced by fasting, dieting, or starvation.

10. ____ Corticotropin-releasing hormone (CRH) is a hormone manufactured primarily by the hypothalamus that reduces eating behavior and increases metabolism, promoting negative energy balance and weight loss.

Check your answers and review any areas of weakness before going on to the next section.

Excess Weight and Obesity: The Epidemic

Preview Questions

Consider the following questions as you study this section of the chapter.

- What is the body mass index (BMI), and what is the difference between being obese and being overweight?

- What seven factors contribute to people becoming overweight?

- How do genetics and environment interact in people who are susceptible to obesity?

- What factors are involved in obesity, and what are the problems associated with dieting?

Read the section "Excess Weight and Obesity: The Epidemic" and **write** *your answers to the following:*

1. The body mass index (BMI) is a _____

_____

_____

2. Obesity is a condition characterized by

_____

_____

_____

In contrast, someone who is overweight has

_____

_____

_____

3. A number of factors are involved in creating a positive energy balance (when caloric intake consistently exceeds energy expenditure) and in becoming overweight:

(a) the positive incentive value of certain foods, defined as_____

_____

(b) the "SuperSize It" syndrome, a relatively recent phenomenon in which _____

_____

(c) the cafeteria diet effect, which is_____

_____

(d) snacks and appetizers between meals (pre-loading calories) are also a problem because, contrary to popular belief, _____

_____

_____

(e) individual differences and lifespan changes are involved because _____

_____

_____

(f) and finally, the sedentary lifestyle of many people (40 percent of Americans) who never

_____

_____

4. Several factors contribute to obesity:

(a) Nature and nurture interact; although susceptibility to obesity is influenced by

_____

_____

_____

(b) Leptin resistance refers to _____

_____

_____

(c) Many overweight or obese dieters experience weight cycling (yo-yo dieting), which refers to

_____

_____

(d) Obese people's brains tend to have fewer

_____

_____

which may lead to _____

_____

Eating Disorders: Anorexia and Bulimia

Preview Questions

Consider the following questions as you study this section of the chapter.

- How are eating disorders defined and what gender differences exist in susceptibility to them?
- What behaviors and symptoms are associated with anorexia nervosa, bulimia nervosa, and binge-eating disorder?
- What factors have been implicated in the development of each eating disorder?

*Read the section "Eating Disorders: Anorexia and Bulimia" and **write** your answers to the following:*

1. Eating disorders involve _____

_____

_____

Although the central features of eating disorders are similar for males and females, approximately _____ to _____ percent of people who experience them are female.

2. Anorexia nervosa is an eating disorder characterized by_____

_____

_____

The two subtypes are _____

_____

and _____

_____

3. Bulimia nervosa is an eating disorder characterized by_____

_____

_____

4. Binge-eating disorder is an eating disorder characterized by_____

_____

_____

5. The type of characteristics associated with anorexia include_____

_____

People with bulimia share many of the characteristics of anorexia (binge–purge subtype), with the main differences being that _____

_____

_____

_____

6. The main factors implicated in the development of eating disorders are _____   _____

_____

_____

After you have carefully studied the preceding section, complete the following exercises.

Concept Check 3

Read the following and write the correct term in the space provided.

1. Feeling a little hungry in the late afternoon, Shasta had a small snack. Eating this snack two hours before her regular dinner time is likely to _____ .

2. Mikka multiplied her weight in pounds by 704.5 and divided the product by her height in inches squared. She has just calculated her _____ and if the resulting number was 30.0, or greater, she would be considered _____ .

3. During his afternoon statistics lecture Dimitri's mind wandered as he contemplated the pleasure of having souvlaki, salad, olives, feta cheese, tzatsiki, and pita bread for dinner. These foods obviously have a high _____ for Dimitri.

4. Mobina consumes about the same number of calories as her husband, keeps physically active at about the same level, and so on, yet she has gained more weight over time than he has. The reason for their weight differences is that

_____ .

5. Alice is a chronic dieter and has experienced weight cycling (yo-yo dieting) throughout most of the time she has been attempting to lose weight. Her inability to maintain weight loss may be due in part to _____

_____ .

6. Trina often feels that she cannot control her need to eat and goes on bouts of overeating a couple of times a week; although embarrassed by her behavior and the fact that she is overweight, she does not compensate for it by engaging in self-induced vomiting, misuse of laxatives, or fasting. Trina would probably be classified as having _____ disorder.

7. Whenever Saul and his friends eat at the International Self-Serve Smorgasbord Deli, where there is a great variety of wonderful foods, they tend to consume substantially more food than they would at the school cafeteria. This phenomenon is called the

_____ .

8. Although Claire is of average height and weighs only 85 pounds, she has an irrational fear of gaining weight and has a distorted body-self perception. She has lost 30 pounds over the past eight or nine months by eating very little and going to aerobics classes twice a day. Claire probably suffers from _____ .

Review of Terms and Concepts 3

Use the terms in this list to complete the Matching Test, then to help you answer the True/False items correctly.

body mass index (BMI)
obese
cafeteria diet effect
leptin resistance
weight cycling
 (yo-yo dieting)
eating disorders
anorexia nervosa

anorexia—restricting
 subtype
anorexia—binge–purge
 subtype
lanugo
bulimia nervosa
binge-eating disorder

Matching Exercise

Match the appropriate term/name with its definition or description.

1. _____ A numerical scale indicating adult height in relation to weight that is calculated by multiplying weight in pounds by 704.5 and dividing the product by height in inches squared.

2. _____ A category of mental disorders characterized by severe disturbances in eating behavior.

3. _____ A condition in which higher than normal blood levels of the hormone leptin does not produce the expected physiological response.

4. _____ Repeated cycles of dieting, weight loss, and weight regain.

5. _____ A subtype of anorexia nervosa that involves episodes of binge eating, followed by purging the food through self-induced vomiting or misusing laxatives to induce diarrhea and flush the food from the system.

6. _____ An eating disorder characterized by recurring episodes of binge eating that are not followed by purging.

True/False Test

Indicate whether each statement is true or false by placing T or F in the blank space next to each item.

1. ____ Obesity is a condition characterized by excessive body fat and a body mass index (BMI) equal to or greater than 30.0.

2. ____ Lanugo is the soft, downy, fine hair that normally occurs during the later stages of human fetal development but can also develop in severe cases of anorexia nervosa or starvation.

3. ____ Anorexia nervosa is an eating disorder characterized by binges of extreme overeating followed by self-induced vomiting, misuse of laxatives, or other inappropriate methods to purge the excessive food and prevent weight gain.

4. ____ The tendency to eat more when a wide variety of palatable foods is available is called the cafeteria diet effect.

5. ____ The restricting subtype of anorexia nervosa involves severe food restriction, maladaptive dieting, excessive fluid intake, fasting, overactivity, and compulsive exercising to burn off calories.

6. ____ Bulimia nervosa is an eating disorder characterized by excessive weight loss, an irrational fear of gaining weight, and distorted body self-perception.

Check your answers and review any areas of weakness before going on to the next section.

Psychological Needs as Motivators

Preview Questions

Consider the following questions as you study this section of the chapter.

- What are the key questions associated with theories that emphasize the motivation to satisfy fundamental psychological needs?

- How does Maslow's hierarchy of needs explain human motivation?

- What are some of the important criticisms of Maslow's theory?

- Who is primarily associated with self-determination theory and what are its basic premises?

- What roles do intrinsic and extrinsic motivation play in human behavior?

*Read the section "Psychological Needs as Motivators" and **write** your answers to the following:*

1. Some of the key questions associated with motivational theories that emphasize fundamental psychological needs are

   (a) _____

   (b) _____

   _____

   (c) _____

   _____

2. Maslow's hierarchy of needs divides motivation into _____

   _____

   _____

   _____

Maslow believed that people_____

_____

_____

_____

3. Criticisms of Maslow's model of motivation are that

(a) the concept of self-actualization is _____

_____

_____

(b) Maslow's initial studies on self-actualization

_____

_____

(c) Despite the claim that self-actualization is an innate motivational goal of all people,

_____

_____

(d) Maslow's notion that we must satisfy needs at one level before moving to the next level

_____

_____

4. Self-determination theory is associated with psychologists _____

_____, who contend that in order to realize optimal psychological functioning three innate and universal psychological needs must be met:

(a) autonomy, which is _____

_____

(b) competence, which is _____

_____

(c) relatedness, which is _____

_____

_____

5. Intrinsic motivation refers to _____

_____

_____

Extrinsic motivation refers to _____

_____

_____

Competence and Achievement Motivation

Preview Questions

Consider the following questions as you study this section of the chapter.

*   How does competence motivation differ from achievement motivation, and how is achievement motivation measured?
*   What characteristics are associated with a high level of achievement motivation, and how does culture affect achievement motivation?

Read the section "Competence and Achievement Motivation" and **write** *your answers to the following:*

1. Competence motivation is displayed when

_____

_____

2. Achievement motivation refers to _____

_____

_____

3. People who score high in achievement motivation tend to _____

_____

_____

_____

_____

4. In individualistic cultures, the need to achieve emphasizes _____

_____

_____

whereas in collectivistic cultures _____

_____

_____

_____

After you have carefully studied the preceding sections, complete the following exercises.

Concept Check 4

Read the following and write the correct term in the space provided.

1. Young Alec practices at the golf range for one or two hours most days because he plans to become a professional golfer. His goal and behavior suggest that Alec has a high level of _____ motivation.

2. Yen Shih and her fellow students believe that it is unacceptable to express pride for personal achievements, but it is acceptable to feel pride in achievements that benefit others. Yen Shih most likely lives in a _____ culture.

3. Young Mindy loves painting and spends many enjoyable hours carefully drawing and coloring flowers, butterflies, and birds. Her focused behavior is most likely a result of _____ motivation.

4. Allison wants to prove to herself that she is capable of mastering basic mathematical con-

cepts, so she enrolls in an algebra course and an introductory statistics course. Allison is demonstrating _____ motivation.

5. Dr. Rosenbaum believes that people are actively growth-oriented and that to realize optimal psychological functioning and growth, three innate and universal psychological needs must be satisfied. Dr. Rosenbaum's views are most consistent with _____ theory.

6. Sarah studies and rehearses her spelling list because those children who get 100 percent on the weekly test receive a gold star and have their name and prize posted on the bulletin board. Sarah's studying behavior appears to be a function of _____ motivation.

7. In her counseling practice, Dr. Harrar is often interested in her clients' achievement motivation; to measure their need for achievement (nAch) she is likely to use _____ .

Graphic Organizer 1

Identify the theory associated with each of the following statements:

Statement	Theory
1. I support the view that behavior is motivated by the desire to reduce internal tension caused by unmet biological needs that push us to behave in certain ways.	
2. I believe in the importance of psychological and cognitive factors in motivation, and especially the notion that people are motivated to realize their personal potential.	
3. I take my lead from Charles Darwin and support the perspective that we are motivated to engage in certain behaviors because of evolutionary programming.	
4. We are of the opinion that people are actively growth-oriented and that optimal human functioning can occur only if the psychological needs of autonomy, competence, and relatedness are satisfied.	
5. We do what we do because of the pull of external goals, such as obtaining rewards, money, or recognition. I believe that learning and cognitive theorists have it right when they say reinforcement, and the expectation of reinforcement, are key factors in motivation.	
6. In my view, people are motivated to maintain an optimal level of arousal that is neither too high nor too low. When arousal is too low, we experience boredom and try to increase arousal by seeking out stimulating experiences; when it is too high, we seek to reduce arousal in less stimulating environments.	

Review of Terms, Concepts, and Names 4

Use the terms in this list to complete the Matching Test, then to help you answer the True/False items correctly.

Abraham Maslow
hierarchy of needs
self-actualization
Edward L. Deci
Richard M. Ryan
self-determination
  theory (SDT)
autonomy
competence

relatedness
intrinsic motivation
extrinsic motivation
internalize
competence motivation
achievement motivation
Thematic Apperception
  Test (TAT)
power motivation

Matching Exercise

Match the appropriate term with its definition or description:

1. _____ The theory that optimal functioning can occur only if the psychological needs for autonomy, competence, and relatedness are satisfied.

2. _____ Maslow's hierarchical division of motivation into levels that progress from basic physical needs to psychological needs to self-fulfillment needs.

3. _____ To adopt or accept the beliefs, values, standards, attitudes, or practices of others as one's own.

4. _____ A projective test developed by Henry Murray and his colleagues that involves creating stories about vague scenes that can be interpreted in a variety of ways.

5. _____ Behavior motivated by the desire to attain power or control or influence the behavior of other people or groups.

6. _____ American psychologist who founded humanistic psychology and developed a hierarchical model of human motivation in which basic needs must first be satisfied before people can strive for self-actualization.

7. _____ In self-determination theory (SDT) the need to effectively learn and master appropriately challenging tasks.

8. _____ In self-determination theory (SDT), the need to determine, control, and organize one's own behavior and goals so that they are in harmony with one's own interests and values.

True/False Test

Indicate whether each statement is true or false by placing T or F in the blank space next to each item.

1. ____ Richard M. Ryan and Edward L. Deci developed self-determination theory, which contends that optimal psychological functioning and growth can occur only if the psychological needs of autonomy, competence, and relatedness are satisfied.

2. ____ Extrinsic motivation refers to behavior motivated by the desire to engage in tasks that the person finds inherently satisfying and enjoyable, novel, or optimally challenging.

3. ____ Self-actualization was defined by Maslow as "the full use and exploitation of talents, capacities, and potentialities."

4. ____ In self-determination theory (SDT), the need to feel attached to others and experience a sense of belongingness, security, and intimacy is called relatedness.

5. ____ Motivated behavior directed toward demonstrating competence and exercising control in a situation is called achievement motivation.

6. ____ Intrinsic motivation refers to behavior motivated by external factors or influences, such as rewards, consequences, or social expectations.

7. ____ Motivated behavior directed toward excelling, succeeding, or outperforming others at some task is called competence motivation.

Check your answers and review any areas of weakness before going on to the next section.

Emotion

Preview Questions

Consider the following questions as you study this section of the chapter.

- How is emotion defined, and what are the three components of emotion?

- How do emotions and moods differ, what functions do emotions serve, and what is emotional intelligence?

- How do evolutionary psychologists view emotions?
- What are the basic emotions, and how are they classified?
- How do culture and individual differences influence emotional experience?

*Read the section "Emotion" and **write** your answers to the following:*

1. Emotion is defined as _____
   _____
   _____

2. Emotions tend to be _____
   _____
   _____

   Moods involve _____
   _____

3. Emotions have many functions, including triggering _____
   _____
   _____
   _____

4. Emotional intelligence is the capacity to
   _____
   _____
   _____

5. According to evolutionary psychologists, emotions are the _____
   _____
   _____
   _____

6. The most common basic emotions that all humans, in every culture, experience are
   _____
   _____

7. Cross-cultural research has shown that
   _____
   _____
   _____

8. Cross-cultural researchers have noted that Japanese subjects also categorized emotions along a dimension of _____
   _____

   which reflects _____
   _____
   _____

The Neuroscience of Emotion

Preview Questions

Consider the following questions as you study this section of the chapter.

- How is the sympathetic nervous system involved in intense emotional responses?
- What brain structures are involved in emotional experience, and what neural pathways make up the brain's fear circuit?
- How does the evolutionary perspective explain the dual brain pathways for transmitting fear-related information?
- How do each of the two neural pathways work and what adaptive function do they play?

*Read the section "The Neuroscience of Emotion" and **write** your answers to the following:*

1. The physiological component of emotions such as fear and anger involves the _____
   _____
   _____
   _____

2. The amygdala is part of the limbic system and is an _____
   _____
   _____

3. From an evolutionary perspective, evidence of a direct thalamus-amygdala pathway makes adaptive sense because the amygdala can be activated by _____
   _____
   _____

When the amygdala is activated, it sends information to _____

_____

4. The second (indirect) pathway, thalamus-cortex-amygdala, allows more complex stimuli to be

_____

_____

_____

5. Comparative brain-imaging studies of the basic emotions indicate that each emotion involves

_____

_____

_____

The Expression of Emotions

Preview Questions

Consider the following questions as you study this section of the chapter.

- What evidence supports the notion that facial expressions for basic emotions are universal?
- How does culture affect the behavioral expression of emotion?
- How can emotional expression be explained in terms of evolutionary theory?

Read the section "The Expression of Emotions" and **write** *your answers to the following:*

1. Research on facial expressions (and emotions expressed vocally) suggests that _____

_____

_____

2. Display rules are social and cultural rules that

_____

_____

3. Display rules can vary greatly from culture to culture (and even for different groups within a given culture, such as males and females); consequently, _____

_____

_____

4. From an evolutionary perspective, the expression of emotions serves the _____

_____

_____

_____

_____

Concept Check 5

Read the following and write the correct term in the space provided.

1. Since the end of the semester, Ellen had been feeling very content and relaxed. When she received her transcript in the mail and discovered that she had received an A+ in statistics, she was overwhelmed with excitement and relief. Ellen's two different states (contentment and excitement) illustrate the difference between _____ and

_____ .

2. Walking to the parking lot late at night, Camellia suddenly hears footsteps behind her. Her heartbeat and blood pressure increase, her muscles tense, her mouth goes dry, and she begins to perspire. These physiological reactions were activated by her _____ nervous system and are called the

_____ response.

3. Mr. Hashimoto is very careful to hide his true feelings and control his facial expressions when in the presence of his company's chief executive officers. This example illustrates the _____ of his culture.

4. Pat and Terry both experience emotions in much the same way, but Pat tends to be inhibited in the expression of emotions, whereas Terry is typically emotionally expressive. Considering research presented in the text, you would be justified in assuming that Pat is _____ (male/female) and that Terry is _____ (male/female).

5. Although Kasper is known for his superior reasoning skills, he appears to lack the ability to manage his own emotions and does not seem to understand or respond appropriately to the emotions of others. It is probable that Kasper is low in _____ .

6. When Pavel got his lay-off notice after five years with the company, he simultaneously experienced a number of emotions—anger, sadness, anxiety, and even relief and a degree of excitement about what the future would hold for him. Pavel has experienced _____ emotions.

7. Opening what he thought was simply a can of peanuts, generously given to him by his older sister, young Kyle was totally startled and alarmed by the "jack-in-the-box" snake that flew out of the can. His instantaneous startle response was most likely the result of stimulation of the _____ neural pathway in his brain.

8. When Keiho first arrived in North America from Japan, she was surprised to find that people vigorously nodded their heads in answer to a question to indicate the affirmative "yes" instead of "maybe" or "no way." Nodding the head is a specific gesture, called _____ , that can have a different meaning in different cultures.

Graphic Organizer 2

Identify the emotion (relaxation, alarm, annoyance, boredom, astonishment) associated with each of the following descriptions and indicate where it should go on the matrix below.

1. Natasha receives an A+ in her third-year history course and can hardly believe it.

   _____

2. In the middle of the night, Harry, who lives alone, is startled out of a deep sleep by strange noises coming from the basement.

   _____

3. During his three o'clock calculus class Nathan finds the topic totally uninteresting and starts losing his concentration. _____

4. On Saturday Dawn sleeps in and spends most of the morning propped up on comfortable pillows reading a romantic novel.

   _____

5. Five minutes after the meter has expired Dhillon arrives at his car only to find he has been given a $20 ticket. _____

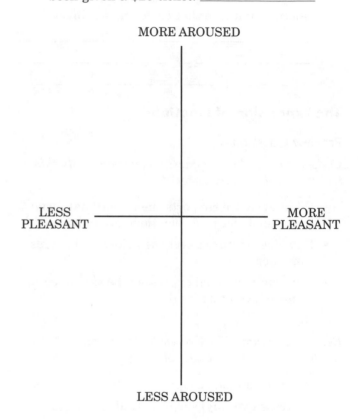

Review of Terms, Concepts, and Names 5

Use the terms in this list to complete the Matching Test, then to help you answer the True/False items correctly.

mood
emotional intelligence
Charles Darwin
basic emotions
mixed emotions
interpersonal
  engagement
fight-or-flight response
amygdala

Paul Eckman
emblem
display rules
polygraph
microexpressions
brain fingerprinting
P300 wave
galvanic skin response

Matching Exercise

Match the appropriate term / name with its definition or description:

1. _____ English naturalist and scientist whose theory of evolution through natural selection was first published in *On the Origin of the Species by Natural Selection* in 1859.

2. _____ The most fundamental set of emotion categories, which are biologically innate, evolutionarily determined, and culturally universal.

3. _____ Fleeting facial expressions, lasting no more than about 1/25 of a second, that "leak" through when people try to control their facial expressions or disguise their true emotions.

4. _____ The capacity to understand and manage your own emotional experiences and to perceive, comprehend, and respond appropriately to the emotional responses of others.

5. _____ The almond-shaped cluster of neurons in the brain's temporal lobe, involved in memory and emotional responses, especially fear.

6. _____ Emotion dimension reflecting the degree to which emotions involve a relationship with another person or people.

7. _____ American psychologist and emotion researcher who is best known for his work in classifying basic emotions, analyzing facial expressions, and demonstrating that basic emotions and facial expressions are culturally universal.

8. _____ Device that measures several indexes of physiological arousal, including heart rate, blood pressure, respiration, and galvanic skin response, and is also known as a lie detector.

True/False Test

Indicate whether each item is true or false by placing T or F in the space next to each item.

1. ___ The fight-or-flight response is a rapidly occurring series of automatic physical reactions, including accelerated breathing and heart rate, a surge in blood pressure, increased perspiration, dilation of the pupils, and dryness of the mouth.

2. ___ Display rules are specific gestures or other nonverbal behaviors that have a particular meaning in a given culture.

3. ___ The P300 wave involves a decrease in the skin's capacity to conduct electricity which is associated with perspiration and increased blood flow and is used as an indicator of physiological arousal.

4. ___ Emblems are social and cultural rules that regulate the expression of emotions, especially facial expressions.

5. ___ In more complex situations we may experience mixed emotions, in which very different emotions are experienced simultaneously or in rapid succession.

6. ___ In comparison to an emotion, a mood involves a milder emotional state that is more general and pervasive and may last for a few hours or even days.

7. ___ The galvanic skin response is a type of brain wave emitted when a person is presented with a stimulus that is in some way distinctive or unexpected.

8. ___ Brain fingerprinting is a technique used to detect lies or deception, which involves the analysis of brain waves by an electroencephalograph, and determines whether a stimulus is familiar (i.e., recognized because it is stored in the suspect's memory) or unfamiliar.

Check your answers and review any areas of weakness before going on to the next section.

Theories of Emotion: Explaining Emotion

Preview Questions

Consider the following questions as you study this section of the chapter.

- What are the basic principles and key criticisms of the James–Lange theory of emotion.
- What challenges did Cannon present to the James–Lange theory?
- What is the facial feedback hypothesis, and how do it and other contemporary research support aspects of the James–Lange theory?
- How does the two-factor theory account for emotions, what is the cognitive-mediational theory of emotion, and how do the two theories of emotion differ?

Read the section "Theories of Emotion: Explaining Emotion" and write your answers to the following:

1. The James–Lange theory of emotions states that _____

   _____

   _____

2. Walter Cannon criticized the James–Lange theory on a number of grounds:

   (a) Bodily reactions are _____

   _____

   _____

   (b) Our emotional reaction to a stimulus is

   _____

   _____

   (c) When physiological changes are artificially induced, _____

   _____

   (d) People cut off from feeling bodily changes

   _____

   _____

3. Support for some aspects of the James–Lange theory come from

   (a) Damasio's work, which demonstrated that

   _____

   _____

   _____

   _____

   (b) the facial feedback hypothesis, which states that _____

   _____

   _____

4. Schachter and Singer's two-factor theory of emotion suggests that _____

   _____

   _____

5. Richard Lazarus's cognitive-mediational theory proposes that _____

   _____

   _____

6. Although both two-factor theory and the cognitive-mediational theory emphasize the importance of cognitive appraisal, two-factor theory states _____

   _____

   _____

   while the cognitive-mediational model stresses that _____

   _____

   _____

   _____

After you have carefully studied the preceding sections, complete the following exercises.

Concept Check 6

Read the following and write the correct term in the space provided.

1. In an experiment testing the two-factor theory of emotion, Milbourne was injected with a hormone called _____ that activated his sympathetic nervous system, causing accelerated heartbeat, rapid breathing, trembling, and so on.

2. Dr. Rhienhard believes that the cognitive interpretation of an event or situation and the personal meaning of that appraisal for the individual determine both the emotion experienced and the intensity of that emotion. Dr. Rhienhard's view is most consistent with the _____ theory of emotion.

3. As the result of an accident that damaged her spinal cord, Gerri is paralyzed from the waist down. The fact that her experience of fear, anger, grief, sentimentality, and joyfulness has not been affected by her injury is _____ (consistent/not consistent) with the proposal made by William James.

4. Whenever she feels a bit gloomy, Danica sings the song "Pretend you're happy when you're blue"; if she follows the advice of the song, she actually experiences an elevation in her mood. This example is consistent with the

_____ .

5. When Harbinder first rode on the High Peak ski lift, he looked down at the steep slopes beneath him and became aware of his high level of physiological arousal. Suddenly, he felt fearful. Harbinder's experience is best explained by the _____ theory of emotion.

6. Cecelia decided to tackle the challenging task of becoming a proficient piano player. Although she knew that progress would likely be gradual and that there would be some setbacks along the way, she nevertheless felt that engaging in what Bandura called a _____ would help strengthen her sense of self-efficacy.

Review of Terms, Concepts, and Names 6

Use the terms in this list to complete the Matching Test, then to help you answer the True/False items correctly.

William James
James–Lange theory of
  emotion
Walter B. Cannon
epinephrine (adrenaline)
Cannon–Bard theory of
  emotions
facial feedback
  hypothesis

two-factor theory of
  emotion
cognitive-mediational
  theory of emotion
Richard Lazarus
anthropomorphism
self-efficacy

Matching Exercise

Match the appropriate term with its definition or description:

1. _____ View that expressing a specific emotion, especially facially, causes the subjective experience of that emotion.

2. _____ American psychologist who promoted the cognitive perspective in the study of emotion, and proposed the cognitive-mediational theory of emotion.

3. _____ The theory that emotions arise from the simultaneous activation of the sympathetic nervous system, which causes physical arousal, and the cortex, which causes the subjective experience of emotion.

4. _____ Schachter and Singer's theory that emotion is the interaction of physiological arousal and the cognitive label that we apply to explain the arousal.

5. _____ The attribution of human traits, motives, emotions, or behaviors to non-human animals or inanimate objects.

6. _____ Hormone secreted by the adrenal glands that is released into the bloodstream in response to physical or emotional stress or excitement.

True/False Test

Indicate whether each statement is true or false by placing T or F in the blank space next to each item.

1. ___ Walter B. Cannon was an American psychologist who developed an influential theory of emotion called the Cannon–Bard theory of emotion.

2. ___ The James–Lange theory suggests that emotions arise from the perception of bodily changes.

3. ___ The cognitive-mediational theory of emotion proposes that emotions result from the cognitive appraisal of a situation's effect on personal well-being.

4. ___ Self-efficacy refers to the degree to which a person is convinced of his or her ability to effectively meet the demands of a particular situation.

5. ___ William James was an American psychologist who developed an influential theory of emotion called the James–Lange theory of emotion.

Check your answers and review any areas of weakness before doing the progress tests.

Something to Think About

1. Many Americans are obsessed with achieving, or at least getting closer to, the socially desirable goal of thinness. Approximately one-third of all American women and one-fifth of all American males are trying to lose weight, and the weight-loss industry is a multibillion-dollar-a-year enterprise. Based on what you have read in your text, what advice would you give to a friend who is trying to lose weight?

2. Most people have heard about the polygraph, or lie detector, as it is commonly called. Reports in the media discuss the use of polygraph testing to screen employees for drug use, suitability for security work, and so on. There is an intense debate about the validity and reliability of test results obtained in police investigations, and whether they should be admissible as evidence in courts of law. In addition, people who claim to have been abducted by aliens have taken polygraph tests to prove that they are not lying. What would you say to someone who is confused by all these reports?

Check your answers and review any areas of weakness before doing the progress tests.

Progress Test 1

Review the complete chapter (including Concept Reviews and the boxed inserts), review all your study notes, and then test yourself on the following progress test. Check your answers. If you make a mistake, review your notes, review the relevant section of the study guide, and, if necessary, go back and read the appropriate part of your textbook.

1. It is an innate characteristic of the European cuckoo to lay her eggs in other birds' nests. This behavior is called _____ and is an example of _____ .
   - (a) a fixed action pattern; an instinct
   - (b) energy homeostasis; a drive
   - (c) a drive; incentive motivation
   - (d) anthropomorphism; competence motivation

2. Harland got up in the middle of the night to go to the bathroom and in the dark accidentally tripped over his sleeping dog. Both the dog and Harland were instantaneously startled and frightened; the dog barked and Harland screamed. In this instance it is very probable that the neural pathway involved in their immediate emotional reactions was the
   - (a) thalamus-cortex-amygdala pathway.
   - (b) hypothalamus-pituitary-cortex pathway.
   - (c) thalamus-amygdala pathway.
   - (d) amygdala-cortex-thalamus pathway.

3. About ten or fifteen minutes into his weightlifting routine Scott usually begins to perspire heavily. His body's tendency to maintain a steady temperature through the cooling action of sweating is a function of
   - (a) instinct.
   - (b) incentive motivation.
   - (c) energy homeostasis.
   - (d) self-actualization.

4. Dr. Range's views are consistent with self-determination theory (SDT). He believes that for people to realize optimal psychological functioning and growth throughout the lifespan, a number of innate and universal needs must be met, namely,
   - (a) autonomy, competence, and relatedness.
   - (b) competence, interpersonal engagement, and self-efficacy.
   - (c) self-actualization, mastery, and self-efficacy.
   - (d) relatedness, satiation, and homeostasis.

5. Morrie is a very successful stock market consultant. His success, in part at least, is due to his capacity to manage and understand his own emotional experiences, and his ability to correctly perceive, comprehend, and respond appropriately to the emotional reactions of his clients. Morrie has a high level of
   - (a) emotional intelligence.
   - (b) self-determination.
   - (c) interpersonal engagement.
   - (d) power motivation.

6. Tim buys a lottery ticket every Friday with the expectation that he is going to win some money. His behavior illustrates
   - (a) competence motivation.
   - (b) incentive motivation.
   - (c) drive theory.
   - (d) self-actualization.

7. Nicole feels that she has all the material possessions she needs in life and is now determined to devote all her energy to her art. According to Maslow's hierarchy of needs, Nicole is probably striving

   (a) to fulfill her fundamental biological need to paint.
   (b) to fulfill her basic safety needs.
   (c) toward the realization of her personal potential.
   (d) toward the realization of her social needs.

8. Fast-Fat-Fuds offer a double helping of fries with their Sooper Dooper Whooper Burger for only an extra fifteen cents, not surprisingly, many people buy the larger meal. This phenomenon is referred to as

   (a) the "SuperSize It" syndrome.
   (b) the cafeteria diet effect.
   (c) positive incentive value.
   (d) the "lanugo" syndrome.

9. Whenever he sees Amanda, Richard's heart beats faster and he gets a trembling feeling inside. Richard's personal interpretation of his physiological reaction to the sight of Amanda led him to experience the emotion of romantic love. Which theory of emotion is represented in this example?

   (a) self-determination theory (SDT)
   (b) Cannon–Bard theory
   (c) facial feedback theory
   (d) cognitive-mediational theory

10. Erin has been diagnosed with bulimia nervosa. The main symptoms of her eating disorder are

    (a) being 15 to 20 percent below the ideal body weight and having an irrational fear of gaining weight.
    (b) having a body mass index (BMI) in excess of 30.0 and engaging in frequent episodes of binge eating that are not followed by purging.
    (c) binges of extreme overeating and purging by self-induced vomiting and misuse of laxatives or other methods to purge the excessive food and prevent weight gain.
    (d) severe food restriction, maladaptive dieting, and the development of lanugo.

11. Zomobia is easily bored and constantly seeks new and stimulating situations; she loves the outdoors and includes among her many interests skydiving, downhill skiing, white water kayaking, and hang-gliding. Based on this information about her, it is most probable that Zomobia would be classified as

    (a) a sensation seeker.
    (b) fully self-actualized.
    (c) emotionally intelligent.
    (d) having high extrinsic motivation.

12. As part of his overall vocational assessment Bertram took the Thematic Apperception Test (TAT). His score on this test is most likely to reveal his level of

    (a) competence motivation.
    (b) need for achievement (nAch).
    (c) self-actualization.
    (d) emotional intelligence.

13. When Willard's relationship with Rebecca ended, he felt pretty confused and experienced a combination of relief, sadness, nostalgia, anger, and jealousy. Willard's experience illustrates

    (a) basic emotions.
    (b) mixed emotions.
    (c) mood fluctuations.
    (d) interpersonal engagement.

14. Some people claim that subliminal self-help tapes will quickly and easily produce changes in our motivation, learning ability, attitudes, and other behaviors. According to Science Versus Pseudoscience 8.2,

    (a) all these claims have been supported by empirical evidence.
    (b) subliminal self-help tapes are effective but only for highly suggestible people.
    (c) because university and college bookstores sell subliminal self-help tapes, they probably work for improving study habits and passing exams.
    (d) there is no scientific support for the claims made by promoters of subliminal self-help tapes.

15. Tracylynne usually starts the semester with the intention of studying hard, achieving high grades, eating a properly balanced diet, and getting lots of exercise. Unfortunately, these good intentions are rarely translated into actual behavior. According to the Application, which of the following strategies might help Tracylynne?
    (a) Transform general intentions into specific, concrete, measurable goals.
    (b) Create implementation intentions, such as specifying exactly where, when, and how the behaviors will be carried out.
    (c) Use mental rehearsal by visualizing successful outcomes.
    (d) Strengthen self-efficacy through mastery experiences and by observing and imitating the behavior of those already competent at these tasks.
    (e) All of the above would be useful.

Progress Test 2

After you have checked your understanding of the material in Progress Test 1 and reviewed the chapter with special focus on any areas of weakness, you are ready to assess your knowledge on Progress Test 2. Check your answers. If you make a mistake, review your notes, the relevant section of the study guide, and, if necessary, the appropriate part of your textbook.

1. Sidney firmly believes that women are more emotional than men. According to research presented in the text
    (a) women are more emotionally expressive than men are.
    (b) males and females do not differ in their experience of emotion.
    (c) men are more likely than women to mask their emotions.
    (d) all of the above are true.

2. Farina was curious about the physiological changes that correlate with eating behavior. A review of the relevant literature would likely reveal that
    (a) eating is triggered by a drastic drop in blood glucose levels and a drastic increase in blood levels of insulin.
    (b) about thirty minutes before eating there is a *slight* decrease in blood glucose levels and a *slight* increase in blood levels of insulin.

    (c) eating is triggered by a drastic increase in blood glucose levels and a drastic decrease in blood levels of insulin.
    (d) about thirty minutes before eating there is a *slight* increase in blood glucose levels and a *slight* decrease in blood levels of insulin.

3. If he's feeling sad or unhappy, Milton "puts on a happy face." When he does this, his mood often improves. This result is best predicted by the
    (a) cognitive-mediational theory.
    (b) two-factor theory.
    (c) self-determination theory.
    (d) facial feedback hypothesis.

4. After his fifth slice of pizza, Massimo felt quite full. His feeling of satiation was most likely triggered by
    (a) his taste buds, stretch receptors in his stomach, and cholecystokinin (CCK).
    (b) leptin, insulin, neuropeptide Y (NPY), and corticotropin-releasing hormone (CRH).
    (c) homeostasis, adipose, and insulin.
    (d) glycogen, leptin, lanugo, and insulin.

5. Professor DeVoir's area of research is concerned with the long-term signals that regulate body weight. The chemical messengers of most interest to the professor are likely to be
    (a) leptin, insulin, neuropeptide Y (NPY), and corticotropin-releasing hormone (CRH).
    (b) glucose, insulin, glycogen, and adipose.
    (c) CCK, BMR, BMI, and SDT.
    (d) CRH, lanugo, and CCK.

6. During a trip to Bulgaria, Connor was surprised when the smiling waiter brought him a cup of coffee after he had indicated, by shaking his head, that he did not want one. This slight confusion probably resulted from the failure to recognize that a specific gesture, such as shaking or nodding the head, can have a different meaning in different cultures. Connor would be wise to study the function of various _____ in the countries he plans to visit next.
    (a) interpersonal engagements
    (b) microexpressions
    (c) emblems
    (d) levels of anthropomorphism

7. Dr. Zascow conducts research on the facial feed-back hypothesis. Her results are consistent with previous research which showed that expressing a specific emotion, especially facially, causes people to subjectively experience that emotion. Collectively, this evidence provides support for the _____ theory of emotion.
   (a) Cannon–Bard
   (b) cognitive-mediational
   (c) two-factor
   (d) James–Lange

8. While writing a term paper for her motivation course, Oara notes that the majority of people do not experience or achieve self-actualization, despite the claim that it is a goal common to all people. She decides that this is an important limitation of
   (a) instinct theories.
   (b) drive theories.
   (c) incentive theories.
   (d) Maslow's hierarchy of needs.

9. Set-point theory provides the best explanation for which of the following?
   (a) Gladys finds that when she is alone and feeling bored her arousal level is uncomfortably low; in order to regain her normal or optimal level of arousal she seeks out a more stimulating environment.
   (b) At age sixty Edwina noted that her weight had fluctuated over the years and had progressively increased to the point where she is now about twenty-five pounds heavier than she was thirty-five years ago.
   (c) After eating a very filling and satisfying main meal, Ken manages to eat and enjoy a delicious slice of banana cream pie.
   (d) Although she leads a somewhat sedentary lifestyle, 40-year-old Andrea has been about the same weight, give or take a pound or two, since her late teens.

10. In an investigation of culture and emotional experience, researchers discovered that Japanese subjects categorize emotions not only along pleasantness and activation dimensions but also along a third dimension. This dimension, called _____ , reflects the idea that some emotions result from relationships and interactions with other people.
    (a) interpersonal engagement
    (b) the self-efficacy dimension
    (c) anthropomorphism
    (d) emotional intelligence

11. Nithya has had a body mass index (BMI) in excess of 30.0 for many years. If she is like most of the obese experimental subjects examined by neuroscientists (as described in the Focus on Neuroscience), a PET scan is likely to reveal _____ in her brain, compared to normal-weight control subjects.
    (a) higher levels of leptin and insulin
    (b) more dopamine receptors
    (c) lower levels of neuropeptide Y (NPY)
    (d) fewer dopamine receptors

12. About six months ago, fifteen-year-old Kirsten went on a drastic weight-loss diet that caused her to drop from 115 to 85 pounds. Although she is dangerously underweight and undernourished, she continues to think she looks fat. Kirsten probably suffers from
    (a) binge-eating disorder.
    (b) a very high metabolic rate.
    (c) bulimia nervosa.
    (d) anorexia nervosa.

13. Researchers using the electroencephalograph (EEG) were able to determine whether or not a stimulus was familiar to a subject by looking for a distinctive brain-wave response, called a P300 wave. According to In Focus 8.3, the researchers are using a technique referred to as
    (a) the Thematic Apperception Test (TAT).
    (b) the galvanic skin conductance test.
    (c) the body mass index test.
    (d) brain fingerprinting.

14. According to Critical Thinking 8.1, the tendency for people in industrialized countries to be overweight or obese is the result of
    (a) the high positive incentive value of many of our foods.
    (b) an evolutionary propensity to eat a wide variety of foods.
    (c) a tendency, that was adaptive in our ancestral past, to overeat when food is available.
    (d) all of the above.

15. Doyne typically approaches any difficult task as a challenge to be mastered, he exerts a strong motivational effort, persists in the face of obstacles, and looks for creative ways to solve the problem. According to the Application section, Doyne has a high level of
    (a) self-efficacy.
    (b) self-actualization.
    (c) power motivation.
    (d) interpersonal engagement.

Progress Test 3

After you have checked your understanding of the material in Progress Tests 1 and 2, and have done a complete chapter review with special focus on any areas of weakness, you are ready to further assess your knowledge on Progress Test 3. Check your answers. If you make a mistake, review your notes, the appropriate parts of the study guide, and, if necessary, the relevant sections of your textbook.

1. Safana experiences very intense positive emotions and is generally considered to be a very emotionally expressive person. It is likely that Safana
    (a) also tends to experience very intense negative emotions.
    (b) is very unpopular compared to people who are emotionally inhibited.
    (c) almost never experiences negative emotions.
    (d) is very low in both achievement and competence motivation.

2. Five-year-old Nemanja was excited and very curious about the various animals he saw when he was taken to the zoo for the first time. His exploratory behavior and curiosity were quickly inhibited, however, when he was suddenly startled and frightened by a loud roar from the lion's enclosure. According to the _____ theory of emotion, Nemanja's negative emotions were the result of cognitive appraisal of the meaning of the event or stimulus, whereas the _____ theory would say that they were the result of the perception of the physiological response to the event or stimulus.
    (a) Cannon–Bard; two-factor
    (b) James–Lange; Cannon–Bard
    (c) cognitive-mediational; James–Lange
    (d) two-factor; cognitive-mediational

3. The desire to drink when thirsty is to _____ as the desire to avoid boredom is to _____ .
    (a) sensory-specific satiety; sensation seeking
    (b) set-point theory; settling-point theory
    (c) drive theory; arousal theory
    (d) two-factor theory; cognitive-mediational theory

4. As Leopold aged he had to pay more attention to how much he ate in order to maintain his typical weight. One factor that may be involved in this tendency to gain weight as we age is that
    (a) the positive incentive value of food increases substantially over time.
    (b) leptin resistance increases with age.
    (c) as age increases the basal metabolic rate (BMR) decreases.
    (d) as age increases the basal metabolic rate (BMR) increases.

5. Dr. Fleming studies how food is converted into energy in the body. She is very likely to be interested in
    (a) glucose.
    (b) insulin.
    (c) basal metabolic rate (BMR).
    (d) all of the above.

6. Lazy Lou's food intake tends to exceed the amount of calories he expends on energy. On the other hand, Frenetic Frank's caloric intake is often less than the calories he expends on energy. It is likely that Lou has _____ and Frank has _____ .
    (a) a low set-point weight; a high set-point weight
    (b) a positive energy balance; a negative energy balance
    (c) a low settling-point weight; a high settling point weight
    (d) a negative energy balance; a positive energy balance

7. Despite minor seasonal fluctuations, Phil's weight has been fairly consistent all his adult life. One reason for this stability over time is that the number of calories he consumed tended to match the number of calories he expended, a process called
    (a) positive incentive value.
    (b) satiation.
    (c) fixed action pattern.
    (d) energy homeostasis.

8. Neuropeptide Y (NPY) and corticotropin-releasing hormone (CRH) are to _____ as classical and operant conditioning are to _____ .
   (a) set-point theory; settling-point theory
   (b) long-term signals that regulate body weight; short-term psychological factors that regulate body weight
   (c) positive incentive value; sensory-specific satiety
   (d) becoming overweight; becoming obese

9. Graham, an assistant manager, has a strong need to attain more power and status so that he can control and influence the behavior of other employees; he has his heart set on becoming general manager. It is probable that Graham has a high level of
   (a) self-actualization.
   (b) emotional intelligence.
   (c) anthropomorphism.
   (d) power motivation.

10. Before the guests went to the dining room for dinner, plates of delicious appetizers were served to them. The probable net effect of the guests eating these hors d'oeuvres will be that
    (a) much less food will be eaten during dinner.
    (b) appetites will be stimulated and more food than normal will be consumed at dinner.
    (c) most guest will feel satiated and will skip dinner entirely.
    (d) most guests will become restrained eaters.

11. Ulricke lost twenty pounds on her latest diet and her weight fell below her set-point weight. She is likely to experience a(n) _____ in her basal metabolic rate and energy level, and when she goes off the diet she is likely to

    _____ .
    (a) increase; maintain her weight loss
    (b) decrease; regain the lost pounds
    (c) increase; regain the lost pounds
    (d) decrease; maintain her weight loss

12. When Bryce was too afraid to jump off the top diving board at the pool, his friends accused him of having "cold feet." Later, when he was telling his Dad about the episode, he became angry and "hot under the collar." The two different descriptions of these basic emotions could have arisen because
    (a) anger produces an increase in skin temperature and fear produces a decrease in skin temperature.

    (b) anger is associated with an decrease in heart rate and blood pressure, and fear is associated with an increase in heart rate and blood pressure.
    (c) anger produces an decrease in skin temperature and blood pressure and fear produces an increase in skin temperature.
    (d) anger is associated with a decrease in heart rate and blood pressure, and fear is associated with an increase in heart rate and blood pressure.

13. Miguella was born blind and deaf. Despite her inability to observe or hear others, she still expresses joy, anger, and pleasure using the same expressions as sighted children. This example provides support for
    (a) the idea that basic emotions are innate.
    (b) the notion that emotional expressions are culturally determined.
    (c) the idea that both genetics and the environment are involved in the expression of basic emotions.
    (d) all of the above.

14. April is convinced that her cats experience the same emotions as humans. She argues that they can be happy or sad, anxious or content, frightened or fearless, and they can feel embarrassment, grief, love, and shame. According to Critical Thinking Box 8.4, April is engaging in
    (a) interpersonal engagement.
    (b) anthropomorphism.
    (c) sensation seeking behavior.
    (d) homeostasis.

15. When Alfie applied for a job with a government agency, he was told that he would have to take a polygraph test as part of his evaluation. According to In Focus 8.3, which of the following is true?
    (a) The polygraph test will reliably determine if he is lying or telling the truth.
    (b) The polygraph can readily detect if he regularly uses drugs.
    (c) It is possible that he could be judged guilty of lying even when he is telling the truth.
    (d) The test will accurately determine whether or not he suffers from aphasia.

Answers

Introduction: Motivation and Emotion

1. *Motivation refers to* the biological, emotional, cognitive, or social forces that activate and direct behavior.

2. *The three characteristics associated with motivation are* activation (the initiation of behavior), persistence (continued efforts to achieve a goal), and intensity (the vigor of responding).

3. *Emotions are closely tied to motivational processes (and vice versa) because both topics involve* the complex interaction of physical, behavioral, cognitive, and social factors. We may be motivated to achieve certain emotions, and emotions may motivate us to take action.

Motivational Concepts and Theories

1. *According to the earliest theories of motivation, instinct theories, people are motivated to* engage in certain behaviors because of evolutionary programming. *The limitation of these theories is* that they merely describe and label behaviors rather than actually explaining them.

2. *According to drive theories, behavior is motivated by* the desire to reduce internal tension caused by unmet biological needs such as hunger or thirst. *Their limitations are* that people engage in behaviors that are not a reflection of internal drives (we sometimes eat when we are not hungry or don't eat when we are hungry) and that many behaviors involve psychological influences, such as buying a lottery ticket, that are not related to filling unmet biological needs.

3. *Incentive theories proposed that behavior is motivated by* the pull of external goals, such as rewards. *Their limitation is* that many behaviors are not primarily motivated by any kind of external incentive (we sometimes engage in behaviors for their own sake without any obvious reinforcement).

4. *Arousal theory is based on the notion that people are motivated* to maintain an optimal level of arousal. When arousal is too low, we are motivated to seek stimulation, and when it is too high we seek to reduce arousal in a less stimulating environment. *The limitation of this theory is that* what constitutes an optimal level of arousal varies from person to person, time to time, and from one situation to another. For example, some people (called sensation seekers) seek out varied, novel, and unique sensory experiences because they find high levels of arousal pleasurable.

5. *Humanistic theories emphasize the importance of* psychological and cognitive factors in motivation, especially the notion that people are motivated to realize their personal potential.

6. *The key ideas and concepts from these theories that were incorporated in later models include* evolutionary programming, drive, homeostasis, incentive, and arousal.

Concept Check 1

1. motivation
2. homeostasis
3. sensation seeker
4. incentive
5. instinct
6. emotions

Matching Exercise 1

1. humanistic theories of motivation
2. motivation
3. persistence
4. fixed action patterns
5. drive
6. instinct theories
7. sensation seeking
8. evolutionary perspective

True/False Test 1

1. T	3. F	5. T	7. T
2. T	4. T	6. F	

Biological Motivation: Hunger and Eating

1. *Eating behavior reflects the complex interaction of* psychological, biological, social, and cultural factors.

2. *Energy homeostasis refers to* the long-term matching of food intake to energy expenditure.

3. *Energy balance or homeostasis involves (a) glucose (blood sugar), which is a* simple sugar that provides energy and is primarily produced by the conversion of carbohydrates and fats;
   (b) insulin, which is a hormone produced by the pancreas that regulates blood levels of glucose and signals the hypothalamus, regulating hunger and eating behavior;

(c) basal metabolic rate (BMR), which is the rate at which your body uses energy for vital body functions such as generating body heat, heartbeat, respiration, and brain activity; *(d) adipose tissue, which is* body fat that is the main source of stored or reserve energy.

4. *A positive energy balance occurs when* caloric intake exceeds the amount of calories expended for energy and the excess glucose is stored as fat (reserve energy). *A negative energy balance occurs when* caloric intake falls short of the calories expended as energy, and if continued, body fat stores will shrink.

5. *In terms of physiological changes, about 30 minutes before eating there is* a slight increase in blood levels of insulin, a slight decrease in blood levels of glucose, body temperature increases, and metabolism decreases. *Once a meal has begun,* blood glucose levels return to baseline, body temperature decreases, and metabolism increases.

6. *Psychological factors that trigger eating behavior involve*
   (a) classical conditioning, in which the CS (the time you normally eat, the setting, the sight of food cues, etc.) elicits the CR (internal physiological changes, such as slight changes in blood levels of insulin and glucose, increased body temperature, and decreased metabolism).
   (b) operant conditioning, in which voluntary eating behaviors are followed by a reinforcing stimulus (food) and are thus positively reinforced (they acquire positive incentive value).

7. *Satiation refers to* the feeling of fullness and diminished desire to eat that accompanies eating a meal. *Satiation involves signals from (a)* taste buds *on the tongue, roof of the mouth, and throat; (b)* stretch receptors *in the stomach; and (c)* cholecystokinin (CCK), *a hormone/neurotransmitter that promotes satiety effects.*

8. *Sensory-specific satiety refers to* the reduced desire to continue consuming a particular food, especially the food that is being eaten; this may be due to a decline in the food's positive incentive value.

9. *Four long-term chemical signals that regulate body weight are*
   (a) leptin, a hormone produced by fat cells that influences the hypothalamus (both ventromedial and lateral areas) in the regulation of eating behavior;
   (b) insulin, which also varies in response to positive and negative energy balance and can trig-

ger an increase or decrease in eating;
(c) neuropeptide Y (NPY), a neurotransmitter manufactured throughout the brain, and most notably in the hypothalamus, that triggers eating behavior, reduces metabolism, promotes positive energy balance, and fat storage; and
(d) corticotropin-releasing hormone (CRH), a hormone manufactured primarily in the hypothalamus that reduces eating behavior, increases metabolism, promotes negative energy balance and weight loss.

10. *According to set-point theory,* the body has a natural or optimal body weight, called the set-point weight, that the body defends from becoming higher or lower by regulating feelings of hunger and body metabolism. *According to settling-point models of weight regulation,* the body weight tends to settle, or stabilize, around the point at which an equilibrium, or balance, is achieved between energy expenditure and food consumption; settling-point weight may go up or down depending on whether the factors affecting food consumption and energy expenditure change.

Concept Check 2

1. the basal (or resting) metabolic rate (BMR)
2. satiation; cholecystokinin (CCK)
3. sensory-specific
4. baseline body weight; set-point
5. energy homeostasis or energy balance
6. leptin, insulin, neuropeptide Y (NPY), and corticotropin-releasing hormone (CRH)
7. neuropeptide Y; corticotropin-releasing hormone (CRH)
8. settling-point

Matching Exercise 2

1. baseline body weight
2. basal (or resting) metabolic rate (BMR)
3. glycogen
4. neuropeptide Y (NPY)
5. adipose tissue
6. insulin
7. set-point weight
8. stretch receptors
9. energy homeostasis (energy balance)

10. settling-point weight
11. sensory-specific satiety

True/False Test 2

1. F	5. T	9. F
2. T	6. T	10. T
3. F	7. F	
4. T	8. T	

Excess Weight and Obesity: The Epidemic

1. *The body mass index (BMI) is a* numerical scale indicating adult height in relation to weight and is calculated as 704.5 x weight (in pounds) divided by height in inches squared.

2. *Obesity is a condition characterized by* excessive body fat and a body mass index equal to or greater than 30.0; *in contrast, someone who is overweight has* excess weight that may be attributable to muscle, bone, body water, or fat (and has a BMI lower than 30.0).

3. *A number of factors are involved in creating a positive energy balance (when caloric intake consistently exceeds energy expenditure) and in becoming overweight:*
   (a) the positive incentive value of certain foods, defined as the anticipated pleasure of consuming particular highly palatable foods.
   (b) the "SuperSize It" syndrome, a relatively recent phenomenon in which restaurants, fast food outlets, etc., offer substantially increased portions of food for very little extra money, an offer many find hard to resist.
   (c) the cafeteria diet effect, which is the tendency to eat more when a wide variety of palatable foods is available.
   (d) snacks and appetizers between meals (preloading calories) are also a problem because, contrary to popular belief, they do not curb the appetite and reduce consumption during the later meal; in fact, having a small but scrumptious appetizer shortly before a meal may stimulate the appetite and increase consumption during the subsequent meal.
   (e) individual differences and lifespan changes are involved because people vary greatly in their basal metabolic rate (which accounts for about two-thirds of energy expenditure), females have a slightly lower BMR than males, metabolism decreases slightly over the lifespan (2.5% per decade), and weight gain will occur over time if food intake is not reduced.
   (f) and finally, the sedentary lifestyle of many people (40 percent of Americans) who never exercise, play sports, or engage in physically active hobbies.

4. *Several factors contribute to obesity:*
   (a) Nature and nurture interact; although susceptibility to obesity is influenced by genetic factors, environmental factors also play a role (a genetic predisposition combined with an environment characterized by ample and easily obtainable high-fat, high-calorie, palatable foods will lead to obesity).
   (b) Leptin resistance refers to a condition in which higher than normal blood levels of the hormone leptin does not produce the expected physiological response of reduced eating behavior and weight loss.
   (c) Many overweight or obese dieters experience weight cycling (yo-yo dieting), which refers to the repeated cycles of dieting, weight loss, and weight regain.
   (d) Obese people's brains tend to have fewer dopamine receptors than normal-weight individuals, *which may lead to* compulsive eating to stimulate brain reward centers.

Eating Disorders: Anorexia and Bulimia

1. *Eating disorders involve* serious and maladaptive disturbances in eating behavior and can include extreme reduction of food intake, severe bouts of overeating, and obsessive concerns about body shape and weight. *Although the central features of eating disorders are similar for males and females, approximately 90 to 95 percent of people who experience them are female.*

2. *Anorexia nervosa is an eating disorder characterized by* excessive weight loss, an irrational fear of gaining weight, and distorted body self-perception. *The two subtypes are* restricting subtype (severe food restriction and maladaptive dieting), *and* binge–purge subtype (episodes of binge eating and purging).

3. *Bulimia nervosa is an eating disorder characterized by* binges of extreme overeating followed by self-induced vomiting, misuse of laxatives, or other inappropriate methods to purge excessive food and prevent weight gain.

4. *Binge-eating disorder is an eating disorder characterized by* recurring episodes of binge eating (at least two days a week over six months or more) that are *not* followed by purges.

5. *The type of characteristics associated with anorexia include* perfectionism, rigid thinking, poor peer relations, social isolation, and low self-esteem. *People with bulimia share many of the characteristics of anorexia (binge–purge subtype), with the main differences being that* people with bulimia stay within a normal weight range, or may be slightly overweight, and they usually recognize that they have an eating disorder.

6. *The main factors implicated in the development of eating disorders are* genetics, decreases in brain activity of serotonin, disruptions in chemical signals that normally regulate eating behavior, and contemporary Western cultural attitudes about thinness and dieting.

Concept Check 3

1. cause little change in the number of calories she will consume at dinnertime (eating the snack will simply add more calories to her overall caloric intake for the day)

2. Body Mass Index (BMI); obese

3. positive incentive value

4. their basal metabolic weight may differ (in addition, females' BMRs are 3 to 5 percent lower than males).

5. her body defending against weight loss by decreasing her basal metabolic rate and energy level.

6. binge-eating

7. cafeteria diet effect

8. anorexia nervosa

Matching Exercise 3

1. body mass index (BMI)

2. eating disorder

3. leptin resistance

4. weight cycling

5. anorexia, binge–purge subtype

6. binge-eating disorder

True/False Test 3

1. T	3. F	5. F
2. T	4. T	

Psychological Needs as Motivators

1. *Some of the key questions associated with motivational theories that emphasize fundamental psychological needs include*
(a) Are there universal psychological needs?
(b) Are we internally or externally motivated to satisfy psychological needs?
(c) What psychological needs must be satisfied for optimal human functioning?

2. *Maslow's hierarchy of needs divides motivation into* levels that progress from basic physical needs to psychological needs to self-fulfillment needs; *Maslow believed that people* are motivated to satisfy the needs at each level of the hierarchy before moving up to the next level, and that they are ultimately motivated by the desire to achieve self-actualization (the full use and exploitation of talents, capacities, and potentialities).

3. *Criticisms of Maslow's model of motivation are that*
(a) the concept of self-actualization is very vague and difficult to define in a way that would allow it to be tested scientifically;
(b) Maslow's initial studies on self-actualization had limited samples and many were based on biographical and autobiographical accounts of famous historical figures that Maslow selected;
(c) despite the claim that self-actualization is an innate motivational goal of all people, most people do not experience or achieve self-actualization;
(d) Maslow's notion that we must satisfy needs at one level before moving to the next level has not been supported (has not stood the test of time).

4. *Self-determination theory is associated with psychologists* Edward L. Deci and Richard M. Ryan, *who contend that in order to realize optimal psychological functioning three innate and universal psychological needs must be met:*
(a) autonomy, which is the need to determine, control, and organize one's own behavior and goals so that they are in harmony with one's own interests and values. *(b) competence, which is* the need to effectively learn and master appropriately challenging tasks. *(c) relatedness, which is* the need to feel attached to others and experience a sense of belongingness, security, and intimacy.

5. *Intrinsic motivation refers to* behavior motivated by the desire to engage in tasks that the person finds inherently satisfying and enjoyable, novel, or optimally challenging (the desire to do something for its own sake). *Extrinsic motivation refers to* behavior motivated by external factors or influences, such as rewards, consequences, or social expectations.

Competence and Achievement Motivation

1. *Competence motivation is displayed when* a person strives to use his/her cognitive, social, and behavioral skills to be capable and exercise control in a situation (provides much of the "push" for tackling new challenges).

2. *Achievement motivation refers to* motivated behavior directed toward excelling, succeeding, or outperforming others at some task and is measured by the Thematic Apperception Test (TAT).

3. *People who score high in achievement motivation tend to* expend their greatest efforts when faced with moderately challenging tasks, work long hours, display original thinking, seek expert advice, value feedback about their performance, and have the capacity to delay gratification. They also tend to be independent and to attribute their successes to their own abilities and efforts and explain their failures as being due to external factors or bad luck.

4. *In individualistic cultures, the need to achieve emphasizes* personal, individual success rather than the success of the group, *whereas in collectivistic cultures* there is a social orientation with a focus on the well-being of others and a desire to fulfill the expectations of family members and to fit into the larger group.

Concept Check 4

1. achievement
2. collectivistic
3. intrinsic
4. competence
5. self-determination theory (SDT)
6. extrinsic
7. Thematic Apperception Test (TAT)

Graphic Organizer 1

1. drive theory
2. humanistic theory
3. instinct theory
4. self-determination theory (SDT)
5. incentive theory
6. arousal theory

Matching Exercise 4

1. self-determination theory (SDT)
2. hierarchy of needs

3. internalize
4. Thematic Apperception Test (TAT)
5. power motivation
6. Abraham Maslow
7. competence
8. autonomy

True/False Test 4

1. T	4. T	7. F
2. F	5. F	
3. T	6. F	

Emotion

1. *Emotion is defined as* a complex psychological state involving three distinct components: subjective experience, a physiological response, and a behavioral or expressive response.

2. *Emotions tend to be* intense, rather short lived, have a specific cause, be directed toward a particular object, and motivate a person to take some form of action. *Moods involve* a milder emotional state that is more general and pervasive, such as gloominess or contentment, and they may last for a few hours or days.

3. *Emotions have many functions, including triggering* motivational behavior, and they contribute to rational decision making, guide purposeful behavior, and are essential to successful living (people who have lost the capacity to feel emotion tend to make disastrous decisions).

4. *Emotional intelligence is the capacity to* understand and manage your own emotional experiences, and to perceive, comprehend, and respond appropriately to the emotions of others.

5. *According to evolutionary psychologists, emotions are the* product of evolution, they help us solve important adaptive problems posed by the environment, they move us towards potential resources and away from potential dangers, and ultimately help survival and reproductive success.

6. *The most common basic emotions that all humans, in every culture, experience are* happiness, sadness, anger, fear, surprise, and disgust.

7. *Cross-cultural research has shown that* people from different cultures tend to arrange emotions in much the same way as Americans, with general agreement among cultures regarding

the "pleasant/unpleasant" and "activated/not activated" emotional dimensions.

8. *Cross-cultural researchers have noted that Japanese subjects also categorized emotions along a dimension of* interpersonal engagement, *which reflects* the degree to which emotions involve a relationship with another person or other people.

The Neuroscience of Emotion

1. *The physiological component of emotions such as fear and anger involves the* activation of the sympathetic division of the autonomic nervous system, which gears people for action, affecting heart rate, blood pressure, respiration, perspiration, and other bodily activities (the fight-or-flight response).

2. *The amygdala is part of the limbic system and is an* almond-shaped cluster of neurons in the brain's temporal lobe, is involved in memory and emotional responses, and has connections with other brain structures, including the cortex, the thalamus, and the hypothalamus.

3. *From an evolutionary perspective, evidence of a direct thalamus-amygdala pathway makes adaptive sense because the amygdala can be activated by* a threatening stimulus, even before we become consciously aware of the stimulus, an adaptive response. *When the amygdala is activated, it sends information to* the hypothalamus, then to the medulla, which, in combination, trigger arousal of the sympathetic nervous system and the release of stress hormones.

4. *The second (indirect) pathway, thalamus-cortex-amygdala, allows more complex stimuli to be* evaluated in the cortex before triggering the amygdala's alarm system, providing a way for cognitive processes to inhibit instinctive emotional responses; in addition, because the amygdala also sends information to the cortex, instinctive emotional responses can affect cognitive processes.

5. *Comparative brain-imaging studies of the basic emotions indicate that each emotion involves* distinct neural circuits in the brain, activating different combinations of brain regions.

The Expression of Emotions

1. *Research on facial expressions (and emotions expressed vocally) suggests that* expressions of the basic emotions are innate and probably hard-wired in the brain, and appear to be universal across different cultures.

2. *Display rules are social and cultural rules that* regulate the expression of emotions, particularly facial expressions.

3. *Display rules can vary greatly from culture to culture (and even for different groups within a given culture, such as males and females); consequently,* the expression of different emotions may vary depending on the culture and its display rules.

4. *From an evolutionary perspective, the expression of emotions serves the* adaptive function of communicating internal states to friends and enemies, helps us recognize and respond quickly to the emotional state of others, and ultimately helps in survival and reproductive success.

Concept Check 5

1. a mood; an emotion
2. sympathetic; fight-or-flight
3. display rules
4. male; female
5. emotional intelligence
6. mixed
7. thalamus-amygdala
8. an emblem

Graphic Organizer 2

1. astonishment
2. alarm
3. boredom
4. relaxation
5. annoyance

```
                              MORE AROUSED
                                    |
                  2                 |             1
                                    |
                              5     |
                                    |
        LESS _____|_____ MORE
      PLEASANT                      |             PLEASANT
                                    |
                  3                 |             4
                                    |
                              LESS AROUSED
```

Matching Exercise 5

1. Charles Darwin
2. basic emotions
3. microexpressions
4. emotional intelligence
5. amygdala
6. interpersonal engagement
7. Paul Eckman
8. polygraph

True/False Test 5

1. T   4. F   7. F
2. F   5. T   8. T
3. F   6. T

Theories of Emotion: Explaining Emotion

1. *The James–Lange theory of emotions states that* emotions arise from the perception and interpretation of bodily changes; in other words, the experience of emotion results from the perception of the internal physical responses to a stimulus—you feel afraid because your heart pounded.

2. *Walter Cannon criticized the James-Lange theory on a number of grounds:*
   (a) Bodily reactions are similar for many emotions, yet our subjective experience of various emotions is very different.
   (b) Our emotional reaction to a stimulus is often faster than our physiological reaction, but the subjective experience of emotion is often virtually instantaneous.
   (c) When physiological changes are artificially induced, people do not necessarily report feeling a related emotion.
   (d) People cut off from feeling bodily changes do experience true emotions (the perception of physical arousal does not seem to be essential to the experience of emotion).

3. *Support for some aspects of the James–Lange theory come from (a) Damasio's work, which demonstrated that* each of the basic emotions produced a distinct pattern of neural responses and that the subjective sense of feeling an emotion follows from physiological feedback from the skin, muscles, internal organs, and the sympathetic nervous system, and *(b) the facial feedback hypothesis, which states that* expressing a specific emotion, especially facially, causes the subjective experience of that emotion.

4. *Schachter and Singer's two-factor theory of emotion suggests that* emotion is a result of the interaction of physiological arousal and the cognitive label that we apply to explain the arousal.

5. *Richard Lazarus's cognitive-mediational theory proposes that* the most important aspect of an emotional experience is our cognitive interpretation, or appraisal, of the personal meaning of events and experiences—the more personally important the outcome, the more intense the emotion.

6. *Although both two-factor theory and the cognitive-mediational model emphasize the importance of cognitive appraisal, two-factor theory states that* emotion results from physiological arousal plus a cognitive label, *while the cognitive-mediational model stresses that* appraisal is the essential trigger for an emotional response, and all other components of emotion, including physiological arousal, follow from the initial cognitive appraisal.

Concept Check 6

1. epinephrine
2. cognitive-mediational
3. not consistent
4. facial feedback hypothesis
5. James–Lange
6. mastery experience

Matching Exercise 6

1. facial feedback hypothesis
2. Richard Lazarus
3. Cannon–Bard theory of emotion
4. two-factor theory of emotion
5. anthropomorphism
6. epinephrine (adrenaline)

True/False Test 6

1. T   4. T
2. T   5. T
3. T

Something to Think About

1. Losing weight and keeping it off is a big problem for many people. You might begin your discussion by noting that our motivation to eat is influenced by psychological, biological, social, and cultural factors. For example, biologically, hunger and satiation are regulated by oral signals from taste buds, stretch receptors in the stomach, and chemicals such as CCK, insulin, NPY, CRH, and leptin. Of course, genetic factors also play a role. Psychological factors include classically conditioned stimuli, the positive incentive value of certain foods acquired through operant conditioning and reinforcement, and memory of previous meals eaten. Socially, people are affected by the cultural norms and attitudes about what constitutes the ideal weight.

   First, knowing a little about how food is converted to energy in the body is useful in understanding the regulation of hunger and eating behavior. Food provides glucose, the main source of the body's energy, which is regulated by insulin. Excess glucose is stored in adipose tissue (fat) and the basal metabolic rate reflects the rate at which your body uses energy for vital body functions. Energy homeostasis helps people maintain their baseline body weight, which tends to remain stable over time unless conditions of positive or negative energy balance occur. When the former happens, we gain weight. Body mass index (BMI) is one way to calculate weight status, and someone with a BMI of 30.0 or more is classified as obese.

   So what are the major factors involved in becoming overweight and what might we do to minimize or prevent weight gain?

   First, there is the positive incentive value of many easily available and very palatable foods, which can easily lead to overeating. You have to become aware of this factor and try to avoid these foods.

   Second, when faced with the opportunity of a double portion of a tasty food for only a few cents more (the "SuperSize It" syndrome) most people can't resist. These situations are optimized to pack on those extra calories, so do your best to stay away from them.

   Third, there is the cafeteria diet effect. This happens when a wide variety of highly palatable foods are offered, such as at a cafeteria or an all-you-can-eat buffet. Your "eyes are bigger than your stomach," as the expression goes, and sure enough people tend to pile up their plates with food, a sure-fire formula for packing on the pounds.

   Fourth, snacks and appetizers between and before meals do not reduce the caloric intake of the later meal. The snacks simply add more calories on top of those subsequently consumed. Worse yet is the finding that having a small but delicious appetizer shortly before your meal may simply stimulate your appetite, increasing the amount later eaten. So try to avoid snacks and appetizers, stick to the usual fare, and don't load up your plate at the buffet.

   Fifth, there are individual difference in BMR. Two people, matched on all the essential variables can maintain the same approximate weight even though one of the pair consumes twice as much as the other. Yes, it's true, and no, life is not fair. In addition, your BMR decreases with age, so as you get older you have to watch carefully what you eat or you'll gain weight (the old "middle-age spread" idea). People also differ in the amount of energy they use for normal daily activities.

   Finally, weight gain for many people is a result of a sedentary life style. Forty percent of Americans report that they never exercise, play sports, or engage in physical activities such as walking the dog or gardening. Make exercise a regular part of your routine and give the time spent doing some physical activity the highest priority. When you get busy and anxiety levels are high, the very last thing you should give up is your regular exercise program.

   Having said all that, it is important to note that this is a complex problem with no magic bullet or easy solution. For example, obesity certainly involves genetic susceptibility, but environmental factors also play a role. Obese people also develop leptin resistance, a condition in which higher than normal blood levels of the hormone leptin do not produce the expected physiological response of reduced hunger and eating. Frequent dieting may lead to weight cycling, a phenomenon in which the weight lost during dieting is regained in a matter of weeks or months and is then maintained until the next attempt at dieting begins. Research has also shown that obese people tend to have fewer dopamine receptors in their brains than normal weight people, which may lead some individuals to engage in compulsive eating to stimulate brain reward centers. And, as Critical Thinking 8.1 points out, we may be programmed by evolution for the propensity to overeat and store energy as fat. Obviously, obesity is not a simple problem with a simple solution.

So, the best advice for losing weight is to become aware of all the factors (especially those mentioned above) that can contribute to weight gain, modify your eating patterns accordingly, and follow a regular exercise program. It's an uphill battle, and despite the gloomy statistics, many people have successfully kept weight off by following this advice.

2. The first thing to note about the polygraph is that it does not detect lies. It might be more accurate to refer to the polygraph as an "emotion detector" because it measures physiological arousal. Changes in heart rate, blood pressure, respiration, and perspiration, which are all associated with emotional arousal, can be detected by the polygraph. These changes may be associated with many different emotional states, such as anxiety, fear, irritation, and general nervousness. There is no specific pattern of responding associated with lying, and the polygraph can't specify which response is which. In addition, some people are able to lie without experiencing anxiety or arousal, whether they are guilty or not. Even if someone "passes" a polygraph test, as some alien abductees have, it does not necessarily mean that they are telling the truth; it may simply indicate that they believe they are.

Research suggests that polygraph experts are prone to error in interpretation; innocent people may be judged guilty and guilty people may be declared innocent. In fact, polygraph testing is more likely to indicate that innocent people are guilty than guilty people are to be found out. Because of the high error rate, many states do not allow polygraph results to be used as evidence in court, and it is now illegal for nongovernmental agencies and companies to use a lie detector to routinely screen prospective employees for drug use or theft. Ironically, the U.S. government uses polygraph testing in several agencies, including the CIA and the Department of Energy. Because of the controversy over government's continued use of the polygraph, the National Association of Science is reviewing the scientific evidence for the reliability and validity of polygraph testing. A number of prominent scientific psychologists are participating in this review.

Progress Test 1

1. a	6. b	11. a
2. c	7. c	12. b
3. c	8. a	13. b
4. a	9. d	14. d
5. a	10. c	15. e

Progress Test 2

1. d	6. c	11. d
2. b	7. d	12. d
3. d	8. d	13. d
4. a	9. d	14. d
5. a	10. a	15. a

Progress Test 3

1. a	6. b	11. b
2. c	7. d	12. a
3. c	8. b	13. a
4. c	9. d	14. b
5. d	10. b	15. c

chapter 9

Lifespan Development

PREVIEW
Reading the section below first will give you a general sense of the chapter's contents and an initial introduction to some of the major concepts and terms. This will prime you for what you are about to read and help you to develop a "cognitive map" that will guide your study of the material in this chapter. Likewise, reading the **preview questions** at the beginning of each major section will improve your ability to understand, learn, and retain the information.

CHAPTER 9 . . . AT A GLANCE

Chapter 9 examines the scope of developmental psychology and major themes such as the stages of lifespan development, the nature of change, and the interaction between heredity and environment. The first two sections describe genetic contributions to development and the stages of prenatal development.

Development during infancy and childhood and the capacities and capabilities of the newborn are explored, including social and personality development, with special attention paid to the nature of temperament and the concept of attachment. This is followed by a description of the stages of language development. The section concludes with a detailed analysis of Piaget's theory of cognitive development and an examination of Vygotsky's information-processing model.

Adolescence marks the transition from childhood to adulthood. Important changes in adolescent–parent relationships take place during this period, and relationships with peers and peer influence become increasingly relevant. Erikson's theory of psychosocial development and Kohlberg's theory of the development of moral reasoning are discussed next.

The final sections describe the three phases of adult development as well as the contributions of genetics, environment, and the individual's lifestyle. Love and work are the key themes that dominate adult development. Late adulthood does not necessarily involve a steep decline in physical and cognitive functioning. In discussing dying and death, which can occur at any point in the lifespan, the text outlines Kübler-Ross's five-stage model of dying, noting that dying is an individual process, much as any other during the lifespan.

The Application presents some basic principles of parenting that have been shown to foster the development of psychologically well-adjusted and competent children who are in control of their own behavior.

Introduction: Your Life Story

Preview Questions

Consider the following questions as you study this section of the chapter.

- What do developmental psychologists study?
- What are the major themes in developmental psychology?

*Read the section "Introduction: Your Life Story" and **write** your answers to the following:*

1. Developmental psychology is the _____
   _____
   _____

2. The major themes in developmental psychology
   are _____
   _____
   _____
   _____
   _____

Genetic Contributions to Your Life Story

Preview Questions

Consider the following questions as you study this section of the chapter.

- What are chromosomes, DNA, and genes, and what role do they play in determining each individual's unique genetic makeup?
- What role does the environment play in the relationship between genotype and phenotype?
- How do dominant and recessive genes differ, and what are sex-linked recessive characteristics?

*Read the section "Genetic Contributions to Your Life Story" and **write** your answers to the following:*

1. Chromosomes are_____
   _____

2. DNA (deoxyribonucleic acid) is_____
   _____

3. Genes are _____
   _____
   _____

4. Genotype refers to the _____
   _____

   Phenotype refers to the _____
   _____

5. In a pair of genes, the dominant gene is _____
   _____
   _____

   A recessive gene is _____
   _____

6. We inherit from our biological parents _____
   _____

7. The sex chromosomes are _____
   _____
   _____

   Sex-linked recessive characteristics are traits
   determined by _____
   _____

Prenatal Development

Preview Questions

Consider the following questions as you study this section of the chapter.

- What happens to the single-cell zygote during prenatal development?
- What are the three phases of prenatal development?
- What are teratogens?

*Read the section "Prenatal Development" and **write** your answers to the following:*

1. During prenatal development, the single-cell
   zygote _____
   _____
   _____

2. The three phases of the prenatal stage are_____
   _____
   _____
   _____
   _____

3. Teratogens are _____

_____

_____

*After you have carefully studied the preceding
sections, complete the following exercises.*

Concept Check 1

*Read the following and write the correct term in the
space provided.*

1. Dr. Dalliwhal's research focuses on the relationship between various teratogens and birth
defects. Dr. Dalliwhal is most likely a
_____ psychologist.

2. From the day Franco was born, people have
always responded very positively to his good
looks. Now that he is growing older, it is clear
that he is developing a socially confident and
outgoing personality. This best illustrates the
interaction of _____ and

_____ .

3. Paul and Paula are brother and sister; in terms
of chromosomes, Paul received a(n)
_____ from his mother and a(n)
_____ from his father, and Paula
received a(n) _____ from her mother and a(n) _____ from her father.

4. It is now six weeks since Jennifer conceived.
The human organism she is carrying is called
a(n) _____ ; by the third month, it
will be called a(n) _____ .

5. When Myra became pregnant, she decided that
she would not drink any alcohol because she
did not want to risk causing abnormal development or birth defects in her unborn child. Myra
is aware that alcohol is a _____ .

6. Dr. Zhang conceptualizes the lifespan in terms
eight basic stages of development. She is most
likely to label the stage from birth to 2 years of
age as _____ , the stage from 2 to 6
years as _____ , and the stage
from 6 to 12 years as _____ .

7. When answering an exam question about what
makes each individual unique, Phillipa is most
likely to note that every cell in the body has 23
pairs of _____ , each of which is a
long threadlike structure composed of twisted
strands of _____ , which are
arranged in thousands of segments called

_____ .

8. Sarina has red-green color blindness. This trait
is called a _____
because it is determined by a _____
gene on each of her X chromosomes in the 23rd
pair of chromosomes.

Graphic Organizer 1

*There is a dominant gene (D) for "dimples" and a
recessive gene (r) for "no dimples." The following
matrix shows the four possible combinations. Decide
which combinations (genotype) will result in "dimples" or "no dimples" (phenotype).*

	Dominant (D)	Recessive (r)
Dominant (D)	Cell 1 DD	Cell 2 Dr
Recessive (r)	Cell 3 Dr	Cell 4 rr

Cell 1: The genotype DD results in the phenotype of

_____ .

Cell 2: The genotype Dr results in the phenotype of

_____ .

Cell 3: The genotype Dr results in the phenotype of

_____ .

Cell 4: The genotype rr results in the phenotype of

_____ .

Review of Terms and Concepts 1

Use the terms in this list to complete the Matching Test, then to help you answer the True/False items correctly.

developmental
   psychology
critical period
nature–nurture issue
chromosome
deoxyribonucleic acid
   (DNA)
gene
genotype
phenotype
dominant gene
dominant characteristics
recessive gene
recessive characteristics
sex chromosomes
X chromosome

Y chromosome
sex-linked recessive
   characteristics
prenatal stage
zygote
germinal period
   (zygotic period)
embryo
embryonic period
amniotic sac
umbilical cord
placenta
teratogens
fetal period
quickening
fetus

Matching Exercise

Match the appropriate term with its definition or description.

1. _____ The stage of development before birth; divided into the germinal, embryonic, and fetal periods.

2. _____ The basic unit of heredity that directs the development of a particular characteristic; the individual unit of DNA instructions on a chromosome.

3. _____ The branch of psychology that studies how people change over the lifespan.

4. _____ Traits determined by recessive genes located on the X chromosome; in males, these characteristics require only one recessive gene to be expressed.

5. _____ Harmful agents or substances that can cause malformations or defects in an embryo or a fetus.

6. _____ Long, threadlike structure composed of twisted parallel strands of DNA; found in the nucleus of the cell.

7. _____ In a pair of genes, the gene containing genetic instructions that will not be expressed unless paired with another recessive gene.

8. _____ The first two weeks of prenatal development.

9. _____ Cluster of cells that develop from the single-cell zygote by the end of the two-week germinal period.

10. _____ Traits whose expression requires two identical recessive genes, like those for light hair and being dimple-free.

11. _____ Chromosomes designated as X or Y that determine biological sex; the 23rd pair of chromosomes in humans.

12. _____ Disk-shaped tissue on the mother's uterine wall that the embryo is attached to.

13. _____ The larger of the two types of sex chromosomes that carries more genes than its smaller counterpart, including genes for traits unrelated to sex.

14. _____ Lifeline through which the embryo receives nutrients.

True/False Test

Indicate whether each statement is true or false by placing T or F in the blank space next to each item.

1. ____ The fetus is the name given to the growing organism at the beginning of the third month.

2. ____ A critical period during development is a time during which the child is maximally sensitive to environmental influences.

3. ____ Deoxyribonucleic acid (DNA) is the chemical basis of heredity; carries genetic instructions in the cell.

4. ____ The fetal period is the second period of prenatal development, extending from the third week through the eighth week.

5. ____ At conception, chromosomes from the biological mother and father combine to form a single cell called the fertilized egg, or zygote.

6. ____ In a pair of genes, the gene containing genetic instructions that will be expressed whether paired with another dominant gene or with a recessive gene is called the dominant gene.

7. ____ The embryonic period is the third and longest period of prenatal development, extending from the ninth week until birth.

8. ____ An important theme in developmental psychology is the interaction between heredity and environment; traditionally called the nature–nurture issue.

9. ___ Genotype refers to observable traits or characteristics of an organism determined by the interaction of genetic and environmental factors.

10. ___ Traits such as freckles, dark eyes, dark hair, and dimples are referred to as dominant characteristics because they require only one member of a gene pair to be present in order for the trait to be displayed.

11. ___ Phenotype refers to the underlying genetic makeup of a particular organism, including the genetic instructions for traits that are not actually displayed.

12. ___ The embryo is protectively housed in the fluid filled *amniotic sac*.

13. ___ The smaller of the two sex chromosomes is called the Y chromosome.

14. ___ During the fourth month of pregnancy, the mother can feel the fetus moving, an experience called quickening.

Check your answers and review any areas of weakness before going on to the next section.

Development During Infancy and Childhood: Physical Development

Preview Questions

Consider the following questions as you study this section of the chapter.

- What reflexes and sensory capabilities are physically helpless infants equipped with that enhance their chances for survival?
- How do the sensory capabilities of the newborn promote the development of relationships with caregivers?
- How does the brain develop after birth?

*Read the section "Development During Infancy and Childhood" and **write** your answers to the following:*

1. Newborn infants enter the world equipped with

_____

_____

Their senses of vision, hearing, smell, and touch are _____

_____

_____

2. The infant's sensory capabilities promote the development of relationships with caregivers, as evidenced by the fact that they _____

_____

_____

_____

_____

3. After birth, a number of changes take place in the infant's brain: _____

_____

_____

Development During Infancy and Childhood: Social and Personality Development

Preview Questions

Consider the following questions as you study this section of the chapter.

- What is temperament, and what is attachment?
- What temperamental patterns have been identified?
- How is attachment measured?
- What is the basic premise of attachment theory?

*Read the section "Social and Personality Development" and **write** your answers to the following:*

1. Temperament refers to _____

_____

Attachment is the _____

_____

2. The three broad temperamental patterns are

_____

3. Attachment is measured using a procedure called the _____

In this technique _____

_____

_____

_____

_____

4. The basic premise of attachment theory is

_____

_____

_____

_____

Development During Infancy and Childhood: Language Development

Preview Questions

Consider the following questions as you study this section of the chapter.

- How does a biological predisposition to learn language function in language development?
- How is language development encouraged by caregivers?
- What are the stages of language development?

Read the section "Language Development" and **write** *your answers to the following:*

1. According to Noam Chomsky _____

_____

_____

_____

2. Language development is encouraged by _____

_____

3. The stages of language development are _____

_____

_____

_____

_____

After you have carefully studied the preceding sections, complete the following exercises.

Concept Check 2

Read the following and write the correct term in the space provided.

1. Dr. Snow is interested in the abilities of newborn children. While testing visual perception, she is likely to find that newborns will look longer at the image of a(n) _____ compared to other visual patterns.

2. In order to determine whether a child is securely or insecurely attached, researchers are likely to use _____ .

3. Kathy gave birth to a normal, healthy, eight-and-a-half-pound baby. In terms of brain development, the baby's brain weighs _____ (25 percent/50 percent/75 percent/100 percent) of its adult weight.

4. When Kathy touched her newborn's right cheek, the baby turned to the right and opened her mouth, a response called the _____ ; touching her lips elicited the _____ ; and when Kathy put a finger on each of the baby's palms, she grasped them tightly, a response called the _____ .

5. Like most newborns, Kathy's baby entered the world with about _____ neurons. After birth, her brain continued to develop with the number of _____ increasing dramatically during the first two years, and the axons of many neurons acquiring _____ , the white, fatty covering that increases a neuron's communication speed.

6. As Kathy's baby develops, it becomes apparent that she readily adapts to new experiences, displays positive moods and emotions, and has regular sleeping and eating patterns. She is likely to be classified as a temperamentally _____ baby.

7. Kathy and her husband are consistently warm, responsive, and sensitive to their infant's needs, and the baby has developed the expectation that her needs will be met. It is very probable that the baby will form a(n) _____ attachment to her parents.

8. When Kathy tells 12-month-old Kaila to "Bring Mommy the dolly," Kaila immediately does so, even though she cannot say the words "bring," "Mommy," or "dolly." This suggests that Kaila's _____ vocabulary is larger than her _____ vocabulary.

Review of Terms, Concepts, and Names 2

Use the terms in this list to complete the Matching Test, then to help you answer the True/False items correctly.

rooting reflex
sucking reflex
grasping reflex
temperament
easy temperament
difficult temperament
slow-to-warm-up
  temperament
attachment
attachment theory
multiple attachments
secure attachment
insecure attachment

Strange Situation
Mary D. Salter
  Ainsworth
Noam Chomsky
motherese (infant-
  directed speech)
cooing and babbling
  stage
comprehension
  vocabulary
production vocabulary
one-word stage
two-word stage

Matching Exercise

Match the appropriate term/name with its definition or description.

1. _____ Theory that an infant's ability to thrive physically and psychologically depends in part on the quality of the emotional bond that forms between infant and caregiver(s).

2. _____ Measure of attachment devised by Mary Ainsworth, typically used with infants who are between 1 and 2 years old.

3. _____ Automatic response elicited by touching a newborn's lips.

4. _____ Temperamental category for babies who have a low activity level, who withdraw from new situations and people, and who adapt to new experiences very gradually.

5. _____ Universal style of speech used with babies and characterized by very distinct pronunciation, a simplified vocabulary, short sentences, a high pitch, and exaggerated intonation and expression.

6. _____ Biologically programmed stage in language development that occurs between about 3 and 9 months of age.

7. _____ Emotional bond that forms between infants and their caregiver(s), especially parents.

8. _____ Words that are understood by an infant or child.

9. _____ Form of attachment that may develop when parents are neglectful, inconsistent, or insensitive to their infant's moods or behaviors and reflects an ambivalent or detached emotional relationship between infant and his or her parents.

10. _____ Universal stage in language development, starting around 2 years of age, in which infants combine two words to construct simple "sentences" that reflect the first understanding of grammar.

11. _____ Bonds that are formed between the infant and other consistent caregivers in his or her life, such as relatives or workers at day-care centers.

True/False Test

Indicate whether each statement is true or false by placing T or F in the blank space next to each item.

1. ____ Noam Chomsky is the psychologist who devised the Strange Situation procedure to measure attachment; contributed to attachment theory.

2. ____ Production vocabulary refers to the words that an infant or child can speak.

3. ____ An infant's response to having his or her palms touched is called the rooting reflex.

4. ____ Babies with a difficult temperament tend to be intensely emotional, are irritable and fussy, cry a lot, and have irregular sleeping and eating patterns.

5. ____ During the one-word stage, babies use a single word and vocal intonation to stand for an entire sentence.

6. ____ Secure attachment is likely to develop when parents are consistently warm, responsive, and sensitive to their infant's needs.

7. ____ Mary D. Salter Ainsworth is the American linguist who proposed that people have an innate understanding of the basic principles of language, which is called a universal grammar.

8. ____ Babies with an easy temperament readily adapt to new experiences, generally display positive moods and emotions, and have regular sleeping and eating patterns.

9. ____ Touching the newborn's cheek elicits the grasping reflex; the infant turns toward the source of the touch and opens the mouth.

10. ___ Temperament is the inborn predisposition to consistently behave and react in a certain way.

Check your answers and review any areas of weakness before going on to the next section.

Development During Infancy and Childhood: Cognitive Development

Preview Questions

Consider the following questions as you study this section of the chapter.

- What are Piaget's four stages of cognitive development, and what are the characteristics of each stage?
- What are the main criticisms of Piaget's theory?

Read the section "Cognitive Development" and **write** *your answers to the following:*

1. The four stages (and their characteristics) in Piaget's theory are

   (a) _____

   _____

   _____

   (b) _____

   _____

   _____

   (c) _____

   _____

   _____

   (d) _____

   _____

   _____

2. Piaget's theory has been criticized because ____

   _____

   _____

   _____

   _____

   _____

3. The information-processing model of cognitive development views cognitive development as

   _____

   _____

   _____

   _____

After you have carefully studied the preceding sections, complete the following exercises.

Concept Check 3

Read the following and write the correct term in the space provided.

1. Four-year-old Tiborg is not completely egocentric, and 5-year-old Natasha exhibits some understanding of conservation. Observations such as these suggest that Piaget may have _____ (overestimated/underestimated) the cognitive abilities of infants and children.

2. Eight-year-old Nadia has the ability to think logically about visible and tangible objects and situations. She is in the

   _____ stage of cognitive development.

3. Young Adrienne attempts to retrieve her toy bear after her father hides it under a blanket. This suggests that Adrienne has developed a sense of _____ .

4. When Mrs. Goodley cut Janet's hot dog into eight pieces and Simon's into six pieces, Simon started to cry and complained that he wasn't getting as much hot dog as Janet. Piaget would say that Simon doesn't understand the principle of _____ .

5. Three-year-old Rita calls all unfamiliar four-legged animals "doggies." She appears to be _____ these new experiences into her existing concept of a dog.

6. Piaget would call Rita's mental representation or concept of dog a _____ .

7. During a tutorial devoted to the pros and cons of genetic engineering, Vasilis raised some important issues about the ownership of fertilized eggs and whether destroying them constitutes taking a life. Piaget would say that Vasilis is in the _____ operational stage of cognitive development.

8. While Coral was still in high school, she imagined that most of her college professors would be older bearded males. During her first year, she was surprised to find that many were relatively young females. Because of these new experiences, she has changed her way of thinking about college professors, a process Piaget called _____ .

9. Dr. Ramenian believes that infants have limited physical coordination and are therefore incapable of clearly demonstrating their mental abilities in tasks involving manual responses. The results of Dr. Ramenian's research using visual tasks suggest that Piaget confused _____ limitations with _____ limitations.

10. Dr. Ramenian also believes that cognitive development is a process of continuous change over the lifespan, not a series of distinct stages, as Piaget proposed. His views are consistent with the _____ model of cognitive development.

Review of Terms, Concepts, and Names 3

Use the terms in this list to complete the Matching Test, then to help you answer the True/False items correctly.

Jean Piaget	irreversibility
qualitative difference in thinking	centration
	conservation
assimilation	concrete operational
accommodation	stage
sensorimotor stage	formal operational stage
object permanence	Renée Baillargeon
schemas	information-processing
preoperational stage	model of cognitive
operations	development
symbolic thought	Lev Vygotsky
egocentrism	

Matching Exercise

Match the appropriate term/name with its definition or description.

1. _____ The ability to use words, images, and symbols to represent the world.

2. _____ Canadian-born psychologist whose studies of cognitive development during infancy using visual rather than manual tasks challenged beliefs about the age at which object permanence first appears.

3. _____ The understanding that an object continues to exist even when it can no longer be seen.

4. _____ Piaget's fourth stage of cognitive development, which lasts from adolescence through adulthood and is characterized by the ability to think logically about abstract principles and hypothetical situations.

5. _____ Swiss child psychologist whose influential theory proposed that children progress through distinct stages of cognitive development.

6. _____ The model that views cognitive development as a continuous process over the lifespan and that studies the development of basic mental processes such as attention, memory, and problem solving.

7. _____ Piaget's term for the mental representations of the world that children acquire as their memories improve and as they gain an understanding of object permanence.

8. _____ Piaget's first stage of cognitive development, from birth to about age 2; the period during which the infant explores the environment and acquires knowledge through sensing and manipulating objects.

9. _____ In Piaget's theory, the inability to take another person's perspective or point of view.

10. _____ Russian psychologist who stressed the importance of social and cultural influences on cognitive development.

True/False Test

Indicate whether each statement is true or false by placing T or F in the blank space next to each item.

1. ___ In Piaget's theory, the word *operations* refers to logical, mental activities.

2. ___ Changing one's mental representation of the world, and the way one thinks about things on the basis of new information and experiences, is a process Piaget called accommodation.

3. ___ In Piaget's theory, the concrete operational stage is the second stage of cognitive development, which lasts from about age 2 to age 7 and is characterized by increasing use of symbols and prelogical thought processes.

4. ___ In Piaget's theory, irreversibility is the inability to reverse a sequence of events or logical operations mentally.

5. ___ In Piaget's theory, centration refers to the understanding that two equal quantities remain equal even though the form or appearance is rearranged, as long as nothing is added or subtracted.

6. ___ According to Piaget, as children advance to a new stage, their thinking is qualitatively different from that used in the previous stage; each new stage represents a fundamental shift in *how* children think and understand the world.

7. ___ In Piaget's theory, the tendency to focus on only one aspect of a situation and ignore other important aspects of the situation is called conservation.

8. ___ Assimilation is the process of incorporating and interpreting new information in terms of existing mental representations of the world.

9. ___ In Piaget's theory, the preoperational stage is the third stage of cognitive development, which lasts from about age seven to adolescence and is characterized by the ability to think logically about concrete objects and situations.

Check your answers and review any areas of weakness before going on to the next section.

Adolescence

Preview Questions

Consider the following questions as you study this section of the chapter.

- How is adolescence defined?
- What characterizes adolescent relationships with parents and peers?

- How do adolescents begin the process of identity formation?
- What is Erikson's psychosocial theory of lifespan development?
- What are the stages and levels in Kohlberg's theory of moral development?
- What are some criticisms of Kohlberg's theory?

*Read the section "Adolescence" and **write** your answers to the following:*

1. Adolescence is _____
_____

2. The relationship between parents and their adolescent children is _____
_____

3. Identity refers to _____
_____
_____

4. Adolescents begin the process of identity formation by _____
_____
_____

5. According to Erikson's psychosocial theory of lifespan development _____
_____

The key psychosocial conflict facing adolescents is _____
_____

6. Kohlberg's levels (and stages) of moral development include _____
_____
_____
_____
_____
_____
_____

7. Criticisms of Kohlberg's theory are _____

_____

_____

_____

_____

After you have carefully studied the preceding section, complete the following exercises.

Concept Check 4

Read the following and write the correct term in the space provided.

1. Delbert resists stealing cookies from the cookie jar because he is afraid his mother will punish him if he does. According to Kohlberg's theory, Delbert is demonstrating stage _____ of the _____ level of moral reasoning.

2. In her studies of women's moral reasoning, Dr. Haydari found that women tend to stress the importance of maintaining interpersonal relationships and responding to the needs of others, rather than focusing primarily on individual rights. Her findings are consistent with those of psychologist _____ who developed a model of women's moral development that is based on the ethic of _____ .

3. Thomas, who is now a young adult, had a typical adolescent period of conflict over identity issues but now feels comfortable with the choices and commitments he has made. According to Erikson, Thomas has achieved an _____ and the next psychosocial task he is facing is likely to be _____ .

4. When her daughter chided her about driving slowly, Mrs. Estafani replied that she would not drive faster than the posted speed limit because responsible, law abiding citizens should always obey traffic laws. According to Kohlberg's theory of moral development, Mrs. Estafani is probably at stage _____ of the _____ level of moral development.

5. Seventeen-year-old Brendan questions his parents' values but is not sure that his peer group's standards are totally correct either. His confusion about what is really important in life suggests that Brendan is struggling with the problem of _____ .

6. Prior to adolescence, Brendan very likely struggled with other conflicts. According to Erikson, his first psychosocial conflict during infancy was about _____ ; his second, during toddlerhood (18 months to 3 years), involved _____ ; his third, which is likely to have happened during early childhood (3 to 6 years), was concerned with _____ ; and his fourth psychosocial conflict in middle to late childhood (6 to 12 years) dealt with _____ .

7. Mr. and Mrs. Atkins have three adolescent children. If they are like most American parents, their relationships with their children are likely to be generally _____ (negative/positive).

Graphic Organizer 2

For each of the following, identify the appropriate stage of Piaget's theory and the stage and level of Kohlberg's theory.

Statement	Theory	Stage/Level
1. Jeremy refuses to pay taxes and risks going to jail because he does not believe in supporting a government that spends so many tax dollars on weapons of mass destruction. Jeremy enjoys discussing his position and is very articulate in developing logical arguments.	Piaget	
	Kohlberg	
2. Mary is convinced that her older sister Natalie has more soda than she does after her mother pours Natalie's can of soda into a long, thin glass and hers into a short, fat one. Despite being tempted to take a big drink out of Natalie's glass when she is in the washroom, Mary refrains because she thinks she might get punished.	Piaget	
	Kohlberg	
3. While playing a game of cards with his friends, Mark insists that everyone should have a chance to be dealer because that is the fair thing to do. Mark is also able to explain the rules to everyone by dealing a couple of practice hands; later, he has difficulty trying to explain the game to his Dad without using the cards.	Piaget	
	Kohlberg	
4. During a discussion with her therapist, Mrs. Bradshaw is asked to describe her husband. Among other things, she notes that he is very law abiding, always drives with extreme care, and frequently boasts that he has never received a ticket. He never completed high school because he couldn't handle all that abstract, hypothetical stuff and is fairly content working as a custodian in an office building.	Piaget	
	Kohlberg	

Review of Terms, Concepts, and Names 4

Use the terms in this list to complete the Matching Test, then to help you answer the True/False items correctly.

adolescence
identity
Erik Erikson
identity diffusion
moratorium period
integrated identity
moral reasoning
Lawrence Kohlberg
levels and stages
  of moral reasoning

preconventional level
conventional level
postconventional level
ethic of individual rights
  and justice
ethic of care and
  responsibility

Matching Exercise

Match the appropriate term/name with its definition or description.

1. _____ American psychologist who proposed an influential theory of moral development.

2. _____ A person's self-definition or description, including the values, beliefs, and ideals that guide the individual's behavior.

3. _____ Carol Gilligan's categorization of women's moral development and reasoning, based on her research that showed women tended to stress the importance of maintaining interpersonal relationships and of responding to the needs of others, rather than focusing primarily on individual rights.

4. _____ The aspect of cognitive development related to the way an individual reasons about moral decisions.

5. _____ In Erikson's theory, the period following identity diffusion during which the adolescent experiments with different roles, values, and beliefs.

6. _____ Transitional stage between late childhood and the beginning of adulthood, during which sexual maturity is reached.

7. _____ Kohlberg's level of moral reasoning that begins in late childhood and continues through adolescence and adulthood; characterized by moral reasoning that emphasizes social roles, rules, and obligations.

True/False Test

Indicate whether each item is true or false by placing T or F in the space next to each item.

1. ____ Erik Erikson was the German-born American psychoanalyst who proposed an influential theory of psychosocial development throughout the lifespan.

2. ____ In Kohlberg's theory, the postconventional level is characterized by moral reasoning that reflects self-chosen ethical principles that are universally applied.

3. ____ In Erikson's theory, the adolescent's path to successfully achieving an identity begins with identity diffusion, which is characterized by little sense of commitment to the various issues he or she has to grapple with and the social demands made on him or her.

4. ____ The ethic of individual rights and justice is Carol Gilligan's term for the ethic that she believes is the basis for Kohlberg's theory and that she suggests is a more common perspective for males.

5. ____ Following the moratorium period, during which the adolescent experiments with different roles, values, and beliefs, he or she may then choose among alternatives and make commitments and gradually arrive at an *integrated identity*.

6. ____ In Kohlberg's theory, there are three distinct *levels* of moral reasoning, and each level has two *stages* that represent different degrees of sophistication in thinking about moral dilemmas.

7. ____ In Kohlberg's theory, the preconventional level is characterized by moral reasoning based on self-interest and is guided by external consequences, such as avoiding punishment and maximizing personal gain, rather than by internalized values and rules.

Check your answers and review any areas of weakness before going on to the next section.

Adult Development

Preview Questions

Consider the following questions as you study this section of the chapter.

- What physical changes take place in adulthood?
- What general patterns of social development occur?
- How does the transition to parenthood affect adults?
- What are some of the variations in the paths of adult social development?

Read the section "Adult Development" and **write** *your answers to the following:*

1. The physical changes that take place during adulthood include _____

_____

_____

2. According to Erikson, the primary psychosocial conflict of middle adulthood is _____

_____

3. The most general pattern of social development includes _____

_____

_____

4. In relation to having children, marital satisfaction _____

_____

_____

5. The nature of intimate relationships and family structures varies widely in the United States. For example, _____

_____

_____

_____

_____

In terms of careers in adulthood, _____

_____

_____

_____

_____

_____

Late Adulthood and Aging

Preview Questions

- What cognitive changes take place in late adulthood?
- What factors can influence social development during this period?

Read the section "Late Adulthood and Aging" and **write** *your answers to the following:*

1. Regarding mental abilities in late adulthood

_____

_____

2. According to the activity theory of aging _____

_____

_____

_____

3. According to Erikson, the psychosocial task of late adulthood is _____

The Final Chapter: Dying and Death

Preview Question

- How did Kübler-Ross describe the stages of dying, and how valid is her theory?

Read the section "The Final Chapter: Dying and Death" and **write** *your answers to the following:*

1. According to Kübler-Ross's theory of dying and death, the five stages are _____

_____

_____

_____

_____

_____

2. Problems with Kübler-Ross's theory are that

_____

_____

_____

After you have carefully studied the preceding sections, complete the following exercises.

Concept Check 5

Read the following and write the correct term in the space provided.

1. Forty-eight-year-old Dr. Gretinger has three grown children, a thriving dental practice, and is very involved in local community activities. Dr. Gretinger is in the _____ stage of life and, according to Erikson, has achieved the psychosocial task of

_____ .

2. Compared with their grandparents, Mr. and Mrs. Belmont's children are likely to marry for the first time at _____ (an earlier/a later) age.

3. David, a 65-year-old retired civil servant, feels that his life has been unproductive and ultimately meaningless. David is in the

_____ stage of life and, according to Erikson, is experiencing

_____ .

4. Andrew, a 45-year-old accountant, has just learned he has a terminal illness. According to Kübler-Ross, as soon as Andrew gets over his initial denial, he will experience

   _____ .

5. Sarah is a 25-year-old, white, middle-class, well-educated, moderately religious person. If she is typical, she will marry someone very _____ (different from/similar to) herself.

6. The last of the Sandwells' four children has just left home to pursue a career with NASA. If the Sandwells are like most parents whose children have left home, they are likely to experience a steady _____ (decline/increase) in marital satisfaction.

7. Mort and Harry, who are in their seventies, belong to a club called the "Active Ancients Association." Both men feel that their lives have been meaningful and satisfying and feel no disappointment about their accomplishments. Erikson would say that Mort and Harry have achieved _____ .

8. Harry and Mort pursue hobbies, such as fishing, golf, and chess, travel occasionally, take an interest in their grandchildren and great-grandchildren, and do occasional volunteer work. Mort and Harry appear to epitomize the _____ theory of aging.

Graphic Organizer 3

Identify the theorist related to each of the following statements.

Statement	Theorist
1. I believe that social and cultural influences are the most important factors in cognitive development.	
2. I study attachment, and I have devised a measure of attachment called the Strange Situation.	
3. In my view people have an innate understanding of the basic principles of language, which I call a "universal grammar."	
4. I believe that development continues throughout the lifespan and that individuals pass through eight distinct stages during which they are faced with resolving important psychosocial conflicts.	
5. My primary interest is in how children develop intellectually and cognitively, and my theory proposes that children progress through four distinct stages in succession, each stage characterized by a qualitatively different way of thinking from the previous stage.	
6. The primary goal of my research has been to map out the development of moral reasoning in humans; it is my view that there are three levels, each consisting of two stages, and that humans progress through these stages in sequence, until reaching the highest level.	
7. As a result of my research on cognitive development in infants, using visual rather than manual tasks, I have concluded that Piaget was incorrect about the age at which object permanence first appears.	

Review of Terms and Concepts 5

Use the terms in this list to complete the Matching Test, then to help you answer the True/False items correctly.

menopause
early adulthood
middle adulthood
late adulthood
generativity
activity theory of aging
ego integrity
despair
life review

Kübler-Ross's stages of dying (denial, anger, bargaining, depression, acceptance)
authoritarian parenting style
permissive parenting style
authoritative parenting style
induction

Matching Exercise

Match the appropriate term/name with its definition or description.

1. _____ Discipline technique that combines parental control with explaining why a behavior is prohibited.

2. _____ The natural cessation of menstruation and the end of reproductive capacity in women.

3. _____ Baumrind's term for a parenting style in which parents are extremely tolerant and not demanding.

4. _____ Stage of adulthood, roughly from the forties to the mid-sixties, when physical strength and endurance gradually decline.

5. _____ Psychosocial theory that life satisfaction in late adulthood is highest when people maintain the level of activity they displayed earlier in life.

6. _____ Erikson's eighth psychosocial task that involves the feeling that one's life has been meaningful.

7. _____ Process through which the themes of ego integrity or despair emerge as older adults think about or retell their life story to others.

True/False Test

Indicate whether each item is true or false by placing T or F in the space next to each item.

1. ____ In Erikson's theory, the primary psychosocial task of middle adulthood in which the person contributes to future generations through children, career, and other meaningful activity is called generativity.

2. ____ Early adulthood refers to the stage of development during the twenties and thirties when physical strength typically peaks.

3. ____ *Authoritarian parenting style* is Baumrind's term for describing parents who set clear standards for their children's behavior but are also responsive to the children's needs and wishes.

4. ____ Late adulthood refers to the stage of development beginning in the mid-sixties, when physical stamina and reaction time tend to decline further and faster.

5. ____ According to Baumrind, authoritative parents are demanding and unresponsive toward their children's needs or wishes.

6. ____ According to Kübler-Ross, people who are facing death go through five stages—denial, anger, bargaining, depression, and acceptance.

7. ____ During Erikson's eighth stage of psychosocial development, older adults who are filled with regrets or bitterness about past mistakes, missed opportunities, or bad decisions, experience despair.

Check your answers and review any areas of weakness before going on to the next section.

Something to Think About

1. A popular and controversial topic in any discussion of raising children is the effect of day care on a child's development. Discussions like this can become quite heated, with people holding strong views on both sides of the debate. On the basis of what you have read in this chapter, what light could you shed on this controversial topic?

2. You may be planning to have a family one day if you haven't already done so. For most people this is quite a responsibility and a lot of work. Unlike many other areas in life, no formal training is available or required for the job of parent. You, however, are fortunate because you are taking an introductory psychology course and have learned a few things about child development. What advice would you give to people who are planning to have a family?

Check your answers and review any areas of weakness before doing the progress tests.

Progress Test 1

Review the complete chapter (including Concept Reviews and the boxed inserts), review all your study notes, and then test yourself on the following progress test. Check your answers. If you make a mistake, review your notes, review the relevant section of the study guide, and, if necessary, go back and read the appropriate part of your textbook.

1. When Thomas was conceived, he was a single fertilized egg called a(n)

   (a) zygote.   (c) fetus.
   (b) embryo.   (d) infant.

2. Young Misty has dark curly hair and freckles; her friend Paige has straight blonde hair and no freckles. In both children, the underlying genetic makeup and genetic instructions for these traits are their _____ , and the observable traits that they actually display are their _____ .

   (a) dominant characteristics; recessive characteristics
   (b) phenotypes; genotypes
   (c) recessive characteristics; dominant characteristics
   (d) genotypes; phenotypes

3. In her research, Dr. Joacim found that a pregnant mother's use of a certain chemical substance caused harm to the fetus. The chemical substance could be classified as

   (a) deoxyribonucleic acid.
   (b) a chromosome.
   (c) a phenotype.
   (d) a teratogen.

4. Kalbiar has dimples, which is a dominant characteristic determined by a single pair of genes. Kalbiar's genotype

   (a) could be a dimples/no dimples combination.
   (b) could be a no dimples/no dimples combination.
   (c) could be expressed phenotypically as no dimples, depending on the amount of sunlight she was exposed to.
   (d) could be all of the above.

5. When Mrs. Euland touched her newborn's lips, he produced an automatic response called the _____ reflex.

   (a) rooting   (c) grasping
   (b) sucking   (d) greedy

6. It has become apparent to Mr. and Mrs. Euland that their baby has a low activity level, tends to withdraw from new situations and people, and adapts to new experiences very gradually. The baby would be classified as a(n) _____ baby.

   (a) easy   (c) slow-to-warm-up
   (b) difficult   (d) securely attached

7. When 2-year old Kerry was tested in the Strange Situation, she did not explore the environment even when her mother was present. She appeared very anxious, and she became extremely distressed when her mother left the room. Kerry is a(n)

   (a) insecurely attached infant.
   (b) securely attached infant.
   (c) conventional infant.
   (d) concrete operational infant.

8. When she was almost 11 months old, Jessica said "ba ba" when she pointed at her bottle and "ma ma" when she pointed at her Mom. Jessica is in the _____ stage of language development.

   (a) cooing   (c) one-word
   (b) babbling   (d) two-word

9. When Neil's mother hides his favorite toy under a blanket, Neil acts as though it no longer exists and makes no attempt to retrieve it. Neil is in Piaget's _____ stage, and his behavior suggests that he _____ .

   (a) sensorimotor; has developed object permanence
   (b) preoperational; has not developed object permanence
   (c) concrete operational; is capable of reversible thinking
   (d) formal operational; understands the principle of conservation

10. Darlene and Mike have been married for three years and have a 9-month-old infant. If they are like most young married couples, their level of marital satisfaction is probably

    (a) declining.
    (b) increasing dramatically.
    (c) the same as it was when they first got married.
    (d) increasing steadily year after year.

11. Danielle has switched college majors four times and does not know what she wants to do after she gets her degree. Erikson would suggest that Danielle has not achieved
    (a) an integrated identity.
    (b) a sense of generativity.
    (c) the conventional level of moral reasoning.
    (d) the concrete operational stage of development.

12. According to Kohlberg's theory of moral development, preconventional morality is to postconventional morality as_____ is to _____ .
    (a) social approval; ethical principle
    (b) self-interest; social approval
    (c) self-interest; ethical principle
    (d) social approval; self-interest

13. Gordon, a 50-year-old lawyer, has just learned from his physician that he has only one year to live. According to Kübler-Ross, his first reaction to hearing the news is likely to be
    (a) "No, it's not possible, there's obviously been some mix-up, some terrible mistake."
    (b) "Life is not worth living any more."
    (c) "Why me? This is very unfair and makes me mad."
    (d) "Well, that's the way it goes, I guess."

14. According to the Application, a parenting style in which parents set clear standards for their children's behavior but are also responsive to the children's needs and wishes is called
    (a) authoritarian.
    (b) permissive-indulgent.
    (c) permissive-indifferent.
    (d) authoritative.

15. According to Culture and Human Behavior 9.1, infants typically sleep in their own bed and in a separate room from their parents in
    (a) all cultures.
    (b) all Western cultures.
    (c) the United States.
    (d) all Latin cultures.

Progress Test 2

After you have checked your understanding of the material in Progress Test 1 and have done a complete chapter review with special focus on any areas of weakness, you are ready to assess your knowledge on Progress Test 2. Check your answers. If you make a mistake, review your notes, the relevant section of the study guide, and, if necessary, the appropriate part of your textbook.

1. Dr. Strayer is conducting longitudinal research on factors that correlate with getting older. She is likely to find that
    (a) intelligence declines sharply with age.
    (b) there is severe memory impairment as people reach late adulthood.
    (c) most people maintain their intellectual abilities as they age.
    (d) no matter how much older people practice their mental skills, they still do very poorly on intellectual tasks.

2. Mr. Danzig is a 68-year-old retired accountant. If he is typical of people his age, he is probably living
    (a) in his own home.
    (b) in a nursing home.
    (c) with his grown-up children.
    (d) in a mental health facility.

3. Which of the following utterances is 2-year-old Quentin likely to have used during his recent birthday party?
    (a) "Please Mama, may I have another cookie."
    (b) "ah-ah-ah, ba-ba-ba, ca-ca-ca!"
    (c) "Mama cookie."
    (d) "Quentin wants another cookie now, and if he doesn't get one he's going to throw a tantrum!"

4. Miguel is a 25-year-old, college-educated middle-class engineer. Like his Mexican parents, he is a devout Catholic. If Miguel is like most people, he will probably marry someone who is
    (a) completely different from him in every way as long as she is Catholic.
    (b) very much like he is.
    (c) much older than he is.
    (d) much richer than he is.

5. Mrs. Grant is 49 years old and has recently ceased to menstruate. Mrs. Grant has experienced
    (a) moratorium.   (c) induction.
    (b) menopause.   (d) centration.

6. According to Erikson's psychosocial theory of development, late adulthood is to _____ as adolescence is to _____ .
    (a) ego integrity; generativity
    (b) generativity; intimacy
    (c) intimacy; ego integrity
    (d) ego integrity; integrated identity

7. Mr. Gates believes in law and order, obeys all rules and regulations, and has respect for authorities just because they are authorities. Mr. Gates is likely at Kohlberg's _____ level of moral reasoning.
   (a) conventional
   (b) preconventional
   (c) concrete operational
   (d) formal operational

8. Sixteen-year-old Jade is reading books about different religions and philosophies and is trying out different approaches to how one should live one's life. Jade is in Erikson's
   (a) moratorium period.
   (b) generativity stage.
   (c) ego integrity period.
   (d) formal operational stage.

9. The Atwells have two teenage children. If they are like most parents, their relationship with their kids
   (a) is very negative and getting worse.
   (b) is full of fights, arguments, anger, and hostility.
   (c) is just about as positive as it was when the children were younger.
   (d) was positive at first but has deteriorated as the children aged.

10. Marcel is researching a paper for his child development course and discovers the work of Lev Vygotsky. In summarizing Vygotsky's contribution to developmental psychology, Marcel is likely to note that the theorist emphasized
    (a) genetic factors.
    (b) clearly defined biological stages of cognitive development.
    (c) clearly defined biological stages of moral development.
    (d) social and cultural factors in cognitive development.

11. Kelly is 5 years old and has a good imagination. Recently, for example, she used a discarded box as a make-believe castle and made up a very interesting dialogue between the "king" and "queen" of her castle. This illustrates
    (a) centration.
    (b) conservation.
    (c) symbolic thought.
    (d) object permanence.

12. In the Strange Situation procedure, little Anthony used his mother as a safe base from which to explore the environment, showed distress when she left the room, and greeted her warmly when she returned. Anthony would be classified as a(n)
    (a) difficult baby.
    (b) securely attached baby.
    (c) insecurely attached baby.
    (d) slow-to-warm-up baby.

13. During a class debate on the issue of whether war is ever justified, Dominique argued that it is never justified because war involves killing people and killing people is against the law. Dominique is in the conventional stage of
    (a) Kohlberg's model of moral development.
    (b) Piaget's model of cognitive development.
    (c) Erikson's model of psychosocial development.
    (d) Chomsky's model of language development.

14. According to Critical Thinking 9.2, putting young children in a high-quality day-care facility
    (a) is detrimental to their physical health.
    (b) severely disrupts the attachment process.
    (c) has no detrimental effect on the children.
    (d) is detrimental to their psychological health.

15. According to the Application, psychologist Diana Baumrind has described a number of basic parenting styles. In her research, she found that children of _____ parents were likely to be moody, unhappy, fearful, withdrawn, unspontaneous, and irritable.
    (a) permissive-indulgent
    (b) permissive-indifferent
    (c) authoritative
    (d) authoritarian

Progress Test 3

After you have checked your understanding of the material in Progress Tests 1 and 2, and have done a complete chapter review with special focus on any areas of weakness, you are ready to further assess your knowledge on Progress Test 3. Check your answers. If you make a mistake, review your notes, the appropriate parts of the study guide, and, if necessary, the relevant sections of your textbook.

1. In looking back at his life, 70-year-old Redner experiences regret, dissatisfaction, and disappointment about his accomplishments. According to Erikson, Redner, who is in late adulthood, is experiencing _____ and has failed to achieve a sense of
   _____ .
   (a) inferiority; generativity
   (b) despair; ego integrity
   (c) stagnation; ego identity
   (d) isolation; intimacy

2. Nine-year-old Adam has acquired the mental operations to comprehend such things as conservation and reversibility and can solve tangible problems in a logical manner. Adam is in Piaget's _____ stage of development.
   (a) sensorimotor   (c) concrete operational
   (b) preoperational   (d) formal operational

3. Piaget is to _____ development as Erikson is to _____ development.
   (a) cognitive; moral
   (b) psychosocial; physical
   (c) moral; emotional
   (d) cognitive; psychosocial

4. Despite the fact that he uses only one word utterances when he attempts to talk, one-year-old Vincent immediately does what he is told when his mother says, "Bring Mommy the teddy bear, Vincent." This suggests that
   (a) Vincent's comprehension vocabulary is much larger than his production vocabulary.
   (b) Vincent is in the embryonic stage of language development.
   (c) Vincent has a sex-linked recessive characteristic that has retarded his development.
   (d) Vincent's production vocabulary is much larger than his comprehension vocabulary.

5. When Kiran was born, his brain was about 25 percent of its adult weight; during infancy, it reached about 75 percent of its adult weight. This increase in weight is due to the fact that
   (a) millions of new neurons were formed daily during this period.
   (b) the number of dendrites increased dramatically and the axons of many neurons acquired myelin.
   (c) neurons grew bigger in size and the dendrites acquired a white fatty covering called myelin.
   (d) the number of new neurons increased dramatically and the original neurons increased in size and weight.

6. Nine months after conception, baby Tracy is born. The stages of her prenatal development, from first to last, were
   (a) embryonic, fetal, germinal.
   (b) fetal, embryonic, germinal.
   (c) germinal, embryonic, fetal.
   (d) germinal, fetal, embryonic.

7. Mrs. Hoff uses very distinct pronunciation, a simplified vocabulary, short sentences, a high pitch, and exaggerated intonation and expression whenever she interacts with her baby. This is an example of
   (a) motherese, or infant-directed speech.
   (b) a sex-linked recessive characteristic.
   (c) an insecurely attached mother.
   (d) cooing and babbling.

8. Michael has red-green color blindness, which is a sex-linked recessive characteristic, but his sister Eileen has normal color vision. It is likely that
   (a) Eileen has the recessive gene for red-green color blindness on each of her X chromosomes.
   (b) Michael has the recessive gene for red-green color blindness on each of his X chromosomes.
   (c) Eileen has the recessive gene for red-green color blindness on each of her Y chromosomes.
   (d) Michael has the recessive gene for red-green color blindness on the X chromosome of his XY chromosomes.

9. During Mr. Guerno's seventieth birthday party his grandchildren had a chance to ask him about some of his many adventures and travels. It was apparent while listening to his colorful stories that their grandfather had lived a very meaningful life and was very satisfied with his many accomplishments. Mr. Guerno is in the _____ stage of life and has achieved what Erikson called _____ .
   (a) middle adulthood; generativity
   (b) late adulthood; ego integrity
   (c) middle adulthood; initiative
   (d) late adulthood; ego identity

10. Neuroscientists studying brain changes during childhood are likely to find that between age 6 and early adolescence
   (a) there is a steady increase in the actual number of neurons in the brain.
   (b) unused dendrites, synaptic connections, and neurons are selectively pruned and discarded, and those neurons that are most used strengthen their interconnections with other neurons.
   (c) the neurons that are least used tend to proliferate and those that are most used tend to wear out and decrease in number.
   (d) there is an explosive proliferation of synaptic connections in all neurons regardless of whether they are used or not.

11. Young Allison doesn't understand that adding together one and three is the same as adding together three and one. Allison is demonstrating _____ and is in Piaget's _____ stage of development.
   (a) conservation; concrete operational
   (b) egocentrism; preoperational
   (c) centration; sensorimotor
   (d) irreversibility; preoperational

12. Fourteen-year-old Jason has the ability to reason abstractly and think logically even about hypothetical situations. Jason is in Piaget's _____ stage of cognitive development.
   (a) sensorimotor
   (b) preoperational
   (c) concrete operational
   (d) formal operational

13. Gretchen is freckle-free, which is a recessive characteristic determined by a single gene pair. She hopes that she will have a child who is also freckle-free. In order for this to happen, her daughter will need to inherit
   (a) the phenotype combination of freckles/no freckle.
   (b) the genotype combination of freckles/no freckles.
   (c) the genotype combination of no freckles/no freckles.
   (d) the genotype combination of freckles/ freckles.

14. According to Culture and Human Behavior 9.3
   (a) the level of conflict between parents and adolescents tends to be higher in Chinese families, compared with European-American families.
   (b) although the level of conflict may vary, parent–adolescent conflict is a common dimension of family life in all cultures.
   (c) regardless of which culture they belonged to, adolescents showed a high level of respect for parental authority, a strong sense of family obligation, and a keen desire for harmony within the family.
   (d) there is significantly less parent–adolescent conflict in individualistic cultures, compared with collectivistic cultures.

15. According to the Application, which of the following is *not* recommended for raising psychologically healthy children?
   (a) Work with your children's temperamental qualities.
   (b) Use induction to teach as you discipline.
   (c) Let your children know that you love them.
   (d) Strive to be an authoritarian parent.
   (e) Listen to your children.

Answers

Introduction: Your Life Story

1. *Developmental psychology is the* study of how people change physically, mentally, and socially over the lifespan.

2. *The major themes in developmental psychology are* the common patterns of growth and development people share and how they differ in terms of social, occupational, and interpersonal accomplishment; the abrupt age-related stages people go through over the lifespan and those aspects of development that reflect gradually

unfolding changes; and the nature of the interaction between heredity (nature) and environment (nurture) throughout development.

Genetic Contributions to Your Life Story

1. *Chromosomes are* long, threadlike structures
   composed of twisted parallel strands of DNA;
   they are found in the nucleus of the cell.

2. *DNA (deoxyribonucleic acid) is* the chemical
   basis of heredity and carries genetic instructions in the cell.

3. *Genes are* the basic units of heredity that direct
   the development of a particular characteristic;
   each gene is a unit of DNA instructions pertain-
   ing to some characteristic such as eye or hair
   color, height, or handedness.

4. *Genotype refers to the* underlying genetic makeup of a particular organism, including the
   genetic instructions for traits that are not actually displayed. *Phenotype refers to the* observable traits or characteristics of an organism as
   determined by the interaction of genetics and
   environmental factors.

5. *In a pair of genes, the dominant gene is* the
   gene that contains genetic instructions that will
   be expressed whether paired with another dominant gene or with a recessive gene. *A recessive
   gene is* the gene that contains genetic instructions that will not be expressed unless paired
   with another recessive gene.

6. *We inherit from our biological parents* a genetic
   potential, the expression of which can be influenced by environmental conditions.

7. *The sex chromosomes are* chromosomes designated as X or Y that determine biological sex;
   they are the 23rd pair of chromosomes in
   humans. *Sex-linked recessive characteristics are
   traits determined by* recessive genes located on
   the X chromosome; in males, these characteristics require only one recessive gene to be
   expressed.

Prenatal Development

1. *During prenatal development, the single-cell
   zygote* undergoes rapid cell divison before
   becoming implanted on the mother's uterine
   wall. Eventually, it develops into a full-term
   fetus.

2. *The three phases of the prenatal stage are* the
   germinal period (the first two weeks), the
   embryonic period (from the third to eighth
   week), and the fetal period (from the ninth
   week until birth).

3. *Teratogens are* harmful agents or substances
   that can cross the placenta and cause malformations or defects in an embryo or fetus. The
   greatest vulnerability to teratogens is during
   the embryonic stage.

Concept Check 1

1. developmental
2. nature (heredity); nurture (environment)
3. X; Y; X; X
4. embryo; fetus
5. teratogen
6. infancy; early childhood; middle childhood
7. chromosomes; deoxyribonucleic acid (DNA);
   genes
8. sex-linked recessive characteristic; recessive

Graphic Organizer 1

Cell 1: dimples

Cell 2: dimples

Cell 3: dimples

Cell 4: no dimples

Matching Exercise 1

1. prenatal stage
2. gene
3. developmental psychology
4. sex-linked recessive characteristics
5. teratogens
6. chromosome
7. recessive gene
8. germinal period (zygotic period)
9. embryo
10. recessive characteristics
11. sex chromosomes
12. placenta
13. X chromosome
14. umbilical cord

True/False Test 1

1. T	5. T	9. F	13. T
2. T	6. T	10. T	14. T
3. T	7. F	11. F	
4. F	8. T	12. T	

Development During Infancy and Childhood: Physical Development

1. *Newborn infants enter the world equipped with* the rooting reflex, the sucking reflex, and the grasping reflex. *Their senses of vision, hearing, smell, and touch are* keenly attuned to people, and this ability helps them differentiate between their mothers and other people.

2. *The infant's sensory capabilities promote the development of relationships with caregivers, as evidenced by the fact that they* stare at human faces longer than other images, make eye contact with adults who position themselves close to the newborn (6 to 12 inches), respond with increased alertness to the sound of human voices, and quickly become sensitized to the scent of their mothers.

3. *After birth, a number of changes take place in the infant's brain:* during infancy, the brain will go from being 25 percent of its adult weight to 75 percent; the number of dendrites will increase dramatically during the first two years; and the axons of many neurons will acquire myelin.

Development During Infancy and Childhood: Social and Personality Development

1. *Temperament refers to* the inborn predispositions to consistently behave and react in a certain way. *Attachment is the* emotional bond that forms between the infant and his or her caregivers, especially the parents.

2. *The three broad temperamental patterns are* easy, difficult, and slow-to-warm-up.

3. *Attachment is measured using a procedure called the* Strange Situation. *In this technique* the baby and mother are brought into an unfamiliar room with a variety of toys, and a few minutes later a stranger enters. The mother stays with the child for a few moments, then departs and returns a short time later, she spends a little time with the child, and then departs and returns again. Observers record the infant's behavior through a one-way mirror.

4. *The basic premise of attachment theory is* that an infant's ability to thrive physically and psychologically depends in part on the quality of attachment. When parents are consistently warm, responsive, and sensitive to their infant's needs, the infant develops a secure attachment; if parents are neglectful, inconsistent, or insensitive, an infant may suffer insecure attachment.

Development During Infancy and Childhood: Language Development

1. *According to Noam Chomsky,* all children are born with a biological predisposition to learn language; in effect, they possess a "universal grammar," which allows them to easily extract grammatical rules from what they hear.

2. *Language development is encouraged by* the use of infant-directed speech (motherese) that adults instinctively use with babies.

3. *The stages of language development are* the cooing and babbling stage, the one-word stage (in which comprehension vocabulary is usually much larger than production vocabulary), the two-word stage, and finally, fully developed language comprehension and production.

Concept Check 2

1. human face
2. the Strange Situation
3. 25 percent
4. rooting reflex; sucking reflex; grasping reflex
5. 100 billion; dendrites; myelin
6. easy
7. secure
8. comprehension; production

Matching Exercise 2

1. attachment theory
2. Strange Situation
3. sucking reflex
4. slow-to-warm-up temperament
5. motherese (infant-directed speech)
6. cooing and babbling stage
7. attachment
8. comprehension vocabulary
9. insecure attachment
10. two-word stage
11. multiple attachments

True/False Test 2

1. F	5. T	9. F
2. T	6. T	10. T
3. F	7. F	
4. T	8. T	

Development During Infancy and Childhood: Cognitive Development

1. *The four stages (and their characteristics) in Piaget's theory are*

    (a) the sensorimotor stage, from birth to about age 2, during which the infant explores the environment and acquires knowledge through sensing and manipulating objects. The development of object permanence is characteristic of this stage.

    (b) the preoperational stage, from about age 2 to age 7, during which the use of symbols and prelogical thought processes increase. Characteristics of this stage include the increasing use of symbolic thought; the tendency for egocentrism, irreversibility, and centration; and the inability to understand conservation.

    (c) the concrete operational stage, from about age 7 to adolescence, during which the child develops the ability to think logically about concrete objects and situations. Characteristics of this stage are the tendency to be less egocentric in their thinking, the ability to reverse mental problems, and the ability to understand the principle of conservation.

    (d) the formal operational stage, from adolescence through adulthood, during which the person acquires the ability to think logically about abstract principles and hypothetical situations. This stage is characterized by more systematic and logical problem solving abilities.

2. *Piaget's theory has been criticized because* he underestimated the cognitive abilities of infants and children, confusing motor skill limitations with cognitive limitations; his notion that the stages unfold universally has not been supported by research; and he underestimated the impact of social and cultural factors on cognitive development.

3. *The information-processing model of cognitive development views cognitive development as* a continuous process over the lifespan. Researchers in this area focus on the development of basic mental processes, such as attention, memory, and problem solving.

Concept Check 3

1. underestimated
2. concrete operational
3. object permanence
4. conservation

5. assimilating
6. schema
7. formal
8. accommodation
9. motor skill; cognitive
10. information processing

Matching Exercise 3

1. symbolic thought
2. Renée Baillargeon
3. object permanence
4. formal operational stage
5. Jean Piaget
6. information-processing model of cognitive development
7. schemas
8. sensorimotor stage
9. egocentrism
10. Lev Vygotsky

True/False Test 3

1. T	5. F	9. F
2. T	6. T	
3. F	7. F	
4. T	8. T	

Adolescence

1. *Adolescence is* the transitional stage between late childhood and the beginning of adulthood, during which sexual maturity is reached.

2. *The relationship between parents and their adolescent children is* generally positive, but relationships with friends and peers become increasingly important.

3. *Identity refers to* a person's definition or description of himself or herself, including the values, beliefs, and ideals that guide the individual's behavior.

4. *Adolescents begin the process of identity formation by* evaluating themselves on several different dimensions, such as social acceptance by peers, academic and athletic abilities, work abilities, personal appearance, and romantic appeal.

5. *According to Erikson's psychosocial theory of lifespan development,* each of the eight stages of life is associated with a particular psychosocial

conflict that can be resolved in either a positive or negative direction. *The key psychosocial conflict facing adolescents is* identity versus identity diffusion.

6. *Kohlberg's levels (and stages) of moral development include* the preconventional level (stage 1: punishment and obedience and stage 2: mutual benefit), the conventional level (stage 3: interpersonal expectations and stage 4: law and order), and the postconventional level (stage 5: legal principles and stage 6: universal moral principles).

7. *Criticisms of Kohlberg's theory are* that it reflects a male perspective and does not accurately depict the development of moral reasoning in women, that it is based on the ethic of individual rights and justice, and that aspects of moral reasoning in other cultures do not appear to be reflected in the theory.

Concept Check 4

1. 1; preconventional
2. Carol Gilligan; care and responsibility
3. integrated identity; intimacy versus isolation
4. 4; conventional
5. identity
6. trust versus mistrust; autonomy versus doubt; initiative versus guilt; industry versus inferiority
7. positive

Graphic Organizer 2

1. Piaget: formal operational stage;   Kohlberg: postconventional level, stage 6
2. Piaget: preoperational stage; Kohlberg: preconventional level, stage 1
3. Piaget: concrete operational stage; Kohlberg: preconventional level, stage 2
4. Piaget: concrete operational stage; Kohlberg: conventional level, stage 4

Matching Exercise 4

1. Lawrence Kohlberg
2. identity
3. ethic of care and responsibility
4. moral reasoning
5. moratorium period
6. adolescence
7. conventional level

True/False Test 4

1. T	4. T	7. T
2. T	5. T	
3. T	6. T	

Adult Development

1. *The physical changes that take place during adulthood include* genetically influenced changes such as menopause (the cessation of menstruation) and thinning, graying hair; and environmentally influenced changes such as the formation of wrinkles, a decrease in the efficiency of various body organs, and a decline in physical strength and endurance.

2. *According to Erikson, the primary psychosocial conflict of middle adulthood is* generativity versus stagnation.

3. *The most general pattern of social development includes* love and work, which means forming a long-term committed relationship, becoming parents, and pursuing a career or careers. However, there is great variability in the path to intimacy.

4. *In relation to having children, marital satisfaction* tends to decline after the first child is born and to increase after children leave home.

5. *The nature of intimate relationships and family structures varies widely in the United States. For example,* the number of unmarried couples living together has increased dramatically in the last 20 years; more than 30 percent of children are being raised by a single parent; more than half of all first marriages end in divorce and remarrying and starting a second family later in life is not uncommon; among married couples an increasing number are opting for a child-free life together; and there are many gay and lesbian couples committed to a long-term monogamous relationship.

In terms of careers in adulthood, about one-third of people in their late twenties and early thirties not only change jobs within a particular field, but completely switch occupational fields; dual-career families have become more common; and although the combination of work and family roles can be demanding, especially for women, multiple roles can lead to increased personal satisfaction.

Late Adulthood and Aging

1. *Regarding mental abilities in late adulthood,* there is not necessarily a steep decline in physical or cognitive abilities; mental abilities only begin to decline at around age 60, and these declines can be minimized or eliminated with an active and mentally stimulating lifestyle.

2. *According to the activity theory of aging,* life satisfaction in late adulthood is highest when you maintain your previous level of activity, either by continuing old activities or by finding new ones.

3. *According to Erikson, the psychosocial conflict of late adulthood is* ego integrity versus despair.

The Final Chapter: Dying and Death

1. *According to Kübler-Ross's theory of death and dying, the five stages are* denial (people deny that death is imminent); anger (people feel and express indignation and rage); bargaining (people try to work out a deal with doctors, relatives, or God); depression (people become despondent about their fate); and acceptance (people realize what lies ahead and resign themselves to their fate).

2. *Problems with Kübler-Ross's theory are that* dying individuals do not progress through a predictable sequence of stages. Dying is as individual a process as living; people cope with the prospect of dying much as they have coped with other stresses in their lives.

Concept Check 5

1. middle adulthood; generativity
2. a later
3. late adulthood; despair
4. anger
5. similar to
6. increase
7. ego integrity
8. activity

Graphic Organizer 3

1. Lev Vygotsky
2. Mary D. Salter Ainsworth
3. Noam Chomsky
4. Erik Erikson
5. Jean Piaget
6. Lawrence Kohlberg
7. Renée Baillargeon

Matching Exercise 5

1. induction
2. menopause
3. permissive parenting style
4. middle adulthood
5. activity theory of aging
6. ego integrity
7. life review

True/False Test 5

1. T	4. T	7. T
2. T	5. F	
3. F	6. T	

Something to Think About

1. Most psychologists today agree that the *quality* of the child-care arrangements is the key factor in promoting secure attachment in early childhood and preventing problems in later childhood. In fact, many studies have found that children who experience high-quality day care tend to be more sociable, better adjusted, and more academically competent than children who experience poor-quality day care. In addition, some researchers have found that grade school children enrolled in high-quality day care from infancy experience no negative effects of their day-care experience. Research in Sweden has supported these findings.

   High-quality day care is characterized by a number of key factors: caregivers should be warm and responsive, developmentally appropriate activities and a variety of play materials should be available, caregivers should have some training and education in child development, low staff turnover is important, and the ratio of caregivers to children should be low.

2. A short discussion of the various stages of cognitive, psychosocial, and moral development would be appropriate. Raising psychologically healthy children is possible if parents adopt some of the strategies suggested by the experts. Psychologist Diana Baumrind has described three basic parenting styles: authoritarian, permissive, and authoritative. Research has shown that the authoritative style produces the best

results. Can parents learn to be authoritative in their parenting style? The Application has a number of practical suggestions: let your children know that you love them, listen to your children, use induction to teach as you discipline, work with your children's temperamental qualities, and understand your child's age-related cognitive abilities and limitations.

Although all children inherit genetic predispositions from both parents, research has shown that environmental factors, such as the social and cultural influences, educational experiences, and parenting style have very powerful effects on a child's development.

Progress Test 1

1. a	6. c	11. a
2. d	7. a	12. c
3. d	8. c	13. a
4. a	9. b	14. d
5. b	10. a	15. c

Progress Test 2

1. c	6. d	11. c
2. a	7. a	12. b
3. c	8. a	13. a
4. b	9. c	14. c
5. b	10. d	15. d

Progress Test 3

1. b	6. c	11. d
2. c	7. a	12. d
3. d	8. d	13. c
4. a	9. b	14. b
5. b	10. b	15. d

chapter 10

Gender and Sexuality

PREVIEW	Reading the section below first will give you a general sense of the chapter's contents and an initial introduction to some of the major concepts and terms. This will prime you for what you are about to read and help you to develop a "cognitive map" that will guide your study of the material in this chapter. Likewise, reading the **preview questions** at the beginning of each major section will improve your ability to understand, learn, and retain the information.

CHAPTER 10 . . . AT A GLANCE

To help you distinguish between sex and gender, the text first defines all the relevant terms *sex, gender, gender roles, gender identity, sexual orientation,* and *gender-role stereotype*. Similarities and differences in the cognitive abilities and sexual attitudes and behaviors of men and women are discussed. Gender-role development and the influence of social and cultural factors are examined. Two theories of gender-role development—social learning theory and gender schema theory—explain current thinking about how gender roles develop.

Human sexuality is discussed next. The four phases of the human sexual response cycle are presented, and sexual motivation in both humans and other animals is explored. Sexual orientation appears to develop at an early age, and genetics and brain structure may be involved. During early and middle childhood, children become increasingly aware of their own bodies and increasingly curious about sexual matters. At puberty adolescents reach sexual maturity, and this is when they must deal with a number of physical changes as well as romantic and sexual relationships. Details of human sexuality in early, middle, and late adulthood are presented, including the frequency and type of sexual behavior people engage in, and people's fantasies about sexual activity.

The chapter ends with a discussion of various sexual disorders and problems, including the paraphilias and gender identity disorder. The most common types of sexual dysfunctions in men and women are described. Sexually transmitted diseases (STDs) and AIDS are discussed. The Application looks at communication differences and conflicts people in intimate relationships experience, and offers some important practical tips for dealing with them.

Introduction: Gender and Sexuality

Preview Questions

Consider the following questions as you study this section of the chapter.

- How is sex defined, and how does it differ from gender?
- How do the terms *gender role, gender identity,* and *sexual orientation* differ in meaning?

*Read the section "Introduction: Gender and Sexuality" and **write** your answers to the following:*

1. Sex refers to _____

   _____

   _____

   gender refers to _____

   _____

   _____

2. Gender roles consist of _____

   _____

   _____

   gender identity refers to_____

   _____

   _____

   and sexual orientation refers to _____

   _____

   _____

Gender Stereotypes and Gender Roles

Preview Questions

Consider the following questions as you study this section of the chapter.

- What are gender-role stereotypes?
- How do men and women compare in terms of personality characteristics, cognitive abilities, and sexual attitudes and behaviors?
- What important qualifications about gender differences need to be made?

*Read the section "Gender Stereotypes and Gender Roles" and **write** your answers to the following:*

1. Gender-role stereotypes are _____

   _____

   _____

   _____

2. Important qualifications about gender

   differences are as follows:_____

   _____

   _____

   _____

   _____

   _____

   _____

3. Research on gender differences has shown that

   (a) _____

   _____

   (b) _____

   _____

   _____

   _____

   (c) _____

   _____

Gender-Role Development: Blue Bears and Pink Bunnies

Preview Questions

Consider the following questions as you study this section of the chapter.

- What role does gender play in our culture?
- How are boys and girls treated differently, and what gender differences develop during childhood?
- How do social learning theory and gender schema theory explain the development of gender roles?

Read the section "Gender-Role Development: Blue Bears and Pink Bunnies" and **write** *your answers to the following:*

1. Some gender differences that develop during childhood in our culture are _____

   _____

   _____

   _____

   _____

   _____

   _____

2. According to social learning theory_____

   _____

   _____

3. Gender schema theory contends that _____

   _____

   _____

   _____

After you have carefully studied the preceding section, complete the following exercises.

Concept Check 1

Read the following and write the correct term in the space provided.

1. During a sex education talk, the teacher describes the differences in genetic composition and reproductive anatomy that are biologically determined characteristics that define a person as being male or female. The teacher is describing_____ .

2. Sheila contends that children actively develop cognitive categories for masculinity and femininity, and that these mental representations influence how children perceive, interpret, and remember relevant aspects of what is appropriate for boys and girls. Sheila's views are most consistent with _____ theory.

3. Liam describes his girlfriend as gentle, caring, empathetic, and very feminine. Liam is referring to his girlfriend's _____ .

4. Pat and Les are fraternal twins. Pat consistently scores higher than Les on tests of verbal fluency, reading comprehension, and basic writing skills; Les outscores Pat on spatial skills and tests of mathematical ability. It is very probable that Pat is _____ (male/female) and Les is _____ (male/female).

5. As part of an experiment investigating gender-role development, Dr. Beach decides to dress a number of male and female one-year-olds in identical clothes. It is very likely that adults _____ (will/will not) be able to tell male and female infants apart but that other one-year-olds _____ (will/will not) be able to do so.

6. Frank is very fit and works out in the gym almost every day. He is considered by many to be very masculine, especially by his boyfriend. Frank's sense of maleness is his _____ , and his attraction to members of the same sex is his _____ .

7. Mr. and Mrs. Morganthaler were window shopping in the mall when they saw the devastating aftermath of a terrorist attack on TV. Both were overcome with emotion. Mrs. Morganthaler started to cry but Mr. Morganthaler masked his feelings. This gender difference in the *expression* of emotion is probably a result of _____ .

8. After watching an action-packed movie on TV, young Ho Wai started practicing kung fu kicks and karate chops. According to _____ theory, Ho Wai's present behavior is the result of observing and imitating the movie characters, a process called _____ .

Review of Terms, Concepts, and Names 1

Use the terms in this list to complete the Matching Test, then to help you answer the True/False items correctly.

sex
gender
gender roles
gender identity
sexual orientation
gender-role stereotypes

social learning theory
benevolent sexism
Sandra Bem
gender schema theory
schemas

Matching Exercise

Match the appropriate term/name with its definition or description.

1. _____ American psychologist who has conducted extensive research on sex roles and gender identity; proposed gender schema theory to explain gender-role development.

2. _____ The cultural, social, and psychological meanings that are associated with masculinity and femininity.

3. _____ The direction of a person's emotional and erotic attraction toward members of the opposite sex, the same sex, or both sexes.

4. _____ The beliefs and expectations that people hold about the typical characteristics, preferences, and behavior of men and women.

5. _____ In gender schema theory, the mental categories or representations of masculinity and femininity.

6. _____ Form of prejudice that results from accepting positive stereotypes of women.

True/False Test

Indicate whether each statement is true or false by placing T or F in the blank space next to each item.

1. ___ Social learning theory contends that gender roles are acquired through the basic processes of learning, including reinforcement, punishment, and modeling.

2. ___ Sex refers to (1) the biological category of male or female as defined by physical differences in genetic composition and in reproductive anatomy and function and (2) the behavioral manifestations of the sexual urge; sexual intercourse.

3. ___ Gender identity refers to the behaviors, attitudes, and personality traits that are designated as either masculine or feminine in a given culture.

4. ___ Gender schema theory states that gender-role development is influenced by the formation of schemas, or mental representations, of masculinity and femininity.

5. ___ Gender roles refer to people's psychological sense of being male or female.

Check your answers and review any areas of weakness before going on to the next section.

Human Sexuality

Preview Questions

Consider the following questions as you study this section of the chapter.

- What factors are involved in human sexuality?

- What are the four stages of the human sexual response?

- How does sexual motivation differ for lower and higher animals?

- What biological factors are involved in sexual motivation?

*Read the section "Human Sexuality" and **write** your answers to the following:*

1. The scientific study of sexuality is _____
   _____
   _____

2. The four stages of the human sexual response (and the characteristics of each) are _____
   _____
   _____
   _____
   _____
   _____
   _____
   _____

3. In nonhuman animals, sexual behavior is _____
   _____
   _____

In higher animals, sexual behavior is _____

_____

_____

Sexual Orientation

Preview Questions

Consider the following questions as you study this section of the chapter.

- What does sexual orientation refer to?
- Why is sexual orientation sometimes difficult to identify?
- What factors have been associated with sexual orientation?

*Read the section "Sexual Orientation" and **write** your answers to the following:*

1. Sexual orientation refers to _____

   _____

   _____

2. Sexual orientation is difficult to identify because _____

   _____

   _____

   _____

   _____

3. Factors associated with sexual orientation are as follows: _____

   _____

   _____

   _____

   _____

   _____

Sexual Behavior over the Lifespan

Preview Questions

Consider the following questions as you study this section of the chapter.

- What elementary forms of sexuality appear during infancy and childhood?
- What is puberty, and what are primary and secondary sex characteristics?

- What is the adolescent growth spurt and, in females, what is menarche?
- What characterizes the sexual relationships that develop in adolescence?
- What have neuroscientist shown about activity in the brains of people in love?
- What characterizes the sexual behavior patterns of adults, and what are some important aspects of sexual relationships in late adulthood?

*Read the section "Sexual Behavior over the Lifespan" and **write** your answers to the following:*

1. Sexuality is expressed in infancy and childhood in a number of ways: _____

   _____

   _____

   _____

2. Puberty is the _____

   _____

3. Puberty involves the development of primary sex characteristics, which are_____

   _____

   _____

   _____

   and secondary sex characteristics, which are

   _____

   _____

   _____

4. The adolescent growth spurt is_____

   _____

   _____

5. Menarche refers to _____

   _____

   _____

   _____

   _____

6. Factors involved in romantic and sexual relationships during adolescence include _____

_____

_____

_____

_____

_____

_____

7. Neuroscientists have shown that romantic love activates _____

_____

_____

_____

8. The most general conclusions about sexuality in early and middle adulthood are

(a) _____

_____

(b) _____

_____

(c) _____

_____

(d) _____

_____

9. In late adulthood, people experience _____

_____

_____

_____

After you have carefully studied the preceding section, complete the following exercises.

Concept Check 2

Read the following and write the correct term in the space provided.

1. Mary and her husband James have just shared a fulfilling sexual experience. Unlike Mary, James is not likely to be able to experience another orgasm for a period of time; this is called the _____ period.

2. Mrs. Jacobson had her ovaries removed because of cancer and is now in perfect health. As a result of the operation, the level of the female sex hormone estrogen will _____ ; the level of her interest in sexual activity will _____ (increase/decrease/stay the same).

3. Dr. Jamison surgically removed the testes of an experimental laboratory rat. It is very probable that the rat will experience a(n) _____ in sexual activity and interest.

4. Hamish, a twenty-five-year-old medical student, is heterosexual; his brother Stuart, a twenty-one-year-old philosophy major, is homosexual. The two brothers differ in their

_____ .

5. When she was almost thirteen, Manjit experienced her first menstrual period. She has reached _____ .

6. Adam is fifteen and has gained both height and weight, some body hair, and a deeper voice during the past year. These changes are referred to as _____ sex characteristics.

7. Mr. and Mrs. Dempster are in their seventies and enjoy good health and an active lifestyle. If they are like many adults in their age range, they are very _____ (unlikely/likely) to have an interest in sex.

8. Twelve-year-old Sonia is taller than most of her classmates, has been wearing a bra for more than a year and a half, and had her first menstrual period when she was only ten. Compared with late-maturing girls, Sonia is likely to have had some _____ (positive/negative) experiences related to her early maturation.

9. Young Simon has a rather passive, weak-willed father and a strong-willed, assertive mother. Research on early life experiences and sexual orientation indicates that such atypical family relationships _____ (are/are not) one of the main causes of homosexuality.

Review of Terms, Concepts, and Names 2

Use the terms in this list to complete the Matching Test, then to help you answer the True/False items correctly.

William H. Masters
Virginia E. Johnson
excitement phase
plateau phase
orgasm
resolution phase
refractory period
estrus
estrogen
testosterone
sexual orientation
heterosexual
homosexual

bisexual
lesbian
gay
retrospective study
prospective study
puberty
genital play
primary sex
  characteristics
secondary sex
  characteristics
adolescent growth spurt
menarche

Matching Exercise

Match the appropriate term/name with its definition or description.

1. _____ American behavioral scientist who, along with William H. Masters, conducted pioneering research in the field of human sexuality and sex therapy.

2. _____ The second stage in the human sexual response cycle in which physical arousal builds as pulse and breathing rates continue to rise; the penis becomes fully erect, the testes enlarge, the clitoris withdraws but remains sensitive, the vaginal entrance tightens, and vaginal lubrication continues.

3. _____ The stage of adolescence in which an individual reaches sexual maturity and becomes physiologically capable of sexual reproduction.

4. _____ A female's first menstrual period, which occurs during puberty.

5. _____ A person who is sexually attracted to individuals of the other sex.

6. _____ Period of accelerated growth during puberty, involving rapid increases in height and weight.

7. _____ For a male, a period of time following orgasm during which he is incapable of having another erection or orgasm.

8. _____ A person who is attracted to individuals of the same sex.

9. _____ American physician who, along with Virginia E. Johnson, conducted pio-

neering research in the field of human sexuality and sex therapy.

10. _____ The first stage in the human sexual response cycle that marks the beginning of sexual arousal and can occur in response to sexual fantasies or other sexually arousing stimuli, physical contact with another person, or masturbation.

11. _____ Term typically used by male homosexuals to describe their sexual orientation.

12. _____ Type of study in which a group of people are systematically observed over time in order to discover what factors are associated with a particular trait, characteristic, or behavior.

True/False Test

Indicate whether each statement is true or false by placing T or F in the blank space next to each item.

1. ____ Secondary sex characteristics are the sexual organs that are directly involved in reproduction, such as the uterus, ovaries, penis, and testicles.

2. ____ Estrus refers to the cyclical period during which a nonhuman female animal is fertile and receptive to male sexual advances.

3. ____ The fourth stage of the sexual response cycle, during which both sexes tend to experience a warm physical glow and sense of well-being and arousal returns to normal, is called the resolution phase.

4. ____ A bisexual is sexually attracted to individuals of both sexes.

5. ____ Testosterone, the female sex hormone produced by the ovaries, influences a woman's monthly reproductive cycle.

6. ____ Orgasm is the third and shortest phase of the sexual response cycle, during which blood pressure and heart rate reach their peak and muscles in the vaginal walls and uterus contract rhythmically, as do the muscles in and around the penis as the male ejaculates.

7. ____ Primary sex characteristics are sexual characteristics that develop during puberty and are not directly involved in reproduction but differentiate between the sexes, such as male facial hair and female breasts.

8. ____ Estrogen, the male sex hormone produced by the testes, is responsible for male sexual development.

9. ___ Sexual orientation refers to the direction of a person's emotional and erotic attraction toward members of the opposite sex, the same sex, or both sexes.

10. ___ Female homosexuals are usually called lesbians.

11. ___ A retrospective study involves asking people to recall or remember childhood events and behaviors.

12. ___ Infants as young as three or four months of age will smile or coo as they engage in genital play, and by the first birthday genital play is a common occurrence.

Check your answers and review any areas of weakness before going on to the next section.

Sexual Disorders and Problems

Preview Questions

Consider the following questions as you study this section of the chapter.

- What are sexual dysfunctions, and what characterizes these disorders?
- What are the paraphilias, and how do they differ from dysfunctions?
- What is gender identity disorder?
- What are sexually transmitted diseases (STDs), and what causes AIDS

*Read the section "Sexual Disorders and Problems" and **write** your answers to the following:*

1. A sexual dysfunction is _____

   _____

   _____

2. The eight categories of sexual dysfunctions and their characteristics are

   (a) _____

   _____

   (b) _____

   _____

   (c) _____

   _____

   (d) _____

   (e) _____

   (f) _____

   (g) _____

   (h) _____

3. A paraphilia is

   _____

   _____

4. The eight most common paraphilias and their characteristics are

   (a) _____

   _____

   (b) _____

   _____

   _____

   (c) _____

   _____

   (d) _____

   _____

   (e) _____

   _____

   (f) _____

   _____

   (g) _____

   _____

   (h) _____

   _____

5. Unlike a person with a sexual dysfunction, a person who has a paraphilia is _____

   _____

   _____

   _____

   _____

6. Gender identity disorder (formerly called transsexualism) involves _____

    _____

    _____

7. Sexually transmitted diseases (STDs) are

    _____

    _____

    They include _____

    _____

    _____

    _____ — _____

    _____

8. AIDS (acquired immune deficiency syndrome) is a disease caused by _____

    _____

    _____

    _____

    _____

After you have carefully studied the preceding section, complete the following exercises.

Concept Check 3

Read the following and write the correct term in the space provided.

1. Marshall went to his doctor because his complete lack of sexual desire was causing interpersonal problems with his wife. He is most likely to be diagnosed as having a disorder called _____ disorder.

2. Recently, Herbert was arrested when he was caught peering through the window of a woman who was getting undressed. It turned out that Herbert had a long history of similar behavior. Herbert suffers from _____ .

3. Axel uses public transport during rush hour because he gets sexually aroused from touching and rubbing against strangers. Axel has a paraphilia called _____ .

4. When Julian was a child, he loved playing with dolls and joining in girls' games; as a teenager, he shaved his legs and under his arms. Now, he frequently dresses in women's clothes and hopes one day to undergo sex-reassignment surgery. Julian has _____ disorder, formerly called _____ .

5. Margorie went to her doctor when she experienced symptoms that included vaginal discharge and painful urination. If she is diagnosed with a bacterial sexually transmitted disease (STD) it is likely to be _____ or _____ .

6. Jennifer sought medical help for a problem she noticed after she started living with her boyfriend. After she described her symptoms of chronic genital pain during intercourse, her doctor diagnosed her condition as _____ .

7. Marek has been diagnosed with AIDS. When the HIV virus became active, it selectively attacked a key component of his immune system called _____ , which mobilize other immune system cells to fight off diseases and infections. Most likely, the first drug prescribed for him was _____ . Now, he is taking newer antiviral drugs called _____ , which interfere with the last stage of HIV's reproductive cycle.

Graphic Organizer 1

Identify the following paraphilias.

1. Sexual arousal achieved by exposing one's genitals to shocked strangers:

    _____

2. Sexual arousal from touching and rubbing against a nonconsenting person, usually in a crowded public situation, such as a crowded bus or subway car:

    _____

3. Sexual arousal in response to inanimate objects or body parts that are not primarily associated with sexual arousal:

_____

4. For a heterosexual male, sexual arousal from cross-dressing in women's clothes:

_____

5. Sexual fantasies, urges, or behavior involving sexual activity with a prepubescent child (generally age 13 or younger):

_____

6. Sexual arousal from observing an unsuspecting person who is disrobing, naked, or engaged in sexual activity:

_____

7. Sexual arousal achieved through intentionally inflicting psychological or physical suffering on another person:

_____

8. Sexual arousal in response to actually being humiliated, beaten, bound, or otherwise made to suffer:

_____

Graphic Organizer 2

Read the following and decide whether the statement is more characteristic of a paraphilia (P) or a sexual dysfunction (SD):

Statement	P	SD
1. Consistent disturbances in sexual desire, arousal, or orgasm.		
2. Much more prevalent among men than women.		
3. Is not usually accompanied by psychological distress.		
4. Sexual gratification is almost always dependent on fantasies, urges, or behaviors that fall outside the socially accepted range of sexual behavior.		
5. Is usually accompanied by psychological distress and interpersonal difficulties.		
6. Typically come to the attention of mental health professionals when a person's behavior causes problems for his or her partner, family member, or coworker or has resulted in the person's arrest.		
7. Can be successfully treated by psychologists and physicians who have received specialized training in sex therapy.		
8. Some forms of the disturbance are illegal.		
9. Although biological and psychological theories have been proposed, the cause or causes remain obscure.		
10. While there is no reliable data on the prevalence of these problems, it is known that they affect both men and women about equally.		

Review of Terms and Concepts 3

Use the terms in this list to complete the Matching Test, then to help you answer the True/False items correctly.

sexual dysfunction
hypoactive sexual desire
  disorder
sexual aversion disorder
dyspareunia
male erectile disorder
male orgasmic disorder
premature ejaculation
female orgasmic
  disorder
vaginismus
paraphilia
exhibitionism
frotteurism
fetishism
transvestic fetishism
pedophilia
voyeurism
sexual sadism

sexual masochism
gender identity disorder
  (transsexualism)
sex-reassignment
  surgery
sexually transmitted
  diseases (STDs)
gonorrhea, syphilis, and
  chlamydia
pubic lice
genital herpes
AIDS (acquired immune
  deficiency syndrome)
human immunode-
  ficiency virus (HIV)
helper T cells
AZT
protease inhibitors

Matching Exercise

Match the appropriate term with its definition or description.

1. _____ Paraphilia characterized by sexual arousal in response to inanimate objects (for example, female undergarments, shoes, leather) or body parts that are not typically associated with sexual arousal (for example, feet, hair, legs).

2. _____ Infectious diseases that are transmitted primarily through sexual intercourse or other intimate sexual contact.

3. _____ In males, sexual dysfunction characterized by a recurring inability to achieve or maintain an erect penis.

4. _____ In females, sexual dysfunction characterized by consistent delays in achieving orgasm or the inability to achieve orgasm.

5. _____ Paraphilia in which a heterosexual male achieves sexual arousal from cross-dressing in women's clothes.

6. _____ Sexual dysfunction characterized by persistent, involuntary contractions or spasms of the vaginal muscles, which result in uncomfortable or painful intercourse.

7. _____ Nontraditional sexual behavior in which a person's sexual gratification depends on an unusual sexual experience, object, or fantasy.

8. _____ Virus that enters the bloodstream through the exchange of bodily fluids, primarily semen, blood, and blood products, and causes the disease called acquired immune deficiency syndrome, or AIDS.

9. _____ Consistent disturbance in sexual desire, arousal, or orgasm that causes psychological distress and interpersonal difficulties.

10. _____ In males, sexual dysfunction characterized by delayed orgasm during intercourse or the inability to achieve orgasm during intercourse.

11. _____ In males, sexual dysfunction characterized by orgasm occurring before it is desired, often immediately or shortly after penetration.

12. _____ Newer antiviral drugs used in the treatment of AIDS that interfere with the last stage of HIV's reproductive cycle.

13. _____ Medical procedure performed on people with gender identity disorder in which the existing genitalia are removed and the genitals of the opposite sex are surgically constructed.

14. _____ Parasitic sexually transmitted disease (STD).

15. _____ Cells that mobilize other immune system cells to fight off diseases or infections and are selectively attacked by the HIV virus, weakening the immune system.

True/False Test

Indicate whether each item is true or false by placing T or F in the space next to each item.

1. ____ A paraphilia in which sexual arousal is achieved through intentionally inflicting psychological or physical suffering on another person is called sexual masochism.

2. ____ A paraphilia in which sexual fantasies, urges, or behaviors involve sexual activity with a prepubescent child is called pedophilia.

3. ____ Dyspareunia is a sexual dysfunction characterized by active avoidance of genital sexual contact because of extreme anxiety, fear, or disgust.

4. ___ The disease caused by the exchange of body fluids (semen, blood, or blood products) containing the human immunodeficiency virus (HIV), which attacks and weakens the immune system, is called AIDS (acquired immune deficiency syndrome).

5. ___ Voyeurism is a paraphilia in which sexual arousal is obtained from observing an unsuspecting person disrobing, naked, or engaging in sexual activity.

6. ___ Hypoactive sexual desire disorder is a sexual dysfunction characterized by abnormally high and persistent levels of sexual desire.

7. ___ A paraphilia in which sexual arousal is achieved by exposing one's genitals to shocked strangers is called exhibitionism.

8. ___ Sexual sadism is a form of paraphilia in which sexual arousal is achieved in response to actually being humiliated, beaten, bound, or otherwise made to suffer.

9. ___ Frotteurism is a paraphilia in which the person achieves sexual arousal from touching and rubbing against a nonconsenting person, usually in a crowded public situation, such as a crowded bus or subway car.

10. ___ Persons who express persistent discomfort about their assigned gender and repeatedly express a desire to be a member of the opposite sex are said to have gender identity disorder (formerly called transsexualism).

11. ___ A sexual dysfunction characterized by genital pain before, during, or after sexual intercourse is called sexual aversion disorder.

12. ___ Gonorrhea, syphilis, and chlamydia are bacterial sexually transmitted diseases (STDs).

13. ___ AZT is a drug used in the treatment of AIDS which disrupts the early stage of the HIV cycle, slowing the progression of the disease.

14. ___ Genital herpes is a viral sexually transmitted disease (STD) in which painful blisters on or inside the genitals may sometimes be accompanied by fever, swollen lymph nodes, and bodily aches or pains.

Check your answers and review any areas of weakness before going on to the next section.

Something to Think About

1. Just about everyone experiences some kind of relationship problem at one time or another. Most frequently, problems tend to arise in intimate relationships between men and women. Imagine you are a therapist and a couple comes to you for help in resolving their ongoing interpersonal conflicts. Based on what you have discovered in this chapter, what advice would you give them?

2. The French saying "Vive la différence!" refers to the differences between men and women. When people use it, they may simply be celebrating the most obvious anatomical features and behaviors associated with masculinity and femininity. Male-female differences, however, continue to be a topic of debate. For instance, some popular books and the media have suggested that male and female brains are fundamentally different and that men and women are like creatures from two different planets (Mars and Venus, respectively). Now that you know quite a bit about gender and sexuality, what would you add to a discussion of the issue?

Check your answers and review any areas of weakness before doing the progress tests.

Progress Test 1

Review the complete chapter (including Concept Reviews and the boxed inserts), review all your study notes, and then test yourself on the following progress test. Check your answers. If you make a mistake, review your notes, review the relevant section of the study guide, and, if necessary, go back and read the appropriate part of your textbook.

1. In a recent tutorial discussion, Michael stated that women are more nurturing, patient, and emotional than men, and that men are more logical, rational, and aggressive than women. Michael's beliefs about male and female differences best illustrates

    (a) sexual orientation.
    (b) gender identity.
    (c) sex.
    (d) gender-role stereotypes.

2. Aldred believes that gender roles develop as young children observe others modeling particular gender-appropriate behaviors and that children are rewarded when they behave accordingly and are punished when they don't. Aldred's view is most consistent with the _____ theory of gender-role development.
   - (a) gender schema
   - (b) Masters and Johnson's
   - (c) social learning
   - (d) evolutionary

3. When Kathy's baby was born, the doctor took one look at its genitals and said "It's a girl!" By definition, the doctor was referring to the newborn's
   - (a) gender.
   - (b) sex.
   - (c) sexual orientation.
   - (d) gender role.

4. In order to avoid the potential problems of memory bias in recall of childhood events, researchers followed the development of two groups of boys for approximately 15 years, then compared them on a number of different traits and characteristics. These researchers are trying to avoid the problems associated with _____ by conducting a(n) _____ .
   - (a) prospective studies; retrospective study
   - (b) correlational research; experimental study
   - (c) retrospective studies; prospective study
   - (d) experimental research; correlational study

5. Because of an illness, thirty-year-old Mandy had her ovaries surgically removed. As a result of this operation, Mandy is likely to experience
   - (a) homosexual feelings and urges.
   - (b) an increase in estrogen production.
   - (c) a steep drop in sexual activity and interest.
   - (d) a decrease in estrogen production.

6. Laureen is a lesbian. It is very probable that
   - (a) her sexual orientation was determined before adolescence and before any sexual activity occurred.
   - (b) she experienced some early childhood sexual abuse by a member of the opposite sex.
   - (c) her father was overly domineering and her mother was ineffectual and provided her with a poor feminine role model.
   - (d) her first sexual experience occurred in childhood with a member of the same sex.

7. Thomas and Shauna have just completed a number of tests of cognitive abilities. If they are typical, Thomas is likely to score _____ than Shauna on spatial skills, and Shauna is likely to score _____ than Thomas on verbal, reading, and writing skills.
   - (a) lower; higher
   - (b) lower; lower
   - (c) higher; lower
   - (d) higher; higher

8. When he was eighteen months old, Garreth had sex-reassignment surgery after his penis was accidentally severed during a routine medical procedure. Although he was given hormone treatments and brought up as a girl, he has never been comfortable with the role; he was dressed and treated in every way like a female but he always felt like a male. Garreth's psychological sense of being a male is his _____ , and the way he was dressed and treated represents his _____ .
   - (a) gender identity; gender role
   - (b) sex; sexual orientation
   - (c) gender role; gender identity
   - (d) gender role stereotype; sex

9. After her husband died, sixty-eight-year-old Mrs. Jaspers started dating seventy-year-old Sidney. At their age
   - (a) it is very unlikely that they will engage in sexual activity.
   - (b) they will want to get married almost immediately.
   - (c) dating fills their needs for companionship and sexual intimacy.
   - (d) all of the above are true.

10. Frank and his wife Joanne have not managed to start a family yet because Frank is unable to achieve orgasm during intercourse but is able to do so through other means. Frank has a problem called
    - (a) premature ejaculation.
    - (b) male erectile disorder.
    - (c) dyspareunia.
    - (d) male orgasmic disorder.

11. Nancy and Bruce are newlyweds. They are going to a sex therapist because Nancy experiences persistent, involuntary contraction of the vaginal muscles, resulting in painful intercourse. Nancy suffers from
    (a) female orgasmic disorder.
    (b) vaginismus.
    (c) hypoactive sexual desire disorder.
    (d) frotteurism.

12. When Desmond and Mona met, they found that they shared certain sexual interests. Desmond achieves sexual arousal through intentionally inflicting psychological or physical suffering on another person, and Mona is sexually aroused by being humiliated, beaten, bound, or otherwise made to suffer. Desmond is a(n) _____ and Mona is a(n) _____ .
    (a) exhibitionist; voyeur
    (b) sexual sadist; sexual masochist
    (c) pedophiliac; frotteurist
    (d) sexual masochist; sexual sadist

13. Steve is uncomfortable with his own assigned gender, fantasizes about being a woman, frequently dresses in female clothes, and displays the mannerisms typical of an "extremely feminine" female. Steve suffers from
    (a) exhibitionism.
    (b) fetishism.
    (c) hypoactive sexual desire disorder.
    (d) gender identity disorder (transsexualism).

14. According to the Application, a key ingredient in successful intimate relationships is
    (a) suppressing one's true emotions.
    (b) resolving conflict.
    (c) stonewalling.
    (d) flooding.

15. According to Critical Thinking 10.2, which discusses brain differences in males and females, which of the following is true?
    (a) Even the best-substantiated brain differences are small and inconsistent.
    (b) The meaning and practical significance of any known brain differences are unclear. and open to many different interpretations.
    (c) Male and female brains are much more alike than they are dissimilar.
    (d) All of the above are true.

Progress Test 2

After you have checked your understanding of the material in Progress Test 1 and have done a complete chapter review with special focus on any areas of weakness, you are ready to assess your knowledge on Progress Test 2. Check your answers. If you make a mistake, review your notes, the relevant section of the study guide, and, if necessary, the appropriate part of your textbook.

1. Julian is a heterosexual male who has a transvestic fetishism. Cross-dressing in women's clothes and wearing women's cosmetics sexually arouses him. Because his behavior falls outside the socially accepted range of sexual behaviors, he is likely to be classified as having
    (a) dyspareunia.
    (b) male orgasmic disorder.
    (c) hypoactive sexual desire disorder.
    (d) a paraphilia.

2. Elsie is thinking of going to a sex therapist. She is worried because she has never experienced an orgasm during sexual intercourse with her husband, despite having an otherwise very warm and loving relationship. Elsie probably has a sexual dysfunction called
    (a) dyspareunia.
    (b) sexual aversion disorder.
    (c) female orgasmic disorder.
    (d) vaginismus.

3. Mary and Martin are fraternal twins who will be celebrating their sixth birthday very soon. If they are typical of children at this age, Mary will ask for _____ and Martin will ask for _____ as birthday presents.
    (a) dolls and a dollhouse; toy cars and trucks
    (b) sports equipment; dolls and a dollhouse
    (c) toy cars and trucks; sports equipment
    (d) toy guns and soldiers; sports equipment

4. Psychologists at State University's Gerontology Center are conducting research on sexual behavior over the lifespan. They are most likely to discover that by the time people reach their seventies and eighties
    (a) they have no interest in sexual activity.
    (b) women outnumber men by a margin of almost two to one.
    (c) they are usually confined to old age homes.
    (d) men outnumber women by a margin of almost two to one.

5. Keith will be twenty-one years old next month. If he is like most young people his age, he
   (a) is still a virgin.
   (b) had sexual intercourse for the first time before he was fourteen.
   (c) has been married for about a year.
   (d) has already lost his virginity.

6. Harry and Helen were both early-maturing children. Their respective experiences, as a result of early puberty, were likely to have been
   (a) very similar in all respects.
   (b) very negative for both.
   (c) very different in many respects.
   (d) very positive for both.

7. Between the ages of fifteen and sixteen, Sean grew almost five inches. Sean experienced _____ during this year.
   (a) the development of primary sex characteristics
   (b) the adolescent growth spurt
   (c) the development of mammary glands
   (d) menarche

8. Whenever eight-month-old Tristan is being bathed, he fondles his own genitals and smiles and gurgles with apparent delight. Tristan is
   (a) engaging in genital play.
   (b) behaving normally.
   (c) not experiencing sexual arousal.
   (d) not expressing a desire for erotic contact
   (e) doing all of the above.

9. When he was thirteen, Kyle experienced several physical changes: his testicles started to enlarge, his height and weight increased, and his voice deepened. Kyle experienced
   (a) menarche.
   (b) puberty.
   (c) sexual dysfunction.
   (d) paraphilia.

10. In a term paper on child development, Sima made the case that children actively develop categories for masculinity and femininity and suggested that these mental representations influence how children perceive, interpret, and remember relevant aspects of what is appropriate for girls and boys. Sima's position is most consistent with the _____ theory of gender-role development.
    (a) gender schema   (c) Masters and Johnson
    (b) evolutionary   (d) social learning

11. Barney and Bailey are identical twins. Barney is gay. Therefore, there is
    (a) about a 50 percent chance that Bailey will also be homosexual.
    (b) almost 100 percent chance that Bailey will also be homosexual.
    (c) about a 20 percent chance that Bailey will also be homosexual.
    (d) no way to predict Bailey's sexual orientation because there is no correlation between genetic factors and sexual behavior.

12. In the human sexual response cycle, the first phase is _____ and the last phase is _____ .
    (a) plateau; resolution
    (b) excitement; orgasm
    (c) orgasm; plateau
    (d) excitement; resolution

13. Dr. MacKinnon is doing cross-cultural research on gender-role stereotypes. She is likely to discover that
    (a) across cultures, there is a high degree of agreement on the characteristics associated with each sex.
    (b) in every culture, the characteristics associated with the male stereotype are identical.
    (c) across cultures, there is a high degree of disagreement on the characteristics associated with each sex.
    (d) in every culture, the female stereotype is more widely believed than is the male stereotype.

14. According to In Focus 10.4, which of the following is true?
    (a) Sexual fantasies are psychologically unhealthy.
    (b) Male and female sexual fantasies are almost identical in content and frequency.
    (c) Sexual fantasies are a sign of sexual frustration and dissatisfaction with a relationship.
    (d) All of the above are true.
    (e) None of the above are true.

15. One of the most persistent and pervasive gender stereotypes is that women are more emotional than men. Critical Thinking 10.1 concludes that
    (a) women are more emotionally *expressive* than men.
    (b) males and females do not differ in their *experience* of emotion.
    (c) the expression of emotions is strongly influenced by culturally determined display rules.
    (d) men mask their emotions more than women do.
    (e) all of the above are true

Progress Test 3

After you have checked your understanding of the material in Progress Tests 1 and 2, and have done a complete chapter review with special focus on any areas of weakness, you are ready to further assess your knowledge on Progress Test 3. Check your answers. If you make a mistake, review your notes, the appropriate parts of the study guide, and if necessary, the relevant sections of your textbook.

1. When Oliver played with dolls and domestic toys, his mother would show her disapproval; when he played with toy vehicles and building blocks, his mother would respond in a positive manner. As Oliver grew older, he played less and less with dolls, dollhouses, and domestic toys and more and more with stereotypical "boys'" toys. This description of gender-role development illustrates
    (a) gender identity theory.
    (b) gender schema theory.
    (c) social learning theory.
    (d) evolutionary theory.

2. When Rex was a young pup, his owners took him to the vet to have him neutered. If Rex is like most animals, the removal of his testes will very likely result in a(n) _____ in the levels of the hormone testosterone, and a(n) _____ in sexual interest and sexual activity.
    (a) increase; decrease
    (b) decrease; decrease
    (c) decrease; increase
    (d) increase; increase

3. Dr. LaSage conducted twin studies on sexual orientation. If his findings are consistent with previous research on this topic, he is likely to conclude that
    (a) sexual orientation is at least partly influenced by genetics.
    (b) having an inadequate male role model or having an overly dominant mother is the primary cause of homosexuality.
    (c) sexual orientation is almost completely influenced by environmental factors.
    (d) homosexuality is the result of unpleasant early heterosexual experiences.

4. Barbara and Bob have decided to live together. She discovers that he can achieve sexual arousal only from contact with her stockings, shoes, or underwear. It appears that Bob has a disorder called
    (a) voyeurism.   (c) exhibitionism.
    (b) pedophilia.   (d) fetishism.

5. Heinz has a rather passive, weak father who provides a poor masculine role model. His mother, on the other hand, is a very strong, assertive, domineering woman. On the basis of research on early life experiences and sexual orientation, you would be justified in concluding that
    (a) Heinz's experiences with his parents are not likely to cause him to become homosexual.
    (b) by the time he is a young adult Heinz is almost certain to be a homosexual.
    (c) Heinz will be a heterosexual during his teens, a bisexual in his early adult years, and eventually a homosexual in middle to late adulthood.
    (d) by the time he reaches puberty, Heinz will suffer from gender identity disorder and one or more of the paraphilias.

6. Robert is very distressed and embarrassed because he frequently reaches sexual climax within minutes of becoming sexually aroused and before he has intercourse with his partner. Robert's problem is called
    (a) hypoactive sexual desire disorder.
    (b) premature ejaculation.
    (c) male orgasmic disorder.
    (d) male erectile disorder.

7. Doug was infected with HIV from contaminated blood during a blood transfusion many years ago. It is very likely that he will develop
   (a) chlamydia.
   (b) herpes.
   (c) syphilis.
   (d) acquired immune deficiency syndrome (AIDS).

8. Nathan is a homosexual. If the work of neurobiologist Simon LeVay is replicated and confirmed by other researchers, it is likely that Nathan may have a tiny cluster of neurons in a brain area called _____ that is about _____ as the same area in the brains of heterosexual men.
   (a) hypothalamus; half the size
   (b) anterior cingulate cortex; half the size
   (c) hypothalamus; twice the size
   (d) anterior cingulate cortex; twice the size

9. Larry is married, but he and his wife rarely have intercourse because the thought of any genital contact with his wife fills him with fear, anxiety, and disgust. Larry suffers from
   (a) hypoactive sexual desire disorder.
   (b) dyspareunia.
   (c) sexual aversion disorder.
   (d) male orgasmic disorder.

10. Noreen is almost thirteen and has just had her first menstrual period. Noreen has experienced
    (a) menopause.   (c) vaginismus.
    (b) menarche.   (d) a refractory period.

11. Sharina is writing a term paper on human sexuality. Her library research is likely to indicate that the normal order of the four stages in the human sexual response cycle is
    (a) excitement, resolution, plateau, and orgasm.
    (b) excitement, orgasm, plateau, and resolution.
    (c) plateau, excitement, resolution, and orgasm.
    (d) excitement, plateau, orgasm, and resolution.

12. Elizabeth has had to seek treatment because of persistent itching due to pubic lice. Elizabeth has contracted
    (a) a parasitic STD.
    (b) AIDS (acquired immune deficiency syndrome).
    (c) a bacterial STD.
    (d) chlamydia.

13. John is now serving a long jail sentence after his third conviction for engaging in sexual activities with prepubescent girls. John suffers from a paraphilia called
    (a) frotteurism.   (c) voyeurism.
    (b) fetishism   (d) pedophilia.

14. In order to break the vicious circle of flooding-stonewalling-flooding, the Application suggests that couples should
    (a) become aware of the gender differences in handling emotion.
    (b) call a time-out whenever either one begins to feel overwhelmed or in danger of flooding.
    (c) spend the time-out period thinking about ways to resolve the conflict, not about ways to mount a more effective counterattack.
    (d) recognize that males need to try to stop avoiding conflict and females should try to raise issues in need of resolution in a calm manner and without personal attack.
    (e) do all of the above.

15. According to research by David Buss (Culture and Human Behavior 10.3)
    (a) mutual attraction and love are the most important factors in selecting a mate in all cultures studied.
    (b) men are more likely than women to value youth and physical attractiveness in a potential mate.
    (c) women value financial security, access to material resources, and high status and education in a potential mate.
    (d) all of the above are true.

Answers

Introduction: Gender and Sexuality

1. *Sex refers to* biologically determined physical characteristics, such as differences in genetic composition and reproductive anatomy and function; *gender refers to* the cultural, social, and psychological meanings that are associated with maleness and femaleness.

2. *Gender roles consist of* the behaviors, attitudes, and personality traits that a given culture designates as either masculine or feminine; *gender identity refers to* a given person's psychological sense of being either male or female; *and sexual orientation refers to* whether a person's emotional and erotic attraction is directed toward members of the opposite sex, the same sex, or both sexes.

Gender Stereotypes and Gender Roles

1. *Gender-role stereotypes are* the beliefs and expectations that people have about the typical characteristics, preferences, and behaviors of each sex.

2. *Important qualifications about gender differences are as follows:* First, gender differences are not gender deficiencies. Second, differences between men and women are average differences, not absolute differences (no single finding applies to all men and women, there is a wide range of individual variation within each group, and there is a great deal of overlap between the two groups). Third, finding that a gender difference exists does not explain what caused the difference (differences are not necessarily natural, inevitable, or unchangeable).

3. *Research on gender differences has shown that (a)* Men are more assertive than women and women are more nurturant than men, but men and women are otherwise similar in their personality characteristics. *(b)* On average, women outscore men on tests of verbal fluency, spelling, reading comprehension, and writing; men outscore women on mental rotation tasks. The average difference between males and females on math scores is very small, but twice as many males as females score in the very highest range. *(c)* Men and women are largely similar in their sexual attitudes and behaviors, except that men masturbate more often and are more accepting of casual sex than are women.

Gender-Role Development: Blue Bears and Pink Bunnies

1. *Some gender differences that develop during childhood in our culture are:* First, girls and boys are treated differently from birth (pink for girls and blue for boys.) Second, toddler girls play more with soft toys and dolls and ask for adult help, whereas toddler boys play more with blocks and trucks or wagons, and play more actively than do girls. Third, between the ages of two and three, preschoolers start acquiring gender-role stereotypes for toys, clothes, household objects, games, and work; they also develop a strong preference for playing with members of their own sex, tendencies that continue throughout childhood. Finally, girls tend to be less rigid than boys in adhering to gender stereotypes.

2. *According to social learning theory,* gender roles are developed through the basic processes of learning, including reinforcement, punishment, and modeling.

3. *Gender schema theory contends that* children actively develop mental categories, or schemas, for masculinity and femininity, and these mental representations influence gender-role development.

Concept Check 1

1. sex
2. gender schema
3. gender role
4. female; male
5. will not; will
6. gender identity; sexual orientation
7. culturally determined display rules
8. social learning; modeling

Matching Exercise 1

1. Sandra Bem
2. gender
3. sexual orientation
4. gender-role stereotypes
5. schemas
6. benevolent sexism

True/False Test 1

1. T   3. F   5. F
2. T   4. T

Human Sexuality

1. *The scientific study of sexuality is* multidimensional and involves biological, psychological, social, and cultural factors.

2. *The four stages of the human sexual response (and the characteristics of each) are* excitement (which can occur in response to sexual fantasies or other sexually arousing stimuli, physical contact with another person, or masturbation), plateau (physical arousal builds as pulse and breathing rates continue to increase), orgasm (blood pressure and heart rate reach their peak), and resolution (arousal slowly subsides and returns to normal; at this point, males experience a refractory period during which they are incapable of having another erection or orgasm).

3. *In nonhuman animals, sexual behavior is* biologically determined and typically triggered by hormonal changes in the female (during estrus, females are fertile and receptive to male sexual advances). *In higher animals, sexual behavior is* more strongly influenced by learning and environmental factors and is less limited to the goal of reproduction; in some species sexual interactions serve important social functions.

Sexual Orientation

1. *Sexual orientation refers to* whether a person is sexually aroused by members of the same sex, the opposite sex, or both sexes; a heterosexual is sexually attracted to individuals of the other sex, a homosexual is attracted to individuals of the same sex, and a bisexual is attracted to individuals of both sexes.

2. *Sexual orientation is difficult to identify because* there is not always a perfect correspondence between a particular person's sexual identity, sexual desires, and sexual behaviors. In addition, determining accurate numbers depends on how researchers structure survey questions, how they define their criteria, where the survey is conducted, and how survey participants are selected.

3. *Factors associated with sexual orientation are as follows:* First, twin studies suggest genetics play a role in determining a homosexual orientation. Second, research on brain structures, (such as a small cluster of neurons in the hypothalamus) demonstrated a correlation with sexual orientation. Third, cross-gender play patterns in children seem to be related to a later homosexual orientation, and finally, it has been shown that sexual orientation develops at an early age and is difficult to change.

Sexual Behavior over the Lifespan

1. *Sexuality is expressed in infancy and childhood in a number of ways:* Infants experience reflexive sexual responses, and genital play is common, especially during bathing; during early and middle childhood, children demonstrate increased curiosity about their own bodies and gradually begin to notice the anatomical differences between males and females.

2. *Puberty is the* physical process of attaining sexual maturation and reproductive capacity that begins during the early adolescent years.

3. *Puberty involves the development of primary sex characteristics, which are* the sexual organs that are directly involved in reproduction, such as the uterus, ovaries, penis, and testicles, *and secondary sex characteristics, which are* not directly involved in reproduction but differentiate between the sexes and include male facial hair and female breasts.

4. *The adolescent growth spurt is* the period of accelerated growth during puberty, involving rapid increases in height and weight (occurs about two years earlier in females than in males).

5. *Menarche refers to* a female's first menstrual period (typically occurs around 12 or 13, but can be as early as 9 or 10, or as late as 16 or 17).

6. *Factors involved in romantic and sexual relationships during adolescence include* the physical changes of puberty, which prime the adolescent's interest in sexuality; social and cultural factors also have an influence on when, why, and how adolescents initiate sexual behavior; age is a good predictor of when teenagers typically begin various sexual behaviors such as dating, kissing, petting, and having sexual intercourse; peer groups gradually replace parents as a source of sexual information, and by the end of the teen years the majority of males and females have had sexual intercourse.

7. *Neuroscientists have shown that romantic love activates* brain areas (anterior cingulate cortex, caudate nucleus, putamen, and insula) that are involved in positive emotions, such as happiness, and that respond to euphoria-producing drugs, such as opiates and cocaine.

8. *The most general conclusions about sexuality in early and middle adulthood are (a)* Most adults are involved in an intimate relationship by the age of 30. *(b)* Young adults today tend to have more sexual partners than previous generations. *(c)* Married people tend to have the most active sex lives and are the most satisfied with their sex lives. *(d)* Vaginal intercourse is the most preferred sexual activity.

9. *In late adulthood, people experience* physical changes that affect the sexual response, but satisfying sexual relationships can continue throughout the lifespan.

Concept Check 2

1. refractory
2. decrease; stay the same
3. decrease
4. sexual orientation
5. puberty
6. secondary
7. likely
8. negative
9. are not

Matching Exercise 2

1. Virginia E. Johnson
2. plateau phase
3. puberty
4. menarche
5. heterosexual
6. adolescent growth spurt
7. refractory period
8. homosexual
9. William H. Masters
10. excitement phase
11. gay
12. prospective study

True/False Test 2

1. F	4. T	7. F	10. T
2. T	5. F	8. F	11. T
3. T	6. T	9. T	12. T

Sexual Disorders and Problems

1. *A sexual dysfunction is* a consistent disturbance in sexual desire, arousal, or orgasm that causes psychological distress.

2. *The eight categories of sexual dysfunctions and their characteristics are (a)* hypoactive sexual desire disorder (characterized by little or no sexual desire); *(b)* sexual aversion disorder (characterized by active avoidance of genital sexual contact because of extreme anxiety, fear, or disgust); *(c)* dyspareunia (characterized by genital pain before, during, or after intercourse); *(d)* male erectile disorder (characterized by a recurring inability to achieve or maintain an erect penis); *(e)* male orgasmic disorder (characterized by delayed orgasm during intercourse or the inability to achieve orgasm during intercourse); *(f)* premature ejaculation (characterized by orgasm occurring before it is desired, often immediately or shortly after sexual stimulation or penetration); *(g)* female orgasmic disorder (characterized by consistent delays in achieving orgasm or the inability to achieve orgasm); *(h)* vaginismus (characterized by persistent, involuntary contractions or spasms of the vaginal muscles, which result in uncomfortable or painful intercourse).

3. *A paraphilia is* any of several forms of nontraditional sexual behavior in which a person's sexual gratification depends on an unusual sexual experience, object, or fantasy.

4. *The eight most common paraphilias and their characteristics are (a)* exhibitionism (sexual arousal achieved by exposing one's genitals to shocked strangers); *(b)* frotteurism (sexual arousal from touching or rubbing against a nonconsenting person, usually in a crowded public situation, such as a crowded bus or subway car); *(c)* fetishism (sexual arousal in response to inanimate objects, or body parts that are not typically associated with sexual arousal); *(d)* transvestic fetishism (in heterosexual males, sexual arousal from cross-dressing in women's clothes); *(e)* pedophilia (sexual fantasies, urges, or behavior involving sexual activity with a prepubescent child, generally age 13 or younger); *(f)* voyeurism (sexual arousal from observing an

unsuspecting person who is disrobing, naked, or engaged in sexual activity); *(g)* sexual sadism (sexual arousal achieved through intentionally inflicting psychological or physical suffering on another person); *(h)* sexual masochism (sexual arousal in response to actually being humiliated, beaten, bound, or otherwise made to suffer).

5. *Unlike a person with a sexual dysfunction, a person who has a paraphilia is* often not psychologically distressed by it. In addition, these individuals typically come to the attention of mental health professionals only when their behavior has created a conflict with their sexual partner, has been discovered by a family member or coworker, or has resulted in arrest (some paraphilias, such as voyeurism and pedophilia are illegal).

6. *Gender identity disorder (formerly called* transsexualism) *involves* a persistent discomfort about one's assigned gender along with the desire to be a member of the opposite sex (in some instances, the person may undergo sex-reassignment surgery).

7. *Sexually transmitted diseases (STDs)* are any of several infectious diseases that are transmitted primarily through sexual intercourse or other intimate sexual contact. *They include* bacterial infections (gonorrhea, syphilis, and chlamydia), parasitic infections (pubic lice), and viral infections (herpes and AIDS).

8. *AIDS (acquired immune deficiency syndrome) is a disease caused by* the exchange of bodily fluids (semen, blood, or blood products) containing the human immunodeficiency virus (HIV), which attacks and weakens the immune system.

Concept Check 3

1. hypoactive sexual desire
2. voyeurism
3. frotteurism
4. gender identity; transsexualism
5. gonorrhea; chlamydia
6. dyspareunia
7. helper T cells; AZT; protease inhibitors

Graphic Organizer 1

1. exhibitionism
2. frotteurism
3. fetishism

4. transvestic fetishism
5. pedophilia
6. voyeurism
7. sexual sadism
8. sexual masochism

Graphic Organizer 2

1. SD	5. SD	9. P
2. P	6. P	10. SD
3. P	7. SD	
4. P	8. P	

Matching Exercise 3

1. fetishism
2. sexually transmitted diseases (STDs)
3. male erectile disorder
4. female orgasmic disorder
5. transvestic fetishism
6. vaginismus
7. paraphilia
8. human immunodeficiency virus (HIV)
9. sexual dysfunction
10. male orgasmic disorder
11. premature ejaculation
12. protease inhibitors
13. sex-reassignment surgery
14. pubic lice
15. helper T cells

True/False Test 3

1. F	5. T	9. T	13. T
2. T	6. F	10. T	14. T
3. F	7. T	11. F	
4. T	8. F	12. T	

Something to Think About

1. Resolving conflicts is a key ingredient in successful intimate relationships. Men and women differ significantly in the way they communicate, especially when they are trying to deal with emotional issues and interpersonal conflicts; these fundamental differences can sabotage conflict resolution. There is hope, however. John Gottman's research provides evidence of a number of constructive ways for overcoming these communication differences.

First, conflict can play a key role in a healthy, happy relationship; a couple's relationship will grow if the couple successfully reconciles the inevitable differences that occur. Men and women react differently to conflict, particularly if it involves strong emotions. Typically, men have learned to suppress and contain their emotions, whereas women tend to be more comfortable with emotional expression. During emotional conflicts, people may experience flooding (the feeling of being overwhelmed emotionally); in reaction to this intense physiological arousal, they may engage in stonewalling (withdrawing to contain their uncomfortable emotions). Men tend to get more physiologically aroused during relationship conflicts than do women and are therefore more likely to engage in stonewalling. Women tend to experience stonewalling as disapproval and rejection and typically react by flooding. And that's how the vicious circle of flooding-stonewalling-flooding begins.

A number of things can be done to break this vicious circle. First, both parties need to become aware of the gender differences in handling emotion. Men need to remember that women experience stonewalling as rejection, disapproval, and abandonment, and women need to accept men's need to temporarily withdraw from the situation. Second, calling for a 20- to 30-minute time-out period during a conflict is a good idea so long as both parties use the time to think about ways to resolve the conflict, rather than rehearsing or preparing vengeful comments and counterattack strategies. Third, men need to make a conscious effort to embrace, rather than avoid, the problem; sidestepping the issue won't make it go away. If the woman didn't care about the relationship, she wouldn't keep confronting her partner; generally, she wants both people to resolve the issue together. Fourth, women should try raising the issue in a more calm and less emotionally confrontational manner. Frame the problem in the context of maintaining a loving relationship and avoid personal attacks. Finally, tell the couple to buy, read, and discuss John Gottman's book—together!

2. The first point to make in any discussion of differences between men and women is that the sexes are much more alike than they are different. The similarities extend across many different and important aspects of behavior and ability, including brain structure. We tend to over-

look these similarities when we focus on the differences that have been found between men and women. In addition, if the data on sex differences are examined, there is often a great deal of overlap between men and women.

Second, note that any sex differences in behavior and cognitive functioning are not necessarily because male and female brains are structurally different. There is considerable *individual* variation in brain structure and function; thus, the average range of differences *within* each sex is larger than the average differences between the sexes. Indeed, some individual females are found to be more similar to the average male pattern than average female pattern, and vice versa. There are more similarities than differences between male and female brains.

Third, even if we assume, for the sake of argument, that there are reliable sex differences in brain structure, no one knows the functional significance of those differences. The human brain is incredibly complex, and researchers have not yet managed to unravel all the interrelated organizational and functional aspects of this complicated organ. Clearly, we know a lot more than we used to, but we are still a long way from being able to specify the precise significance of any subtle sex difference that has been found or may be found in the future. It certainly can't be concluded that male and females "think differently" because of structural differences in their brains, as some headlines have claimed.

If we accept that there may be some small and inconsistent differences in the structure of male and female brains, it does not necessarily follow that we are born with these differences. The brain's structure changes in response to experience, so it is entirely possible that any sex differences in the brain could be due to men's and women's different environmental and learning experiences.

Finally, and worth repeating, male and female brains are much more alike than they are dissimilar.

Progress Test 1

1.	d	6.	a	11.	b
2.	c	7.	d	12.	b
3.	b	8.	a	13.	d
4.	c	9.	c	14.	b
5.	d	10.	d	15.	d

Progress Test 2

1. d	6. c	11. a
2. c	7. b	12. d
3. a	8. e	13. a
4. b	9. b	14. e
5. d	10. a	15. e

Progress Test 3

1. c	6. b	11. d
2. b	7. d	12. a
3. a	8. a	13. d
4. d	9. c	14. e
5. a	10. b	15. d

Personality

PREVIEW

Reading the section below first will give you a general sense of the chapter's contents and an initial introduction to some of the major concepts and terms. This will prime you for what you are about to read and help you to develop a "cognitive map" that will guide your study of the material in this chapter. Likewise, reading the **preview questions** at the beginning of each major section will improve your ability to understand, learn, and retain the information.

CHAPTER 11 . . . AT A GLANCE

Chapter 11 focuses on the four major perspectives on personality. Freud's psychoanalysis stresses the unconscious, the importance of sex and aggression, and the influences of early childhood experiences. The major defense mechanisms, as well as the psychosexual stages of development and the various conflicts associated with each, are examined. The contributions of Freud's early followers, the neo-Freudians, are explored, and criticisms of Freud's theory are discussed.

Carl Rogers's humanistic theory and his optimistic view of human nature are examined, including his ideas about the self-concept, unconditional positive regard, the actualizing tendency, and the fully functioning person.

The social cognitive perspective stresses the role of conscious thought processes, goals, self-regulation, and reciprocal determinism. The influence of self-efficacy on behavior, performance, motivation, and persistence is explored. The notion that the interaction of multiple factors determines personality and behavior is examined.

The trait perspective focuses on measuring and describing individual differences. Cattell initially suggested sixteen basic personality factors, then Eysenck proposed three dimensions. The five-factor model is the current view of the number of source traits. The text concludes that traits are generally stable across time and across situations.

Behavioral genetics research uses twin and adoption studies to measure the relative influences of genetics and environment. Personality factors that appear to have a genetic basis are identified.

The final section examines projective tests and self-report inventories, as well as their strengths and weaknesses. The Application discusses the concept of "possible selves" and explains how we can apply research findings regarding this concept to our own lives.

Introduction: What Is Personality?

Preview Questions

Consider the following questions as you study this section of the chapter.

- How is personality defined, and what is a personality theory?
- What are the four major theoretical perspectives on personality?

*Read the section "Introduction: What Is Personality?" and **write** your answers to the following:*

1. Personality is defined as _____
   _____

2. A personality theory is _____
   _____
   _____

3. The four basic perspectives on personality (and the main emphasis of each) are _____
   _____
   _____
   _____
   _____
   _____
   _____
   _____

The Psychoanalytic Perspective on Personality

Preview Questions

Consider the following questions as you study this section of the chapter.

- Who was the founder of psychoanalysis, and what did he consider to be the main factors that influenced personality development?
- What were some of the key influences on Freud's thinking?

*Read the section "The Psychoanalytic Perspective on Personality" and **write** your answers to the following:*

1. Psychoanalysis—Freud's theory of personality—stresses _____
   _____
   _____

2. Some of the key factors in the development of Freud's ideas were _____
   _____
   _____
   _____
   _____

The Psychoanalytic Perspective on Personality: Freud's Dynamic Theory of Personality

Preview Questions

Consider the following questions as you study this section of the chapter.

- How do we access unconscious mental processes?
- What are the three basic structures of personality, and what are their functions?
- What are the main defense mechanisms, and what role do they play?

*Read the section "The Psychoanalytic Perspective: Freud's Dynamic Theory of Personality" and **write** your answers to the following:*

1. The content of the unconscious can surface in disguised form in _____
   _____

2. The three basic structures of personality (and their functions) are _____
   _____
   _____
   _____
   _____
   _____
   _____

3. The three main ego defense mechanisms (and the roles they play) are _____

_____

_____

_____

The Psychoanalytic Perspective: Personality Development

Preview Questions

Consider the following questions as you study this section of the chapter.

- What are the five psychosexual stages of personality development, and what is the focus of each?
- What are the consequences of fixation?
- What role does the Oedipus complex play in personality development?

Read the section "The Psychoanalytic Perspective: Personality Development" and **write** *your answers to the following:*

1. The psychosexual stages are age-related development periods _____

_____

_____

2. The five psychosexual stages (and the focus of each) are _____

_____

_____

_____

_____

3. If the developmental conflict of a particular stage is not resolved _____

_____

_____

4. The Oedipus complex refers to _____

_____

_____

5. Identification (which is one result of the Oedipus complex) is an ego defense mechanism that _____

_____

_____

After you have carefully studied the preceding sections, complete the following exercises.

Concept Check 1

Read the following and write the correct term in the space provided.

1. Birkley was feeling irritable and bad-tempered all day. When she arrived home from work, she accused her husband of being moody and grumpy. According to Freud, Birkley may be using an ego defense mechanism called

_____ .

2. Colleen, who is suffering from some puzzling physical and psychological symptoms that don't appear to have any physiological cause, has decided to seek help from a Freudian psychoanalyst. The therapist is most likely to use

_____ in an attempt to explore Colleen's unconscious.

3. During a heated argument, David inadvertently called his wife Joanne by his mother's name. From the psychoanalytic perspective, this "Freudian slip" reveals something about David's

_____ (conscious/preconscious/ unconscious) motivation.

4. Amelia had a very strange dream in which she was with a very handsome man on a train traveling through the Swiss Alps. The train kept going in and out of tunnels and going faster and faster as it made its way through the mountains. According to Freudian theory, the

_____ (manifest/latent) content of the dream should give some clue as to what is going on in Amelia's unconscious.

5. When 2-year-old Tyler was told that he would get no dessert unless he finished eating all his vegetables, he turned the plate upside down and said he hated his Mom and Dad. Freud would have said that Tyler was responding to the demands of the _____ .

6. Kato found a wallet containing $200 in cash. For just a moment he was tempted to keep the money, but the thought of doing so made him feel guilty and anxious, and he immediately took the wallet to the lost-and-found office. According to Freud, Kato's good deed was motivated by his _____ .

7. Leslie sometimes thinks that the real reason her husband became a psychotherapist was to provide himself with a socially acceptable way to indulge his excessive inquisitiveness about other people's private lives. Leslie is suggesting that her husband is using a special form of displacement called _____ .

8. Nine-year-old Danny looks up to his father and wants to be an engineer just like him. Freud would suggest that Danny is exhibiting signs of the process of _____ .

9. When Gregory did not get the promotion he applied for, he told his family and colleagues that, in retrospect, he was much happier staying in his present position and glad he didn't have to deal with all the hassles associated with the higher-paying position. It appears that Gregory is using an ego defense mechanism called _____ .

Graphic Organizer 1

Read the following and match each one with the appropriate stage of psychosexual development:

Description	Stage
1. Sixteen-year-old Graham has started going steady with Julie and is experiencing all the sensations of being in love.	
2. Five-year-old Annette has become very competitive with her mother for her father's affections and quite defiantly states that she is "Going to marry Daddy when I grow up!"	
3. Vivian is eight years old and does not like boys very much. In fact, she plays with her girlfriends almost exclusively.	
4. It seems that no matter what Marie gives her baby to play with, she immediately puts it in her mouth.	
5. Darcy is not quite two but seems to take great pleasure in refusing to obey his parents and by asserting his control and independence. His favorite word is "No!"	

Review of Terms, Concepts, and Names 1

Use the terms in this list to complete the Matching Test, then to help you answer the True/False items correctly.

personality
personality theory
Sigmund Freud
psychoanalysis
catharsis
free association
conscious

preconscious
unconscious
id
Eros
libido
Thanatos
pleasure principle

ego
reality principle
superego
ego defense mechanisms
repression
displacement
sublimation
psychosexual stages
oral stage

anal stage
phallic stage
fixation
Oedipus complex
castration anxiety
identification
penis envy
latency stage
genital stage

Matching Exercise

Match the appropriate term/name with its definition or description.

1. _____ In Freud's theory, the psychological and emotional energy associated with expressions of sexuality; the sex drive.

2. _____ An individual's unique and relatively consistent patterns of thinking, feeling, and behaving.

3. _____ In Freud's theory, the partly conscious self-evaluative, moralistic component of personality that is formed through the internalization of parental and societal rules.

4. _____ In Freud's theory, a child's unconscious sexual desire for the opposite-sex parent, usually accompanied by hostile feelings toward the same-sex parent.

5. _____ Latin for "I"; in Freud's theory, the partly conscious rational component of personality that regulates thoughts and behavior and is most in touch with the demands of the external world.

6. _____ Level of awareness that contains information not currently in conscious awareness but easily accessible.

7. _____ Psychosexual stage of development during which the child derives pleasurable and gratifying sensations through feeding and exploring objects with his or her mouth.

8. _____ In psychoanalytic theory, the ego defense mechanism that involves unconsciously shifting the target of an emotional urge to a substitute target that is less threatening or dangerous.

9. _____ Austrian neurologist who founded psychoanalysis and emphasized the role of unconscious determinants of behavior and early childhood experiences in the development of personality and psychological problems.

10. _____ Psychosexual stage of development during which the infant derives pleasurable sensations through acquiring control over elimination via toilet training.

11. _____ Theory that attempts to describe and explain individual similarities and differences.

12. _____ Latin for "the it"; in Freud's theory, the completely unconscious, irrational component of personality that seeks immediate satisfaction of instinctual urges and drives; ruled by the pleasure principle.

13. _____ Psychosexual stage of development during which sexual urges become repressed and dormant as the child develops same-sex friendships with peers and focuses on school, sports, and other activities.

14. _____ Sigmund Freud's theory of personality, which emphasizes unconscious determinants of behavior, sexual and aggressive instinctual drives, and the enduring effects of early childhood experiences on later personality development.

15. _____ In psychoanalytic theory, largely unconscious distortions of thought or perception that act to reduce anxiety.

16. _____ In Freud's theory, age-related developmental periods in which the child's sexual urges are expressed through different areas of the body and the activities associated with those areas.

True/False Test

Indicate whether each statement is true or false by placing T or F in the blank space next to each item.

1. ____ During the phallic psychosexual stage of development, the adolescent reaches physical sexual maturity and the genitals become the primary focus of pleasurable sensations, which the person seeks to satisfy in heterosexual relationships.

2. ____ As the Oedipus complex unfolds, the little boy feels affection for his mother and hostility and jealousy toward his father but realizes that his father is more physically powerful than he is; the boy experiences castration anxiety, or the fear that his father will punish him by castrating him.

3. ____ Fixation occurs if the child is frustrated or overindulged in his or her attempts to resolve the conflict associated with a psychosexual stage, and the individual will continue to seek pleasure through behaviors that are similar to those associated with that stage.

4. ____ In Freud's theory, the death instinct, reflected in aggressive, destructive, and self-destructive actions, is called Eros.

5. ___ In psychoanalytic theory, repression refers to the unconscious exclusion of anxiety-provoking thoughts, feelings, and memories from conscious awareness; the most fundamental ego defense mechanism.

6. ___ The term *unconscious* is used in Freud's theory to describe thoughts, feelings, wishes, and drives that are operating below the level of conscious awareness.

7. ___ Catharsis is a phenomenon that occurs when puzzling physical and psychological problems disappear after a person expresses pent-up emotions associated with traumatic events that may have been related to his or her problems.

8. ___ As part of the resolution of her Oedipus complex, the little girl discovers that little boys have a penis and that she does not; she experiences a sense of loss, or deprivation, that Freud referred to as *penis envy*.

9. ___ During the genital stage of psychosexual development, the genitals are the primary focus and the child derives pleasurable sensations through sexual curiosity, masturbation, and sexual attraction toward the opposite-sex parent.

10. ___ In psychoanalytic theory, sublimation is an ego defense mechanism that involves reducing anxiety by modeling the behavior and characteristics of another person.

11. ___ The reality principle refers to the awareness of environmental demands and the capacity to accommodate them by postponing gratification until the appropriate time or circumstances exist.

12. ___ In Freud's theory, Thanatos refers to the self-preservation, or life, instinct, reflected in the expression of basic psychological urges that perpetuate the existence of the individual as well as the species.

13. ___ Free association is a psychoanalytic technique in which the patient spontaneously reports all thoughts, feelings, and mental images as they come to mind.

14. ___ All thoughts, feelings, and sensations that a person is aware of at any given moment represent the conscious level of awareness.

15. ___ The pleasure principle refers to the motive to obtain pleasure and avoid tension or discomfort; the most fundamental human motive and the guiding principle of the id.

16. ___ In psychoanalytic theory, an ego defense mechanism that involves redirecting sexual urges toward productive, socially acceptable, nonsexual activities is called identification.

Check your answers and review any areas of weakness before going on to the next section.

The Psychoanalytic Perspective: The Neo-Freudians

Preview Questions

Consider the following questions as you study this section of the chapter.

- What are the similarities and differences in the approaches taken by Freud and the neo-Freudians?
- What are the key ideas of Jung, Horney, and Adler?

*Read the section "The Psychoanalytic Perspective: The Neo-Freudians" and **write** your answers to the following:*

1. The neo-Freudians followed Freud in stressing

_____

_____

However, they developed independent personality theories, because they disagreed with Freud on three key points:

(a) _____

_____

(b) _____

_____

(c) _____

_____

2. Carl Jung emphasized _____

_____

_____

3. Karen Horney stressed _____

_____

_____

4. Alfred Adler believed _____

_____

_____

The Psychoanalytic Perspective: Evaluating Freud and the Psychoanalytic Perspective on Personality

Preview Questions

Consider the following questions as you study this section of the chapter.

- What are three criticisms of Freud's theory and, more generally, the psychoanalytic perspective?
- Which Freudian ideas have been substantiated by empirical research?

Read the section "Evaluating Freud and the Psychoanalytic Perspective on Personality" and **write** *your answers to the following:*

1. Although Sigmund Freud's ideas have had a profound and lasting effect on psychology and on society, the main criticisms of Freud's theory and psychoanalysis are

   (a) _____

   _____

   (b) _____

   _____

   _____

   _____

   (c) _____

   _____

   _____

2. Several of Freud's ideas have been substantiated by empirical evidence, including

   _____

   _____

   _____

   _____

After you have carefully studied the preceding sections, complete the following exercises.

Concept Check 2

Read the following and write the correct term in the space provided.

1. Wilfred suffered a lot of physical hardship and abuse as a child; as an adult, he lacks confidence, can't hold a job for long, and feels that nothing is really worth striving for. Adler would have said that Wilfred suffers from feelings of

   _____ .

2. In a class discussion, Louanne disputed Freud's assumption that women are inferior to men and that they suffer from penis envy; instead, she suggested that men suffer from womb envy and feel inadequate because they are incapable of bearing children. Louanne's views are most consistent with those of personality theorist

   _____ .

3. During a lecture on personality, Dr. Shornagel suggested that the deepest aspect of the individual psyche is a part inherited from previous generations, which contains universally shared experiences and ideas called archetypes. Dr. Shornagel is describing the

   _____ , which is

   central to _____ theory of personality.

4. Terry has an excessive need to exert power over people; his competitiveness and need to feel superior to others stem from the feeling he had as a child of being isolated and helpless in a potentially hostile world. Horney would have suggested that Terry is attempting to deal with

   _____ .

5. Frank is very sociable and outgoing and has a keen interest in sports and outdoor activities. Jung would probably describe Frank as a(n) _____ personality type.

6. The therapist suggested that to achieve psychological harmony, Adrian has to recognize and accept the feminine aspect of his personality. The therapist is referring to the

_____ , an important archetype in

_____ theory of personality.

Review of Terms, Concepts, and Names 2

Use the terms in this list to complete the Matching Test, then to help you answer the True/False items correctly.

neo-Freudians	Karen Horney
Carl Jung	basic anxiety
collective unconscious	womb envy
archetypes	Alfred Adler
anima	striving for superiority
animus	feelings of inferiority
introvert	inferiority complex
extravert	superiority complex

Matching Exercise

Match the appropriate term/name with its definition or description.

1. _____ German-born American psychoanalyst who emphasized the role of social relationships and culture in personality; sharply disagreed with Freud's characterization of female psychological development, especially his notion that women suffer from penis envy.

2. _____ In Jung's theory, the inherited mental images of universal human instincts, themes, and preoccupations that are the main components of the collective unconscious.

3. _____ In Adler's theory, the desire to improve oneself, master challenges, and move toward self-perfection and self-realization, considered to be the most fundamental human motive.

4. _____ Fundamental emotion that Horney described as a child's feeling of being isolated and helpless in a potentially hostile world.

5. _____ Adler's term for the personality characteristic that people who are unable to compensate for specific weaknesses develop; a general sense of inadequacy, weakness, and helplessness.

6. _____ In Jung's theory, the basic personality type that focuses attention and energy toward the outside world.

7. _____ In Jung's theory, the hypothesized part of the unconscious mind that is inherited from previous generations and that contains universally shared ancestral experiences and ideas.

8. _____ An important archetype that, according to Jung, represents the feminine side in every person.

True/False Test

Indicate whether each statement is true or false by placing T or F in the blank space next to each item.

1. ____ The term *neo-Freudians* was given to the early followers of Freud who developed their own theories yet still recognized the importance of many of Freud's basic notions, such as the influence of unconscious processes and early childhood experiences.

2. ____ Alfred Adler was an Austrian physician who broke with Freud and developed his own psychoanalytic theory of personality, which emphasized social factors and motivation toward self-improvement and self-realization, and overcoming feelings of inferiority.

3. ____ According to Adler's theory, people can overcompensate for their feelings of inferiority and develop a superiority complex, which is characterized by exaggeration of one's accomplishments and importance in an effort to cover up weaknesses and limitations.

4. ____ Horney used the term *womb envy* to describe the envy that men feel about women's capacity to bear children.

5. ____ In Jung's theory, the introvert is a basic personality type that focuses attention inward.

6. ____ Carl Jung was the Swiss psychiatrist who broke with Freud to develop his own psychoanalytic theory of personality, which stressed striving toward psychological harmony and included the key ideas of the collective unconscious and archetypes.

7. ____ According to Adler's theory, striving for superiority arises from universal feelings of inferiority that are experienced during infancy and childhood, when the child is helpless and dependent on others.

8. ___ The animus is the archetype in Jung's theory that represents the masculine side in every person.

Check your answers and review any areas of weakness before going on to the next section.

The Humanistic Perspective on Personality

Preview Questions

Consider the following questions as you study this section of the chapter.

- What is the focus of the humanistic perspective?
- What role do the self-concept, the actualizing tendency, and unconditional positive regard play in Rogers's personality theory?
- What are the key strengths and weaknesses of the humanistic perspective?

*Read the section "The Humanistic Perspective on Personality" and **write** your answers to the following:*

1. The humanistic perspective emphasizes

2. The actualizing tendency is _____

3. The self-concept is _____

4. Conditional positive regard is_____

   Unconditional positive regard is _____

5. The fully functioning person experiences _____

6. The humanistic perspective has been criticized on two particular points: _____

The Social Cognitive Perspective on Personality

Preview Questions

Consider the following questions as you study this section of the chapter.

- What is the focus of the social cognitive perspective?
- What is the principle of reciprocal determinism, and what is the role of self-efficacy beliefs in personality, according to this perspective?
- What are the key strengths and weaknesses of the social cognitive perspective?

*Read the section "The Social Cognitive Perspective on Personality" and **write** your answers to the following:*

1. The social cognitive perspective stresses _____

2. Bandura's social cognitive theory emphasizes

3. Reciprocal determinism suggests that human functioning and personality _____

4. Self-efficacy is _____

5. Key strengths of the social cognitive perspective are _____

6. Some weaknesses of the social cognitive perspective are that _____

The Trait Perspective on Personality

Preview Questions

Consider the following questions as you study this section of the chapter.

- What is the focus of trait theories?
- How are traits defined, and what is the difference between surface traits and source traits?
- What models of personality did Cattell and Eysenck propose, and what is the five-factor model of personality?
- What is the focus of behavioral genetics?
- To what degree are personality traits inherited?
- What are the key strengths and weaknesses of the trait perspective?

Read the section "The Trait Perspective on Personality" and **write** *your answers to the following:*

1. Trait theories focus on _____

   _____

2. Traits are _____

   _____

   Surface traits are _____

   _____

   Source traits are _____

   _____

3. Cattell believed that _____

   _____

4. Hans Eysenck proposed that _____

   _____

   _____

5. According to the five-factor model _____

   _____

   _____

6. The field of behavioral genetics studies _____

   _____

7. Factors that seem to have a significant genetic component are _____

   _____

   _____

   _____

8. The trait perspective is useful in _____

   _____

9. Some criticisms of the trait theories are _____

   _____

   _____

   _____

   _____

   _____

After you have carefully studied the preceding sections, complete the following exercises.

Concept Check 3

Read the following and write the correct term in the space provided.

1. Dunja is confident in her ability to service her own car but is less sure of her ability to bake cakes and cookies. According to Bandura, Dunja's different beliefs about her own abilities are her _____ beliefs.

2. Eileen is consistently cheerful, optimistic, talkative, and impulsive. These traits, which are inferred from her observable behavior, are referred to as _____ traits.

3. Navi is viewed by her family and friends as a flexible, creative, spontaneous, open, caring person who likes and is liked by most people. Carl Rogers would probably describe her as a(n) _____ person.

4. Alfred believes that from an early age we develop a set of perceptions and beliefs about ourselves, our nature, and our personal qualities and are motivated to act in accordance with these perceptions. Alfred's belief about personality development is most consistent with _____ theory.

5. Dr. Bhatt is concerned with describing, classifying, and measuring the numerous ways in which individuals may differ from one another. Her approach is most characteristic of the _____ perspective on personality.

6. Whenever her son misbehaves, Rochelle's disciplinary strategy is to make sure he clearly understands that his behavior is not acceptable while taking care to reassure him that he is loved and valued. Rachel is using Rogers's concept of _____ .

7. Dr. Lavalle studies the effects of heredity on behavior. In his research, he studies identical and fraternal twins who were separated at birth, identical and fraternal twins raised together, and the similarities and differences between adopted children and their adoptive and biological parents. Dr. Lavalle works in the field of _____ .

Graphic Organizer 2

Read the following statements and match the personality theorist and theory/perspective associated with each:

Statement	Theorist	Theory/Perspective
1. I believe that people can be classified into four basic types: introverted-neurotic, introverted-stable, extraverted-neurotic, and extraverted-stable.		
2. It is my belief that people have an innate drive to maintain and enhance themselves. This actualizing tendency is the most basic human motive, and all other motives, whether biological or social, are secondary.		
3. I reduced Allport's 4,000 terms to 171, and then, by using factor analysis, I eventually came up with 16 personality factors that represent the essential source of human personality.		
4. My theory of personality stresses the influence of unconscious mental processes, the importance of sexual and aggressive instincts, and the enduring effects of early childhood experiences on personality.		
5. For me the most fundamental human motive is striving for superiority, which arises from universal feelings of inferiority. Depending on how people deal with these feelings, they may develop either an inferiority complex or a superiority complex.		
6. My research suggests that human functioning is caused by the interaction of behavioral, cognitive, and environmental factors, a process I call reciprocal determinism.		
7. For me the impact of social relationships and the nature of the parent–child interaction are the main determinants of personality. Different patterns of behavior develop as people try to deal with their basic anxiety. Males have an additional problem to deal with, womb envy.		

Statement	Theorist	Theory/Perspective
8. I am most well known for my theory of motivation and the notion of a hierarchy of needs. I also identified the qualities most associated with self-actualized people.		
9. It is apparent to me, from my observations of different cultures and my own patients, that the deepest part of the individual psyche is the collective unconscious, which contains universal archetypes. Personality can be described on two basic dimensions, introversion and extraversion.		

Review of Terms, Concepts, and Names 3

Use the terms in this list to complete the Matching Test, then to help you answer the True/False items correctly.

humanistic psychology
Abraham Maslow
Carl Rogers
actualizing tendency
self-concept
positive regard
conditional positive
  regard
incongruence
unconditional positive
  regard
fully functioning person
congruence
Albert Bandura
self-efficacy
social cognitive theory

reciprocal determinism
self-system
trait
trait theory
surface trait
source traits
Raymond Cattell
Hans Eysenck
introversion
extraversion
neuroticism
stability
psychoticism
five-factor model of
  personality
behavioral genetics

Matching Exercise

Match the appropriate term/name with its definition or description.

1. _____ A relatively stable, enduring predisposition to consistently behave in a certain way.

2. _____ People's beliefs about their ability to meet the demands of a specific situation; feelings of self-confidence or self-doubt.

3. _____ Contemporary American psychologist who is best known for his research on observational learning and his social cognitive theory of personality.

4. _____ In Rogers's theory, the innate drive to maintain and enhance the human organism.

5. _____ Trait theory of personality that identifies five basic source traits (extraversion, neuroticism, agreeableness, conscientiousness, and openness to experience) as the fundamental building blocks of personality.

6. _____ American psychologist who was one of the founders of humanistic psychology and emphasized the study of healthy personality development; developed a hierarchical theory of motivation based on the idea that people will strive for self-actualization, the highest motive, only after more basic needs have been met.

7. _____ In Eysenck's theory, a third dimension of personality; a person high on this trait is antisocial, cold, hostile, and unconcerned about others, whereas a person low on this trait is warm and caring toward others.

8. _____ In Rogers's theory, the term for the sense of being loved and valued by other people, especially one's parents.

9. _____ Bandura's theory of personality, which emphasizes the importance of observational learning, conscious cognitive processes, social experiences, self-efficacy beliefs, and reciprocal determinism.

10. _____ Theory of personality that focuses on identifying, describing, and measuring individual differences in attributes.

11. _____ In Eysenck's theory, the dimension of personality that describes people who direct their energies outward toward the environment and other people; a person high on this dimension would be outgoing and sociable, enjoying new experiences and stimulating environments.

12. _____ American psychologist who was one of the founders of humanistic psychology; developed a theory of personality and form of psychotherapy that emphasized the inherent worth of people, the innate tendency to strive toward one's potential, and the importance of the self-concept in personality development.

13. _____ Theoretical viewpoint on personality that generally emphasizes the inherent goodness of people, human potential, self-actualization, the self-concept, and healthy personality development.

14. _____ Albert Bandura's model that explains human functioning and personality as caused by the interaction of behavioral, cognitive, and environmental factors.

15. _____ In Eysenck's theory, a personality dimension in which the person directs his or her energies inward, toward inner, self-focused experiences; a person high on this dimension might be quiet, solitary, and reserved, avoiding new experiences.

True/False Test

Indicate whether each statement is true or false by placing T or F in the blank space next to each item.

1. ____ Behavioral genetics is an interdisciplinary field that studies the effects of genes and heredity on behavior.

2. ____ In Rogers's theory, people are in a state of congruence when their feelings and experiences are denied and distorted because they contradict or conflict with their self-concept.

3. ____ Raymond Cattell was a British-born American psychologist who developed a trait theory that identifies 16 essential source traits or personality factors; also developed the widely used self-report personality test, the Sixteen Personality Factor Questionnaire (16PF).

4. ____ Personality characteristics or attributes that can easily be inferred from observable behavior are called source traits.

5. ____ In Rogers's theory, the sense that you will be valued and loved only if you behave in a way that is acceptable to others is called conditional positive regard.

6. ____ Self-concept is the set of perceptions and beliefs that you hold about yourself.

7. ____ In Eysenck's theory, neuroticism refers to a person's predisposition to become emotionally upset.

8. ____ In Rogers's theory, the fully functioning person has a flexible, constantly evolving self-concept and is realistic, open to new experiences, and capable of changing in response to new experiences.

9. ____ Unconditional positive regard, in Rogers's theory, is the sense that you will be valued and loved even if you don't conform to the standards and expectations of others.

10. ____ A surface trait is the most fundamental dimension of personality; these broad basic traits are hypothesized to be universal and relatively few in number.

11. ____ In Rogers's theory, people are in a state of incongruence when their sense of self (their self-concept) is consistent with their emotions and experiences.

12. ____ Hans Eysenck was a German-born British psychologist who developed a trait theory of personality that identifies the three basic dimensions of personality as neuroticism, extraversion, and psychoticism.

13. ____ In Eysenck's theory, stability reflects a person's predisposition to be emotionally even.

14. ____ Cognitive skills, abilities, and attitudes that emerge through developmental experiences involving the interaction of behavioral, cognitive, and environmental factors represent the person's self-system.

Check your answers and review any areas of weakness before going on to the next section.

Assessing Personality: Psychological Tests

Preview Questions

Consider the following questions as you study this section of the chapter.

- What are projective tests and self-report inventories, and how are they used to measure personality?

- What are the key strengths and weaknesses of projective tests and self-report inventories?

Read the section "Assessing Personality: Psychological Tests" and **write** *your answers to the following:*

1. A psychological test is _____
_____
_____

2. A projective test is _____
_____
_____

3. A self-report inventory is _____
_____
_____

4. Projective tests provide qualitative data but their weaknesses are that _____
_____
_____
_____

5. The strengths of self-report inventories are that
_____
_____
_____

6. Problems with self-report inventories are that
_____
_____
_____

After you have carefully studied the preceding section, complete the following exercises.

Concept Check 4

Read the following and write the correct term in the space provided.

1. Michelle was given a psychological test in which she was asked to look at a series of cards with ambiguous scenes and make up stories for each one. She was told to give as much detail as possible about what the characters are feeling and how the story ends. Michelle was given a(n) _____ test called the _____ .

2. When Roger was assessed for his suitability to be a police officer, he was given a 500-item test that was used to evaluate his mental health. The test he was given was most likely the _____ .

3. Mr. and Mrs. Sheldrake want to get some idea of how their son is going to do in high school.

The test that is best at predicting their son's high school grades is the _____ .

4. In his psychoanalytic practice, Dr. Coles tries to understand his client's unconscious conflicts, motives, psychological defenses, and personality traits. It is very probable that Dr. Coles uses a(n) _____ test called the _____ .

5. Dr. Cera sees a lot of married couples in his counseling practice. In an effort to help them resolve their conflicts, he frequently administers a test to each partner, which generates a profile of their personality characteristics. Dr. Cera most likely uses the _____ .

Review of Terms and Concepts 4

Use the terms in this list to complete the Matching Test, then to help you answer the True/False items correctly.

psychological test
projective test
Rorschach Inkblot Test
Thematic Apperception Test (TAT)
self-report inventory
Minnesota Multiphasic Personality Inventory (MMPI)
California Personality Inventory (CPI)
Sixteen Personality Factor Questionnaire (16PF)
graphology
possible selves

Matching Exercise

Match the appropriate term with its definition or description.

1. _____ Type of psychological test in which a person's responses to standardized questions are compared with established norms.

2. _____ Projective test that uses inkblots, developed by Swiss psychiatrist Hermann Rorschach in 1921.

3. _____ Self-report inventory that assesses personality characteristics in normal populations.

4. _____ Test that assesses a person's abilities, aptitudes, interests, or personality, based on a systematically obtained sample of behavior.

5. _____ Self-report inventory developed by Raymond Cattell that generates a personality profile with ratings on 16 trait dimensions.

True/False Test

Indicate whether each statement is true or false by placing T or F in the blank space next to each item.

1. ___ A projective test is a type of personality test that involves a person's interpreting an ambiguous image and is used to assess unconscious motives, conflicts, psychological defenses, and personality traits.

2. ___ Possible selves refers to an aspect of the self-concept that includes images of the selves that you hope, fear, or expect to become in the future.

3. ___ The Minnesota Multiphasic Personality Inventory (MMPI) is a projective personality test that involves creating stories about each of a series of ambiguous scenes.

4. ___ The Thematic Apperception Test (TAT) is a self-report inventory that assesses personality characteristics and psychological disorders; used to assess both normal and disturbed populations.

5. ___ Graphology is a pseudoscience that claims to assess personality as well as social and occupational attributes based on a person's distinctive handwriting, doodles, and drawing style.

Check your answers and review any areas of weakness before going on to the next section.

Something to Think About

1. The use of psychological tests has been and will continue to be an interesting topic of discussion for most people. Almost everyone has heard of the famous inkblot test, but not everyone knows its purpose or its limitations. Considering what you have learned about psychological tests in this chapter, what would you tell someone about the inkblot test and psychological tests in general?

2. The history of astrology can be traced back over 4,000 years. Astrology's basic premise is that the positions of the planets and stars at the time and place of your birth determine your personality and destiny. Today, belief in astrological predictions remains widespread. Indeed, you probably know a number of people who, even if they are not true believers, at least read their daily horoscope in the paper. How might you enlighten these people about scientific research on astrology?

Check your answers and review any areas of weakness before completing the progress tests.

Progress Test 1

Review the complete chapter (including Concept Reviews and the boxed inserts), review all your study notes, and then test yourself on the following progress test. Check your answers. If you make a mistake, review your notes, review the relevant section of the study guide, and, if necessary, go back and read the appropriate part of your textbook.

1. Marvin is angry and upset after an argument with his boss. At home that evening he is harshly and unreasonably critical of his son for not getting all his homework assignments completed. According to Freud, Marvin is using an ego defense mechanism called
   (a) identification.   (c) rationalization.
   (b) repression.   (d) displacement.

2. Seven-year old Salvatore prefers to play with his male friends and does not like playing with girls very much. Salvatore is probably in the _____ stage of psychosexual development.
   (a) anal   (c) latency
   (b) phallic   (d) genital

3. Although Tim has many fond memories of his college days, he only vaguely remembers the girl he was engaged to but who left him suddenly for another man. Tim's unconscious forgetting is an ego defense mechanism called
   (a) identification.   (c) displacement.
   (b) sublimation.   (d) repression.

4. Every time 2-year-old Kate is given a bath, she plays with her genital area. If her parents chastise or punish her, she is likely to experience frustration, which could lead to an unresolved developmental conflict called
   (a) fixation.   (c) displacement.
   (b) undoing.   (d) denial.

5. Zachary considers himself to be an outgoing, fun-loving type of person, and he goes to a lot of parties. Sondra, on the other hand, thinks of herself as fairly quiet and shy, and enjoys being by herself, reading a book and listening to classical music. In Jung's theory, Zachary's and Sondra's different behaviors reflect

   (a) the two basic personality types, the extravert and the introvert.
   (b) the two important archetypes, the hero and the nurturing mother.
   (c) a superiority complex and an inferiority complex.
   (d) penis envy and womb envy.

6. Read the example in question 5 again. According to social cognitive theory, the different personalities of Zachary and Sondra reflect the interaction of behavioral, cognitive, and environmental factors, a process Bandura called

   (a) identification.
   (b) striving for superiority.
   (c) the actualizing tendency.
   (d) reciprocal determinism.

7. As part of a research project, Jasbinder was given the same psychological test three times at 2-month intervals by three different therapists. Her results on the tests were all very different. It is most probable that she was given the

   (a) MMPI.   (c) CPI.
   (b) 16PF.   (d) TAT.

8. The actualizing tendency and the self-concept are to _____ as reciprocal determinism and self-efficacy are to _____ .

   (a) Abraham Maslow; Hans Eysenck
   (b) Alfred Adler; Albert Bandura
   (c) Raymond Cattell; Carl Jung
   (d) Carl Rogers; Albert Bandura

9. When asked to describe her husband, Mrs. Roech said that he is prone to exaggerating his accomplishments and importance, seems unaware of the reality of his limitations, and tends to overcompensate for his feelings of inferiority and weakness. Adler would probably have said that Mr. Roech has

   (a) an inferiority complex.
   (b) an extraverted personality.
   (c) a superiority complex.
   (d) an anal fixation.

10. Katrina thinks of herself as fairly laid back, easygoing, and relatively calm. She believes that she is above average academically and intellectually and sees herself as very conscientious at work and caring and loving with her family. Carl Rogers's term for Katrina's perceptions and beliefs about herself would be

    (a) self-efficacy.   (c) self-system.
    (b) self-concept.   (d) possible selves.

11. Miguel is giving a lecture on the five-factor model of personality. Which of the following personality dimensions is not likely to be included in his talk?

    (a) anal retentiveness
    (b) extraversion
    (c) neuroticism
    (d) agreeableness
    (e) openness to experience

12. Dr. Markowitz studies the effects of heredity on behavior. One of his areas of research focuses on similarities and differences in identical twins who were separated at birth or early infancy and raised by different families. Dr. Markowitz is most probably a(n)

    (a) psychoanalyst.
    (b) humanistic psychologist.
    (c) social cognitive psychologist.
    (d) behavioral geneticist.

13. Zintyre was very impressed when told by an astrologer that, "You are gregarious, outgoing, and fond of travel. You tend to react negatively to authority figures, and you have had a number of confrontations as a result. You enjoy good food and good wine and you don't suffer fools gladly." According to Science Versus Pseudoscience 11.4, which of the following is true?

    (a) The astrologer probably has an extraordinary gift for accurately assessing personality.
    (b) The astrologer is probably operating at chance level in assessing personality.
    (c) The astrologer is using a proven scientific method in assessing Zintyre's personality.
    (d) Zintyre is probably extremely accurate in assessing the truthfulness of the astrologer's personality description.

14. According to the Application, the term *possible selves* refers to
    (a) the unconscious part of the mind that motivates our behavior.
    (b) the major symptom of a fixated personality.
    (c) the aspect of the self-concept that includes images of the selves that you hope, fear, or expect to become in the future.
    (d) delusional thought processes.

15. According to Critical Thinking 11.1, which of the following is true?
    (a) Freud's view of human nature was deeply pessimistic.
    (b) Rogers's view of human nature was deeply pessimistic.
    (c) Freud believed that humans are positive, forward-moving, constructive, realistic, and trustworthy.
    (d) Rogers believed that the essence of human nature is destructive but that societal, religious, and cultural restraints make people behave in good and moral ways.

Progress Test 2

After you have checked your understanding of the material in Progress Test 1 and have done a complete chapter review with special focus on any areas of weakness, you are ready to assess your knowledge on Progress Test 2. Check your answers. If you make a mistake, review your notes, the relevant section of the study guide, and, if necessary, the appropriate part of your textbook.

1. Nathan chews the end of his pen, bites his nails, overeats, smokes cigarettes, and talks incessantly. According to Freud, Nathan has probably fixated at the _____ stage of psychosexual development due to some unresolved conflict.
   (a) oral   (c) phallic
   (b) anal   (d) genital

2. Dr. Jivraj, like many contemporary trait theorists, believes that the 16 trait model is too complex, and that the three-dimensional trait theory is too limited. Instead, he favors a model in which five basic dimensions represent the structural organization of personality traits. These five factors are
   (a) extraversion, neuroticism, agreeableness, conscientiousness, and openness to experience.
   (b) submissiveness, apprehensiveness, dominance, sociability, and venturesomeness.
   (c) inferiority, superiority, introversion, extraversion, and actualizing tendencies.
   (d) self-efficacy, self-concept, reciprocal determining tendencies, defensiveness, and openness to experience.

3. Shelly was often rejected by her parents; as a result, she mistrusts other people and treats them with hostility, which leads to their rejection of her. This cycle of rejection, mistrust, hostility, and further rejection illustrates what Bandura called
   (a) self-efficacy.
   (b) identification.
   (c) displacement.
   (d) reciprocal determinism.

4. During a class discussion of various perspectives on personality, Sasha points to all the evidence that human beings are destructive and aggressive. He points to the millions who died in two world wars and the ongoing killings and massacres that continue in many parts of the world today. Sasha's observation about basic human nature supports the _____ perspective and is a criticism of the _____ perspective.
   (a) humanistic; psychoanalytic
   (b) trait; social cognitive
   (c) social cognitive; trait
   (d) psychoanalytic; humanistic

5. Dr. Sheenan is a clinical psychologist who wants to assess the extent to which a client is suffering from depression, delusions, and other mental health problems. Dr. Sheenan is most likely to use the
   (a) 16PF.   (c) MMPI.
   (b) CPI.   (d) TAT.

6. When Cindy was given the Rorschach Inkblot Test, she reported seeing a number of inanimate objects and some animal figures and tended to concentrate on very small details in each inkblot. Her therapist observed her behavior, gestures, and reactions as she responded to each card. It is most probable that her therapist is
   (a) interested in her unconscious conflicts, motives, and psychological defenses.
   (b) assessing her suitability for a particular occupation, such as police officer or pilot.
   (c) trying to generate a personality profile based on a number of personality traits.
   (d) trying to predict how she will perform academically when she goes to college.

7. Lukasz was given a forced-choice personality test in which he was required to respond to each item by choosing one of three alternatives. The results generated a personality profile with ratings on a number of trait dimensions that helped Lukasz decide which career path he should pursue. Lukasz was most likely given the
   (a) Thematic Apperception Test (TAT).
   (b) Minnesota Multiphasic Personality (MMPI).
   (c) California Personality Inventory (CPI).
   (d) Sixteen Personality Factor Questionnaire (16PF).

8. Five-year-old Dunstan has recently become very possessive of his mother and appears to be jealous of his father. He is sometimes openly hostile, telling his father, "Don't kiss my Mommy!" According to Freud, Dunstan is in the _____ stage of psychosexual development and showing manifestations of _____ .
   (a) oral; fixation
   (b) anal; fixation
   (c) phallic; the Oedipus complex
   (d) latency; the Oedipus complex

9. Wendy believes that the most fundamental human motive is striving for superiority. She thinks that this drive arises from global feelings of inferiority and that human personality and behavior reflect our attempts to compensate for or overcome our perceived weaknesses. Which personality theorist is most likely to agree with Wendy's views?
   (a) Freud   (c) Horney
   (b) Jung   (d) Adler

10. David is very quiet, pessimistic, anxious, and moody and becomes emotionally upset very easily. In terms of Eysenck's four basic personality types, he would be classified as
    (a) introverted-neurotic.
    (b) introverted-stable.
    (c) extraverted-neurotic.
    (d) extraverted-stable.

11. In a term paper on Carl Jung's theory of personality, Justin quoted Jung as saying that the _____ contains "the whole spiritual heritage of mankind's evolution, born anew in the brain structure of every individual."
    (a) personal preconscious
    (b) collective conscious
    (c) personal unconscious
    (d) collective unconscious

12. Ursula's therapist instructs her to relax, close her eyes, and state aloud whatever thoughts come to mind no matter how trivial, silly, or absurd they seem. The therapist is using a technique called
    (a) free association.
    (b) displacement.
    (c) unconditional positive regard.
    (d) repression.

13. Leanne studies very hard, but she always feels that she hasn't studied enough. If she takes a break to socialize with her friends, she starts feeling guilty and anxious. Freud would say that Leanne has a
    (a) strong superego.   (c) weak superego.
    (b) strong id.   (d) weak id.

14. According to In Focus 11.3, which of the following is true?
    (a) Any two randomly chosen people of the same age, sex, and culture will likely have absolutely no similarities.
    (b) Some similarities between separated identical twins may be genetically influenced.
    (c) Personality is almost completely determined by genes.
    (d) Personality is almost completely determined by environmental factors.

15. According to Science Versus Pseudoscience 11.5, graphologists' claims that handwriting reveals temperament, personality traits, intelligence, and reasoning ability
    (a) have been empirically tested and supported by numerous scientific studies.
    (b) have not been supported by scientific research.
    (c) should be believed because thousands of U.S. companies have used graphologists to assist in hiring new employees.
    (d) have much greater validity and reliability than similar claims made by astrologers.

Progress Test 3

After you have checked your understanding of the material in Progress Tests 1 and 2, and have done a complete chapter review with special focus on any areas of weakness, you are ready to further assess your knowledge on Progress Test 3. Check your answers. If you make a mistake, review your notes, the appropriate parts of the study guide, and if necessary, the relevant sections of your textbook.

1. During a class reunion Adeil reminisced with some of his high school friends about their last year at school and had no problem recalling many of the fun times they had together. In terms of Freud's theory of personality, Adeil's ability to recall these events would suggest that they are stored at the _____ level of awareness.
    (a) unconscious   (c) latency
    (b) conscious   (d) preconscious

2. Researchers conducting twin and adoption studies are likely to conclude that
    (a) in general, the influence of environmental factors on personality traits is at least equal to the influence of genetic factors.
    (b) certain personality traits, such as extraversion and neuroticism, are significantly influenced by genetics.
    (c) identical twins are more alike early in life, but as they grow up, leave home, and encounter different experiences and environments, their personalities become more different.
    (d) all of the above are true.

3. Juan is an experienced car mechanic who believes he can fix just about any problem in any make of car or truck. According to Bandura, Juan's confidence in his ability to handle mechanical problems is his
    (a) self-concept.
    (b) superiority complex.
    (c) self-efficacy.
    (d) actualizing tendency.

4. When Romwaldo was given the results of his psychological test, he was told that he scored high on the extraverted-stable dimension and that he has a tendency to be sociable, outgoing, talkative, and responsive. This description of Romwaldo's source and surface traits is most consistent with
    (a) Hans Eysenck's view of personality.
    (b) Rorschach's theory of personality.
    (c) Alfred Adler's model of personality.
    (d) Carl Rogers's humanistic approach to personality.

5. The pleasure principle is to _____ as the reality principle is to _____ .
    (a) the oral stage; the anal stage
    (b) Thanatos; Eros
    (c) the id; the ego
    (d) the ego; the superego

6. When Kaysone was researching a term paper for her history of psychology course, she was intrigued by the ideas of neo-Freudian Alfred Adler. She noted that for Adler the most fundamental human motive was _____ , which arises from universal _____ .
    (a) driven by basic anxiety; feelings of womb and penis envy
    (b) the need to achieve psychological growth, self-realization, and psychic harmony; archetypes in the collective unconscious
    (c) sexual and aggressive in nature; feelings of guilt and anxiety repressed in the unconscious
    (d) striving for superiority; feelings of inferiority

7. Dr. Selnick believes in the importance of unconscious psychological conflicts, sexual and aggressive drives, and the formative influence of early childhood experiences. Dr. Selnick's views are most consistent with the _____ perspective.
   (a) psychoanalytic   (c) social cognitive
   (b) humanistic   (d) trait

8. Raffi is shown a series of cards with ambiguous scenes and is told to make up a story about each one, describing the characters' feelings and their motives. Raffi has been given the
   (a) Thematic Apperception Test (TAT).
   (b) Rorschach Inkblot Test.
   (c) California Personality Inventory (CPI).
   (d) Minnesota Multiphasic Personality Inventory (MMPI).

9. Sheldon has frequently been rebellious, inconsiderate, and self-centered. His parents are consistent in disciplining him for his inappropriate behaviors while communicating to him that they value and love him. The person most likely to agree with their parenting approach and use of unconditional positive regard is
   (a) Sigmund Freud.   (c) Joseph Breuer.
   (b) Carl Rogers.   (d) Carl Jung.

10. Dr. Welch is a clinical psychologist who uses the MMPI and the 16PF. If asked to identify the key strength of these tests, he is most likely to note that
    (a) they provide a wealth of qualitative information about the individual.
    (b) scoring relies on the examiner's subjective judgment and clinical experience and expertise.
    (c) they accurately measure the individual's unconscious motives and conflicts.
    (d) they are standardized and objectively scored.

11. Research participants were first given a personality test; then, as they viewed very positive or very negative images, they underwent fMRI brain scans. It is very probable that those who scored high on extraversion showed _____ and those who scored high on neuroticism showed _____ .
    (a) less activity in the brain areas that control emotion; more activity in the brain areas that control emotion
    (b) damage to the frontal and temporal cortical areas; damage to the temporal lobe and the amygdala
    (c) more activity in the brain areas that control emotion; less activity in the brain areas that control emotion
    (d) damage to the temporal lobe and the amygdala; damage to the frontal and temporal cortical areas

12. Dr. Sharma stresses the importance of identifying, measuring, and describing individual differences in terms of various personality characteristics. His views are most representative of the _____ perspective on personality.
    (a) psychoanalytic   (c) social cognitive
    (b) humanistic   (d) trait

13. According to the Application , which of the following is *false*?
    (a) A person's self-concept is a multifaceted system of related images and ideas.
    (b) Possible selves influence our behavior in important ways.
    (c) We're often unaware of how possible selves we've mentally constructed influence our beliefs, actions, and self-evaluations.
    (d) A person's self-concept is a singular mental self-image.

14. According to Critical Thinking 11.2, which of the following is true?
    (a) Freud viewed aggression as a universal, unconscious human instinct.
    (b) Bandura believed that the essence of human nature is aggressive but that societal, religious, and cultural restraints make people behave in nonaggressive ways.
    (c) Freud believed that human aggression, like other human behavior, is driven by conscious, rational goals and motives.
    (d) Bandura viewed aggression as a universal, unconscious human instinct.

15. Science Versus Pseudoscience 11.4, which discusses astrology and personality, concluded that
    (a) the position of the planets and stars at the time and place of your birth determines your personality and destiny.
    (b) today, virtually nobody believes in astrological interpretations and predictions.
    (c) science has not been able to refute the claims, predictions, and interpretations of astrology.
    (d) neither popular nor serious astrology has any reliable basis in scientific fact.

Answers

Introduction: What Is Personality?

1. *Personality is defined as* an individual's unique and relatively consistent pattern of thinking, feeling, and behaving.

2. *A personality theory is* an attempt to describe and explain how people are similar, how they are different, and why every individual is unique.

3. *The four basic perspectives on personality (and the main emphasis of each) are* the psychoanalytic perspective, which emphasizes the importance of unconscious processes and the influence of early childhood experience; the humanistic perspective, which represents an optimistic look at human nature, emphasizing the self and the fulfillment of a person's unique potential; the social cognitive perspective, which emphasizes learning and conscious cognitive processes, including the importance of beliefs about the self, goal-setting, and self-regulation; and the trait perspective, which emphasizes the description and measurement of specific personality differences among individuals.

The Psychoanalytic Perspective on Personality

1. *Psychoanalysis—Freud's theory of personality— stresses* the influence of unconscious mental processes, the importance of sexual and aggressive instincts, and the enduring effects of early childhood experiences on later personality development.

2. *Some of the key factors in the development of Freud's ideas were* his collaboration with Joseph Breuer on the cause of hysteria, the concept of catharsis; the development of free association to study the unconscious; the importance of dreams and their interpretation; and the impact of war on culture and society.

The Psychoanalytic Perspective: Freud's Dynamic Theory of Personality

1. *The content of the unconscious can surface in disguised form in* free association, dreams, slips of the tongue, and what, on the surface, appear to be accidents.

2. *The three basic structures of personality (and their functions) are* the id (the completely unconscious, irrational component of personality that seeks immediate satisfaction of instinctual urges and is ruled by the pleasure princi-

ple); the ego (the partly conscious rational component of personality that regulates thoughts and behavior, that is most in touch with the real world, and that is governed by the reality principle); and the superego (the partly conscious, self-evaluative, moralistic component of personality that is formed through the internalization of parental and societal rules).

3. *The three main ego defense mechanisms (and the roles they play) are* repression (the unconscious exclusion of anxiety-provoking thoughts, feelings, and memories from conscious awareness, which is involved in all other ego defense mechanisms); displacement (unconscious shifting of the target of an emotional urge to a substitute target that is less threatening or dangerous), and sublimation (a form of displacement in which sexual urges are rechanneled into productive, nonsexual activities). Other ego defense mechanisms include rationalization, projection, reaction formation, denial, undoing, and regression.

The Psychoanalytic Perspective: Personality Development

1. *The psychosexual stages are age-related developmental periods* in which the child's sexual impulses are expressed through different bodily zones and the activities associated with these areas.

2. *The five psychosexual stages (and the focus of each) are* the oral stage (the mouth is the primary focus of pleasurable and gratifying sensations which are achieved via feeding and exploring objects with the mouth); the anal stage (the anus is the primary focus of pleasurable sensations, which are derived from developing control over elimination via toilet training); the phallic stage (the genitals are the primary focus of pleasurable sensations derived through sexual curiosity, masturbation, and sexual attraction toward the opposite sex parent); the latency stage (sexual impulses become repressed and dormant and same-sex friendships with peers develop and the focus is on school, sport, and other activities); and the genital stage (at physical sexual maturity the genitals become the focus of pleasurable sensations, which are satisfied in a heterosexual relationship).

3. *If the developmental conflict of a particular stage is not resolved,* the result may be fixation, and the person will continue to seek pleasure

through behaviors that are similar to those associated with that psychosexual stage.

4. *The Oedipus complex refers to* a child's unconscious sexual desire for the opposite-sex parent, usually accompanied by hostile feelings toward the same-sex parent.

5. *Identification (which is one result of the Oedipus complex) is an ego defense mechanism that* involves reducing anxiety by modeling the behavior and characteristics of another person.

Concept Check 1

1. projection
2. free association
3. unconscious
4. latent
5. id
6. superego
7. sublimation
8. identification
9. rationalization

Graphic Organizer 1

1. genital
2. phallic
3. latency
4. oral
5. anal

Matching Exercise 1

1. libido
2. personality
3. superego
4. Oedipus complex
5. ego
6. preconscious
7. oral stage
8. displacement
9. Sigmund Freud
10. anal stage
11. personality theory
12. id
13. latency stage
14. psychoanalysis
15. ego defense mechanisms
16. psychosexual stages

True/False Test 1

1. F	6. T	11. T	16. F
2. T	7. T	12. F	
3. T	8. T	13. T	
4. F	9. F	14. T	
5. T	10. F	15. T	

The Psychoanalytic Perspective: The Neo-Freudians

1. *The neo-Freudians followed Freud in stressing* the importance of the unconscious and early childhood. *However, they developed independent personality theories, because they disagreed with Freud on three key points: (a)* They took issue with Freud's belief that behavior was primarily motivated by sexual desires. *(b)* They disagreed with Freud's contention that personality is fundamentally determined by early childhood experiences; instead, they believed that personality can also be influenced by experiences throughout the lifespan. *(c)* They departed from Freud's generally pessimistic view of human nature and society.

2. *Carl Jung emphasized* psychological growth and self-realization. He proposed the existence of the collective unconscious, which contains archetypes of universal human instincts, themes, and preoccupations. He was the first to describe two basic personality types: introverts and extraverts.

3. *Karen Horney stressed* the role of social relationships in protecting against basic anxiety; she objected to Freud's views of female development, particularly his idea of penis envy (she proposed that males have womb envy).

4. *Alfred Adler believed* that the most fundamental human motive was to strive for superiority, which arose from universal feelings of inferiority. He proposed the notions of the inferiority complex and the superiority complex.

The Psychoanalytic Perspective: Evaluating Freud and the Psychoanalytic Perspective on Personality

1. *Although Sigmund Freud's ideas have had a profound and lasting effect on psychology and on society, the main criticisms of Freud's theory and psychoanalysis are*

   (a) Freud's theory relies wholly on data derived from a relatively small sample of patients and

from his self-analysis. He did not take notes during his private therapy sessions, and so we have only Freud's interpretations of the cases; this problem has to do with the ability to objectively evaluate the evidence.

(b) Many psychoanalytic concepts, because they are so vague and ambiguous, are very difficult to measure or confirm scientifically. In addition, because even seemingly contradictory information can be used to support Freud's theory, psychoanalytic concepts are often impossible to disprove. Psychoanalysis is also better at explaining past behavior than at predicting future behavior.

(c) Many people feel that Freud's theories reflect a sexist view of women. Freud's theory uses male psychology as a prototype, and women are essentially viewed as a deviation from the norm of masculinity.

2. *Several of Freud's ideas have been substantiated by empirical evidence, including* the idea that much of mental life is unconscious; that early childhood experiences have a critical influence on interpersonal relationships and psychological adjustment in adulthood; and that people differ significantly in the degree to which they are able to regulate their impulses, emotions, and thoughts toward adaptive and socially acceptable ends.

Concept Check 2

1. inferiority
2. Karen Horney
3. collective unconscious; Jung's
4. basic anxiety
5. extravert
6. anima; Jung's

Matching Exercise 2

1. Karen Horney
2. archetypes
3. striving for superiority
4. basic anxiety
5. inferiority complex
6. extravert
7. collective unconscious
8. anima

True/False Test 2

1. T
2. T
3. T
4. T
5. T
6. T
7. T
8. T

The Humanistic Perspective on Personality

1. *The humanistic perspective emphasizes* free will, self-awareness, and psychological growth.
2. *The actualizing tendency is* the innate drive to maintain and enhance the human organism.
3. *The self-concept is* the set of perceptions and beliefs that you have about yourself, including your nature, your personal qualities, and your typical behavior.
4. *Conditional positive regard is* the sense that you will be loved and valued only if you behave in a way that is acceptable to others; this can cause a person to deny or distort aspects of experience, leading to a state of incongruence with regard to the self-concept. *Unconditional positive regard is* the sense that you will be valued and loved even if you don't conform to the standards and expectations of others; this leads to a state of congruence, where your sense of self is consistent with your emotions and experiences.
5. *The fully functioning person experiences* congruence, the actualizing tendency, and psychological growth.
6. *The humanistic perspective has been criticized on two particular points*: first, humanistic theories are hard to validate or test scientifically; second, according to many psychologists, the humanistic perspective's view of human nature is too optimistic.

The Social Cognitive Perspective on Personality

1. *The social cognitive perspective stresses* the role of conscious thought processes, self-regulation, and the importance of situational influences.
2. *Bandura's social cognitive theory emphasizes* the importance of observational learning, conscious cognitive processes, social experiences, self-efficacy beliefs, and reciprocal determinism.
3. *Reciprocal determinism suggests that human functioning and personality* are caused by the interaction of behavioral, cognitive, and environmental factors.

4. *Self-efficacy is* a person's belief about his or her ability to meet the demands of a specific situation (feelings of self-confidence or self-doubt); self-efficacy influences behavior, performance, motivation, and persistence.

5. *Key strengths of the social cognitive perspective are* that it is grounded in empirical, laboratory research; it is built on research in learning, cognitive psychology, and social psychology rather than on clinical impressions. Unlike the vague psychoanalytic and humanistic concepts, the concepts of social cognitive theory are scientifically testable; they can be operationally defined and measured.

6. *Some weaknesses of the social cognitive perspective are that* real-life, everyday situations are not adequately captured in the typical laboratory research situation because they are more complex, with multiple factors converging to affect behavior and personality. Other psychologists argue that the social cognitive perspective ignores unconscious conflicts and emotions.

The Trait Perspective on Personality

1. *Trait theories focus on* identifying, measuring, and describing individual differences.

2. *Traits are* relatively stable, enduring predispositions to consistently behave in certain ways. *Surface traits are* personality characteristics or attributes that can easily be inferred from observing behavior. *Source traits are* the most fundamental dimensions of personality and are thought to be universal and relatively few in number.

3. *Cattell believed that* there are 16 basic personality factors (he developed the 16PF test).

4. *Hans Eysenck proposed that* there are three personality dimensions, introversion-extraversion, neuroticism-stability, and psychoticism.

5. *According to the five-factor model,* there are five basic personality dimensions: extraversion, neuroticism, agreeableness, conscientiousness, and openness to experience.

6. *The field of behavioral genetics studies* the effects of genes and heredity on behavior.

7. *Factors that seem to have a significant genetic component are* extraversion, neuroticism, openness to experience, and conscientiousness, but the influence of environmental factors on personality traits is at least equal to the influence of genetic factors.

8. *The trait perspective is useful in* describing and comparing people.

9. *Some criticisms of the trait theories are* that they don't really explain human personality or how or why individual differences develop, and they generally fail to address other important personality factors, such as the basic motives that drive human personality, the role of unconscious mental processes, how beliefs about the self influence personality, or how psychological change and growth occur.

Concept Check 3

1. self-efficacy
2. surface
3. fully functioning
4. social cognitive
5. trait
6. unconditional positive regard
7. behavioral genetics

Graphic Organizer 2

1. Hans Eysenck; trait
2. Carl Rogers; humanistic
3. Raymond Cattell; trait
4. Sigmund Freud; psychoanalytic
5. Alfred Adler; psychoanalytic (neo-Freudian)
6. Albert Bandura; social cognitive
7. Karen Horney; psychoanalytic (neo-Freudian)
8. Abraham Maslow; humanistic
9. Carl Jung; psychoanalytic (neo-Freudian)

Matching Exercise 3

1. trait
2. self-efficacy
3. Albert Bandura
4. actualizing tendency
5. five-factor model of personality
6. Abraham Maslow
7. psychoticism
8. positive regard
9. social cognitive theory
10. trait theory
11. extraversion
12. Carl Rogers

13. humanistic psychology

14. reciprocal determinism

15. introversion

True/False Test 3

1. T	6. T	11. F
2. F	7. T	12. T
3. T	8. T	13. T
4. F	9. T	14. T
5. T	10. F	

Assessing Personality: Psychological Tests

1. *A psychological test is* a test that assesses a person's abilities, aptitudes, interests, or personality, based on a systematically obtained sample of behavior.

2. *A projective test is* a type of personality test that involves the client's interpreting an ambiguous image; it is used to assess unconscious motives, conflicts, psychological defenses, and personality traits. The Rorschach Inkblot Test and the Thematic Apperception Test are examples.

3. *A self-report inventory is* a type of psychological test in which a person's responses to standardized questions are compared to established norms. The MMPI, the CPI, and the 16PF are examples.

4. *Projective tests provide qualitative data but their weaknesses are that* responses may be affected by the examiner or the situation, scoring is very subjective, results may be inconsistent, and they do not predict behavior well.

5. *The strengths of self-report inventories are that* they are objectively scored, they differentiate among people on particular personality characteristics, they have high reliability, validity, and predictive value.

6. *Problems with self-report inventories are that* people do not always respond honestly or accurately, people can successfully fake responses and answer in socially desirable ways, and some people may respond in a set way to all questions.

Concept Check 4

1. projective; Thematic Apperception Test (TAT)

2. MMPI

3. CPI

4. projective; Rorschach Inkblot Test

5. 16PF

Matching Exercise 4

1. self-report inventory

2. Rorschach Inkblot Test

3. California Personality Inventory (CPI)

4. psychological test

5. Sixteen Personality Factor Questionnaire (16PF)

True/False Test 4

1. T	3. F	5. T
2. T	4. F	

Something to Think About

1. In any discussion of psychological testing it is always a good idea to point out the important characteristics of a good test, namely, reliability and validity. In terms of personality testing, you should first describe the two categories of tests, projective tests and self-report inventories.

   The famous Rorschach Inkblot Test is, of course, a projective test. In other words, it is assumed that people will project their unconscious feelings, motives, drives, thoughts, and so on in their responses to the series of inkblots. Similarly, the Thematic Apperception Test (TAT) gives subjects an opportunity to project unconscious information into the stories they make up about ambiguous scenes. Both tests developed out of the psychoanalytic approaches to personality, and scoring involves the subjective interpretations of the examiner. A brief discussion of Freud's theory as it relates to personality would probably be in order. A review of the most damaging criticisms of psychoanalysis may shed light on the topic, and the issue of the validity and reliability of projective tests should not be overlooked. Despite the criticisms, projective tests are widely used and can provide a wealth of qualitative data about an individual.

   Self-report inventories are used by clinical psychologists to evaluate both normal and abnormal populations in a variety of settings and for a variety of purposes. The most common are the MMPI, the CPI, and the 16PF. These are often called objective personality tests because they are standardized and objectively scored and measured against established norms. Self-report inventories are far more reliable and valid than are projective tests. These tests do have some drawbacks, including a person's ability to fake responses and answer in a socially desirable manner, some people's tendency to answer in a set way to all questions, and the fact that people are not always the best judges of their own behavior.

Personality tests are generally useful strategies that can provide insights about the psychological makeup of a person. However, no personality test, by itself, is likely to provide a definitive description of a given individual. In addition, because people can and often do change over time, any personality test provides a profile of the person only at the time of the test.

2. Many people believe in astrology, and a large number consult professional astrologers to find out what they should do and to predict the future. Belief in astrology is not restricted to any class or group of individuals. People from all walks of life, from senior managers to assembly line workers, from government leaders to junior clerks, consult their horoscopes on a regular basis. As is the case with many strongly held beliefs, it is often difficult to get true believers in astrology to listen to any information that might contradict what they feel is a valid point of view. It is always important to be aware of this and to respect their right to believe whatever they wish. However, if the opportunity does arise to have an open-minded discussion, presenting the results of Shawn Carlson's (1985) carefully designed study could be useful. Remember, a panel of astrological advisers were involved in helping Carlson design the study, and thirty of the top American and European astrologers were involved. All the participating astrologers agreed beforehand that Carlson's study was a fair test of astrological claims. Although the astrologers who

approved the design predicted that 50 percent was the minimum effect they would expect to see, the results showed that astrologers performed at a chance level. In other words, anybody simply guessing would have done as well as the astrologers. Carlson's results are consistent with those of many other researchers. A careful review of the scientific research on astrology came to the conclusion that astrology has absolutely no reliable basis in scientific fact and cannot stand up to any valid statistical test. Of course, if the astrologers had any real insight from their reading of the planets, they could easily have foreseen the outcome of Carlson's study!

Progress Test 1

1. d	6. d	11. a
2. c	7. d	12. d
3. d	8. d	13. b
4. a	9. c	14. c
5. a	10. b	15. a

Progress Test 2

1. a	6. a	11. d
2. a	7. d	12. a
3. d	8. c	13. a
4. d	9. d	14. b
5. c	10. a	15. b

Progress Test 3

1. d	6. d	11. c
2. d	7. a	12. d
3. c	8. a	13. d
4. a	9. b	14. a
5. c	10. d	15. d

chapter 12

Social Psychology

PREVIEW

Reading the section below first will give you a general sense of the chapter's contents and an initial introduction to some of the major concepts and terms. This will prime you for what you are about to read and help you to develop a "cognitive map" that will guide your study of the material in this chapter. Likewise, reading the **preview questions** at the beginning of each major section will improve your ability to understand, learn, and retain the information.

CHAPTER 12 . . . AT A GLANCE

Chapter 12 discusses social psychology—the scientific study of the way individuals think, feel, and behave in social situations—as broadly divided into two major research areas: social cognition and social influence. The chapter first explores person perception, including the factors that influence our perceptions of others. This is followed by a discussion of the process of attribution, including three important attributional biases and the influence of culture on attributional processes.

Once we form impressions of people, we tend to interpret their behavior in terms of our attitudes about them. The conditions under which attitudes determine behavior are identified. The role of cognitive dissonance in behavior and cognition is explored. In discussing prejudice, the text describes such cognitive influences as stereotypes, in-groups, out-groups, the out-group homogeneity effect, in-group bias, and ethnocentrism. The emotional roots of prejudice and techniques for reducing prejudice are also considered.

Conformity occurs when people change their behavior, attitudes, or beliefs in response to real or imagined group pressure. The original experimental design and the results of Stanley Milgram's research on obedience are presented in detail. Conditions that influence people to obey and to resist obeying authority figures are identified.

Latané and Darley's research on helping behavior, bystander intervention, and diffusion of responsibility is discussed, and their model, which identifies the factors that increase and decrease the likelihood of bystander intervention, is presented. In this context, individual behavior can be strongly influenced by the presence of others. The phenomena of social loafing, social striving, social facilitation, and deindividuation are examined. The Application discusses various techniques used by professional persuaders and provides some practical suggestions that will help you to avoid being taken in by such techniques.

Introduction: Social Psychology

Preview Questions

Consider the following questions as you study this section of the chapter.

- What is social psychology?
- What is meant by social cognition and social influence?

*Read the section "Introduction: Social Psychology" and **write** your answers to the following:*

1. Social psychology is _____

   _____

2. Social cognition refers to _____

   _____

3. Social influence focuses on _____

   _____

Person Perception: Forming Impressions of Other People

Preview Questions

Consider the following questions as you study this section of the chapter.

- What is person perception?
- What four principles does the mental process of forming judgments of others follow?
- How do social categories, implicit personality theories, and physical attractiveness influence person perception?

*Read the section "Person Perception: Forming Impressions of Other People" and **write** your answers to the following:*

1. Person perception refers to _____

   _____

   _____

2. The four basic principles of person perception are

   (a) _____

   (b) _____

   (c) _____

   (d) _____

3. In combination, these four basic principles underscore that person perception is _____

   _____

   _____

   _____

4. Social categorization is_____

   _____

   _____

   Its advantages and disadvantages are _____

   _____

   _____

5. An implicit personality theory is _____

   _____

   _____

   Like social categories, implicit personality theories are useful _____

   _____

   _____

6. Physical attractiveness is correlated with _____

   _____

   _____

   and it is not correlated with _____

   _____

   _____

   Neuroscientists have shown that when people make direct eye contact with a physically attractive person _____

   _____

   _____

   _____

Attribution: Explaining Behavior

Preview Questions

Consider the following questions as you study this section of the chapter.

- How is attribution defined?
- What are the fundamental attribution error, blaming the victim, the just-world hypothesis, the actor–observer discrepancy, and the self-serving bias?

*Read the section "Attribution: Explaining Behavior" and **write** your answers to the following:*

1. Attribution is _____
   _____
   _____

2. The fundamental attribution error is the tendency to _____
   _____
   _____

3. Blaming the victim is the tendency to _____
   _____
   _____

4. The just-world hypothesis is _____
   _____
   _____

5. The actor–observer discrepancy is the tendency to _____
   _____

6. The self-serving bias is the tendency to _____
   _____
   _____

   _____

After you have carefully studied the preceding sections, complete the following exercises.

Concept Check 1

Read the following and write the correct term in the space provided.

1. Adam earned an A in his philosophy class and concluded that he had quite a talent for writing coherently and thinking logically. When he earned a C in his sociology class, he expressed dissatisfaction with the course content, the teaching ability of the professor, and the quality and clarity of the exams. This best illustrates the _____ .

2. Rachel has just learned that her neighbor's teenage son, Brad, was involved in an automobile accident at a nearby intersection. She said to her husband, "Well, Brad's recklessness has finally got him into trouble!" Rachel's comment suggests that she has made the _____ .

3. When Allen observed Mark miss what looked to him like an easy point, Allen concluded that Mark was not a skilled basketball player. Later, in an identical position, Allen also failed to score. However, this time he concluded that it was the strong opposing team that prevented him from scoring. It would appear that Allen is committing the _____ .

4. When Cheryl first met Charles, who is an archivist in the university library, she concluded that he was probably very quiet, introverted, and introspective. She was later surprised to learn that he was the lead singer in a heavy metal band. Cheryl's surprise is probably the result of using a(n) _____ to judge people on the basis of certain traits and characteristics associated with certain types of people.

5. After learning about some interesting social psychology phenomena in his introductory class, Patrick decided he would like to test one of the concepts by facing the back instead of the front while riding the elevator. Much to his surprise, he found that he could not carry out his plan. After a second or two, he was overcome with embarrassment and ended up facing the front like everyone else. Patrick's behavior was governed by the _____ of the situation.

6. Grover does not support any charities because he believes that people who are poor, hungry, or homeless did something to deserve their situation. Grover's explanatory style is called _____ ; it probably reflects his strong need to believe the world is fair, an assumption called the _____ .

7. Byron is tall, dark, and handsome. Like most physically attractive people, he is likely to be *perceived* as being _____ _____ than less attractive people.

8. When people make direct eye contact with Byron, an area of the brain called the ventral striatum is likely to_____ ; if he disengages from eye contact and averts his gaze it is likely _____ .

Graphic Organizer 1

The following statements represent attributional processes. Decide which is (A) the fundamental attribution error, (B) the actor–observer discrepancy, or (C) the self-serving bias, and decide whether the attribution is to the self or to others or to both and whether it is internal (INT) or external (EXT).

Statement	Process	Attribution
1. I solved the local newspaper puzzle because I'm smart; I couldn't solve the *Times* puzzle because it was tricky and unfair and asked questions about facts unknown to most people.		
2. My sister had a fender-bender because she is a typical female driver; when I had a fender-bender, it was because the other driver was an idiot.		
3. I don't care what he said about his car breaking down; he was fifteen minutes late for the first class, so he must be one of those inconsiderate professors who is more concerned with his research than with his students.		

Review of Terms and Concepts 1

Use the terms in this list to complete the Matching Test, then to help you answer the True/False items correctly.

social psychology
social cognition
social influence
person perception
interpersonal context
social norms
social categorization
implicit personality
   theory
attribution

fundamental attribution
   error
blaming the victim
just-world hypothesis
actor–observer
   discrepancy
self-serving bias
self-effacing bias
   (modesty bias)

Matching Exercise

Match the appropriate term with its definition or description.

1. _____ The "rules," or expectations, for appropriate behavior in a particular social situation.

2. _____ Mental process of inferring the causes of people's behavior, including one's own. Also used to refer to the explanation made for a particular behavior.

3. _____ Tendency to attribute successful outcomes of one's own behavior to internal causes and unsuccessful outcomes to external, situational causes.

4. _____ Branch of psychology that studies how people think, feel, and behave in social situations.

5. _____ Network of assumptions or beliefs about the relationships among various types of people, traits, and behaviors.

6. _____ Tendency to attribute one's own behavior to external, situational causes while attributing the behavior of others to internal, personal causes; especially likely to occur with regard to behaviors that lead to negative outcomes.

7. _____ Tendency to blame an innocent victim of misfortune for having somehow caused the problem or for not having taken steps to avoid or prevent it.

8. _____ The assumption that the world is fair and that therefore people get what they deserve and deserve what they get.

True/False Test

Indicate whether each statement is true or false by placing T or F in the blank space next to each item.

1. ____ The effect that situational factors and other people have on an individual's behavior is called social cognition.

2. ____ The fundamental attribution error refers to the tendency to attribute the behavior of others to internal, personal characteristics while ignoring or underestimating the effects of external, situational factors; an attributional bias that is common in individualistic cultures.

3. ____ Person perception refers to the mental processes we use to form judgments and draw conclusions about the characteristics and motives of others.

4. ____ Social categorization refers to the mental process of classifying people into groups (or categories) on the basis of their shared characteristics.

5. ____ Social influence is the study of the mental processes people use to make sense of their social environment; it includes the study of person perception, attribution, attitudes, and prejudice.

6. ____ The self-effacing bias (modesty bias) involves blaming failure on internal, personal factors while attributing success to external, situational factors; more common in collectivistic cultures than in individualistic cultures.

7. ____ Interpersonal context has three components: the characteristics of the person being perceived, your own characteristics, and the specific situation in which the process occurs.

Check your answers and review any areas of weakness before going on to the next section.

The Social Psychology of Attitudes

Preview Questions

Consider the following questions as you study this section of the chapter.

- How is the term *attitude* defined, and what are its three components?
- Under what conditions are attitudes most likely to determine behavior?
- What is cognitive dissonance, and how does it affect behavior?

Read the section "The Social Psychology of Attitudes" and **write** *your answers to the following:*

1. An attitude is defined as _____
   _____

2. The three components of an attitude are
   (a) _____
   (b) _____
   (c) _____

3. You are most likely to behave in accordance with your attitudes in any of five conditions:
   (a) _____
   (b) _____
   (c) _____
   (d) _____
   (e) _____

4. Cognitive dissonance is _____
   _____
   _____

   It commonly occurs in situations in which
   _____
   _____
   _____
   _____

5. Cognitive dissonance can also change _____
   _____

6. Cognitive dissonance also operates when you have to choose _____
   _____
   _____
   _____
   _____

Understanding Prejudice

Preview Questions

Consider the following questions as you study this section of the chapter.

- How is prejudice defined?
- What are in-groups, out-groups, the out-group homogeneity effect, the in-group bias, and ethnocentrism?
- What is contact theory, and what conditions are necessary for reducing tension between groups?
- How can prejudice be overcome, and what are the three steps that help reduce prejudice on an individual level?

Read the section "Understanding Prejudice" and **write** *your answers to the following:*

1. Prejudice is defined as _____

_____

2. A stereotype is _____

_____

_____

3. An in-group is _____

_____

An out-group is _____

_____

4. The out-group homogeneity effect refers to ____

_____

The in-group bias is _____

_____

5. Ethnocentrism is the belief _____

_____

_____

6. Contact theory suggests that _____

_____

_____

7. In his classic study on overcoming prejudice, psychologist Muzafer Sherif demonstrated that

_____

_____

_____

In the educational system _____

_____

_____

_____

8. Prejudice reduction at the individual level involves three steps:

(a) _____

_____

_____

(b) _____

_____

_____

(c) _____

_____

_____

_____

After you have carefully studied the preceding sections, complete the following exercises.

Concept Check 2

Read the following and write the correct term in the space provided.

1. In Zeegland, where Majib grew up, women manage all the household finances, make all the major decisions regarding the family, and earn most of the family income. The men, on the other hand, tend to spend their time "hanging out" and trying to impress each other with the way they dress. Majib's belief that all women are naturally more assertive and domineering than men reflects her _____ about gender.

2. In a discussion about gun control laws, Jerrilee said, "In my opinion, easy access to guns is the major contributing factor to the high homicide rate in the United States." This statement reflects the _____ component of Jerrilee's attitude about gun control.

3. At lunch one day, a group of fine arts majors happened to sit next to a group of engineering students. During a discussion after lunch, one of the fine arts students remarked, "Boy, those engineering students are all alike. They are so loud, pushy, and aggressive, and, unlike us, they haven't got a scrap of creativity among them!" This statement reflects the

_____

effect.

4. During a sociology class, the instructor mentioned that the Heckawe tribe considers chopped-up earthworms, sheep's eyeballs, water buffalo testicles, and live caterpillars to be delicacies. Later, while having a hamburger and fries for lunch, a student remarked that the Heckawe diet was disgusting and repulsive. Another suggested that the tribe would someday become civilized and maybe even start eating good food "just like us." These remarks illustrate a form of in-group bias called

_____ _____ .

5. Sylvester was having a tough time deciding which computer to buy: the model Z5000 Spartan or its equivalent, the LX5000 MBI. With a toss of a coin, he chose the Z5000 Spartan. Initially, he was worried about his choice; however, after talking with many enthusiastic Z5000 Spartan owners, he is now very pleased that he chose the better of the two options. It is very likely that Sylvester experienced _____ when he purchased his PC, and his subsequent behavior was an attempt to _____ this unpleasant state of psychological tension.

6. Miss Graham's elementary class is made up of students from a variety of backgrounds and cultures. In order to increase cooperation and decrease negative stereotypes and intergroup hostility, Miss Graham has students cooperate in small ethnically diverse groups in which each individual has responsibility for one aspect of the overall project. This is called the

_____ .

7. Dr. Gandham argues that bringing members of different groups together with the goal of creating intergroup harmony, can, under some circumstances, actually increase prejudice by confirming negative stereotypes. Dr. Gandham is arguing against _____ theory.

8. In a class discussion, Klarissa points out that negative attitudes toward people who belong to a specific group are ultimately based on the exaggerated notion that members of other social groups are very different from members of our own social group. Klarissa is discussing the topic of _____ .

9. In response to Klarissa's comment, Selena suggests that certain groups *are* different from others. She notes that Italians are emotional and passionate, the English are cold and aloof, the Japanese are inscrutable, and the Scots are hairy and argumentative. These comments indicate that Selena is engaging in

_____ about these particular groups.

Graphic Organizer 2

The following statements reflect attitudes about certain topics. Decide which component—cognitive, affective, or behavioral— is represented by each statement.

Statement	Component
1. I believe that the automobile is the single most destructive element on this planet.	
2. I consistently recycle paper, plastic, soda cans, glass, and other waste.	
3. I vote for antigun control advocates and give them my full support.	
4. I get really angry when I see people carelessly throwing their litter on the ground.	
5. I don't want to contribute to the pollution of our city, so I ride my bicycle or take public transportation.	
6. I am very happy when I see women doing well in what used to be male-dominated occupations.	
7. In my opinion, a woman's place is in the home, raising the kids and doing housework.	
8. I get really upset when motorists are rude and inconsiderate.	
9. I believe that the automobile is the greatest invention ever and that we need to elect politicians who will promise to build more roads and freeways.	

Review of Terms, Concepts, and Names 2

Use the terms in this list to complete the Matching Test, then to help you answer the True/False items correctly.

attitude
cognitive component
affective component
behavioral component
cognitive dissonance
prejudice
stereotype
in-group
out-group
out-group homogeneity
   effect

heterogeneous
in-group bias
ethnocentrism
discrimination
contact theory
Muzafer Sherif
jigsaw classroom
   technique

Matching Exercise

Match the appropriate term/name with its definition or description.

1. _____ American social psychologist who is best known for his "Robbers Cave" experiments to study prejudice, conflict resolution, and group processes.

2. _____ The belief that one's own culture or ethnic group is superior to all others and the related tendency to use one's own culture as a standard by which to judge other cultures.

3. _____ Learned tendency to evaluate some object, person, or issue in a particular way; such evaluations may be positive, negative, or ambivalent.

4. _____ A social group to which one belongs.

5. _____ Unpleasant state of psychological tension or arousal that occurs when two thoughts or perceptions are inconsistent; typically results from awareness that attitudes and behavior are in conflict.

6. _____ A social group to which one does not belong.

7. _____ Theory that bringing members of different groups together would inevitably reduce prejudice and that positive stereotypes would naturally replace negative ones.

8. _____ Component of an attitude that involves thoughts, ideas, and conclusions about a given topic or object.

9. _____ Cluster of characteristics that are associated with all members of a specific social group, often including qualities that are unrelated to the objective criteria that define the group.

True/False Test

Indicate whether each statement is true or false by placing T or F in the blank space next to each item.

1. ____ Prejudice is a negative attitude toward people who belong to a specific social group.

2. ____ When prejudice is displayed behaviorally, it is called discrimination.

3. ____ The out-group homogeneity effect refers to the tendency to judge the behavior of in-group members favorably and out-group members unfavorably.

4. ____ The jigsaw classroom technique is a teaching technique that stresses cooperative, rather than competitive, learning situations.

5. ____ The in-group bias refers to the tendency to see members of out-groups as very similar to one another.

6. ____ The affective component of an attitude is reflected in the feelings that people have about a given event, object, or topic.

7. ____ Members of an in-group typically see themselves as being quite varied, or *heterogeneous*.

8. ____ The behavioral component of an attitude is reflected in people's actions.

Check your answers and review any areas of weakness before going on to the next section.

Conformity: Following the Crowd

Preview Questions

Consider the following questions as you study this section of the chapter.

- What is social influence, and how is conformity defined?
- Which psychologist first studied conformity, and what did he find?
- Why do people conform, and what factors influence the degree to which people conform?
- How does culture affect conformity?

Read the section "Conformity: Following the Crowd" and ***write*** *your answers to the following:*

1. Social influence is _____
_____
_____

2. Conformity is the tendency to _____
_____
_____

3. In studying the degree to which people would conform to the group even when the group opinion was clearly wrong, Asch found that _____
_____
_____

4. We conform to the larger group for two basic reasons:
(a) _____
_____
(b) _____
_____

5. In a cross-cultural meta-analysis, British psychologists found that _____
_____
_____

Obedience: Just Following Orders

Preview Questions

Consider the following questions as you study this section of the chapter.

- How is obedience defined?
- What was the basic procedure in Milgram's original obedience experiment, and what were the results?
- What aspects of the experimental situation increased the likelihood of obedience?
- What factors did Milgram later discover that decreased the level of obedience?

Read the section "Obedience: Just Following Orders" and **write** *your answers to the following:*

1. Obedience is defined as _____
   _____

2. The basic design of Milgram's obedience experiment was as follows: _____
   _____
   _____
   _____

3. In contrast to predictions, the results of Milgram's original experiment showed that
   _____
   _____

4. Aspects of the experimental situation that had a strong impact on the subjects' willingness to continue obeying the experimenter's orders were as follows: _____
   _____
   _____
   _____
   _____
   _____

5. Some of the situational factors that made people less willing to obey were_____
   _____
   _____
   _____
   _____
   _____

Helping Behavior: Coming to the Aid of Strangers

Preview Questions

Consider the following questions as you study this section of the chapter.

- What is altruism and how does it differ from prosocial behavior?
- What factors increase or decrease the likelihood that people will help a stranger?
- What is the bystander effect, and what causes it?
- What factors decrease the likelihood that people will help a stranger?

Read the section "Helping Behavior: Coming to the Aid of Strangers" and **write** *your answers to the following:*

1. Altruism is _____
   _____

   whereas prosocial behavior is _____
   _____
   _____

2. According to Latané and Darley's general model, six factors increase the likelihood of bystander intervention:
   (a) _____
   _____
   (b) _____
   _____
   (c) _____
   _____
   (d) _____
   _____
   (e) _____
   _____
   (f) _____
   _____

3. The bystander effect refers to _____
   _____
   _____

4. There are two reasons for the bystander effect:

    (a) _____

    _____

    _____

    (b) _____

    _____

    _____

5. Factors that decrease the likelihood of helping behavior are

    (a) _____

    _____

    (b) ___ _____

    _____

    (c) _____

    _____

    (d) _____

    _____

The Influence of Groups on Individual Behavior

Preview Questions

Consider the following questions as you study this section of the chapter.

- What is social loafing, and what factors reduce or eliminate it?
- What is social striving, and how is it affected by cultural factors?
- What are social facilitation and deindividuation?

Read the section "The Influence of Groups on Individual Behavior" and **write** *your answers to the following:*

1. Social loafing is _____

    _____

    _____

    Social loafing is reduced or eliminated when

    (a) _____

    (b) _____

    (c) _____

    (d) _____

2. Social striving is _____

    _____

    _____

Cross-cultural psychologists have found that

_____

_____

_____

3. Social facilitation is _____

_____

_____

4. Deindividuation refers to _____

_____

_____

After you have carefully studied the preceding sections, complete the following exercises.

Concept Check 3

1. Trent hates to wear ties but wears one to his sister's wedding to avoid the disapproval of his family. Trent's behavior illustrates the importance of _____ social influence.

2. Harold is a subject in a replication of Milgram's obedience experiment. If he is like most of the subjects in the experiment, he _____ (will/will not) administer high levels of shock to the learner.

3. If Harold was allowed to act as his own authority and freely choose the shock level, it is very _____ (likely/unlikely) that he will use a shock over 150 volts, the first point at which the learner is likely to protest.

4. At the end of a music concert featuring his favorite group, Jamal joined everyone else in giving the group a standing ovation. Jamal's behavior _____ (is/is not) an example of conformity.

5. Carmichael was elated when he won $1,000 in the lottery. Later that day, he gladly volunteered to spend a few hours on the weekend to help collect food for the local food bank. This illustrates the "_____" effect.

6. While about twenty subjects were filling out a questionnaire in a classroom, an odorless vapor started seeping into the room from one of the heating vents. The room slowly began to fill with the vapor, yet nobody stopped what he was doing, and nobody went to report the incident. This bystander effect occurred because the presence of other people creates a(n)

_____ .

7. Keith and his friends, who are normally law-abiding teenagers, put on masks and costumes on Halloween and smashed a number of pumpkins in the neighborhood. Social psychologists suggest that acts of vandalism such as this may be the result of _____ .

8. While practicing for an upcoming bike race, Leonarda completed the route in 47 minutes and 12 seconds. In the actual race, she improved her time by almost 3 minutes. Leonarda's improvement in front of a large audience may be the result of

_____ .

9. In a social psychology experiment, college students pulled less hard on a rope if they believed others were also pulling on the same rope compared to a situation in which they thought they were pulling alone. This example illustrates the phenomenon of _____ . In a replication of this experiment in a collectivistic culture, the reverse pattern, called

_____ , was observed.

10. Bryan is short of cash and needs about another $20 for an evening out with his girlfriend. He asks his friend Jared if he can borrow $150; before Jared can say no, Bryan appears to back off and makes a much smaller request—to borrow $20. Jared says, "OK, I can't lend you $150, but I guess I can cough up $20." Bryan has cleverly utilized a strategy called the

_____

technique, which is based on the rule of

_____ .

Graphic Organizer 3

Describe the main research findings of the following social psychologists.
(For example, Zimbardo's grasshopper study showed how behavior
can change attitude through the process of cognitive dissonance.)

Researcher	Main Research Findings
1. Asch	
2. Sherif	
3. Milgram	
4. Latané and Darley	

Review of Terms, Concepts, and Names 3

Use the terms in this list to complete the Matching Test, then to help you answer the True/False items correctly.

conformity
Solomon Asch
normative social
 influence
informational social
 influence
Stanley Milgram
obedience
Bibb Latané
John M. Darley
altruism

prosocial behavior
"feel good, do good"
 effect
bystander effect
diffusion of
 responsibility
social loafing
social striving
social facilitation
deindividuation
persuasion

Matching Exercise

Match the appropriate term/name with its definition or description.

1. _____ American social psychologist who is best known for his controversial investigation of destructive obedience to an authority figure.

2. _____ The tendency to adjust one's behavior, attitudes, or beliefs to group norms in response to real or imagined group pressure.

3. _____ Contemporary American social psychologist who, along with co-researcher John M. Darley, is best known for his pioneering studies of bystander intervention in emergency situations.

4. _____ Performance of an action in response to the direct orders of an authority or person of higher status.

5. _____ American social psychologist who is best known for his pioneering studies of conformity.

6. _____ Contemporary American social psychologist who, along with co-researcher Bibb Latané, is best known for his pioneering studies of bystander intervention in emergency situations.

7. _____ The reduction of self-awareness and inhibitions that can occur when a person is part of a group whose members feel anonymous.

8. _____ Helping another person with no expectation of personal reward or benefit.

9. _____ The tendency for the presence of other people to enhance individual performance.

True/False Test

Indicate whether each item is true or false by placing T or F in the space next to each item.

1. ____ Persuasion is the deliberate attempt to influence the attitudes or behavior of another person in a situation in which that person has some freedom of choice.

2. ____ The bystander effect refers to the phenomenon in which the greater the number of people present, the less likely each individual is to help someone in distress.

3. ____ The phenomenon in which the presence of other people makes it less likely that any individual will help someone in distress because the obligation to intervene is shared among all the onlookers is called diffusion of responsibility.

4. ____ Source of behavior that is motivated by the desire to gain social acceptance and approval is called informational social influence.

5. ____ The "feel good, do good" effect refers to the fact that when people feel good, successful, happy, or fortunate, they are more likely to help others.

6. ____ Source of behavior that is motivated by the desire to be correct is called normative social influence.

7. ____ Social loafing refers to the tendency of individuals working alone to expend much less effort on a task compared to when they are working as part of a group.

8. ____ Prosocial behavior refers to any behavior that helps another person, whether the underlying motive is self-serving or selfless.

9. ____ The tendency for individuals working in a group to expend less effort on a the task compared to when they are working alone is called social striving.

Check your answers and review any areas of weakness before going on to the next section.

Something to Think About

1. People often ask, "Why are so many people reluctant to help others who are in distress and need help?" The most usual responses are that people suffer from apathy and that big cities alienate and depersonalize people. What would you say if someone asked you that question?

2. We are subjected to a wide variety of situations and stimuli that are designed to influence our attitudes or behavior. The most obvious of these are media advertisements, but we regularly encounter many other more subtle sources of attempted influence. These attempts to influence us all use techniques of persuasion. Imagine that you are hired by a company, and management wants you to write a brief summary of the factors that are most powerful in changing people's attitudes or behaviors. What would you put in your report?

Check your answers and review any areas of weakness before completing the progress tests.

Progress Test 1

Review the complete chapter (including Concept Reviews and the boxed inserts), review all your study notes, and then test yourself on the following progress test. Check your answers. If you make a mistake, review your notes, review the relevant section of the study guide, and, if necessary, go back and read the appropriate part of your textbook.

1. Dr. Lopez is a social psychologist who studies the mental processes people use to make sense of their social environment, including person perception, attribution, attitudes, and prejudice. His specific area of research is called
   (a) social cognition.
   (b) perception.
   (c) social influence.
   (d) personality.

2. About a dozen students were sitting in a small research laboratory room filling out a questionnaire when they heard a crash followed by groaning from the room next door. While many of them appeared to notice, nobody went to inform the researcher, who said he would be in his office just down the hall. This example illustrates
   (a) the actor–observer discrepancy.
   (b) diffusion of responsibility.

   (c) obedience.
   (d) informational social influence.

3. Michael, who is an accountant, often wonders why people are surprised when they find out that he is also a skydiving instructor on the weekends. The most obvious explanation is that people form cognitive schemas for different types of people and occupations. The use of these types of assumptions is called
   (a) the fundamental attribution error.
   (b) ethnocentrism.
   (c) implicit personality theory.
   (d) the self-serving bias.

4. In her field research, Dr. Safarian observes that people generally do not sit next to strangers on trains. She also notices a similar pattern in movie theaters, airport lounges, and cafeterias. Dr. Safarian is documenting the effects of _____ on behavior.
   (a) stereotypes
   (b) ethnocentrism
   (c) prejudice
   (d) social norms

5. Sally did very poorly on her last math test. If her fifth-grade teacher concludes that Sally did poorly because she is not motivated to do well in school, the teacher may be committing the
   (a) fundamental attribution error.
   (b) actor–observer discrepancy.
   (c) self-serving bias.
   (d) social categorization error.

6. When Allison landed a big contract for her firm, she accepted the credit for her hard work and smart "wheeling and dealing." When she failed to get the contract in another situation, she blamed the sneaky and dishonest tactics of the competition. This illustrates
   (a) informational social influence.
   (b) the self-serving bias.
   (c) the self-effacing bias.
   (d) the actor–observer discrepancy.

7. During a discussion on fast food and fast-food outlets, Reginald stated, "Fast food is great. I just love southern fried chicken, fries, coleslaw, and milkshakes." This statement represents the _____ component of Reginald's positive attitude toward fast-food restaurants.
   (a) cognitive   (c) behavioral
   (b) affective   (d) ambivalent

8. Faced with the equally attractive choice of either a baconburger or a cheeseburger, Jill finally decided on the cheeseburger. Shortly after she made her choice, she decided that the cheeseburger was a healthier choice and probably had fewer calories than the baconburger. Her tendency to emphasize the positive aspects of her choice and the negative aspects of the choice she rejected illustrates the effect of

   (a) diffusion of responsibility.
   (b) conformity.
   (c) prejudice.
   (d) cognitive dissonance.

9. One of Manfred's college classmates was from Turkey, and he loved turkey sandwiches, turkey pizza, turkey burgers, and turkey sausages. Manfred now believes that the main diet of all people from Turkey is centered around meals made from turkey meat, and he has little doubt why the country is called Turkey. Manfred's beliefs about the culture of Turkey reflect

   (a) ethnic stereotyping.
   (b) ethnocentrism.
   (c) informational social influence.
   (d) in-group bias.

10. Jackson joined the Alpine cross-country ski club because he couldn't afford the cost of downhill skiing. Many members of his club think that downhill skiing is destroying the natural environment, and they often make derogatory remarks about downhillers. Since joining the club, Jackson has changed his attitude about downhill skiing; he now promotes the benefits of cross-country skiing and joins his new buddies in categorizing all downhill skiers as self-centered, uncaring destroyers of the environment. This example illustrates

   (a) the out-group homogeneity effect.
   (b) in-group bias.
   (c) stereotyping.
   (d) all of the above.

11. Greg, who is a new faculty member, is on a college committee concerned with student evaluation. Greg disagrees with the proposal to institute a collegewide percentage system for grading. The other five members have already stated that they are in favor of the proposal. Greg decides that it would be in his best interests to

go along with his colleagues and not risk antagonizing them, so he votes in favor of the proposed policy. This example best illustrates

   (a) obedience.
   (b) informational social influence.
   (c) in-group bias.
   (d) normative social influence.

12. All the members of the MacGregor household are enthusiastic supporters of the new community recycling program. They consistently sort their garbage by placing paper, plastic, glass, and aluminum in their respective bins. The actions of the MacGregors best illustrates the _____ component of attitudes.

   (a) emotional
   (b) behavioral
   (c) biological
   (d) cognitive

13. Just moments after dozens of people get off a crowded bus, a badly dressed man stumbles and falls on the sidewalk near the bus stop. Research on bystander intervention would suggest that

   (a) he will get immediate help from many people.
   (b) the presence of others will decrease the diffusion of responsibility.
   (c) if one person stops to help him, other people are likely to help as well.
   (d) no one in the crowd will perceive that he may need help.

14. According to Critical Thinking 12.2, which of the following is true of Milgram's experiment?

   (a) Two-thirds of the subjects completely obeyed the experimenter's destructive demands and progressed to the full 450-volt level.
   (b) Milgram was criticized because he failed to debrief the subjects after the experiment was over.
   (c) Less than 1 percent of the subjects obeyed the experimenter's destructive demands and progressed to the full 450-volt level.
   (d) The vast majority of Milgram's subjects experienced long-term traumatic reactions, such as depression, decreased self-esteem, and psychotic episodes.

15. According to the Application, which of the following is correct?
    (a) Persuasion refers to the deliberate attempt to influence the attitudes or behaviors of another person in a situation in which the person has some freedom of choice.
    (b) Persuasion techniques are not effective in manipulating people in any way.
    (c) Professional persuaders can easily manipulate and change the attitudes and behaviors of the vast majority of people.
    (d) Because of the flexible nature of social norms, the vast majority of people can resist conforming to any societal standards.

Progress Test 2

After you have checked your understanding of the material in Progress Test 1 and have done a complete chapter review with special focus on any areas of weakness, you are ready to assess your knowledge on Progress Test 2. Check your answers. If you make a mistake, review your notes, the relevant section of the study guide, and, if necessary, the appropriate part of your textbook.

1. Jake lost his job two months ago when his company downsized its operations; despite his efforts, he has not yet found another job. One of his neighbors stated that Jake is just like most unemployed people—irresponsible, unmotivated, and basically lazy. The neighbor has committed the
   (a) self-serving bias.
   (b) actor–observer discrepancy.
   (c) social categorization error.
   (d) fundamental attribution error.

2. When their town was threatened by a flood, two families who had been enemies for years ended up working together to try to save the town from the overflowing river. Generalizing from Sherif's findings, you might conclude that this act of cooperative behavior may lead to
   (a) increased antagonism once the danger has passed.
   (b) an increase in cognitive dissonance.
   (c) reduced conflict and increased harmony between the two families.
   (d) diffusion of responsibility.

3. Liliana thinks that people her parents' age are old-fashioned, critical, intolerant, and unconcerned about important social issues. Liliana is assuming that people in a particular age category have certain characteristics, even though these qualities may be unrelated to the objective criteria that define this particular age group. This example illustrates
   (a) the just-world hypothesis.
   (b) stereotyping.
   (c) ethnocentrism.
   (d) the self-effacing (modesty) bias.

4. When Rachel found out that she had straight As in all her courses, she was elated. Later that day, when she was asked if she could donate some money to the restore-the-church fund, she readily made a donation, even though she is not religious and does not go to church. This illustrates
   (a) cognitive dissonance.
   (b) the "feel good, do good" effect.
   (c) conformity.
   (d) informational social influence.

5. Wolfgang's best typing speed was 50 words a minute during practice. However, in a typing competition with 10 other people, he improved his speed to 55 words a minute. His improved performance in the presence of others reflects
   (a) social striving.
   (b) normative social influence.
   (c) social facilitation.
   (d) informational social influence.

6. When Inge was first elected to the student finance committee, she was asked to make a decision on some important financial matter with which she was not familiar. All the other members of the committee stated that they were going to vote against the proposal. Inge voted with the group because she assumed that they must have the correct information. This example illustrates
   (a) the bystander effect.
   (b) normative social influence.
   (c) informational social influence.
   (d) diffusion of responsibility.

7. Martha is participating in a replication of Milgram's original obedience experiment that involves female subjects only. Compared with a similar study involving only male subjects,

    (a) at least 60 percent of the females will refuse to continue with the experiment at the 300-volt level.

    (b) a much higher percentage of the females will obey the experimenter and progress to the 450-volt level.

    (c) only about 10 percent of the female subjects will obey the experimenter and progress to the 450-volt level.

    (d) the results of the all-female replication will be the same as the all-male condition.

8. In the study described in question 7, if the experimenter leaves the room and gives the directions over the phone, it is very likely that

    (a) the level of compliance will be the same as if the experimenter were in the room.

    (b) the level of compliance will be greater than if the experimenter were in the room.

    (c) the level of compliance will be significantly lower than if the experimenter were in the room.

    (d) none of the subjects will follow the experimenter's instructions and progress to the 450-volt level.

9. In preparing a term paper on conformity and obedience, Quincy has reviewed all the relevant literature. He is most likely to conclude that

    (a) virtually nobody is capable of resisting group or authority pressure.

    (b) all people are innately predisposed to be cruel and aggressive.

    (c) conformity and obedience are not necessarily bad in and of themselves and are important for an orderly society.

    (d) all of the above are true.

10. Jorge thought that either horse, Con Brio or White Lightning, had an equal chance of winning the next race and was debating which one to bet on. After he placed his money on Con Brio, however, he felt very confident that he had backed the winner. This example illustrates the effect of

    (a) cognitive dissonance.

    (b) the self-serving bias.

    (c) conformity.

    (d) social influence.

11. Jenny got 90 percent on her biology midterm exam, Jean got 60 percent, and Jackie got 75 percent. On the basis of their scores on the exam, Jackie thinks to herself that Jenny must be really intelligent and that Jean must be a little slow. Which of the following is true?

    (a) Jackie has made an attribution.

    (b) Jackie's assessment of her classmates' intelligence is accurate.

    (c) Jackie's evaluation reflects the in-group bias.

    (d) Jackie's assessment of her classmates' intelligence reflects her prejudice.

12. During a discussion about gun-control laws, Marylou said, "I believe it is every American's fundamental right to own a gun and that the government has no right to pass laws banning the ownership of guns under any circumstances." This statement reflects the _____ component of Marylou's attitude about guns and gun-control laws.

    (a) cognitive   (c) behavioral

    (b) affective   (d) dissonant

13. As part of a social psychology experiment, a group of male college students are asked to wear masks and clothes that hide their identities. Compared with a similar group wearing name tags and no masks, the anonymous group demonstrated significantly more aggression. This example illustrates

    (a) social facilitation.

    (b) social striving.

    (c) the rule of reciprocity.

    (d) deindividuation.

14. Yoko was late for work because the traffic was particularly heavy. When she arrived at the office, she apologized to her boss, insisting that it was her fault for being late; if she were less lazy, it wouldn't have happened. According to Culture and Human Behavior, 12.1, blaming an accidental occurrence on an internal, personal disposition rather than on situational factors is called the

    (a) self-serving bias.

    (b) self-effacing bias (modesty bias).

    (c) actor–observer discrepancy.

    (d) fundamental attribution error.

15. A number of persuasion techniques are used by professional marketers. According to the Application, which of the following is *not* one of those techniques?

    (a) the door-in-the-face technique
    (b) the that's-not-all technique
    (c) the foot-in-the-mouth technique
    (d) the low-ball technique
    (e) the foot-in-the-door technique

Progress Test 3

After you have checked your understanding of the material in Progress Tests 1 and 2, and have done a complete chapter review with special focus on any areas of weakness, you are ready to further assess your knowledge on Progress Test 3. Check your answers. If you make a mistake, review your notes, the appropriate parts of the study guide, and, if necessary, the relevant sections of your textbook.

1. Dr. Saroya is a social psychologist whose research interests focus on how our behavior is affected by situational factors and other people, and in particular why we conform to group norms and why we help or don't help strangers. The basic area of social psychology that Dr. Saroya studies is called

    (a) social cognition.
    (b) social perception.
    (c) social influence.
    (d) social categorization.

2. When Ruby stepped into the subway car, she quickly looked around and decided it would be safer to sit next to the middle-aged, well-dressed woman than the man with bright orange hair and earrings. Ruby has engaged in the process of

    (a) blaming the victim.
    (b) person perception.
    (c) ethnocentrism.
    (d) cognitive dissonance.

3. When Mr. Denbridge was asked to donate to a fund to help people infected with hepatitis B and the HIV virus, he responded that he would not help these people because they caused their own misfortunes. It appears that Mr. Denbridge is

    (a) blaming the victim.
    (b) demonstrating the out-group homogeneity effect.
    (c) responding to normative social influence.
    (d) reducing his cognitive dissonance.

4. During a tour of a Latin American country, Susanne was surprised to find that almost everyone took a three-hour break in the middle of the day. She concluded that, compared with the United States, this country was not doing well economically because everyone was lazy, lacked motivation, and spent too much time sleeping. Susanne's conclusion reflects a form of in-group bias called

    (a) ethnocentrism.
    (b) the self-effacing bias.
    (c) the self-serving bias.
    (d) the actor–observer discrepancy.

5. In her fifth grade class, Miss Tausig uses a technique for improving cooperation that involves students working together in small, ethnically diverse groups on a mutual project. Miss Tausig is using the

    (a) out-group homogeneity procedure.
    (b) jigsaw classroom technique.
    (c) normative social influence technique.
    (d) actor–observer discrepancy technique.

6. Rita volunteers three or four evenings a week at a local shelter for the homeless because she believes in helping those less fortunate than herself. Richard also volunteers at the shelter because he believes the work experience will increase his chances of getting accepted in the master's degree program in social work. In this situation, Rita's motivation is guided by _____ and Richard's motivation reflects _____ .

    (a) prosocial behavior; altruism
    (b) social striving; social loafing
    (c) altruism; prosocial behavior
    (d) social facilitation; the self-serving bias

7. Kyle is in sixth grade and, like most children in his school, believes that his school is better than all the other schools in town. This best illustrates

    (a) in-group bias.
    (b) ethnic stereotyping.
    (c) cognitive dissonance.
    (d) the fundamental attribution error.

8. Seeing a skier wipe out on a steep section of the run, Jenny comments, "A klutz like that shouldn't be allowed on the slopes!" Later, when Jenny wipes out in the same place, she blames the icy conditions. This is an example of
   (a) the self-serving bias.
   (b) the actor–observer discrepancy.
   (c) social categorization.
   (d) stereotyping.

9. Pietro notices that when there are empty seats on the bus, nobody ever sits beside a stranger; however, when the bus is crowded, people sit beside strangers all the time. He noticed that the same thing happens in movie theaters, the cafeteria, and even the classroom. Pietro's observation suggests that people's behavior in these situations is governed by
   (a) prejudice.   (c) stereotypes.
   (b) social categorization. (d) social norms.

10. Fraser loves wearing sandals or thongs and hates wearing shoes. However, when he went out to dinner with his girlfriend's family, he wore shoes because he did not want to evoke their disapproval. Fraser's behavior best illustrates the importance of
    (a) informational social influence.
    (b) normative social influence.
    (c) diffusion of responsibility.
    (d) obedience.

11. Lyle is studying alone late Friday night in the almost deserted library. His concentration is interrupted when he notices another student nearby slumped over his desk, making sounds that suggest he might be in pain. In this situation, it is very likely that Lyle will engage in _____ , because he is not constrained by _____ .
    (a) prosocial behavior; the bystander effect
    (b) social categorization; social norms
    (c) blaming the victim; diffusion of responsibility
    (d) social loafing; deindividuation

12. When Maryjane steps into the elevator, she quickly looks at the other passengers and decides that the gray-haired man with the beard must be a professor at the college. Maryjane has engaged in the process of
    (a) prejudicial thinking.
    (b) discrimination.
    (c) social categorization.
    (d) ethnocentrism.

13. During cross-examination, a witness repeatedly offers his opinion in answer to the lawyer's questions, so the judge orders him to confine his answers to a simple "yes" or "no." Following the judge's rebuke, the witness stops offering his opinions. This example best illustrates
    (a) obedience.   (c) persuasion.
    (b) conformity.   (d) prejudice.

14. According to Critical Thinking 12.2, which of the following is true of Milgram's research?
    (a) It created a controversy that led to the establishment of ethical safeguards by the American Psychological Association and the federal government regarding experiments involving human subjects.
    (b) It was criticized for causing the subjects emotional stress, tension, and loss of dignity.
    (c) It demonstrated, much to everyone's surprise, that the majority of subjects would obey an authority figure even if it apparently meant hurting another person.
    (d) All of the above are true.

15. In the run-up to a fiercely contested local election, Birkley believes she can win if she can only get enough people to display her large poster on their front lawns. First, her supporters ask homeowners if they would be willing to put a very small poster in their window. Later, when they asked these same people if they could put a large poster on their front lawn, most agreed to the request. Birkley is using a technique called the _____ , which capitalizes on a powerful social norm, the
    _____ .
    (a) door-in-the-face technique; rule of reciprocity
    (b) foot-in-the-door-technique; rule of commitment
    (c) low-ball technique; rule of reciprocity
    (d) foot-in-the-mouth technique; rule of commitment

Answers

Introduction: Social Psychology

1. *Social psychology is* the branch of psychology that studies how people think, feel, and behave in social situations.

2. *Social cognition refers to* the study of the mental processes people use to make sense out of their social environment.

3. *Social influence focuses on* the study of the effects of situational factors and other people on an individual's social behavior.

Person Perception: Forming Impressions of Other People

1. *Person perception refers to* the mental processes we use to form judgments and draw conclusions about the characteristics and motives of others; it is an active and subjective process that always occurs in some interpersonal context.

2. *The four basic principles of person perception are (a)* Your reactions to others are determined by your perceptions of them, not by who or what they really are. *(b)* Your goals in a particular situation determine the amount and kind of information you collect about others. *(c)* In every situation, how you expect people to act in that situation partly determines how you evaluate them (you make reference to the social norms for the appropriate behavior in a particular social situation). *(d)* Your self-perception also influences how you perceive others and how you act on your perceptions.

3. *In combination, these four basic principles underscore that person perception is* not a one-way process in which we objectively survey other people, then logically evaluate their characteristics. Instead, the context, our self-perceptions, and the perception we have of others all interact.

4. *Social categorization is* the mental process of classifying people into groups (or categories) on the basis of their shared characteristics. This is mostly automatic and spontaneous and occurs outside of conscious awareness. *Its advantages and disadvantages are,* respectively, that it is cognitively efficient, natural, and adaptive, but that it ignores a person's unique qualities.

5. *An implicit personality theory is* a network of assumptions or beliefs about the relationships among various types of people, traits, and behaviors. *Like social categories, implicit personality theories are useful* as mental shortcuts in perceiving other people; however, they are not always accurate and in some instances can be dangerously misleading.

6. *Physical attractiveness is correlated with* being more popular, less lonely, and less anxious in social situations; *and it is not correlated with* intelligence, mental health, or self-esteem.
   Neuroscientists have shown that when people make direct eye contact with a physically attrac- *tive person* a brain area that predicts rewards, the ventral striatum, is activated, and when the attractive person's gaze is averted away from the viewer, activity in this brain area decreases.

Attribution: Explaining Behavior

1. *Attribution is* the mental process of inferring the causes of people's behavior, including one's own (also refers to the explanation made for a particular behavior).

2. *The fundamental attribution error is the tendency to* attribute the behavior of others to internal, personal characteristics, while ignoring or underestimating the effects of external, situational factors.

3. *Blaming the victim is the tendency to* blame an innocent victim of misfortune for having somehow caused the problem or for not having taken steps to avoid or prevent it.

4. *The just-world hypothesis is* the assumption that the world is fair and that therefore people get what they deserve and deserve what they get.

5. *The actor–observer discrepancy is the tendency to* attribute one's own behavior to external, situational causes, while attributing the behavior of others to internal, personal causes, especially when the outcome is likely to be negative.

6. *The self-serving bias is the tendency to* attribute successful outcomes of our own behavior to internal causes and unsuccessful outcomes to external, situational causes.

Concept Check 1

1. self-serving bias
2. fundamental attribution error
3. actor–observer discrepancy
4. implicit personality theory
5. social norms
6. blaming the victim; just-world hypothesis
7. more intelligent, happier, better adjusted, more socially competent, and sexier
8. become activated; that activity will decrease in this area of the brain

Graphic Organizer 1

1. C; INT for own success; EXT for own failure
2. B; EXT for self; INT for other
3. A; INT for other

Matching Exercise 1

1. social norms
2. attribution
3. self-serving bias
4. social psychology
5. implicit personality theory
6. actor–observer discrepancy
7. blaming the victim
8. just-world hypothesis

True/False Test 1

1. F	3. T	5. F	7. T
2. T	4. T	6. T	

The Social Psychology of Attitudes

1. *An attitude is defined as* a learned tendency to evaluate some object, person, or issue in a particular way; such evaluations may be positive, negative, or ambivalent.

2. *The three components of an attitude are (a)* cognitive (your thoughts and conclusions about a given topic or object); *(b)* affective (your feelings or emotions about a given topic or object); and *(c)* behavioral (your attitude is reflected in your actions).

3. *You are most likely to behave in accordance with your attitudes in any of five conditions:* (a) your attitudes are extreme or are frequently expressed; (b) your attitudes have been formed through direct experience; (c) you are very knowledgeable about the subject; (d) you have a vested interest in the subject; and (e) you anticipate a favorable outcome or response from others.

4. *Cognitive dissonance is* an unpleasant state of psychological tension or arousal (dissonance) that occurs when two thoughts or perceptions (cognitions) are inconsistent. *It commonly occurs in situations in which* you become uncomfortably aware that your behavior and your attitudes conflict with each other. If you can easily change your behavior to make it consistent with your attitude, then any dissonance can be quickly and easily resolved. When your behavior cannot be easily changed, you will tend to change your attitude to make it consistent with your behavior.

5. *Cognitive dissonance can also change* the strength of an attitude so that it is consistent with some behavior you've already performed.

6. *Cognitive dissonance also operates when you have to choose* between two basically equal alternatives; each choice has desirable and undesirable features, creating dissonance. Once you make a choice, however, you immediately bring your attitudes more closely into line with that commitment, reducing the dissonance; you emphasize the negative features of the choice you rejected and the positive features of the choice you made.

Understanding Prejudice

1. *Prejudice is defined as* a negative attitude toward people who belong to a specific social group.

2. *A stereotype is* a cluster of characteristics that are associated with all members of a specific social group, often including qualities that are unrelated to the objective criteria that define the group.

3. *An in-group is* a social group to which one belongs. *An out-group is* a social group to which one does not belong.

4. *The out-group homogeneity effect refers to* the tendency to see members of out-groups as very similar to one another. *The in-group bias is* the tendency to judge the behavior of in-group members favorably and out-group members unfavorably.

5. *Ethnocentrism is the belief* that one's own culture or ethnic group is superior to all others and the related tendency to use one's own culture as a standard by which to judge other cultures.

6. *Contact theory suggests that* simply bringing members of different groups into contact with one another will inevitably reduce prejudice among groups and positive attitudes will replace negative ones once different groups get to know one another as individuals (this theory has not been supported).

7. *In his classic study on overcoming prejudice, psychologist Muzafer Sherif demonstrated that* prejudice can be overcome when rival groups cooperate to achieve a common goal.

   In the educational system cooperative learning, as used in the jigsaw classroom technique, is one way of reducing prejudice in the classroom.

8. *Prejudice reduction at the individual level involves three steps: (a)* Individuals must decide that prejudiced responses are wrong and con-

sciously reject prejudice and stereotyped thinking. *(b)* They must internalize their nonprejudiced beliefs so that those beliefs become an integral part of their personal self-concept. *(c)* Individuals must learn to inhibit automatic prejudicial reactions and deliberately replace them with nonprejudiced responses that are based on their personal standards.

Concept Check 2

1. stereotype
2. cognitive
3. out-group homogeneity
4. ethnocentrism
5. cognitive dissonance; reduce
6. jigsaw classroom technique
7. contact
8. prejudice
9. stereotyical thinking

Graphic Organizer 2

1. cognitive
2. behavioral
3. behavioral
4. affective
5. behavioral
6. affective
7. cognitive
8. affective
9. cognitive

Matching Exercise 2

1. Muzafer Sherif
2. ethnocentrism
3. attitude
4. in-group
5. cognitive dissonance
6. out-group
7. contact theory
8. cognitive component
9. stereotype

True/False Test 2

1. T	3. F	5. F	7. T
2. T	4. T	6. T	8. T

Conformity: Following the Crowd

1. *Social influence is* the study of the effects of situational factors and other people on an individual's behavior.

2. *Conformity is the tendency to* adjust one's behavior, attitudes, or beliefs to group norms in response to real or imagined group pressure.

3. *In studying the degree to which people would conform to the group even when the group opinion was clearly wrong, Asch found that* the vast majority conformed with the group judgment on at least one of the critical trials in the line judgment task.

4. *We conform to the larger group for two basic reasons: (a).* normative social influence (we want to be liked and accepted by the group); *(b)* informational social influence (we want to be right; when we're uncertain or doubt our own judgment, we may look to the group as a source of accurate information).

5. *In a cross-cultural meta-analysis, British psychologists found that* conformity is generally higher in collectivistic cultures than in individualistic cultures.

Obedience: Just Following Orders

1. *Obedience is defined as* the performance of an action in response to the direct orders of an authority or person of higher status.

2. *The basic design of Milgram's obedience experiment was as follows:* the subject (the teacher) thought he was delivering ever-increasing levels of electric shock to another person (the learner); if the teacher protested that he wished to stop, he was instructed by the experimenter to continue with the experiment.

3. *In contrast to predictions, the results of Milgram's original experiment showed that* most of the subjects (two-thirds) obeyed the experimenter and progressed to the maximum shock level.

4. *Aspects of the experimental situation that had a*

strong impact on the subjects' willingness to continue obeying the experimenter's orders were as follows: the subjects had a previously well-established mental framework to obey; the context or situation influenced them (they believed the experiment would advance scientific knowledge and may have felt that defying the experimenter's orders would make them appear arrogant, rude, disrespectful, or uncooperative); the gradual, repetitive escalation of the task; the experimenter's behavior and reassurances (the experimenter took responsibility for the learner's well-being); and the physical and psychological separation from the learner.

5. *Some of the situational factors that made people less willing to obey were* when the buffers that separated the teacher from the learner were lessened or removed, such as when both of them were put in the same room; when subjects (teachers) were allowed to act as their own authority and freely choose the shock level, 95 percent of them did not go beyond 150 volts; and if the teacher observed two other teachers rebel and refuse to continue, then the obedience rate dropped to 10 percent.

Helping Behavior: Coming to the Aid of Strangers

1. *Altruism is* the act of helping another person with no expectation of personal reward or benefit, *whereas prosocial behavior is* any behavior that helps another person, whether the underlying motive is self-serving or selfless.

2. *According to Latané and Darley's general model, six factors increase the likelihood of bystander intervention: (a)* We tend to be more helpful when we're feeling good, successful, happy, or fortunate (the "feel good, do good" effect). *(b)* We tend to be more helpful when we're feeling guilty, such as after telling a lie or inadvertently causing an accident. *(c)* Seeing others who are willing to help increases the likelihood that we will help. *(d)* We're more likely to help people who are perceived as deserving, such as people who are in need through no fault of their own. *(e)* Knowing how to help contributes greatly to the decision to help someone else. *(f)* Any sort of personal relationship (even the most minimal social interaction, such as making eye contact or engaging in small talk) increases the likelihood that one person will help another.

3. *The bystander effect refers to* the phenomenon in which the greater the number of people pres-

ent, the less likely each individual is to help someone in distress.

4. *There are two reasons for the bystander effect: (a)* The presence of other people creates a diffusion of responsibility, which means that the responsibility to intervene is shared (or diffused) among the other onlookers (because no one person feels all the pressure to respond, each bystander becomes less likely to help). *(b)* Each of us is motivated to some extent by the desire to behave in a socially acceptable way (normative social influence) and to appear correct (informational social influence), and consequently we often rely on the reactions of others to help us define the situation and guide our responses.

5. *Factors that decrease the likelihood of helping behavior are (a)* the presence of other people (if other people are present, helping behavior declines, a phenomenon called the *bystander effect*); *(b)* being in a big city or a very small town (people are less likely to help a stranger in very big cities [300,000 people or more] or in very small towns [5,000 people or less], but you are more likely to get help in towns with populations in between these two extremes); *(c)* when situations are vague or ambiguous and people are not certain that help is needed, such as in domestic disputes or a lovers' quarrel; and, *(d)* as a general rule, we tend to weigh the costs as well as the benefits in deciding whether to help others (when the cost of helping outweighs the benefit, we tend not to help).

The Influence of Groups on Individual Behavior

1. *Social loafing is* the tendency to expend less effort on a task when it is a group effort.
   Social loafing is reduced or eliminated when (a) the group is composed of people who know each other, *(b)* the members belong to a highly valued group, *(c)* the task is meaningful or unique, and *(d)* when the group members are female rather than male.

2. *Social striving is* a pattern in which individuals work harder when they are part of a group than when they are alone. *Cross-cultural psychologists have found that* social striving is very common in many collectivistic cultures, and social loafing is generally absent. Factors that influence this phenomenon are that in collectivistic cultures group success is more highly valued than individual success and social norms encourage a sense of social responsibility and hard work by individuals within groups.

3. *Social facilitation is* the tendency for the presence of other people to enhance individual performance, especially on a task that is relatively simple or well rehearsed.

4. *Deindividuation refers to* the reduction of self-awareness and inhibitions that can occur when a person is part of a group whose members feel anonymous.

Concept Check 3

1. normative
2. will
3. unlikely
4. is not
5. feel good, do good
6. diffusion of responsibility
7. deindividuation
8. social facilitation
9. social loafing; social striving
10. door-in-the-face; reciprocity

Graphic Organizer 3

1. Naive subjects yielded to group pressure in the line-judging task, even though the group opinion was wrong.

2. The Robbers Cave study helped clarify the conditions that produce intergroup conflict and harmony and led to the use of the jigsaw classroom technique to promote cooperative behavior.

3. Dramatic illustration of the pressure to obey an authority figure's request to shock another person in a mock learning experiment.

4. Showed the conditions under which people are more likely to help a stranger in distress as well as the factors that decrease helping behavior.

Matching Exercise 3

1. Stanley Milgram
2. conformity
3. Bibb Latané
4. obedience
5. Solomon Asch
6. John M. Darley
7. deindividuation

8. altruism
9. social facilitation

True/False Test 3

1. T	4. F	7. F
2. T	5. T	8. T
3. T	6. F	9. F

Something to Think About

1. Why is it that people do not help others who are in obvious distress? What prevents bystanders from intervening? In some instances, such as in the Kitty Genovese case, people could easily help by simply making a phone call, but often they don't. Latané and Darley have conducted extensive research that addresses the question of why people don't intervene.

   Latané and Darley's final model identifies six specific factors that increase the likelihood that bystanders will help: (1) the "feel good, do good" effect, (2) feeling guilty, (3) seeing others who are willing to help, (4) perceiving others as deserving help, (5) knowing how to help, and (6) a personal relationship with the person who needs help.

   A number of factors decrease the likelihood of bystanders helping: (1) the presence of others, called the *bystander effect,* and the resulting diffusion of responsibility; (2) being in a big city or a very small town; (3) a vague or ambiguous situation; and (4) when the personal costs for helping outweigh the benefits. In a discussion of this issue it is important to be able to explain and give examples of each factor.

2. The summary in the Application "The Persuasion Game" provides the information you need to answer this question. First, define persuasion, then paraphrase the main strategies that professional persuaders use to manipulate people's attitudes and behaviors. These include the role of reciprocity, the door-in-the-face technique, the that's-not-all technique, the rule of commitment, the foot-in-the-door technique, and the low-ball technique. You might also want to integrate material from the chapter, such as the role of cognitive dissonance in changing cognitions and behavior, and various aspects of conformity and obedience research. Finally, you should discuss the ways in which people can defend themselves against professional persuasion techniques—for example,

sleeping on it, playing the devil's advocate, and paying attention to gut feelings.

Progress Test 1

1. a	6. b	11. d
2. b	7. b	12. b
3. c	8. d	13. c
4. d	9. a	14. a
5. a	10. d	15. a

Progress Test 2

1. d	6. c	11. a
2. c	7. d	12. a
3. b	8. c	13. d
4. b	9. c	14. b
5. c	10. a	15. c

Progress Test 3

1. c	6. c	11. a
2. b	7. a	12. c
3. a	8. b	13. a
4. a	9. d	14. d
5. b	10. b	15. b

chapter 13

Stress, Health, and Coping

<table>
<tr>
<td>PREVIEW</td>
<td>Reading the section below first will give you a general sense of the chapter's contents and an initial introduction to some of the major concepts and terms. This will prime you for what you are about to read and help you to develop a "cognitive map" that will guide your study of the material in this chapter. Likewise, reading the preview questions at the beginning of each major section will improve your ability to understand, learn, and retain the information.</td>
</tr>
</table>

CHAPTER 13 . . . AT A GLANCE

Chapter 13 deals with the effects of stress on health and the ways that people cope with stress. Health psychologists study stress and other psychological factors that influence health, illness, and treatment and are guided by the biopsychosocial model. The life events approach to stress, first developed in the 1960s, is critically examined. More recently, researchers have focused on the importance of daily hassles, conflict, and social and cultural factors as sources of stress.

The physical effects of stress are discussed. Walter Cannon's fight-or-flight response and Hans Selye's three-stage general adaptation syndrome are described. Ader and Cohen's research on conditioning the immune system, and its influence on the foundation of psychoneuroimmunology, is presented along with research findings on the effects of stress on the immune system.

Psychological factors can also influence our response to stress. People's sense of personal control and their explanatory style—optimistic or pessimistic—are important in determining how a person responds to stress. The text notes that chronic negative emotions are related to the development of some chronic diseases and that the hostility component of the Type A behavior pattern can predict the development of heart disease. The role of social support in how people deal with stressful situations is explored.

The final section covers coping strategies. Depending on the situation, people use problem-focused or emotion-focused coping. Culture affects the choice of coping strategies; individualistic and collectivistic coping strategies are compared and contrasted. The Application offers some important advice for providing effective social support.

Introduction: What Is Stress?

Preview Questions

Consider the following questions as you study this section of the chapter.

- How is stress defined, and what is the main focus of health psychology?
- What is the biopsychosocial model?

Read the section "Introduction: What Is Stress?" and **write** *your answers to the following:*

1. Stress is defined as _____

   _____

2. Health psychologists focus on_____

   _____

   _____

3. The biopsychosocial model is _____

   _____

   _____

What Is Stress? Sources of Stress

Preview Questions

Consider the following questions as you study this section of the chapter.

- What are stressors, and what are some of the most important sources of stress?
- What is the life events approach, and what problems are associated with this approach?
- What are daily hassles and conflict, and how do they contribute to stress?
- How can social and cultural factors become sources of stress?

Read the section "What Is Stress? Sources of Stress" and **write** *your answers to the following:*

1. Stressors are _____

   _____

2. Early stress researchers Holmes and Rahe believed that _____

   _____

   _____

3. Several problems with the life events approach have been pointed out:

   (a) _____

   _____

   (b) _____

   _____

   (c) _____

   _____

   (d) _____

   _____

   _____

4. Daily hassles are _____

   _____

5. Conflict is the _____

   _____

6. The three basic types of conflict are

   (a) _____

   _____

   (b) _____

   _____

   (c) _____

   _____

7. Social factors that are a source of stress include

   _____

   _____

8. In terms of culture, stress can result when

   _____

   _____

After you have carefully studied the preceding sections, complete the following exercises.

Concept Check 1

Read the following and write the correct term in the space provided.

1. Dr. Woodworth studies stress and how biological, behavioral, and social factors influence health, illness, medical treatment, and health-related behaviors. Dr. Woodworth is a

   _____ psychologist.

2. If Dr. Woodworth is like most psychologists in his specialty area, he adheres to the theory that health and illness are determined by the complex interaction of biological, psychological, and social factors. In other words, he is guided by the _____ model.

3. In the past year, Frank has been divorced, moved twice, and started a new relationship. In addition, he has received a promotion and a big raise at work but now has many more responsibilities. His score on the Social Readjustment Rating Scale is likely to be _____ (high/low); according to the scale's developers, Holmes and Rahe, Frank has a(n) _____ (increased/decreased) likelihood of developing serious physical or psychological problems.

4. According to Richard Lazarus, Frank's major life events may create a ripple effect and generate a host of _____ that may accumulate to cause even greater stress.

5. Janet can take only one course this semester because of work commitments. She is torn between two courses she really wants to take, each of which fits her work schedule. Janet is probably experiencing an _____ conflict.

6. When Kailen got a speeding ticket, he complained bitterly about the unfairness of it all. When Kylie got a ticket for a similar infraction, he perceived it as a lesson learned and decided that if he didn't want to waste his scarce resources, he should stop speeding. The two reactions to the same stressor were due, in part at least, to Kailen and Kylie's different _____ of getting a speeding ticket.

7. When Serena married Hiroyuki and went to live in Japan, she continued to value her North American customs and way of life, but she was also very determined to become part of her new culture. She now speaks fluent Japanese and moves comfortably between her new society and her original culture and feels almost equally at home in both countries. In terms of acculturation, Serena would be classified as _____ and her level of acculturative stress would be _____ (high/low).

8. Godfrey was very excited about an upcoming blind date. However, as the day of his dinner date approached, his level of anxiety and stress escalated and he vacillated between going and canceling the date. Godfrey could eliminate his _____ conflict by adopting a _____ strategy.

9. Pat has more daily hassles (mainly from family demands and interpersonal conflicts) and experiences higher levels of psychological stress than Les (whose main sources of stress are job-related and financial). It is very probable that Pat is _____ (male/female) and Les is _____ (male/female).

Graphic Organizer 1

Read the following descriptions and decide which type of stress-producing conflict is involved: approach-approach, avoidance-avoidance, or approach-avoidance. In addition, label each one as producing either a high, medium, or low level of stress.

Description	Type of Conflict/ Level of Stress (low/medium/high)
1. Lyndle wants to maintain a high grade-point average and needs to study hard before his exam tomorrow, but he has been asked by his girlfriend to go with her to a party this evening.	
2. A rat in the start box of a Y-shaped maze with two separate goal boxes at the end of each prong will receive an equally desirable food pellet in each one.	
3. Annalee is very happy to be doing well on her diet but now has to decide whether to go for lunch with her friends at her favorite Greek taverna or stay in the lunchroom and eat her low-calorie snack.	
4. In order to be allowed to borrow the family car for the evening, Jason has to decide between doing two equally unappealing chores: the family laundry or washing and waxing the bathroom and kitchen floors.	
5. Virginia entered her name in a contest and was overwhelmed when she won a seven-day Caribbean cruise. She has to decide between a seven-day eastern Caribbean cruise or a seven-day western Caribbean cruise.	
6. Melvin is overweight and out of shape and is given a choice of two daily exercise regimens by his doctor, one involving 40 minutes of running, riding an exercise bike, and weightlifting and the other involving 40 minutes of rowing machine, step-up machine, and weightlifting.	

Review of Terms, Concepts, and Names 1

Use the terms in this list to complete the Matching Test, then to help you answer the True/False items correctly.

stress
cognitive appraisal
health psychology
  (behavioral medicine
  or medical psychology)
biopsychosocial model
stressors
Social Readjustment
  Rating Scale
life change units
Richard Lazarus
daily hassles

Daily Hassles Scale
conflict
approach–approach
  conflict
avoidance–avoidance
  conflict
approach–avoidance
  conflict
partial-approach
  strategy
chronic stress
acculturative stress

Matching Exercise

Match the appropriate term/name with its definition or description.

1. _____ American psychologist who helped promote the cognitive perspective in the study of emotion and stress; developed the cognitive appraisal model of stress and coping with coresearcher Susan Folkman.

2. _____ Basic type of conflict in which you're faced with a choice between two equally appealing outcomes. As a rule, these conflicts are usually easy to resolve and don't produce much stress.

3. _____ Situation in which a person feels pulled between two or more opposing desires, motives, or goals.

4. _____ Everyday minor events that annoy and upset people.

5. _____ The branch of psychology that studies how biological, behavioral, and social factors influence health, illness, and medical treatment as well as health-related behaviors.

6. _____ Model that guides the work of health psychologists. According to this model, health and illness are determined by the complex interaction of biological, psychological, and social factors.

7. _____ On the Social Readjustment Rating Scale, the numerical rating assigned to each life event that estimates its relative impact on a person.

8. _____ Scale developed by Richard Lazarus that measures the occurrence of everyday annoyances and irritations.

9. _____ Type of stress that is persistent and ongoing.

True/False Test

Indicate whether each statement is true or false by placing T or F in the blank space next to each item.

1. ___ Stress refers to events or situations that are perceived as harmful, threatening, or challenging.

2. ___ The Social Readjustment Rating Scale was developed by Thomas Holmes and Richard Rahe in an attempt to measure the amount of stress people experienced as a function of life events that are likely to require some level of adaptation.

3. ___ An approach–avoidance conflict has a single goal with both desirable and undesirable aspects. When faced with this conflict, people often vacillate, or repeatedly go back and forth in their minds, unable to decide to approach or avoid the goal.

4. ___ Stressors refer to negative emotional states that occur in response to events that are perceived as taxing or exceeding a person's resources or ability to cope.

5. ___ An avoidance–avoidance conflict involves choosing between two unappealing or undesirable outcomes. People often delay making a decision when faced with this conflict, or they may bail out altogether.

6. ___ The stress that results from the pressure of adapting to a new culture is called acculturative stress.

7. ___ One way of dealing with the stress and anxiety of being stuck in an approach-avoidance conflict is to adopt a *partial approach strategy* in which you test the waters but leave yourself a way out before making a final decision or commitment.

8. ___ Whether or not people experience stress depends largely on the role played by their perception of the event or situation, a factor called *cognitive appraisal*.

Check your answers and review any areas of weakness before going on to the next section.

Physical Effects of Stress: The Mind–Body Connection

Preview Questions

Consider the following questions as you study this section of the chapter.

- How can stress contribute to health problems both directly and indirectly?

- What is the fight-or-flight response, and what role do catecholamines play?

- What is the general adaptation syndrome, and what endocrine pathways are involved?

- What have neuroscientists demonstrated about the role of placebos in the perception of pain?

*Read the section "Physical Effects of Stress: The Mind–Body Connection" and **write** your answers to the following:*

1. Stress can indirectly affect a person's health by

_____

_____

2. High levels of stress can also interfere with

_____

_____

3. Stress can directly affect physical health by

_____

_____

4. The fight-or-flight response refers to _____

_____

_____

_____

5. Catecholamines are _____

_____

_____

6. The general adaptation syndrome is _____

_____

_____

_____

7. Selye found that prolonged stress activates a

_____

_____

_____

8. Using positron emission tomography (PET), neuroscientists have shown that _____

_____

_____

_____

Physical Effects of Stress: Stress and the Immune System

Preview Questions

Consider the following questions as you study this section of the chapter.

- What is the immune system, and what is its function?

- What did the work of Ader and Cohen demonstrate, and what new interdisciplinary field was created?

- What is psychoneuroimmunology, and how does the immune system interact with the nervous system?

- What kinds of stressors affect immune system functioning?

*Read the section "Physical Effects of Stress: Stress and the Immune System" and **write** your answers to the following:*

1. The elements of the immune system are _____

_____

_____

The function of this system is _____

_____

_____

2. Psychologist Robert Ader and immunologist Nicholas Cohen demonstrated that _____

_____

_____

3. Psychoneuroimmunology is _____

_____

_____

4. The three main findings of psychoneuroimmunological research are

(a) _____

_____

(b) _____

_____

(c) _____

_____

5. Extremely stressful events reduce _____

_____

_____

_____

6. Psychologist Janice Kiecolt-Glaser, immunologist Ronald Glaser, and others have found that

_____

_____

_____

After you have carefully studied the preceding sections, complete the following exercises.

Concept Check 2

Read the following and write the correct term in the space provided.

1. When Hans was hiking on a trail in the wilderness, he unexpectedly encountered a large brown bear and her two cubs. Hans froze in his tracks, and his heartbeat, blood pressure, and pulse increased dramatically. Fortunately, the bear and the cubs took off into the bush. The rapidly occurring chain of internal physical reactions that Hans experienced was described by Walter Cannon as the _____ response.

2. The physiological changes that Hans experienced when he was startled resulted from his sympathetic nervous system stimulating the _____ to secrete hormones called _____ .

3. After overcoming the initial shock of finding her new car badly damaged by a hit-and-run driver, Wilma phones the police and becomes actively involved in seeking witnesses to the incident. At this point, it is most likely that Wilma is in the _____ stage of the general adaptation syndrome.

4. Dr. Laslo believes that there is an interaction among psychological processes, the nervous and endocrine systems, and the immune system and that each system influences and is influenced by the other systems. It is very likely that Dr. Laslo works in the new interdisciplinary field called _____ .

5. When Georgia was under a lot of stress, she became ill due to a viral infection. In response to this infection, the most important elements in her immune system, called _____ , will try to defend against the foreign invader.

6. Dr. Batisic gave a painkilling drug to half the group of participants who were exposed to a painful stimulus and a placebo to the other half. A PET scan of their brains is likely to reveal that _____ (a different/the same) area of the brain was activated in each group.

7. In a replication of Selye's work on the effects of prolonged stress, researchers confirmed the existence of a second endocrine pathway that involves the hypothalamus, the pituitary gland, and the adrenal cortex. Like Selye, they found that in response to a stressor the hypothalamus signals the pituitary gland to secrete a hormone called _____ , which in turn stimulates the adrenal cortex to release stress-related hormones called _____ , the most important of which is _____ .

8. Eng-Seng had a tooth extracted just before going on summer vacation. Yihong had his tooth removed just before taking very stressful final exams. Research by Kiecolt-Glaser and her colleagues suggests that Eng-Seng's gum will heal _____ (faster/slower) than Yihong's.

9. Researchers investigating factors that are linked to susceptibility to respiratory infections, the common cold, and influenza, for example, are likely to discover that _____ is(are) related to becoming ill.

Review of Terms, Concepts, and Names 2

Use the terms in this list to complete the Matching Test, then to help you answer the True/False items correctly.

fight-or-flight response
Walter Cannon
catecholamines
Hans Selye
general adaptation
  syndrome
alarm stage
resistance stage
exhaustion stage

adrenocorticotropic
  hormone (ACTH)
corticosteroids
cortisol
immune system
lymphocytes
Robert Ader
psychoneuroimmunology
Janice Kiecolt-Glaser

Matching Exercise

Match the appropriate term/name with its definition or description.

1. _____ American psychologist who made several important contributions to psychology, especially in the study of emotions; he described the fight-or-flight response, which involves the sympathetic nervous system and the endocrine system.

2. _____ Specialized white blood cells that are responsible for immune defenses.

3. _____ Hormones, including adrenaline and noradrenaline, secreted by the adrenal medulla that cause rapid physiological arousal.

4. _____ Canadian endocrinologist who was a pioneer in stress research; described a three-stage response to prolonged stress that he called the general adaptation syndrome.

5. _____ Hormones released by the adrenal cortex that play a key role in the body's response to long-term stressors.

6. _____ The first stage of the general adaptation syndrome, during which intense arousal occurs as the body mobilizes internal physical resources to meet the demands of the stress-producing event.

7. _____ Body system that produces specialized white blood cells that protect the body from viruses, bacteria, and tumor cells.

8. _____ The most important of the stress-related hormones called corticosteroids.

True/False Test

Indicate whether each statement is true or false by placing T or F in the blank space next to each item.

1. ____ Robert Ader is the American psychologist who, with immunologist Nicholas Cohen, first demonstrated that immune system responses could be classically conditioned; helped establish the new interdisciplinary field of psychoneuroimmunology.

2. ____ The rapidly occurring chain of internal physical reactions that prepare people to either fight or take flight from an immediate threat is called the general adaptation syndrome.

3. ____ In the resistance stage of the general adaptation syndrome, the body actively tries to resist or adjust to the continuing stressful situation.

4. ____ Janice Kiecolt-Glaser is the American psychologist who, with immunologist Ronald Glaser, conducted extensive research on the effect of stress on the immune system.

5. ____ The fight-or-flight response is Hans Selye's term for the three-stage progression of physical changes that occur when an organism is exposed to intense and prolonged stress.

6. ____ Psychoneuroimmunology is an interdisciplinary field that studies the interconnections among psychological processes, nervous and endocrine system functions, and the immune system.

7. ____ In the exhaustion stage of the general adaptation syndrome, the symptoms of the alarm stage reappear, only this time irreversibly; as the body's energy reserves become depleted, adaptation begins to break down, leading to exhaustion, physical disorders, and, potentially, death.

8. ____ In response to stress, a hormone called adrenocorticotropic hormone (ACTH) is released by the pituitary gland after it receives a signal from the hypothalamus.

Check your answers and review any areas of weakness before going on to the next section.

Individual Factors That Influence the Response to Stress: Psychological Factors

Preview Questions

Consider the following questions as you study this section of the chapter.

- What psychological factors can affect our response to stress?
- How do feelings of control, explanatory style, and negative emotions influence stress and health?
- What is Type A behavior, and what role does hostility play in its relationship to health?

*Read the section "Individual Factors That Influence the Response to Stress" (up to "Social Factors") and **write** your answers to the following:*

1. Psychological factors that influence responses to stressful events include _____

_____

_____

_____

2. According to psychologist Martin Seligman, how people characteristically explain _____

_____

_____

_____

3. Explanatory style is related to health consequences in that _____

_____

_____

4. Two effects of chronic negative emotions on health are that_____

_____

_____

5. The Type A behavior pattern refers to _____

_____

_____

The critical component (and the strongest predictor of cardiac disease) in this type of behavior pattern is _____

_____

6. High levels of hostility are associated with

_____

_____

_____

_____

Individual Factors That Influence the Response to Stress: Social Factors

Preview Questions

Consider the following questions as you study this section of the chapter.

- What is meant by social support, and how does it benefit health?
- How can social support sometimes increase stress?
- What gender differences have been found in the effects of social support?

*Read the section "Individual Factors That Influence the Reaction to Stress: Social Factors" and **write** your answers to the following:*

1. Social support refers to _____

_____

2. Social support may benefit our health and improve our ability to cope with stressors by

(a) _____

_____

(b) _____

_____

(c) _____

_____

3. Conversely, relationships with others can also be a significant source of stress for two reasons:

(a) _____

_____

(b) _____

_____

4. Some of the main gender differences in social support are

(a) _____

_____

(b) _____

(c) _____

_____

(d) _____

_____

Coping: How People Deal with Stress

Preview Questions

Consider the following questions as you study this section of the chapter.

- How is *coping* defined?
- What are the two basic forms of coping, and when is each typically used?
- What are some of the most common coping strategies, and how does culture affect coping style?

Read the section "Coping: How People Deal with Stress" and **write** *your answers to the following:*

1. Coping refers to _____

_____

2. The two basic types of coping (and their uses) are _____

_____

_____

_____

3. Problem-focused coping strategies include

(a) _____

_____

(b) _____

_____

4. Emotion-focused coping strategies include

(a) _____

_____

(b) _____

_____

(c) _____

_____

(d) _____

_____

_____

(e) _____

5. In terms of coping strategy, members of individualistic cultures tend to

_____

_____

_____

_____

Members of collectivistic cultures tend to

_____

_____

_____

_____

_____

After you have carefully studied the preceding sections, complete the following exercises.

Concept Check 3

Read the following and write the correct term in the space provided.

1. When Marie turned down Massimo's offer to go out for dinner on Friday night, he was very disappointed. Upon reflection, however, he decided that Marie was really not his type anyway, and he'd be better off going out with someone else. Massimo's rationalization of the situation reflects a(n) _____ explanatory style.

2. When asked by her therapist to describe her husband, Cheryl said that he was very competitive and ambitious, he was always very busy, and any demands made on his time angered and irritated him. Cheryl's description suggests that her husband may have a(n)

_____ behavior pattern.

3. In the case of Cheryl's husband, the critical component and the strongest predictor of cardiac disease in his particular type of behavior pattern is _____ .

4. Irene constantly complains about her health, her job, and in general everything about her life. She tends to dislike most of the people she meets and always seems to be in a grouchy mood. It appears that Irene suffers from _____ emotions.

5. Masayuki is an engineer in a large industrial plant in Tokyo. When things get stressful, Masayuki tries to control the outward expression of his emotions and endeavors to accept the situation with maturity, serenity, and flexibility. Masayuki is using a(n) _____ coping strategy, which is more characteristic of collectivistic cultures than of individualistic cultures.

6. Shortly after he lost his job and his relationship with his girlfriend ended, Jim went to visit his family. Unfortunately, being with his family made him feel worse. The only time he felt better was when he was with the family dog. It is possible that Jim perceived his family as being _____ and the dog as being _____ and unconditionally supportive.

7. Although Lambert was very disappointed when he didn't even come close to winning his first mountain bike race, he concluded that all his training and the knowledge he gained from the experience were beneficial. Lambert is using a very constructive emotion-focused strategy called _____ .

8. Researchers have found some gender differences in the stress response. The evolutionary perspective suggests that women have developed a "_____" behavioral response to stress, because this response is more likely to promote the survival of both the individual and the individual's offspring. The researchers have speculated that the effects of the hormone _____ , which is higher in females that in males, may be a factor.

9. Most evenings after work—especially if she has had a stressful day—Laureena deals with her high level of tension by swimming and exercising in the pool. Laureena is using a(n) _____-focused coping strategy called _____ .

10. The Bickersons have been married for five difficult years. When asked about his marriage, Mr. Bickerson admits that he and his wife have some "disagreements," but he thinks the fights are "no big deal." He also jokes about the relationship, saying about women: "You can't live with them but you can't live without them." On the other hand, Mrs. Bickerson thinks their marriage is not going well and openly discusses her problems with friends and family. Mr. Bickerson appears to be using a coping strategy called _____ , and his wife deals with her marital problems by _____ .

Graphic Organizer 2

Read the following statements and decide which researcher(s) is (are) most likely to have expressed these views:

Statement	Researcher(s)
1. I believe that when we are faced with danger or any threatening or stress-producing situation, we have an immediate physical reaction that involves the sympathetic nervous system and the endocrine system and the release of catecholamines. I call these internal physical changes the fight-or-flight response.	
2. When we published the results of our research, we realized that we were challenging the prevailing scientific view that the immune system operates independently of the brain and psychological processes. However, our results, which demonstrated that the immune response in rats could be classically conditioned, have been replicated by many other researchers.	
3. We were two of the earliest researchers to study stress. In an attempt to measure the amount of stress people experienced, we developed the Social Readjustment Rating Scale. Our view at the time was that any changes, either positive or negative, would cause stress and that high levels of stress, as measured by life change units, would lead to the development of serious physical and psychological problems.	
4. My research on stress led me to postulate a three-stage model to prolonged stress, called the general adaptation syndrome. I believe that the stress response involves the hypothalamus, pituitary gland, adrenal cortex, and release of hormones such as ACTH and corticosteroids.	
5. My view is that what causes us problems in the long run is not so much the major life events, which do cause stress, but the cumulative effect of daily hassles that annoy, irritate, and upset people. I have developed a scale to measure these hassles. The number of daily hassles is a better predictor of physical illness and symptoms than the number of major life events experienced.	
6. In my view, it is the way people characteristically explain their failures and defeats that determines who will persist and who will not. I think there are two basic types of explanatory style, an optimistic explanatory style and a pessimistic explanatory style. Those who use a pessimistic explanatory style experience more stress than those who use an optimistic explanatory style.	
7. We are a husband-and-wife team who collected immunological and psychological data from medical students, who face three-day exam periods several times each academic year. We have consistently found that even the rather commonplace stress of exams adversely affects the immune system.	

Review of Terms, Concepts, and Names 3

Use the terms in this list to complete the Matching Test, then to help you answer the True/False items correctly.

Martin Seligman
optimistic explanatory
　style
pessimistic explanatory
　style
Type A behavior pattern
Type B behavior pattern
hostility
social support
stress contagion effect
coping
problem-focused coping

emotion-focused coping
confrontive coping
planful problem solving
escape–avoidance
seeking social support
distancing
denial
positive reappraisal
emotional support
tangible support
informational support

Matching Exercise

Match the appropriate term/name with its definition or description.

1. _____ Behavioral and cognitive responses used to contend with stressors; involves efforts to change circumstances, or one's interpretation of circumstances, to make them more favorable and less threatening.

2. _____ Problem-focused coping strategy in which the person relies on aggressive or risky efforts to change the situation.

3. _____ American psychologist who conducted research on explanatory style and the role it plays in stress, health, and illness.

4. _____ Emotion-focused coping strategy in which the person shifts his or her attention away from the stressor and toward other activities.

5. _____ Behavioral and emotional style characterized by a sense of time urgency, hostility, and competitiveness.

6. _____ Category of social support that includes the expression of concern, empathy, and positive regard.

7. _____ Gender difference in the effects of social support that results from women becoming upset about negative life events that happen to other people.

8. _____ Resources provided by other people in times of need, including emotional support, tangible support, and informational support.

9. _____ Emotion-focused coping strategy that involves turning to friends, relatives, or other people for emotional, tangible, or informational support.

10. _____ Emotion-focused coping strategy that involves the refusal to acknowledge that the problem exists.

11. _____ The critical component of the type A behavior pattern that is the strongest predictor of cardiac disease and other health problems.

True/False Test

Indicate whether each item is true or false by placing T or F in the space next to each item.

1. ____ An optimistic explanatory style involves accounting for negative events or situations with internal, stable, and global explanations.

2. ____ The Type B behavior pattern is a behavioral and emotional style characterized by a relatively relaxed and laid-back approach to situations and problems.

3. ____ Informational social support involves direct assistance, such as providing transportation, lending money, or helping with meals, child care, or household tasks.

4. ____ Emotion-focused coping efforts are aimed primarily at relieving or regulating the emotional impact of a stressful situation.

5. ____ The most constructive emotion-focused coping strategy is positive reappraisal, which involves not only minimizing the negative emotional aspects of the situation but also trying to create positive meaning by focusing on personal growth.

6. ____ A pessimistic explanatory style involves accounting for negative events or situations with external, unstable, and specific explanations.

7. ____ An emotion-focused coping strategy in which the individual acknowledges the stressor but attempts to minimize or eliminate its emotional impact is called distancing.

8. ____ Problem-focused coping efforts are aimed primarily at directly changing or managing a threatening or harmful stressor.

9. ___ A problem-focused coping strategy that involves efforts to rationally analyze the situation, identify potential solutions, and then implement them is called planful problem solving.

10. ___ Tangible social support involves offering helpful suggestions and advice to a person in distress.

Check your answers and review any areas of weakness before going on to the next section.

Something to Think About

It sometimes seems that everyone you meet is stressed out. There are things to be done, deadlines to be met, social and family obligations, financial pressures, work-related problems, and so on. How can people cope with all this stress? Is there anything that can be done? Fortunately, there are several strategies for coping with stress. What advice would you give someone who is experiencing stress?

Check your answers and review any areas of weakness before completing the progress tests.

Progress Test 1

Review the complete chapter (including Concept Reviews and the boxed inserts), review all your study notes, and then test yourself on the following progress test. Check your answers. If you make a mistake, review your notes, review the relevant section of the study guide, and, if necessary, go back and read the appropriate part of your textbook.

1. Natasha experienced a great deal of anxiety when she had three exams on the same day. In this situation the exams are _____ and her response is called _____ .
   (a) stress; stressor
   (b) the biological component; the cognitive component
   (c) stressors; stress
   (d) the social component; the biological component

2. Dr. Turnbull uses the biopsychosocial model to guide his research into how psychological factors influence health, illness, and treatment. Dr. Turnbull is most likely a
   (a) developmental psychologist.
   (b) health psychologist.
   (c) psychoneuroimmunologist.
   (d) psychiatrist.

3. Donald scored 300 points on the Social Readjustment Rating Scale. What does that mean?
   (a) It is absolutely certain that Donald will develop physical and psychological problems.
   (b) It is impossible to accurately predict whether Donald will develop physical and psychological problems.
   (c) Donald has probably experienced very few daily hassles during the past year.
   (d) Donald's subjective appraisal of the events in his life during the previous year will have no bearing on his health and well-being.

4. Del got up late and nicked himself three times while shaving. When he poured his coffee, he found that there was no cream in the fridge; then, as he was tying his shoe laces, one of them broke. Richard Lazarus would call these incidents
   (a) major life events.   (c) minor life events.
   (b) daily hassles.   (d) life change units.

5. To earn money so that he can buy a ticket to a rock concert, Ken has to either wash and wax the two family cars or wash and wax the kitchen and bathroom floors. In trying to decide between these two equally unappealing choices, Ken is likely to experience an _____ conflict.
   (a) approach–avoidance
   (b) approach–approach
   (c) avoidance–avoidance
   (d) escape–avoidance

6. Yui is leaving Japan to work and live in the United States and is very excited about the move. When Yui arrives and starts work in the United States, she is likely to
   (a) be much more relaxed and laid back than she was in Japan.
   (b) experience increased levels of stress due to the acculturation process.
   (c) become physically and psychologically ill within weeks.
   (d) adapt to the new environment without experiencing any stress whatsoever.

7. When Nibras was chased and attacked by a dog during his regular morning run, he experienced the classic symptoms of the fight-or-flight response. According to Walter Cannon, it is likely that his sympathetic nervous system stimulated his adrenal medulla to secrete hormones called
   (a) catecholamines.   (c) corticosteroids.
   (b) ACTH.   (d) lymphocytes.

8. After overcoming the initial shock of having his house broken into and many of his personal possessions stolen, Vincent calls the police for help and starts thinking of ways to help catch the burglar and retrieve his belongings. At this point, Vincent is most likely in the _____ stage of the general adaptation syndrome.
   (a) alarm   (c) exhaustion
   (b) resistance   (d) denial

9. When Claudia became ill because of a viral infection, her immune system kicked into high gear to defend her by producing
   (a) lymphocytes.   (c) catecholamines.
   (b) corticosteroids. (d) noradrenaline.

10. Dr. Blackman studies the interconnections among psychological processes, the nervous and endocrine systems, and the immune system. Like other specialists in the field of psychoneuroimmunology, Dr. Blackman is aware that researchers have discovered that
   (a) the central nervous system and the immune system are directly linked.
   (b) the surfaces of lymphocytes contain receptor sites for neurotransmitters and hormones, including catecholamines and cortisol.
   (c) lymphocytes themselves produce neurotransmitters and hormones.
   (d) all of the above are true.

11. When Darcy was taking his statistics exam, he was very anxious and nervous. According to researchers such as Janice Kiecolt-Glaser, the stress of exams
   (a) adversely affects the immune system.
   (b) has no effect on the immune system.
   (c) has a beneficial effect on the immune system.
   (d) does none of the above.

12. Whenever anything goes wrong in his life, Dean typically feels that it must be something about him that causes the problem; he also believes that no amount of personal effort will improve his situation. Martin Seligman would say that Dean has
   (a) a Type A behavior pattern.
   (b) an optimistic explanatory style.
   (c) a Type B behavior pattern.
   (d) a pessimistic explanatory style.

13. After his third month of low sales, Allen is called into the sales manager's office and told that he had better start meeting his quota or he will be laid off. The manager appears to be coping with the problem of low sales by using a(n) _____ strategy called _____ .
   (a) problem-focused; confrontive coping
   (b) emotion-focused; escape-avoidance
   (c) problem-focused; planful problem solving
   (d) emotion-focused; distancing

14. According to In Focus 13.4, there are some gender differences in responding to stress. Males tend to adopt the _____ response, and females typically engage in the _____ behavioral pattern of responding.
   (a) fight-or-flight; escape–avoidance
   (b) tend-and-befriend; fight-or-flight
   (c) fight-or-flight; tend-and-befriend
   (d) escape–avoidance; fight-or-flight

15. Critical Thinking 13.3, which discusses personality and disease, points out that psychologists and other scientists are cautious in reaching conclusions about the connection between personality and health for which of the following reasons?

(a) Many studies investigating the role of psychological factors in disease are correlational.

(b) Personality factors might indirectly lead to disease via poor health habits.

(c) It may be that the disease influences a person's emotions, rather than the other way around.

(d) All of the above factors are true.

Progress Test 2

After you have checked your understanding of the material in Progress Test 1 and have done a complete chapter review with special focus on any areas of weakness, you are ready to assess your knowledge on Progress Test 2. Check your answers. If you make a mistake, review your notes, the relevant section of the study guide, and, if necessary, the appropriate part of your textbook.

1. When Janeen was caught in a large traffic jam, she experienced a severe headache. In this case, the traffic jam is to _____ as her headache is to _____ .

(a) fight; flight   (c) flight; fight
(b) stressor; stress   (d) stress; stressor

2. For his birthday, Liam has to decide between a snowboard and a mountain bike. In trying to decide between these two equally attractive alternatives, Liam is likely to experience an _____ conflict.

(a) approach–avoidance
(b) approach–approach
(c) avoidance–avoidance
(d) escape–avoidance

3. Fifty-five-year-old Maxwell is a very impatient and competitive defense lawyer who feels that he must be the best in his field. In addition, he has a reputation for being hostile toward judges and prosecuting attorneys. Maxwell is likely to be classified as having a(n)

(a) Type A behavior pattern.
(b) pessimistic explanatory style.
(c) Type B behavior pattern.
(d) optimistic explanatory style.

4. In the above example, it is very likely that Maxwell is at high risk for developing heart disease. The component of his behavior that is most likely to contribute to health problems is his

(a) impatience.
(b) competitiveness.
(c) achievement orientation.
(d) hostility.

5. Heloise is an emergency room nurse. Whenever she has a particularly hectic and stressful shift, she and some of the other nurses find themselves making fun of the patients and the doctors. Heloise is using an emotion-focused coping strategy called

(a) confrontive coping.   (c) distancing.
(b) denial.   (d) positive reappraisal.

6. Madge wants advice on how to cope with the stress of returning to college after being out of school for a number of years. She would be best advised to approach her classes

(a) with a sense of personal control and optimism.
(b) with a realistic but pessimistic attitude.
(c) using an emotion-focused coping strategy called distancing.
(d) using an emotion-focused coping strategy called denial.

7. Whenever Beth experiences problems in her relationship with her fiancee, she typically talks to her family about her troubles. Beth is using a(n) _____ strategy called _____ .

(a) problem-focused; confrontive coping
(b) emotion-focused; distancing
(c) problem-focused; planful problem solving
(d) emotion-focused; seeking social support

8. While researching a paper for her psychology class, Joyce came across the research of Ader and Cohen on conditioning and immune system functioning. She is likely to conclude that their work was important for which of the following reasons?

   (a) It challenged the prevailing scientific view that the immune system operates independently of the brain and psychological processes.
   (b) It demonstrated that humans could be conditioned to salivate just like Pavlov's dogs.
   (c) Before their research was published, everyone believed that there was a strong interconnectedness among psychological processes, nervous and endocrine system functions, and the immune system.
   (d) It proved conclusively that the immune system could not be classically conditioned.

9. After a bank was robbed, the bank tellers and the customers got up off the floor, where they had been held at gunpoint. Because it was such a frightening experience, they are likely to have experienced a rapidly occurring chain of internal physical reactions called

   (a) daily hassles.
   (b) the fight-or-flight response.
   (c) the general adaptation syndrome.
   (d) the stress contagion effect.

10. Following the bank robbery, the people who were very frightened probably experienced increased activation of the sympathetic nervous system, stimulation of the adrenal medulla, and the release of hormones called

    (a) lymphocytes.   (c) testosterone.
    (b) catecholamines.   (d) estrogen.

11. During her final year of medical training, Lissette was under constant pressure; she never seemed to get enough sleep, was anxious and nervous most of the time, and experienced many physical symptoms and disorders. As a result of this prolonged stress, it is likely that her hypothalamus, pituitary gland, and adrenal cortex will work together to release stress-related hormones called

    (a) lymphocytes.   (c) corticosteroids.
    (b) catecholamines.   (d) acetylcholine.

12. Gregory was very disappointed when he wasn't accepted in the graduate program at State University. Upon reflection, however, he decided that the preparations he made in putting his application together and the knowledge he gained from the interview were very beneficial experiences. Gregory is using a(n) _____ strategy called

    _____ .

    (a) problem-focused; confrontive coping
    (b) emotion-focused; positive reappraisal
    (c) problem-focused; planful problem solving
    (d) emotion-focused; escape-avoidance

13. According to the Application, which of the following is *not* recommended for helping someone in distress?

    (a) Express affection for the person, whether by a warm hug or simply a pat on the arm.
    (b) Be a good listener and show concern and interest.
    (c) Ask questions that encourage the person under stress to express his or her feelings and emotions.
    (d) Give advice that the person has not asked for.
    (e) Be willing to invest time and attention in helping.

14. In Focus 13.2, which discusses the relationship between stress and the common cold, concludes that

    (a) stress reduces the effectiveness of the immune system and its ability to fight off viruses, bacteria, and other foreign invaders.
    (b) factors such as health-compromising behaviors provide the underlying stress–illness connection.
    (c) highly stressed people get sick more often because they interact with more people than do people with little stress.
    (d) all of the above are true.

15. When Sanjeev went to Britain to attend one of the top universities in the country he was enthralled by all things English and decided that he would like to live there permanently. He took up cricket, lawn bowling, and polo, preferred to be called Sandy rather than Sanjeev, and enthusiastically embraced the "pub" culture of his adopted home. According to Culture and Human Behavior 13.1, it appears that Sanjeev has adopted a pattern of acculturation called _____ and has probably experienced a _____ degree of stress as a result of abandoning his old cultural identity.
    (a) integration; low
    (b) separation; high
    (c) assimilation; moderate
    (d) marginalization; high

Progress Test 3

After you have checked your understanding of the material in Progress Tests 1 and 2, and have done a complete chapter review with special focus on any areas of weakness, you are ready to further assess your knowledge on Progress Test 3. Check your answers. If you make a mistake, review your notes, the appropriate parts of the study guide, and, if necessary, the relevant sections of your textbook.

1. Following a bitter divorce and a long-fought custody battle over her two children, Luzmilda is in the exhaustion stage of the general adaptation syndrome. According to Selye, this prolonged stress is likely to activate an endocrine pathway that involves _____ and the release of _____ .
    (a) the hypothalamus, the pituitary gland, the adrenal cortex; corticosteroids
    (b) the hypothalamus, the sympathetic nervous system, the adrenal medulla; catecholamines
    (c) the sympathetic nervous system, the adrenal medulla, the immune system; oxytocin
    (d) classical conditioning, the adrenal cortex, the immune system; lymphocytes

2. When Argento encountered a wild cougar on the hiking trail, he experienced acute stress. Which of the following would Walter Cannon consider the correct sequence involved in Argento's fight-or-flight response?
    (a) pituitary, hypothalamus, ACTH release, sympathetic nervous system.
    (b) secretion of corticosteroids, ACTH release, perspiration, cognitive appraisal.
    (c) hypothalamus, sympathetic nervous system, adrenal medulla, secretion of catecholamines
    (d) perspiration, ACTH release, respiration, parasympathetic nervous system, secretion of catecholamines

3. If Dr. Penman is like most researchers in the field of psychoneuroimmunology, he is likely to hold the view that
    (a) it is impossible to classically condition the immune system.
    (b) the immune system works independently of other body systems.
    (c) the endocrine system and the immune system are interconnected, but psychological processes operate independently.
    (d) there are interconnections among psychological processes, nervous and endocrine system functions, and the immune system.

4. Rita and Richard both have a large network of social relationships, including close friends and family members. Compared with Richard, Rita may be potentially vulnerable to some of the problematic aspects of social support because
    (a) women are less likely than men to serve as providers of support.
    (b) women, in general, are more likely than men to suffer from the stress contagion effect.
    (c) women tend to rely on a close personal relationship with their spouse and place less importance on relationships with other people.
    (d) women are less likely than men to become upset about what happens to their friends and relatives.

5. Reena has a very successful accounting practice and frequently works sixty hours or more a week. She has to manage her time efficiently in order to keep up with the demands of her career and family life. Despite all the pressure, Reena loves her job, is always kind and considerate to her employees, and has a very cheerful personality. Which of the following is most likely to be true of Reena?
    (a) Because of her very stressful lifestyle, she is likely to have very high levels of corticosteroids.
    (b) She is at a very high risk for coronary disease and other health problems.

(c) She is very likely to develop coronary disease because of her Type A behavior pattern.

(d) Because she is low in hostility, her risk of developing coronary disease is no higher than that of anyone else.

6. Forty-year-old Lannie is a widow, lives alone, has very few friends, and rarely interacts with other people except at work. Research suggests that compared with people who have many social contacts and relationships, social isolation such as Lannie's is correlated with
   (a) higher-than-normal levels of catecholamines.
   (b) poor health and higher death rates.
   (c) lower-than-normal levels of corticosteroids.
   (d) good health and lower death rates.

7. In replicating Ader and Cohen's original research, Dr. Andrews and his colleagues also found that the suppression of the immune system was influenced by
   (a) Type A behavior.
   (b) the general adaptation syndrome.
   (c) classical conditioning.
   (d) aerobic exercise.

8. Kari is a very laid-back, easygoing mail carrier. She loves her job because it allows her to meet people and get daily exercise. Kari is likely to be classified as having a
   (a) Type A behavior pattern.
   (b) high risk of heart disease.
   (c) Type B behavior pattern.
   (d) stress contagion syndrome.

9. Jacob was one of the unsuccessful candidates for a job, and naturally he was disappointed. However, in his habitual manner, he thought that he would have better luck next time, especially if he took some additional training to make himself more qualified for the position. Martin Seligman would say that Jacob has a(n)
   (a) Type A behavior pattern.
   (b) optimistic explanatory style.
   (c) problem-focused coping style.
   (d) pessimistic explanatory style.

10. Helga, a college student, was offered a new job. On the plus side, the higher salary and increased benefits are appealing; on the down side, she will have to work longer hours, take on extra responsibilities, and have a longer commute to work. She needs the extra money but she also needs to keep her high GPA at college. Helga is likely experiencing a type of conflict called _____ conflict.
    (a) approach–approach
    (b) avoidance–avoidance
    (c) escape–avoidance
    (d) approach–avoidance

11. Anders, a fifty-two-year-old insurance salesman, is unexpectedly called into the sales manager's office and told that he is going to be laid off because the company is downsizing. Which stage of the general adaptation syndrome is Anders likely experiencing?
    (a) alarm stage   (c) exhaustion stage
    (b) resistance stage   (d) denial stage

12. Dr. Chambers has a very busy clinical practice. To clear his mind of all the problems he faces each day and to cope with the high level of stress, he goes to the gym for a workout four or five times a week. Dr. Chambers is using a(n) _____ coping strategy called

    _____ .
    (a) emotion-focused; escape–avoidance
    (b) problem-focused; denial
    (c) emotion-focused; wishful thinking
    (d) problem-focused; confrontive coping

13. When Lester was having personal and academic problems in college, he went to see one of the counselors, who provided some helpful suggestions to improve his study habits and advised him to enroll in a remedial course to improve his writing skills. According to the Application, the type of social support that Lester received is called _____ support.
    (a) emotional   (c) informational
    (b) tangible   (d) confrontive

14. According to In Focus 13.5, which of the following strategies is recommended for minimizing stress?
    (a) Exercise regularly.
    (b) Avoid or minimize stimulants.
    (c) Regularly practice a relaxation technique.
    (d) All of the above are recommended.

15. Having moved to the United States from China two years ago, Mi-Ling still does not feel comfortable with Americans, mainly because of her poor command of English. She prefers to work in a Chinese neighborhood and socialize with other Chinese immigrants and Chinese-Americans. According to Culture and Human Behavior 13.1, Mi-Ling has adopted the acculturation pattern of
    (a) assimilation.   (c) marginalization.
    (b) separation.   (d) integration.

Answers

Introduction: What Is Stress?

1. *Stress is defined as* a negative emotional state occurring in response to events that are perceived as taxing or exceeding a person's resources or ability to cope.

2. *Health psychologists focus on* how biological, behavioral, and social factors influence health, illness, medical treatment, and health-related behaviors (health psychology is also called behavioral medicine or medical psychology).

3. *The biopsychosocial model is* the belief that physical health and illness are determined by the complex interaction of biological factors, psychological and behavioral factors, and social conditions.

What Is Stress? Sources of Stress

1. *Stressors are* events or situations that are perceived as harmful, threatening, or challenging.

2. *Early stress researchers Holmes and Rahe believed that* any change, whether positive or negative, that required you to adjust your behavior or lifestyle would cause stress (they developed the Social Readjustment Rating Scale in an attempt to measure the amount of stress people experienced).

3. *Several problems with the life events approach have been pointed out: (a)* The link between scores on the Social Readjustment Rating Scale and the development of physical and psychological problems is relatively weak. *(b)* Most people don't develop physical or mental problems as a result of major life events. *(c)* The Social Readjustment Rating Scale does not take into account a person's subjective appraisal of an event, response to that event, or ability to cope with the event (it assumes that a given life event will have the same impact on virtually everyone). *(d)* The life events approach assumes change in itself, whether good or bad, produces stress (research has shown that health is most adversely affected by negative life events, especially when they are unexpected or uncontrollable, whereas positive or desirable events are much less likely to affect health adversely). Recently, efforts have been made to revise and update the SRRS in an attempt to address these problems.

4. *Daily hassles are* everyday minor events that annoy and upset people. The frequency of daily hassles is linked to psychological distress and physical symptoms: The number of daily hassles people experience is a better predictor of physical illness and symptoms than is the number of major life events experienced.

5. *Conflict is the* feeling of being pulled between two or more opposing desires, motives, or goals.

6. *The three basic types of conflict are (a)* approach–approach conflict (a win-win situation in which the choice is between two equally appealing outcomes); *(b)* avoidance–avoidance conflict (in which the choice is between two unappealing or undesirable outcomes); and *(c)* approach–avoidance conflict (a very stressful situation in which the goal has both desirable and undesirable aspects).

7. *Social factors that are a source of stress include* crowding, crime, unemployment, poverty, racism and discrimination (real or suspected), inadequate health care, and substandard housing (people in the lowest socioeconomic levels of society tend to have the highest levels of psychological distress, illness, and death).

8. *In terms of culture, stress can result when* cultures clash; for refugees, immigrants, and their children, adapting to a new culture can be extremely stress producing.

Concept Check 1

1. health
2. biopsychosocial
3. high; increased
4. daily hassles
5. approach–approach
6. cognitive appraisals
7. integrated; low
8. approach–avoidance; partial-approach
9. female; male

Graphic Organizer 1

1. approach–avoidance; high
2. approach–approach; low
3. approach–avoidance; high
4. avoidance–avoidance; medium
5. approach–approach; low
6. avoidance–avoidance; medium

Matching Exercise 1

1. Richard Lazarus
2. approach–approach conflict
3. conflict
4. daily hassles
5. health psychology
6. biopsychosocial model
7. life change units
8. Daily Hassles Scale
9. chronic stress

True/False Test 1

1. F	3. T	5. T	7. T
2. T	4. F	6. T	8. T

Physical Effects of Stress: The Mind–Body Connection

1. *Stress can indirectly affect a person's health by* prompting behavior that jeopardizes physical well-being; people under chronic stress are more likely to use alcohol, coffee, and cigarettes than are people under less stress.

2. *High levels of stress can also interfere with* cognitive abilities, such as attention, concentration, and memory; in turn, such disruptions can increase the likelihood of accidents and injuries.

3. *Stress can directly affect physical health by* altering body functions, leading to symptoms, illness, or disease (for example, stress can cause neck and head muscles to contract and tighten, resulting in stress-induced headaches).

4. *The fight-or-flight response refers to* a rapidly occurring chain of internal physical reactions that prepare people to either fight or take flight from an immediate threat (involves both the sympathetic nervous system and the endocrine system).

5. *Catecholamines are* hormones secreted by the adrenal medulla that cause rapid physiological arousal (they include adrenaline and noradrenaline).

6. *The general adaptation syndrome is* Selye's term for the three-stage progression of physical changes that occur when an organism is exposed to intense and prolonged stress; the three stages are alarm, resistance, and exhaustion.

7. *Selye found that prolonged stress activates a* second endocrine pathway that involves the hypothalamus, the pituitary gland, and the secretion of a hormone called adrenocorticotropic hormone (ACTH), which in turn stimulates the adrenal cortex to release stress-related hormones called corticosteroids, the most important being cortisol.

8. *Using positron emission tomography (PET), neuroscientists have shown that* both a genuine painkilling drug and a placebo activated the same brain area, the anterior cingulate cortex, which is known to contain many opioid receptors. Although exactly how placebos produce their results is not clear, these researchers concluded that this substantiated the mind–body connection, and that higher mental processes (expectations, learned associations, and emotional responses) can have a profound effect on the perception of pain.

Physical Effects of Stress: Stress and the Immune System

1. *The elements of the immune system are* the bone marrow, the spleen, the thymus, and lymph nodes. Most important are the lymphocytes, which are manufactured in the bone marrow. *The function of this system is* to detect and battle foreign invaders, such as bacteria, viruses, and tumor cells.

2. *Psychologist Robert Ader and immunologist Nicholas Cohen demonstrated that* the immune system response in rats could be classically conditioned; their research helped establish a new interdisciplinary field called psychoneuroimmunology.

3. *Psychoneuroimmunology is* the scientific study of the interconnections among psychological processes (psycho-), the nervous system (-neuro-), and the immune system (-immunology).

4. *The three main findings of psychoneuroimmunological research are (a)* The central nervous system and the immune system are directly linked; the sympathetic nervous system fibers go into virtually every organ of the immune system, directly influencing the production and functioning of lymphocytes. *(b)* The surfaces of lymphocytes contain receptor sites for neurotransmitters and hormones, including catecholamines and cortisol. *(c)* Lymphocytes themselves produce neurotransmitters and hormones, which in turn influence the nervous and endocrine systems.

5. *Extremely stressful events reduce* immune system functioning. Thus, common negative life events, such as the end or disruption of important interpersonal relationships and chronic stressors that continue for years, can diminish immune system functioning.

6. *Psychologist Janice Kiecolt-Glaser, immunologist Ronald Glaser, and others have found that* even the rather commonplace stress of exams adversely affects the immune system and that reduced immune system functioning as a result of stress puts us at greater risk for health problems, with slower recovery times for illnesses and injuries.

Concept Check 2

1. fight-or-flight

2. adrenal medulla; catecholamines

3. resistance

4. psychoneuroimmunology

5. lymphocytes

6. the same

7. adrenocorticotropic hormone (ACTH); corticosteroids; cortisol

8. faster

9. high levels of stress and chronic stress

Matching Exercise 2

1. Walter Cannon

2. lymphocytes

3. catecholamines

4. Hans Selye

5. corticosteroids

6. alarm stage

7. immune system

8. cortisol

True/False Test 2

1. T	5. F
2. F	6. T
3. T	7. T
4. T	8. T

Individual Factors That Influence the Response to Stress: Psychological Factors

1. *Psychological factors that influence responses to stressful events include* people's appraisal of the event and their resources for coping with it; having a sense of control over the stressful situation; and being able take steps to minimize or avoid the stressor (in contrast, feeling a lack of control over events produces all the landmarks of the stress response: Levels of catecholamines and corticosteroids increase, and the effectiveness of the immune system decreases).

2. *According to psychologist Martin Seligman, how people characteristically explain* their failures and defeats makes the difference: People who have an optimistic explanatory style tend to use external, unstable, and specific explanations for negative events; people who have a pessimistic explanatory style use internal, stable, and global explanations for negative events.

3. *Explanatory style is related to health consequences in that* explanatory style in early adulthood predicts physical health status decades later; those with optimistic explanatory styles have significantly better health than those with pessimistic explanatory styles.

4. *Two effects of chronic negative emotions on health are that* people who are habitually anxious, depressed, angry, and hostile are more likely to develop chronic diseases such as arthritis or heart disease, and people who are tense, angry, and unhappy experience more stress than happier people (they also report more frequent and intense daily hassles and react much more intensely to the stressful events they encounter).

5. *The Type A behavior pattern refers to* a behavioral and emotional style characterized by a sense of time urgency, hostility, and competitiveness. *The critical component (and the strongest predictor of cardiac disease) in this type of behavior pattern is* hostility, which refers to the tendency to feel anger, annoyance, resentment, and contempt and to hold negative beliefs about human nature in general.

6. *High levels of hostility are associated with* suspiciousness, mistrust, cynicism, and pessimism; an increased likelihood of dying from all natural causes, including cancer; increased blood pressure, heart rate, and the production of stress-related hormones; more intense reactions to stressors and a tendency to create more stress; and more severe negative life events and daily hassles than other people.

Individual Factors That Influence the Response to Stress: Social Factors

1. *Social support refers to* the resources provided by other people in times of need.

2. *Social support may benefit our health and improve our ability to cope with stressors by* (a) modifying our appraisal of a stressor's significance, including the degree to which we perceive it as threatening or harmful (simply knowing that support and assistance are readily available may make the situation seem less threatening); (b) decreasing the intensity of physical reactions to a stressor; and (c) making us less likely to experience negative emotions (in contrast, loneliness and depression are unpleasant emotional states that increase levels of stress hormones and adversely affect immune system functioning).

3. *Conversely, relationships with others can also be a significant source of stress for two reasons:* (a) Negative interactions with other people are more effective in creating psychological distress than positive interactions are in improving well-being. (b) When people are perceived as being judgmental, their presence may increase the individual's physical reaction to a stressor.

4. *Some of the main gender differences in social support are* (a) Women are more likely than men to serve as providers of support, which can be a very stressful role. (b) Women may be more likely to suffer from the stress contagion effect, becoming upset about negative life events that happen to other people whom they care about. (c) Men are more likely to be distressed only by negative events that happen to their immediate family—their wives and children. (d) Men generally tend to rely heavily on a close relationship with their spouse, placing less importance on relationships with other people (women, in contrast, are more likely to list close friends along with their spouses as confidants).

Coping: How People Deal with Stress

1. *Coping refers to* behavioral and cognitive responses used to deal with stressors; it involves efforts to change circumstances, or our interpretations of circumstances, to make them more favorable and less threatening.

2. *The two basic types of coping (and their uses) are* problem-focused coping (aimed at managing or changing a threatening or harmful stressor) and emotion-focused coping (aimed at relieving or regulating the emotional impact of the stressful situation).

3. *Problem-focused coping strategies include (a)* confrontive coping (relying on aggressive or risky efforts to change the situation) and (b) planful problem solving (rationally analyzing the situation, identifying potential solutions, and then implementing them).

4. *Emotion-focused coping strategies include* (a) escape-avoidance (shifting attention away from the stressor and toward other activities, with the basic goal of escaping or avoiding the stressor and neutralizing distressing emotions), (b) seeking social support (turning to friends, relatives, or other people for emotional, tangible, or informational support), (c) distancing (acknowledging the stressor while attempting to minimize or eliminate its emotional impact), (d) denial (the refusal to acknowledge that the problem even exists), and (e) positive reappraisal (minimizing the negative emotional aspects of the situation but also trying to create positive meaning by focusing on personal growth).

5. *In terms of coping strategies, members of individualistic cultures tend to* emphasize personal autonomy and personal responsibility in dealing with problems (they are less likely to seek social support in stressful situations than are members of collectivistic cultures) and to favor problem-focused strategies, such as confrontive coping and planful problem solving. *Members of collectivistic cultures tend to* be more oriented toward their social group, family, or community and to seek help with their problems; they also place greater emphasis on controlling personal reactions to a stressful situation rather than trying to control the situation itself.

Concept Check 3

1. optimistic

2. Type A

3. hostility

4. chronic negative

5. emotion-focused

6. judgmental; nonjudgmental

7. positive reappraisal

8. "tend-and-befriend"; oxytocin

9. emotion-focused; escape–avoidance

10. distancing; seeking social support

Graphic Organizer 2

1. Walter Cannon

2. Robert Ader and Nicholas Cohen

3. Thomas Holmes and Richard Rahe

4. Hans Selye

5. Richard Lazarus

6. Martin Seligman

7. Janice Kiecolt-Glaser and Ronald Glaser

Matching Exercise 3

1. coping

2. confrontive coping

3. Martin Seligman

4. escape–avoidance

5. Type A behavior pattern

6. emotional support

7. stress contagion effect

8. social support

9. seeking social support

10. denial

11. hostility

True/False Test 3

1. F	5. T	9. T
2. T	6. F	10. F
3. F	7. T	
4. T	8. T	

Something to Think About

A good place to start in giving advice to someone is to explain what stressors are and what the stress reaction is. Identifying potential sources of stress, from major life events to daily hassles, is useful, and noting how our subjective cognitive appraisal of stressors influences our reactions is also important. It is also helpful to know about physical reactions and psychological and social factors that influence our response to stress.

People vary a great deal in the way they respond to distressing events. Psychologists have identified several different factors that influence an individual's response to stressful events. Having a sense of control reduces the impact of stressors and decreases feelings of anxiety and depression. The type of explanatory style we use—optimistic, pessimistic, or, as in most cases, somewhere in between—can also have an effect on our health. People with a pessimistic explanatory style tend to have poorer physical health, whereas people with an optimistic, confident, and generally positive outlook have better immune system responses and better physical health. Furthermore, chronically grouchy people experience more stress, have more frequent and intense daily hassles, and generally react with far greater distress to stressful events.

Many different strategies can be used to deal with stress, some of which are more adaptive than others. Having good social support is beneficial, but so too are the types of strategies that we adopt to cope with distressing events. Problem-focused and emotion-focused coping strategies are two that the text discusses in detail. In addition, we can minimize the impact of stressors by exercising regularly, avoiding or minimizing stimulants such as coffee, tea, or cigarettes, and by regularly practicing a relaxation technique such as meditation or progressive muscle relaxation. Stress is an unavoidable part of life and can influence both our physical and psychological well-being. How we choose to cope with stress can reduce and minimize its destructive effects.

Progress Test 1

1. c	6. b	11. a
2. b	7. a	12. d
3. b	8. b	13. a
4. b	9. a	14. c
5. c	10. d	15. d

Progress Test 2

1. b	6. a	11. c
2. b	7. d	12. b
3. a	8. a	13. d
4. d	9. b	14. a
5. c	10. b	15. c

Progress Test 3

1. a	6. b	11. a
2. c	7. c	12. a
3. d	8. c	13. c
4. b	9. b	14. d
5. d	10. d	15. b

chapter

14

Psychological Disorders

PREVIEW

Reading the section below first will give you a general sense of the chapter's contents and an initial introduction to some of the major concepts and terms. This will prime you for what you are about to read and help you to develop a "cognitive map" that will guide your study of the material in this chapter. Likewise, reading the **preview questions** at the beginning of each major section will improve your ability to understand, learn, and retain the information.

CHAPTER 14 . . . AT A GLANCE

Chapter 14 begins by addressing the distinction between normal and abnormal behavior and the criteria for diagnosing psychological disorders, according to DSM-IV-TR.

Anxiety is a common experience for all people, but only when it becomes maladaptive is it considered a disorder. The prevalence, course, and possible causes of anxiety disorders, including generalized anxiety disorder (GAD), panic disorder, phobias, posttraumatic stress disorder (PTSD), and obsessive-compulsive disorder (OCD), are discussed.

Mood disorders involve serious, persistent disturbances in emotions that cause psychological discomfort and/or impair the ability to function. The symptoms of major depression, dysthymic disorder, and bipolar disorder are identified, and the course and potential causes of these mood disorders are discussed.

Personality disorders are characterized by inflexible and maladaptive personality traits. Paranoid, antisocial, and borderline personality disorder are discussed in terms of symptoms, causation, and treatment.

Dissociative experiences involve a disruption in awareness, memory, and personal identity. The symptoms and possible causes of dissociative amnesia, dissociative fugue, and dissociative identity disorder (DID) are examined.

The main symptoms of schizophrenia are identified. Positive symptoms represent excesses in normal functioning, and negative symptoms reflect deficits or decreases in normal functioning. Three subtypes of schizophrenia are discussed, and the prevalence and course of the disorder are presented. Various theories of the causes of schizophrenia are explored, and the conclusion is reached that no single factor has emerged as causing this psychological disorder. The Application deals with the topic of suicide.

Introduction: Understanding Psychological Disorders

Preview Questions

Consider the following questions as you study this section of the chapter.

- What is psychopathology, and what characterizes psychological disorders?
- What is DSM-IV-TR, and how was it developed?
- How prevalent are psychological disorders?

*Read the section "Introduction: Understanding Psychological Disorders" and **write** your answers to the following:*

1. Psychopathology is _____

   _____

2. A psychological, or mental, disorder can be defined as _____

   _____

   _____

3. DSM-IV-TR stands for _____

   _____

   This manual describes _____

   _____

   _____

   _____

4. The National Comorbidity Survey found that psychological disorders were more common than previously thought, which can be interpreted to mean_____

   _____

   _____

   _____

Anxiety Disorders

Preview Questions

Consider the following questions as you study this section of the chapter.

- What are the main symptoms of anxiety disorder, and how does pathological anxiety differ from normal anxiety?

- What characterizes generalized anxiety disorder (GAD) and panic disorder?
- What are the phobias, and how have they been explained?

*Read the section "Anxiety Disorders" (up to "Posttraumatic Stress Disorder") and **write** your answers to the following:*

1. Anxiety is defined as _____

   _____

   _____

   It is often adaptive and normal because_____

   _____

2. In the anxiety disorders, the anxiety is _____

   _____

3. The three features that distinguish normal anxiety from pathological anxiety are

   (a) _____

   _____

   (b) _____

   _____

   (c) _____

4. Generalized anxiety disorder (GAD) is characterized by_____

   _____

   _____

5. A panic attack is _____

   _____

6. A panic disorder is _____

   _____

   Its cause is thought to be _____

   _____

   _____

7. A phobia is_____

   _____

   A specific phobia is_____

   _____

   _____

8. Phobias are assumed by some to involve various forms of learning such as _____

_____

_____

_____

_____

Anxiety Disorders: Posttraumatic Stress Disorder and Obsessive-Compulsive Disorder

Preview Questions

Consider the following questions as you study these sections of the chapter.

- How is posttraumatic stress disorder (PTSD) defined?
- What are the main characteristics of PTSD, and what causes the disorder?
- What is obsessive-compulsive disorder (OCD), and what causes it?

Read the sections "Anxiety Disorders: Posttraumatic Stress Disorder" and "Obsessive-Compulsive Disorders" and ***write*** *your answers to the following:*

1. Posttraumatic stress disorder (PTSD) is _____

_____

2. The three core symptoms that characterize PTSD are

(a) _____

_____

(b) _____

_____

(c) _____

_____

3. Factors that influence the likelihood of developing posttraumatic stress disorder are

(a) _____

_____

(b) _____

_____

(c) _____

_____

4. Obsessive-compulsive disorder (OCD) is

_____

_____

Obsessions are _____

_____

_____

Compulsions are _____

_____

_____

5. People with obsessive-compulsive disorder commonly experience _____

_____

_____

6. Two biological factors that seem to be involved in obsessive-compulsive disorder are _____

_____

_____

_____

After you have carefully studied the preceding sections, complete the following exercises.

Concept Check 1

Read the following and write the correct term in the space provided.

1. Dr. Janz is a psychiatrist who assesses and treats patients in a mental institution. Dr. Sloane is a clinical psychologist who works with a similar population of patients in a mental health clinic. Dr. Janz is likely to describe his patients as suffering from _____ disorders, whereas Dr. Sloane is more likely to use the term _____ disorder when referring to his patients' problems.

2. Seventeen-year-old Brad has a shaved head, and he has rings in his nose, ears, and navel. Shortly after purchasing a new pair of jeans, he cut and tore horizontal slits across the thigh and knee areas of each leg. In our present culture, Brad would be classified as

_____ .

3. Mr. and Mrs. Jefferson want to hire a new housekeeper. Mr. Jefferson suggests that the best person would be someone who has an excessive dislike and fear of dirt, germs, and insects and who deals with anxiety about contamination by using a very thorough cleaning, washing, and disinfecting routine. Mrs. Jefferson thinks that any person fitting that description might have a problem called _____ disorder.

4. Mr. Alviro suffers from intense anxiety most of the time. He is nervous and worried and is overly concerned about a wide range of life circumstances with little or no justification. Mr. Alviro probably suffers from _____ disorder.

5. Maurice is very quiet and introverted. He is painfully shy in the presence of other people and has dropped many courses at college sim-ply because they involved oral presentations. He can't get a job because he is intensely afraid and anxious about being interviewed. Maurice would probably be classified as having

_____ .

6. Mr. Ng frequently recalls the horrors he and his family experienced in his native Cambodia. He suffers from sleep disturbances and is often awakened by terrifying nightmares. Mr. Ng is experiencing _____ disorder.

7. Ever since the sudden death of her husband, Mrs. Baxter has experienced a number of terrifying and unexpected episodes in which her heart suddenly starts to pound hard for no apparent reason; she typically feels a choking sensation, has trouble breathing, and starts to sweat and tremble. Mrs. Baxter is probably experiencing _____ .

Graphic Organizer 1

List the main symptoms of each of the following anxiety disorders:

Generalized Anxiety Disorder	Panic Disorder	Phobias

Posttraumatic Stress Disorder	Obsessive-Compulsive Disorder

Review of Terms and Concepts 1

Use the terms in this list to complete the Matching Test, then to help you answer the True/False items correctly.

psychopathology
psychological disorder
  (mental disorder)
DSM-IV-TR
anxiety
anxiety disorders
generalized anxiety
  disorder (GAD)
panic attack
panic disorder
phobia

specific phobia
agoraphobia
social phobia
  (social anxiety
  disorder)
posttraumatic stress
  disorder (PTSD)
obsessive-compulsive
  disorder (OCD)
obsessions
compulsions

Matching Exercise

Match the appropriate term with its definition or description.

1. _____ The scientific study of the origins, symptoms, and development of psychological disorders.

2. _____ Abbreviation for the *Diagnostic and Statistical Manual of Mental Disorders*, Fourth Edition, Text Revision, the book published by the American Psychiatric Association that describes the specific symptoms and diagnostic guidelines for different psychological disorders.

3. _____ Anxiety disorder in which the symptoms of anxiety are triggered by intrusive, repetitive thoughts and urges to perform certain actions.

4. _____ Unpleasant emotional state characterized by physical arousal and feelings of tension, apprehension, and worry.

5. _____ Irrational fear triggered by a specific object or situation.

6. _____ Anxiety disorder in which chronic and persistent symptoms of anxiety develop in response to an extreme physical or psychological trauma.

7. _____ Anxiety disorder involving the extreme and irrational fear of experiencing a panic attack in a public situation and being unable to escape or get help.

8. _____ Anxiety disorder characterized by an extreme or irrational fear of a specific object or situation that interferes with the ability to function in daily life.

True/False Test

Indicate whether each statement is true or false by placing T or F in the blank space next to each item.

1. ____ Compulsions refer to repeated, intrusive, and uncontrollable irrational thoughts or mental images that cause extreme anxiety and distress.

2. ____ A psychological (or mental) disorder is a pattern of behavioral and psychological symptoms that cause significant personal distress, impair the ability to function in one or more important areas of daily life, or both.

3. ____ Generalized anxiety disorder (GAD) is characterized by excessive, global, and persistent symptoms of anxiety; also called free-floating anxiety.

4. ____ Panic disorder is an anxiety disorder in which the person experiences frequent and unexpected panic attacks.

5. ____ Obsessions refer to repetitive behaviors or mental acts that are performed to prevent or reduce anxiety.

6. ____ Social phobia (social anxiety disorder) is an anxiety disorder involving the extreme and irrational fear of being embarrassed, judged, or scrutinized by others in social situations.

7. ____ Anxiety disorders are a category of psychological disorders in which extreme anxiety is the main diagnostic feature and causes significant disruptions in the person's cognitive, behavioral, and interpersonal functioning.

8. ____ A panic attack is a sudden episode of extreme anxiety that rapidly escalates in intensity.

Check your answers and review any areas of weakness before going on to the next section.

Mood Disorders: Emotions Gone Awry

Preview Questions

Consider the following questions as you study this section of the chapter.

- What are mood disorders?
- What characterizes major depression, and what is dysthymic disorder?
- What is seasonal affective disorder (SAD)?

- How is bipolar disorder defined?
- What characterizes a manic episode, and what is cyclothymic disorder?
- How prevalent is bipolar disorder, and what factors contribute to mood disorders?

*Read the section "Mood Disorders: Emotions Gone Awry" and **write** your answers to the following:*

1. Mood disorders are _____
   _____
   _____

2. Major depression is characterized by _____
   _____
   _____

3. Dysthymic disorder is _____
   _____
   _____

4. Seasonal affective disorder is a mood disorder in which _____
   _____

5. Bipolar disorder is defined as _____
   _____
   _____

6. A manic episode is a_____
   _____
   _____

7. Cyclothymic disorder is a mood disorder characterized by_____
   _____

8. Multiple factors appear to be involved in the development of mood disorders. These include
   _____
   _____
   _____

Personality Disorders: Maladaptive Traits

Preview Questions

Consider the following questions as you study this section of the chapter.

- What are the main characteristics of personality disorder, and how are personality disorders grouped into categories?

- What characterizes the behavior of someone with an antisocial, paranoid, or borderline personality disorder?

*Read the section "Personality Disorders: Maladaptive Traits" and **write** your answers to the following:*

1. Personality disorder is defined as _____
   _____
   _____

   The basic clusters that the ten personality disorders are grouped into are _____
   _____
   _____

2. The paranoid personality disorder is characterized by _____
   _____
   _____

3. The antisocial personality disorder is characterized by _____
   _____
   _____

4. Borderline personality disorder is characterized by_____
   _____
   _____

The Dissociative Disorders: Fragmentation of the Self

Preview Questions

Consider the following questions as you study this section of the chapter.

- How is a dissociative experience defined, and what are dissociative disorders?
- What are dissociative amnesia and dissociative fugue?
- What is dissociative identity disorder (DID), and what is thought to cause it?

*Read the section "The Dissociative Disorders: Fragmentation of the Self" and **write** your answers to the following:*

1. The dissociative experience is _____
   _____
   _____

2. Dissociative disorders are _____

   _____

3. Dissociative amnesia is a disorder involving

   _____

   Dissociative fugue is _____

   _____

4. Dissociative identity disorder (DID) involves

   _____

   _____

5. According to one theory, DID is caused by _____

   _____

   _____

After you have carefully studied the preceding sections, complete the following exercises.

Concept Check 2

Read the following and write the correct term in the space provided.

1. Ursula is generally happy about her move to northern Canada six years ago, but at regular intervals since then she has suffered episodes of depression during the fall and winter months. Ursula is probably suffering from _____ disorder.

2. Laura suffers from a mood disorder. Her therapist has taken a family history and found that Laura's mother and two sisters also suffer from the same problem. Although her therapist is aware that multiple factors may be involved in her problem, he is most likely to conclude that Laura may have a(n) _____ predisposition for the disorder.

3. Dr. Markoff has prescribed lithium for Sandro's mood disorder. It is most likely that Sandro suffers from _____ disorder.

4. Nedzad has a chronic disorder involving moderate but frequent mood swings that are not severe enough to qualify as bipolar disorder or major depression. He is perceived as being very moody, unpredictable, and inconsistent; taken together, these symptoms may indicate _____ disorder.

5. Marion Einer, a fifth-grade schoolteacher in Jersey City, disappeared a few days after her husband left her. One year later, she was discovered working as a waitress in a cocktail lounge in San Diego. Calling herself Faye Bartell, she claimed to have no recollection of her past life and insisted that she had never been married. This example illustrates

   _____ .

6. When Vanessa goes to a movie, she tends to become totally absorbed in the plot and loses all track of time and place; she is also often momentarily disoriented when she leaves the theater. These episodes represent

   _____ .

7. Karlson recently survived an airplane crash. Although he escaped from the burning plane with very few injuries, three of his friends were killed in the crash. Karlson is unable to recall any details from the time of the accident until a week later. Karlson has experienced

   _____ .

8. Dr. Rendell studies people who typically disregard and violate the rights of others and who appear to have no remorse or conscience about their destructive behaviors. Her colleague Dr. Gideon studies people who have a personality disorder characterized by instability of interpersonal relationships, self-image, and emotions and marked impulsivity. Dr. Rendell studies _____ personality disorder, and Dr. Gideon studies _____ personality disorder.

9. Without any valid evidence or logical reason, Bruce has an all-consuming distrust and suspiciousness of his coworkers, supervisors, friends, and family members. He is constantly on guard because he thinks other people are out to harm, exploit, or trick him. Bruce is displaying symptoms of _____ disorder.

Graphic Organizer 2

List the main symptoms of the mood disorders:

Major Depression	Bipolar Disorder
1.	1.
2.	2.
3.	3.
4.	
5.	
6.	
Dysthymic Disorder	**Cyclothymic Disorder**
1.	1.

Review of Terms and Concepts 2

Use the terms in this list to complete the Matching Test, then to help you answer the True/False items correctly.

mood disorders
major depression
dysthymic disorder
seasonal affective
   disorder (SAD)
bipolar disorder
manic episode
cyclothymic disorder
personality disorder
antisocial personality
   disorder (psychopath
   or sociopath)
borderline personality
   disorder

dissociative experience
dissociative disorders
dissociative amnesia
dissociative fugue
dissociative identity
   disorder (DID)
paranoid personality
   disorder
spirit possession
trance state
glossolalia

Matching Exercise

Match the appropriate term with its definition or description.

1. _____ Personality disorder characterized by a pervasive pattern of disregarding and violating the rights of others; such individuals are also referred to as psychopaths or sociopaths.

2. _____ Once called manic depression, this mood disorder involves periods of incapacitating depression alternating with periods of extreme euphoria and excitement.

3. _____ Mood disorder in which episodes of depression typically recur during fall and winter and disappear during spring and summer.

4. _____ Mood disorder characterized by extreme and persistent feelings of despondency, worthlessness, and hopelessness, causing impaired emotional, cognitive, behavioral, and physical functioning.

5. _____ Sudden, rapidly escalating emotional state characterized by extreme euphoria, excitement, physical energy, and rapid thoughts and speech.

6. _____ Break or disruption in consciousness during which awareness, memory, and personal identity become separated or divided.

7. _____ Inflexible, maladaptive patterns of thoughts, emotions, behavior, and interpersonal functioning that are stable over time and across situations; they deviate from the expectations of the individual's culture.

8. _____ Nonpathological dissociative experience, usually within a religious context, in which the occupant of the person's body is supposedly displaced by a "spirit" that takes control of the body, and the person often has no memory of the experience.

9. _____ A dissociative disorder involving extensive memory disruptions along with the presence of two or more distinct identities, or "personalities"; *formerly called multiple personality disorder*.

10. _____ A dissociative state that occurs in some cultures in which a person enters an altered state of consciousness and loses his sense of personal identity or is unaware of his surroundings.

True/False Test

Indicate whether each statement is true or false by placing T or F in the blank space next to each item.

1. _____ Mood disorders are a category of mental disorders in which significant and chronic disruption in mood is the predominant symptom, causing impaired cognitive, behavioral, and physical functioning.

2. ___ Dissociative fugue involves the partial or total inability to recall important personal information but does not involve sudden, unexpected travel from home.

3. ___ Dissociative amnesia involves sudden and unexpected travel away from home, extensive amnesia, and identity confusion.

4. ___ Cyclothymic disorder involves chronic, low-grade feelings of depression that produce subjective discomfort but do not seriously impair the ability to function and are not severe enough to qualify as major depression.

5. ___ Dissociative disorders are a category of psychological disorders in which extreme and frequent disruptions of awareness, memory, and personal identity impair the ability to function.

6. ___ Borderline personality disorder is characterized by instability of interpersonal relationships, self-image, and emotions, as well as by marked impulsivity.

7. ___ Dysthymic disorder is a milder but chronic form of bipolar disorder in which the person experiences moderate but frequent mood swings.

8. ___ Paranoid personality disorder is characterized by a pervasive distrust and suspiciousness of the motives of others without sufficient basis.

9. ___ Glossolalia, or speaking in tongues, is common in some North American Christian churches; it is a dissociative state in which the person is said to be temporarily possessed by the Holy Spirit who speaks through the individual in an unknown language.

Check your answers and review any areas of weakness before going on to the next section.

Schizophrenia: A Different Reality

Preview Questions

Consider the following questions as you study this section of the chapter.

- How is schizophrenia characterized?
- How do positive and negative symptoms differ?
- What are the main subtypes of schizophrenia?
- What evidence points to the involvement of genetic factors and brain abnormalities in the development of schizophrenia?
- How do environmental factors affect the development of schizophrenia?

*Read the section "Schizophrenia: A Different Reality"
and **write** your answers to the following:*

1. Schizophrenia is a psychological disorder that
   involves _____

   _____

2. Positive symptoms include _____

   _____

   _____

   _____

   Negative symptoms reflect _____

   _____

   _____

3. The four subtypes of schizophrenia are

   (a) _____

   _____

   (b) _____

   _____

   (c) _____

   _____

   (d) _____

   _____

4. Evidence that genetic factors are involved in
   the development of schizophrenia comes from

   _____

5. Research on parental age and the risk of schizophrenia indicates that _____

   _____

   _____

   _____

6. The idea that schizophrenia is the result of
   abnormal brain chemistry is supported largely
   by two pieces of indirect evidence:

   (a) _____

   _____

   (b) _____

   _____

7. Environmental and psychological factors implicated in the development of schizophrenia
   include _____

   _____

   _____

   _____

   _____

   _____

   _____

*After you have carefully studied the preceding
section, complete the following exercises.*

Concept Check 3

*Read the following and write the correct term in the
space provided.*

1. Franko and Alberto are identical twins. Franko
   has developed schizophrenia. The probability
   that Alberto will also develop schizophrenia is
   about _____ percent.

2. Dr. Hansen is conducting research on the viral
   infection theory. He is likely to find that people
   born in the winter and spring months, when
   upper respiratory infections are most common,
   are _____ (more/less) likely to suffer from schizophrenia than those born at other
   times of the year.

3. Derrick hears voices that tell him to be careful
   because he is being watched by aliens. Kirk
   believes that he is a famous rock star. Derrick
   suffers from _____ , and Kirk suffers from _____ .

4. Quincy falsely believes that others are plotting
   against him and are trying to kill him. He
   believes that these agents are putting poison in
   the hospital's coffee supply and will attack him
   if he ever tries to leave the ward. This example
   illustrates a positive symptom of schizophrenia
   called _____ .

5. Neuroscientists researching changes in the brain structures of normal adolescents and adolescents with schizophrenia took high-resolution brain scans of the participants over a five-year period. Normal teens showed about 1 percent loss of gray matter, while teens with schizophrenia lost more than 5 percent; the amount of loss was directly correlated with clinical symptoms of schizophrenia. More rapid gray matter losses in the temporal lobe were associated with _____ (positive/negative) symptoms; more rapid losses in the frontal lobes were associated with _____ (positive/negative) symptoms.

6. Mrs. Perez usually sits passively in a motionless stupor, but if the nurse moves her arms to a new position, she will stay in that position for a very long time. This symptom of catatonic schizophrenia is called _____ .

7. When Darcy was examined by his psychologist, she noted that he displayed some combination of positive and negative symptoms that did not clearly fit the criteria for _____ , _____ , or _____ types of schizophrenia, so she diagnosed him as having an undifferentiated type of schizophrenia.

Graphic Organizer 3

Write the main positive and negative symptoms of schizophrenia in the spaces provided.

Positive Symptoms	Negative Symptoms
1.	1.
2.	2.
3.	3.

Review of Terms and Concepts 3

Use the terms in this list to complete the Matching Test, then to help you answer the True/False items correctly.

schizophrenia
positive symptoms
negative symptoms
delusion
delusions of reference
delusions of grandeur
delusions of persecution
hallucination
flat affect
alogia (poverty of speech)
avolition

paranoid type of schizophrenia
catatonic type of schizophrenia
waxy flexibility
disorganized type of schizophrenia (hebephrenic schizophrenia)
undifferentiated type of schizophrenia
dopamine hypothesis

Matching Exercise

Match the appropriate term with its definition or description.

1. _____ View that schizophrenia is related to, and may be caused by, excess activity of the neurotransmitter dopamine in the brain.

2. _____ Mental disorder in which the ability to function is impaired by severely distorted beliefs, perceptions, and thought processes.

3. _____ Subtype of schizophrenia that is characterized by the presence of delusions, hallucinations, or both; the person shows virtually no cognitive impairment, disorganized behavior, or negative symptoms; instead, well-organized delusions of persecution or grandeur are operating, and auditory hallucinations are often evident.

4. _____ Unusual symptom of catatonic schizophrenia in which the person can be molded into any position and will hold that position indefinitely.

5. _____ Commonly seen negative symptom of schizophrenia in which an individual consistently shows a dramatic reduction in emotional responsiveness and a lack of normal facial expression; few expressive gestures are made, and the person's speech is slow and monotonous, lacking normal vocal inflections.

6. _____ Falsely held belief that persists despite contradictory evidence.

7. _____ Delusion in which the person believes that other people are constantly talking about her or that everything that happens is somehow related to her.

8. _____ False or distorted perception that seems vividly real to the person experiencing it.

9. _____ Subtype of schizophrenia in which an individual displays some combination of positive and negative symptoms that does not clearly fit the criteria for the paranoid, catatonic, or disorganized type.

True/False Test

Indicate whether each item is true or false by placing T or F in the space next to each item.

1. ____ In schizophrenia, positive symptoms reflect defects or deficits in normal functioning and include flat affect, alogia, and avolition.

2. ____ Avolition refers to the inability to initiate or persist in even simple forms of goal-directed behaviors, such as dressing, bathing, or engaging in social activities.

3. ____ The catatonic type of schizophrenia is marked by highly disturbed movements or actions and may include bizarre postures or grimaces, waxy flexibility, extremely agitated behavior, complete immobility, echoing words spoken by others, and assuming rigid postures that resist being moved.

4. ____ Alogia, which is also referred to as poverty of speech, is used to describe the symptom in which speech production is greatly reduced.

5. ____ The basic theme of delusions of grandeur is that the person is extremely important, powerful, or wealthy.

6. ____ In schizophrenia, negative symptoms reflect excesses or distortions of normal functioning and include delusions, hallucinations, and disorganized thoughts and behaviors.

7. ____ In delusions of persecution, the person believes that others are plotting against him or trying to harm him or someone close to him.

8. ____ The prominent features of the disorganized type of schizophrenia are extremely disorganized behavior, disorganized speech, and flat affect; this subtype is sometimes called hebephrenic schizophrenia.

Check your answers and review any areas of weakness before going on to the next section.

Something to Think About

1. One of the most common misconceptions about mental, or psychological, disorders is that schizophrenia and dissociative identity disorder are the same thing. This myth is fostered by inaccurate portrayals and misinformation in the media. What are the important distinctions between these two disorders, and what would you say to someone who thought they were the same thing?

2. Most people are curious about mental, or psychological, disorders. Students frequently recognize aspects of themselves in the descriptions they read and wonder if they could one day suffer from some form of psychological disorder. What is normal, and what is abnormal? What are the chances of developing symptoms of psychopathology, and what causes such disorders? How would you answer these questions?

3. Suppose a friend says that he read somewhere that cigarette smoking causes psychological disorders. Based on what you know from reading the text, how would you respond to this claim?

Check your answers and review any areas of weakness before completing the progress tests.

Progress Test 1

Review the complete chapter (including Concept Reviews and the boxed inserts), review all your study notes, and then test yourself on the following progress test. Check your answers. If you make a mistake, review your notes, review the relevant section of the study guide, and, if necessary, go back and read the appropriate part of your textbook.

1. Phoebe believes that she is the president of the United States and thinks that her indecipherable scribblings are actually top secret memos. Phoebe is most clearly suffering from a(n)

   (a) delusion.
   (b) panic attack.
   (c) hallucination.
   (d) obsession.

2. Shayna has very erratic, unstable relationships, emotions, and self-image. She is extremely impulsive and goes to great lengths to avoid real or imagined abandonment. It is most probable that Shayna has a disorder called

   (a) agoraphobia.
   (b) borderline personality disorder.
   (c) antisocial personality disorder.
   (d) cyclothymic disorder.

3. Dr. Koopman deals with people who suffer from a variety of problems that cause them significant personal distress and impair their ability to function in one or more important areas of their lives. Like most people in his profession, Dr. Koopman uses the term *mental disorder* to describe these symptoms. Dr. Koopman is most likely a

   (a) clinical psychologist.
   (b) psychiatrist.
   (c) social psychologist.
   (d) developmental psychologist.

4. Kaila often appears nervous and agitated. She frequently talks in a loud voice and giggles at almost everything she hears. Her behavior is most likely to be diagnosed as a psychological disorder if it

   (a) is not caused by some biological dysfunction.
   (b) is the result of a genetic predisposition.
   (c) represents a significant departure from the prevailing social and cultural norms.
   (d) is caused by drugs or medication.

5. Sidney, a college student, complains that he feels nervous and fearful most of the time but doesn't know why. He worries constantly about everything in his life, and if he manages to deal with one problem, he starts worrying about a dozen more things. Sidney most likely suffers from _____ disorder.

   (a) generalized anxiety   (c) dissociative
   (b) bipolar   (d) cyclothymic

6. Imogene, a third-grade teacher, sometimes experiences a pounding heart, rapid breathing, breathlessness, and a choking sensation. She breaks out in a sweat, starts to tremble, and experiences light-headedness and chills. These symptoms last for about ten minutes and are characteristic of

   (a) posttraumatic stress disorder (PTSD).
   (b) dysthymic disorder.
   (c) cyclothymic disorder.
   (d) panic attack.

7. Paula has been diagnosed with agoraphobia. Her symptoms include which of the following?

   (a) an extreme and irrational fear of experiencing a panic attack in a public place and being unable to escape or get help
   (b) a sudden, rapidly escalating emotional state characterized by extreme euphoria, excitement, physical energy, and rapid thoughts and speech
   (c) partial or total inability to recall important personal information
   (d) all of the above

8. Jaime brushes her teeth 12 times every day. Each time, she uses exactly 35 strokes up and 35 strokes down and three different brands of toothpaste. Jaime suffers from a(n) _____ disorder.

   (a) obsessive-compulsive
   (b) panic
   (c) cyclothymic
   (d) bipolar

9. Kevin was working in a building when an explosion occurred; although he escaped with relatively minor injuries, he can't stop thinking about all the dead and seriously injured people he saw. He has frequent nightmares about the event and feels guilty that he survived when many of his coworkers did not. Kevin's symptoms are indicative of
   (a) dissociative fugue.
   (b) dysthymic disorder.
   (c) cyclothymic disorder.
   (d) posttraumatic stress disorder (PTSD).

10. Mrs. Landon has been diagnosed as suffering from major depression. Which of the following symptoms is she most likely to be experiencing?
    (a) feelings of guilt, worthlessness, inadequacy, emptiness, and hopelessness
    (b) awkward and slower than usual speech, movement, and gestures and frequent crying spells for no apparent reason
    (c) dull and sluggish thought processes and problems concentrating
    (d) loss of physical energy and vague aches and pains
    (e) all of the above

11. Karla suffers from a chronic, low-grade depression characterized by many of the symptoms of major depression but less intense; these problems started many years ago when both her parents were killed in a car accident. Karla is likely to be diagnosed as suffering from
    (a) dysthymic disorder.
    (b) agoraphobia.
    (c) cyclothymic disorder.
    (d) dissociative amnesia.

12. After living in Anchorage for a number of years, Juanitta was diagnosed with seasonal affective disorder (SAD). Episodes of depression are most likely to occur
    (a) when she travels south to visit her family in Florida.
    (b) during the fall and winter months.
    (c) during the day but not at night.
    (d) during the spring and summer months.

13. According to the Application, the best way to help prevent someone from committing suicide is to
    (a) use some well-known platitudes like "every cloud has a silver lining."
    (b) not let the person talk too much about what is bothering him because it will only make him more depressed.
    (c) suggest that seeking professional help would be a total waste of time and money in the present situation.
    (d) ask the person to delay his decision and encourage him to seek professional help.

14. According to Critical Thinking 14.1, which of the following is true?
    (a) People with mental disorders are generally portrayed with great accuracy in the media.
    (b) The statistical risk of violent behavior associated with mental illness is far higher than the risks associated with being young, male, or poorly educated.
    (c) The incidence of violent behavior among current or former mental patients is grossly exaggerated in media portrayals.
    (d) The statistical risk of violent behavior is greater among people with catatonic schizophrenia than among those with any other mental disorder.

15. According to Critical Thinking 14.2, which of the following is true?
    (a) Smoking cigarettes is a major cause of mental illness and psychological disorders.
    (b) Mental illness is a major cause of cigarette smoking behavior in both adolescents and adults.
    (c) Although there is a positive correlation between cigarette smoking and the prevalence of mental illness, the exact causal connection has not been clearly established.
    (d) One of the main active ingredients in cigarettes, nicotine, has no known psychoactive properties, nor does it have any effect on brain structures or on the release of various neurotransmitters.

Progress Test 2

After you have checked your understanding of the material in Progress Test 1 and have done a complete chapter review with special focus on any areas of weakness, you are ready to assess your knowledge on Progress Test 2. Check your answers. If you make a mistake, review your notes, the relevant section of the study guide, and, if necessary, the appropriate part of your textbook.

1. Dr. Moretti believes that schizophrenia is the result of abnormal brain chemistry. Her views are consistent with the
   (a) viral infection theory.
   (b) dopamine hypothesis.
   (c) genetic predisposition theory.
   (d) cognitive-behavioral theory.

2. Psychiatrists, psychologists, and other mental health professionals are likely to refer to _____ to determine the criteria for diagnosing a patient.
   (a) pop psychology books
   (b) standard medical textbooks
   (c) DSM-IV-TR
   (d) astrology charts

3. Dr. Crewe believes that people with panic disorder tend to misinterpret the physical signs of arousal as catastrophic and dangerous, and this misinterpretation only adds to the problem by causing even more physiological arousal. Eventually, they become conditioned to respond with fear to the physical symptoms of arousal, and repeated panic attacks lead to panic disorder. Dr. Crewe's explanation is most consistent with the _____ of panic disorder.
   (a) social-cultural explanation
   (b) biological theory
   (c) cognitive-behavioral theory
   (d) genetic predisposition explanation

4. Nima suffers from a type of schizophrenia that is characterized by hallucinations and delusions of grandeur, but she shows virtually no cognitive impairment, disorganized behavior, or negative symptoms. Nima suffers from _____ -type schizophrenia.
   (a) paranoid   (c) disorganized
   (b) catatonic   (d) undifferentiated

5. Tara, a young married woman, has wandered from her home to a distant city where she has completely forgotten her family and her identity. This example illustrates
   (a) undifferentiated-type schizophrenia.
   (b) dissociative fugue.
   (c) disorganized-type schizophrenia.
   (d) dissociative amnesia.

6. Maury repeatedly checks to see if the stove is turned off and frequently turns around on his way to work to go back home to double check. This is an example of a(n)
   (a) delusion.   (c) hallucination.
   (b) obsession.   (d) compulsion.

7. Otis turned down a very high-paying job because it meant he would have to fly to the head office in Tokyo two or three times a year. He doesn't know why, but the thought of flying absolutely terrifies him. Otis may have
   (a) undifferentiated-type schizophrenia.
   (b) a phobia.
   (c) bipolar disorder.
   (d) posttraumatic stress disorder (PTSD).

8. Every semester just before midterm exams, Lilly gets very anxious and worries about how she is going to do. To reduce her apprehension, she studies very hard. Lilly suffers from
   (a) anxiety disorder.
   (b) free-floating disorder.
   (c) panic disorder.
   (d) obsessive-compulsive disorder (OCD).
   (e) none of the above; her symptoms are quite normal.

9. Jessica rarely leaves her home. She doesn't go shopping because she is frightened of having a panic attack and getting lost or trapped in a crowd. Jessica has symptoms that indicate she may have
   (a) agoraphobia.
   (b) cyclothymic disorder.
   (c) posttraumatic stress disorder (PTSD).
   (d) seasonal affective disorder (SAD).

10. Yvette usually stands motionless and will echo words just spoken to her. She resists directions from others and sometimes assumes a rigid posture to prevent people from moving her. These symptoms suggest that Yvette has a type of _____ called _____ type.
    - (a) schizophrenia; catatonic
    - (b) mood disorder; cyclothymic
    - (c) schizophrenia; disorganized
    - (d) mood disorder; dysthymic

11. Brandy's doctor prescribed lithium for her symptoms; as long as she keeps taking the medication, she feels fine. It is very likely that Brandy suffers from
    - (a) schizophrenia.
    - (b) generalized anxiety disorder (GAD).
    - (c) bipolar disorder.
    - (d) dissociative identity disorder (DID).

12. Regardless of the situation, Philip responds in an emotionally flat manner and consistently shows greatly reduced lack of emotional responsiveness or facial expression. His speech is slow and monotonous, and he is unable to initiate even simple forms of goal-directed behavior, such as dressing, bathing, or engaging in social activities. Philip is suffering from _____ , and his symptoms are _____ .
    - (a) schizophrenia; positive
    - (b) anxiety disorder; positive
    - (c) schizophrenia; negative
    - (d) anxiety disorder; negative

13. Perry has dropped out of college because of the extreme distress that being in social situations causes him. He is unemployed because he is unable to bring himself to partake in an interview. Perry has
    - (a) disorganized-type schizophrenia.
    - (b) a dissociative disorder.
    - (c) a generalized anxiety disorder (GAD).
    - (d) social phobia (social anxiety disorder).

14. Within the last two years, John has been fired from four different jobs for stealing money and goods from his employers. He feels no remorse and thinks his bosses were stupid for making it so easy to steal from them. John has a long history of problems with the law, which started in his early teens when he was diagnosed as having a conduct disorder. It is most likely that John has
    - (a) an antisocial personality disorder.
    - (b) an obsessive-compulsive disorder (OCD).
    - (c) paranoid-type schizophrenia.
    - (d) dissociative identity disorder (DID).

15. According to Culture and Human Behavior 14.4, which of the following is true?
    - (a) The content of schizophrenic hallucinations and delusions is virtually identical across cultures.
    - (b) People who suffer from the Jerusalem or Florence syndrome are typically people who have a long history of dissociative identity disorder (DID).
    - (c) The content of schizophrenic hallucinations and delusions can vary from one culture to another and may be influenced by a particular culture's religious beliefs.
    - (d) The Jerusalem and Florence syndromes are personality disorders caused by inherited genetic factors.

Progress Test 3

After you have checked your understanding of the material in Progress Tests 1 and 2, and have done a complete chapter review with special focus on any areas of weakness, you are ready to further assess your knowledge on Progress Test 3. Check your answers. If you make a mistake, review your notes, the appropriate parts of the study guide, and, if necessary, the relevant sections of your textbook.

1. Wendell repeatedly steals small items that he doesn't need and could easily pay for if he wanted to. Harman frequently sets fire to property for no obvious reason other than the pleasure he derives from seeing buildings on fire. According to Table 14.1, Some Key Diagnostic Categories in DSM IV-TR, Wendell suffers from _____ and Harman has a disorder called _____ .
    - (a) kleptomania; pyromania
    - (b) Tourette's disorder; hypochondriasis
    - (c) autistic disorder; fetishism
    - (d) agoraphobia; pyrophobia

2. Fear of having a panic attack in a public situation is to _____ as an extreme and irrational fear of being embarrassed, judged, or scrutinized by others in social situations is to
_____ .

   (a) social phobia (social anxiety disorder); agoraphobia
   (b) bibliophobia; phonophobia
   (c) agoraphobia; social phobia
   (d) phobophobia; ergophobia

3. Shayne suffers from posttraumatic stress disorder (PTSD). If he is similar to most people who have this disorder, he is likely to exhibit which of the following symptoms?

   (a) frequent, intrusive recollections of a traumatic event, numbing of emotional responsiveness, and avoidance of particular situations
   (b) recurrent episodes of unintended sleep in inappropriate situations, such as during a meeting or while driving a car
   (c) repetitive behaviors or mental acts that are performed to prevent or reduce anxiety
   (d) the urge to set fires for pleasure, gratification, or relief of tension
   (e) all of the above

4. Mandy is a 45-year-old administrative assistant. Based on the National Comorbidity Survey (NCS), the chance that Mandy may have experienced the symptoms of a psychological disorder at some point in her life is about _____ percent.

   (a) 10   (c) 80
   (b) 50   (d) 100

5. Dr. Burstein explains the development of phobias in terms of basic learning principles. Which of the following are likely to be included in his explanation?

   (a) classical conditioning
   (b) operant conditioning
   (c) observational learning
   (d) All of the above may be involved in his explanation.

6. After several weeks of feeling very apathetic and dissatisfied with his life, Elmiro has suddenly become extremely euphoric and full of energy. He talks so rapidly that he is hard to understand, sleeps very little, and has gone on a number of very expensive shopping sprees. He gets very irritated when anyone tells him to take it easy and slow down. Elmiro is exhibiting all the signs of

   (a) obsessive-compulsive disorder (OCD).
   (b) catatonic schizophrenia.
   (c) dissociative identity disorder (DID).
   (d) bipolar disorder.

7. Lucille suffers from dissociative identity disorder (DID). If she is like most people diagnosed with this disorder, she is likely to have experienced

   (a) extreme physical or sexual abuse in childhood.
   (b) episodes when she believed she was the reincarnation of some famous and powerful person.
   (c) exposure to a viral infection during prenatal development or early infancy.
   (d) excess dopamine in her brain during childhood.
   (e) all of the above.

8. During a religious ceremony in his local church, Billy Joe suddenly starts speaking very rapidly in what seem to be a number of different languages, and he appears to be in a trancelike state. This form of dissociative experience is called _____ and is classified in DSM-IV-TR as _____ .

   (a) fugue state; pathological
   (b) glossolalia; normal
   (c) fugue state; normal
   (d) glossolalia; pathological

9. Personality disorders are grouped into a number of clusters. The odd, eccentric cluster is to _____ personality disorder, as the dramatic, emotional, erratic cluster is to _____ personality disorder.

   (a) paranoid; antisocial
   (b) borderline; avoidant
   (c) histrionic; obsessive-compulsive
   (d) antisocial; borderline

10. Vera has been diagnosed with cyclothymic disorder. Her symptoms are likely to include
    (a) moderate but frequent mood swings for two years or longer.
    (b) chronic low-grade feelings of depression that produce subjective discomfort but do not seriously impair her ability to function.
    (c) partial or total inability to recall important personal information.
    (d) irrational fears of a specific object or situation.
    (e) all of the above.

11. Nester's sense of self-esteem is wildly inflated, and he exudes supreme self-confidence. He has delusional, grandiose plans for obtaining wealth, power, and fame and is engaged in a frenzy of goal-directed activities that could cost thousands of dollars. This is an example of a(n)
    (a) manic episode.
    (b) obsession.
    (c) social phobia (social anxiety disorder).
    (d) hallucination.

12. Deidre suffers from frequent and unexpected panic attacks. Despite her apprehension about these episodes, Deidre functions fairly well in her job and has a relatively normal social life. Deidre is likely to be diagnosed with
    (a) panic disorder.
    (b) social phobia (social anxiety disorder).
    (c) bipolar disorder.
    (d) dissociative fugue.

13. Scott repeatedly thinks that he might get a gun and kill all his colleagues at work. These thoughts are very disturbing, intrusive, and uncontrollable and cause Scott great distress and anxiety. Scott is experiencing a(n)
    (a) delusion.   (c) hallucination.
    (b) obsession.   (d) compulsion.

14. Konrad has experienced numerous psychiatric and physical symptoms and memory loss, and he has a chaotic personal history. During a session with his therapist, Konrad suddenly began speaking in a very childlike voice and claimed that his name was Arnold and that he was only ten years old. A short time later he reverted to his normal adult voice and claimed to have no recollection of the incident. Konrad is likely to be diagnosed as suffering from
    (a) paranoid-type schizophrenia.
    (b) dissociative identity disorder (DID).
    (c) gender identity disorder.

(d) posttraumatic stress disorder.

15. According to Critical Thinking 14.3, which of the following statements about DID is (are) true?
    (a) Much of the skepticism about DID is related to the fact that the number of reported cases has decreased dramatically in the last two decades.
    (b) Some psychologists suggest that DID patients are consciously or unconsciously faking the symptoms, responding to the therapists' suggestions, or mimicking the symptoms of sensational DID cases portrayed in the media.
    (c) Cross-cultural research has shown that the incidence of DID outside the United States is almost zero.
    (d) Most psychologists believe that DID and schizophrenia are identical disorders.
    (e) All of the above are true.

Answers

Introduction: Understanding Psychological Disorders

1. *Psychopathology is* the scientific study of the origins, symptoms, and development of psychological disorders.

2. *A psychological, or mental, disorder can be defined as* a pattern of behavioral and psychological symptoms that causes significant personal distress, impairs the ability to function in one or more important areas of daily life, or both. These symptoms must represent a serious departure from prevailing social and cultural norms.

3. *DSM-IV-TR stands for the Diagnostic and Statistical Manual of Mental Disorders,* Fourth Edition, Text Revision; it was published by the American Psychiatric Association in 2000 and represents the consensus of a wide range of mental health professionals and organizations. *This manual describes* approximately 250 specific psychological disorders (including the symptoms, the exact criteria that must be met to make a diagnosis, and the typical course for each mental disorder) and provides mental health professionals with a common language to label mental disorders and comprehensive guidelines for diagnosing mental disorders.

4. *The National Comorbidity Survey found that psychological disorders were more common than previously thought, which can be interpreted to mean* that many people who could benefit from treatment do not seek it. However, it seems that most of these people seem to weather the symptoms without becoming completely debilitated.

Anxiety Disorders

1. *Anxiety is defined as* an unpleasant emotional state characterized by physical arousal and feelings of tension, apprehension, and worry that often hits during personal crises and everyday conflicts. *It is often adaptive and normal because* it puts you on physical and mental alert and helps you focus attention on the threatening situation.

2. *In the anxiety disorders, the anxiety is* maladaptive, disrupting everyday activities, moods, and thought processes.

3. *The three features that distinguish normal anxiety from pathological anxiety are (a)* Pathological anxiety is irrational (it is provoked by perceived threats that are exaggerated or nonexistent, and the anxiety response is out of proportion to the actual importance of the situation). *(b)* Pathological anxiety is uncontrollable (the person can't shut off the alarm reaction, even when he or she knows it's unrealistic). *(c)* Pathological anxiety is disruptive (it interferes with relationships, job or academic performance, or everyday activity).

4. *Generalized anxiety disorder (GAD) is characterized by* excessive, global, and persistent symptoms of anxiety (also called free-floating anxiety).

5. *A panic attack is* a sudden episode of extreme anxiety that rapidly escalates in intensity; the most common symptoms are a pounding heart, rapid breathing, breathlessness, and a choking sensation, often accompanied by sweating, trembling, light-headedness, chills, or hot flashes.

6. *A panic disorder is* an anxiety disorder in which the person experiences frequent and unexpected panic attacks. *Its cause is thought to be* both biological and psychological. The cognitive-behavioral theory proposes that people with panic disorder interpret physical symptoms as catastrophic.

7. *A phobia is* an intense, irrational fear that is triggered by a specific object or situation (encountering the feared situation or object can provoke a full-fledged panic attack in some people). *A specific phobia is* characterized by an extreme and irrational fear of a specific object or situation that interferes with the ability to function in daily life (e.g., agoraphobia, social phobia, etc.).

8. *Phobias are assumed by some to involve various forms of learning such as* classical conditioning (the feared object is the conditioned stimulus, and the learned fear is the conditioned response, which can generalize to other similar stimuli); operant conditioning, which can also be involved in the avoidance behavior that characterizes phobias (the conditioned response of avoiding the feared object is negatively reinforced by the relief from anxiety and fear that the behavior brings about); observational learning (people can learn to be phobic of certain objects or situations by observing the fearful reactions of someone else who acts as a model in the situation or through seeing media accounts of disasters and catastrophes), and biological preparedness (humans are predisposed through our evolutionary history to acquire fears of certain animals or situations).

Anxiety Disorders: Posttraumatic Stress Disorder and Obsessive-Compulsive Disorder

1. *Posttraumatic stress disorder (PTSD) is* a long-lasting anxiety disorder in which chronic and persistent symptoms of anxiety develop in response to an extreme physical or psychological trauma (extreme traumas are events that produce intense feelings of horror and helplessness, such as a serious physical injury or threat of injury to yourself or to loved ones).

2. *The three core symptoms that characterize PTSD are (a)* The person frequently recalls the event, replaying it in his or her mind (it is often unwanted or intrusive and interferes with normal thought processes). *(b)* The person avoids stimuli or situations that tend to trigger memories of the experience and undergoes a general numbing of emotional responsiveness. *(c)* The person experiences the increased physical arousal associated with anxiety (he or she may be easily startled, experience sleep disturbances, have problems concentrating and remembering, and be prone to irritability or angry outbursts).

3. *Factors that influence the likelihood of developing posttraumatic stress disorder are (a)* People with a personal or family history of psychological disorders are more likely to develop PTSD when exposed to extreme trauma. *(b)* The magnitude of the trauma plays an important role—more extreme stressors are more likely to produce PTSD. *(c)* When people undergo multiple traumas the incidence of PTSD can be quite high.

4. *Obsessive-compulsive disorder (OCD) is* an anxiety disorder in which the symptoms of anxiety are triggered by intrusive, repetitive thoughts and urges to perform certain actions. *Obsessions are* repeated, intrusive, and uncontrollable irrational thoughts or mental images that cause extreme anxiety and distress (they have little basis in reality and are often extremely far-fetched). *Compulsions are* repetitive behaviors that are performed to prevent or reduce anxiety and are typically ritual behaviors (overtly physical or covertly mental) that must be carried out in a certain pattern or sequence.

5. *People with obsessive-compulsive disorder commonly experience* both obsessions and compulsions, which are often linked in some way, even if the behaviors bear little logical relationship to the feared consequences (in all cases, obsessive-compulsives feel that something terrible will happen if the compulsive action is left undone).

6. *Two biological factors that seem to be involved in obsessive-compulsive disorder are* a deficiency in the neurotransmitter serotonin (drugs that increase the availability of serotonin in the brain decrease symptoms), and dysfunctions in specific brain areas, such as the frontal lobes (which play a key role in our ability to think and plan ahead), or the caudate nucleus (which is involved in regulating movements).

Concept Check 1

1. mental; psychological
2. normal
3. obsessive-compulsive
4. generalized anxiety
5. social phobia (social anxiety disorder)
6. posttraumatic stress
7. panic attacks

Graphic Organizer 1

Generalized Anxiety Disorder
Persistent, chronic, unreasonable worry and anxiety, characterized by general symptoms of anxiety, including persistent physical arousal.

Panic Disorder
Frequent and unexpected panic attacks, with no specific or identifiable trigger.

Phobias
Intense anxiety or panic attack triggered by a specific object or situation leads to persistent avoidance of feared object or situation.

Posttraumatic Stress Disorder
Anxiety triggered by memories of an extreme physical or psychological traumatic experience.

Obsessive-Compulsive Disorder
Anxiety caused by uncontrollable, persistent, recurring, and intrusive thoughts (obsessions) and/or urges to perform certain actions (compulsions).

Matching Exercise 1

1. psychopathology
2. DSM-IV-TR
3. obsessive-compulsive disorder (OCD)
4. anxiety
5. phobia
6. posttraumatic stress disorder (PTSD)
7. agoraphobia
8. specific phobia

True/False Test 1

1. F	4. T	7. T
2. T	5. F	8. T
3. T	6. T	

Mood Disorders: Emotions Gone Awry

1. *Mood disorders are* a category of mental disorders in which significant and chronic disruption in mood is the predominant symptom, causing impaired cognitive, behavioral, and physical functioning.

2. *Major depression is characterized by* extreme and persistent feelings of despondency, worthlessness, and hopelessness, causing impaired emotional, cognitive, behavioral, and physical functioning.

3. *Dysthymic disorder* is a mood disorder involving chronic, low-grade feelings of depression

that produce subjective discomfort but do not seriously impair the ability to function.

4. *Seasonal affective disorder is a mood disorder in which* episodes of depression typically recur during the fall and winter and remit during the spring and summer.

5. *Bipolar disorder is defined as* a mood disorder involving periods of incapacitating depression alternating with periods of extreme euphoria and excitement (often called manic-depression).

6. *A manic episode is a* sudden, rapidly escalating emotional state characterized by extreme euphoria, excitement, physical energy, and rapid thoughts and speech.

7. *Cyclothymic disorder is a mood disorder characterized by* moderate but frequent mood swings that are not severe enough to qualify as bipolar disorder or major depression.

8. *Multiple factors appear to be involved in the development of mood disorders. These include* genetic predispositions, stress, and brain chemistry (the neurotransmitters serotonin and norepinephrine have been implicated in depression, and glutamate may be involved in bipolar disorder).

Personality Disorders: Maladaptive Traits

1. *Personality disorder is defined as* inflexible, maladaptive patterns of thought, emotions, behavior, and interpersonal functioning that are stable over time and across situations and that deviate from expectations of the individual's culture. *The basic clusters that the ten personality disorders are grouped into are* the odd, eccentric cluster (paranoid, schizoid, and schizotypal personality disorders); the dramatic, emotional, or erratic cluster (antisocial, borderline, histrionic, and narcissistic personality disorders); and the anxious, fearful cluster (avoidant, dependent, or obsessive-compulsive personality disorders).

2. *The paranoid personality disorder is characterized by* a pervasive distrust and suspiciousness of the motives of others without sufficient basis.

3. *The antisocial personality disorder is characterized by* a pervasive pattern of disregarding and violating the rights of others (such individuals are often referred to as psychopaths or sociopaths).

4. *Borderline personality disorder is characterized by* instability of interpersonal relationships, self-image, and emotions and marked impulsivity.

The Dissociative Disorders: Fragmentation of the Self

1. *The dissociative experience is* a break or disruption in consciousness during which awareness, memory, and personal identity become separated or divided.

2. *Dissociative disorders are* a category of psychological disorders in which extreme and frequent disruptions of awareness, memory, and personal identity impair the ability to function.

3. *Dissociative amnesia is a disorder involving* the partial or total inability to recall important personal information. *Dissociative fugue is* a disorder involving sudden and unexpected travel away from home, extensive amnesia, and identity confusion.

4. *Dissociative identity disorder (DID) involves* extensive memory disruptions along with the presence of two or more distinct identities, or "personalities"; formerly called *multiple personality disorder.*

5. *According to one theory, DID is caused by* trauma in childhood and represents an extreme form of coping through dissociation.

Concept Check 2

1. seasonal affective
2. genetic
3. bipolar
4. cyclothymic
5. dissociative fugue
6. dissociative experiences
7. dissociative amnesia
8. antisocial; borderline
9. paranoid personality

Graphic Organizer 2

Major Depression

1. Loss of interest or pleasure in almost all activities
2. Despondent mood, feelings of emptiness or worthlessness, or excessive guilt
3. Preoccupation with death or suicidal thoughts
4. Difficulty sleeping or excessive sleeping
5. Diminished ability to think, concentrate, or make decisions

6. Diminished appetite and significant weight loss or excessive eating and weight gain

Bipolar Disorder
1. One or more manic episodes characterized by euphoria, high energy, grandiose ideas, flight of ideas, inappropriate self-confidence, and decreased need for sleep
2. Usually also has one or more episodes of major depression
3. May alternate rapidly between symptoms of mania and major depression

Dysthymic Disorder
1. Chronic, low-grade depressed feelings that are not severe enough to qualify as major depression

Cyclothymic Disorder
1. Moderate, recurring, up-and-down mood swings that are not severe enough to qualify as major depression or bipolar disorder

Matching Exercise 2

1. antisocial personality disorder
2. bipolar disorder
3. seasonal affective disorder (SAD)
4. major depression
5. manic episode
6. dissociative experience
7. personality disorders
8. spirit possession
9. dissociative identity disorder (DID)
10. trance state

True/False Test 2

1. T	4. F	7. F
2. F	5. T	8. T
3. F	6. T	9. T

Schizophrenia: A Different Reality

1. *Schizophrenia is a psychological disorder that involves* severely distorted beliefs, perceptions, and thought processes that impair an individual's ability to function.

2. *Positive symptoms include* delusions (false beliefs that persist despite contradictory evidence), hallucinations (false perceptions that seem vividly real to the person experiencing them), and severely disorganized thought processes, speech, and behavior. *Negative symp-toms reflect* a restriction or disruption of normal functions, including flat affect, alogia, and avolition.

3. *The four subtypes of schizophrenia are (a)* paranoid type (presence of delusions, hallucinations, or both, but no cognitive impairment, disorganized behavior, or negative symptoms); *(b)* catatonic type (highly disturbed movements or actions, such as bizarre postures or grimaces, extremely agitated behavior, complete immobility, echoing words spoken by others or imitating their movements); *(c)* disorganized type (extremely disorganized behavior, disorganized speech, flat affect, and sometimes disorganized delusions and hallucinations; formerly called hebephrenic schizophrenia); and *(d)* undifferentiated type (used to describe individuals who display some combination of positive and negative symptoms but who do not fit the criteria for the other three types).

4. *Evidence that genetic factors are involved in the development of schizophrenia comes from* family, twin, and adoption studies, but studies of identical twins demonstrate that nongenetic factors play at least an equal role.

5. *Research on parental age and the risk of schizophrenia indicates that* the risk of schizophrenia is higher in the offspring of older fathers, but older parental age failed to account for the majority (75%) of cases of schizophrenia in these studies.

6. *The idea that schizophrenia is the result of abnormal brain chemistry is supported largely by two pieces of indirect evidence: (a)* Antipsychotic drugs that reduce schizophrenic symptoms in many people reduce or block dopamine activity in the brain. *(b)* Drugs such as amphetamines or cocaine enhance dopamine activity in the brain (use of these drugs can produce schizophrenia-like symptoms in normal adults or increase symptoms in people who already suffer from schizophrenia).

7. *Environmental and psychological factors implicated in the development of schizophrenia include* exposure to a virus during prenatal development and a psychologically unhealthy family environment (adopted children who were genetically at risk were found to be less likely to develop schizophrenia when raised in a psychologically healthy family).

Concept Check 3

1. 50
2. more
3. hallucinations; delusions
4. delusions of persecution
5. positive; negative
6. waxy flexibility
7. paranoid, catatonic; disorganized

Graphic Organizer 3

Positive Symptoms
1. delusions
2. hallucinations
3. disorganized thoughts and behavior

Negative Symptoms
1. flat effect
2. alogia (poverty of speech)
3. avolition

Matching Exercise 3

1. dopamine hypothesis
2. schizophrenia
3. paranoid type of schizophrenia
4. waxy flexibility
5. flat affect (affective flattening)
6. delusion
7. delusions of reference
8. hallucination
9. undifferentiated type of schizophrenia

True/False Test 3

1. F	4. T	7. T
2. T	5. T	8. T
3. T	6. F	

Something to Think About

1. Dissociative identity disorder (DID), formerly called multiple personality disorder, involves extensive memory disruptions for personal information along with the presence of two or more distinct identities or personalities. Typically, each personality has its own name and each will be experienced as if it has its own personal history and self-image. These alternate personalities, or alters, may be of widely varying ages and of different genders. Typically, the primary personality is unaware of the existence of the alternate personalities. However, the alters may have knowledge of each other's existence and share memories. Sometimes the experiences of one alter are accessible to another alter but not vice versa. From this description of the disorder, it is clear that symptoms of amnesia and memory problems are a central part of DID. In addition, people with DID have numerous psychiatric and physical symptoms as well as a chaotic personal history.

    Contrast DID with a description of schizophrenia and the differences between the two disorders become apparent. Schizophrenia is a psychological disorder that involves severely distorted beliefs, perceptions, and thought processes. During a schizophrenic episode, people lose their grip on reality. The positive symptoms of schizophrenia reflect an excess or distortion of normal functioning and include hallucinations, delusions, and severely disorganized thought processes, speech, and behavior. The negative symptoms reflect a restriction or reduction of normal functions and include flat affect, alogia (poverty of speech), and avolition, or the inability to initiate or persist in even simple forms of goal-directed behavior. There are four different subtypes of schizophrenia: paranoid type, catatonic type, disorganized type, and undifferentiated type. In addition, as noted in the text, the prevalence, course, and cause of schizophrenia are markedly different from those of DID.

2. The first thing to note is that the line that divides normal and abnormal behavior is not clearly defined. In addition, it is affected by the social and cultural context in which the behavior occurs. Psychopathology is the scientific study of the origins, symptoms, and development of psychological disorders, and as you learned in this chapter, DSM-IV-TR is the book that describes about 250 specific disorders, including their symptoms, the exact criteria that must be met to make a diagnosis, and the typical course of each psychological disorder. The main categories of psychological disorders are the anxiety disorders, mood disorders, personality disorders, dissociative disorders, and schizophrenia.

    According to the text, the chance that someone will experience symptoms of psychological disorder some time in his or her lifetime is about fifty-fifty. About one in three people will have experienced the symptoms of psychological disorder during the last year. However, about 80 percent of those people will not have sought professional help. The good news is that most people seem to weather the symptoms without becoming completely debilitated and without professional intervention. It is estimated that 3 to 5 percent of people have really serious symptoms that demand immediate treatment, and these people usually have developed several mental disorders over time, not just one disorder that suddenly appears. Women tend to have a higher prevalence of anxiety and depression, whereas men tend to have a higher prevalence of substance abuse disorders.

Nobody knows for sure what causes psychological disorders. There is no shortage of theories, however. Biological and genetic factors have been implicated, as have abnormalities in brain structure and chemical imbalances. Various environmental and social explanations have also been suggested. Research continues, and someday we may be closer to finding the cause or causes of these abnormalities.

3. The first thing to note about the studies on the relationship between cigarette smoking and the incidence of mental illness is that these studies are correlational in nature. Causality (cause-effect relationships) cannot be inferred on the basis of correlations; properly conducted experimental research is required in order to conclude anything about causality. While there is a positive correlation between cigarette smoking and the prevalence of psychological disorders, it is not clear what the causal factors are. Does smoking cigarettes cause mental illness, does being mentally ill cause people to smoke more, or are other unknown causal factors at work here? Correlational research does not answer these questions.

To make the point even more clear consider the following example. Suppose researchers found that there was a positive correlation between the consumption of chicken soup and the incidence of cold and flu symptoms. Obviously, you would not conclude that chicken soup consumption causes flu or cold symptoms or that having a cold or the flu causes people to eat chicken soup. Other variables, such as cultural factors, traditions, beliefs about natural remedies, and so on could be involved.

However, correlational research does allow predictions to be made. For example, you could predict that when the prevalence of cold and flu symptoms diminish, the consumption of chicken soup should also decrease, and vice versa. Likewise, with cigarette smoking and the level of mental illness. You could predict that if the rate of cigarette smoking declined over a period of a decade or two, then the prevalence of mental illness should also decrease. This, however, has not happened. The level of cigarette smoking has decreased quite dramatically over the last couple of decades but the incidence of mental illness in the population has not. This further illustrates the complex nature of the relationship between these two variables. Further research may shed light on these intriguing correlational research findings.

Progress Test 1

1. a	6. d	11. a
2. b	7. a	12. b
3. b	8. a	13. d
4. c	9. d	14. c
5. a	10. e	15. c

Progress Test 2

1. b	6. d	11. c
2. c	7. b	12. c
3. c	8. e	13. d
4. a	9. a	14. a
5. b	10. a	15. c

Progress Test 3

1. a	6. d	11. a
2. c	7. a	12. a
3. a	8. b	13. b
4. b	9. a	14. b
5. d	10. a	15. b

Therapies

CHAPTER 15 . . . AT A GLANCE

Chapter 15 discusses the use of psychotherapies and biomedical therapies to treat psychological disorders. Psychoanalysis, which is based on Freud's theory of personality, is described, including its basic assumptions and the techniques used in the psychoanalytic process. Contemporary short-term dynamic psychotherapies are based on psychoanalytic theory but differ in that they are typically time-limited and have specific goals, and the therapist's role is active rather than neutral. One example discussed is interpersonal therapy (IPT), in which the focus is on current relationships and social interactions rather than on the client's past history.

Client-centered therapy is discussed as the prime example of the humanistic approach to psychotherapy, and the basic assumptions of this form of insight therapy are explored. Behavior therapy is based on learning principles and assumes that maladaptive behaviors are learned. Techniques based on classical conditioning (counterconditioning, systematic desensitization, bell and pad treatment, and aversive therapy) and operant conditioning (positive reinforcement, extinction, and the token economy) are examined. The cognitive therapies (RET and CT), which assume that psychological problems are caused by maladaptive patterns of thinking, are explored next. Cognitive-behavioral therapy (CBT) is based on the premise that thoughts, moods, and behaviors are functionally interrelated, and this approach combines cognitive and behavioral techniques in an integrated but flexible treatment plan.

Group and family therapies are contrasted with individual therapy, and the advantages and benefits of each are examined. The effectiveness of psychotherapy is explored, and it is concluded that, in general, psychotherapy is better than no treatment at all and that no particular form of psychotherapy is superior to any other.

In introducing the biomedical therapies, the text notes that the most common biomedical therapy is psychoactive medication. The discussion includes the nature of these drugs, their effects on the brain, their side effects, and the disorder for which they are prescribed. The main categories of drugs are antipsychotic, atypical antipsychotic, antianxiety, and antidepressant medications. Lithium is prescribed for bipolar disorder. Electroconvulsive therapy (ECT), a different type of biomedical therapy, is used for treating severe depression.

Introduction: Psychotherapy and Biomedical Therapy

Preview Questions

Consider the following questions as you study this section of the chapter.

- How is psychotherapy defined, and what types of problems are treated using psychotherapy?
- What is the basic assumption common to all forms of psychotherapy?
- What is biomedical therapy, and what is its basic assumption?

*Read the section "Introduction: Psychotherapy and Biomedical Therapy" and **write** your answers to the following:*

1. Psychotherapy refers to _____
   _____
   _____

2. A basic assumption of all psychotherapies is that _____
   _____

3. Biomedical therapies involve _____
   _____
   _____

4. The biomedical therapies are based on the assumption that _____
   _____

Psychoanalytic Therapy

Preview Questions

Consider the following questions as you study this section of the chapter.

- What is psychoanalysis, and who developed this form of therapy?
- What techniques are used in psychoanalysis, and what is their purpose?
- What role does insight play in psychoanalytic techniques?
- What are short-term dynamic therapies?
- What is interpersonal therapy (IPT), and what four categories of personal problems does it deal with?

*Read the section "Psychoanalytic Therapy" and **write** your answers to the following:*

1. Psychoanalysis is a _____
   _____
   _____
   _____

2. The main psychoanalytic techniques (and their purpose) are
   (a) _____
   _____
   (b) _____
   _____
   (c) _____
   _____
   (d) _____
   _____
   (e) _____
   _____

3. Together, these psychoanalytic techniques are designed to _____

_____

4. The various forms of short-term dynamic therapies (all based on traditional psychoanalytic notions) have four features in common:

   (a) _____

   _____

   (b) _____

   _____

   (c) _____

   _____

   (d) _____

   _____

5. Interpersonal therapy (IPT) is _____

   _____

   _____

   The four categories of personal problems in the interpersonal therapy model are

   (a) _____

   _____

   (b) _____

   _____

   (c) _____

   _____

   (d) _____

   _____

_____

After you have carefully studied the preceding sections, complete the following exercises.

Concept Check 1

Read the following and write the correct term in the space provided.

1. During a session with her psychoanalyst, Felicity was asked to elaborate on her negative feelings about her husband. She responded by making a few wisecracks about men and then abruptly changed the subject. Her therapist would say she is engaging in

_____ .

2. When Felicity's therapist urges her to report all her spontaneous thoughts, mental images, and feelings, he is using the technique called

_____ .

3. Felicity's therapist offers a carefully timed explanation of her free associations, hoping to facilitate the recognition of her unconscious conflicts or motivations. This technique is called _____ .

4. Although her therapist has remained neutral and nonjudgmental throughout their sessions, Felicity is beginning to express feelings of hostility and anger toward him. This part of the psychoanalytic process is called

_____ .

5. When Felicity describes a dream she had the previous night, her therapist explores the content and analyzes it for disguised or symbolic wishes and motivations. Her therapist is using

_____ .

6. Rabia's therapist uses medication and other medical treatments to deal with the symptoms associated with her psychological disorder. On the other hand, Dean's therapist uses psychological techniques to help him modify his troubling behavior and to encourage him to understand the basis of his emotional problems. This example illustrates the difference between two broad forms of therapy, _____ and _____ .

7. Dr. Keller believes that depressive symptoms and other psychological problems are caused and maintained by interpersonal problems; thus, his therapy focuses on the person's current relations and social interactions rather than on his past history. Dr. Keller practices a type of psychotherapy called

_____ .

Review of Terms, Concepts, and Names 1

Use the terms in this list to complete the Matching Test, then to help you answer the True/False items correctly.

psychotherapy
biomedical therapies
psychoanalysis
Sigmund Freud
insight
free association
resistance
dream interpretation
manifest content
latent content

interpretation
transference
short-term dynamic
   therapies
interpersonal therapy
   (IPT)
unresolved grief
role disputes
role transitions
interpersonal deficits

Matching Exercise

Match the appropriate term/name with its definition or description.

1. _____ Founder of psychoanalysis who theorized that psychological symptoms are the result of unconscious and unresolved conflicts stemming from early childhood.

2. _____ The treatment of emotional, behavioral, and interpersonal problems through the use of psychological techniques designed to encourage understanding of problems and modify troubling feelings, behaviors, or relationships.

3. _____ Psychoanalytic technique in which the psychoanalyst offers a carefully timed explanation of the patient's dreams, free associations, or behavior to facilitate the recognition of unconscious conflicts or motivations.

4. _____ Type of psychotherapy originated by Sigmund Freud in which free association, dream interpretation, and analysis of resistance and transference are used to explore repressed or unconscious impulses, anxieties, and internal conflicts.

5. _____ The use of medications, electroconvulsive therapy, or other medical treatment to treat the symptoms associated with psychological disorders.

6. _____ Psychotherapies that are based on traditional psychoanalytic notions in which therapeutic contact typically lasts for no more than a few months rather than years.

7. _____ In interpersonal therapy, the inability to come to terms with bereavement or other loss.

8. _____ In Freud's theory, the actual remembered storyline or remembered images of a dream.

9. _____ In interpersonal therapy, absent or faulty social skills that limit the ability to start or maintain healthy relationships with others.

True/False Test

Indicate whether each statement is true or false by placing T or F in the blank space next to each item.

1. ____ Psychoanalysts believe that it is essential to move conflicts from the patient's unconscious to his or her conscious awareness. The process of recognizing and ultimately resolving these long-standing repressed conflicts is called insight.

2. ____ Interpersonal therapy (IPT) is a brief, psychodynamic psychotherapy that focuses on current relationships and assumes that symptoms are caused and maintained by interpersonal problems.

3. ____ In psychoanalysis, the patient's unconscious attempts to block the revelation of repressed memories and conflicts is called resistance.

4. ____ Dream interpretation is a technique used in psychoanalysis in which the content of dreams is analyzed for disguised or symbolic wishes, meanings, and motivations.

5. ____ Free association is a technique used in psychoanalysis in which the patient spontaneously reports all thoughts, feelings, and mental images as they come to mind as a way of revealing unconscious thoughts and emotions.

6. ____ In interpersonal therapy, role transitions refer to repetitive interpersonal conflicts with significant others, such as family members, coworkers, friends, or marital or romantic partners.

7. ____ Freud called the true, hidden, and unconscious meaning of a dream that is disguised in dream symbols the latent content.

8. ____ Transference is the process by which emotions and desires originally associated with a significant person in the patient's life, such as a parent, are unconsciously transferred to the psychoanalyst.

9. ___ In interpersonal therapy, role disputes refer to major life changes such as going away to college, parenthood, marriage, divorce, or retirement.

_____

Check your answers and review any areas of weakness before going on to the next section.

Humanistic Therapy

Preview Questions

Consider the following questions as you study this section of the chapter.

- What is the most influential humanistic therapy, and who developed it?
- What therapeutic conditions and techniques are important in client-centered therapy?
- How do client-centered therapy and psychoanalysis differ as insight therapies?

*Read the section "Humanistic Therapy" and **write** your answers to the following:*

1. The most influential humanistic therapy is _____ ; it was developed by _____ , who deliberately used the word *client* rather than *patient* because

   _____
   _____
   _____
   _____

2. In client-centered therapy, the main conditions are that _____

   _____
   _____
   _____

3. Unlike psychoanalysis, humanistic therapy does not offer _____

   _____
   _____
   _____

Behavior Therapy

Preview Questions

Consider the following questions as you study this section of the chapter.

- What is the goal of behavior therapy?
- What is the basic assumption of behavior therapy?
- How are classical and operant conditioning principles used to treat and modify problem behaviors?

*Read the section "Behavior Therapy" and **write** your answers to the following:*

1. The goal of behavior therapy is to _____

   _____
   _____

2. Behavior therapists assume that maladaptive behaviors are _____

   _____

   Therefore, the basic strategy in behavior therapy involves _____

   _____

3. Behavior therapists employ techniques that are based on the learning principles of _____

   _____
   _____

4. Mary Cover Jones's procedure, called counter-conditioning, involved _____

   _____
   _____
   _____

5. Along with counterconditioning, Jones used ___

   _____
   _____

6. Based on the same premise as counterconditioning, systematic desensitization involves

   _____
   _____

7. The three basic steps of systematic desensitization are

(a) _____

_____

(b) _____

_____

(c) _____

_____

8. The bell and pad treatment uses classical conditioning techniques to help bedwetters by _____

_____

_____

_____

9. Aversive conditioning involves _____

_____

_____

10. B. F. Skinner's operant conditioning model of learning is based on the simple principle that behavior is _____

_____

11. The token economy is a form of behavior therapy in which _____

_____

A modified version of the token economy is called _____

After you have carefully studied the preceding sections, complete the following exercises.

Concept Check 2

Read the following and write the correct term in the space provided.

1. Dr. Soos does not analyze or interpret his clients' motives or problems. Instead, he believes that the client is in the best position to discover his or her own ways of effectively dealing with problems and that the role of the therapist is to provide the right conditions that foster self-awareness, psychological growth, and self-directed change. Dr. Soos is obviously a(n) _____ psychologist who uses _____ therapy.

2. In an attempt to help her husband overcome his deep fear of traveling by sea, Mrs. Bowman brings home travel brochures showing exotic destinations reached by cruise ships. She asks her husband to imagine both of them sitting in their deck chairs enjoying the warm sunshine and cool beverages, and at the same time she reassures him that these big ships are totally safe and comfortable and that he has nothing to worry about. Mrs. Bowman's efforts to reduce her husband's fear most closely resembles techniques used in _____ .

3. To help Trevor overcome his addiction to nicotine, Dr. Clarke asks him to smoke some cigarettes and at the same time administers electric shock to his arm. Dr. Clarke is using a technique called _____ conditioning.

4. Retarded children in a group home are given plastic chips for making their beds, brushing their teeth, washing their hands, and being on time for meals. They are allowed to exchange these chips for candy, cookies, or additional TV time. The group home is using a behavioral technique called the _____ .

5. Eight-year-old Darryl has problems with bedwetting. His mother takes him to a behavior therapist who recommends a procedure that fixes the problem in a matter of weeks. The therapist most likely is using the

_____ .

6. Desiree told her therapist, "I feel so inadequate and useless, and I can't seem to cope with even the smallest things in my life. What should I do?" Her therapist answered, "You are feeling very helpless about things in your life, and sometimes you feel unable to cope. Can you think where these feelings come from?" The therapist is using _____ therapy and appears to be communicating with

_____ .

Review of Terms, Concepts, and Names 2

Use the terms in this list to complete the Matching Test, then to help you answer the True/False items correctly.

humanistic perspective
client- (or person-)
  centered therapy
Carl Rogers
genuineness
unconditional positive
  regard
conditional acceptance
empathic understanding
self-actualization
behavior therapy
Mary Cover Jones
counterconditioning
systematic
  desensitization
progressive relaxation

control scene
bell and pad treatment
aversive conditioning
Antabuse
extinction
reinforcement (positive)
punishment
shaping
baseline rate
token economy
contingency
  management
  interventions
virtual reality (VR)
  therapy

Matching Exercise

Match the appropriate term/name with its definition or description.

1. _____ American psychologist who conducted the first clinical demonstrations of behavior therapy.

2. _____ Psychological perspective that emphasizes human potential, self-awareness, and freedom of choice.

3. _____ Form of behavior therapy in which the therapeutic environment is structured to reward desired behaviors with tokens or points that may eventually be exchanged for tangible rewards.

4. _____ In client-centered therapy, the critical quality of the therapist that involves honestly and openly sharing his or her thoughts and feelings with the client.

5. _____ Type of psychotherapy that focuses on directly changing maladaptive behavior patterns by using basic learning principles and techniques; also called behavior modification.

6. _____ American psychologist who helped found humanistic psychology and developed client-centered therapy.

7. _____ The first step in systematic desensitization, which involves successively relaxing one muscle group after another until a deep state of relaxation is achieved.

8. _____ Behavior therapy technique used to treat nighttime bedwetting by conditioning arousal from sleep in response to bodily signals of a full bladder.

9. _____ Type of psychotherapy developed by humanist Carl Rogers in which the therapist is nondirective and reflective, and the client directs the focus of each therapy session.

10. _____ Medication that causes extreme nausea if alcohol is consumed after it is taken; used as a form of aversive conditioning in the treatment of alcohol abuse.

11. _____ In behavior therapy, the rate of occurrence of a problem behavior before treatment begins; more generally, data or condition used as a reference with which to compare future observations or results.

12. _____ Form of systematic desensitization that uses exposure to computer-generated images rather than exposure to the actual feared object or situation.

13. _____ In behavior therapy, the process of decreasing an undesirable behavior through the presentation of an aversive or unpleasant consequence.

True/False Test

Indicate whether each statement is true or false by placing T or F in the blank space next to each item.

1. ____ Aversive conditioning is a behavior therapy technique based on classical conditioning that involves modifying behavior by conditioning a new response that is incompatible with a previously learned response.

2. ____ In client-centered therapy, empathic understanding involves active listening and reflecting the content and personal meaning of feelings being experienced by the client.

3. ____ Systematic desensitization is a type of behavior therapy in which phobic responses are reduced by pairing relaxation with a series of mental images or real-life situations that the person finds progressively more fear provoking; it is based on the principle of counterconditioning.

4. ___ In behavior therapy, when a behavior decreases because it no longer leads to a reinforcer, extinction has occurred.

5. ___ In systematic desensitization, the therapist may have the client create a very relaxing scene, unrelated to the hierarchy of anxiety-provoking images, called a control scene.

6. ___ In client-centered therapy, unconditional positive regard is created when the therapist values, accepts, and cares for the client, whatever her problems or behaviors.

7. ___ In behavior therapy, the process by which a behavior is increased as the result of a desirable consequence is called positive reinforcement.

8. ___ When a person has received acceptance by significant others only if she conforms to their expectations, she is said to have experienced conditional acceptance.

9. ___ Counterconditioning, a relatively ineffective type of behavior therapy, involves repeatedly pairing an aversive stimulus with the occurrence of undesirable behaviors or thoughts.

10. ___ One application of the token economy, in which a group of clients receives vouchers or other conditioned reinforcers that can be exchanged for prizes to reinforce carefully specified behaviors or behavioral goals, is called contingency management interventions.

11. ___ Self actualization is the realization of a person's unique potentials and talents.

12. ___ Shaping involves reinforcing successive approximations of a desired behavior, and can be used with extremely impaired patients in whom the desired responses do not normally occur.

Check your answers and review any areas of weakness before going on to the next section.

Cognitive Therapies

Preview Questions

Consider the following questions as you study this section of the chapter.

- On what assumption are cognitive therapies based?

- What is rational-emotive therapy (RET), and who developed it?
- What is Beck's cognitive therapy (CT), and how does it differ from rational-emotive therapy?
- What is cognitive-behavioral therapy (CBT)?

*Read the section "Cognitive Therapies" and **write** your answers to the following:*

1. Cognitive therapies assume that _____

_____

_____

2. The goal of cognitive therapy is to _____

_____

_____

3. Rational-emotive therapy (RET) was founded by_____ and it focuses on

_____

_____

_____

4. Beck's cognitive therapy (CT) focuses on

_____

_____

5. Like Ellis, Beck believes that_____

_____

_____

_____

6. In contrast with RET's emphasis on "irrational" thinking, Beck believes that_____

_____

_____

_____

7. Cognitive-behavioral therapy (CBT) is a therapy that_____

_____

_____

_____

It is based on the assumption that _____

_____

_____

_____

Group and Family Therapy

Preview Questions

Consider the following questions as you study this section of the chapter.

- What is group therapy, and what are some of the advantages of this approach?
- What are family therapy and marital or couple therapy?

Read the section "Group and Family Therapy" and **write** *your answers to the following:*

1. Group therapy involves _____
   _____
   _____

2. Some of the key advantages of group therapy are that _____
   _____
   _____
   _____

3. Family therapy is based on the assumption that
   _____
   _____

4. Marital or couple therapy focuses on _____
   _____
   _____

Evaluating the Effectiveness of Psychotherapy

Preview Questions

Consider the following questions as you study this section of the chapter.

- What is meta-analysis, and what has it demonstrated about the general effectiveness of psychotherapy?
- Is one form of psychotherapy superior to another?
- What common factors contribute to effective psychotherapy, and what is eclecticism?

Read the section "Evaluating the Effectiveness of Psychotherapy" and **write** *your answers to the following:*

1. When meta-analysis is used to summarize studies, the researchers consistently arrive at the same conclusion: _____
   _____
   _____

2. Researchers have identified a number of factors that are related to a positive therapy outcome:
   (a) _____
   _____
   (b) _____
   _____
   (c) _____
   _____
   (d) _____
   _____
   (e) _____

3. Eclecticism refers to the _____
   _____
   _____

After you have carefully studied the preceding sections, complete the following exercises.

Concept Check 3

Read the following and write the correct term in the space provided.

1. Dr. McGilvery wants to determine whether psychotherapy is effective for particular psychological disorders. In attempting to analyze the results of numerous published studies on the issue, he should use a technique called
   _____ .

2. Mike, a mental health professional, tries to tailor his therapeutic approach to the problems and characteristics of the person seeking help. Mike's pragmatic and integrated use of diverse psychotherapeutic techniques would classify him as a(n) _____ therapist.

3. Dr. Samson believes that a key aspect of resolving some psychological problems is getting individuals to realize that others have problems similar to their own. To achieve this goal, _____ therapy would be useful.

4. Jay's therapist attacks and openly criticizes Jay's irrational and self-defeating ways of thinking. Jay's therapist is most likely a(n) _____ therapist.

5. Dr. Beaven tries to help her clients learn to recognize and monitor the automatic thoughts that occur without conscious effort or control; she then encourages them to test the reality of these thoughts empirically. Dr. Beaven's approach is most consistent with _____ therapy.

6. Dr. Sidhu believes that in order to understand psychological problems, it is important to investigate interactions among family members within the context of the dynamic family system in which each member plays a unique role. Dr. Sidhu is most likely a(n) _____ therapist.

7. Ivana's therapist believes that thoughts affect behavior and moods, and that behavior, in turn, can affect cognitions and emotional states. His approach to treating her depression involves a flexible, integrated use of diverse behavioral and cognitive techniques tailored to her unique problem. Ivana's therapist is most likely a _____ therapist.

8. Draco has been attending Alcoholics Anonymous meetings and learning about their 12-step program ever since he was cited for DUI (driving under the influence) and his drivers' license was suspended. Draco is seeking help from a(n) _____ .

9. Judd's therapist asks him to focus on the mental image of the traumatic aftermath of the explosion that destroyed his place of work. While Judd is doing this, the therapist moves his finger back and forth in front of Judd's eyes and asks him to visually track the movement. Judd's therapist is using a technique called

_____ ,

a therapeutic approach that is _____ (significantly better/no better) than other forms of psychotherapy.

10. When Fernandez started experiencing a number of psychological problems, he decided that he needed professional help. Before talking with a therapist, however, he discussed his plan with his extended family, including his grandparents and his in-laws, and with some of his closest friends. This tendency of Latinos to stress interdependence over independence and the importance of the extended family network is called _____ .

Graphic Organizer 1

Fill in each of the following with the correct information.

Type of Therapy	Founder	Source of Problems	Treatment Techniques	Goals of Therapy
Psychoanalysis				
Client-Centered Therapy				
Behavior Therapy				
Rational-Emotive Therapy				
Cognitive Therapy				
Cognitive-Behavioral Therapy				

Review of Terms, Concepts, and Names 3

Use the terms in this list to complete the Matching Test, then to help you answer the True/False items correctly.

cognitive therapies
Albert Ellis
rational-emotive therapy
Aaron T. Beck
cognitive therapy
cognitive-behavioral
   therapy (CBT)
group therapy
marital or couple
   therapy
self-help groups and
   support groups
family therapy

spontaneous remission
meta-analysis
empirically supported
   treatments
eclecticism
eye movement desensiti-
   zation reprocessing
   (EMDR) therapy
exposure therapy
network therapy
familismo
Naikan therapy

Matching Exercise

Match the appropriate term/name with its definition or description.

1. _____ Form of psychotherapy that is based on the assumption that the family is a system and that treats the family as a unit.

2. _____ Group of psychotherapies that are based on the assumption that psychological problems are due to maladaptive patterns of thinking; treatment techniques focus on recognizing and altering these unhealthy thinking patterns.

3. _____ Type of therapy, developed by psychiatrist Aaron Beck, that focuses on changing the client's unrealistic beliefs.

4. _____ Form of psychotherapy that involves one or more therapists working simultaneously with a small group of clients.

5. _____ Type of psychotherapy, developed by psychologist Albert Ellis, that focuses on changing the client's irrational beliefs.

6. _____ Therapy approach typically used with Native American clients, in which members of the client's family and community participate in treatment and/or group healing rituals.

7. _____ Therapy that integrates cognitive and behavioral techniques and is based on the assumption that thoughts, moods, and behaviors are interrelated.

8. _____ Therapy technique in which the client holds a vivid mental image of a troubling event or situation while rapidly moving his eyes back and forth in response to the therapist's waving finger, or while the therapist administers some other form of bilateral stimulation such as sounding tones in alternate ears.

9. _____ A statistical technique that involves pooling or combining the results of many studies into a single analysis that essentially creates one large study that can reveal overall trends in the data.

10. _____ Japanese psychotherapy that emphasizes replacing self-absorption with a sense of obligation and gratitude toward others.

True/False Test

Indicate whether each item is true or false by placing T or F in the space next to each item.

1. ____ Albert Ellis founded cognitive therapy (CT), a psychotherapy based on the assumption that depression and other psychological problems are caused by biased perceptions, distorted thinking, and inaccurate beliefs.

2. ____ Eclecticism is the pragmatic and integrated use of techniques from different psychotherapies.

3. ____ Spontaneous remission is the phenomenon in which people eventually improve or recover from psychological symptoms simply with the passage of time.

4. ____ Self-help groups and support groups deal with a wide array of psychological, medical, and behavioral problems through group processes and interactions that are typically organized and led by nonprofessionals.

5. ____ Aaron T. Beck founded the cognitive psychotherapy called rational-emotive therapy (RET), which emphasizes recognizing and changing irrational beliefs.

6. ____ Empirically supported treatments are psychotherapies whose effectiveness has been validated by empirical research.

7. ____ Familismo is the term for the cultural value in Latino cultures that emphasizes the importance of the extended family network.

8. ___ A behavioral therapy, used for phobias, panic disorder, posttraumatic stress disorder, or related anxiety disorder, and in which the person is repeatedly exposed to the disturbing object or situation under controlled conditions, is called exposure therapy.

9. ___ Marital or couple therapy attempts to improve communication and problem-solving skills as well as increase the intimacy between the two people in the relationship.

Check your answers and review any areas of weakness before going on to the next section.

Biomedical Therapies

Preview Questions

Consider the following questions as you study this section of the chapter.

- What is biomedical therapy?
- What are the most important antipsychotic, atypical antipsychotic, antianxiety, and antidepressant medications, how do they achieve their effects, and what are their advantages?
- What are lithium and ECT, and how are they used?

*Read the section "Biomedical Therapies" and **write** your answers to the following:*

1. The biomedical therapies are _____

   _____

2. Antipsychotic medications are _____

   _____

   The most common antipsychotic medications
   include _____

   _____

   _____

3. The new atypical antipsychotic drugs include

   _____

   _____

   and they act by_____

   _____

   _____

   _____

4. Antianxiety medications are _____

   _____

   _____

   The most common antianxiety medications
   include _____

   _____

   _____

5. Lithium is _____

   _____

   _____

   _____

6. The antidepressant medications are _____

   _____

   _____

   The most common antidepressant medications
   include _____

   _____

   _____

   New antidepressants, including _____

   _____

   tend to _____

   _____

7. Electroconvulsive therapy (ECT) is a biomedical therapy used primarily_____

   _____

   _____

   _____

After you have carefully studied the preceding section, complete the following exercises.

Concept Check 4

Read the following and write the correct term in the space provided.

1. For no apparent reason, Mrs. Bell has constant and persistent feelings of anxiety, nervousness, and apprehension that interfere with her ability to eat, sleep, and function. Her psychiatrist is most likely to prescribe a type of psychoactive medication called an _____ medication.

2. Mr. Millis still experiences intense feelings of despondency, hopelessness, and dejection, and has suicidal thoughts, despite extensive psychotherapy and months of psychoactive medication. Because of this lack of responsiveness, his doctor is likely to consider using _____ therapy.

3. After being on antipsychotic medications for many years, Florence has developed a number of serious symptoms, such as severe, uncontrollable facial tics and grimaces, chewing movements, and other involuntary movements of the lips, jaw, and tongue. Florence suffers from _____ .

4. Dwayne has been diagnosed with bipolar disorder. His doctor is most likely to prescribe _____ .

5. To treat Debra's symptoms, which included hallucinations, delusions, and disordered thought processes, the psychiatrist prescribed a psychoactive medication that selectively affected the levels of the neurotransmitter serotonin and as well as dopamine in her brain. To minimize the potential side effects of the first atypical antipsychotics, he is likely to have prescribed either _____ , _____ , or _____ .

6. After 12 weeks of interpersonal therapy (IPT) or 12 weeks of antidepressant medication (Paxil), depressed patients are given PET scans. It is very likely that there will be _____ (a higher/a lower/the same) level of normalization of brain activity in the drug group compared to the therapy group.

Review of Terms and Concepts 4

Use the terms in this list to complete the Matching Test, then to help you answer the True/False items correctly.

psychoactive medications
antipsychotic medications
tardive dyskinesia
atypical antipsychotic medications
antianxiety medications
benzodiazepines

antidepressant medications
lithium
selective serotonin reuptake inhibitors (SSRIs)
electroconvulsive therapy (ECT)
catharsis

Matching Exercise

Match the appropriate term with its definition or description.

1. _____ A naturally occurring substance that is used in the treatment of bipolar disorder.

2. _____ Prescription drugs that alter mental functions and alleviate psychological symptoms.

3. _____ Biomedical therapy used primarily in the treatment of depression that involves electrically inducing a brief brain seizure; also called *shock therapy* and *electric shock therapy*.

4. _____ Prescription drugs used to alleviate the symptoms of anxiety.

5. _____ Prescription drugs used to reduce the symptoms associated with depression.

6. _____ Potentially irreversible motor disorder that results from the long-term use of antipsychotic medications and is characterized by severe, uncontrollable facial tics and grimaces, chewing movements, and other involuntary movements of the lips, jaw, and tongue.

True/False Test

Indicate whether each item is true or false by placing T or F in the space next to each item.

1. ___ Antipsychotic medications (also called neuroleptics) are prescription drugs that are used to reduce psychotic symptoms; frequently used in the treatment of schizophrenia.

2. ___ Catharsis is the reduction of emotional and physical tension that occurs simply as a result of talking about one's psychological problems.

3. ___ Benzodiazepines are a group of addictive antianxiety drugs which increase levels of the neurotransmitter GABA throughout the brain.

4. ___ Atypical antipsychotic medications are newer antipsychotic medications which, in contrast to the early antipsychotic drugs, block dopamine receptors in brain regions associated with psychotic symptoms rather than more globally throughout the brain, resulting in fewer side effects.

5. ___ Selective serotonin reuptake inhibitors (SSRIs) are a class of antidepressant medication, which includes Prozac, Paxil, and Zoloft, that increase the availability of serotonin in the brain and cause fewer side effects than earlier antidepressants.

Check your answers and review any areas of weakness before going on to the next section.

Something to Think About

1. Many people suffer from fear and anxiety about such things as going to the dentist or doctor or to job interviews and taking exams. These kinds of fears are normal, and most people manage to cope with such anxiety-provoking situations. Other fears are more serious and may cause the person intense distress and somehow interfere with his or her normal functioning. Imagine a situation in which a friend or family member comes to you seeking help about how to overcome her fear of flying. Based on what you know about the behavior therapy technique of systematic desensitization, what might you say to this person?

2. Many people with psychological problems do not seek help from mental health professionals. There are many reasons for this. One reason may have to do with a lack of understanding about what to expect in psychotherapy. What are some of the important things a person should know about psychotherapy?

Check your answers and review any areas of weakness before completing the progress tests.

Progress Test 1

Review the complete chapter (including Concept Reviews and the boxed inserts), review all your study notes, and then test yourself on the following progress test. Check your answers. If you make a mistake, review your notes, review the relevant section of the study guide, and, if necessary, go back and read the appropriate part of your textbook.

1. Jacqueline's therapist uses dream interpretation and free association to help her to become more aware of unresolved conflicts in her childhood. The therapist's techniques and goals best reflect the primary aim of
   (a) psychoanalysis.
   (b) client-centered therapy.
   (c) behavior therapy.
   (d) cognitive therapy.

2. Mrs. Alverz gives her third-grade students a silver sticker every time they get a perfect score on their weekly spelling test. At the end of the term, students can exchange their stickers for prizes. Mrs. Alverz is using a strategy based on _____ conditioning called the _____.
   (a) classical; bell and pad method
   (b) classical; token economy
   (c) operant; bell and pad method
   (d) operant; token economy

3. Laurel's therapist uses rational-emotive therapy (RET). After identifying Laurel's core irrational beliefs, her therapist is likely to
   (a) help her formulate an anxiety hierarchy.
   (b) encourage her to use free association so that she can get insight into her unconscious motivations and feelings.
   (c) provide her with a warm, supportive atmosphere, unconditional positive regard, and empathic understanding.
   (d) vigorously dispute and challenge her irrational beliefs.

4. Dr. Whorley offers a number of explanations for his patient's dreams and free associations in order to help the patient recognize unconscious conflicts and motivations. Dr. Whorley is using a psychoanalytic technique called
   (a) interpretation.   (c) resistance.
   (b) transference.   (d) conditional acceptance.

5. Twenty-five-year-old Melissa told her therapist that she felt worthless and unattractive because she didn't have a boyfriend; she was sure she was going to end up single and unloved. Her therapist said, "Your way of thinking is not only irrational but also totally stupid and absurd! You are worthless only if you *think* you are!" Her therapist is most likely

    (a) a behavior therapist.
    (b) a client-centered therapist.
    (c) a rational-emotive therapist.
    (d) a psychoanalyst.
    (e) none of the above; no therapist would talk like that to a client.

6. Once a week, Gardner attends a local health clinic, where he attempts to deal with some of his psychological problems by discussing them with five or six other people and two psychologists. Gardner is involved in

    (a) individual therapy.
    (b) group therapy.
    (c) a biomedical treatment program.
    (d) a self-help group.

7. Mr. Lansdon's intense feelings of despondency and helplessness are periodically interrupted by episodes in which he experiences excessive feelings of personal power and a grandiose optimism that he can change the world to fit his strange ideological beliefs. A biomedical therapist would most likely prescribe

    (a) electroconvulsive therapy.
    (b) lithium.
    (c) antipsychotic medications.
    (d) antidepressant medications.

8. Gabrielle's feelings of unhappiness, despondency, dejection, and hopelessness have become so extreme that she has attempted suicide. Which of the following treatments is likely to provide her with the quickest relief from her misery?

    (a) systematic desensitization
    (b) the bell and pad treatment
    (c) psychoanalysis
    (d) electroconvulsive therapy (ECT)

9. Because of his persistent psychological problems, Werner has been prescribed a benzodiazepine drug called Valium. It is most likely that Werner suffers from

    (a) bipolar disorder.   (c) anxiety.
    (b) schizophrenia.   (d) depression.

10. When Christos was younger, he experienced a very painful tooth extraction. He now has an extreme fear of going to the dentist and has not been for a dental checkup in years. In order to help Christos overcome his irrational fear, a behavioral therapist is likely to use

    (a) rational-emotive therapy.
    (b) systematic desensitization.
    (c) the bell and pad treatment.
    (d) antianxiety medication.

11. Kathleen is on a committee at a community health-care facility that has the task of determining which of the major forms of psychotherapy is most effective. After she reviews studies that used meta-analysis to assess the results of treatment outcomes, she is most likely to conclude that

    (a) behavior therapy is the single most effective therapy available.
    (b) client-centered therapy has been consistently more effective than all the other forms of therapy.
    (c) in general, there is little or no difference in the effectiveness of the different forms of psychotherapy.
    (d) psychoanalysis works best for schizophrenia, and cognitive therapy works best for phobias.

12. Tyler has been diagnosed with schizophrenia. His doctor is most likely to prescribe

    (a) electroconvulsive therapy.
    (b) lithium.
    (c) antipsychotic medication.
    (d) antianxiety medication.

13. According to the Application, which of the following is true?

    (a) Therapy is a collaborative effort.
    (b) Expect therapy to challenge how you think and act.
    (c) Your therapist will not become a substitute friend.
    (d) Your therapist will not make decisions for you.
    (e) All of the above are true.

14. Mr. Keiko, a middle-aged Japanese American, has been referred to a Western-style psychologist because he is displaying the classic symptoms of anxiety and depression. According to Culture and Human Behavior 15.5, Mr. Keiko

    (a) may be reluctant to discuss personal, intimate details of his life with a stranger.

    (b) might try to avoid focusing on upsetting thoughts and resist exploring painful thoughts and feelings that could help resolve his psychological problems.

    (c) may not agree that becoming more assertive, more self-sufficient, less dependent on others, and caring for his own needs first is a good idea.

    (d) might do all of the above.

15. According to In Focus 15.1, Mary Cover Jones

    (a) was a psychoanalyst who pioneered the development of short-term dynamic therapy

    (b) was the first behavior therapist and pioneered a technique called counter-conditioning

    (c) was a cognitive psychologist who was instrumental in promoting cognitive-behavioral therapy (CBT)

    (d) pioneered the use of virtual reality (VR) technology in the treatment of phobias.

Progress Test 2

After you have checked your understanding of the material in Progress Test 1 and have done a complete chapter review with special focus on any areas of weakness, you are ready to assess your knowledge of Progress Test 2. Check your answers. If you make a mistake, review your notes, the relevant section of the study guide, and, if necessary, the appropriate part of your textbook.

1. Dr. Rassmunsen uses medication and other medical procedures, including electroconvulsive therapy, to treat the symptoms of psychological disorders. Dr. Rassmunsen's approach would most likely be classified as

    (a) cognitive therapy.
    (b) behavioral therapy.
    (c) humanistic therapy.
    (d) biomedical therapy.

2. Mr. Damson suffers from auditory hallucinations and falsely believes that his coworkers are not only trying to steal his "secret inventions" but are also plotting to kill him. A biomedical therapist would most likely prescribe

    (a) electroconvulsive therapy.
    (b) lithium.
    (c) antipsychotic medications.
    (d) antidepressant medications.

3. Mervyn's therapist prescribed a medication that is classified as a selective serotonin reuptake inhibitor (SSRI) for his psychological symptoms. It is most likely that Mervyn suffers from

    (a) schizophrenia.   (c) anxiety disorder.
    (b) bipolar disorder.   (d) depression.

4. When Freda told her therapist that she wanted to get his advice on what she should do about her relationship problems, he replied, "It sounds to me like you are experiencing some difficulties with your relationship. Is that right?" The therapist's response reflects the technique of

    (a) transference.
    (b) free association.
    (c) empathic understanding.
    (d) counterconditioning.

5. It is very probable that Freda's therapist is a _____ therapist.

    (a) cognitive   (c) behavior
    (b) psychoanalytic   (d) humanistic

6. When Greta's psychoanalyst asked her to elaborate on certain aspects of her dream, she couldn't think of anything to say. Her lack of responsiveness is likely to be interpreted as

    (a) resistance.
    (b) extinction.
    (c) transference.
    (d) spontaneous remission.

7. Dr. Whelan believes that people can overcome their problems if they learn to recognize and monitor their automatic thoughts and then try to test the reality of those thoughts empirically. Her approach is most consistent with

    (a) behavior therapy.
    (b) biomedical therapy.
    (c) cognitive therapy.
    (d) psychoanalysis.

8. A behavior therapist trains a child who is a frequent bedwetter to awaken and use the bathroom by arranging for an alarm to sound every time the child wets the bed. This technique is called _____ and illustrates the use of _____ conditioning principles.
   (a) aversive therapy; operant
   (b) the bell and pad treatment; classical
   (c) aversive therapy; classical
   (d) the bell and pad treatment; operant

9. For which of the following is Dr. Kelly most likely to prescribe the atypical antipsychotic medication olanzapine, which affects both serotonin and dopamine levels in the brain?
   (a) Celia, who smokes three packs of cigarettes a day
   (b) Garth, who irrationally believes that aliens are trying to steal his thoughts
   (c) Manuel, who fluctuates between extreme moods of euphoria and depression
   (d) Rachel, who suffers from nervous apprehension, intense anxiety, and an inability to relax

10. Quentin has an irrational fear of riding on elevators. His therapist first teaches him to relax completely, then he asks him to come up with a list of anxiety-provoking images associated with elevators. Finally, the therapist asks Quentin to close his eyes and imagine very clearly the least fearful scene on the list. Quentin's therapist is a _____ therapist using
   _____ .
   (a) behavior; systematic desensitization
   (b) cognitive; rational-emotive techniques
   (c) humanistic; empathic understanding
   (d) psychoanalytic; free association

11. Jeneen is taking a prescription drug that contains a naturally occurring substance called lithium. It is most probable that she is suffering from
   (a) schizophrenia.   (c) chronic depression.
   (b) bipolar disorder.   (d) anxiety disorder.

12. Ursula, who lives in a home for the mentally retarded, is able to earn points for getting dressed, maintaining personal hygiene, and engaging in appropriate social interactions. These points can be exchanged for access to desirable items or special privileges. This example illustrates the use of

   (a) aversive conditioning.
   (b) counterconditioning.
   (c) systematic desensitization.
   (d) a token economy.

13. Seven-year-old Niall chews the ends of all his pens and pencils, so his mother paints them with a foul-tasting, but harmless, substance. After a few days of this treatment, Niall stops chewing his pens and pencils. Niall's mother has used a form of
   (a) transference.
   (b) counterconditioning.
   (c) aversive therapy.
   (d) electroconvulsive therapy.

14. According to Science Versus Pseudoscience 15.4, eye movement desensitization reprocessing (EMDR)
   (a) has been used to treat posttraumatic stress disorder (PTSD), panic disorder, addiction, substance abuse, sleep disorders, and other psychological disorders.
   (b) is very popular and lucrative; more than 40,000 trained practitioners have treated close to a million patients since 1990.
   (c) is no more effective than standard approaches, such as exposure therapy, in the treatment of anxiety disorders, including PTSD.
   (d) displays the fundamental characteristics of a pseudoscience, according to some psychologists.
   (e) all of the above are true.

15. According to In Focus 15.2,
   (a) therapy using virtual reality (VR) technology has become an accepted treatment for phobias.
   (b) virtual reality (VR) technology has been banned as a treatment for psychological disorders because of the dangerous side-effects.
   (c) virtual reality (VR) technology has replaced electroconvulsive therapy (ECT) in the treatment of major depression.
   (d) research and therapy using virtual reality (VR) technology can only be conducted by licensed physicians, such as psychiatrists.

Progress Test 3

After you have checked your understanding of the material in Progress Tests 1 and 2, and have done a complete chapter review with special focus on any areas of weakness, you are ready to further assess your knowledge on Progress Test 3. Check your answers. If you make a mistake, review your notes, the appropriate parts of the study guide, and, if necessary, the relevant sections of your textbook.

1. After reviewing the literature on the use of lithium and the mechanism involved in its effectiveness in treating bipolar disorder, Richelle is likely to conclude that lithium

   (a) stabilizes the availability of glutamate, an excitatory neurotransmitter, preventing both abnormal highs and lows.
   (b) boosts the levels of dopamine in the brain.
   (c) selectively inhibits the reuptake of serotonin.
   (d) stabilizes the levels of both dopamine and serotonin in the brain.

2. Aaron Beck is to _____ as Carl Rogers is to _____ .

   (a) cognitive therapy; rational emotive therapy
   (b) behavior therapy; client-centered therapy
   (c) biomedical therapy; psychoanalysis
   (d) cognitive therapy; client-centered therapy

3. Because of Rhian's persistent feelings of hopelessness, dejection, and guilt, and her suicidal thoughts, her doctor prescribes an antidepressant drug. Rhian is most likely to be taking a(n)

   (a) selective serotonin reuptake inhibitor (SSRI) called Prozac.
   (b) benzodiazepine drug called Valium.
   (c) neuroleptic medication called Thorazine.
   (d) anticonvulsant medicine called Depakote.

4. When Clifford decided to pursue a career as an artist instead of complying with his father's wish for him to become a lawyer, both parents were angry, critical, and rejecting. Carl Rogers would say that Clifford's parents are demonstrating

   (a) conditional acceptance.
   (b) empathic understanding.
   (c) unconditional positive regard.
   (d) unconscious motivations and feelings.

5. Mrs. Blonska has been diagnosed with generalized anxiety disorder. Because her doctor is concerned with the long-term treatment of her global and persistent feelings of anxiety, he is likely to prescribe

   (a) Buspar.   (c) Depakote.
   (b) Prozac.   (d) Clozapine.

6. Mr. MacKaskill has a serious drinking problem. In order to reduce his intake of alcohol, a behavior therapist might give Mr. MacKaskill a medication called Antabuse, which induces nausea whenever it is taken with alcohol. This behavioral technique is called

   (a) counterconditioning.
   (b) systematic desensitization.
   (c) aversive conditioning.
   (d) the token economy.

7. For no obvious reason, Mr. Henderson has recently begun to express feelings of annoyance, irritability, and anger toward his therapist, who has been consistently patient, concerned, and supportive. Freud would most likely consider Mr. Henderson's hostility toward his therapist to be an example of

   (a) insight.   (c) aversion.
   (b) counterconditioning.   (d) transference.

8. Dr. Elson uses a therapeutic technique that involves modifying behavior by conditioning a new response that is incompatible with a previously learned undesired response. Dr. Elson is most likely a _____ therapist who is using _____ .

   (a) behavior; counterconditioning
   (b) cognitive; rational-emotive techniques
   (c) psychoanalytic; free association
   (d) biomedical; ECT

9. Nelson's therapist believes that a therapist should be nondirective, providing unconditional positive regard in an open, honest way. Nelson's therapist is most likely a _____ therapist.

   (a) psychoanalytic   (c) cognitive
   (b) behavioral   (d) humanistic

10. During a lecture to students interested in graduate work in clinical psychology, Dr. Barton is asked what factors contribute most to effective psychotherapy. He is most likely to respond that
    (a) mutual respect, trust, and hope in the therapeutic situation are important factors.
    (b) therapists who have warmth, sensitivity, sincerity, and genuineness are usually effective.
    (c) clients who are motivated, expressive, and actively committed to therapy enhance the success of therapy.
    (d) all of the above contribute to effective psychotherapy.

11. Brian's therapist attempts to tailor her approach to his particular problems and characteristics and, in doing so, makes use of techniques from different psychotherapies. Brian's therapist would most likely be classified as a(n) _____ therapist.
    (a) humanistic   (c) behavior
    (b) eclectic   (d) cognitive

12. Which of the following individuals is most likely to benefit from a psychoactive drug that affects the level of the neurotransmitter dopamine in the brain?
    (a) Herman, who hears imaginary voices telling him that he is going to be abducted by aliens
    (b) Marcel, who is very nervous and anxious all the time
    (c) Carla, who feels sad, despondent, dejected, and worthless most of the time
    (d) Faith, who drinks at least a six-pack of beer every day

13. Harriet has asked her psychology professor whether psychotherapy is more effective than no therapy at all. If her professor is familiar with the meta-analytic studies on the topic, he is most likely to answer that
    (a) psychotherapy is no more effective than talking to a friend.
    (b) it is not possible to measure the effectiveness of psychotherapy.
    (c) psychotherapy harms more people than it helps.
    (d) psychotherapy is significantly more effective than no treatment.

14. According to In Focus 15.3, which of the following is true about self-help groups?
    (a) Compared with therapy provided by mental health professionals, self-help groups are generally ineffective for the vast majority of psychological problems.
    (b) All self-help groups are organized and led by nonprofessionals.
    (c) Compared with professional mental health services, self-help groups are much more likely to cause harm to the people involved.
    (d) In order to operate legally, self-help groups must employ at least one registered professional, such as a clinical psychologist, or a licensed physician, such as a psychiatrist.

15. Masahara goes to a therapist who specializes in a Japanese psychotherapy called Naikan therapy. According to Culture and Human Behavior 15.5, it is very probable that he will be advised
    (a) that being self-absorbed is the surest path to psychological suffering.
    (b) to focus on developing a sense of gratitude and obligation toward significant others.
    (c) to meditate on how much his parents and others have done for him and how he may have failed to meet their needs.
    (d) to reflect on the trouble and problems he may have caused significant others.
    (e) to do all of the above.

Answers

Introduction: Psychotherapy and Biomedical Therapy

1. *Psychotherapy refers to* the treatment of emotional, behavioral, and interpersonal problems through the use of psychological techniques designed to encourage understanding of problems and to modify troubling feelings, behaviors, or relationships.

2. *A basic assumption of all psychotherapies is that* psychological factors play a significant role in a person's troubling feelings, behaviors, or relationships.

3. *Biomedical therapies involve* the use of medications, electroconvulsive therapy, or other medical interventions to treat the symptoms associated with psychological disorders.

4. *The biomedical therapies are based on the assumption that* the symptoms of many psychological disorders involve biological factors, such as abnormal brain chemistry.

Psychoanalytic Therapy

1. *Psychoanalysis is a* type of psychotherapy, originated by Sigmund Freud, in which free association, dream interpretation, and analysis of resistance and transference are used to explore repressed or unconscious impulses, anxieties, and internal conflicts.

2. *The main psychoanalytic techniques (and their purpose) are (a)* free association, in which the patient spontaneously reports all her thoughts, mental images, and feelings while lying on a couch; *(b)* resistance, the patient's unconscious attempts to block the process of revealing repressed memories and conflicts; *(c)* dream interpretation, the analysis of dream content for disguised or symbolic wishes, meanings, and motivations; *(d)* interpretation, in which the psychoanalyst offers a carefully timed explanation of the patient's dreams, free associations, or behavior to facilitate the recognition of unconscious conflicts or motivations; and *(e)* transference, the process by which emotions and desires originally associated with a significant person in the patient's life, such as a parent, are unconsciously transferred to the psychoanalyst.

3. *Together, these psychoanalytic techniques are designed to* help uncover unconscious conflicts so the patient attains insight as to the real source of her problems.

4. *The various forms of short-term dynamic therapies (all based on traditional psychoanalytic notions) have four features in common:* (a) Contact lasts for no more than a few months. (b) The patient's problems are quickly assessed at the beginning of therapy (c) The therapist and patient agree on specific, concrete, and attainable goals. (d) In the actual sessions, most psychodynamic therapists are more directive than traditional psychoanalysts, actively engaging the patient in a dialogue.

5. *Interpersonal therapy (IPT) is a* brief, psychodynamic psychotherapy that focuses on current relationships and social interactions and is based on the assumption that symptoms are caused and maintained by interpersonal problems. *The four categories of personal problems in the interpersonal therapy model are (a)* unre-
solved grief (problems dealing with the death of significant others); *(b)* role disputes (repetitive conflicts with others, such as the person's partner, family members, friends, or coworkers); *(c)* role transitions (problems involving major life changes, such as going away to college, becoming a parent, marriage, divorce, or retirement); and *(d)* interpersonal deficits (absent or faulty social skills that limit the ability to start or maintain healthy relationships with others).

Concept Check 1

1. resistance
2. free association
3. interpretation
4. transference
5. dream interpretation
6. biomedical therapies; psychotherapy
7. interpersonal therapy (IPT)

Matching Exercise 1

1. Sigmund Freud
2. psychotherapy
3. interpretation
4. psychoanalysis
5. biomedical therapy
6. short-term dynamic therapies
7. unresolved grief
8. manifest content
9. interpersonal deficits

True/False Test 1

1. T	4. T	7. T
2. T	5. T	8. T
3. T	6. F	9. F

Humanistic Therapy

1. *The most influential humanistic therapy is* client- (or person-) centered therapy; *it was developed by* Carl Rogers *who deliberately used the word* client *rather than* patient *because* he wanted to get away from the idea that the person was sick and was seeking treatment from an all-knowing authority figure. He also wanted to emphasize the client's subjective perception of himself and his environment.

2. *In client-centered therapy, the main conditions are that* the therapist should be nondirective; the client should direct the focus of therapy sessions; and the therapist should be genuine, demonstrate unconditional positive regard, and communicate empathic understanding.

3. *Unlike psychoanalysis, humanistic therapy does not offer* solutions or interpretations about the client's unconscious feelings and motivations, but instead is nondirective, providing active, reflective listening, unconditional positive regard, and empathic understanding, with an emphasis on the client's subjective, conscious perceptions of herself and her environment.

Behavior Therapy

1. *The goal of behavior therapy is to* modify specific problem behaviors, not to change the entire personality.

2. *Behavior therapists assume that maladaptive behaviors are* learned just as adaptive behaviors are. *Therefore, the basic strategy in behavior therapy involves* unlearning maladaptive behaviors and learning more adaptive behaviors in their place.

3. *Behavior therapists employ techniques that are based on the learning principles of* classical conditioning, operant conditioning, and observational learning.

4. *Mary Cover Jones's procedure, called counterconditioning, involved* gradually introducing the feared stimulus and at the same time pairing it with a pleasant stimulus, such as food, which elicits a positive response that is incompatible with the original conditioned response (this procedure also eliminated fear of objects that were similar to the original feared stimulus).

5. *Along with counterconditioning, Jones used* observational learning techniques and demonstrated that seeing others acting in a fearless manner encourages the fearful individual to imitate the fearless behavior.

6. *Based on the same premise as counterconditioning, systematic desensitization involves* learning a new conditioned response (relaxation) that is incompatible with or inhibits the old conditioned response (fear and anxiety).

7. *The three basic steps involved in systematic desensitization are (a)* The patient learns progressive relaxation. *(b)* The therapist helps the client construct a hierarchy of anxiety-provoking images and develop a control scene. *(c)* The process of desensitization begins by getting the deeply relaxed patient to imagine the least threatening scene in the anxiety hierarchy (over several sessions the client gradually works his way up the anxiety hierarchy).

8. *The bell and pad treatment uses classical conditioning techniques to help bedwetters by* pairing the sensation of a full bladder (conditioned stimulus) with a loud bell (the unconditioned stimulus, which is triggered by a wet bed), which wakens the child (the unconditioned response). Eventually, the sensation of a full bladder by itself (conditioned stimulus) will cause the child to waken (conditioned response) before he wets the bed.

9. *Aversive conditioning involves* repeatedly pairing an aversive stimulus with the occurrence of undesirable behaviors or thoughts (a relatively ineffective type of behavior therapy).

10. *B. F. Skinner's operant conditioning model of learning is based on the simple principle that behavior is* shaped and maintained by its consequences. This model uses positive reinforcement for desired behaviors and extinction (or nonreinforcement) for undesired behaviors.

11. *The token economy is a form of behavior therapy in which* the therapeutic environment is structured to reward desired behaviors with tokens or points that may eventually be exchanged for tangible rewards. *A modified version of the token economy is called* contingency management intervention.

Concept Check 2

1. humanistic; client-centered
2. behavior therapy (systematic desensitization)
3. aversive
4. token economy
5. bell and pad treatment
6. client-centered; empathic understanding

Matching Exercise 2

1. Mary Cover Jones
2. humanistic perspective
3. token economy
4. genuineness
5. behavior therapy
6. Carl Rogers
7. progressive relaxation
8. bell and pad treatment
9. client-centered therapy
10. Antabuse
11. baseline rate
12. virtual reality (VR) therapy
13. punishment

True/False 2

1. F	4. T	7. T	10. T
2. T	5. T	8. T	11. T
3. T	6. T	9. F	12. T

Cognitive Therapies

1. *Cognitive therapies assume that* most people blame unhappiness and problems on external events and situations, but the real cause of unhappiness is the way the person thinks about the events, not the events themselves.

2. *The goal of cognitive therapy is to* identify the maladaptive patterns of thinking and then to change them to more adaptive, healthy patterns.

3. *Rational-emotive therapy (RET) was founded by* Albert Ellis *and it focuses on* identifying, disputing, and changing the client's irrational beliefs (explained by the ABC model [Activating events, Beliefs, and Consequences]).

4. *Beck's cognitive therapy (CT) focuses on* changing the client's unrealistic and distorted beliefs, and on correcting the cognitive biases that underlie depression and other psychological disorders.

5. *Like Ellis, Beck believes that* what people think creates their moods and emotions; like RET, CT involves helping clients to identify faulty thinking and to replace unhealthy patterns of thinking with healthier ones.

6. *In contrast with RET's emphasis on "irrational" thinking, Beck believes that* depression and other psychological problems are caused by distorted thinking and unrealistic beliefs, and the cognitive therapist encourages the client to empirically test the accuracy of his or her assumptions and beliefs.

7. *Cognitive-behavioral therapy (CBT) is a therapy that* integrates cognitive and behavioral techniques. *It is based on the assumption that* thoughts, moods, and behaviors are interrelated; changes in thought patterns affect moods and behaviors, and changes in behavior affect cognitions and emotional states.

Group and Family Therapy

1. *Group therapy involves* one or more therapists working simultaneously with a small group of clients (the group may be as small as three or four people or as large as ten or more people).

2. *Some of the key advantages of group therapy are that* it is cost-effective; therapists can observe clients interacting with other group members; clients can benefit from the support, encouragement, and practical suggestions provided by other group members; and people can try out new behaviors in a safe, supportive environment.

3. *Family therapy is based on the assumption that* the family is an interdependent system; it focuses on treating the family as a unit, rather than on treating the individual.

4. *Marital or couple therapy focuses on* improving communication, problem-solving skills, and intimacy between members of a couple.

Evaluating the Effectiveness of Psychotherapy

1. *When meta-analysis is used to summarize studies, the researchers consistently arrive at the same conclusion:* psychotherapy is significantly more effective than no treatment and no particular form of therapy is superior to any other.

2. *Researchers have identified a number of factors that are related to a positive therapy outcome:* (a) The most important factors are those associated with the therapeutic relationship, such as mutual respect, trust, and hope; (b) certain characteristics of the therapist, such as warmth, sensitivity, responsiveness, being perceived as sincere and genuine, and actively helping people to understand and face their problems; (c) therapists' sensitivity to the cultural differences that may exist between themselves and their clients; (d) client

characteristics, such as level of motivation, commitment to therapy, active involvement in the process, along with emotional and social maturity and the ability to express thoughts and feelings; *(e)* external circumstances, such as supportive family members and a stable living situation.

3. *Eclecticism refers to the* pragmatic and integrated use of techniques from different psychotherapies (eclectic psychotherapists carefully tailor their approach to the problems and characteristics of the person seeking help).

Concept Check 3

1. meta-analysis

2. eclectic

3. group

4. rational-emotive

5. cognitive

6. family

7. cognitive-behavioral therapist

8. self-help group

9. eye movement desensitization reprocessing (EMDR); no better

10. familismo

Graphic Organizer 1

Psychoanalysis:
Founder: Sigmund Freud
Source of Problems: Repressed, unconscious conflicts stemming from early childhood experiences
Treatment Techniques: Free association, analysis of dream content, interpretation, and transference
Goals of Therapy: To recognize, work through, and resolve long-standing conflicts

Client-Centered Therapy:
Founder: Carl Rogers
Source of Problems: Conditional acceptance and dependence that cause a person to develop a distorted self-concept and worldview
Treatment Techniques: Nondirective therapy, with therapist displaying unconditional positive regard, genuineness, and empathic understanding
Goals of Therapy: To develop self-awareness, self-acceptance, and self-determination

Behavior Therapy:
Founder: Various; derived from the fundamental principles of learning
Source of Problems: Learned maladaptive behavior patterns

Treatment Techniques: Counterconditioning, systematic desensitization, bell and pad treatment, aversive conditioning, reinforcement and extinction, token economy, and observational learning
Goals of Therapy: To unlearn maladaptive behaviors and learn adaptive behaviors in their place

Rational-Emotive Therapy
Founder: Albert Ellis
Source of Problems: Irrational beliefs
Treatment Techniques: Very directive therapy: identifying, logically disputing, and challenging irrational beliefs
Goals of Therapy: To surrender irrational beliefs and absolutist demands

Cognitive Therapy:
Founder: Aaron T. Beck
Source of Problems: Unrealistic, distorted perceptions and interpretations of events due to cognitive biases
Treatment Techniques: Directive collaboration: teaching client to monitor automatic thoughts; testing accuracy of conclusions; correcting distorted thinking and perception
Goals of Therapy: To accurately and realistically perceive self, others, and external events

Cognitive-Behavioral Therapy:
Founder: Various (derived from both cognitive and behavioral traditions)
Source of Problems: Cognitions, behaviors, and emotional responses are functionally interrelated; negative thoughts affect moods and behaviors, and maladaptive behaviors affect thoughts and moods
Treatment Techniques: Pragmatic approach that integrates the most appropriate cognitive and behavioral therapeutic approaches for each individual's needs and problems
Goals of Therapy: To replace maladaptive behaviors and irrational, distorted, unrealistic perceptions and cognitions with more adaptive healthier ones

Matching Exercise 3

1. family therapy

2. cognitive therapies

3. cognitive therapy

4. group therapy

5. rational-emotive therapy

6. network therapy

7. cognitive-behavioral therapy (CBT)

8. eye movement desensitization reprocessing (EMDR)

9. meta-analysis

10. Naikan therapy

True/False Test 3

1. F	4. T	7. T
2. T	5. F	8. T
3. T	6. T	9. T

Biomedical Therapies

1. *The biomedical therapies are* medical treatments for the symptoms of psychological disorders.

2. *Antipsychotic medications are* prescription drugs that are used to reduce psychotic symptoms (frequently used in the treatment of schizophrenia). *The most common antipsychotic medications include* reserpine and chlorpromazine, which alter dopamine levels in the brain; while they reduce the positive symptoms of schizophrenia, they have little or no effect on the negative symptoms (serious side effects can include tardive dyskinesia after long-term use).

3. *The new atypical antipsychotic medications include* clozapine, risperidone, olanzapine, sertindole, and quetiapine, *and they act by* selectively affecting both serotonin and dopamine levels in the brain (the atypical antipsychotics have fewer side effects and are more effective in treating both positive and negative symptoms of schizophrenia).

4. *Antianxiety medications are* prescription drugs that are used to alleviate the symptoms of anxiety. *The most common antianxiety medications include* the benzodiazepines, which are effective in the treatment of anxiety but are potentially addictive and have many side effects (Buspar is a newer antianxiety drug that has a very low risk of physical addiction).

5. *Lithium is* a naturally occurring substance that is used in the treatment of bipolar disorder; it appears to work by stabilizing the availability of glutamate, an excitatory neurotransmitter, preventing both abnormal highs and lows. (Depakote has recently been introduced as a new drug treatment for bipolar disorder.)

6. *The antidepressant medications are* prescription drugs that are used to reduce the symptoms associated with depression. *The most common antidepressant medications include* the tricyclics, the MAO inhibitors, and the second-generation antidepressants trazodone and bupropion. *New antidepressants, including* the selective serotonin reuptake inhibitors (SSRIs) Prozac, Paxil, and Zoloft; the dual-action antidepressants Serzone, Remeron, and Celexa; and the dual reuptake inhibitor Effexor *tend to* produce fewer side effects than the first and second generation antidepressants.

7. *Electroconvulsive therapy (ECT) is a biomedical therapy used primarily* in the treatment of severe depression; it involves electrically inducing brief brain seizures (also called shock therapy and electric shock therapy).

Concept Check 4

1. antianxiety

2. electroconvulsive

3. tardive dyskinesia

4. lithium

5. olanzapine (Zyprexa), sertindole (Serlect); quetiapine (Seroquel)

6. the same

Matching Exercise 4

1. lithium

2. psychoactive medications

3. electroconvulsive therapy (ECT)

4. antianxiety medications

5. antidepressant medications

6. tardive dyskinesia

True/False Test 4

1. T	3. T	5. T
2. T	4. T	

Something to Think About

1. The first thing to tell someone with a phobia is that there are many different therapeutic approaches in psychology, such as psychoanalysis, client-centered therapy, cognitive therapy, and behavior therapy. It would be appropriate to briefly explain the differences between each of these approaches and to advise the person to seek professional help if she feels that her problem is severe. Having said that, you can then go on to describe an approach that has been relatively effective in dealing with phobias—systematic desensitization.

   The first step in systematic desensitization is for the person to learn how to relax completely. This is because a state of complete relaxation is incompatible with being tense and anxious. The second step is to have the person generate a hierarchy of feared situations associated with flying. For example, the most feared situation the person can imagine might be sitting on the plane during takeoff and the least fearful might be hearing someone talking about flying. Once the person is totally relaxed, she can start imagining the least fearful situation in the hierarchy. When she can do that for a number of times without tensing up, she can move to the next situation in the hierarchy, and so on. It is also helpful for the person to create an unrelated, relaxing control scene, such as lying on the beach watching the waves roll in, which can be used to help her relax. Over a number of sessions, the person works her way up the hierarchy while relaxing completely, until eventually she can approach the real situation.

In practice, systematic desensitization is often combined with other techniques, such as counterconditioning (pairing pleasant associations, such as being able to travel to exotic islands, with the feared situation) and observational learning (using the real situation or a video), which involves watching other people being calm and relaxed in the anxiety-provoking situation.

2. First, people seek help from mental health professionals not only for psychological problems but also for dealing with troubled relationships, coping with transitions in life, and other troubling situations. Second, there should be no stigma attached to getting help when it is needed. The prevalence of psychological disorders and similar types of problems is much higher than most people realize, so we all probably know someone who is or has been in therapy or perhaps needs to be. So, what should we expect from psychotherapy? The Application gives some important guidelines about the therapist–client relationship and the psychotherapy process.

The cornerstone of psychotherapy is the relationship between the therapist and the person seeking help. This relationship is a collaborative endeavor in which the client is actively involved in the therapeutic process. Therapy requires work not only during the therapy sessions but also outside them. So people should expect to be involved and active. In addition, people should not expect the therapist to make decisions for them. Virtually all forms of therapy are designed to increase a person's sense of responsibility, confidence, and mastery in dealing with life's problems. The therapist is there to help.

A therapist is not a substitute friend. Rather, he or she is more of a consultant, responding objectively and honestly to issues and problems. In addition, ethically and legally, everything that goes on in therapy is totally confidential. And, under no circumstances does therapeutic intimacy include sexual intimacy.

A person should also expect therapy to challenge how he or she thinks and acts, which sometimes can be a painful process. But becoming aware that changes are needed is a necessary step toward developing healthier forms of thinking and behavior. It is important, however, not to confuse insight with change. Just because people gain an understanding of the sources and nature of their psychological problems does not mean that they will automatically resolve these problems. Likewise, the catharsis that often results from therapy is not synonymous with change. With some effort and the help of the therapeutic process, people can move toward changing how they think, behave, and react to other people, but this will not happen overnight.

Progress Test 1

1. a	6. b	11. c
2. d	7. b	12. c
3. d	8. d	13. e
4. a	9. c	14. d
5. c	10. b	15. b

Progress Test 2

1. d	6. a	11. b
2. c	7. c	12. d
3. d	8. b	13. c
4. c	9. b	14. e
5. d	10. a	15. a

Progress Test 3

1. a	6. c	11. b
2. d	7. d	12. a
3. a	8. a	13. d
4. a	9. d	14. b
5. a	10. d	15. e

appendix

Statistics:
Understanding Data

A

PREVIEW

Reading the section below first will give you a general sense of the chapter's contents and an initial introduction to some of the major concepts and terms. This will prime you for what you are about to read and help you to develop a "cognitive map" that will guide your study of the material in this chapter. Likewise, reading the **preview questions** at the beginning of each major section will improve your ability to understand, learn, and retain the information.

APPENDIX A . . . AT A GLANCE

Appendix A explains how and when various statistical techniques are used. Descriptive statistics are used to organize and summarize data in a meaningful way. Examples discussed include frequency distributions, which can be presented as a table, histogram, or frequency polygon; measures of central tendency (mode, median, and mean); and measures of variability (range and standard deviation). z scores are explained, and the concept of the normal distribution is presented.

Correlation, which is introduced in Chapter 1, is described, and calculation of the correlation coefficient is explained. The point is made that correlational research is restricted to prediction and cannot be used to identify cause-and-effect relationships. The scatter diagram can be used to depict graphically the relationship between two variables.

Inferential statistics are used to determine whether outcomes of a study can be generalized to a larger population, and they provide information about the probability of a particular result if only random factors are operating. The text notes that if the probability of the outcome resulting from chance factors is small, the findings are said to be statistically significant.

Descriptive Statistics

Preview Questions

Consider the following questions as you study this section of the chapter.

- What are descriptive statistics, and what are they used for?
- What are frequency distributions, histograms, and frequency polygons?
- What is a skewed distribution, and what is a symmetrical distribution?
- What are the three measures of central tendency?
- What are the two measures of variability, and what are z scores?
- What is the standard normal curve (standard normal distribution)?

*Read the section "Descriptive Statistics" and **write** your answers to the following:*

1. Descriptive statistics are used to _____
   _____

2. A frequency distribution is _____
   _____
   _____

3. A histogram is _____
   _____
   _____

4. A frequency polygon is _____
   _____
   _____

5. A skewed distribution is _____
   _____
   _____

6. A symmetrical distribution is _____
   _____
   _____

7. Measures of central tendency are _____
   _____

   The mode is _____
   _____

   The median is _____
   _____

The mean is _____
_____

8. Measures of variability are _____
   _____

   The range is _____
   _____

   The standard deviation is _____
   _____

9. A z score is _____
   _____

10. The standard normal curve (standard normal distribution) is _____
    _____
    _____

    A person with a z score of +1 on a normal distribution (1 SD above the mean) has _____
    _____
    _____

After you have carefully studied the preceding section, complete the following exercises.

Concept Check 1

Read the following and write the correct term in the space provided.

1. Professor Wilson calculated the mode, median, and mean of the scores from the midterm exam. These descriptive statistics are referred to as

   _____ .

2. Professor Wilson noticed that the most frequently occurring score was 73; this score is called the _____ .

3. In order to determine the spread of the scores, Professor Wilson subtracted the lowest score in the distribution from the highest. In this instance, he has calculated a measure of
   _____ called the
   _____ .

4. Next, he subtracted the mean from each score in the distribution, squared each of these deviations, added them up, divided by the number of scores in the distribution, and finally took the square root of the number just calculated. Professor Wilson has calculated a measure of _____ called the

_____ .

5. Finally, Professor Wilson graphically represented the frequency distribution by placing a mark above each score at the point representing its frequency and then connecting these points with straight lines. This type of graph is called a(n) _____ .

Review of Terms and Concepts 1

Use the terms in this list to complete the Matching Test, then to help you answer the True/False items correctly.

descriptive statistics
frequency distribution
histogram
frequency polygon
skewed distribution
positively skewed
  distribution
negatively skewed
  distribution
symmetrical distribution
measure of central
  tendency

mode
median
mean
measure of variability
range
standard deviation
z score
standard normal curve
  (standard normal
  distribution)

Matching Exercise

Match the appropriate term with its definition or description.

1. _____ A number, expressed in standard deviation units, that shows a score's deviation from the mean.

2. _____ Statistics used to organize and summarize data in a meaningful way.

3. _____ A symmetrical distribution forming a bell-shaped curve in which the mean, median, and mode are all equal and fall in the exact middle.

4. _____ A summary of how often various scores occur in a sample of scores. Score values are arranged in order of magnitude, and the number of times each score occurs is recorded.

5. _____ Measure of variability; expressed as the square root of the sum of the squared deviations around the mean divided by the number of scores in the distribution.

6. _____ An asymmetrical distribution; more scores pile up on one side of the distribution than on the other.

7. _____ A single number that presents information about the spread of scores in a frequency distribution.

8. _____ Distribution in which the scores fall equally on both sides of the graph. The normal curve is an example.

9. _____ Measure of variability; the highest score in a distribution minus the lowest score.

True/False Test

Indicate whether each statement is true or false by placing T or F in the blank space next to each item.

1. ___ In a positively skewed distribution, most people have high scores.

2. ___ The mode is the most frequently occurring score in a distribution.

3. ___ A measure of central tendency is a single number that presents some information about the "center" of a frequency distribution.

4. ___ In a negatively skewed distribution, most people have low scores.

5. ___ A histogram is a way of graphically representing a frequency distribution where frequency is marked above each score category on the graph's horizontal axis and the marks are connected by straight lines.

6. ___ The mean is the sum of a set of scores in a distribution divided by the number of scores and is usually the most representative measure of central tendency.

7. ___ A frequency polygon is a way of graphically representing a frequency distribution and is a type of bar chart using vertical bars that touch.

8. ___ The median is the score that divides a frequency distribution exactly in half, so that the same number of scores lies on each side of it.

Check your answers and review any areas of weakness before going on to the next section.

Correlation and Inferential Statistics

Preview Questions

Consider the following questions as you study these sections of the chapter.

- How is correlation defined, and what is the correlation coefficient?
- How are correlations depicted graphically?
- What are inferential statistics, and what is meant by statistical significance?
- What is meant by the terms *population* and *sample*?

*Read the sections "Correlation" and "Inferential Statistics" and **write** your answers to the following:*

1. Correlation is the _____
   _____

2. The correlation coefficient is a measure of ____
   _____
   _____
   A positive correlation coefficient indicates that
   _____
   _____
   A negative correlation coefficient indicates that
   _____
   _____

3. Correlations are depicted graphically_____
   _____
   A positive correlation is indicated by _____
   _____
   A negative correlation is indicated by_____
   _____
   _____

4. Inferential statistics are _____
   _____
   _____

5. Statistical significance refers to the fact that if the results of a study are _____
   _____
   _____
   _____

6. A population is _____
   _____
   Because the entire population of interest usually cannot be studied, researchers use _____
   _____
   _____

After you have carefully studied the preceding section, complete the following exercises.

Concept Check 2

Read the following and write the correct term in the space provided.

1. Dr. Jabul discovers that the more education people have, the more money they tend to earn. Dr. Jabul has discovered a _____ correlation.

2. Based on his research, Dr. Jabul can use one variable to _____ the other, but he cannot say that one variable _____ the other.

3. When Professor Alphonse plotted his data on a scatter plot, he noticed that they clustered in a pattern that extends from the upper lefthand corner of the graph to the lower righthand corner. This pattern suggests that the two variables are _____ correlated.

4. When Kayla analyzed the correlational data for her psychology project, the correlation coefficient was +.07. Kayla can conclude that the two variables _____ (are/are not) correlated.

5. When researchers analyzed the data from their experiment, they found large differences between the control group and the experimental group that were not due to chance. They can conclude that the results are
   _____ .

6. In order to discover how people feel about the level of service provided, the ABC company asks a randomly selected subset of their customers to fill out a brief questionnaire. ABC's customers represent the _____ , and the subset surveyed is a(n)

_____ .

Review of Terms and Concepts 2

Use the terms in this list to complete the Matching Test, then to help you answer the True/False items correctly.

correlation
correlation coefficient
positive correlation
  coefficient
negative correlation
  coefficient

scatter diagram (scatter
  plot)
inferential statistics
statistically significant
population
sample

Matching Exercise

Match the appropriate term with its definition or description.

1. _____ Graph that represents the relationship between two variables.

2. _____ Measure of the magnitude and direction of the relationship (the correlation) between two variables; the closer the number is to +1 or –1, the stronger the relationship.

3. _____ Statistical techniques that allow researchers to determine whether the outcomes in a study are likely to be more than just chance events and whether they can be legitimately generalized to a larger population.

4. _____ A complete set of something—people, nonhuman animals, objects, or events.

5. _____ The relationship between two variables.

True/False Test

Indicate whether each statement is true or false by placing T or F in the blank space next to each item.

1. ___ Results can be considered statistically significant when the probability of obtaining them, if chance factors alone are operating, is less than .05 (5 chances out of 100).

2. ___ A positive correlation coefficient indicates that as one variable increases, the other tends to decrease.

3. ___ A sample is a subset of a population.

4. ___ A negative correlation coefficient indicates that as one variable increases, the other tends to increase.

Check your answers and review any areas of weakness before completing the progress tests.

Progress Test 1

Review the complete chapter, review all your study notes, and then test yourself on the following progress test. Check your answers. If you make a mistake, review your notes, review the relevant section of the study guide, and, if necessary, go back and read the appropriate part of your textbook.

1. Professor Admunson used a scatter diagram to depict the relationship between her students' high school GPA and their first-year GPA in college. She noticed that the data points clustered in a pattern that extends from the lower left-hand corner of the graph to the upper right-hand corner. This pattern suggests that the two variables

  (a) are negatively correlated.
  (b) have no relationship.
  (c) are positively correlated.
  (d) have a cause-and-effect relationship.

2. A measure of variability is to _____ as a measure of central tendency is to _____ .

  (a) mode; median
  (b) correlation; scatter plot
  (c) standard deviation; mean
  (d) histogram; frequency polygon

3. One student in the class got an extremely low score of 10 out of 100 on a test. Which measure of central tendency is most affected by this low score?

  (a) mode   (c) median
  (b) mean   (d) range

4. Following the final exam, Professor Farrar calculated a number of statistics and noticed that the standard deviation was extremely small. This indicates that
   (a) the scores on the exam were clustered around the mean and not spread out.
   (b) the distribution was skewed.
   (c) the scores had a great deal of variability and were not clustered around the mean.
   (d) there were very few students in her class.

5. Mrs. Kodiak has seven children aged 3, 5, 8, 9, 12, 15, and 15. The median age of her children is
   (a) 9.   (c) 12.
   (b) 15.   (d) 67.

6. When the results of an experiment were examined and the appropriate statistics calculated, the researchers concluded that the probability of obtaining these results, if random factors alone were operating, was less than .01. The results are
   (a) probably due to chance.
   (b) statistically insignificant.
   (c) skewed.
   (d) statistically significant.

7. For his class presentation, Liam prepared a graph that depicted a frequency distribution with vertical bars that touched each other. Liam has constructed a
   (a) scatter diagram.
   (b) frequency polygon.
   (c) histogram.
   (d) standard deviation.

8. Liam's graph is a symmetrical distribution with an equal number of scores on each side of the graph. It is very likely that the
   (a) mean is larger than the median.
   (b) mode is larger than the mean.
   (c) mean, mode, and median have the same value.
   (d) median is larger than the mode.

9. When researchers calculated the correlation coefficients for two different sets of data, they discovered that set A had a negative correlation of −.85 and set B had a positive correlation of +.62. They can conclude that
   (a) set A has a stronger correlation than set B.
   (b) set A has a weaker correlation than set B.
   (c) set B has a stronger correlation than set A.
   (d) both (b) and (c) are true.

10. When Gary calculated the mean, median, and mode of the data in his frequency distribution, he was using
   (a) inferential statistics.
   (b) descriptive statistics.
   (c) correlational statistics.
   (d) measures of variability.

Progress Test 2

After you have checked your understanding of the material in Progress Test 1 and have done a complete chapter review with special focus on any areas of weakness, you are ready to assess your knowledge on Progress Test 2. Check your answers. If you make a mistake, review your notes, the relevant section of the study guide, and, if necessary, the appropriate part of your textbook.

1. In addition to calculating the range, Matthew also calculated the standard deviation for his frequency distribution of scores. Matthew is using
   (a) measures of variability.
   (b) inferential statistics.
   (c) measures of central tendency.
   (d) correlational statistics.

2. When Professor Kitahara finished marking the final exams, he plotted the results on a graph by marking the frequency above each score category on the horizontal axis and then connecting the marks using straight lines. Professor Kitahara has constructed a
   (a) frequency distribution.
   (b) histogram.
   (c) frequency polygon.
   (d) scatter diagram.

3. Professor Kitahara observed that the graph was a symmetrical distribution that resembled a bell-shaped curve and that the mean, median, and mode were all equal. A student who scored better than 84 percent of the other students in this distribution would have a z score of

   (a) +1.   (c) +.84.
   (b) −1.   (d) −.84.

4. Hanna has a grade point average of 3.5. What measure of central tendency was used to calculate this statistic?

   (a) median
   (b) standard deviation
   (c) mode
   (d) mean

5. In her research, Dr. Simiak found that the more credit cards people have, the less money they have in their savings accounts. Dr. Simiak has found a _____ correlation between the number of credit cards owned and savings.

   (a) positive   (c) negative
   (b) zero   (d) skewed

6. Range is to mode as _____ is to _____ .

   (a) correlation; scatter diagram
   (b) median; mode
   (c) correlation coefficient; z score
   (d) variability; central tendency

7. Fydor compared two frequency distributions and noticed that in the first distribution most people had low scores and in the second distribution most people had high scores. The first distribution is _____ , and the second distribution is _____ .

   (a) positively skewed; negatively skewed
   (b) symmetrical; normal
   (c) negatively skewed; positively skewed
   (d) a polygon; a histogram

8. When Tyborg calculated the mean and standard deviation for a set of scores, he found that the mean was 55 out of a 100, and the standard deviation was 15. If the scores are normally distributed, Tyborg can conclude that approximately 68 percent of the scores are between

   (a) 40 and 70.   (c) 55 and 70.
   (b) 25 and 85.   (d) 40 and 55.

9. In the above example, a student with a z score of −1 would have a score of

   (a) 55.   (c) 70.
   (b) 40.   (d) 25.

10. During the past month Karianne read 8 books, Kyle read 2 books, Phyllis read 4 books, and Philip read 6 books. The mean number of books read by this group is

    (a) 5.   (c) 8.
    (b) 20.   (d) 6.

Progress Test 3

After you have checked your understanding of the material in Progress Tests 1 and 2, and have done a complete chapter review with special focus on any areas of weakness, you are ready to further assess your knowledge on Progress Test 3. Check your answers. If you make a mistake, review your notes, the appropriate parts of the study guide, and, if necessary, the relevant sections of your textbook.

1. A complete set of something (people, objects, events, etc.) is to a _____ as a representative subset is to a _____ .

   (a) descriptive statistics; inferential statistics
   (b) sample; population
   (c) inferential statistics; descriptive statistics
   (d) population; sample

2. Dr. Soryun carried out the appropriate calculations on her data and noticed that results were more extreme than would be expected by chance. She concluded that the probability of obtaining these results if random factors alone were operating was less than 1 chance out of a 100. Dr. Soryun has used _____ statistics, and the results can be called _____ .

   (a) descriptive statistics; statistically significant
   (b) inferential statistics; positively skewed
   (c) descriptive statistics; positively skewed
   (d) inferential statistics; statistically significant

3. Organizing and summarizing data is to _____ as making inferences and drawing conclusions is to _____ .

   (a) descriptive statistics; inferential statistics
   (b) correlational research; experimental research
   (c) inferential statistics; descriptive statistics
   (d) experimental research; correlational research

4. Researchers at State University are interested in determining to what extent personality variables such as impatience, aggressiveness, and hostility could be used to predict the risk of cardiovascular disease. These researchers are most likely to use _____ in their research.
   (a) a measure of variability
   (b) the correlation coefficient
   (c) the standard normal distribution
   (d) the standard deviation

5. After analyzing his data, Jamie decided to depict his results in a graph. He noticed that the data points clustered in a pattern that extended from the upper lefthand corner to the lower righthand corner on his graph. Jamie has constructed a _____ that shows a _____ .
   (a) polygon; skewed distribution
   (b) scatter diagram; positive correlation
   (c) histogram; symmetrical distribution
   (d) scatter diagram; negative correlation

6. In his survey research, Dr. Khrod discovered that the more education people have, the less television they watch. Dr. Khrod has discovered a(n) _____ between television watching and level of education.
   (a) negative correlation
   (b) illusory correlation
   (c) positive correlation
   (d) cause-and-effect relationship

7. When Harpinder plotted his data, his graph closely resembled the normal curve and had a mean of 50 and a standard deviation of 5. Harpinder can be confident that approximately 68 percent of the scores are between
   (a) +1 and –1 SDs.
   (b) +2 and –2 SDs.
   (c) +3 and –3 SDs.
   (d) correlation coefficients of +1 and –1.

8. Raphael's z-score on the midterm was +1. If the class scores are normally distributed, Raphael has
   (a) scored better than 34.13 percent of the class.
   (b) scored worse than 34.13 percent of the class.
   (c) scored better than 84 percent of the class.
   (d) scored worse than 84 percent of the class.

9. When Professor Exman compared the statistics from her two introductory biology classes, she noticed that the standard deviation was 8.24 in class A and 3.76 in class B. She can conclude that
   (a) the students in class A studied much harder than those in class B.
   (b) the scores in class A had much more variability than those in class B.
   (c) the range for both classes is likely to be identical.
   (d) one very extreme score probably distorted the standard deviation for class A.

10. As a first step in analyzing her data, Tracianne calculated the mean, the mode, and the median. Tracianne has
   (a) used inferential statistics.
   (b) determined the statistical significance of her results.
   (c) used descriptive statistics.
   (d) calculated measures of variability.

Answers

Descriptive Statistics

1. *Descriptive statistics are used to* organize and summarize data in a meaningful way.

2. *A frequency distribution is* a summary of how often various scores occur in a sample of scores. Score values are arranged in order of magnitude, and the number of times each score occurs is recorded.

3. *A histogram is* a way of graphically representing a frequency distribution. It is like a bar chart with two special features: the bars are always vertical, and they always touch.

4. *A frequency polygon is* another way of graphically representing a frequency distribution. In contrast to a histogram, or a frequency distribution, a mark is made above each category at the point representing its frequency, and these marks are then connected by straight lines.

5. *A skewed distribution is* an asymmetrical distribution with more scores piled up on one side of the distribution than on the other. If most people have low scores, the distribution is positively skewed; if most people have high scores, the distribution is negatively skewed.

6. *A symmetrical distribution is* a distribution in which scores fall equally on both halves of the graph (an example of a symmetrical distribution is the normal curve).

7. *Measures of central tendency are* single numbers that present some information about the center of a frequency distribution. *The mode is* the score or category that occurs most frequently in a set of raw scores or in a frequency distribution. *The median is* the score that divides a frequency distribution exactly in half, so that the same number of scores lie on each side of it. *The mean is* the sum of a set of scores in a distribution divided by the number of scores, and is usually the most representative measure of central tendency.

8. *Measures of variability are* single numbers that present information about the spread of scores in a distribution. *The range is* the highest score in a distribution minus the lowest score. *The standard deviation is* expressed as the square root of the sum of the squared deviations around the mean divided by the number of scores in the distribution.

9. *A z score is* a number, expressed in standard deviation units, that shows a score's deviation from the mean.

10. *The standard normal curve (standard normal distribution) is* a symmetrical distribution forming a bell-shaped curve in which the mean, median, and mode are all equal and fall in the exact middle. *A person with a z score of +1 on a normal distribution (1 SD above the mean) has* scored better than 84 percent of the other people in the distribution (34.13 percent between 0 and +1, plus the 50 percent that falls below 0).

Concept Check 1

1. measures of central tendency
2. mode
3. variability; range
4. variability; standard deviation
5. frequency polygon

Matching Exercise 1

1. *z* score
2. descriptive statistics
3. standard normal curve (standard normal distribution)
4. frequency distribution
5. standard deviation
6. skewed distribution
7. measure of variability

8. symmetrical distribution
9. range

True/False Test 1

1. F
2. T
3. T
4. F
5. F
6. T
7. F
8. T

Correlation and Inferential Statistics

1. *Correlation is the* relationship between two variables; it does not indicate causality between the two variables.

2. *The correlation coefficient is a measure of* the magnitude and direction of the relationship between two variables, and the closer the correlation coefficient is to +1 or −1, the stronger the relationship is. *A positive correlation coefficient indicates that* as one variable increases, the other tends to increase. *A negative correlation coefficient indicates that* as one variable increases, the other tends to decrease.

3. *Correlations are depicted graphically* on a scatter diagram (scatter plot), which is a graph that represents the relationship between two variables. *A positive correlation is indicated by* the upward-sloping pattern of dots, from bottom left to top right (when one variable is high, the other tends to be high too, and vice versa). *A negative correlation is indicated by* the downward-sloping pattern of dots, from upper left to lower right (when one variable is high, the other tends to be low, and vice versa).

4. *Inferential statistics are* statistical techniques that allow researchers to determine whether the outcomes in a study are likely to be more than just chance events and whether they can be legitimately generalized to larger populations.

5. *Statistical significance refers to the fact that if the results of a study are more extreme than* would be expected by chance alone, we reject the idea that no real effect has occurred and conclude that the manipulation of the independent variable is the reason for the obtained results; when this happens, the results are statistically significant, and the probability of getting these results, if random factors alone are operating, is less than .05 (5 chances in 100) or .01 (1 chance in 100).

6. *A population is* a complete set of something— people, nonhuman animals, objects, or events.

Because the entire population of interest usually cannot be studied, researchers use a sample, which is a subset of a population.

Concept Check 2

1. positive
2. predict; causes
3. negatively
4. are not
5. statistically significant
6. population; sample

Matching Exercise 2

1. scatter diagram (scatter plot)
2. correlation coefficient
3. inferential statistics
4. population
5. correlation

True/False Test 2

1. T   3. T
2. F   4. F

Progress Test 1

1. c   5. a   9. a
2. c   6. d   10. b
3. b   7. c
4. a   8. c

Progress Test 2

1. a   5. c   9. b
2. c   6. d   10. a
3. a   7. a
4. d   8. a

Progress Test 3

1. d   5. d   9. b
2. d   6. a   10. c
3. a   7. a
4. b   8. c

appendix B
Industrial/Organizational Psychology

PREVIEW

Reading the section below first will give you a general sense of the chapter's contents and an initial introduction to some of the major concepts and terms. This will prime you for what you are about to read and help you to develop a "cognitive map" that will guide your study of the material in this chapter. Likewise, reading the **preview questions** at the beginning of each major section will improve your ability to understand, learn, and retain the information.

APPENDIX B . . . AT A GLANCE

Appendix B identifies and describes six content areas in the field of industrial/organizational (I/O) psychology (selection and placement, training and development, performance management, organizational development, quality of work life, and ergonomics). Work settings, type of training, and employment outlook in the area of I/O psychology are examined.

Personnel psychology (the "I," or industrial, side of I/O psychology) and organizational behavior (the "O," or organizational, side of I/O psychology) are explored in depth. Job analysis, personnel selection, effective job training programs, and accurate evaluation of job performance are all part of the work carried out in personnel psychology. These psychologists use many devices to help with the goal of selecting the best applicants for jobs and are concerned with the validity of these selection devices.

The discussion of organizational behavior begins with the topic of job satisfaction, noting the various hypotheses used to explain different levels of job satisfaction. Leadership and leadership effectiveness are also discussed. A number of approaches to explaining leadership effectiveness are explored, and the text concludes that situational theories seem to do the best job. Research that examines how followers affect leaders' behavior and how leaders emerge in a group is also described. Finally, workplace trends and issues within I/O psychology are presented.

What Is Industrial/Organizational Psychology?

Preview Questions

Consider the following questions as you study this section of the chapter.

- What is industrial/organizational psychology?
- What are the six content areas of industrial/organizational psychology, and what is the main focus of each?

*Read the section "What Is Industrial/Organizational Psychology?" and **write** your answers to the following:*

1. Industrial/organizational psychology is

   _____

   _____

   The "I" side of I/O psychology is called

   _____ and is

   concerned with _____

   _____

   The "O" side of I/O psychology is called

   _____ and is concerned

   with _____

   _____

2. The six content areas of I/O psychology (and the

   focus of each) are

   (a) _____

   which focuses on _____

   _____

   _____

   (b) _____

   which focuses on _____

   _____

   _____

   (c) _____

   is concerned with _____

   _____

   (d) _____

   whose goal is to _____

   _____

   _____

(e) _____

which emphasizes the _____

_____

(f) _____

which focuses on _____

_____

_____

Work Settings, Type of Training, and Employment Outlook

Preview Questions

Consider the following questions as you study this section of the chapter.

- What are the requirements for working in the field of I/O psychology, and what are the principal employment settings of I/O psychologists?
- What is the employment outlook for I/O psychologists?
- What jobs and careers are open to people with bachelor's degrees?

*Read the section "Work Settings, Type of Training, and Employment Outlook" and **write** your answers to the following:*

1. To work in the field of I/O psychology, a _____

   _____

   _____

   The principal employment settings are _____

   _____

   _____

2. The employment outlook for those with Ph.D.s

   and master's degrees _____

   _____

   _____

   People with bachelor's degrees may find work

   as _____

   _____

   _____

   _____

Personnel Psychology

Preview Questions

Consider the following questions as you study this section of the chapter.

- What are the three major goals of personnel psychology?
- What is the definition of job analysis, what are selection devices used for, and what do training program developers do?
- What is selection device validity?
- What are the most common types of psychological tests and personnel selection devices used in personnel psychology?

*Read the section "Personnel Psychology" and **write** your answers to the following:*

1. The three major goals of personnel psychologists are (a) _____
   (b) _____
   (c) _____

2. Job analysis is a technique in which _____

3. Selection devices, such as tests and interviews, are used to _____

   Training program developers begin by _____

4. Selection device validity refers to _____

5. The six most common psychological tests (and their specific uses) are
   (a) _____

   (b) _____

(c) _____

(d) _____

(e) _____

(f) _____

6. The three most common types of personnel selection devices (and their specific uses) are
   (a) _____

   (b) _____

   (c) _____

Organizational Behavior and Workplace Trends and Issues

Preview Questions

Consider the following questions as you study these sections of the chapter.

- What is the focus of organizational behavior (OB)?
- What is the discrepancy hypothesis, the social influence hypothesis, the dispositional factors approach, and how does each explain job satisfaction?
- What is leadership, and how do the trait, behavioral, and situational (or contingency) theories explain leader effectiveness?
- What is the leader–member exchange model?
- What are the main workplace trends and issues in I/O psychology?

*Read the sections "Organizational Behavior" and "Trends for the Future" and **write** your answers to the following:*

1. Organizational behavior focuses on _____

2. The discrepancy hypothesis is _____
_____
_____

3. The social influence hypothesis is the view that
_____
_____

4. The dispositional factors hypothesis is the
position that_____
_____
_____

5. The trait approach to leader effectiveness is
based on _____
_____
_____

6. Behavioral theories of leader effectiveness focus
on_____
_____
_____

Consideration describes leaders who
_____
_____

and initiating structure describes leaders who
are _____
_____

7. Situational (contingency) theories of leader
effectiveness focus on _____
_____
_____

8. The leader–member exchange model of
leadership suggests _____
_____
_____

Research on upward influence (subordinates
influencing supervisors) has shown that
_____
_____
_____
_____

9. Personal qualities related to leader
emergence are _____
_____
_____

The topic of leader emergence differs from that
of leader effectiveness because _____
_____
_____

10. The major workplace trends and issues are

(a) _____
_____

(b) _____
_____
_____

(c) _____
_____

(d) _____
_____

(e) In the future, I/O psychologists will_____
_____
_____
_____

*After you have carefully studied the preceding
sections, complete the following exercises.*

Concept Check 1

*Read the following and write the correct term in the
space provided.*

1. Dr. Lomburg works in an area of
industrial/organizational psychology that is primarily concerned with the "I" side of I/O. This
side of I/O psychology is sometimes called

_____ .

2. Rather than focusing on the impact of leaders
on followers, Dr. Hagan's research is concerned
with the interaction between supervisors and
subordinates and in particular with the unique
relationships between leaders and their followers. Dr. Hagan is interested in the
_____ of leader effectiveness.

3. Ovidiu works for a personnel supply organization; the main focus of his job is matching employers with job applicants and job applicants with employers. Ovidiu is most likely employed as a _____ .

4. When Laleet applied for job as a mechanic, he was given a test in which he had to take apart the car's gearbox and locate and fix an engine problem. Laleet has experienced a _____ personnel selection test.

5. As part of her assessment for a job in a retail outlet, Serena was given a number of tests, one of which asked about her past behavior involving theft, her attitude about punishment for theft, and her perceptions about the prevalence of theft. This selection device is called a(n) _____ .

6. A research team at State University investigated behavioral theories of leader effectiveness. If their findings are consistent with previous research in this area, they are likely to identify two major types of leadership behavior, namely _____ and _____ .

7. In order to discover who emerges as a leader, researchers gave a group of participants some problems to solve and some topics to discuss. This technique is called _____ .

Review of Terms and Concepts

Use the terms in this list to complete the Matching Test, then to help you answer the True/False items correctly.

industrial/organizational
  (I/O) psychology
personnel psychology
organizational behavior
ergonomics
management analysts
  and consultants
employment interviewer
organizational
  development (OD)
job analysis
leader–member
  exchange model

selection device validity
discrepancy hypothesis
social influence
  hypothesis
dispositional factors
  hypothesis
trait approach to leader
  effectiveness
behavioral theories of
  leader effectiveness
situational (or
  contingency) theories
  of leader effectiveness

Matching Exercise

Match the appropriate term with its definition or description.

1. _____ Assessment of the major responsibilities of a particular job and the human characteristics needed to fill it.

2. _____ Subarea of I/O psychology that focuses on bringing about positive change in an organization, such as increased profitability or improved products.

3. _____ Model of leadership emphasizing that the quality of the interactions among supervisors and subordinates varies depending on the unique characteristics of both.

4. _____ Branch of psychology that focuses on the study of human behavior at work.

5. _____ Theories that focus on how a particular situation influences a leader's effectiveness.

6. _____ Approach to explaining job satisfaction that focuses on the discrepancy, if any, between what a person wants from a job and how that person evaluates what is experienced at work.

7. _____ An I/O-related job, typically with personnel supply firms and open to those with bachelor's degrees, that focuses on matching employers with job applicants and job applicants with employers.

8. _____ View that a person's level of job satisfaction is influenced by the job satisfaction levels of other people.

True/False Test

Indicate whether each statement is true or false by placing T or F in the blank space next to each item.

1. ___ The dispositional factors hypothesis is the view that a person's level of job satisfaction may be due in part to a genetically based disposition toward a positive or negative outlook.

2. ___ Personnel psychology is a subarea of I/O psychology that focuses on how the organization and the social environment in which people work affect their attitudes and behaviors.

3. ___ Behavioral theories of leader effectiveness focus on differences in the behaviors of effective and ineffective leaders.

4. ___ Ergonomics is a subarea of I/O psychology that focuses on the design of equipment and the development of work procedures in accordance with human capabilities and limitations.

5. ___ Selection device validity is the extent to which a personnel selection device is successful in distinguishing between those who will become high performers at a certain job and those who will not.

6. ___ Management analysts and consultants deal with a variety of organizational problems, such as helping organizations relocate or restructure; the job involves collecting, reviewing, and analyzing information, making recommendations, and helping to implement those recommendations.

7. ___ The trait approach to leader effectiveness focuses on the personal characteristics displayed by successful leaders.

8. ___ Organizational behavior is a subarea of I/O psychology that focuses on matching people's characteristics to job requirements, accurately measuring job performance, and assessing employee training needs.

Check your answers and review any areas of weakness before completing the progress tests.

Progress Test 1

Review the complete chapter, review all your study notes, and then test yourself on the following progress test. Check your answers. If you make a mistake, review your notes, review the relevant section of the study guide, and, if necessary, go back and read the appropriate part of your textbook.

1. Dr. Garcia is an I/O psychologist who is concerned with developing assessment techniques to help select from a pool of job applicants those who are most likely to be successful in a given job or organization. Dr. Darton, on the other hand, focuses on identifying criteria or standards that determine the degree to which employees are performing their jobs well, accurately measuring their job performance, and honestly conveying performance results to these employees. Dr. Garcia works in the content area called _____ , and Dr. Darton works in _____ .
   (a) training and development; quality of work life

   (b) selection and placement; performance management
   (c) ergonomics; organizational development (OD)
   (d) performance management; ergonomics

2. Dr. Foggerty focuses on the design of equipment and the development of work procedures in accordance with human capabilities and limitations. Dr. Foggerty's area of interest is called
   (a) ergonomics.
   (b) personnel psychology.
   (c) performance management.
   (d) organizational behavior.

3. When Kamal goes to graduate school, she plans to specialize in matching people's characteristics to job requirements, accurately measuring job performance, and assessing employee training needs. Kamal is interested in
   (a) personnel psychology.
   (b) organizational psychology.
   (c) organizational development.
   (d) ergonomics.

4. Helmut has a bachelor's degree and is interested in working in the field of I/O psychology. Which of the following statements about Helmut's prospects is true?
   (a) It will be difficult for him to find employment in the field of I/O.
   (b) Some areas related to I/O, such as personnel, training, and labor relations specialists and managers, are open to him.
   (c) He may find a job as an employment interviewer.
   (d) All of the above are true.

5. Olivia's research focuses on how the organization and the social environment in which people work affect their attitudes and behaviors. Olivia works in a subarea of I/O psychology called
   (a) personnel psychology.
   (b) selection and placement.
   (c) ergonomics.
   (d) organizational behavior.

6. Gulbinder is the chief personnel officer for a large corporation. She is very concerned that the methods and techniques used in personnel selection are successful in distinguishing between applicants who will become high performers and those who will not. Gulbinder's concerns are related to
   (a) quality of work life.
   (b) ergonomics.
   (c) selection device validity.
   (d) organizational development (OD).

7. Bradford believes that leaders are born, not made, and he cites many examples of people who possess certain qualities or characteristics that make them natural leaders. Bradford's views are most consistent with the
   (a) situational (or contingency) theories of leader effectiveness.
   (b) behavioral theories of leader effectiveness.
   (c) leader–member exchange model of leadership.
   (d) trait approach to leader effectiveness.

8. Although most Americans report that they are satisfied with their jobs, they appear less satisfied with some aspects than with others. In order to explain differences in job satisfaction, which of the following approaches is likely to be used?
   (a) discrepancy hypothesis
   (b) social influence hypothesis
   (c) dispositional factors hypothesis
   (d) All of the above are equally likely to be used.

9. Mrs. Afyia uses a technique to determine the major responsibilities of a job and the human characteristics needed to fill it. Her goal is to select appropriate people for a particular position. Mrs Afyia is using a technique called
   (a) ergonomics.
   (b) job analysis.
   (c) selection device validity.
   (d) the leaderless group discussion technique.

10. According to In Focus B.1, which of the following is true?
   (a) Employees perceived as being sincere, consistent, and loyal are likely to receive positive evaluations from their supervisors.

(b) Employees perceived as being "ingratiating" are more likely to be recognized by their supervisors with higher performance evaluations and higher pay raises than those perceived as being merely "good citizens."
(c) The doctrine of employment-at-will means that employees can be legally discharged from their jobs, without restriction, for any reason.
(d) All of the above are true.

Progress Test 2

After you have checked your understanding of the material in Progress Test 1 and have done a complete chapter review with special focus on any areas of weakness, you are ready to assess your knowledge on Progress Test 2. Check your answers. If you make a mistake, review your notes, the relevant section of the study guide, and, if necessary, the appropriate part of your textbook.

1. Dr. Daviduk has just completed a report identifying major workplace trends and issues. Which of the following is not likely to appear in her report?
   (a) telecommuting or telework
   (b) Internet recruiting
   (c) privacy in the workplace
   (d) the issue of work–life balance
   (e) All of the above are likely to be included in the report.

2. Before building their new factory, ABC Manufacturing Company hired an I/O psychologist to help in the design of new equipment, work procedures, and safety standards. This consultant is involved in which content area of I/O psychology?
   (a) quality of work life
   (b) ergonomics
   (c) organizational development
   (d) performance management

3. In his research on leader effectiveness, Dr. Grether focuses on differences in the behavior of effective and ineffective leaders. Dr. Grether's work is most consistent with the _____ of leader effectiveness.
   (a) trait theories
   (b) behavioral theories
   (c) situational theories
   (d) leader–member exchange model

4. Lance wants to become an I/O psychologist but he is not sure what the future holds for this profession. Research on this topic is likely to reveal that
   (a) I/O psychologists will continue to have a significant impact on the workplace.
   (b) most I/O psychologists will become redundant in the near future due to technological advances.
   (c) increased diversity of the workforce, technological advances, and a global economy will mean a gradual decline in the need for I/O psychologists.
   (d) it will be very easy for people with bachelor's degrees to find employment in the field of I/O psychology.

5. Mr. Wentworth wants to bring about positive change in his organization, increase profitability, and improve the products he manufactures. The subarea of I/O psychology most concerned with these issues is
   (a) personnel psychology.
   (b) ergonomics.
   (c) organizational development (OD).
   (d) performance management.

6. Gladys believes that job satisfaction results from the difference between what a person wants from a job and how that person evaluates what is experienced. Wilma disagrees and suggests that people's level of job satisfaction is probably due to their innate tendency to be positive or negative about life and work. Gladys's view supports the _____ hypothesis, and Wilma's position supports the _____ hypothesis.
   (a) discrepancy; social influence
   (b) dispositional; discrepancy
   (c) discrepancy; dispositional
   (d) social influence; dispositional

7. At a party, Justina was asked what she does for a living. She replied that she focuses on the study of human behavior at work. Justina is most likely a(n)
   (a) counseling psychologist.
   (b) social psychologist.
   (c) industrial/organizational psychologist.
   (d) clinical psychologist.

8. When asked to elaborate on the type of work she does, Justina said that she is primarily interested in research on factors that contribute to a productive and healthy workforce, and in particular on the effects of flexible work schedules, telecommuting, and job sharing on job satisfaction. Justina works in the content area of I/O psychology called
   (a) quality of work life.
   (b) training and development.
   (c) selection and placement.
   (d) performance management.

9. In her work, Dr. Tahler uses a variety of psychological tests that measure cognitive ability, mechanical aptitude, motor and sensory ability, and normal and abnormal personality traits. It is most likely that Dr. Tahler is a(n)
   (a) behavioral psychologist.
   (b) personnel psychologist.
   (c) organizational psychologist.
   (d) ergonomics psychologist.

10. According to In Focus B.2, which of the following is *false*?
    (a) Male and female managers tend to be similar in personality and behavior.
    (b) Male and female managers tend to talk about their jobs differently and typically delegate work differently.
    (c) The gender of managers influences how people react to them.
    (d) Male and female managers use the same techniques at work and at home to deal with and resolve conflicts.
    (e) None of the above are false.

Progress Test 3

After you have checked your understanding of the material in Progress Tests 1 and 2, and have done a complete chapter review with special focus on any areas of weakness, you are ready to further assess your knowledge on Progress Test 3. Check your answers. If you make a mistake, review your notes, the appropriate parts of the study guide, and if necessary, the relevant sections of your textbook.

1. When Brock finishes college, he plans to go on to graduate school and focus on the study of human behavior at work. Brock wants to be a(n)
   (a) counseling psychologist.
   (b) statistician.
   (c) clinical psychologist.
   (d) industrial/organizational psychologist.

2. Researchers interested in leader effectiveness believe that the quality of the interactions among supervisors and subordinates varies depending on the unique characteristics of both. Their approach to the topic of leadership is most consistent with
   (a) the trait approach to leader effectiveness
   (b) the leader–member exchange model
   (c) the behavioral theories of leader effectiveness
   (d) the situational (contingency) theories of leadership

3. Gregory believes that a leader's effectiveness most likely results from a particular combination of personality characteristics, rather than from situational factors. Gregory's views are most consistent with _____ theories of leader effectiveness.
   (a) behavioral
   (b) contingency
   (c) dispositional
   (d) trait

4. Professor Kress focuses on the design of equipment and the development of work procedures in light of human capabilities and limitations. Professor Fergus focuses on bringing about positive change in organizations, such as increased profitability or improved products. Professor Kress works in an area of I/O called _____ , and Professor Fergus works in _____ .
   (a) ergonomics; organizational development (OD)

   (b) training and development; performance management
   (c) organizational development (OD); ergonomics
   (d) performance management; selection and placement

5. Breen has a high need for power, believes strongly in the feminist cause, is extremely self-confident, and has highly developed interpersonal skills. Breen fits the profile of a leader who displays
   (a) consideration.
   (b) leader–member exchange traits.
   (c) charisma.
   (d) initiating structure.

6. Zander Corporation is concerned about selecting the appropriate person for the job of production manager. Mrs. Juarez, the personnel manager, assesses and records the position's responsibilities and the personal characteristics required by the job. Mrs. Juarez is using a technique called
   (a) quality of work analysis.
   (b) job analysis.
   (c) ergonomic analysis.
   (d) discrepancy analysis.

7. In a report for the personnel department of Utopia Corporation, Dr. Raimundo makes recommendations regarding the validity and reliability of the company's various selection devices. Which of the following is Dr. Raimundo likely to suggest has the lowest validity?
   (a) work samples
   (b) general unstructured interviews
   (c) psychological testing
   (d) situational exercises

8. Stephanie and Steven both work as resource specialists for the same company. Stephanie is very satisfied with most aspects of her job, but Steven dislikes almost everything about his job. According to research by the Gallup Corporation
   (a) Stephanie is influenced by dispositional traits, and Steven is affected by discrepancy factors.
   (b) Steven is more typical of American workers than Stephanie is.
   (c) Stephanie's attitude is a function of her gender, whereas Steven's attitude is influenced by situational or contingency factors.
   (d) Stephanie is more typical of American workers than Steven is.

9. Hannalee wants to bring about positive changes in her business organization. She is concerned with improving the line of products, streamlining production, and increasing profitability. Hannalee should probably consult an I/O psychologist who specializes in a subarea called

   (a) personnel psychology.
   (b) ergonomics.
   (c) job analysis.
   (d) organizational development (OD).

10. Dr. Addersly conducted research on male and female leadership behavior. According to In Focus B.2, if his findings are consistent with previous research in this area, Dr. Addersly is likely to discover

    (a) that men will tend to use a style of leadership called consideration and women will prefer initiating structure.
    (b) virtually no behavioral or personality differences between male and female managers.
    (c) that the gender of managers does not influence how people react to them.
    (d) vast differences in behavior between male and female managers.

Answers

What Is Industrial/Organizational Psychology?

1. *Industrial/organizational psychology is* the branch of psychology that focuses on the study of human behavior at work.

   The "I" side of I/O psychology is called personnel psychology *and is concerned with* measuring human characteristics, matching those traits with the requirements of the job, accurately measuring job performance, and training employees.

   The "O" side of I/O psychology is called organizational behavior (OB) *and is concerned with* how the organization and the social environment in which people work affect their attitudes and behaviors.

2. The six content areas of I/O psychology (and the focus of each) are *(a)* selection and placement, *which focuses on* the development of selection techniques to help select from a pool of job applicants those who are most likely to be successful in a given job or organization. *(b)* Training and development, *which focuses on* determining what types of skills need to be enhanced to improve job performance, designing training programs (including training programs for managers), and evaluating the effec-

tiveness of these programs. *(c)* Performance management *is concerned with* identifying criteria or standards for determining the degree to which employees are performing their jobs well, accurately measuring their job performance, and motivating managers to find the best way of providing employees with honest performance feedback. *(d)* Organizational development, *whose goal is to* bring about positive change in an organization (such as greater profitability or improvement in the quality of products) by examining the structure of the organization and the social systems within that organization, and to help organizations manage global and workforce diversity. *(e)* Quality of work life, *which emphasizes the* importance of maintaining a healthy and productive workforce and is concerned with such issues as adequate and fair compensation, a safe and healthy work environment, the development of human capacities, and constitutionalism. *(f)* Ergonomics, *which focuses on* the design of equipment and the development of work procedures in light of human capabilities and limitations.

Work Settings, Type of Training, and Employment Outlook

1. *To work in the field of I/O psychology, a* doctorate or master's degree is generally required (some areas that are closely related to I/O are open to those with bachelor's degrees). *The principal employment settings are* academic settings such as universities or colleges (34 percent), consultants to organizations (31 percent), and private or public organizations (23 percent).

2. *The employment outlook for those with Ph.Ds and master's degrees* appears very favorable, with the unemployment rate of those wishing to work consistently less than 1 percent. *People with bachelor's degrees may find work as* personnel, training, and labor-relations specialists and managers, management analysts, management consultants, and employment interviewers.

Personnel Psychology

1. *The three major goals of personnel psychologists are (a)* selecting the best applicants for jobs, *(b)* training employees so that they perform their jobs effectively, and *(c)* accurately evaluating employee performance.

2. *Job analysis is a technique in which* the major

responsibilities of a job, along with the human characteristics needed to fill it, are determined. Information about the job is usually collected from employees who currently hold the job or from their supervisors and this may be done through interviews, observations, or surveys.

3. *Selection devices, such as tests and interviews, are* used to determine which applicants have the knowledge, skills, and abilities specified in a job analysis.

   Training program developers begin by comparing the current work procedures, knowledge, and skills of employees with the information obtained from the job analysis; they then design training programs to eliminate gaps between what currently exists and what is optimal.

4. *Selection device validity refers to* the extent to which a selection device is successful in distinguishing between those applicants who will become high performers at a certain job and those who will not.

5. *The six most common psychological tests (and their specific uses) are (a)* Cognitive ability tests, which measure general intelligence or specific cognitive skills, such as mathematical or verbal ability. *(b)* Mechanical ability tests, which measure mechanical reasoning and may be used to predict job performance for engineering, carpentry, and assembly work. *(c)* Motor ability tests, which include measures of fine dexterity in fingers and hands, accuracy and speed of arm and hand movement, and eye–hand coordination. *(d)* Sensory ability tests, which include measures of visual acuity, color vision, and hearing. *(e)* Personality tests, which may be designed to measure either abnormal or normal personality characteristics; some tests are designed to measure normal personality traits, such as conscientiousness, extraversion, and agreeableness; assessment of abnormal personality characteristics might be appropriate for selecting people for sensitive jobs, such as nuclear plant operator, police officer, and airline pilots. *(f)* Honesty tests, which attempt to assess an applicant's level of honesty by asking about past behaviors involving theft or dishonesty, attitudes about theft and the punishment of it, and perceptions about the prevalence of theft.

6. *The three most common types of personnel selection devices (and their specific uses) are (a)* Work samples, which provide a high degree of realism and require the applicant to complete work-related problems; these are typically used for positions involving the manipulation of objects. *(b)* Situational exercises, which require the candidate to carry out some organizational task; these are typically used for jobs involving managerial or professional skills. *(c)* The general interview, one of the most commonly used selection devices; this typically possesses low validity (that is, assessments of applicants in general interviews are not strongly related to their subsequent job performance). Structured interviews are adequate predictors of job performance if they are developed and conducted properly. One type of structured interview is the situational interview in which the applicant is given a situation and asked how he or she would respond to that situation.

Organizational Behavior and Workplace Trends and Issues

1. *Organizational behavior focuses on* how the organization and social environment in which people work affect their attitudes (especially regarding job satisfaction) and behaviors.

2. *The discrepancy hypothesis is* an approach to explaining job satisfaction that focuses on the discrepancy, if any, between what the person wants from a job and how that person evaluates what is experienced at work.

3. *The social influence hypothesis is the view that* a person's level of job satisfaction is influenced by the job satisfaction levels of other people.

4. *The dispositional factors hypothesis is the position that* a person's level of job satisfaction may be due in part to a genetically based disposition toward a positive or negative outlook.

5. *The trait approach to leader effectiveness is based on* the idea that leaders are born, not made, and focuses on the personal characteristics displayed by successful leaders.

6. *Behavioral theories of leader effectiveness focus on* differences in the behaviors of effective and ineffective leaders. *Consideration describes leaders who* are deeply concerned about their followers and who spend time building trust, respect, and warmth between themselves and their followers, *and initiating structure describes leaders who* are task-oriented, who structure tasks for their followers and who push to get things done.

7. *Situational (contingency) theories of leader effectiveness focus on* how a particular situation influences a leader's effectiveness.

8. *The leader–member exchange model of leadership suggests* that the quality of the interactions between supervisors and subordinates varies depending on the unique characteristics of both. *Research on upward influence (subordinates influencing supervisors) has shown that* tactics such as assertiveness and ingratiation are ineffective, but that rational persuasion seems to enhance the leader's impression of the persuader's potential for promotion.

9. *Personal qualities related to leader emergence are* intelligence, aggressiveness, decisiveness, and dominance. *The topic of leader emergence differs from that of leader effectiveness because* not everyone who emerges as a leader is a good leader.

10. *The major workplace trends and issues are* *(a)* Telecommuting or telework: This refers to employees working from home and it offers advantages such as flexible work schedules, more freedom at work, and less time wasted commuting. For employers, there are reductions in costs associated with renting office space and an increased ability to attract and retain talented personnel. *(b)* Internet recruiting: This has affected the ways in which employers seek job candidates and the ways in which job candidates learn about potential employers. *(c)* Privacy in the workplace: Employees have fewer rights in the workplace than they may realize, and, in general, organizations are free to monitor Internet use. *(d)* Work–life balance: Many employees are concerned about work–life balance, and many organizations have responded by offering flexible work schedules, telecommuting, job sharing, sabbaticals, more vacation/leave-time, concierge services, and on-site health clubs to help employees balance personal activities and work. *(e) In the future, I/O psychologists will* continue to have a significant role in the workplace, and in order to keep pace with the changing needs of employees and rapid technological advances, I/O psychologists continue to adjust the focus of their research and its applications to improve the experiences of people at work.

Concept Check 1

1. personnel psychology
2. leader–member exchange model

3. employment interviewer
4. work sample
5. honesty test
6. consideration; initiating structure
7. leaderless group discussion

Matching Exercise

1. job analysis
2. organizational development (OD)
3. leader–member exchange model
4. industrial/organizational (I/O) psychology
5. situational (or contingency) theories of leader effectiveness
6. discrepancy hypothesis
7. employment interviewer
8. social influence hypothesis

True/False Test

1. T	4. T	7. T
2. F	5. T	8. F
3. T	6. T	

Progress Test 1

1. b	5. d	9. b
2. a	6. c	10. a
3. a	7. d	
4. d	8. d	

Progress Test 2

1. e	5. c	9. b
2. b	6. c	10. e
3. b	7. c	
4. a	8. a	

Progress Test 3

1. d	5. c	9. d
2. b	6. b	10. b
3. d	7. b	
4. a	8. d	